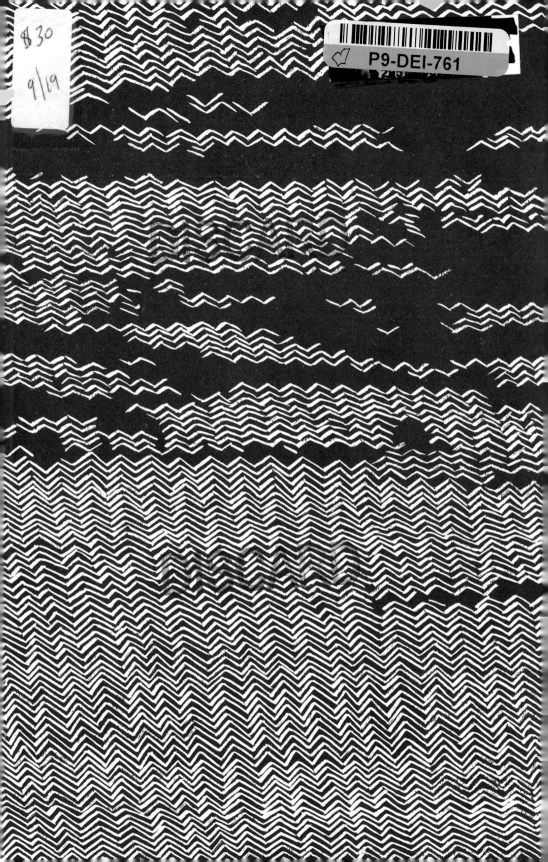

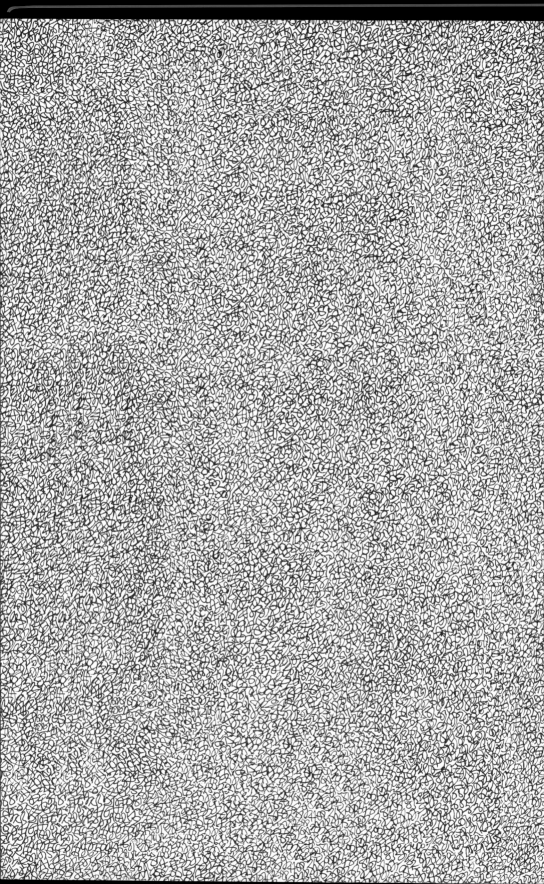

KING OF KING COURT

TRAVIS DANDRO

DRAWN & QUARTERLY

THANK YOU

AMANDA, ISAAC, WYETH, and MILES
TROY, BRIAN, ROBBY, ZUNG, DAD,
AUNT MARY, STEVE, and RHONDA
THE CORNELL DAILY SUN
EVERYONE AT D+Q

SHE DRIVES ME CRAZY (GIFT/STEELE)
PUBLISHED BY VIRGIN MUSIC
PATIENCE (STRADLIN)
PUBLISHED BY UNIVERSAL MUSIC PUBLISHING GROUP
SEPTEMBER MORN (DIAMOND/BÉCAUD)
PUBLISHED BY SONY/ATV MUSIC PUBLISHING LLC, UNIVERSAL MUSIC PUBLISHING GROUP
(MEET) THE FLINTSTONES (CURTIN, BARBERA, HANNA)
PUBLISHED BY WARNER-TAMERLANE PUBLISHING CORP.

DRAWNANDQUARTERLY.COM

978-1-77046-359-2 | FIRST PAPERBACK EDITION AUGUST 2019

978-1-77046-391-2 | FIRST HARDCOVER EDITION AUGUST 2019

PRINTED IN CHINA | 10 9 8 7 6 5 4 3 2 1

CATALOGUING DATA AVAILABLE FROM LIBRARY AND ARCHIVES CANADA

PUBLISHED IN THE USA BY DRAWN & QUARTERLY, A CLIENT PUBLISHER
OF FARRAR, STRAUS AND GIROUX | PUBLISHED IN CANADA BY DRAWN &
QUARTERLY, A CLIENT PUBLISHER OF RAINCOAST BOOKS | PUBLISHED
IN THE UNITED KINGDOM BY DRAWN & QUARTERLY, A CLIENT PUBLISHER
OF PUBLISHERS GROUP UK.

FOR MOM

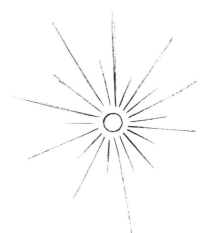

AUBURN, MASSACHUSETTS

AUGUST
1980

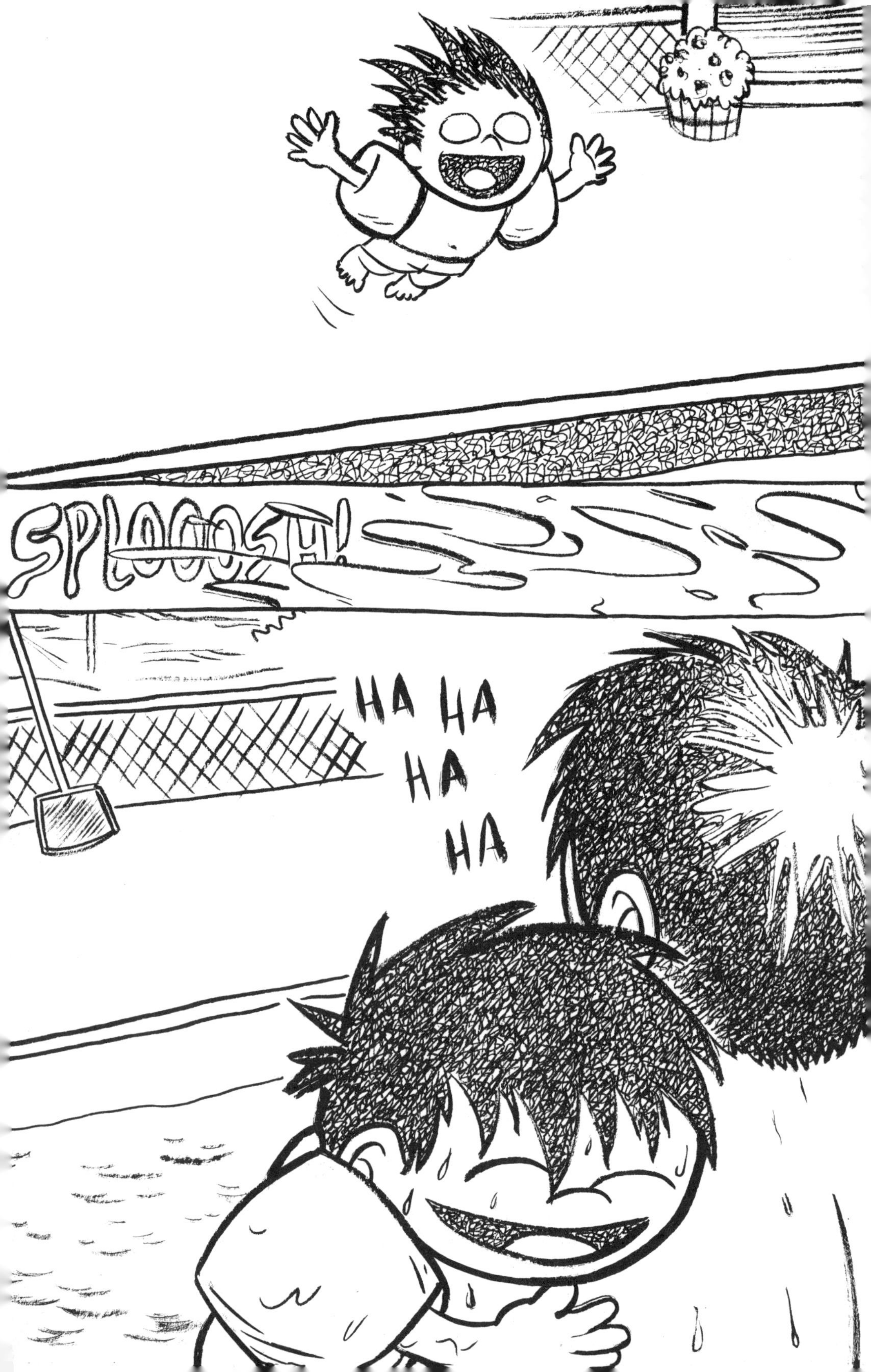
SPLOOOSH!
HA HA
HA
HA

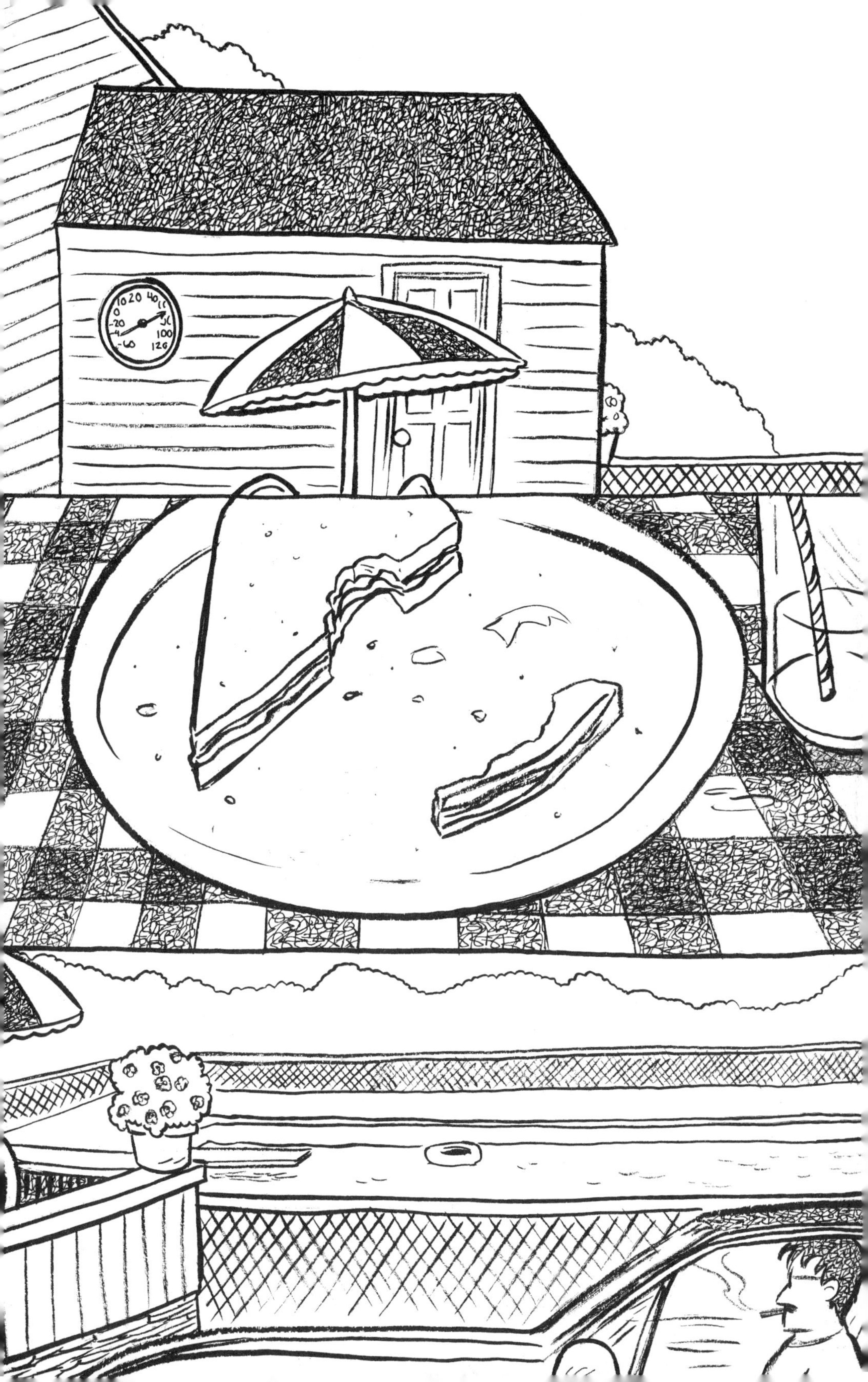

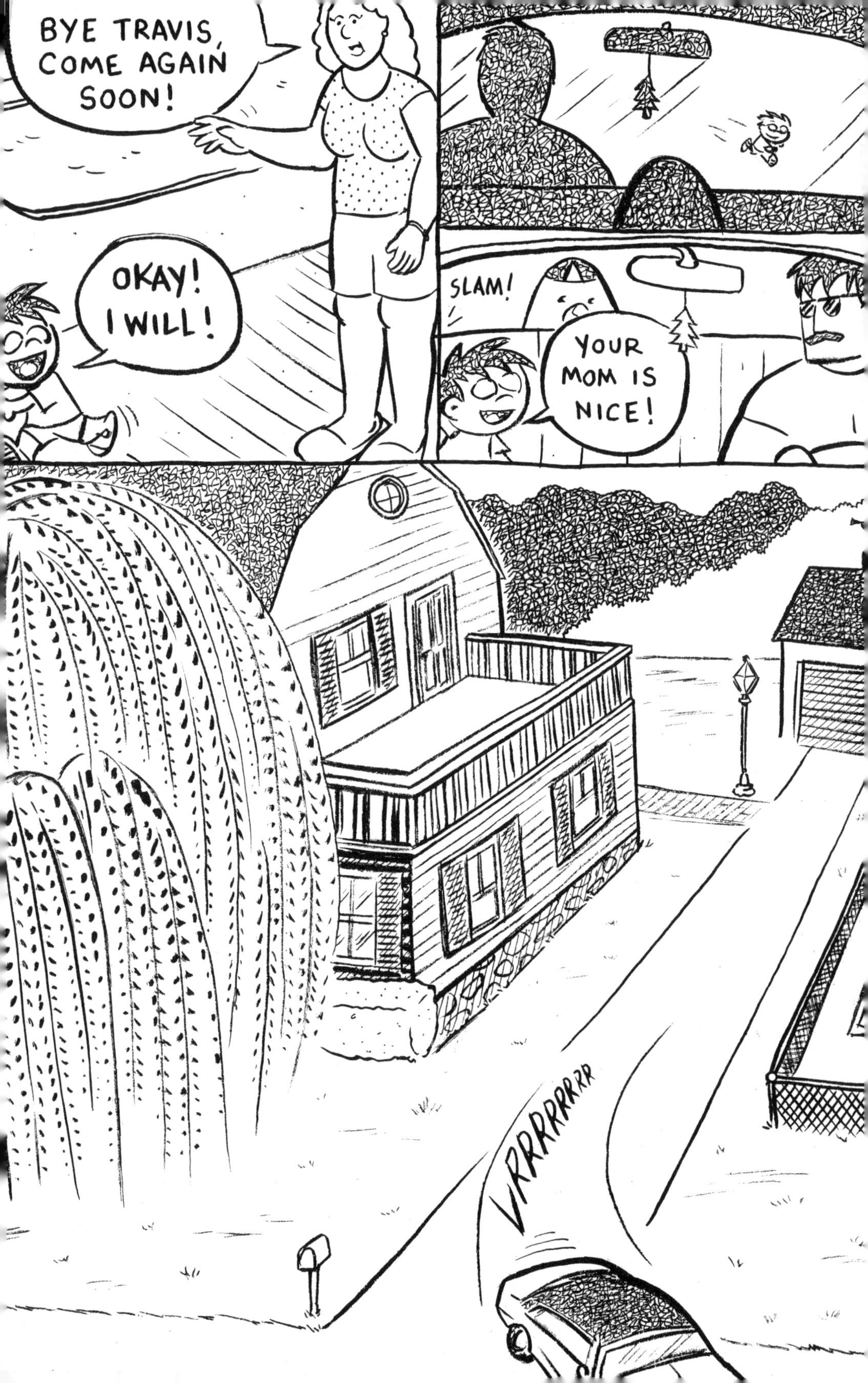
BYE TRAVIS, COME AGAIN SOON!
OKAY! I WILL!
SLAM!
YOUR MOM IS NICE!
VRRRRRRRR

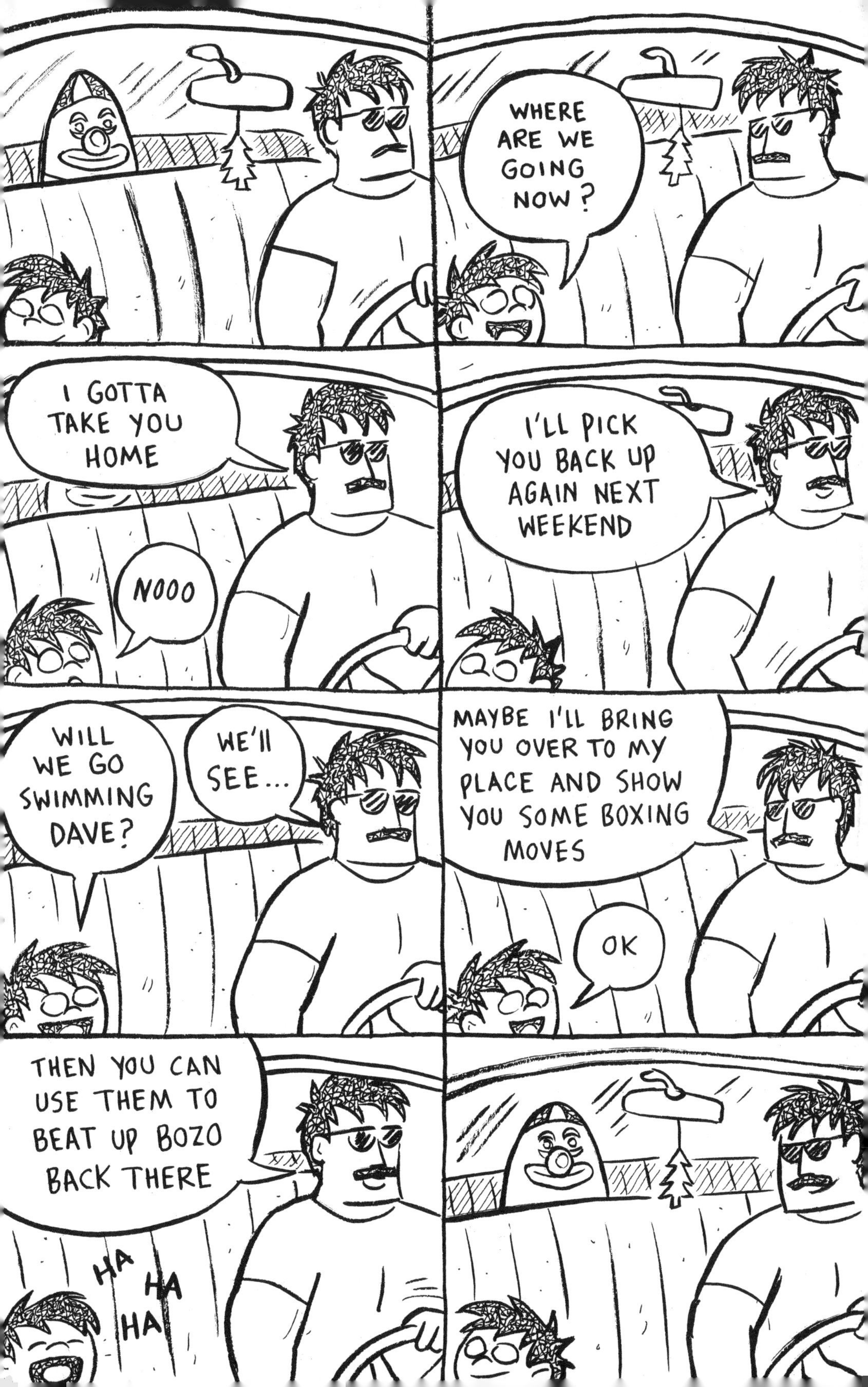
WHERE ARE WE GOING NOW?
I GOTTA TAKE YOU HOME
NOOO
I'LL PICK YOU BACK UP AGAIN NEXT WEEKEND
WILL WE GO SWIMMING DAVE?
WE'll SEE...
MAYBE I'LL BRING YOU OVER TO MY PLACE AND SHOW YOU SOME BOXING MOVES
OK
THEN YOU CAN USE THEM TO BEAT UP BOZO BACK THERE
HA HA HA

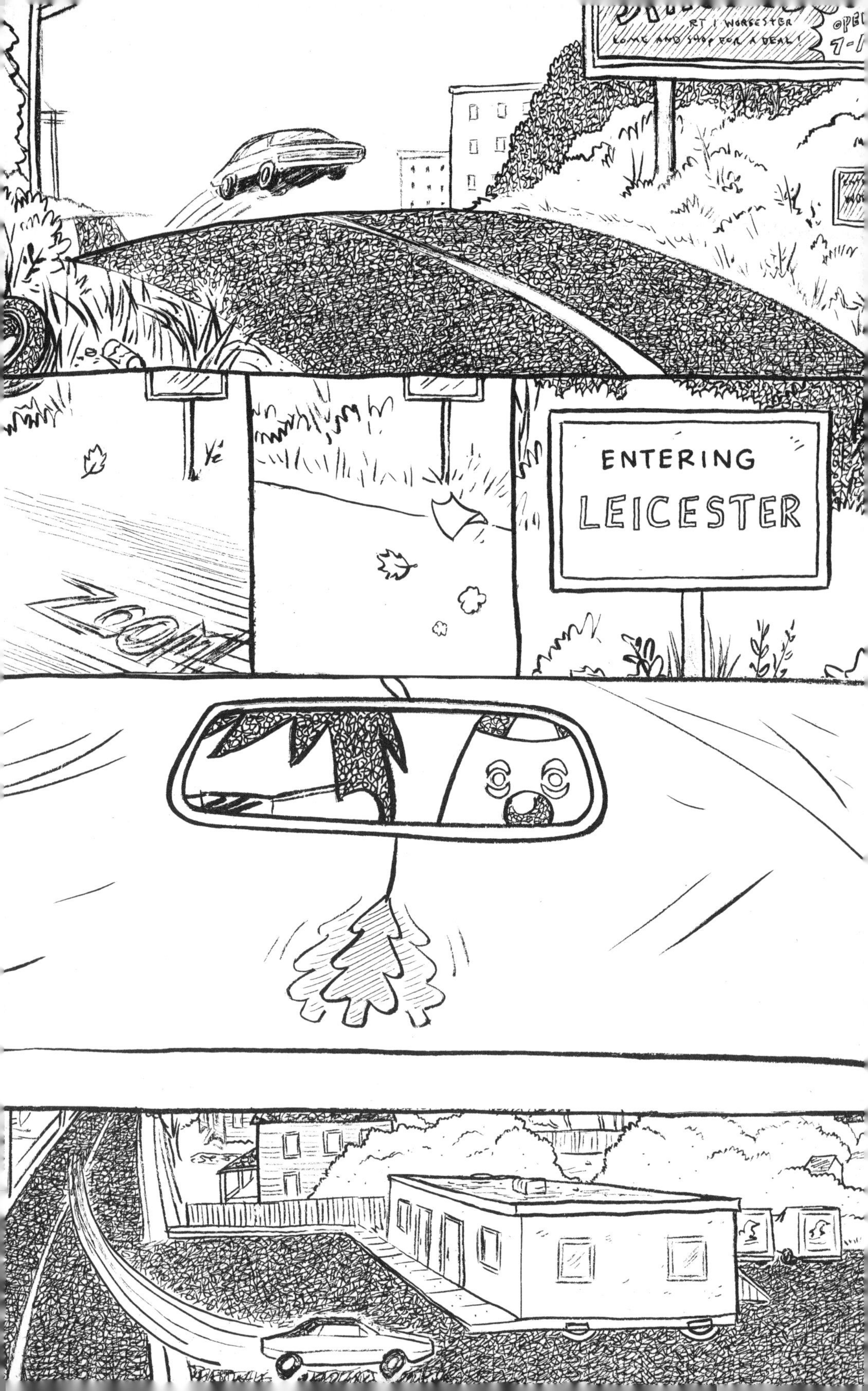
RT 1 WORSESTER
COME AND SHOP FOR A DEAL!
ENTERING LEICESTER
ZOOM!

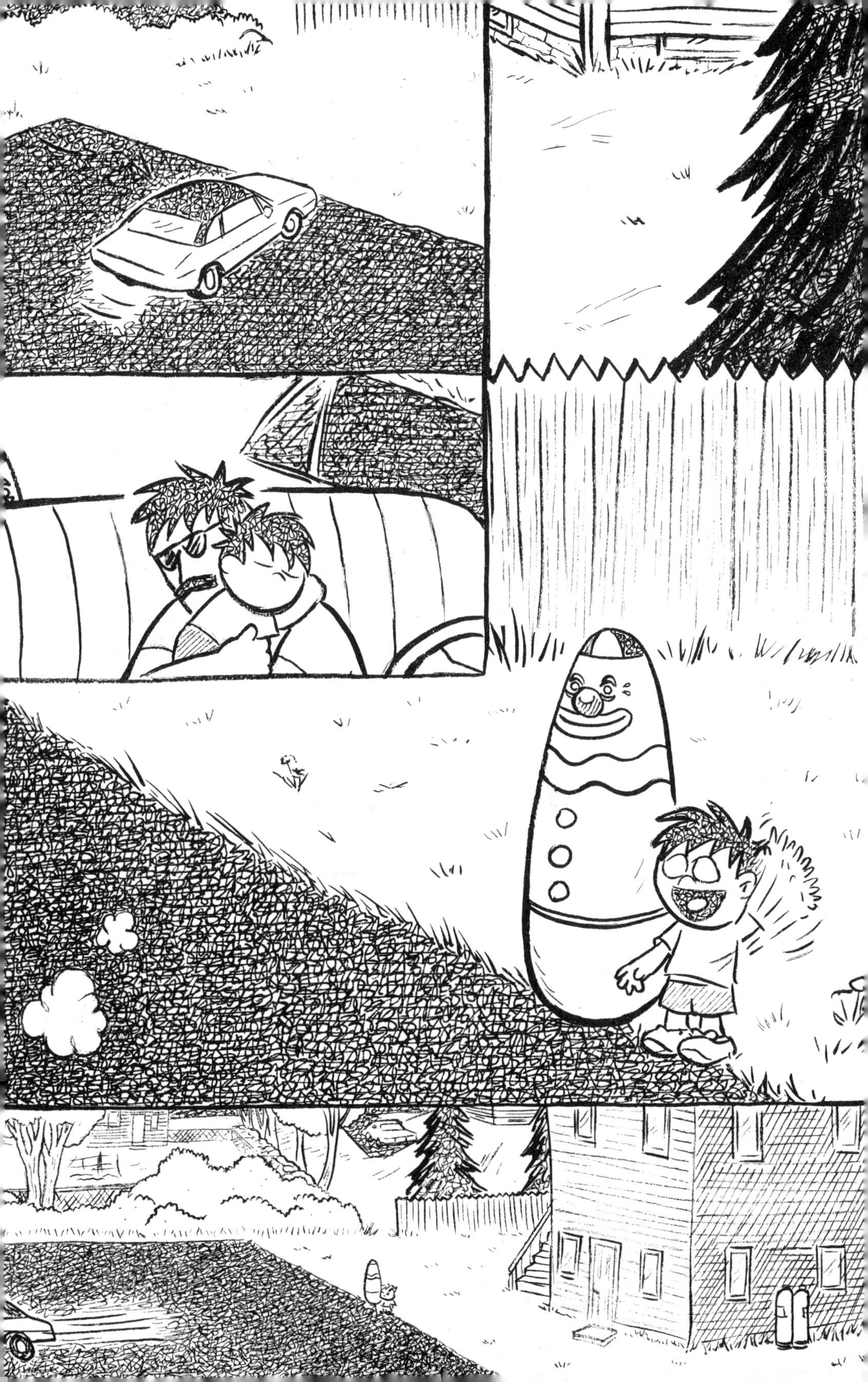

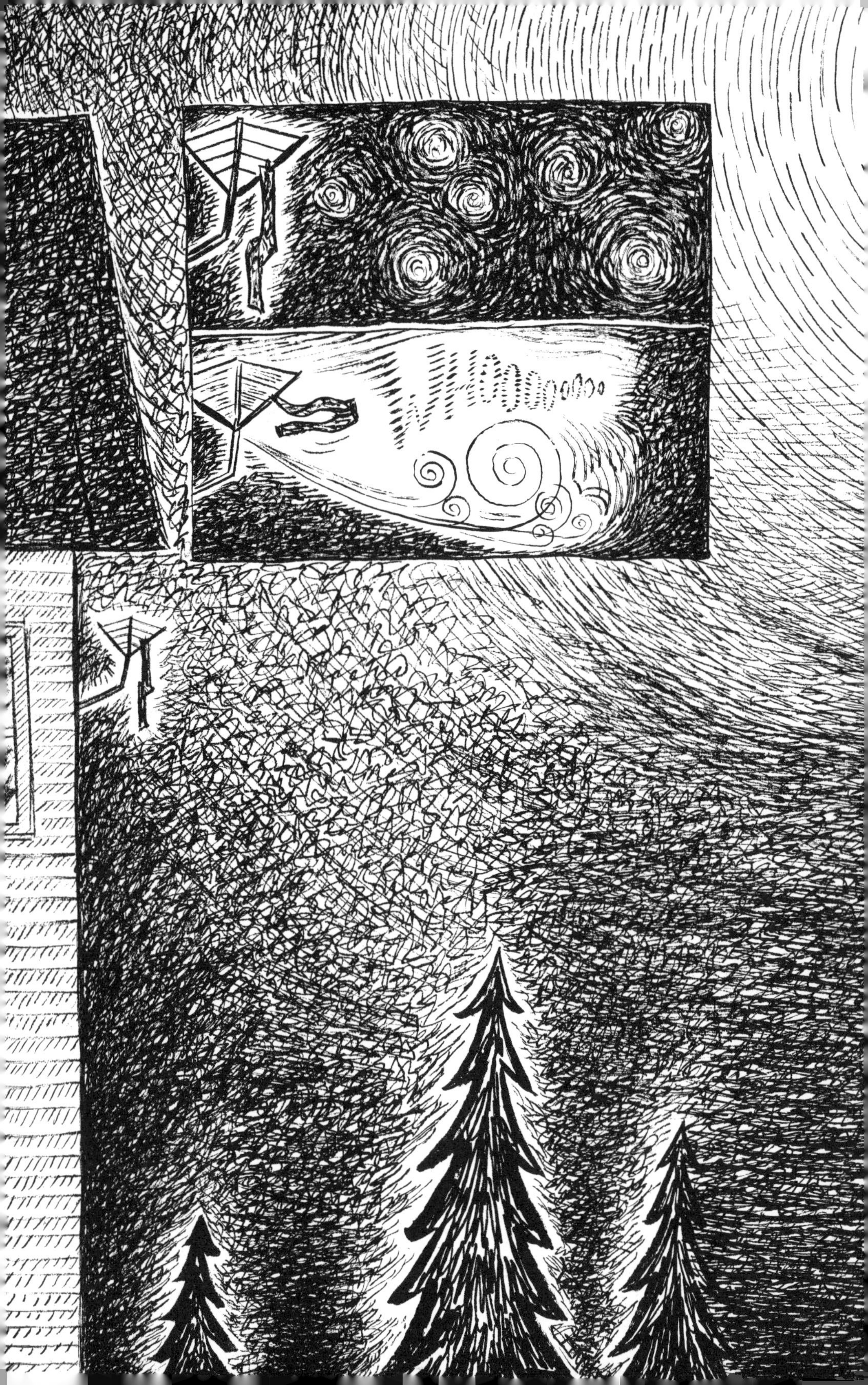
WHOOOooooo

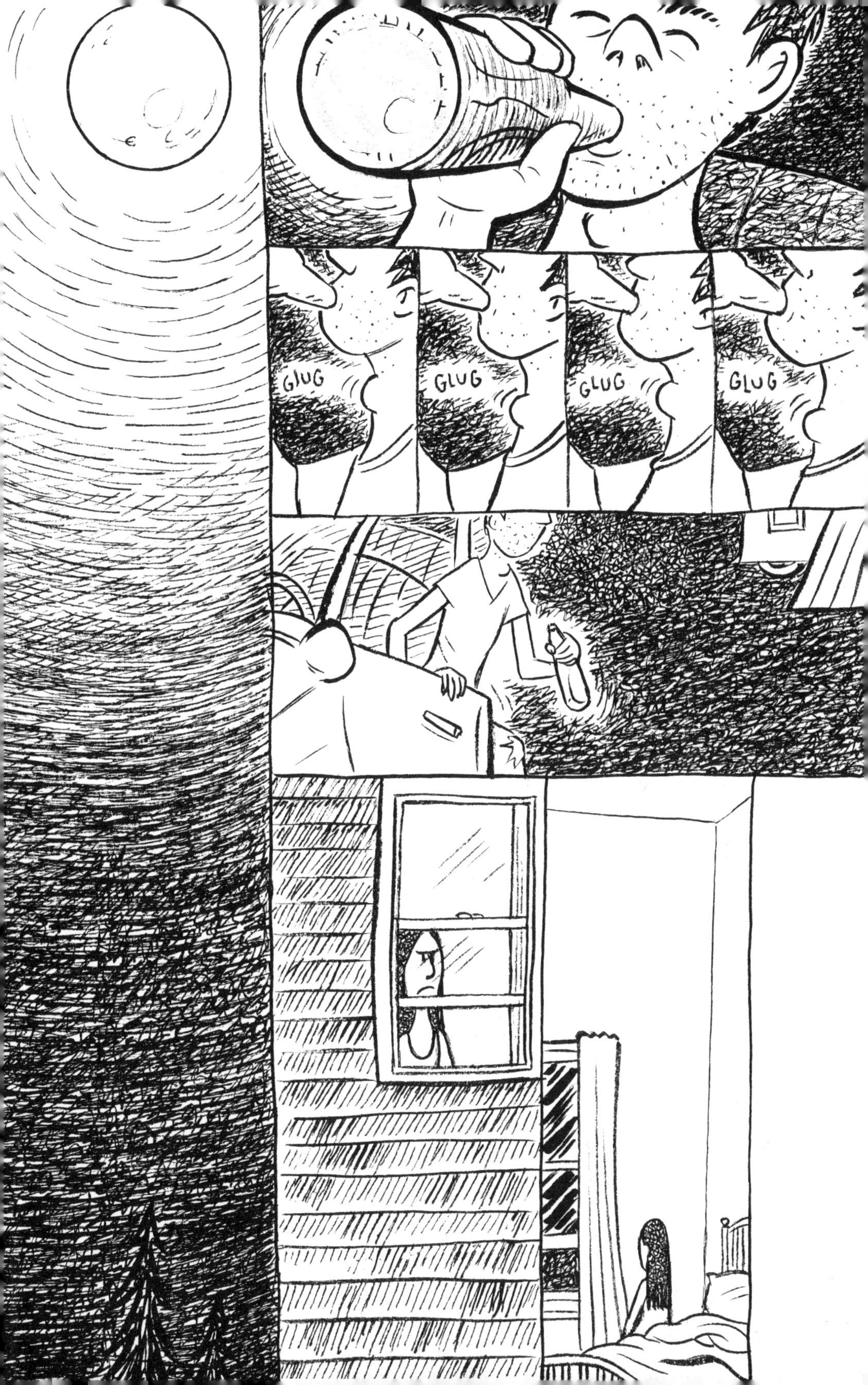
GLUG
GLUG
GLUG
GLUG

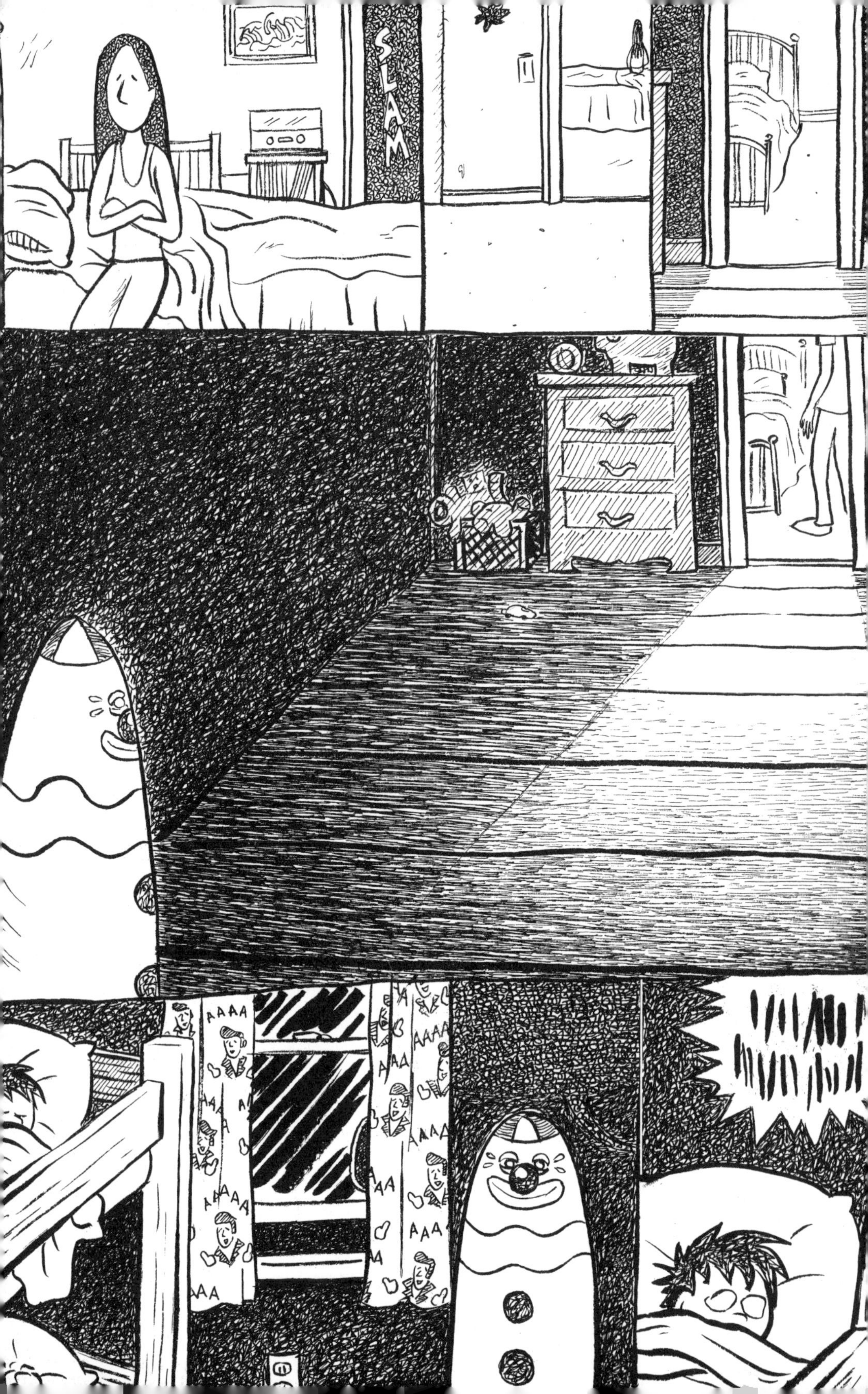
SLAM

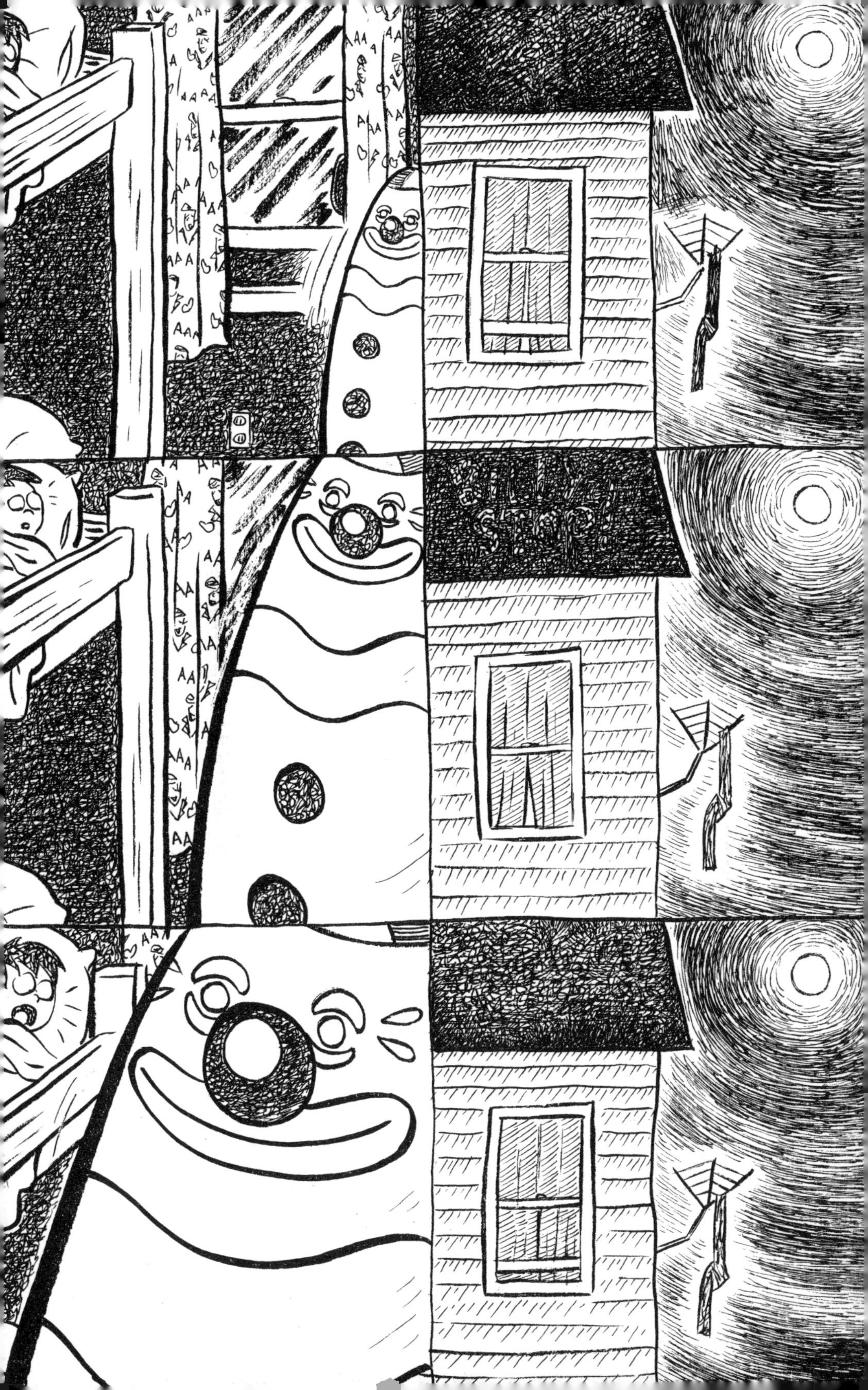
WILLY! STOP!

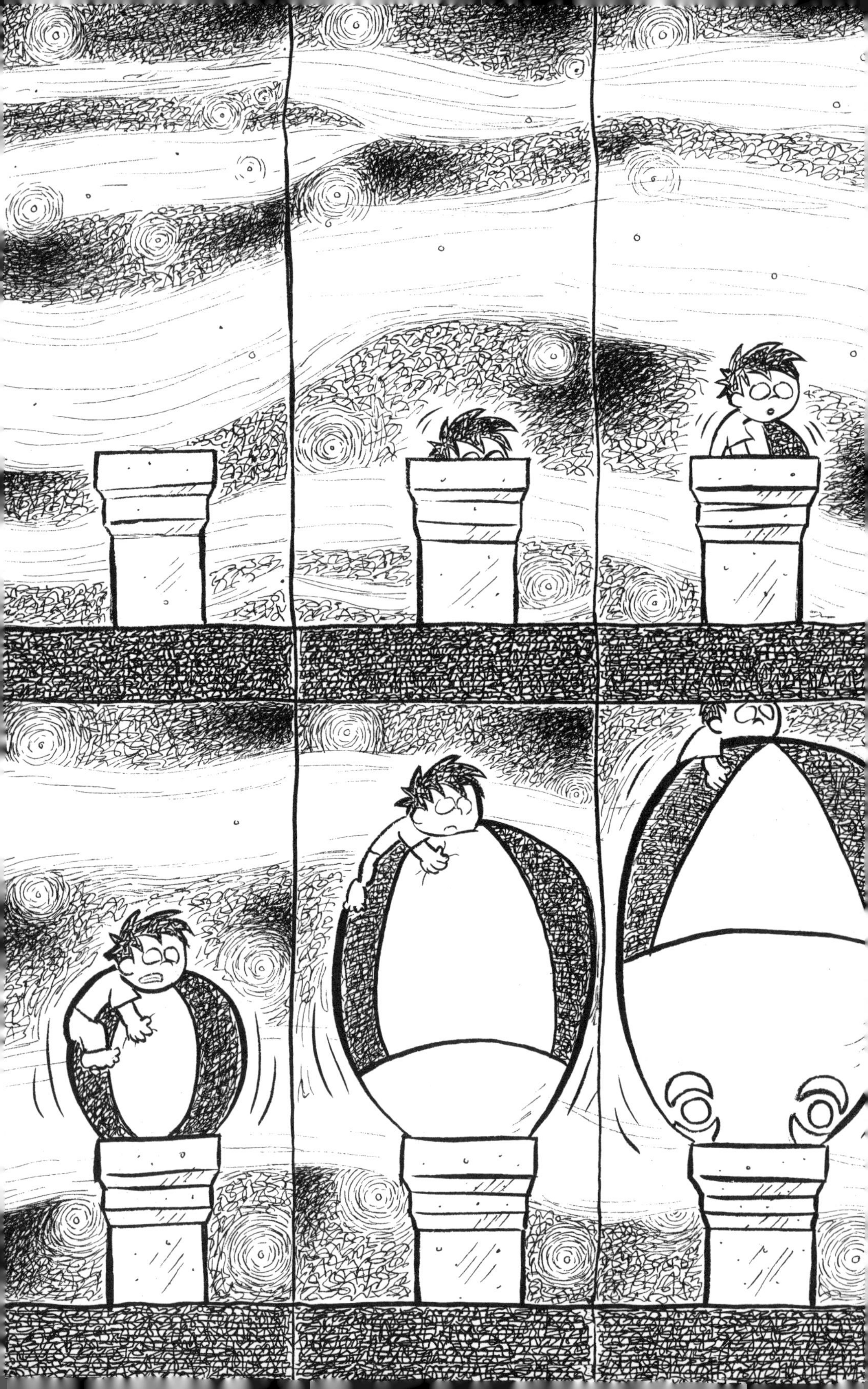

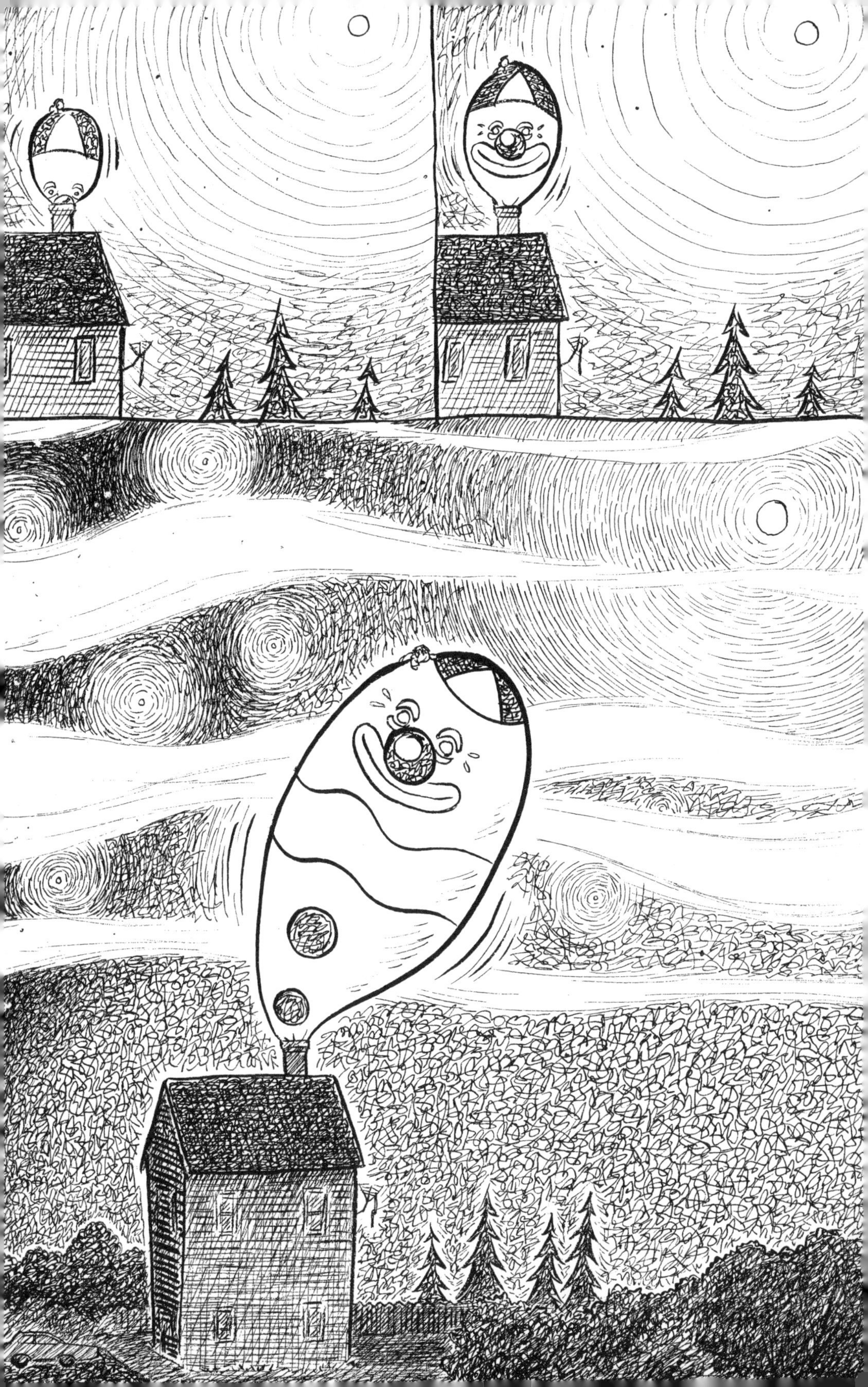

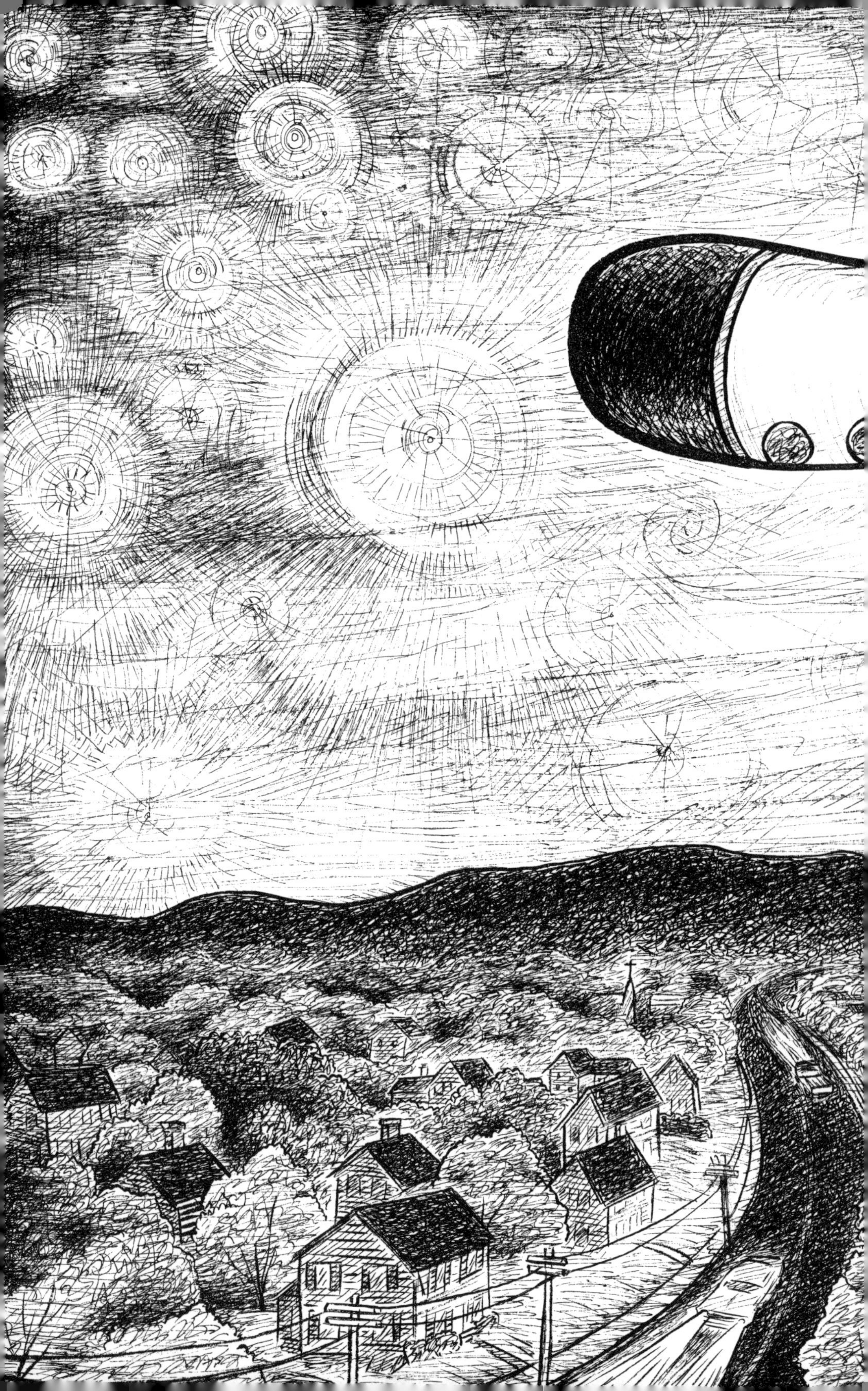

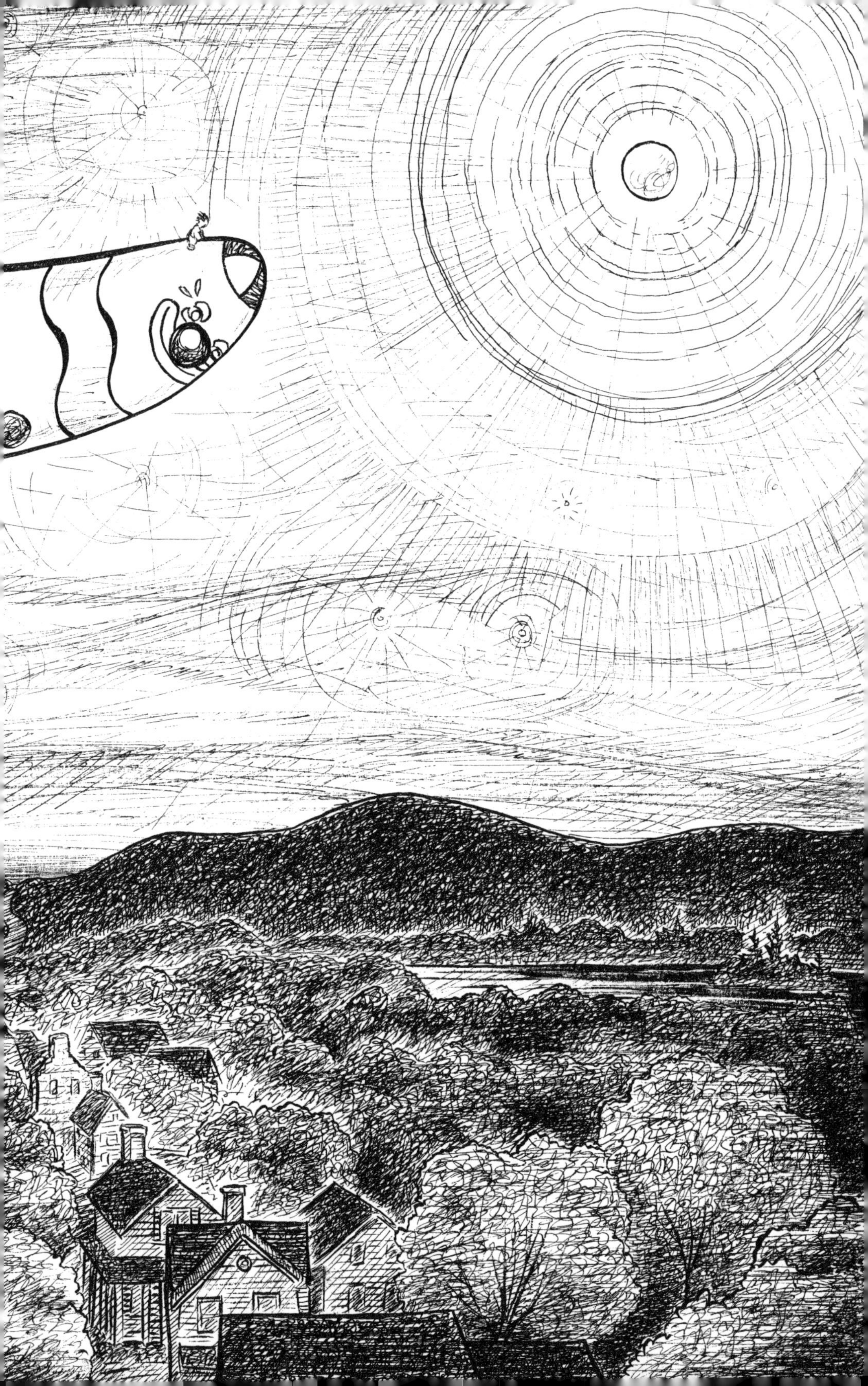

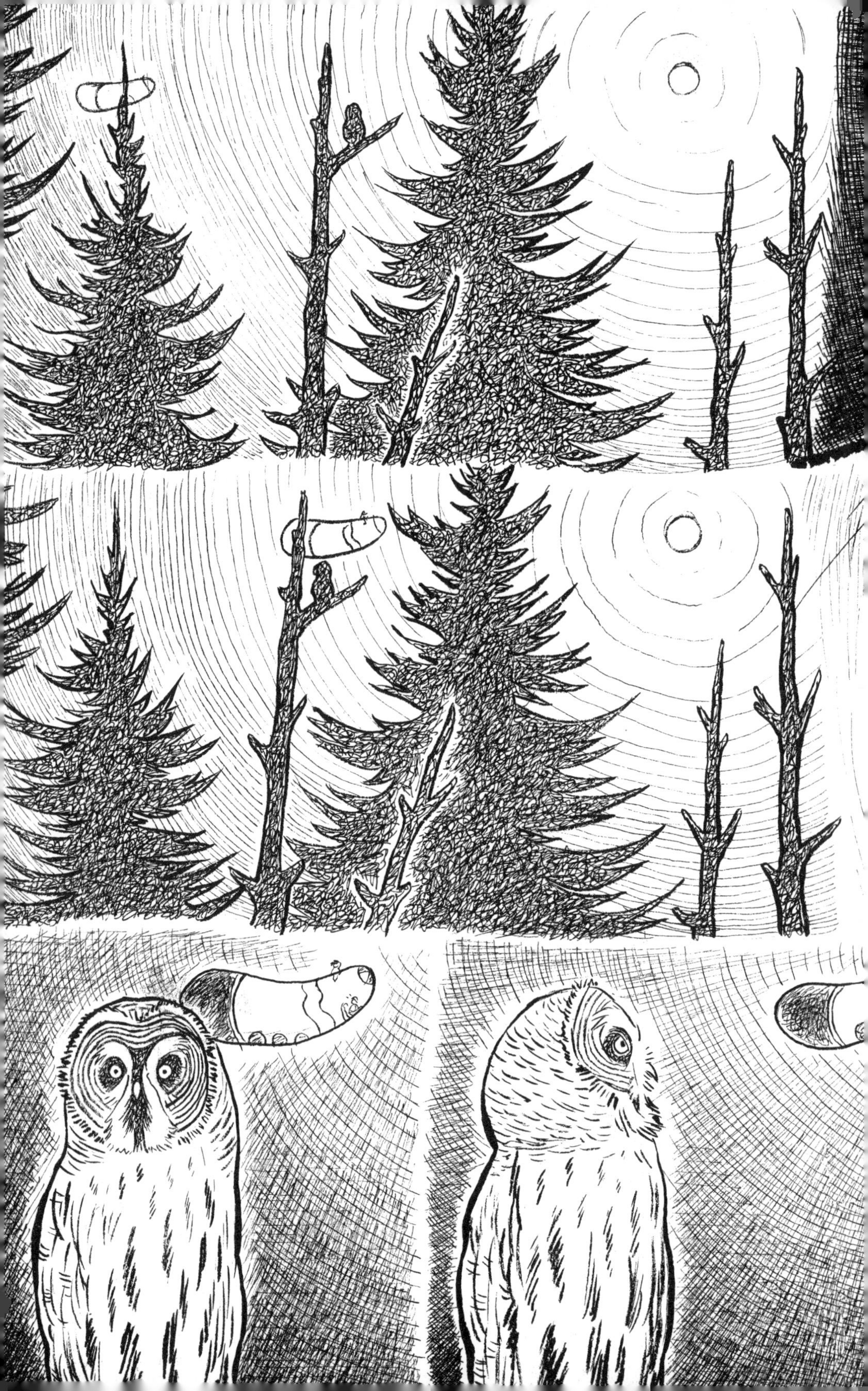

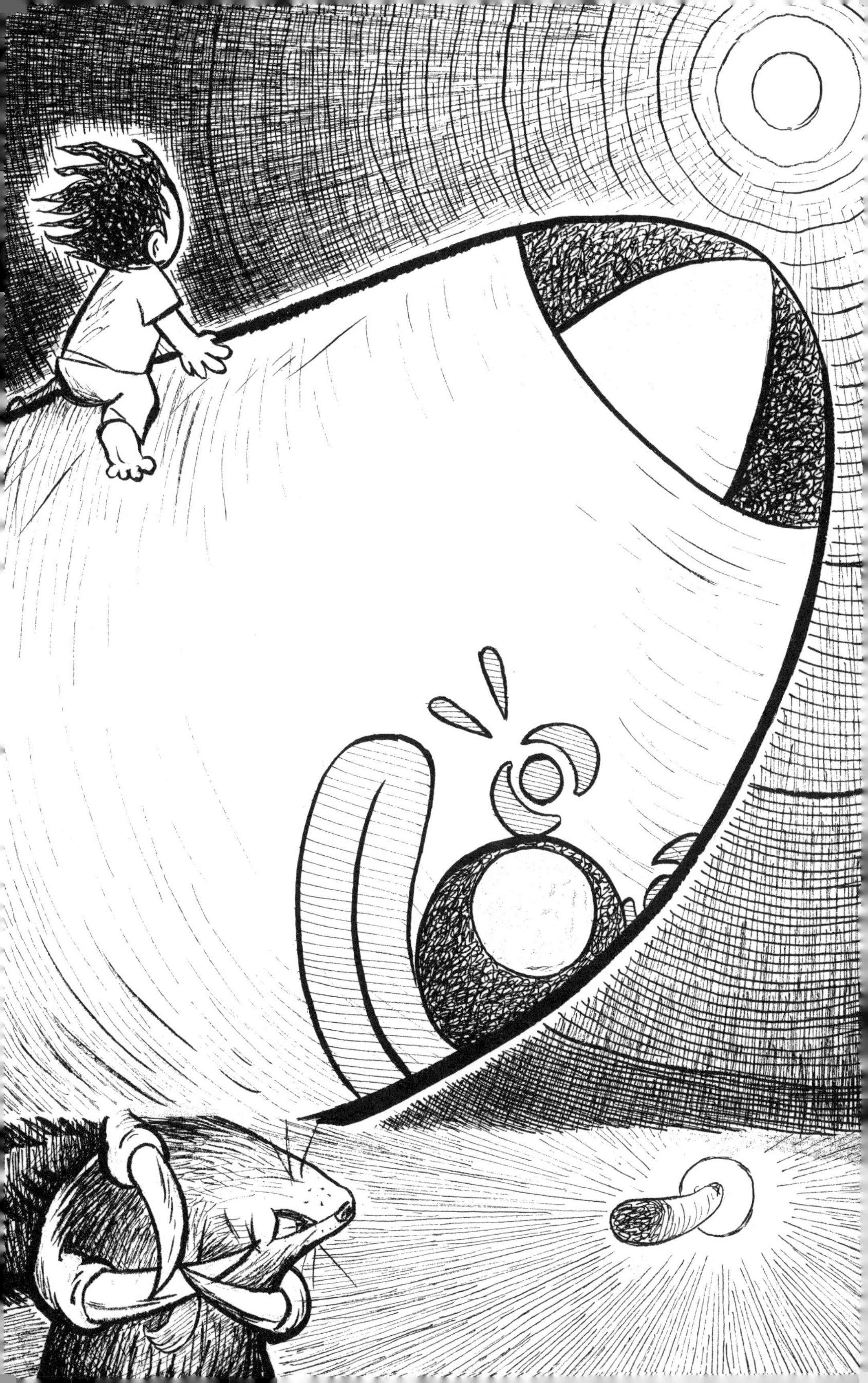

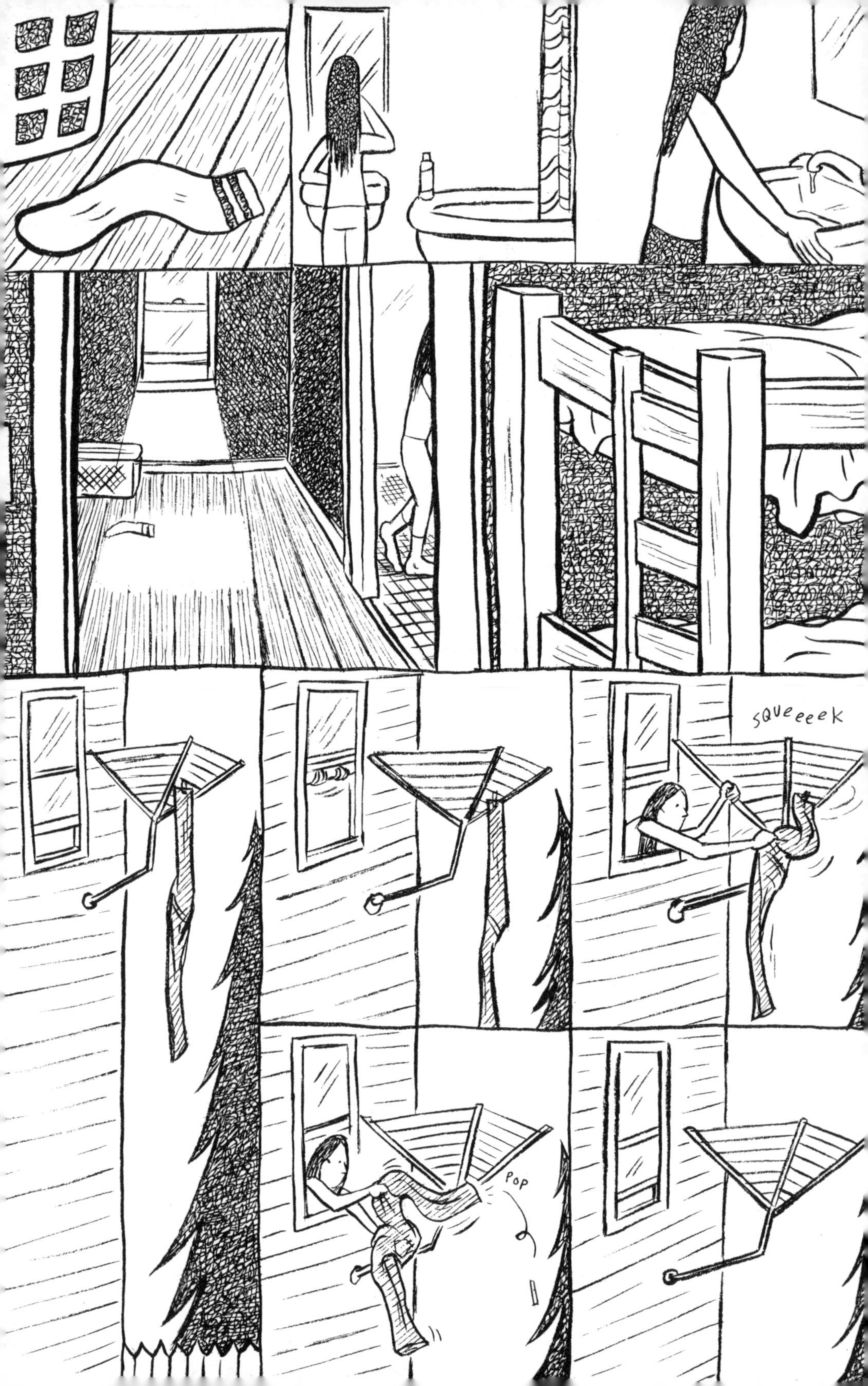
SQUeeeek
POP

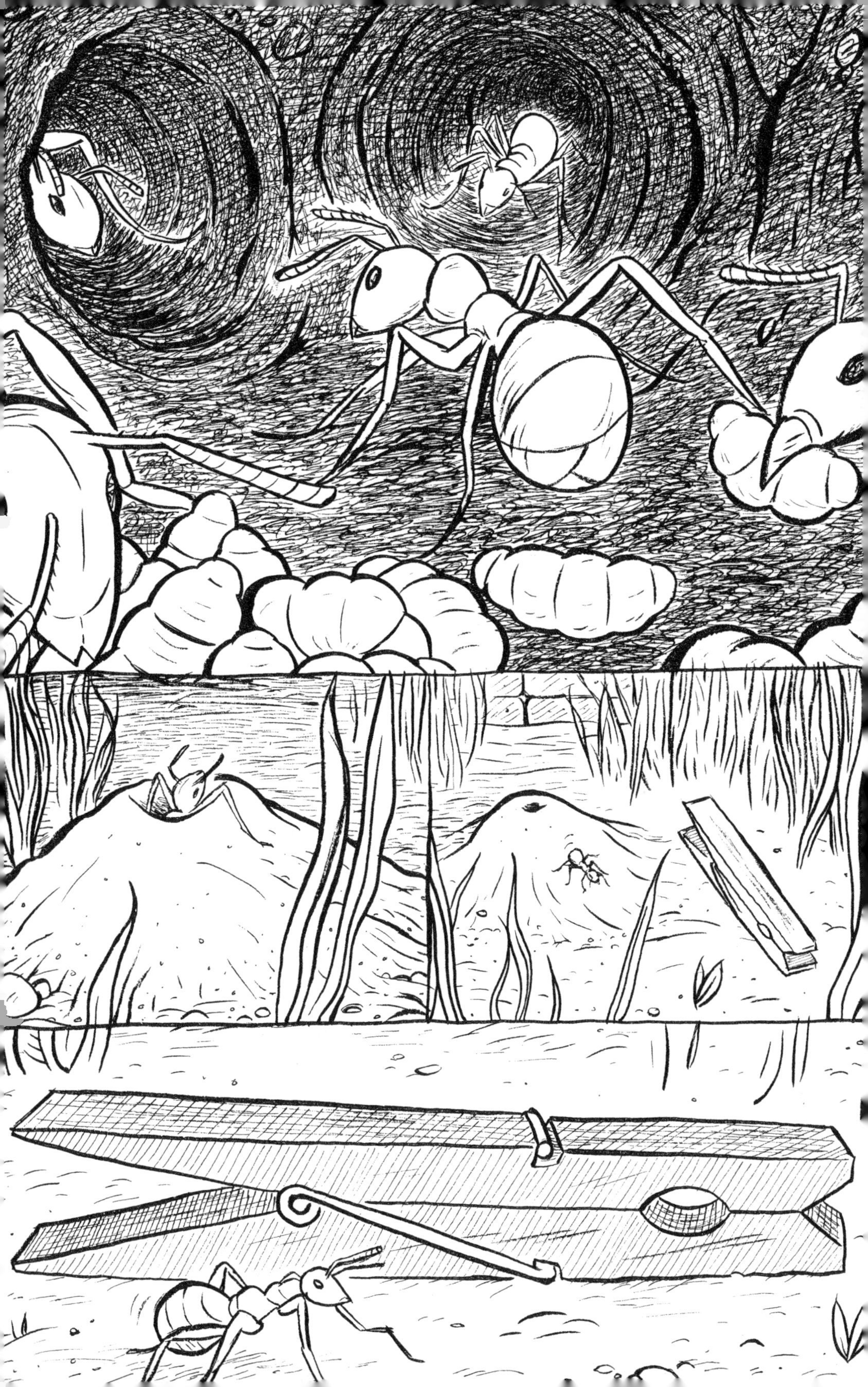

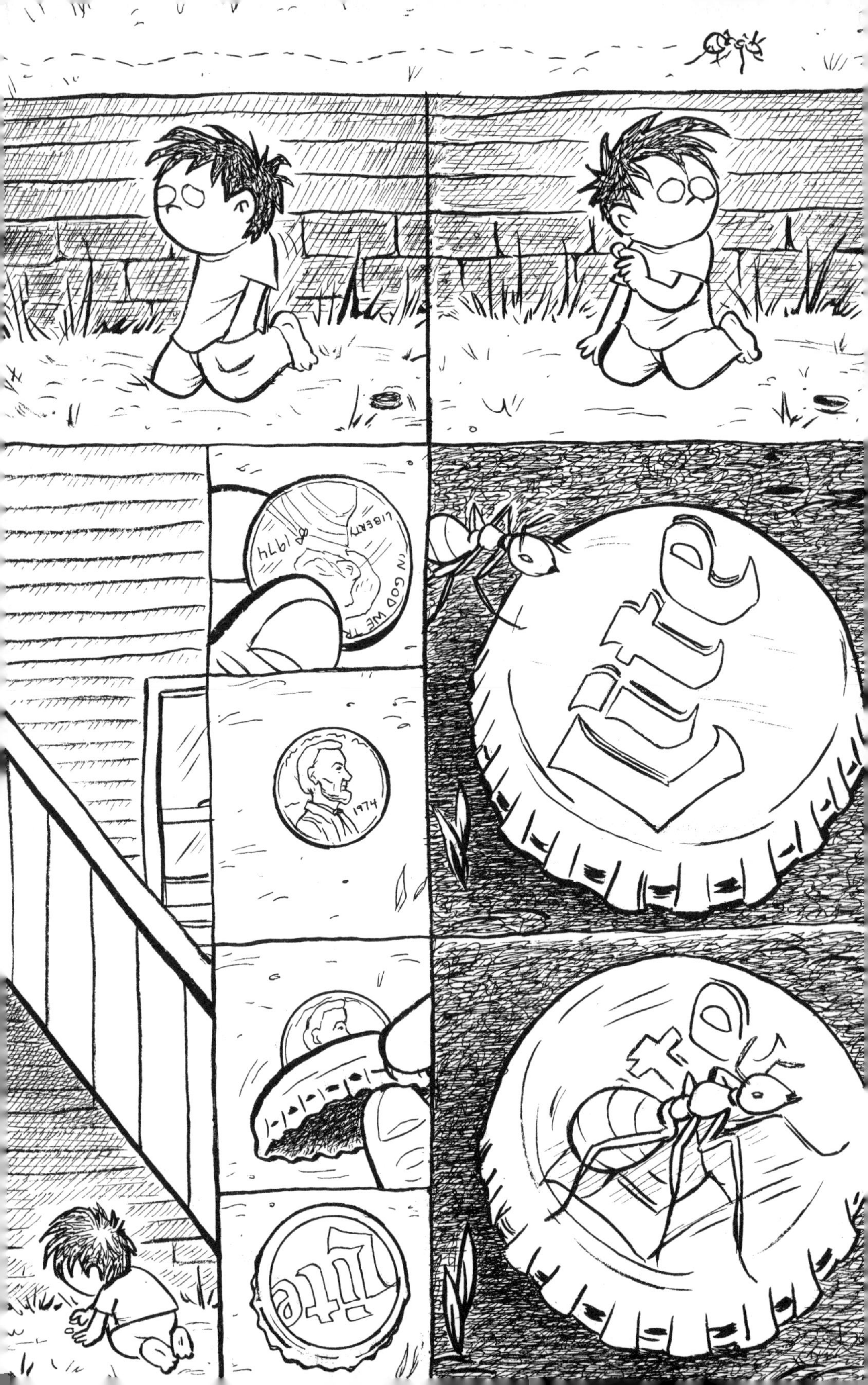
LIBERTY
1974
IN GOD WE TR
1974
lite

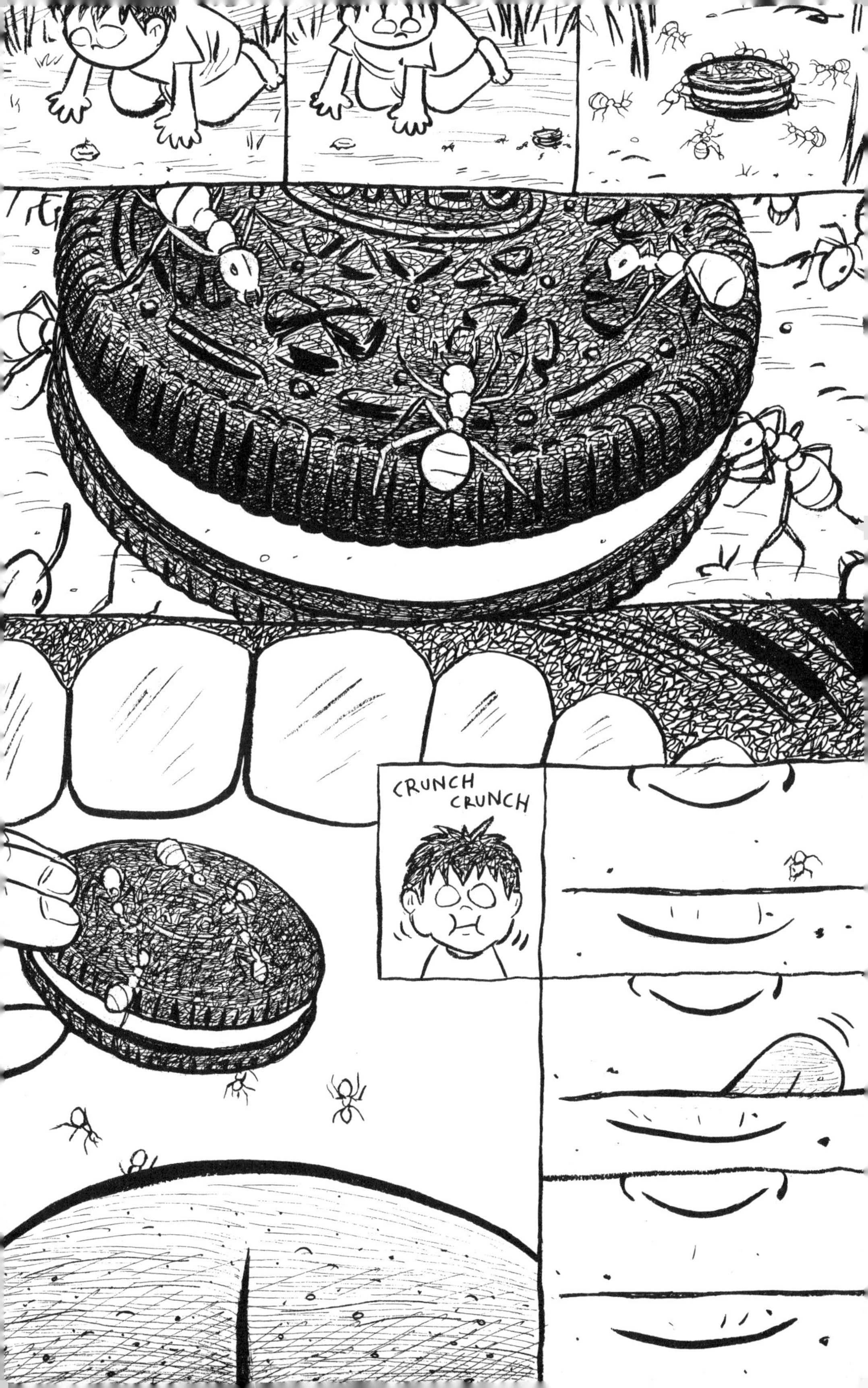
CRUNCH
CRUNCH

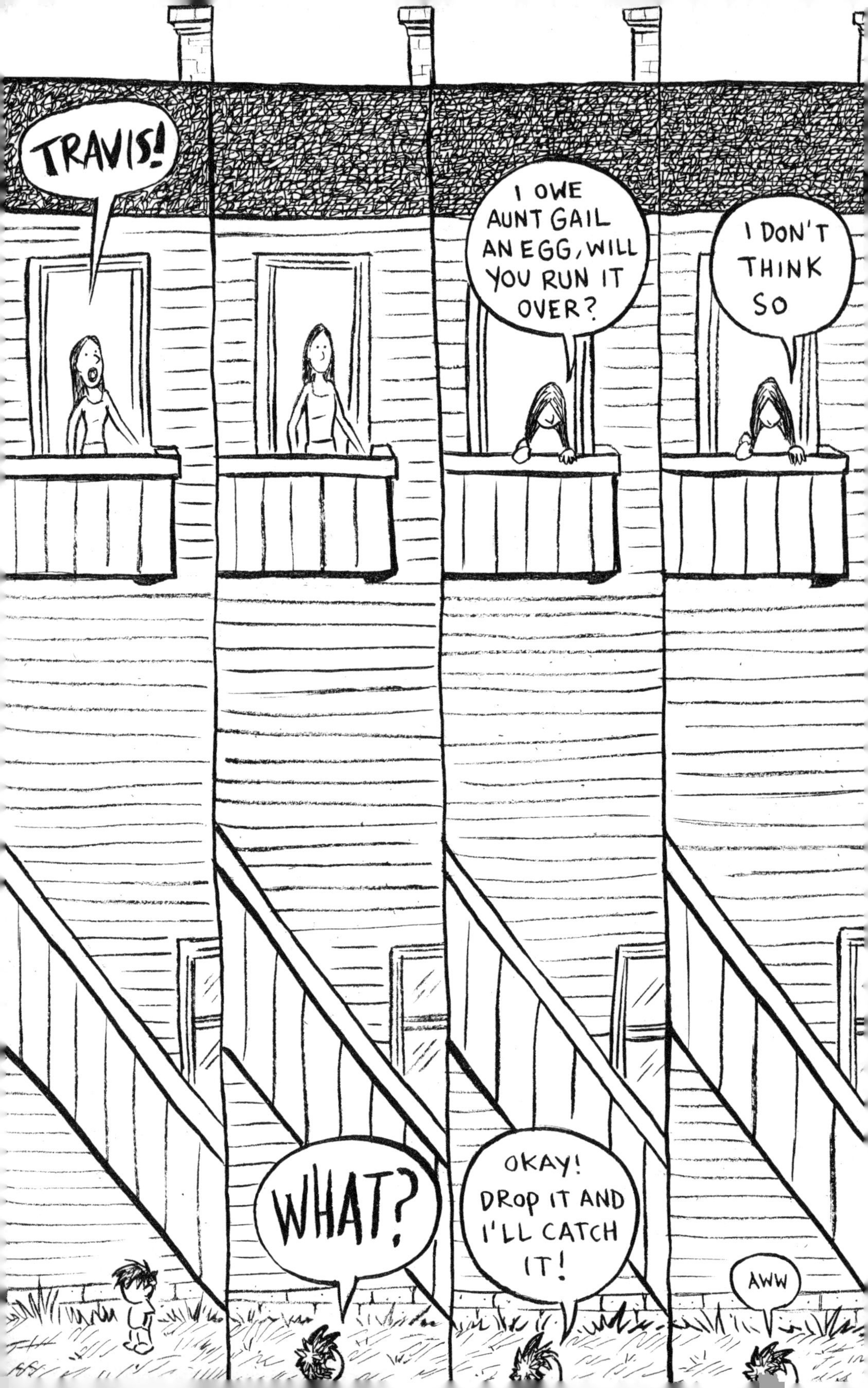
TRAVIS!
WHAT?
I OWE AUNT GAIL AN EGG, WILL YOU RUN IT OVER?
OKAY! DROP IT AND I'LL CATCH IT!
I DON'T THINK SO
AWW

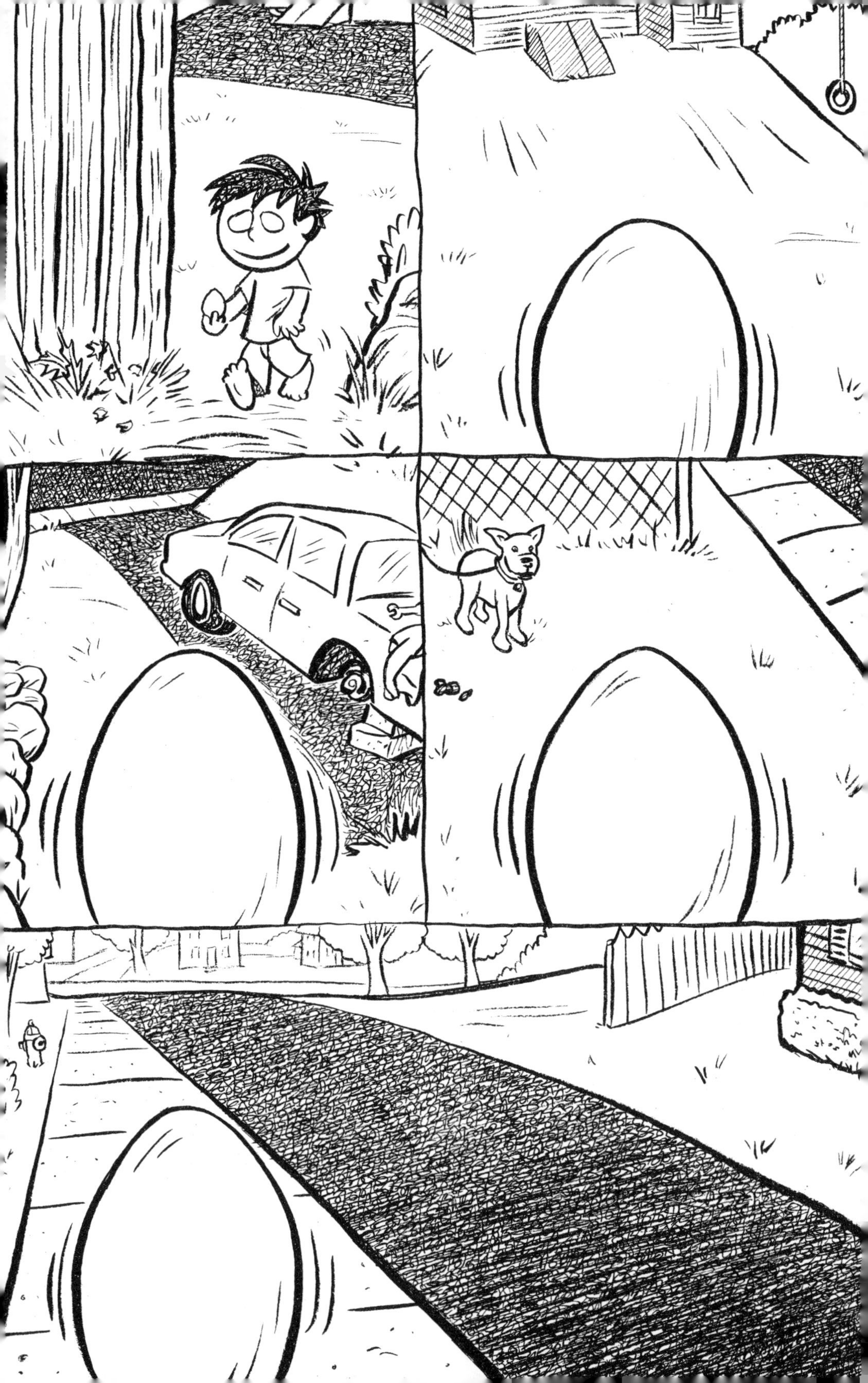

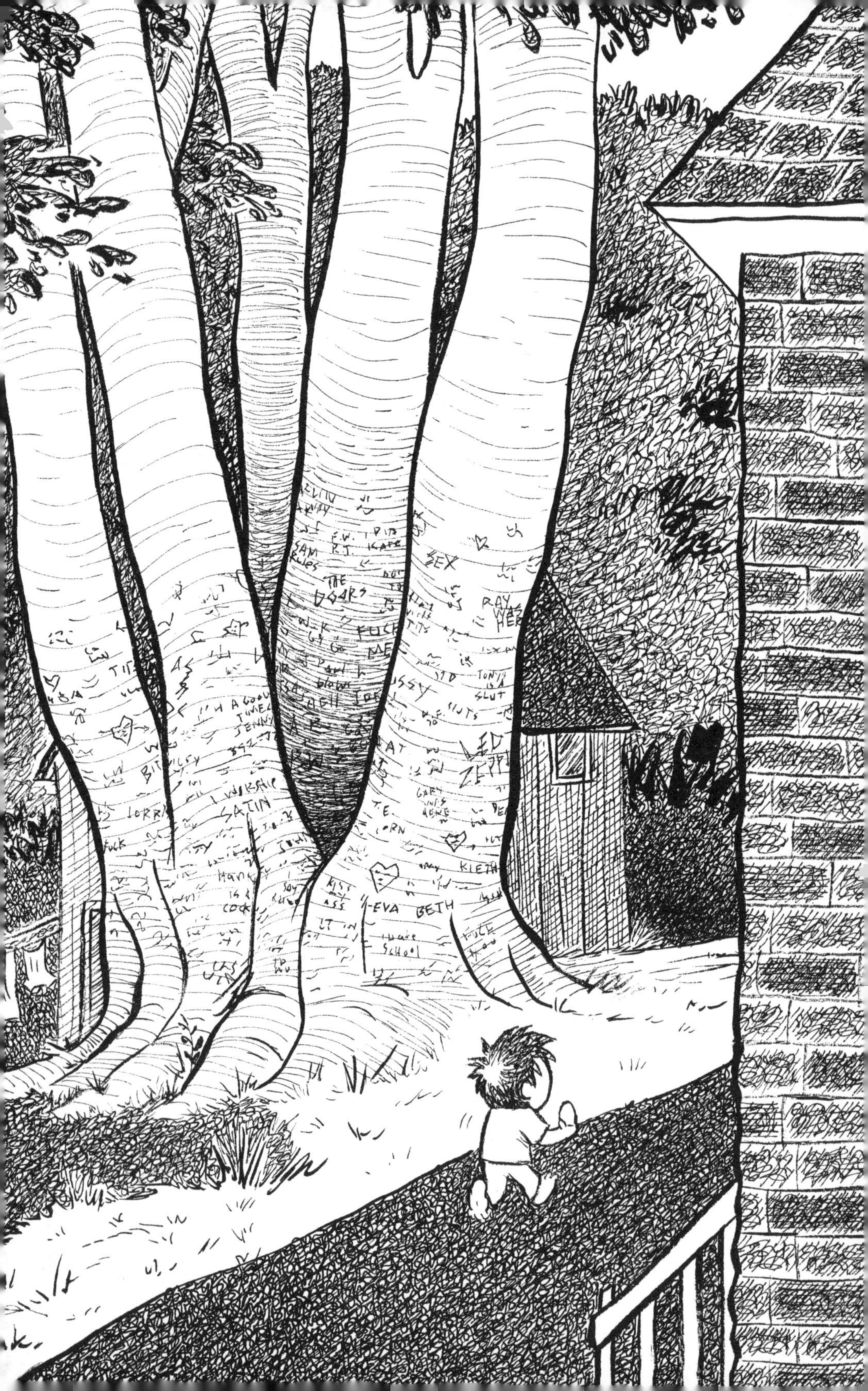
SAM RULES
SEX
THE DOORS
RAY WAS HERE
FUCK ME
TONYA IS A SLUT
SLUTS
LED ZEPP
I WORSHIP SATIN
GARY WAS HERE
T.E.
KLETH
KISS MY ASS
EVA BETH
I hate school
Hank is a cock

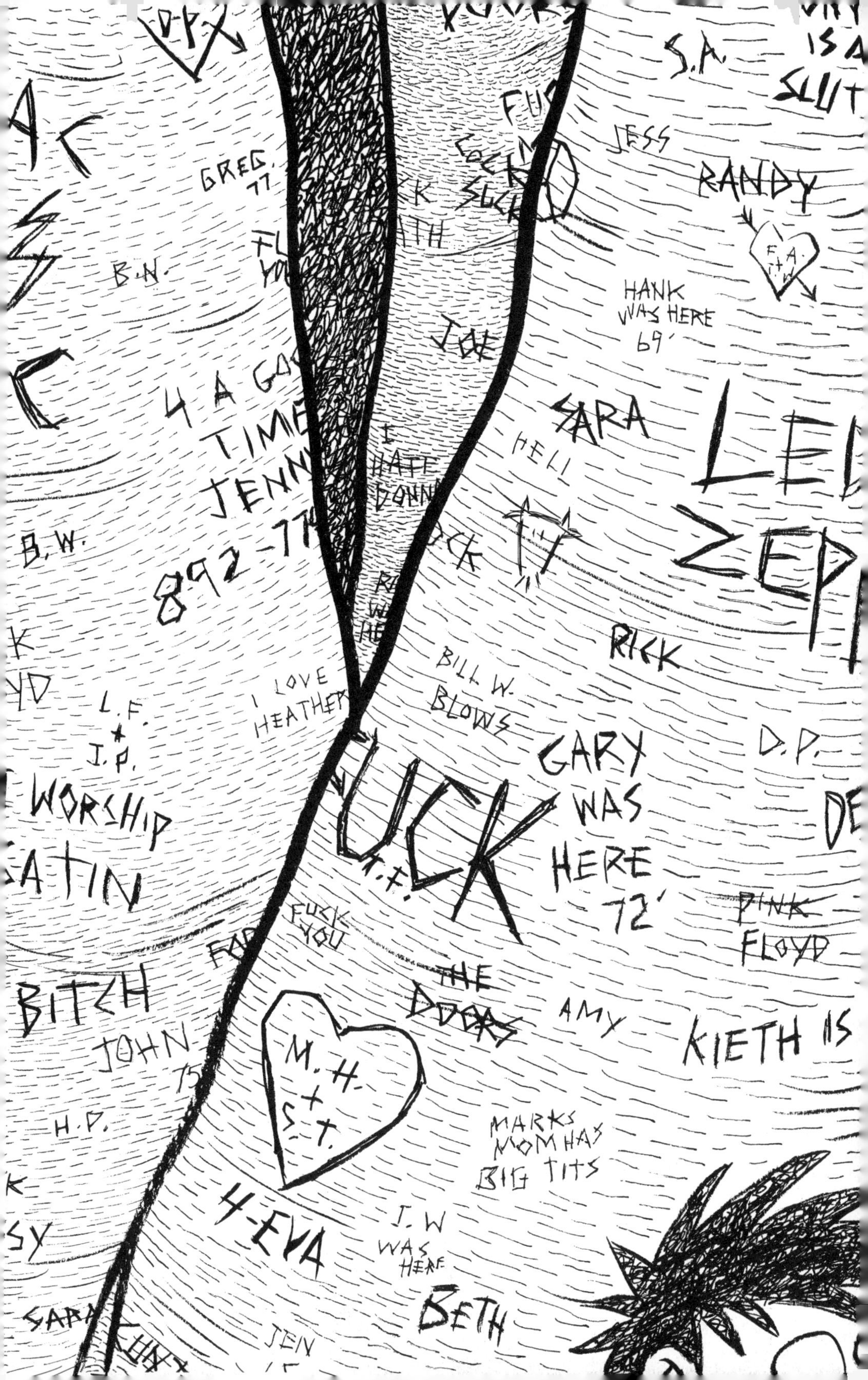
D.P.
S.A.
IS A
SLUT
JESS
RANDY
GREG 77
B.N.
HANK
WAS HERE
69'
JOE
SARA
HELL
B.W.
RICK
BILL W.
BLOWS
I LOVE
HEATHER
L.F.
J.P.
D.P.
GARY
WAS
HERE
72'
WORSHIP
PINK
FLOYD
FUCK
YOU
THE
DOORS
AMY
KIETH IS
BITCH
JOHN
75
H.P.
M.H.
+
S.T.
MARKS
MOM HAS
BIG TITS
4-EVA
T.W
WAS
HERE
BETH
JEN

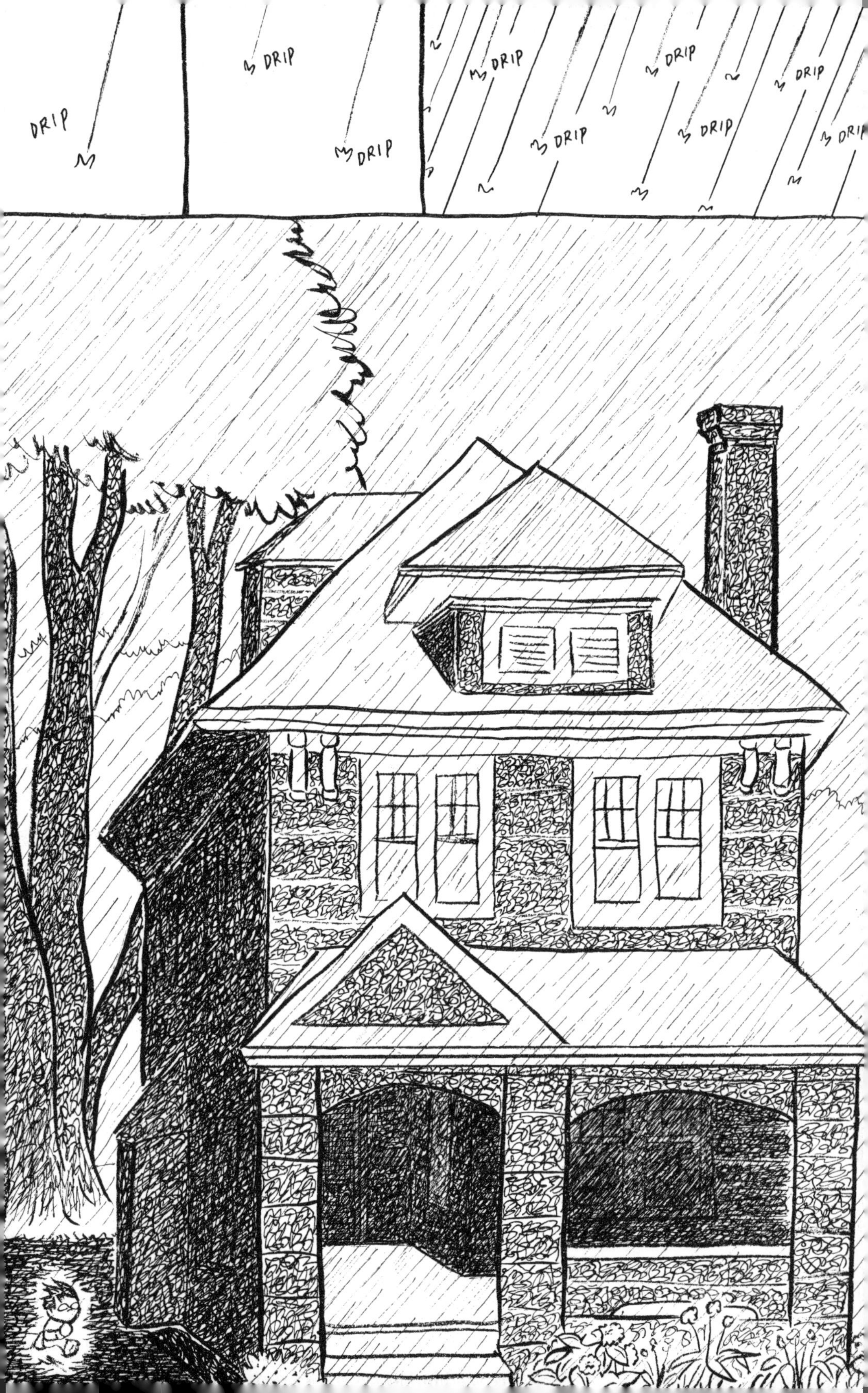
DRIP
DRIP
DRIP
DRIP
DRIP
DRIP
DRIP
DRIP
DRIP

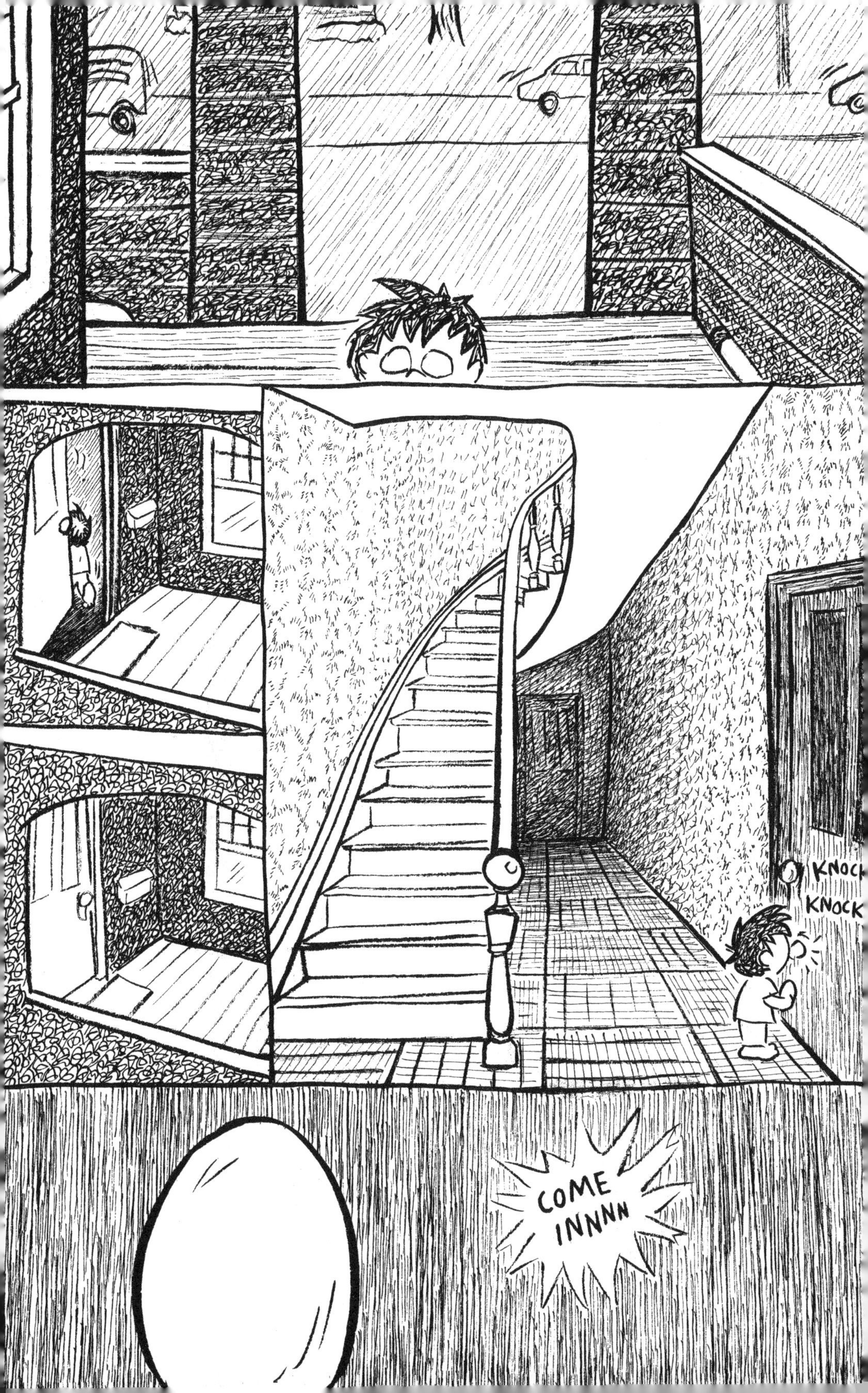
KNOCK
KNOCK
COME INNNN

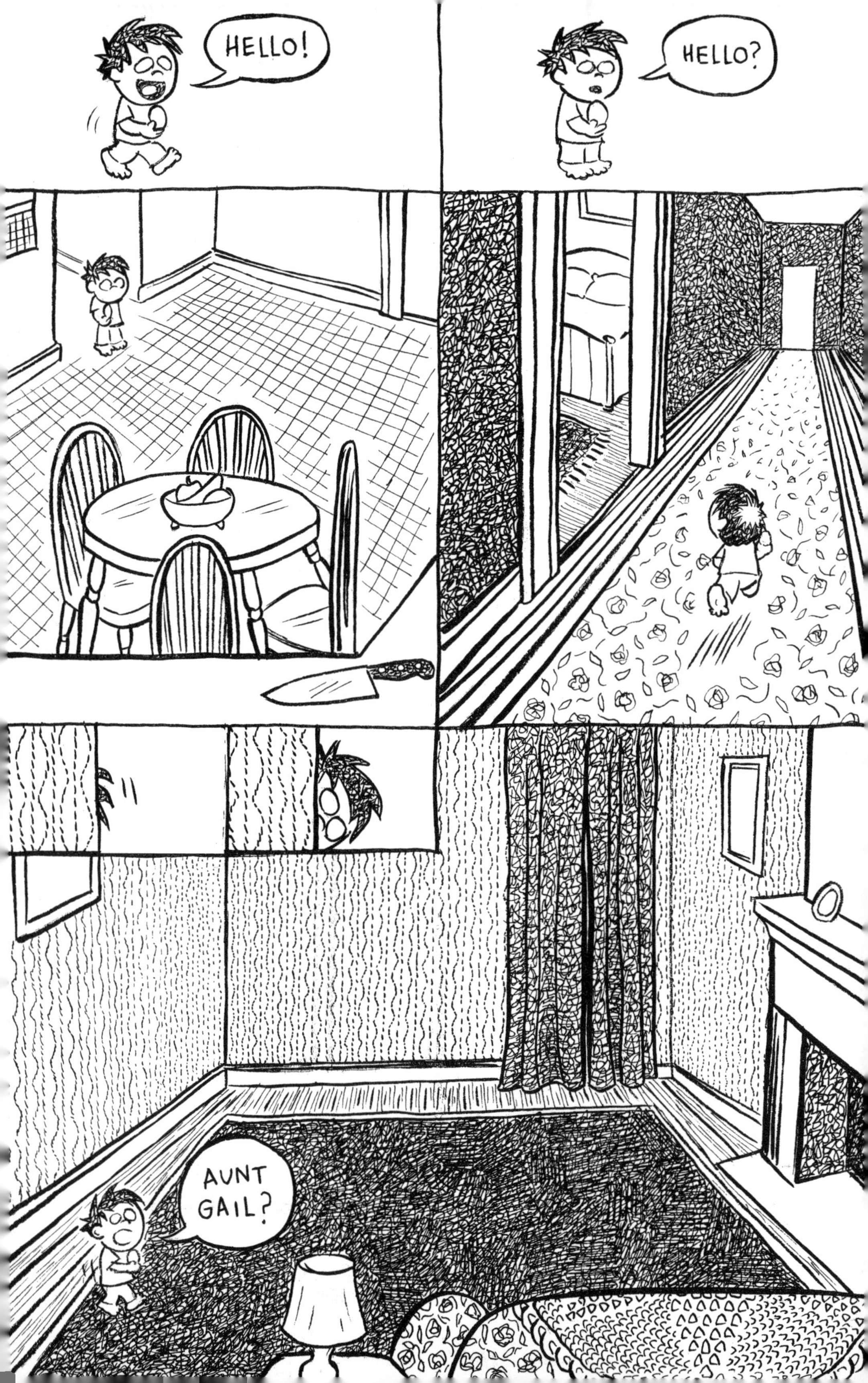
HELLO!
HELLO?
AUNT GAIL?

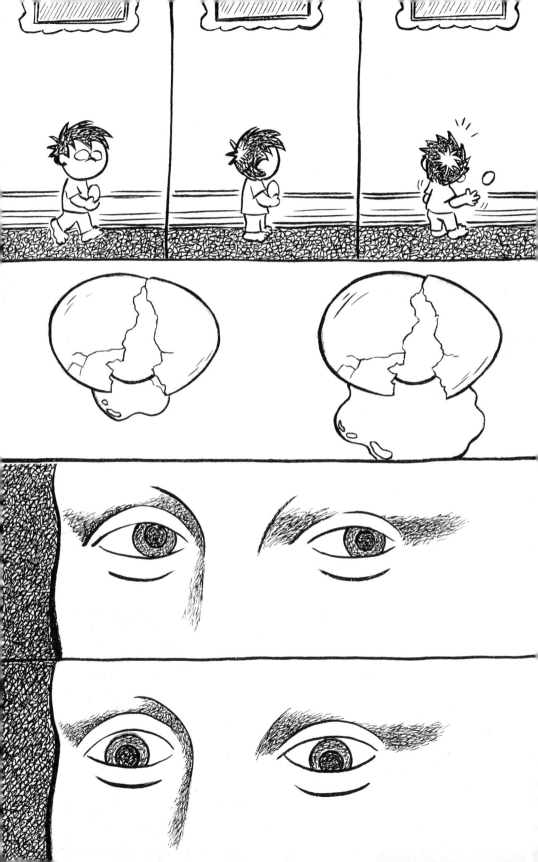

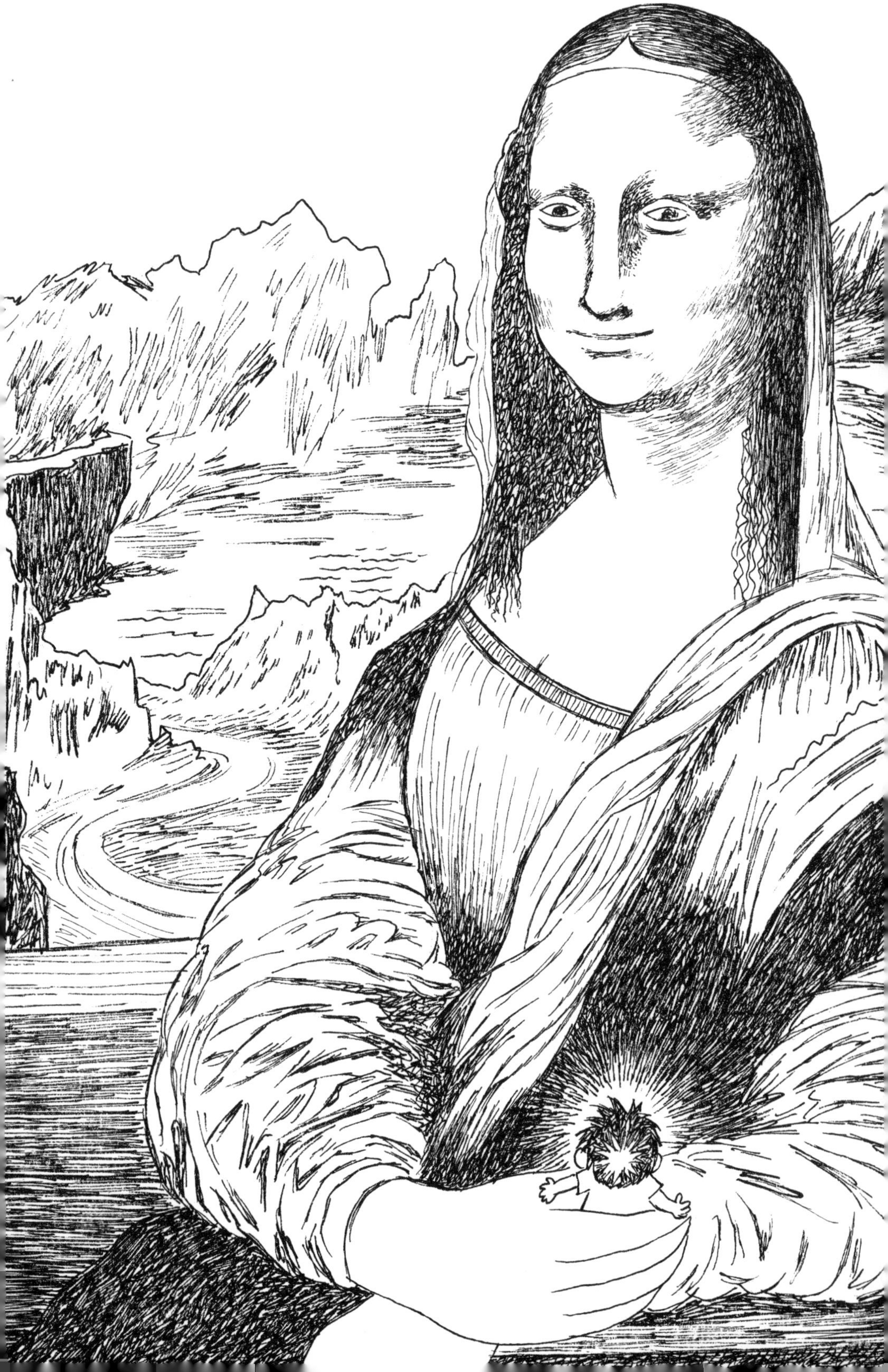

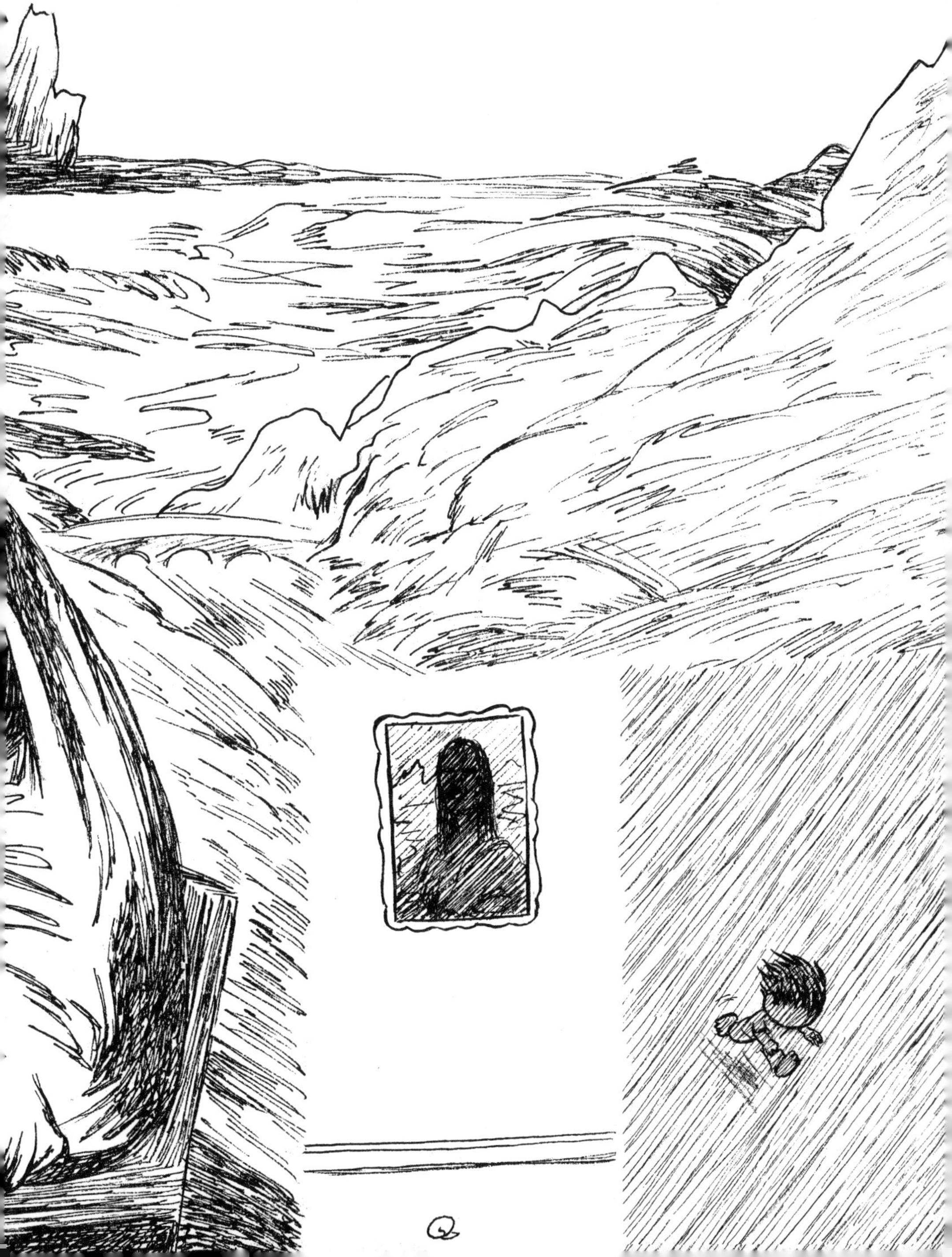

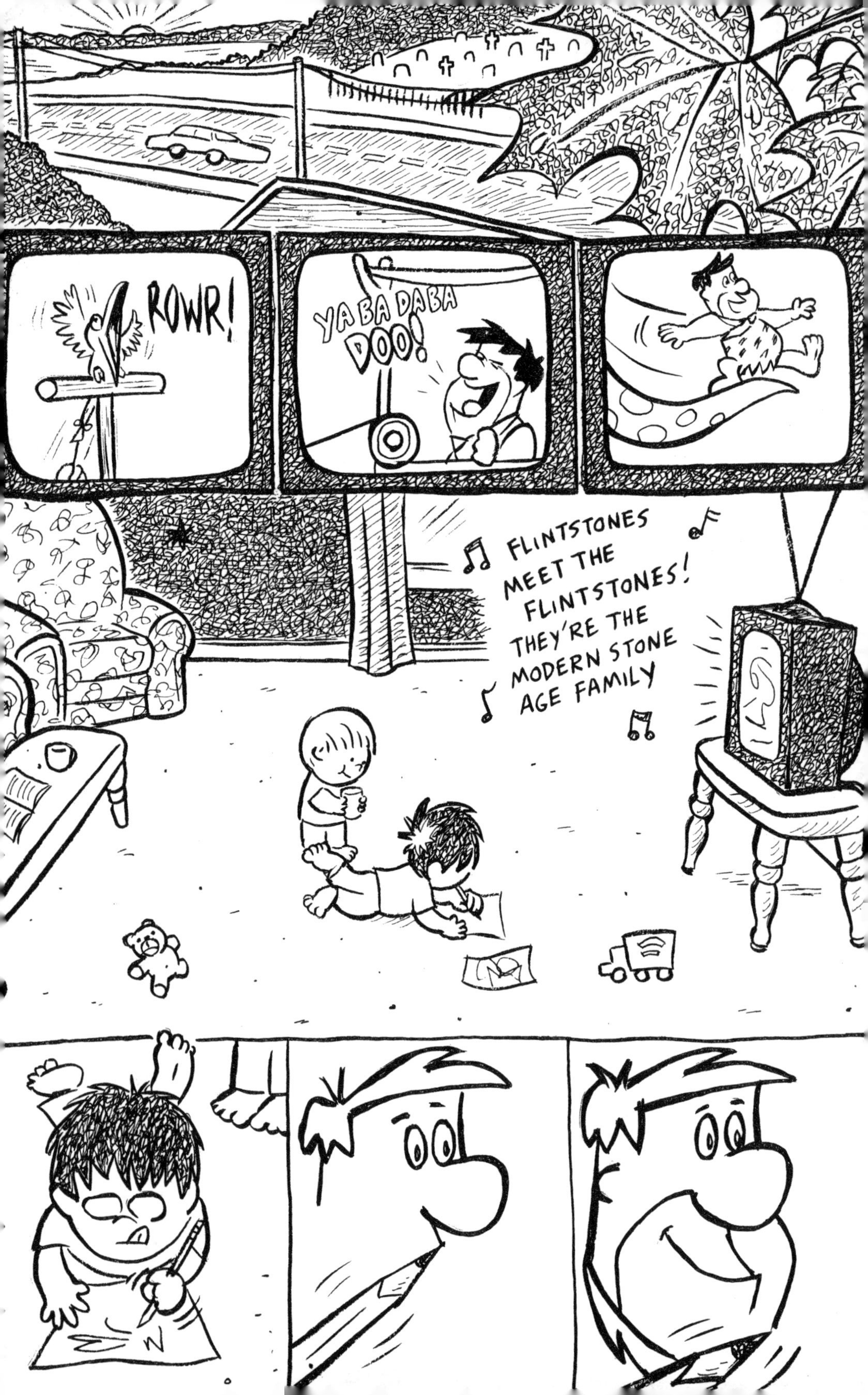
ROWR!
YA BA DABA DOO!
FLINTSTONES MEET THE FLINTSTONES! THEY'RE THE MODERN STONE AGE FAMILY

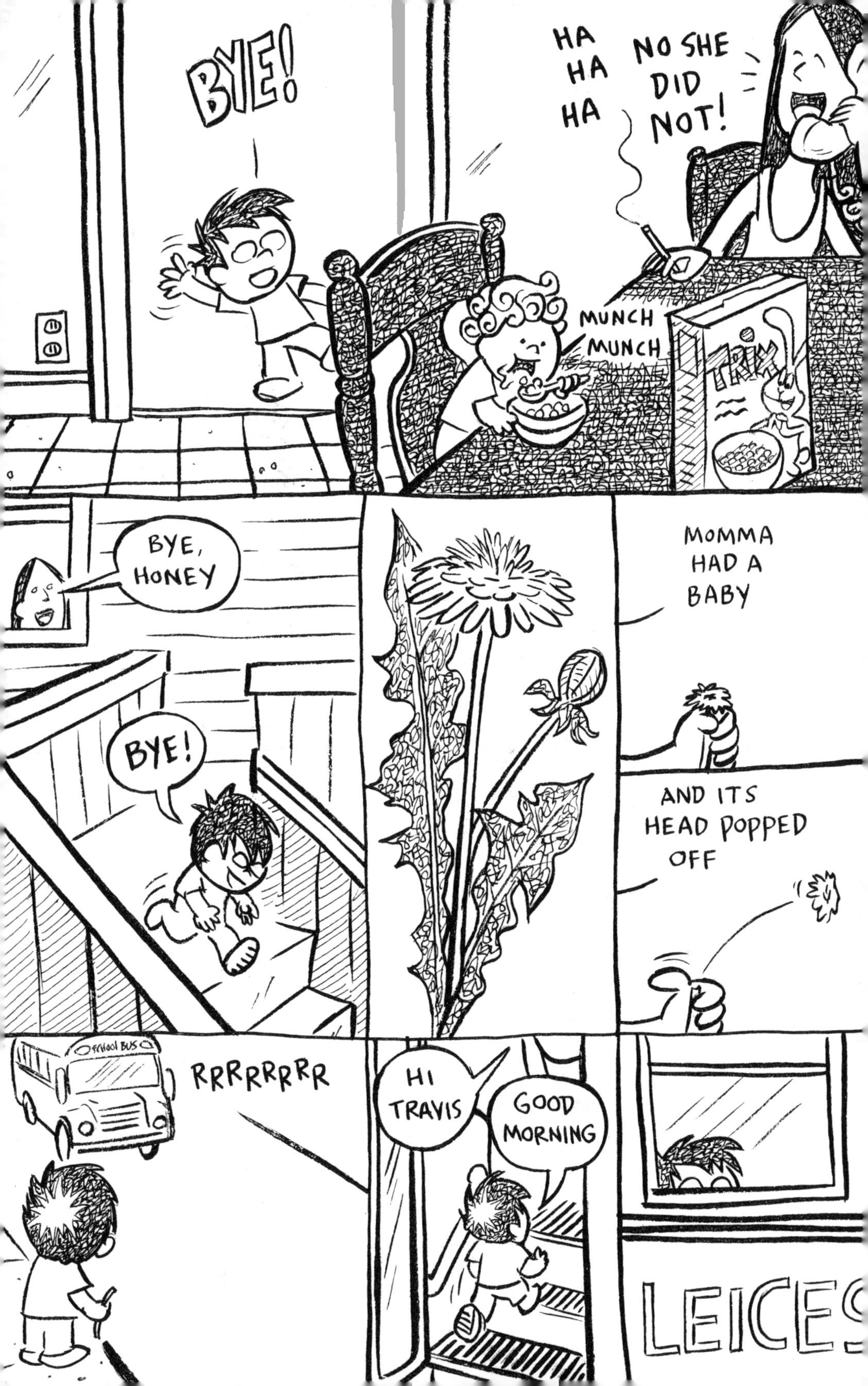
BYE!
HA HA HA
NO SHE DID NOT!
MUNCH MUNCH
TRIX
BYE, HONEY
BYE!
MOMMA HAD A BABY
AND ITS HEAD POPPED OFF
SCHOOL BUS
RRRRRRRR
HI TRAVIS
GOOD MORNING
LEICES

SLUURRP

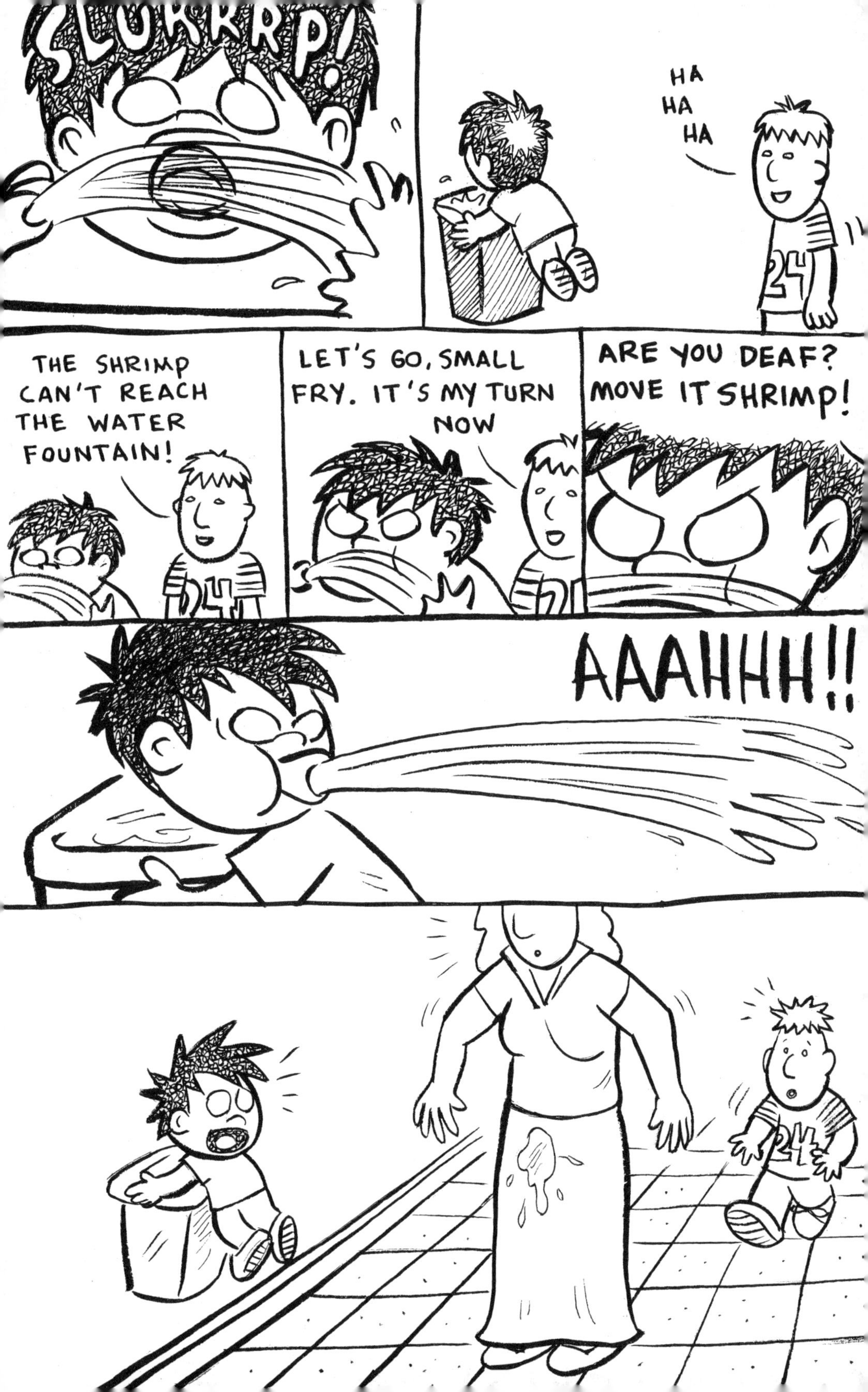
SLURRRP!
HA HA HA
THE SHRIMP CAN'T REACH THE WATER FOUNTAIN!
LET'S GO, SMALL FRY. IT'S MY TURN NOW
ARE YOU DEAF? MOVE IT SHRIMP!
AAAHHH!!

Travis Cormier

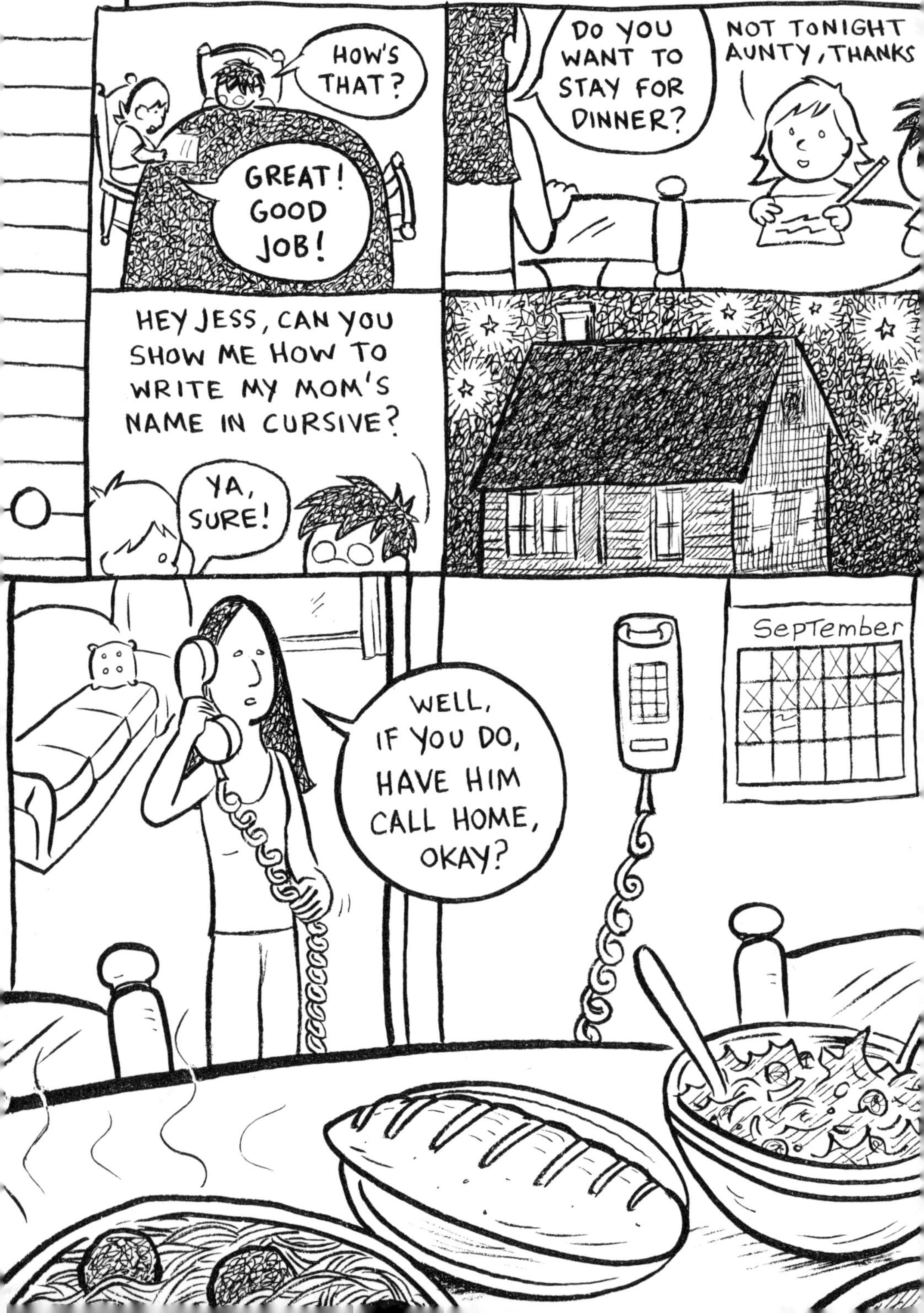
HOW'S THAT?
GREAT! GOOD JOB!
DO YOU WANT TO STAY FOR DINNER?
NOT TONIGHT AUNTY, THANKS
HEY JESS, CAN YOU SHOW ME HOW TO WRITE MY MOM'S NAME IN CURSIVE?
YA, SURE!
WELL, IF YOU DO, HAVE HIM CALL HOME, OKAY?
September

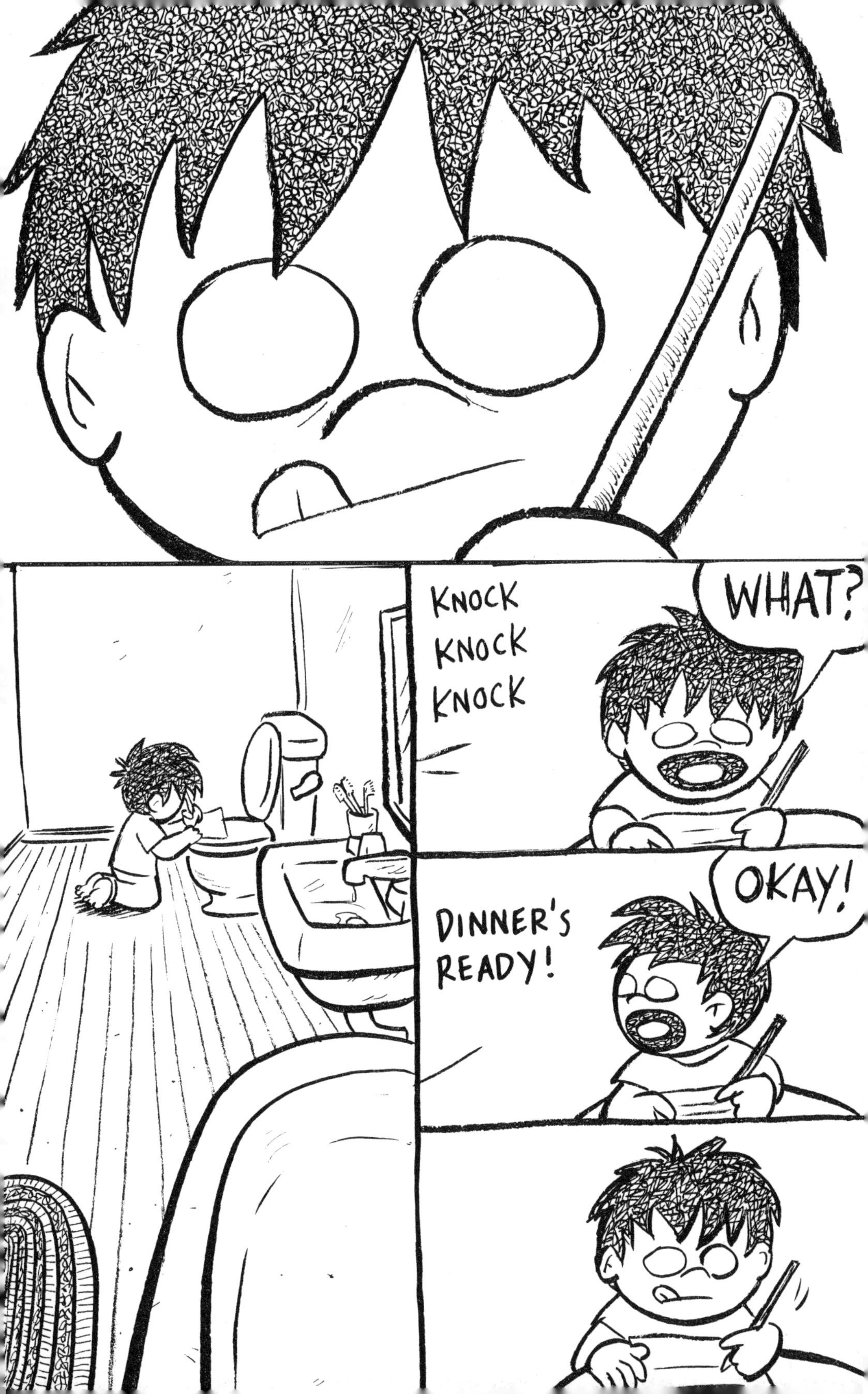
KNOCK
KNOCK
KNOCK
WHAT?
DINNER'S READY!
OKAY!

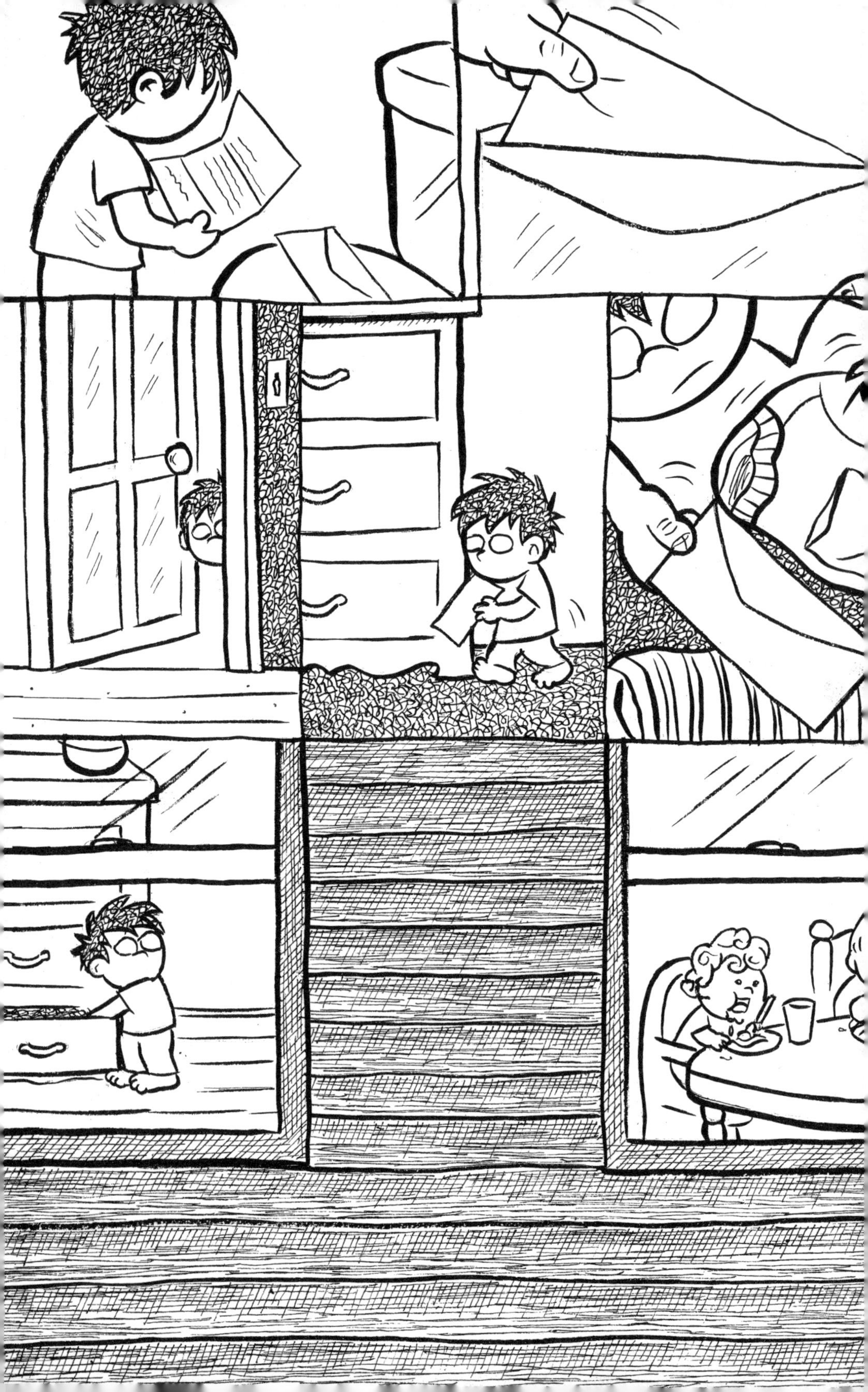

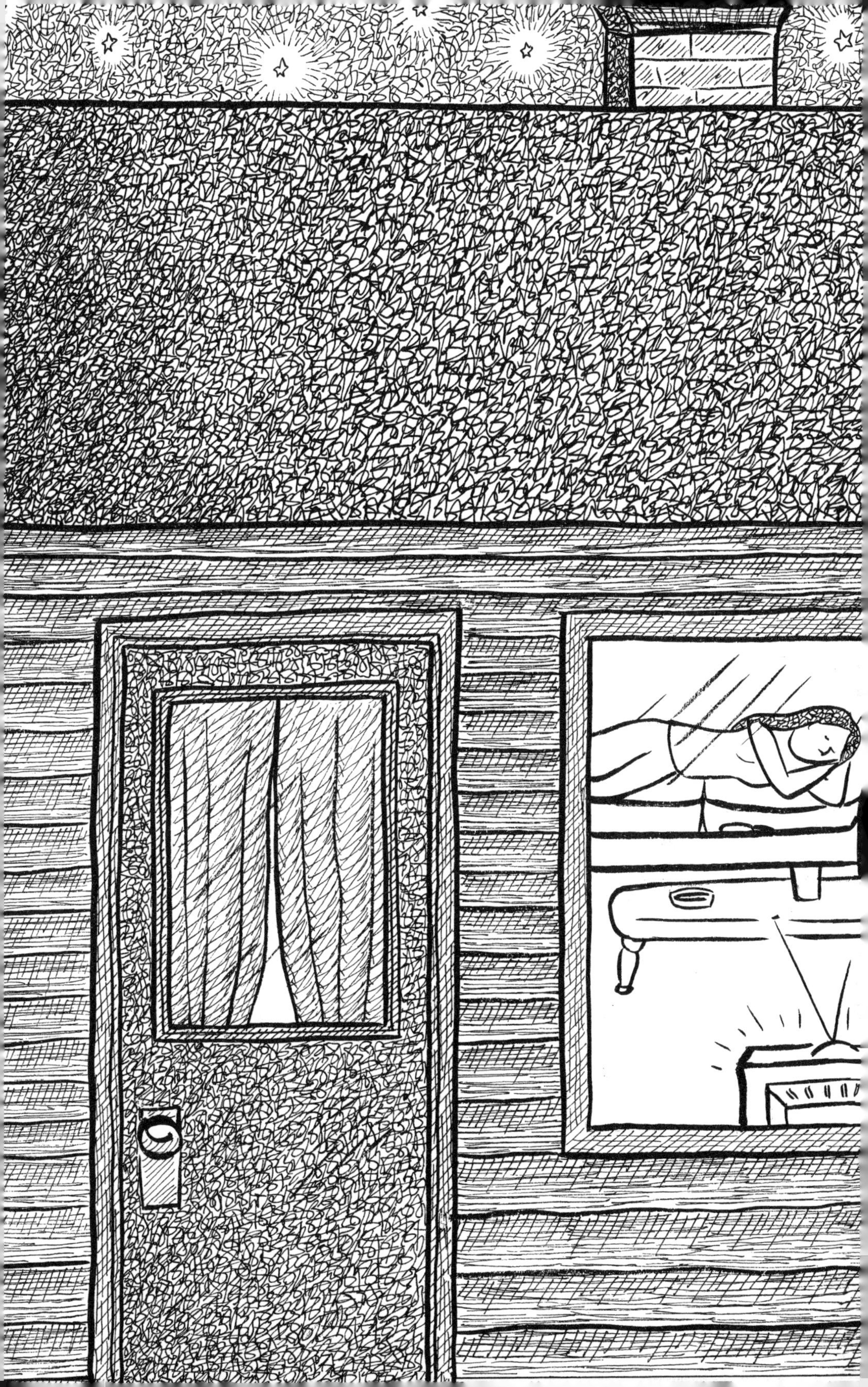

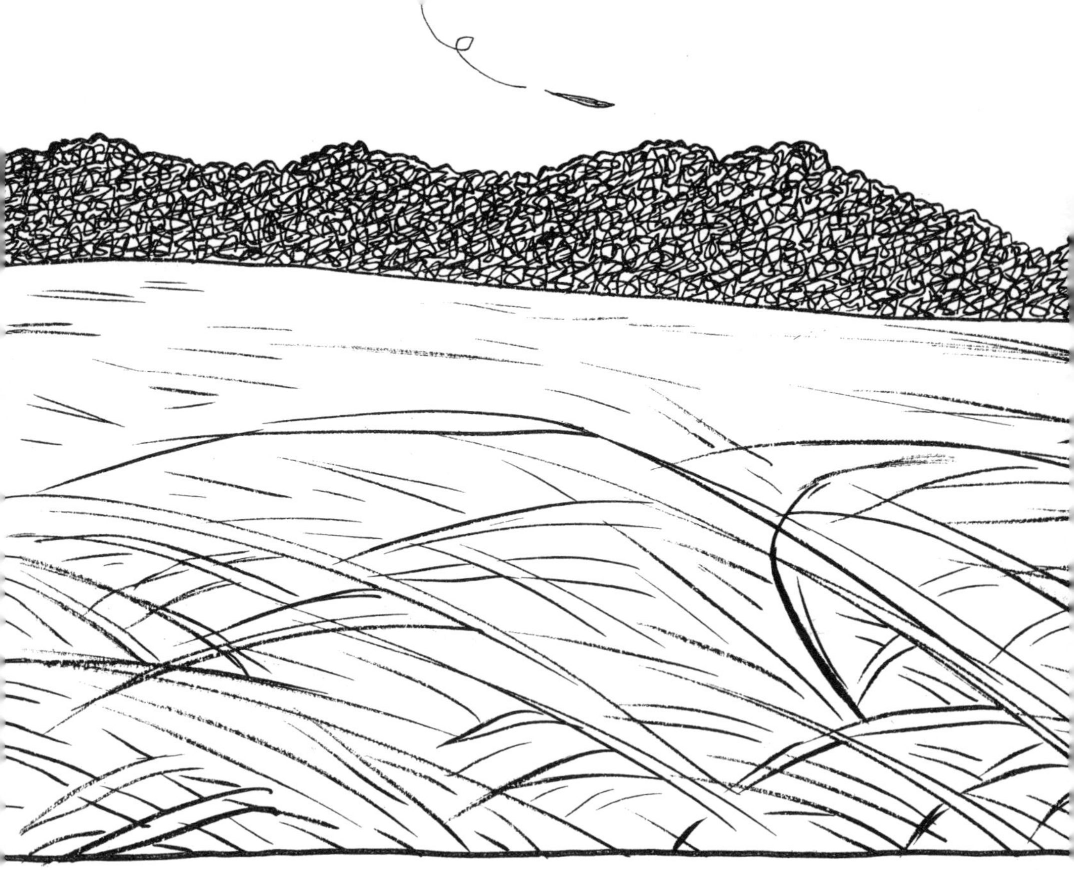
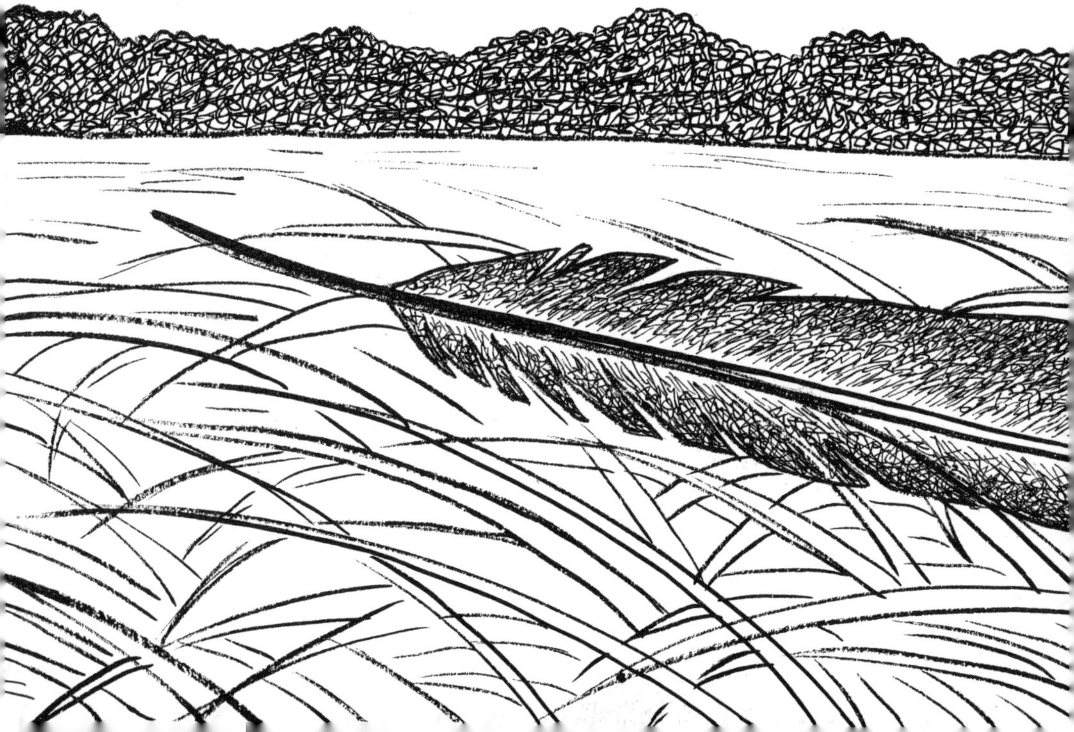

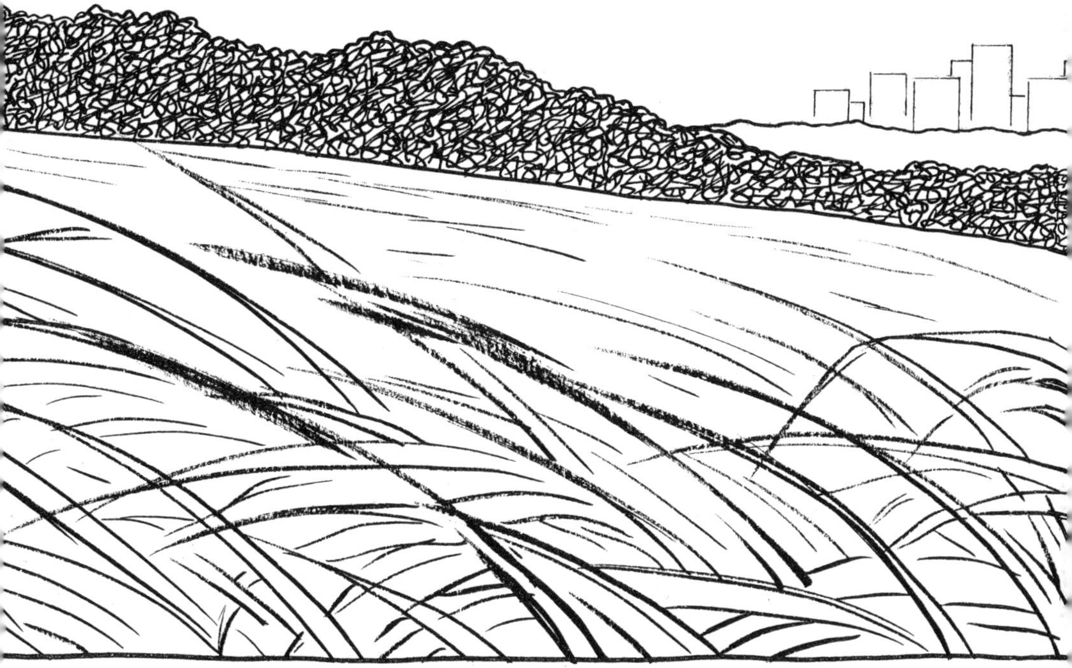

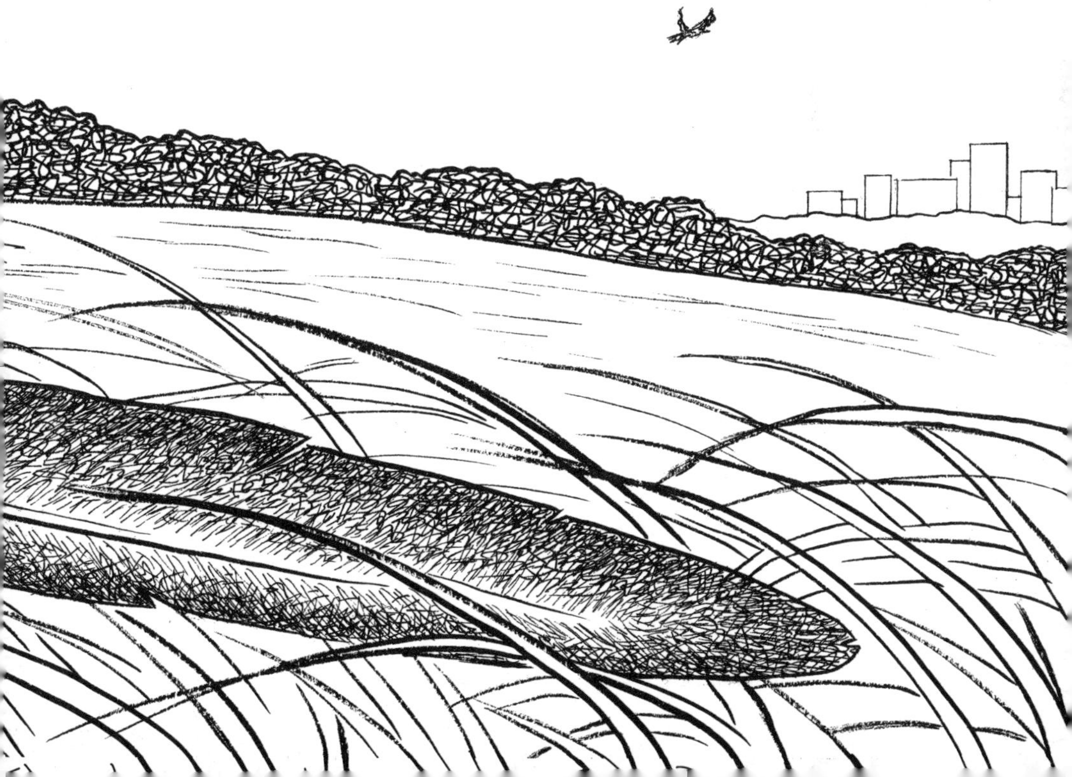

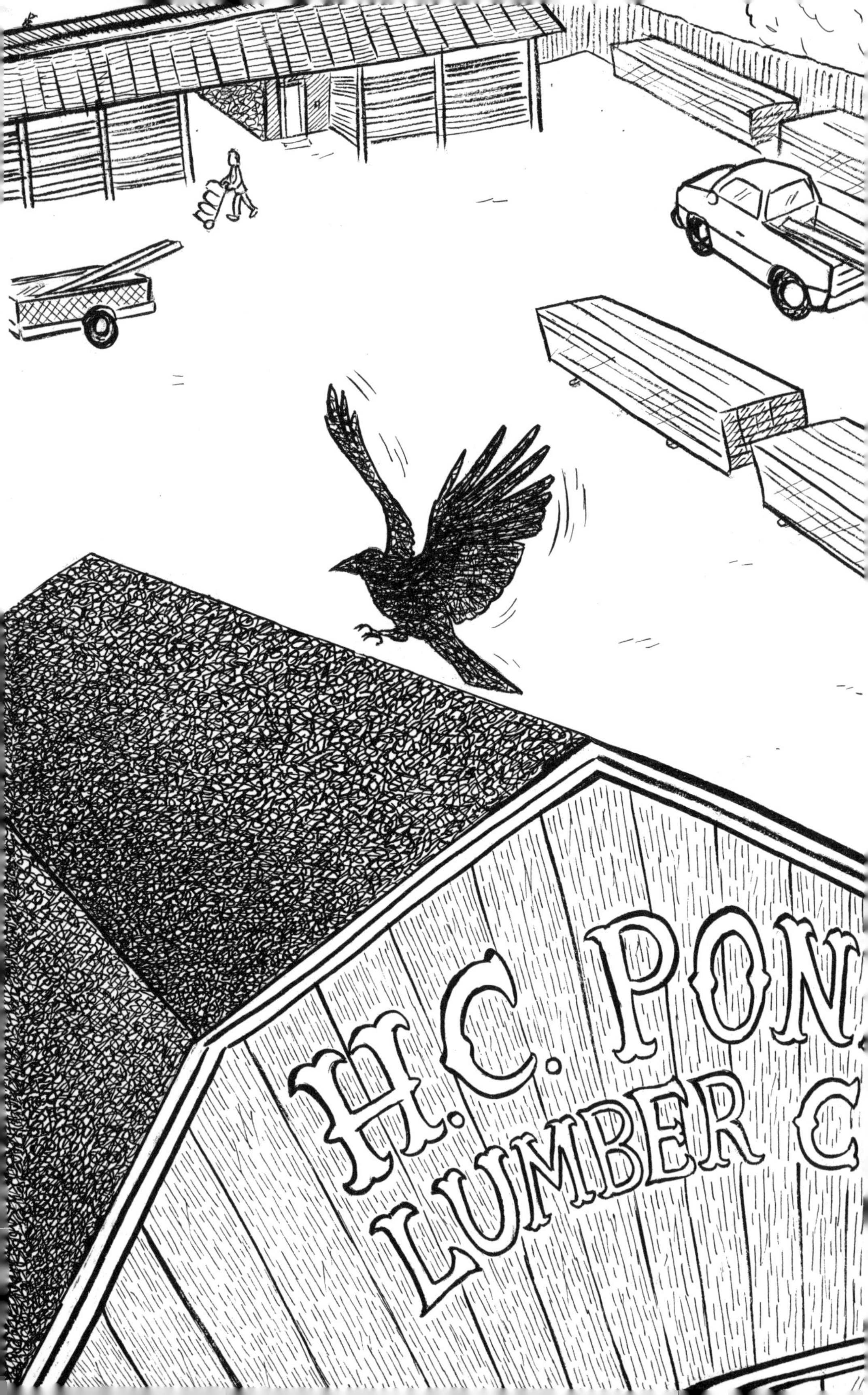
H.C. PON
LUMBER C

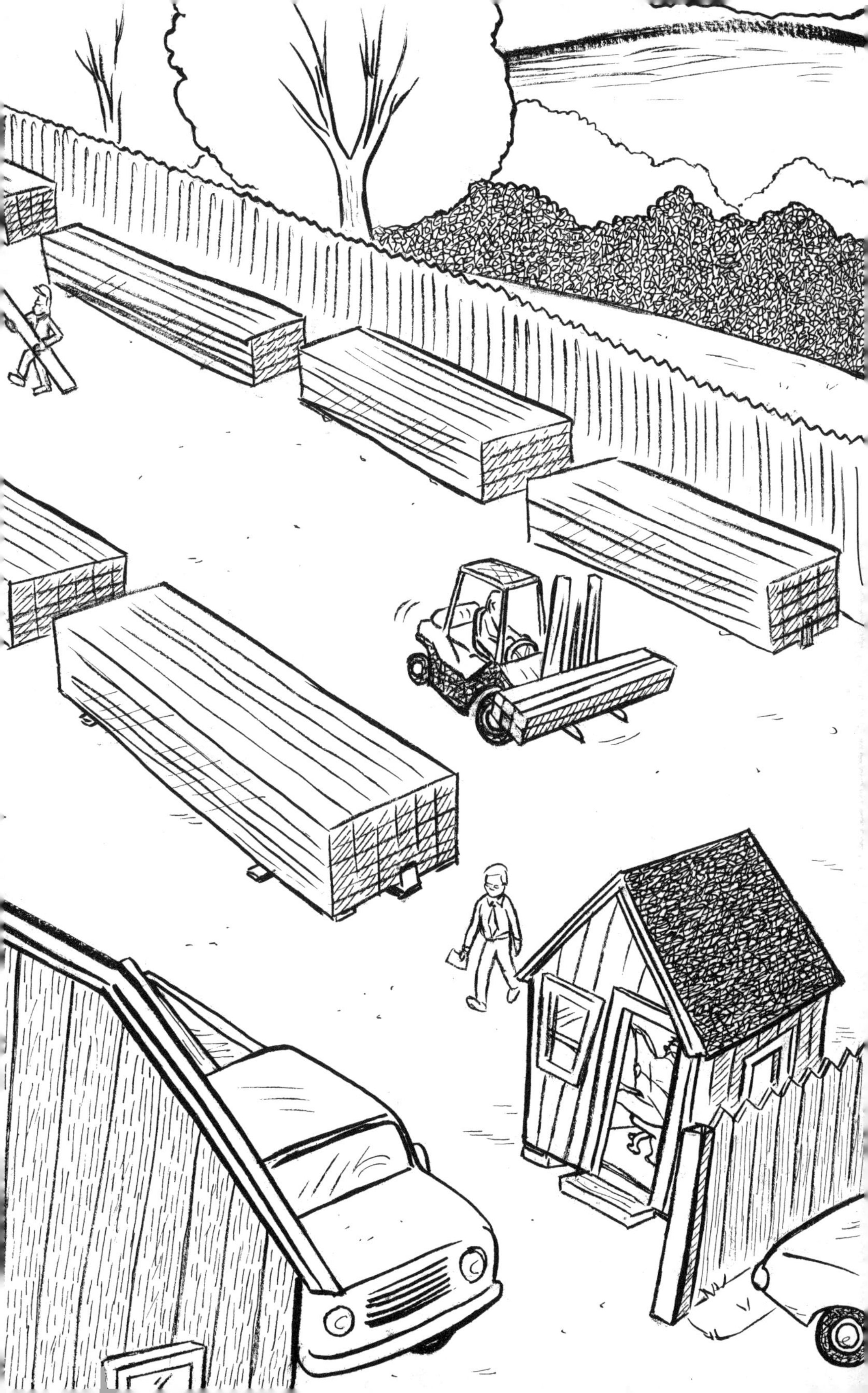

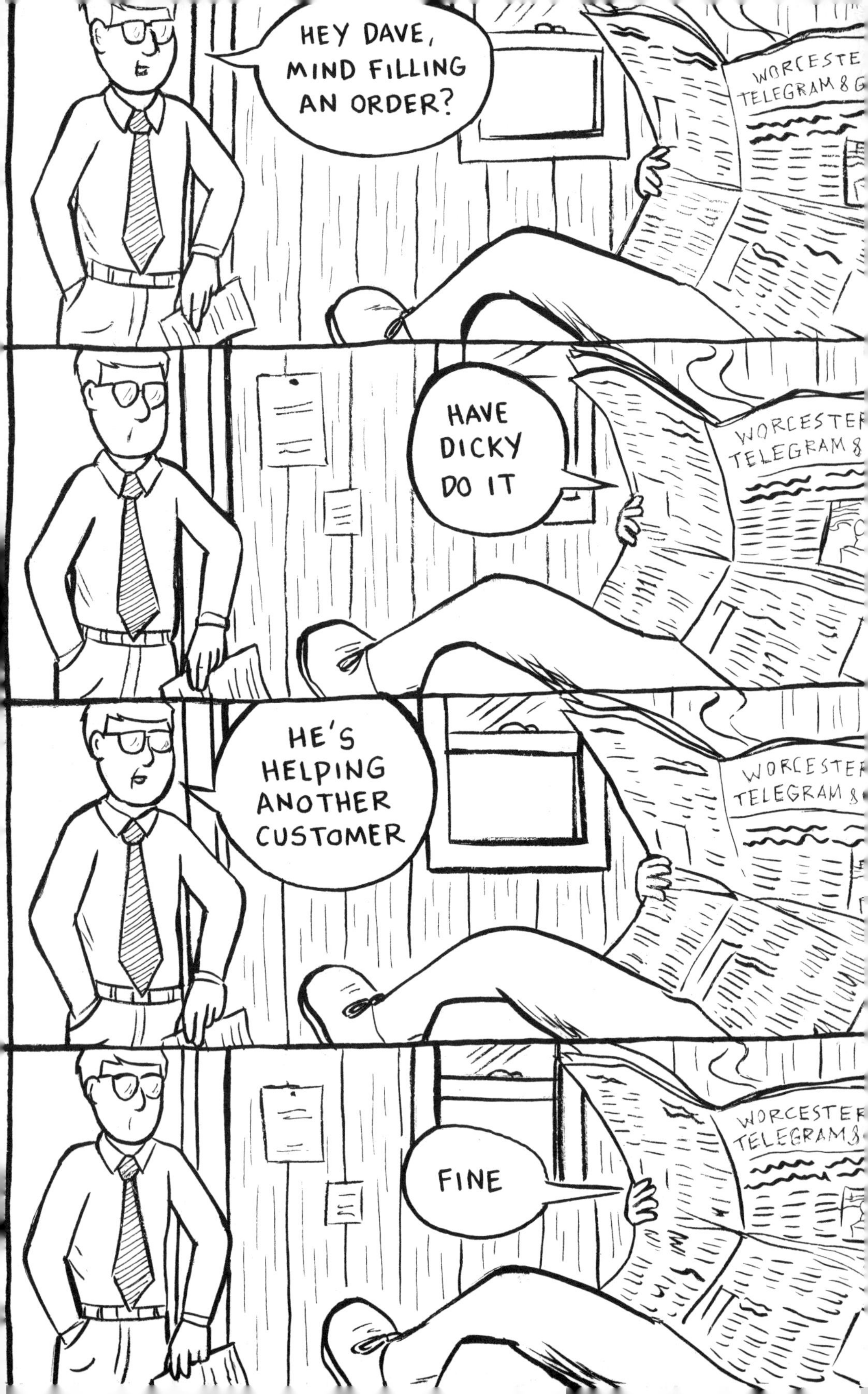
HEY DAVE, MIND FILLING AN ORDER?
WORCESTER TELEGRAM &
HAVE DICKY DO IT
HE'S HELPING ANOTHER CUSTOMER
FINE

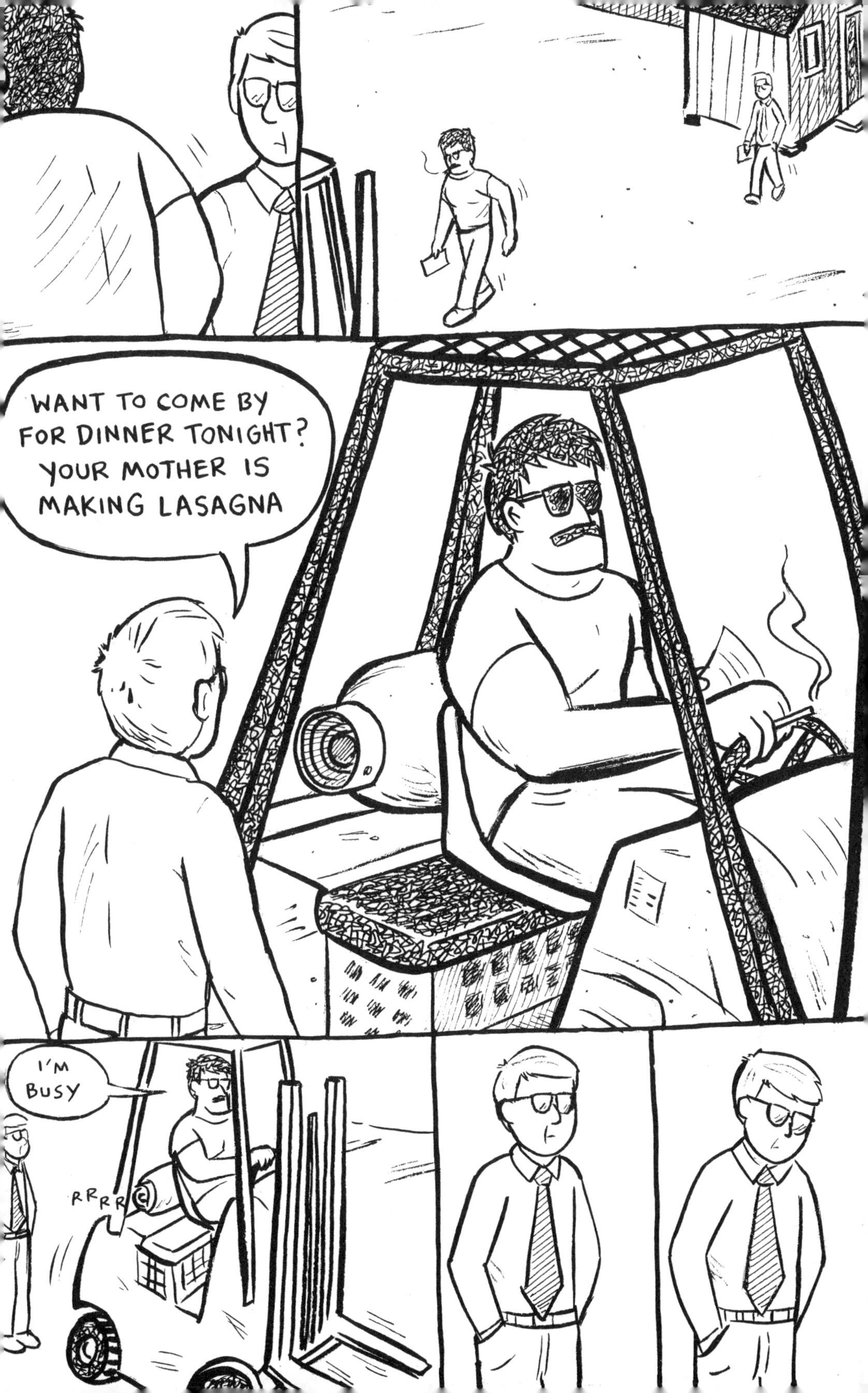
WANT TO COME BY FOR DINNER TONIGHT? YOUR MOTHER IS MAKING LASAGNA
I'M BUSY
RRRR

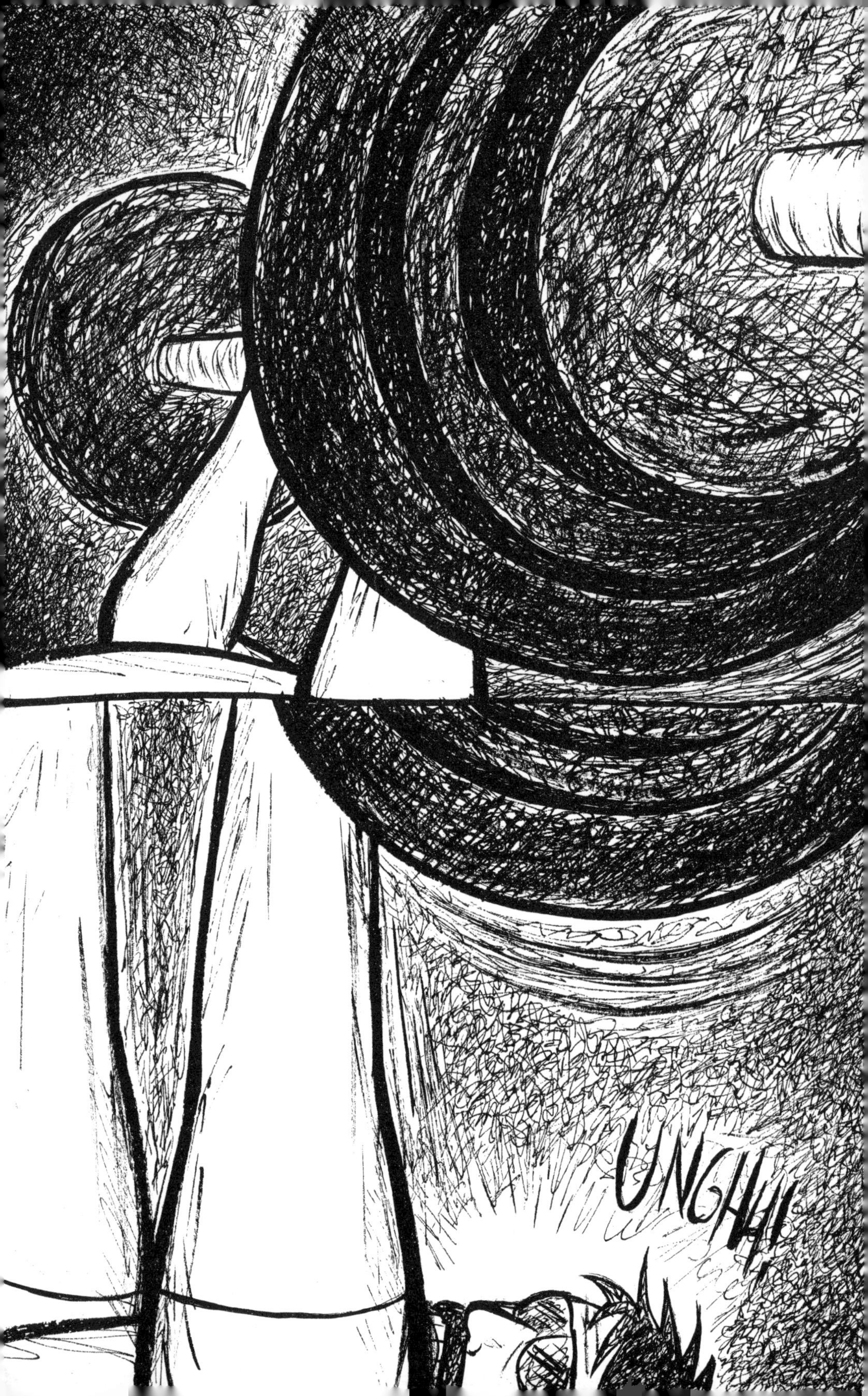
UNGHH!

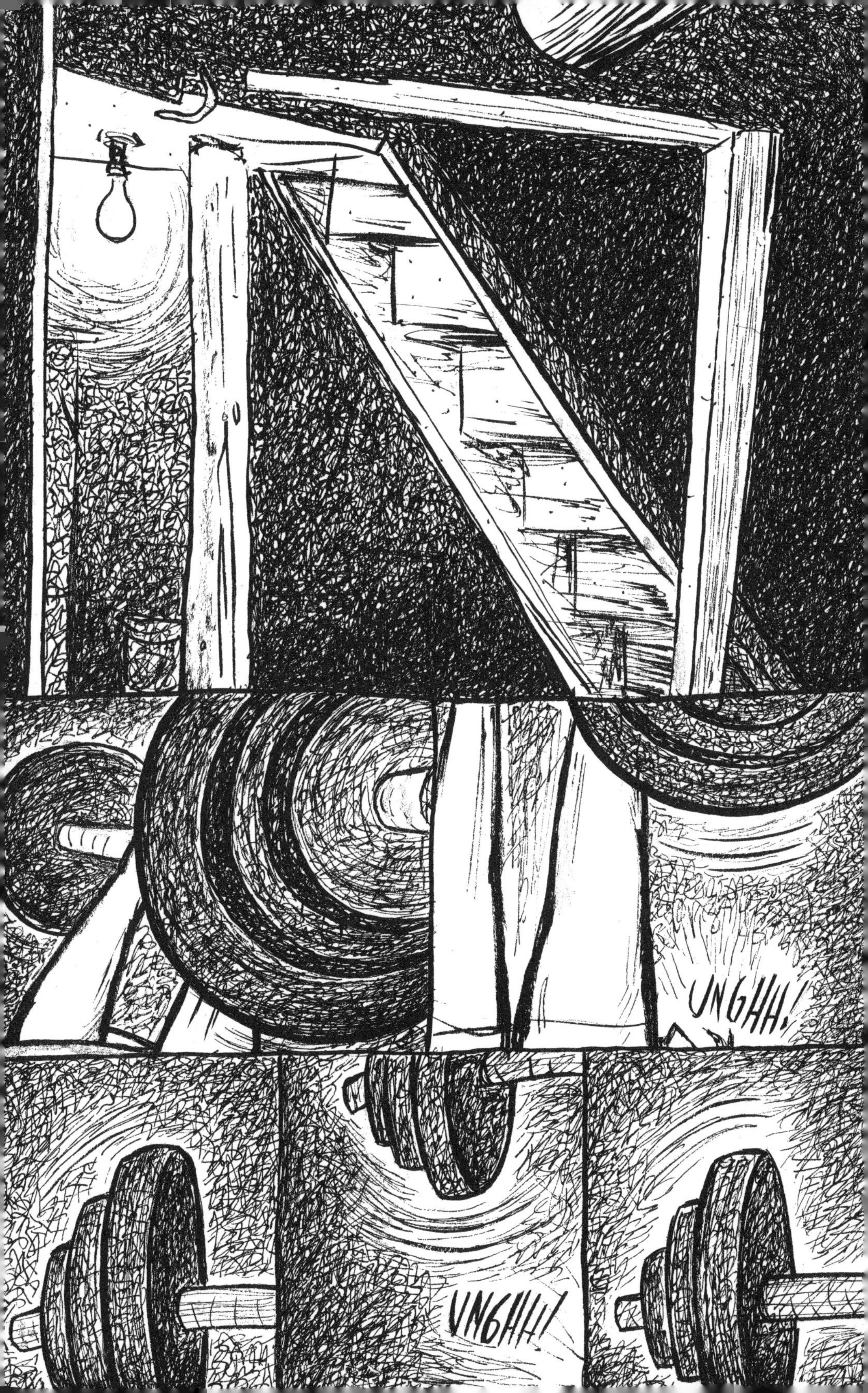
UNGHH!
UNGHH!

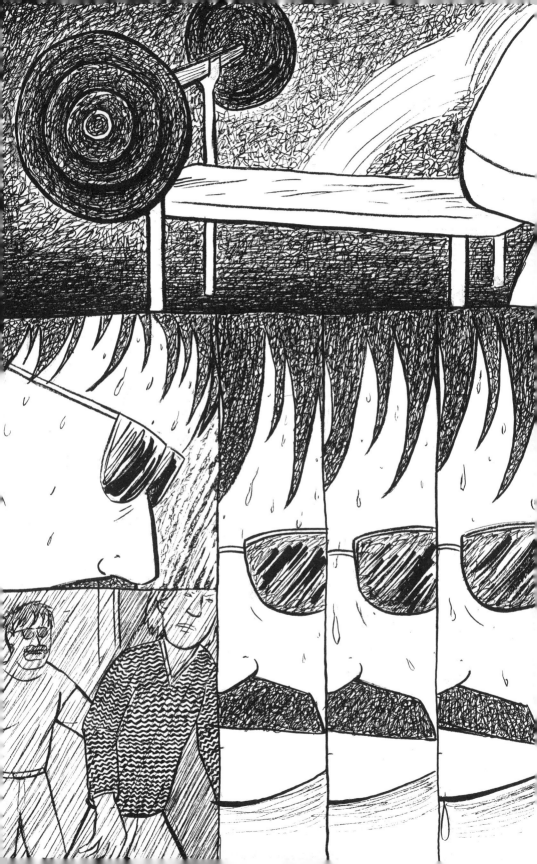

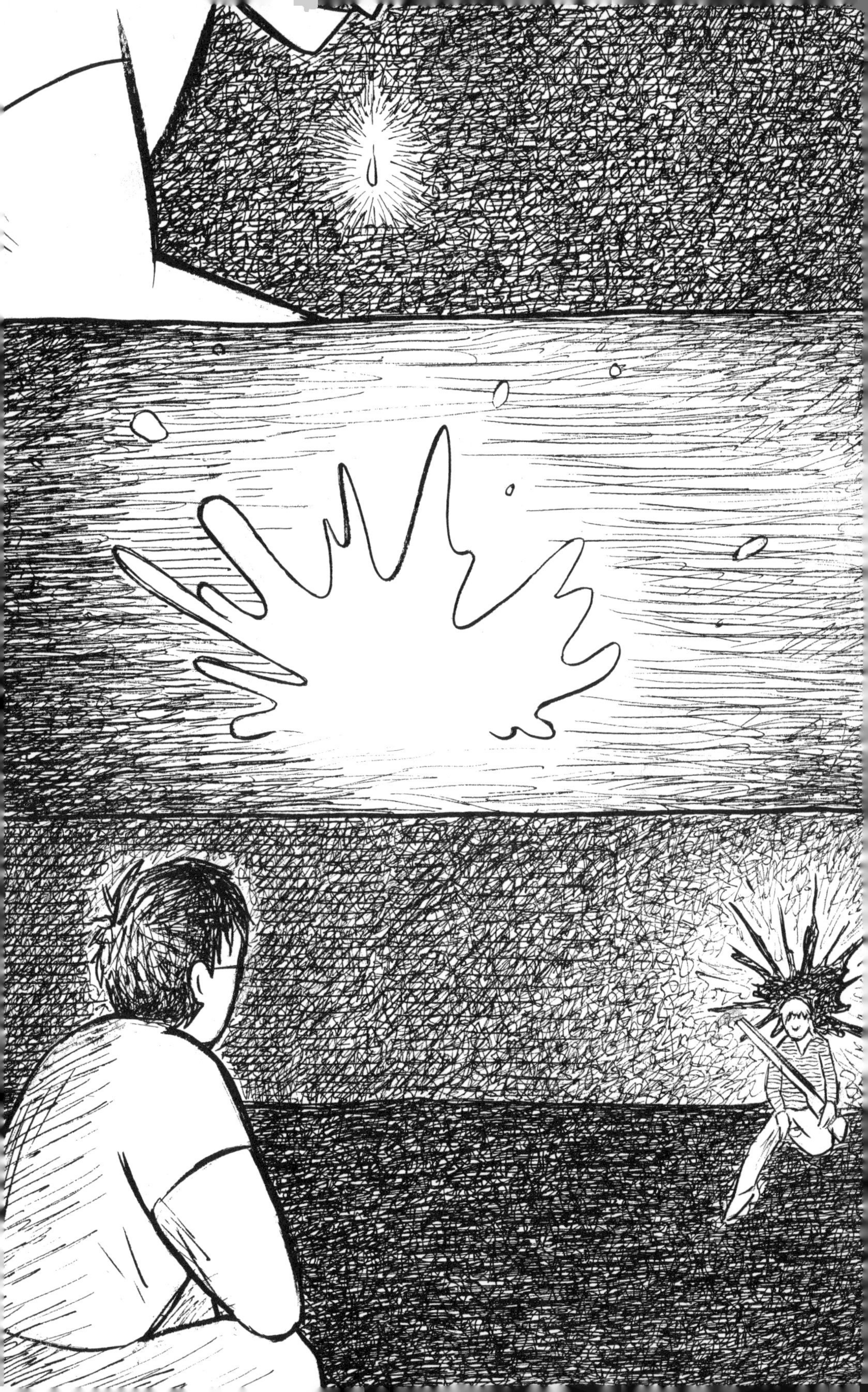

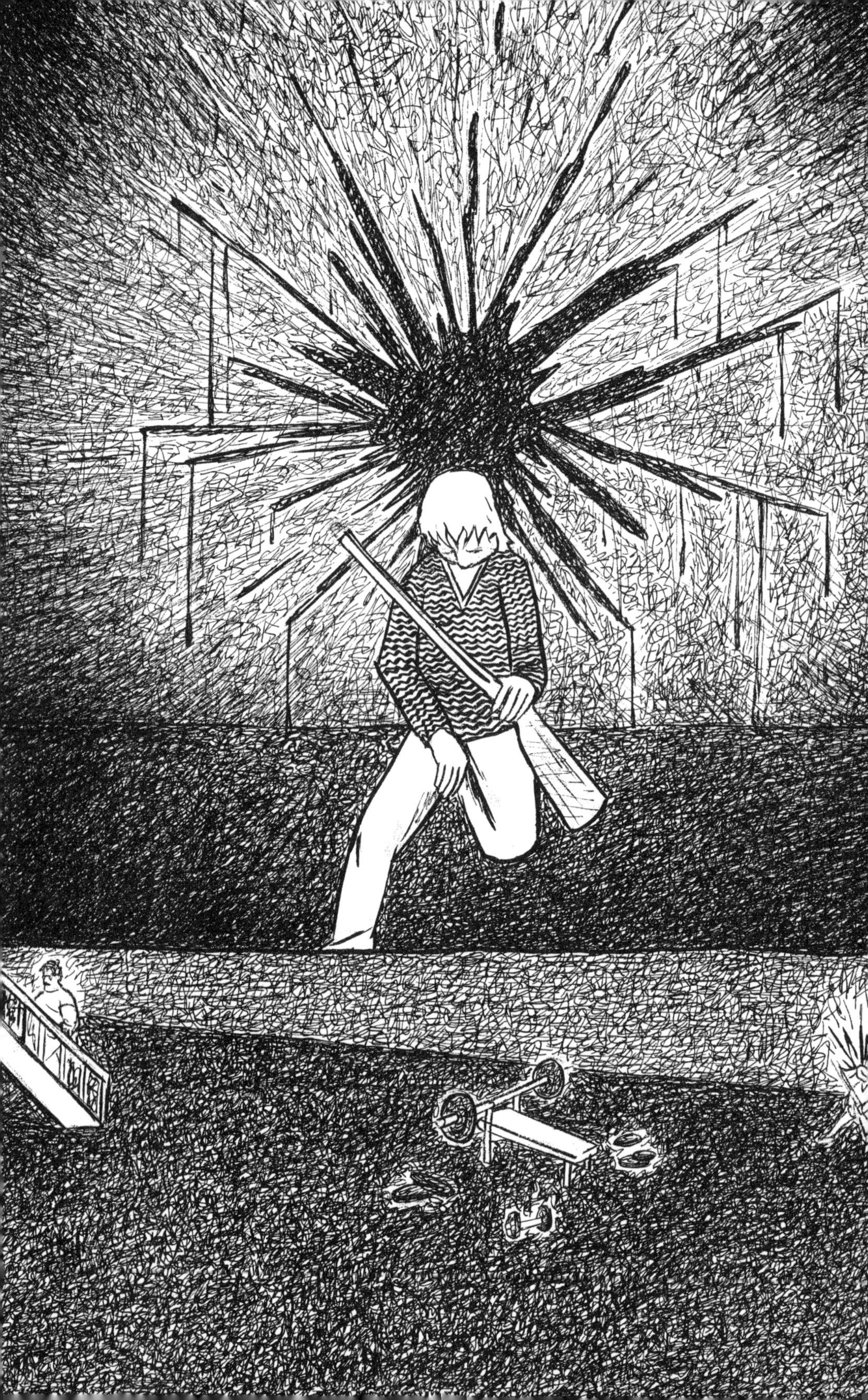

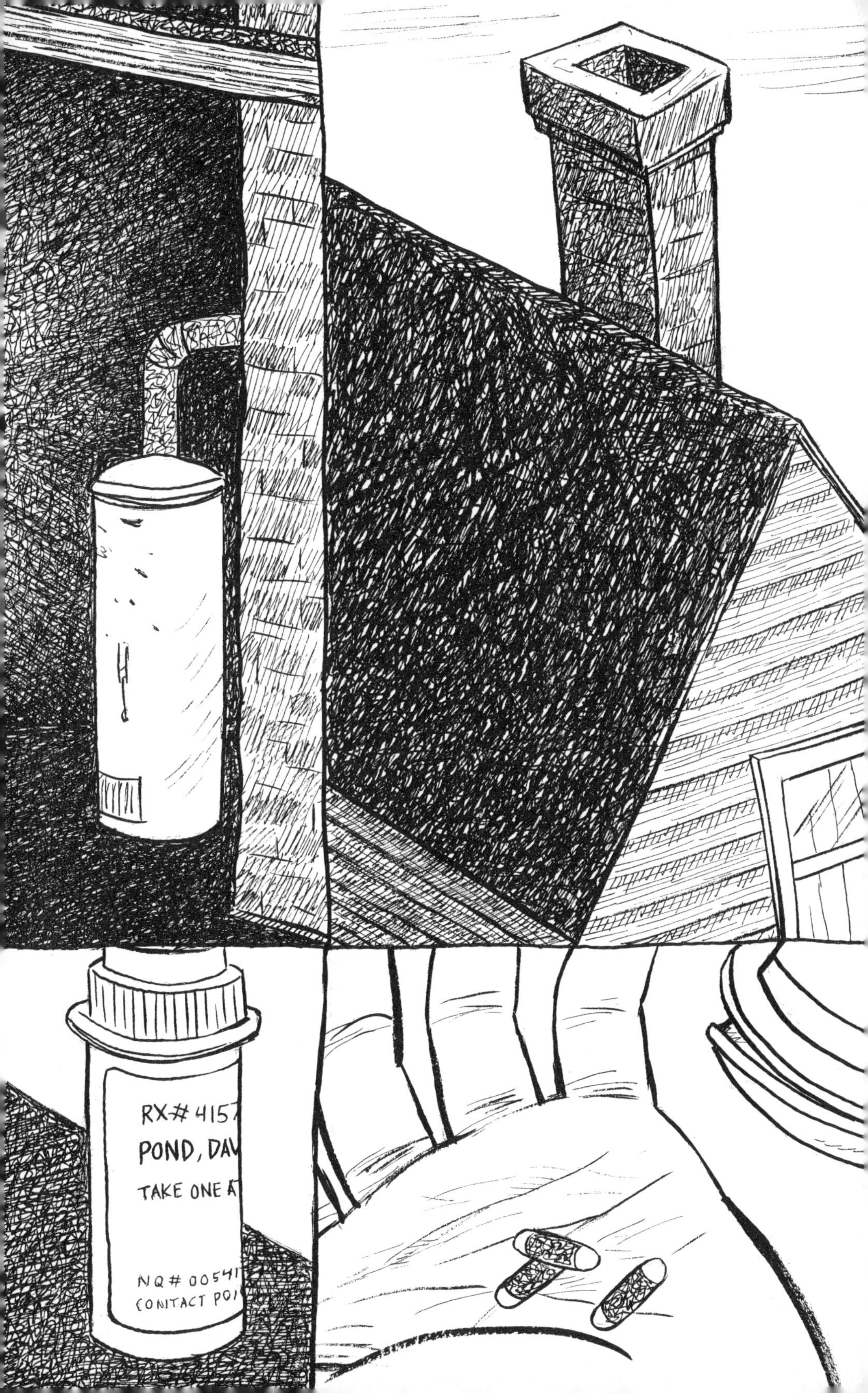
RX# 415
POND, DAV
TAKE ONE A
NQ# 00541
CONTACT PO

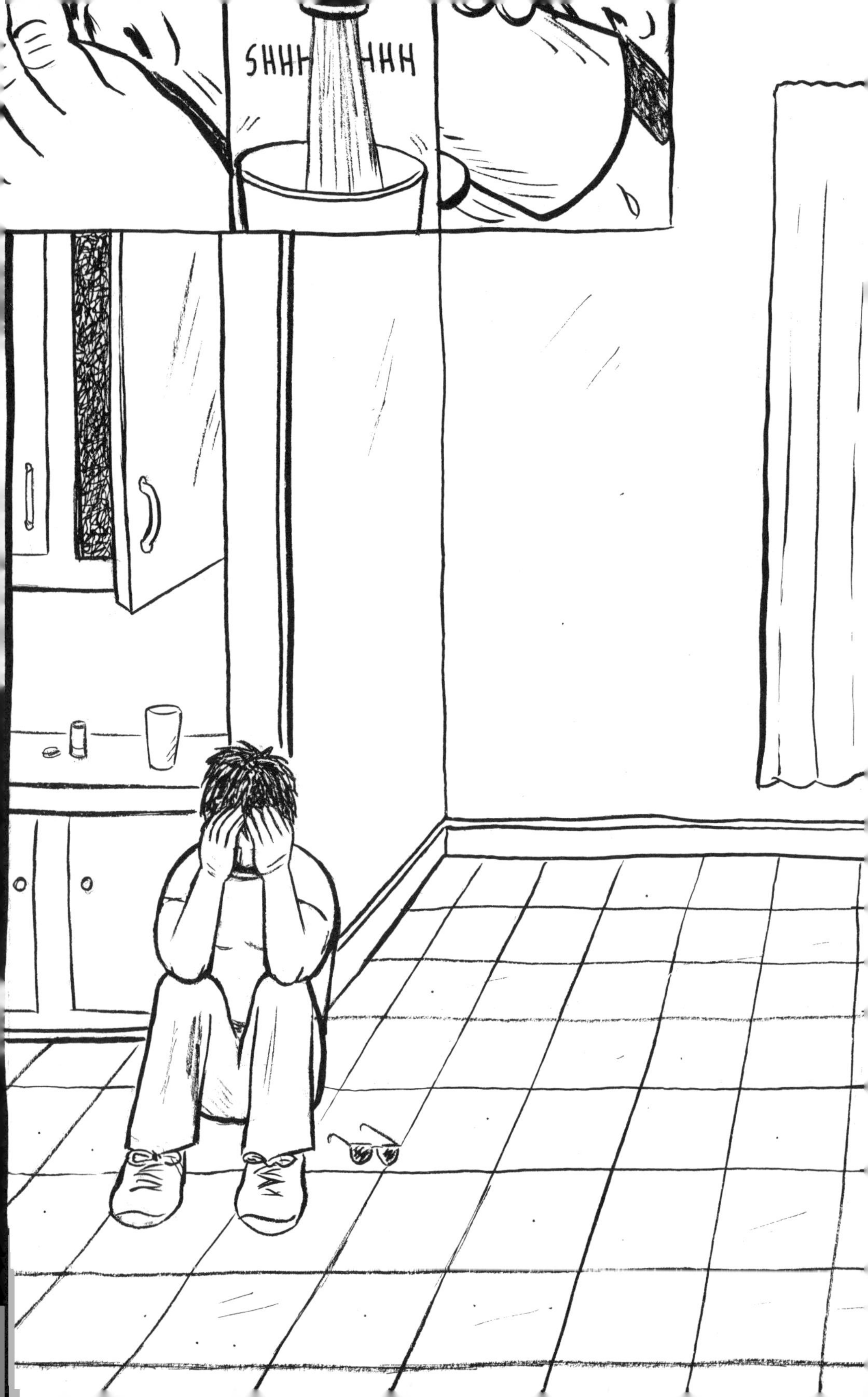
SHHH HHHH

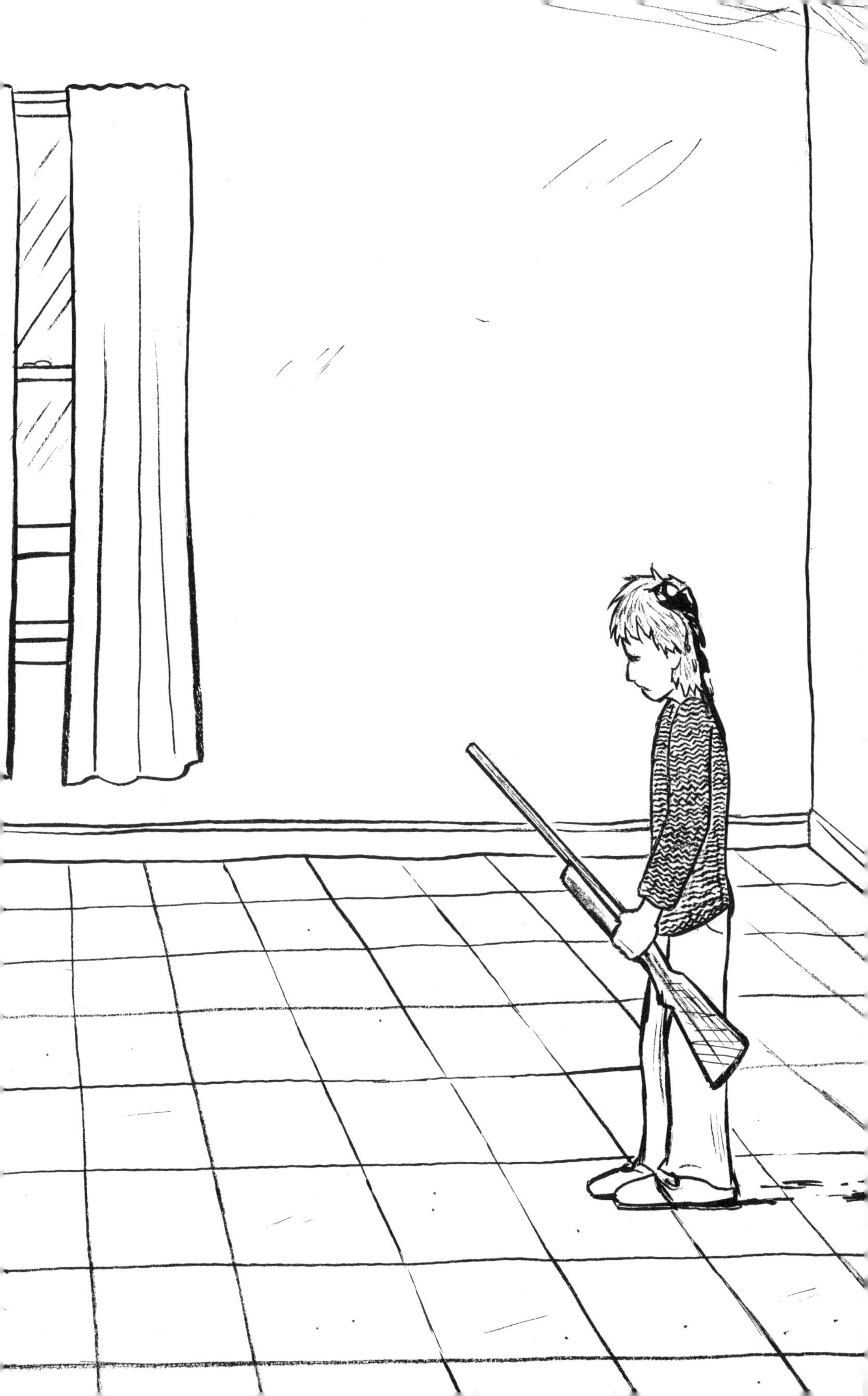

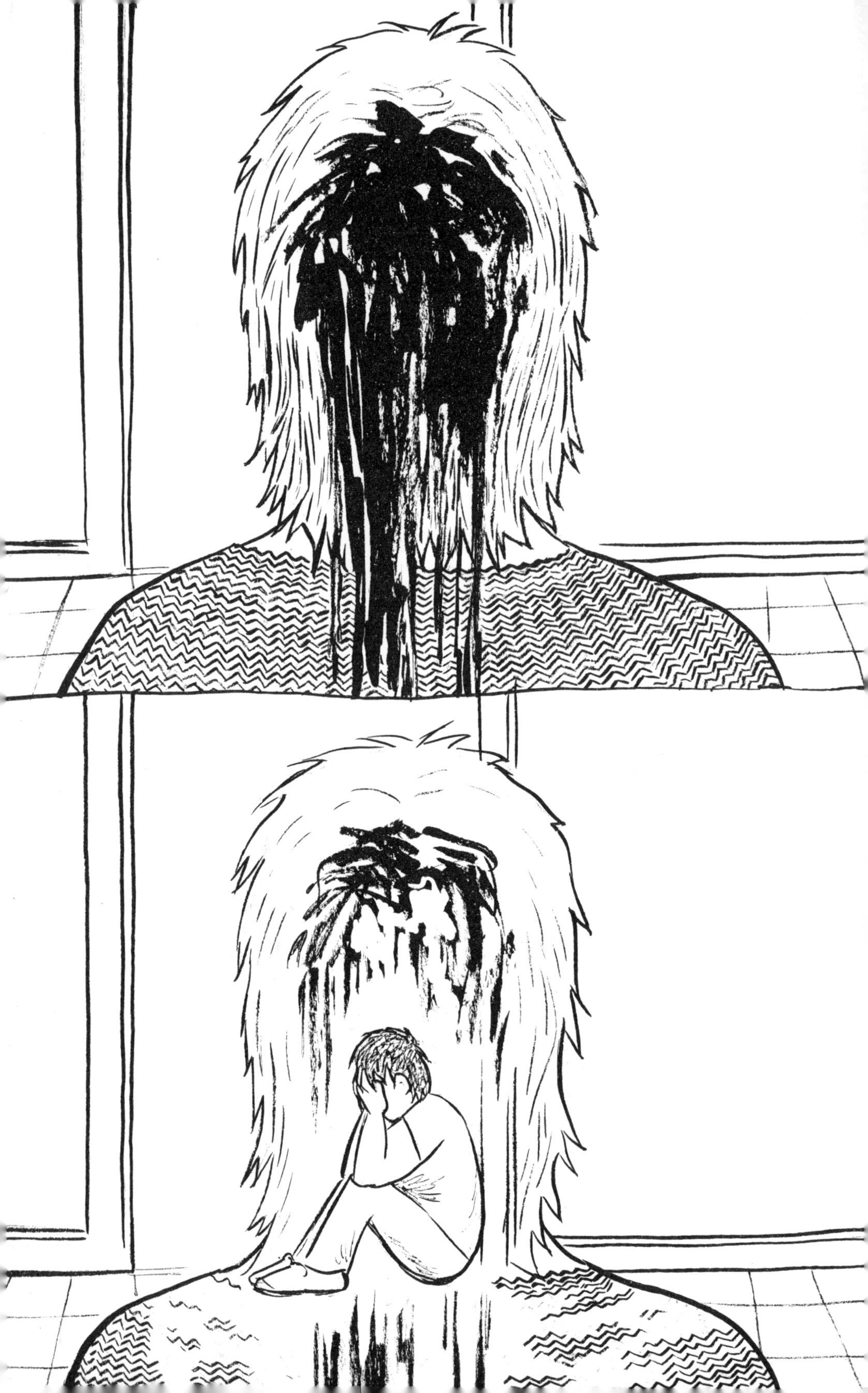

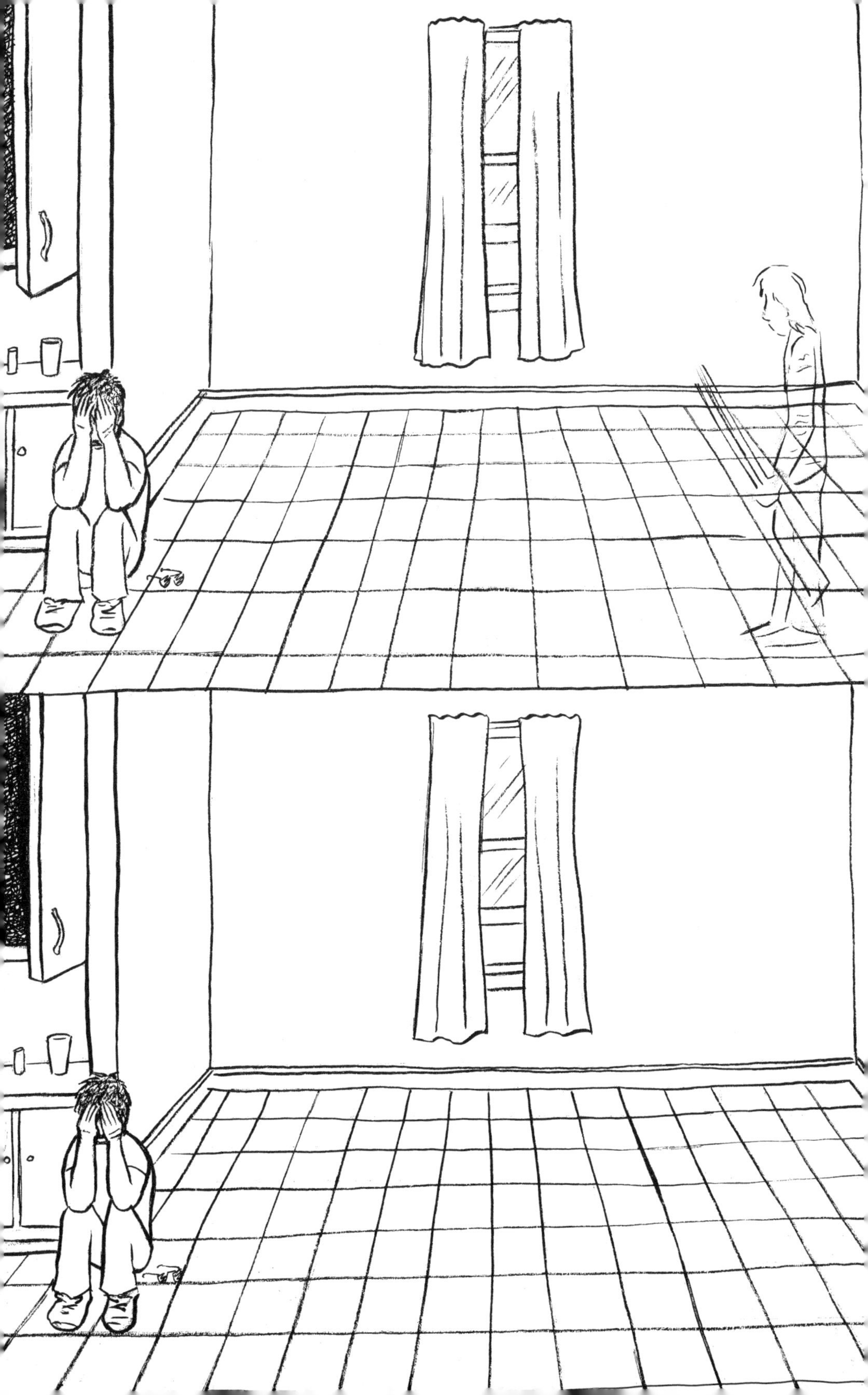

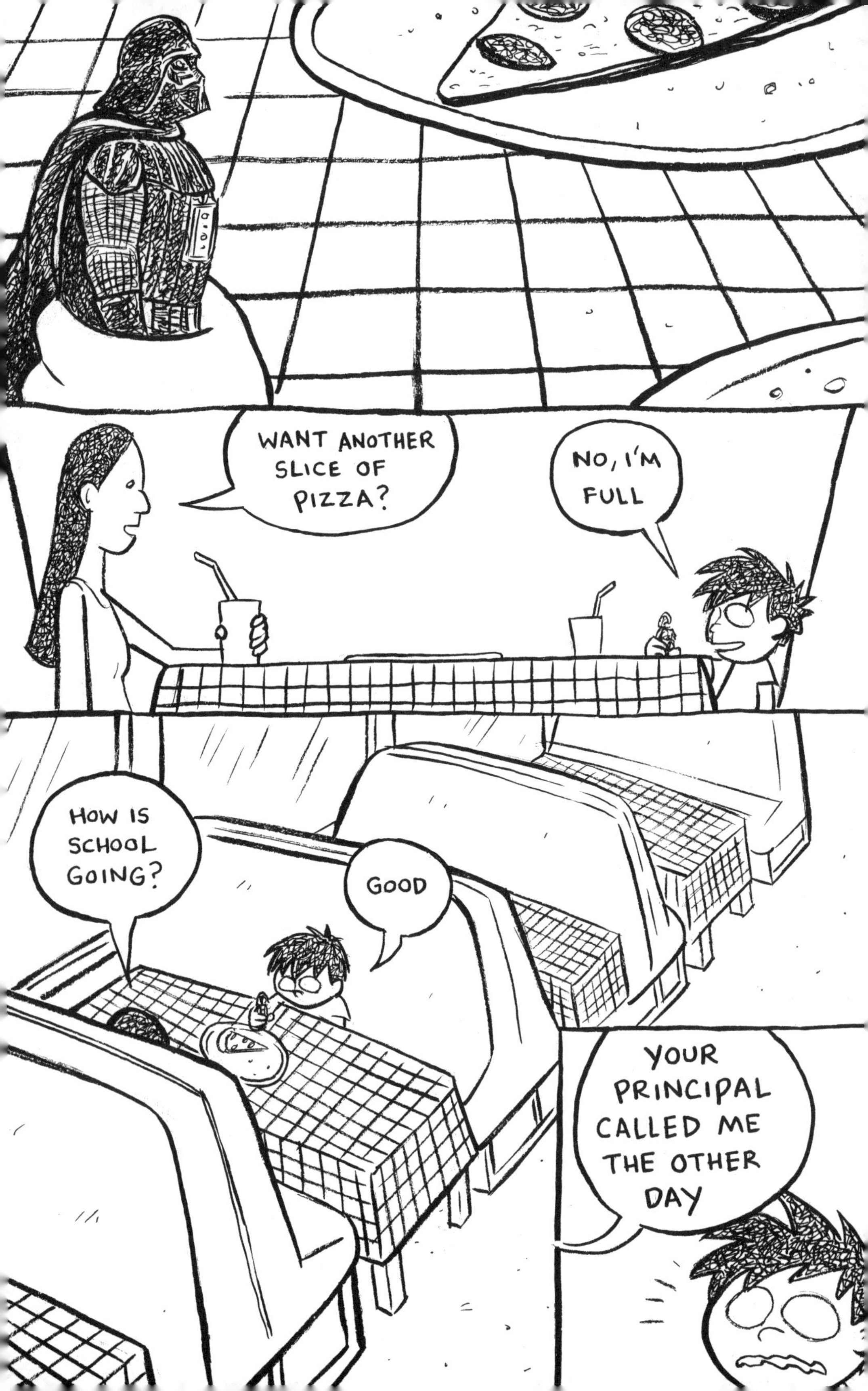
WANT ANOTHER SLICE OF PIZZA?
NO, I'M FULL
HOW IS SCHOOL GOING?
GOOD
YOUR PRINCIPAL CALLED ME THE OTHER DAY

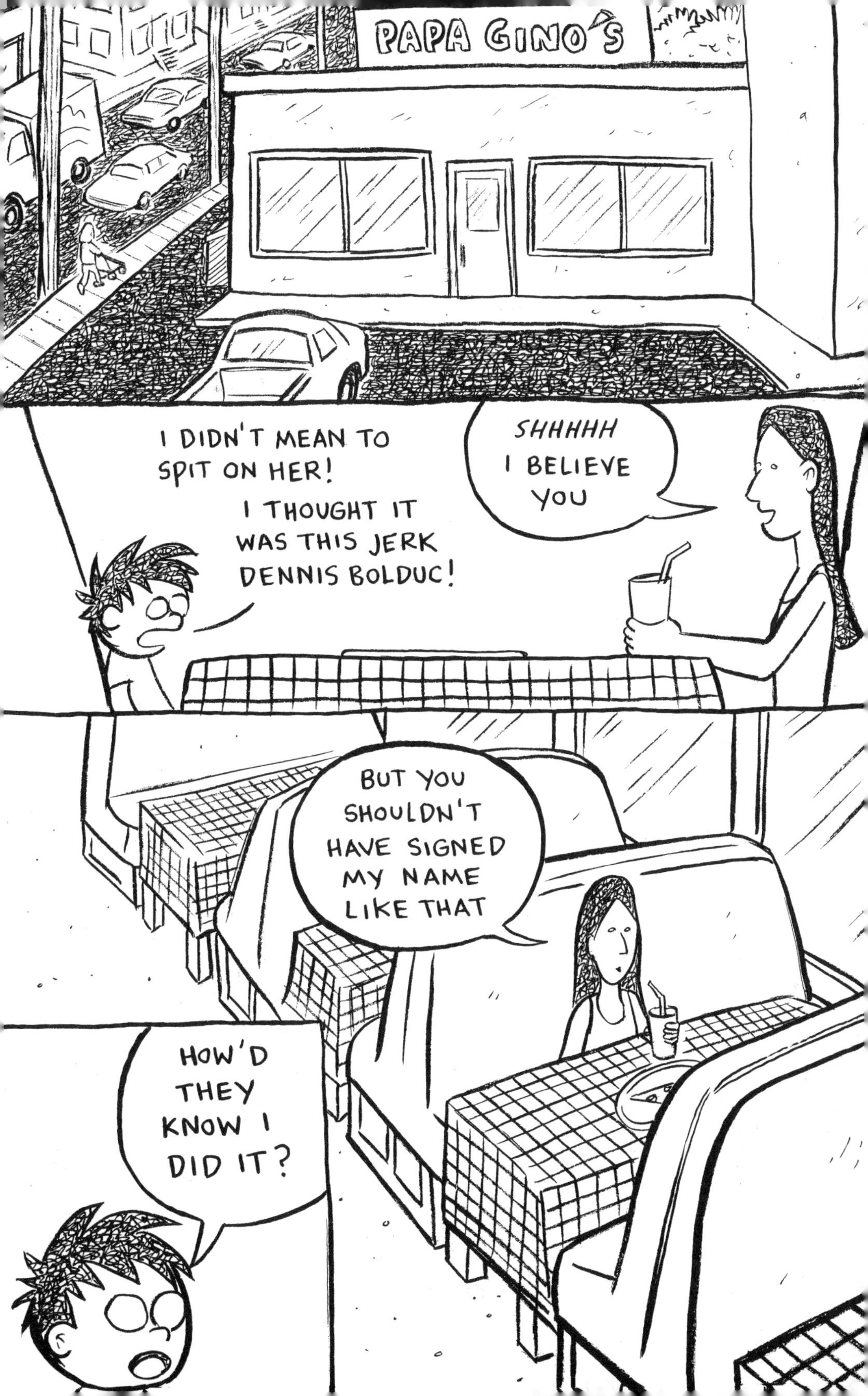
PAPA GINO'S
I DIDN'T MEAN TO SPIT ON HER!
I THOUGHT IT WAS THIS JERK DENNIS BOLDUC!
SHHHHH I BELIEVE YOU
BUT YOU SHOULDN'T HAVE SIGNED MY NAME LIKE THAT
HOW'D THEY KNOW I DID IT?

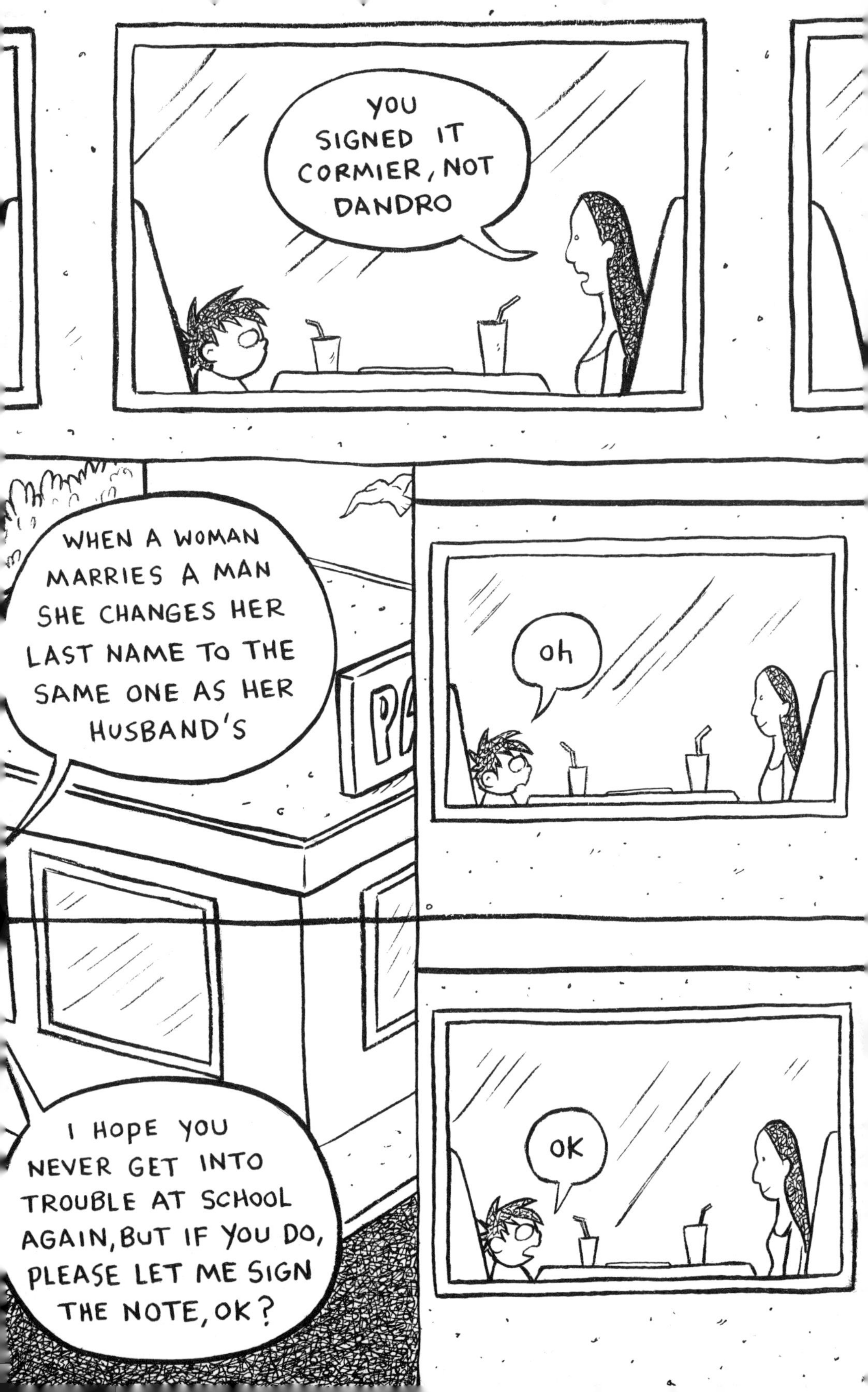
YOU SIGNED IT CORMIER, NOT DANDRO
WHEN A WOMAN MARRIES A MAN SHE CHANGES HER LAST NAME TO THE SAME ONE AS HER HUSBAND'S
oh
I HOPE YOU NEVER GET INTO TROUBLE AT SCHOOL AGAIN, BUT IF YOU DO, PLEASE LET ME SIGN THE NOTE, OK?
OK

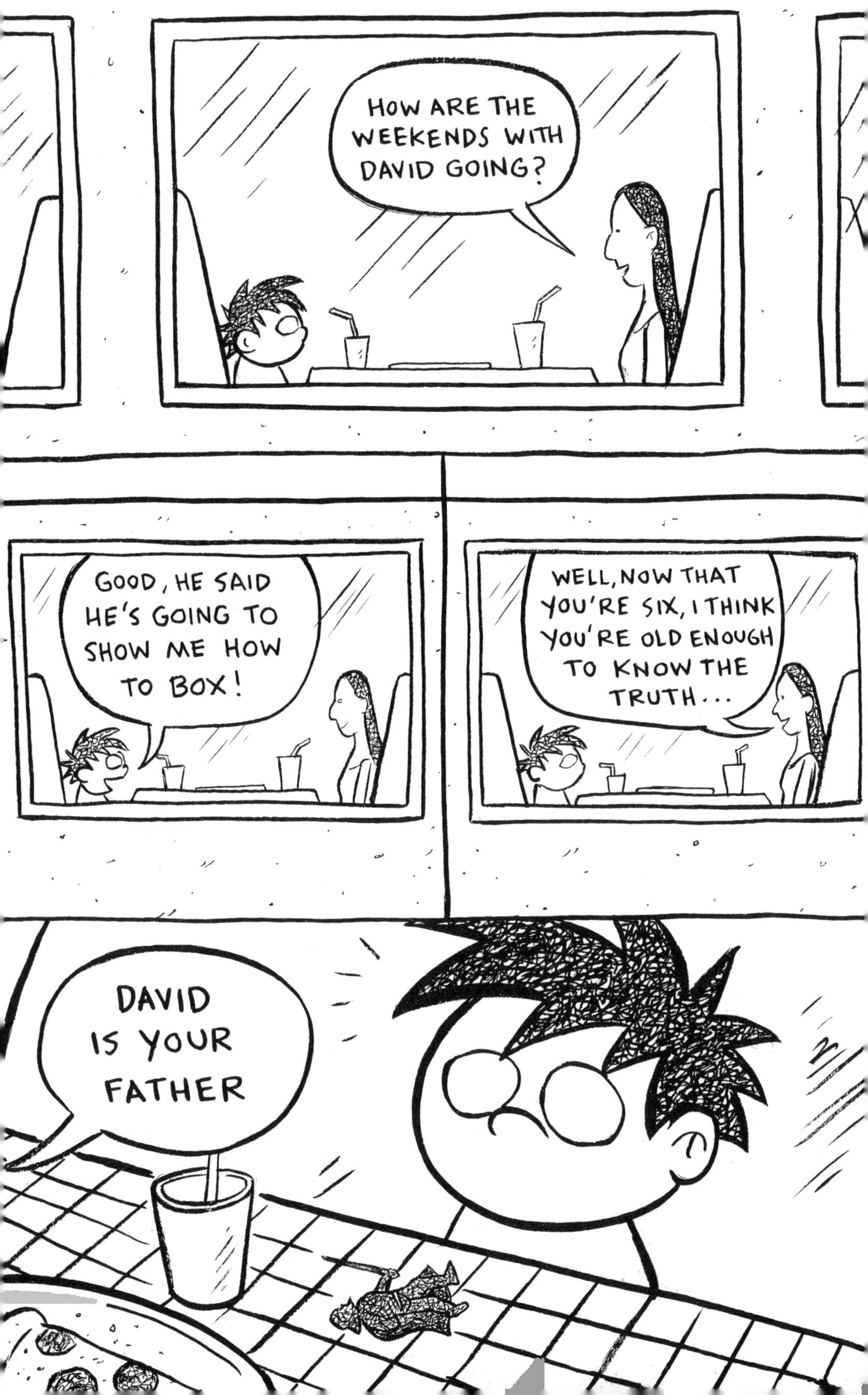
HOW ARE THE WEEKENDS WITH DAVID GOING?
GOOD, HE SAID HE'S GOING TO SHOW ME HOW TO BOX!
WELL, NOW THAT YOU'RE SIX, I THINK YOU'RE OLD ENOUGH TO KNOW THE TRUTH...
DAVID IS YOUR FATHER

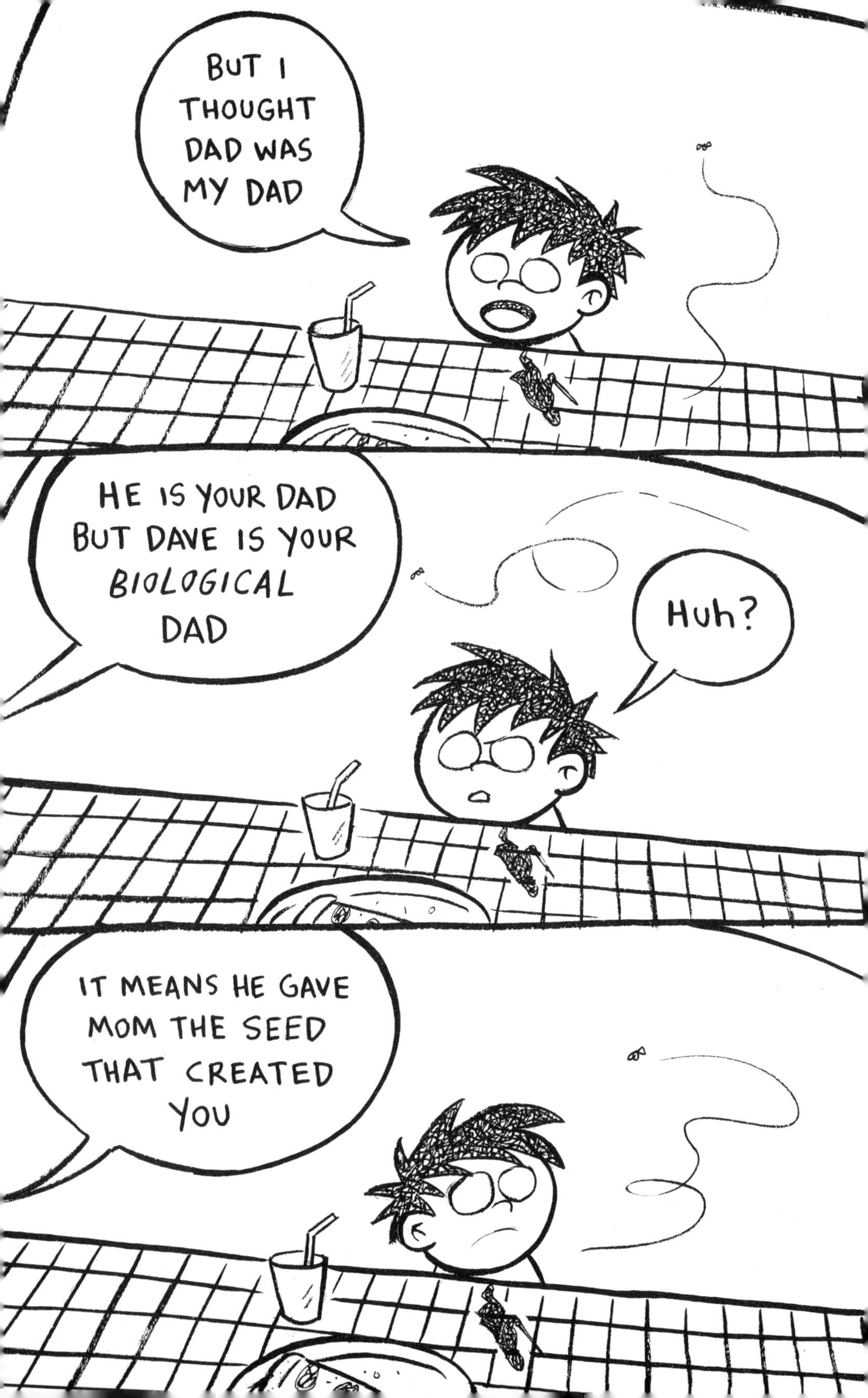
BUT I THOUGHT DAD WAS MY DAD
HE IS YOUR DAD BUT DAVE IS YOUR *BIOLOGICAL* DAD
Huh?
IT MEANS HE GAVE MOM THE SEED THAT CREATED YOU

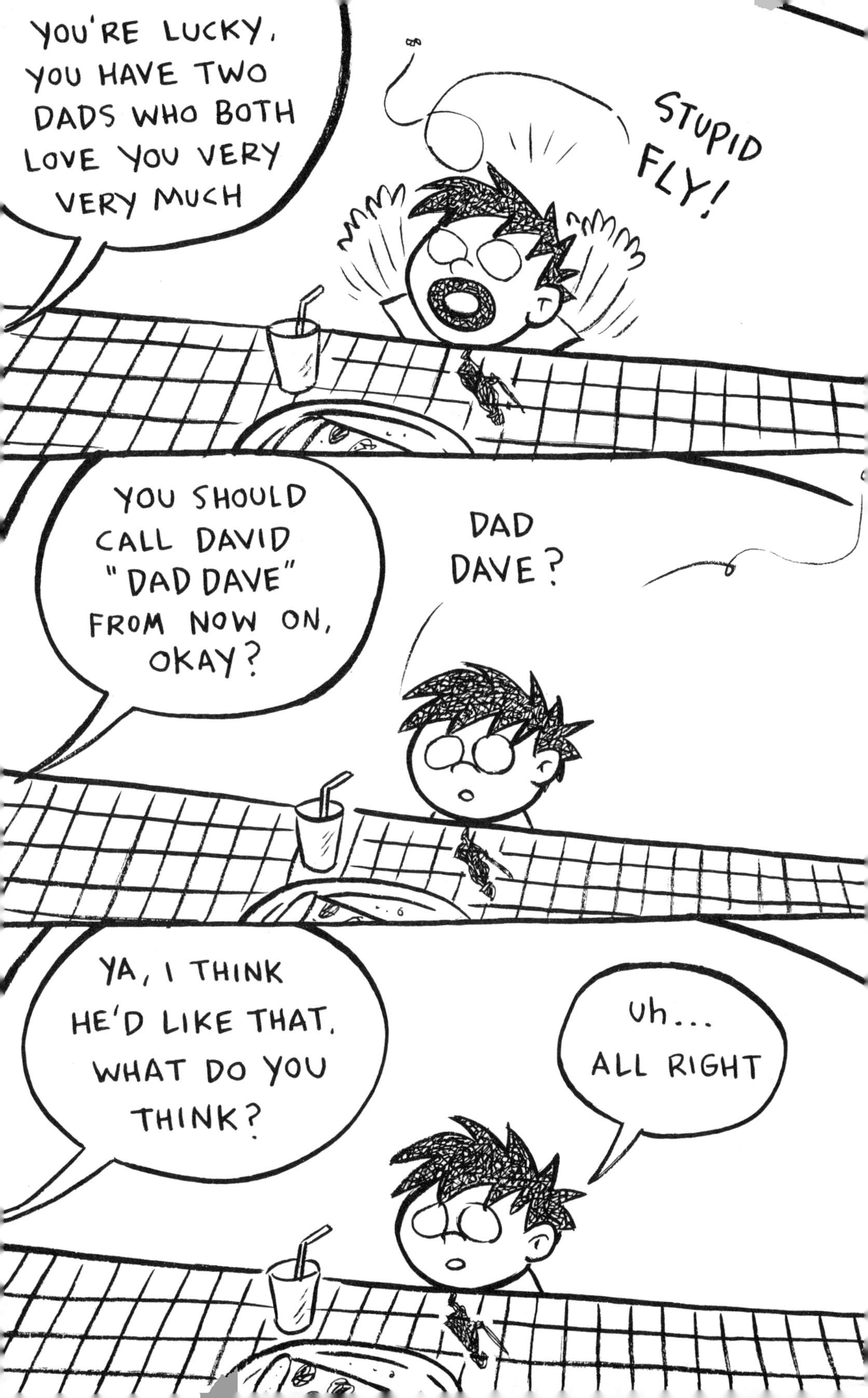
YOU'RE LUCKY, YOU HAVE TWO DADS WHO BOTH LOVE YOU VERY VERY MUCH
STUPID FLY!
YOU SHOULD CALL DAVID "DAD DAVE" FROM NOW ON, OKAY?
DAD DAVE?
YA, I THINK HE'D LIKE THAT. WHAT DO YOU THINK?
uh... ALL RIGHT

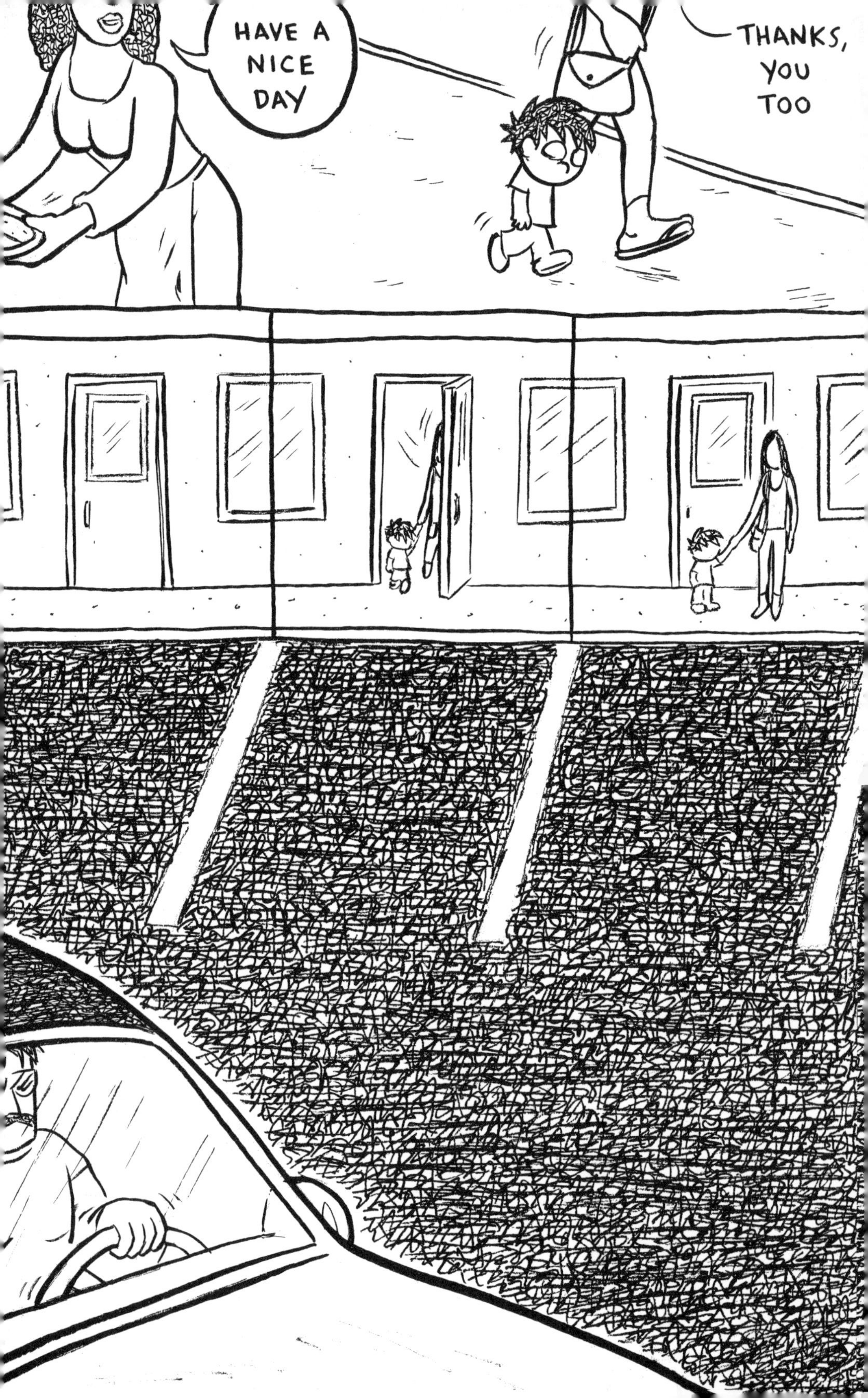
HAVE A NICE DAY
THANKS, YOU TOO

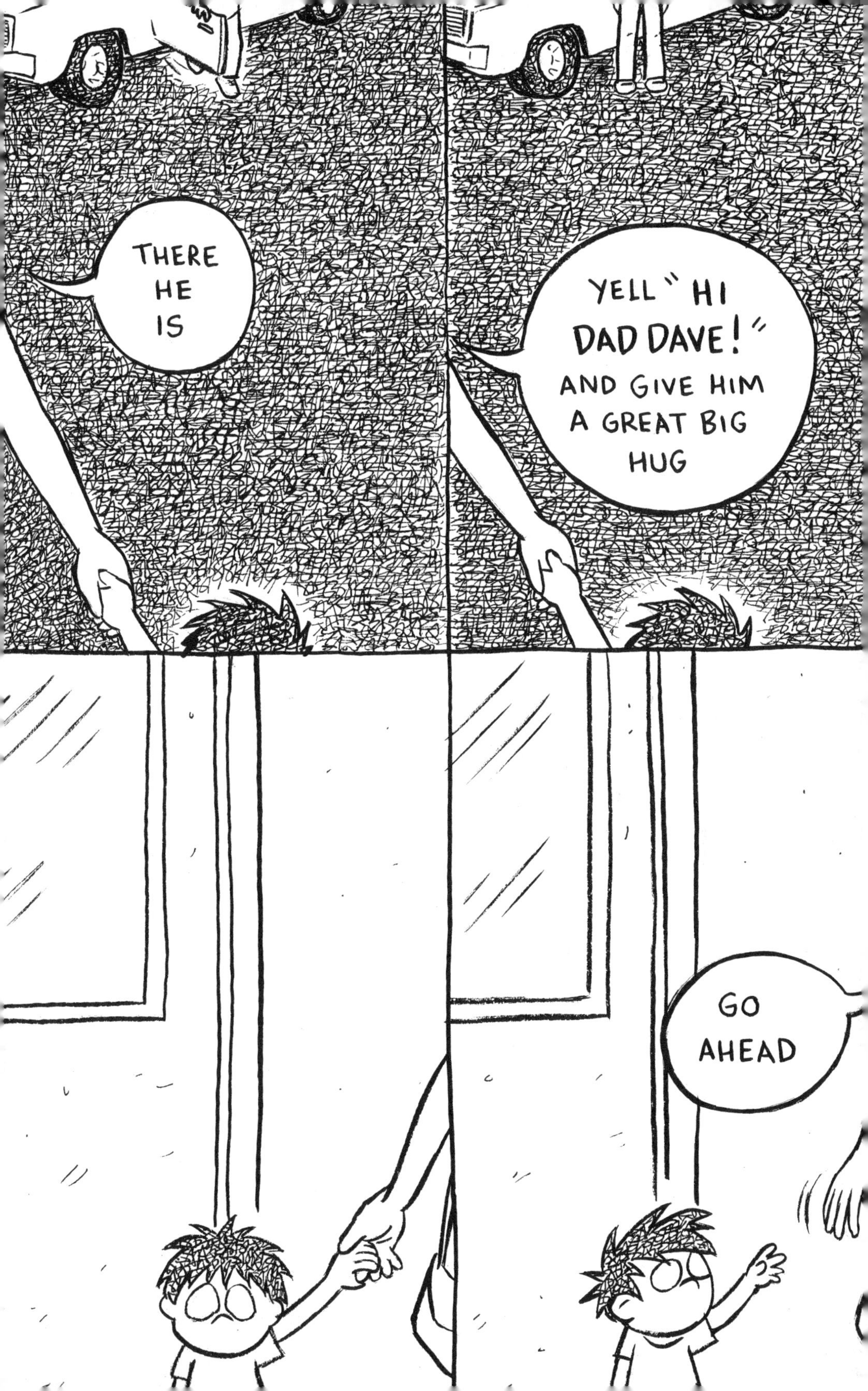
THERE HE IS
YELL "HI DAD DAVE!" AND GIVE HIM A GREAT BIG HUG
GO AHEAD

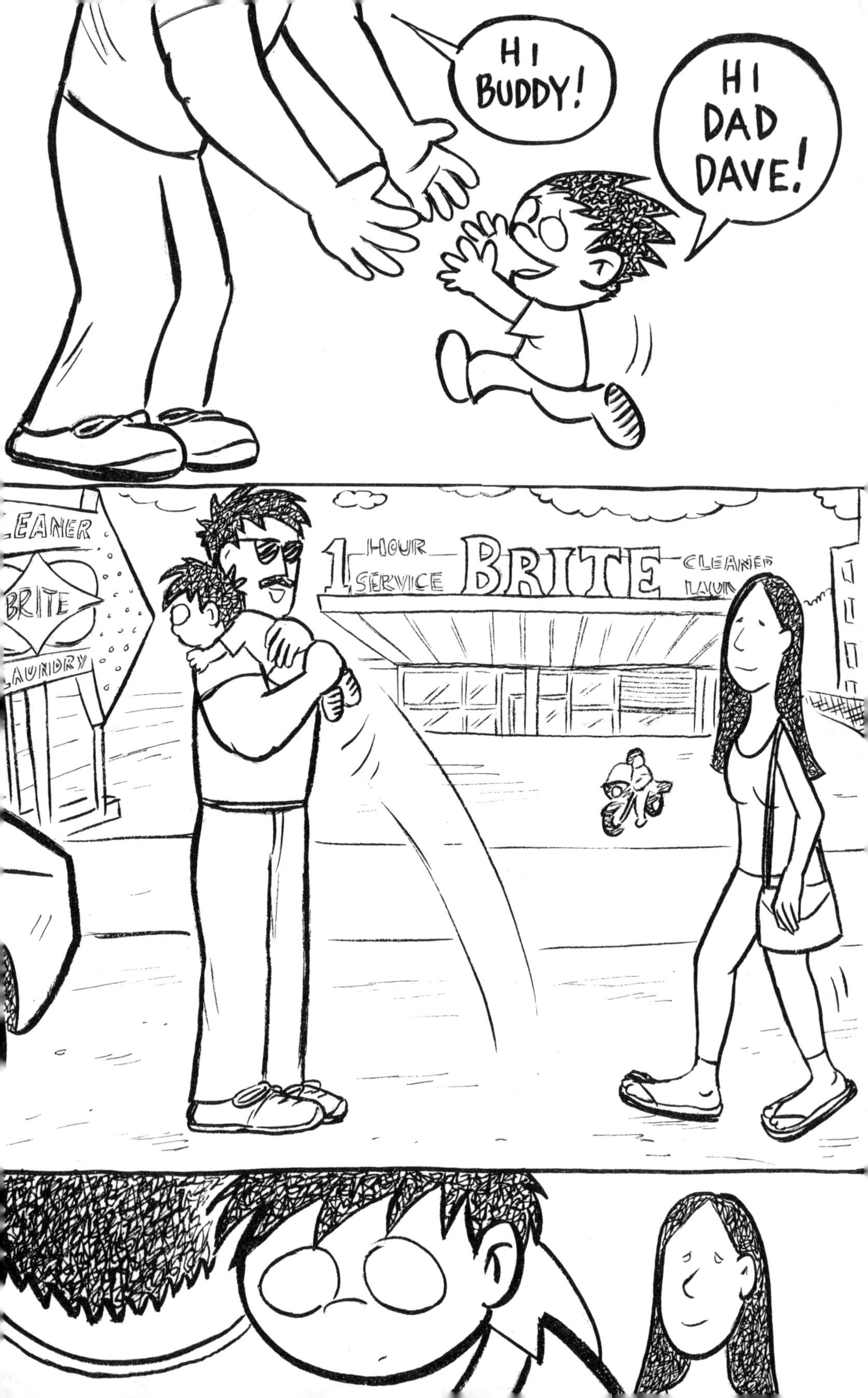
HI BUDDY!
HI DAD DAVE!
BRITE
1 HOUR SERVICE BRITE

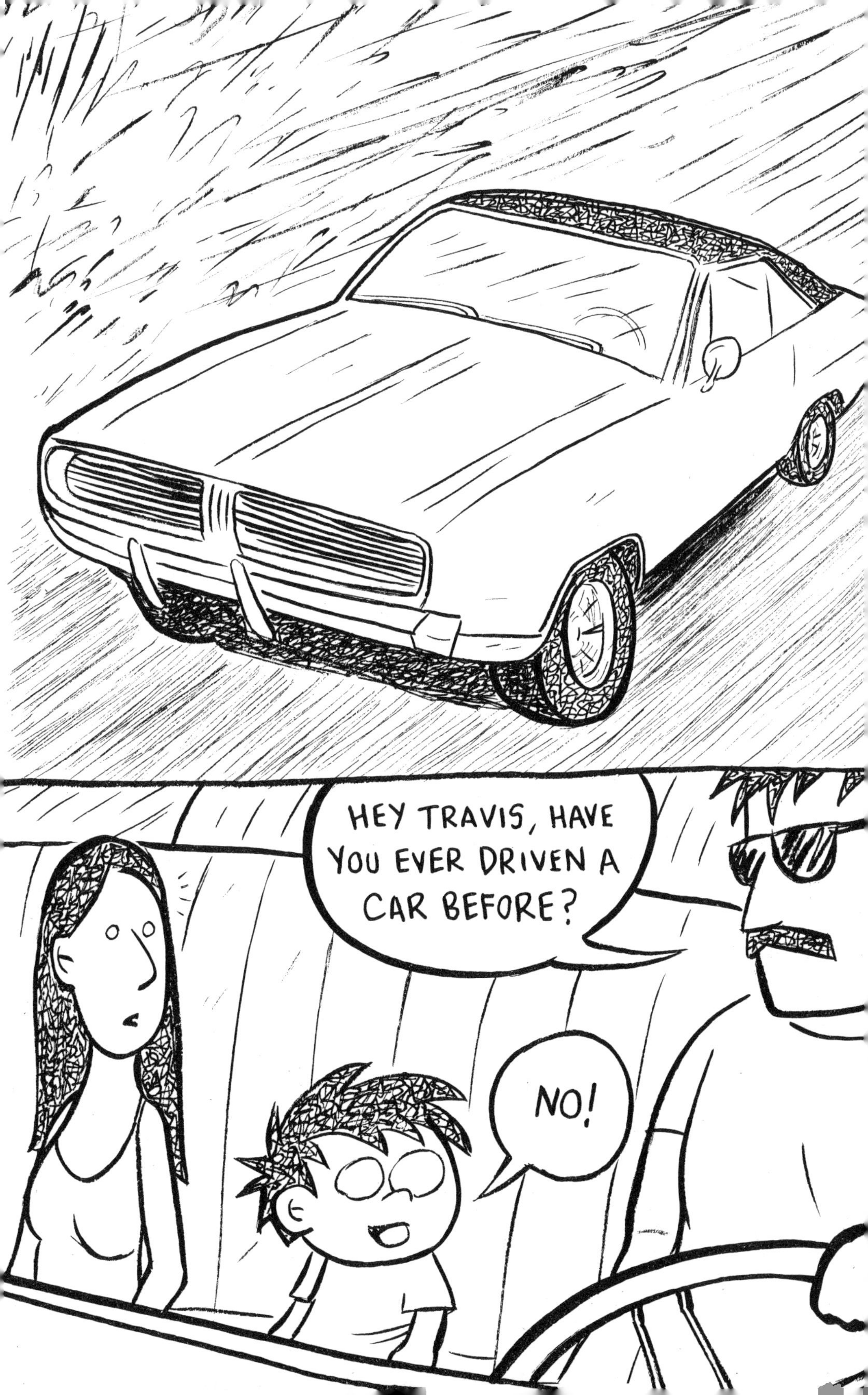
HEY TRAVIS, HAVE YOU EVER DRIVEN A CAR BEFORE?
NO!

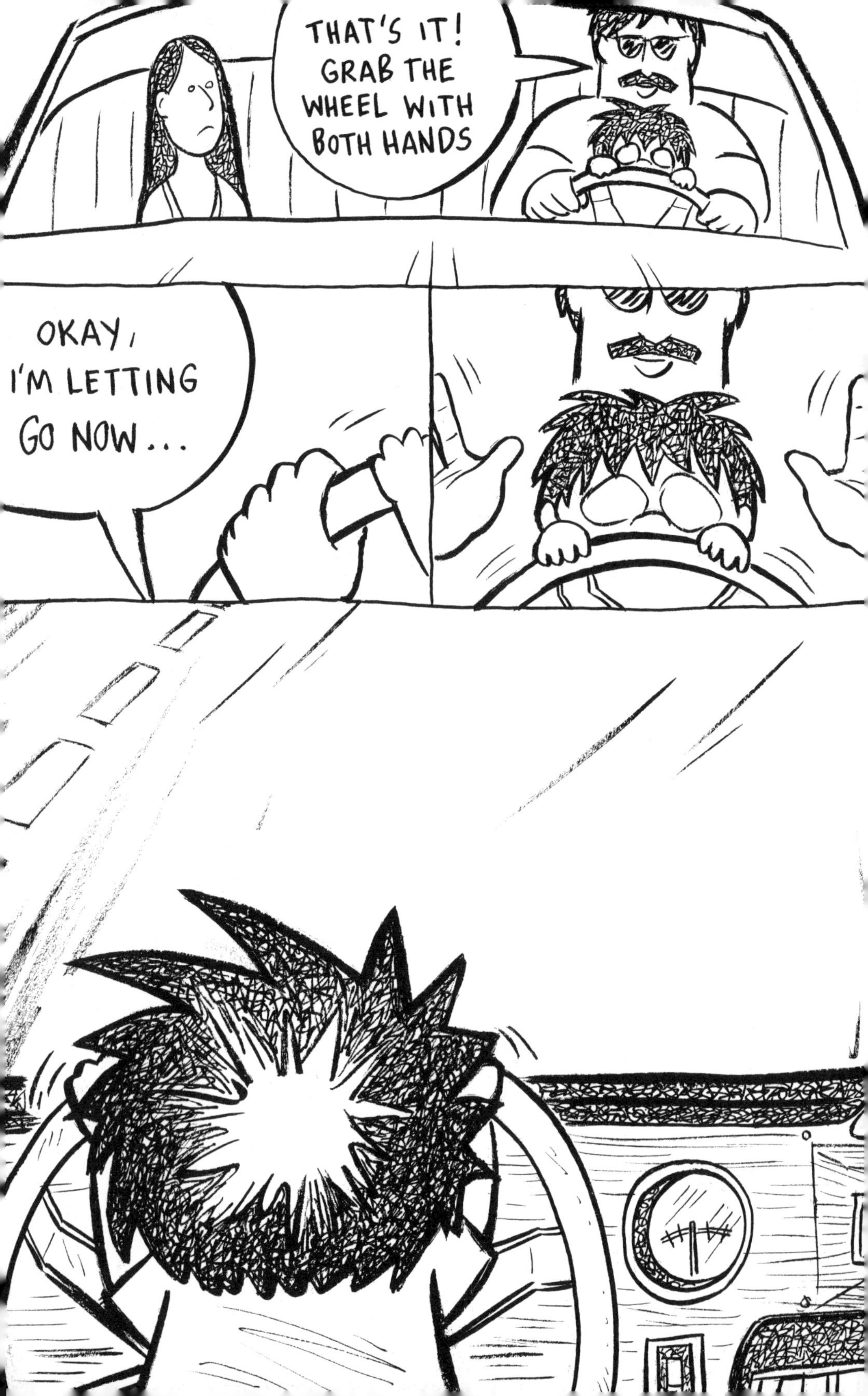
THAT'S IT! GRAB THE WHEEL WITH BOTH HANDS
OKAY, I'M LETTING GO NOW...

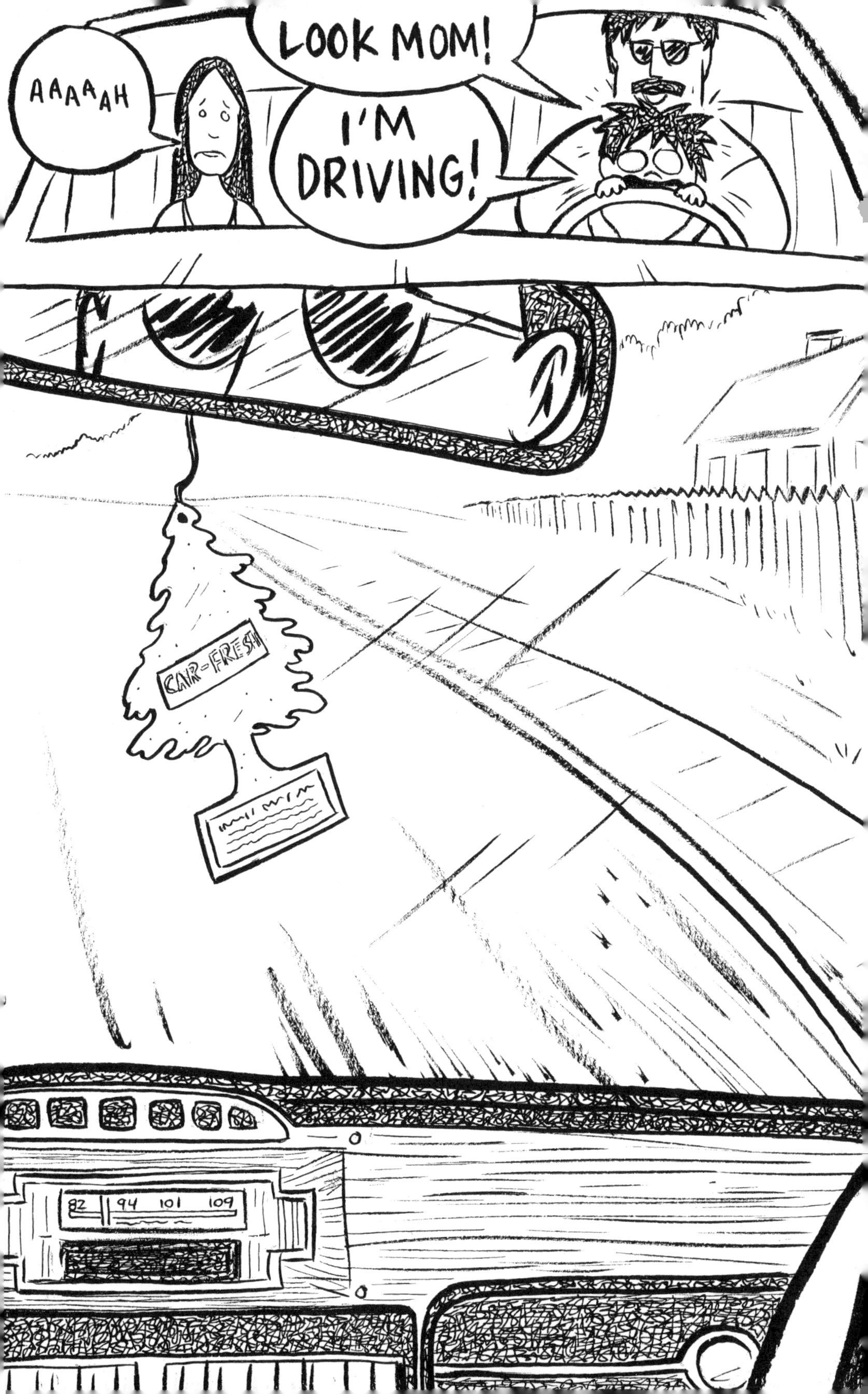
AAAAAH
LOOK MOM!
I'M DRIVING!
CAR-FRESH
82 94 101 109

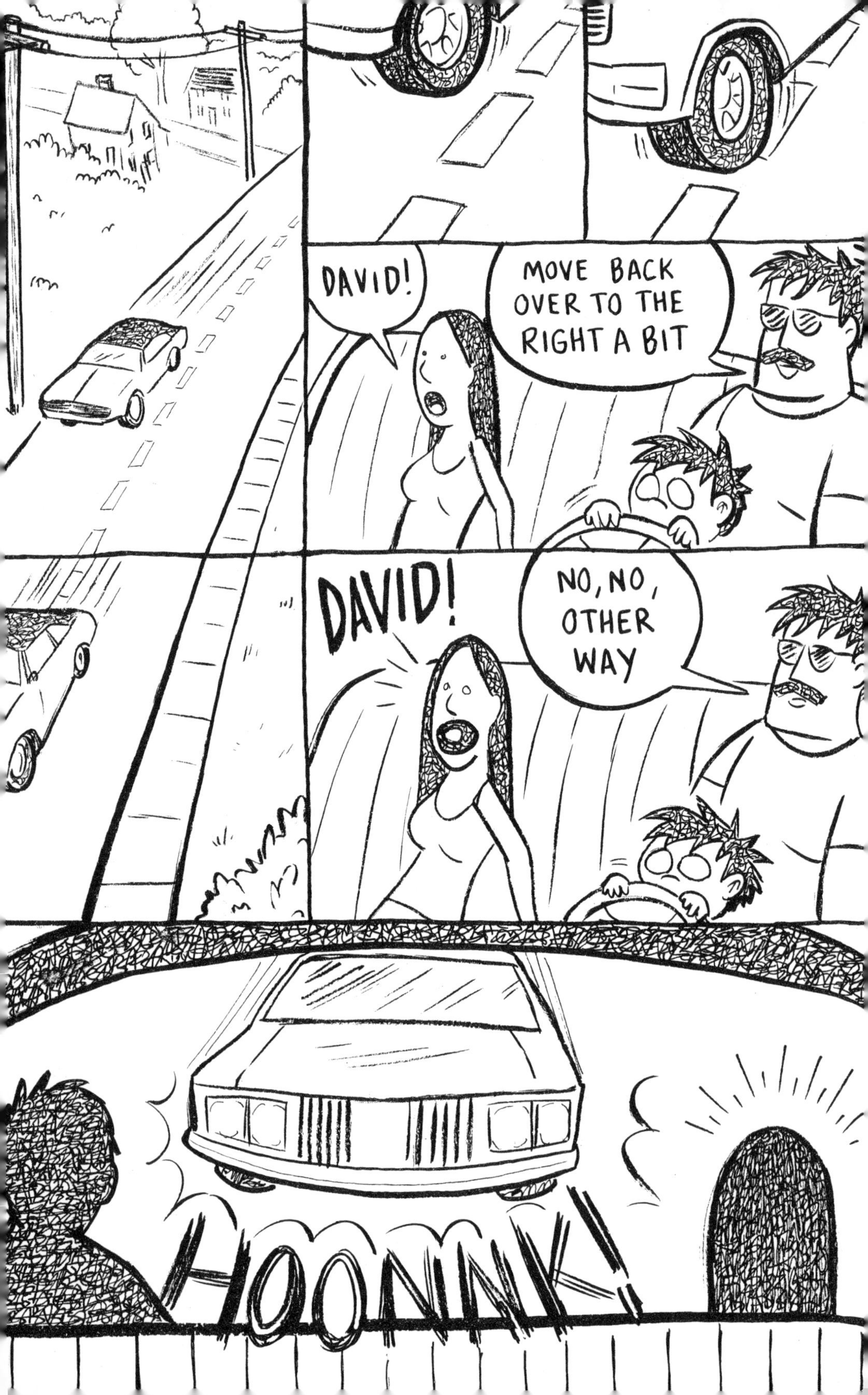
DAVID!
MOVE BACK OVER TO THE RIGHT A BIT
DAVID!
NO, NO, OTHER WAY
HOONNK!

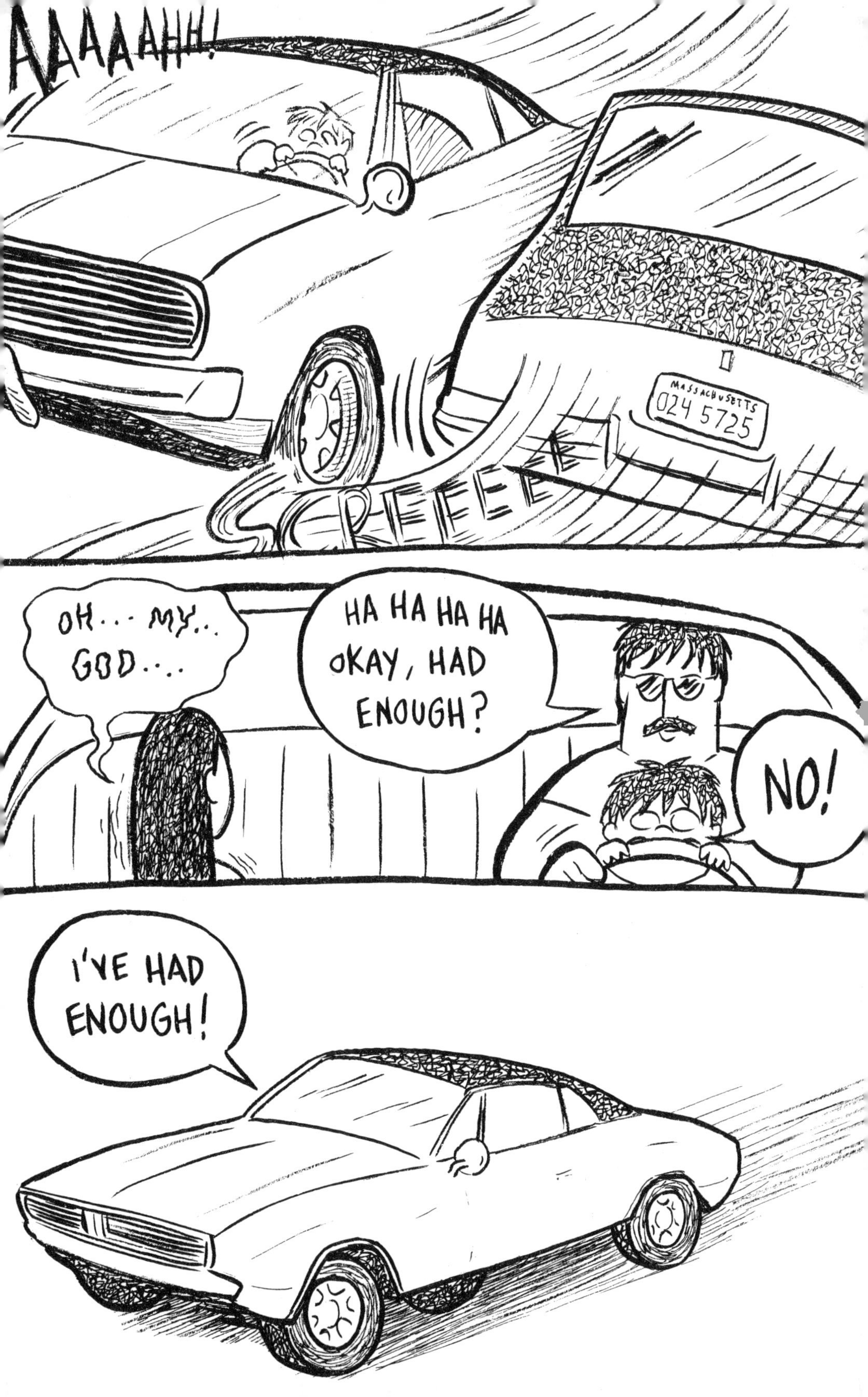
AAAAAHH!
MASSACHUSETTS
024 5725
SCREEEEE
OH... MY... GOD....
HA HA HA HA OKAY, HAD ENOUGH?
NO!
I'VE HAD ENOUGH!

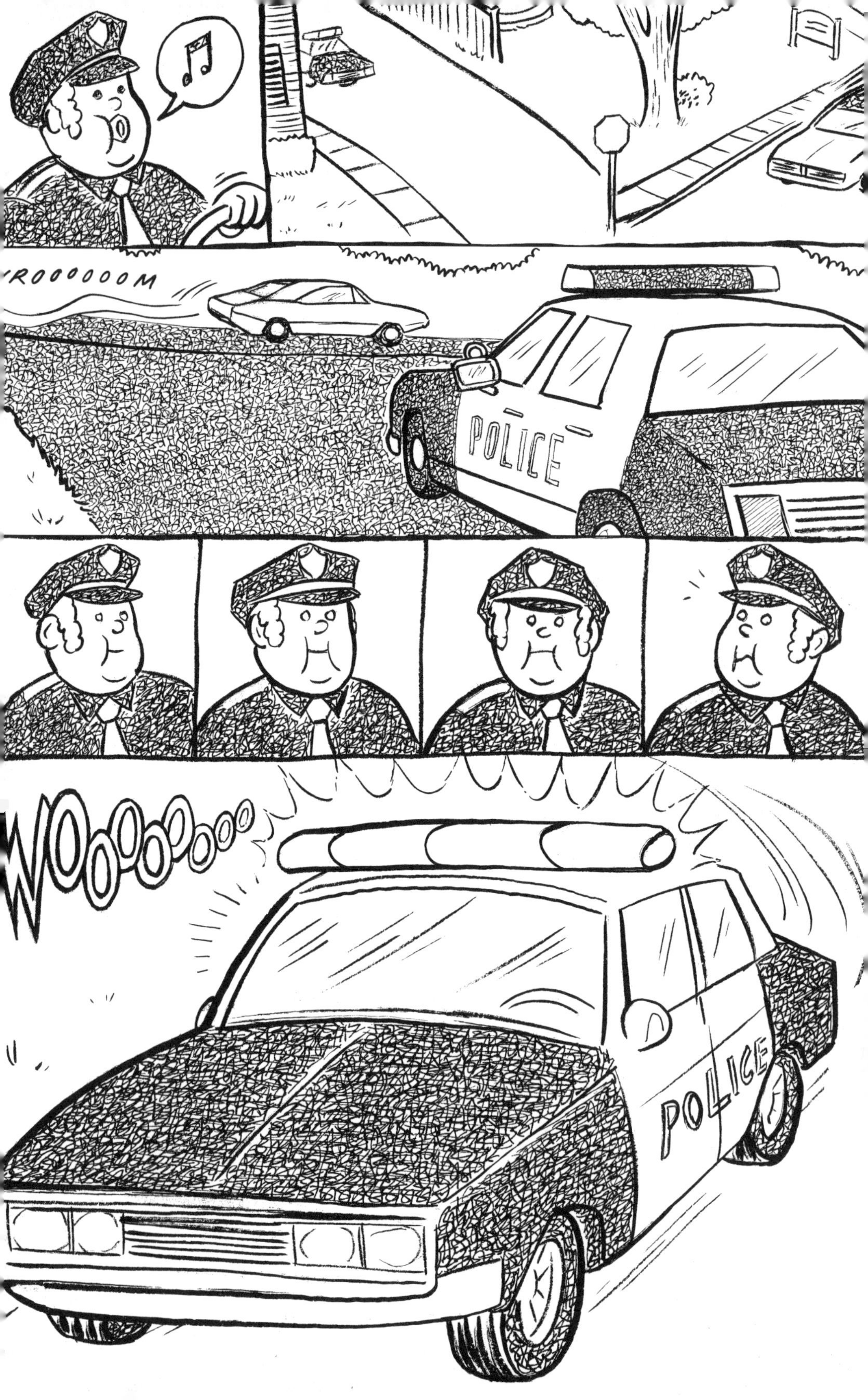
ROOOOOOM
POLICE
WOOOOOOOO
POLICE

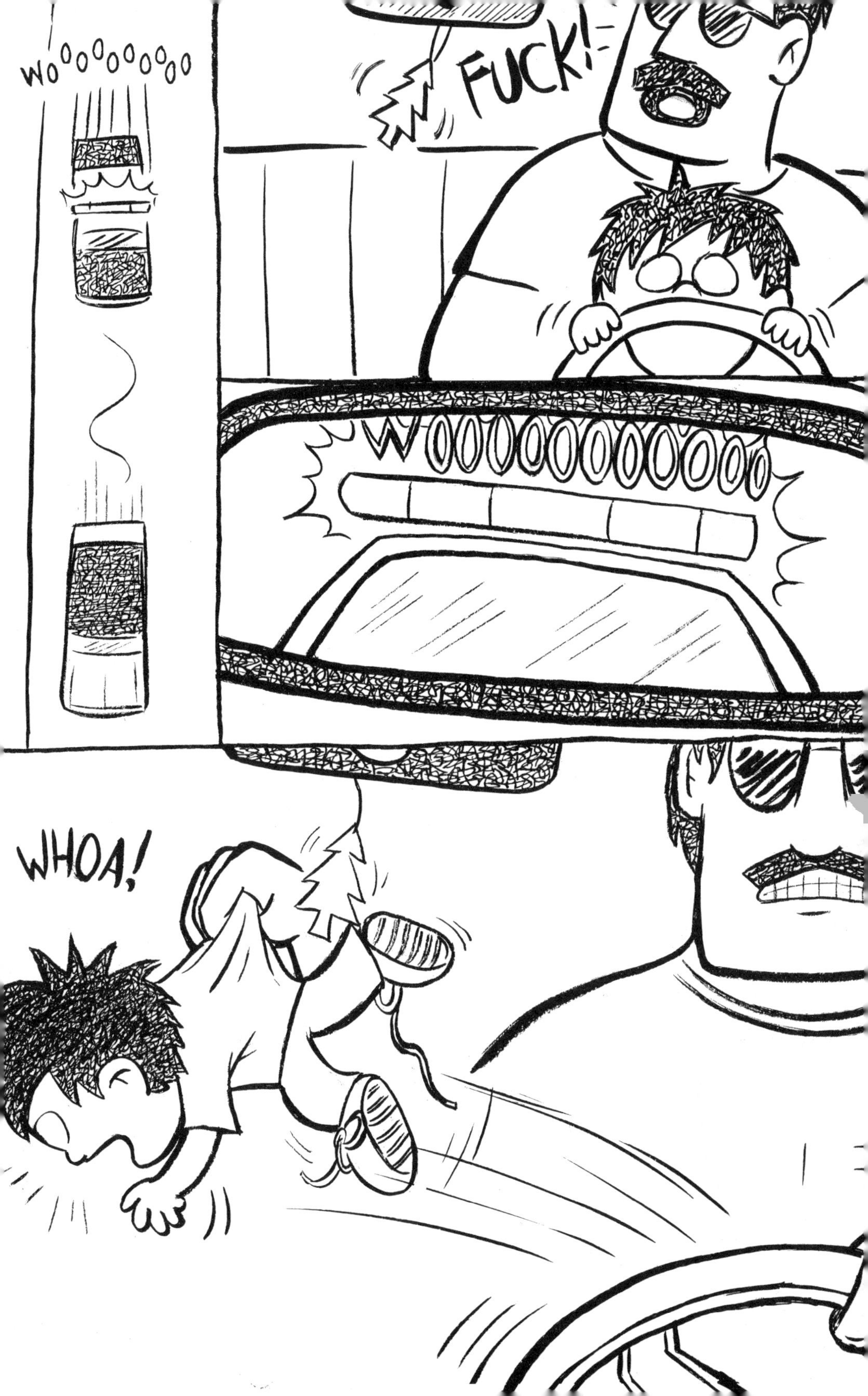
WOOOOOOOOO
FUCK!
WOOOOOOOOOOOO
WHOA!

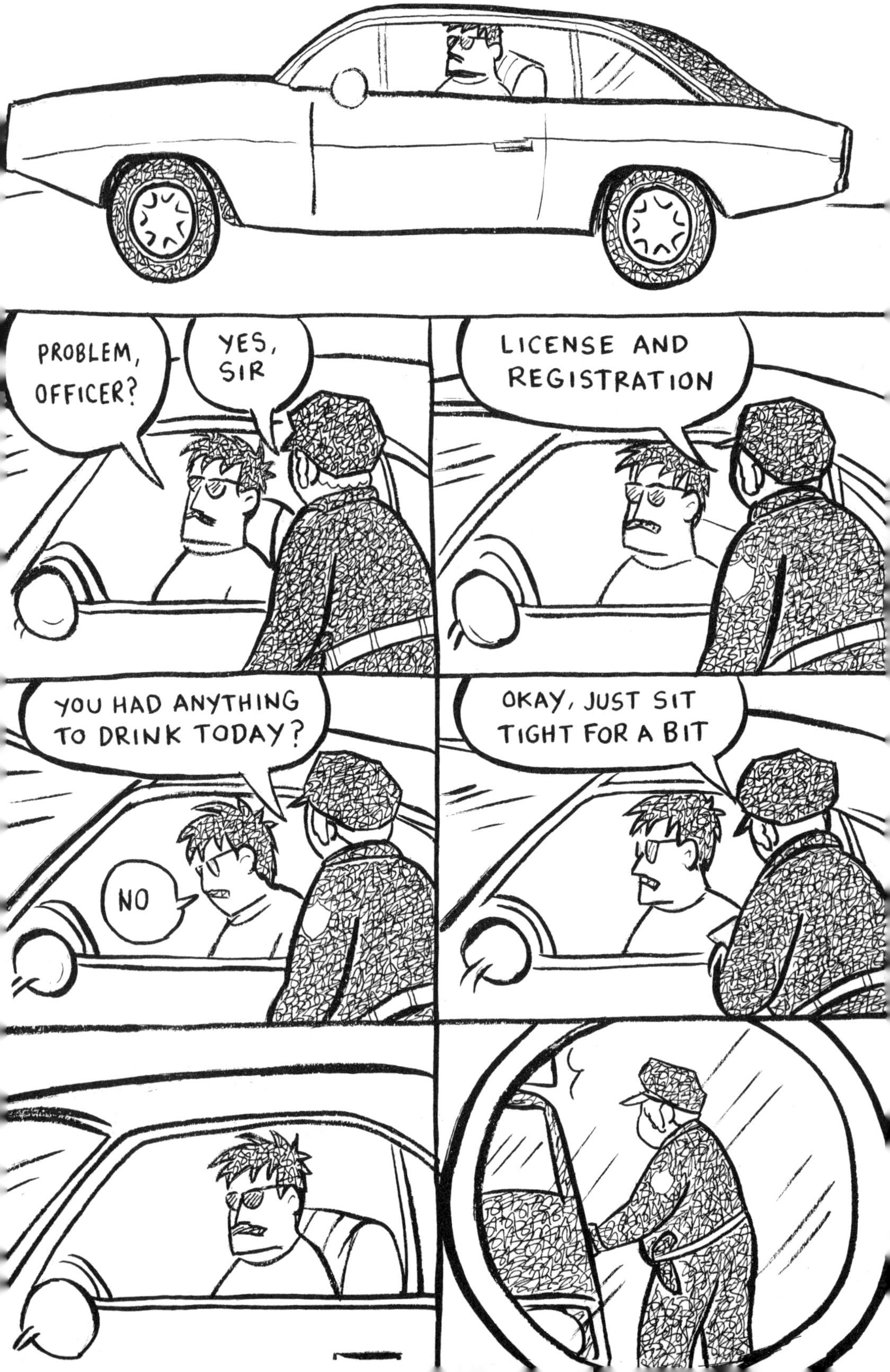
PROBLEM, OFFICER?
YES, SIR
LICENSE AND REGISTRATION
YOU HAD ANYTHING TO DRINK TODAY?
NO
OKAY, JUST SIT TIGHT FOR A BIT

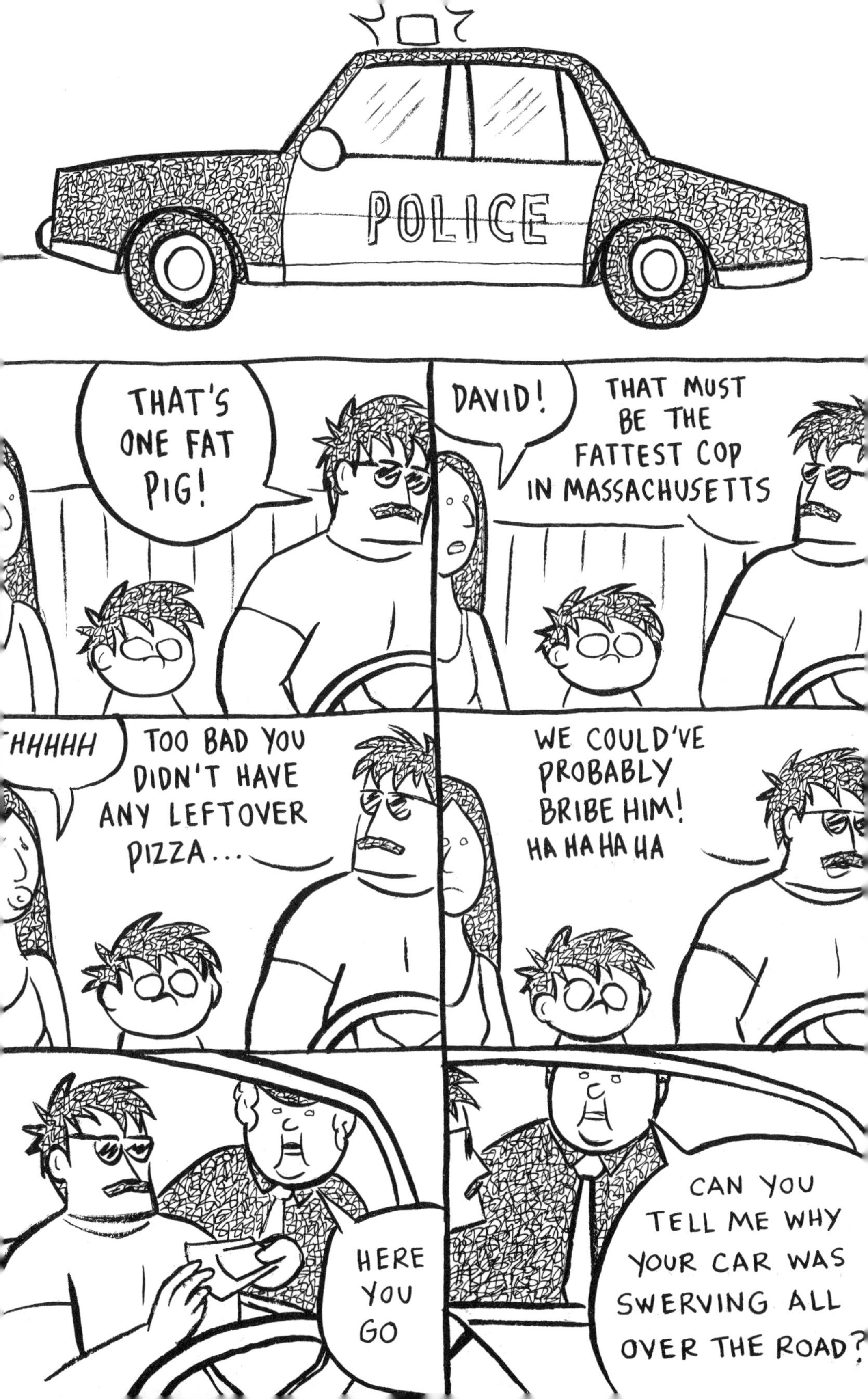
POLICE
THAT'S ONE FAT PIG!
DAVID!
THAT MUST BE THE FATTEST COP IN MASSACHUSETTS
HHHHH
TOO BAD YOU DIDN'T HAVE ANY LEFTOVER PIZZA...
WE COULD'VE PROBABLY BRIBE HIM! HA HA HA HA
HERE YOU GO
CAN YOU TELL ME WHY YOUR CAR WAS SWERVING ALL OVER THE ROAD?

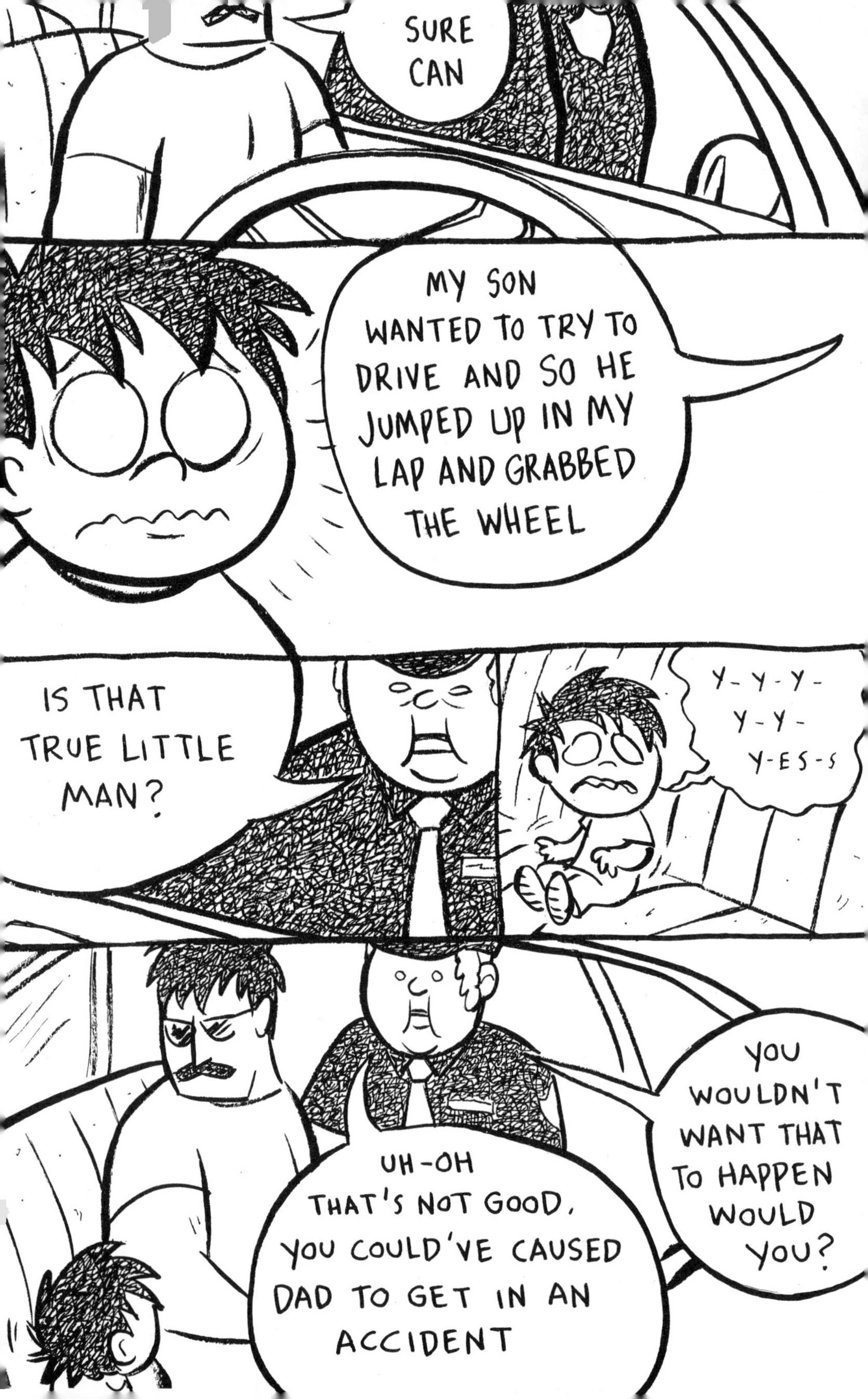
SURE CAN
MY SON WANTED TO TRY TO DRIVE AND SO HE JUMPED UP IN MY LAP AND GRABBED THE WHEEL
IS THAT TRUE LITTLE MAN?
Y-Y-Y-Y-Y-Y-E-S-S
UH-OH THAT'S NOT GOOD. YOU COULD'VE CAUSED DAD TO GET IN AN ACCIDENT
YOU WOULDN'T WANT THAT TO HAPPEN WOULD YOU?

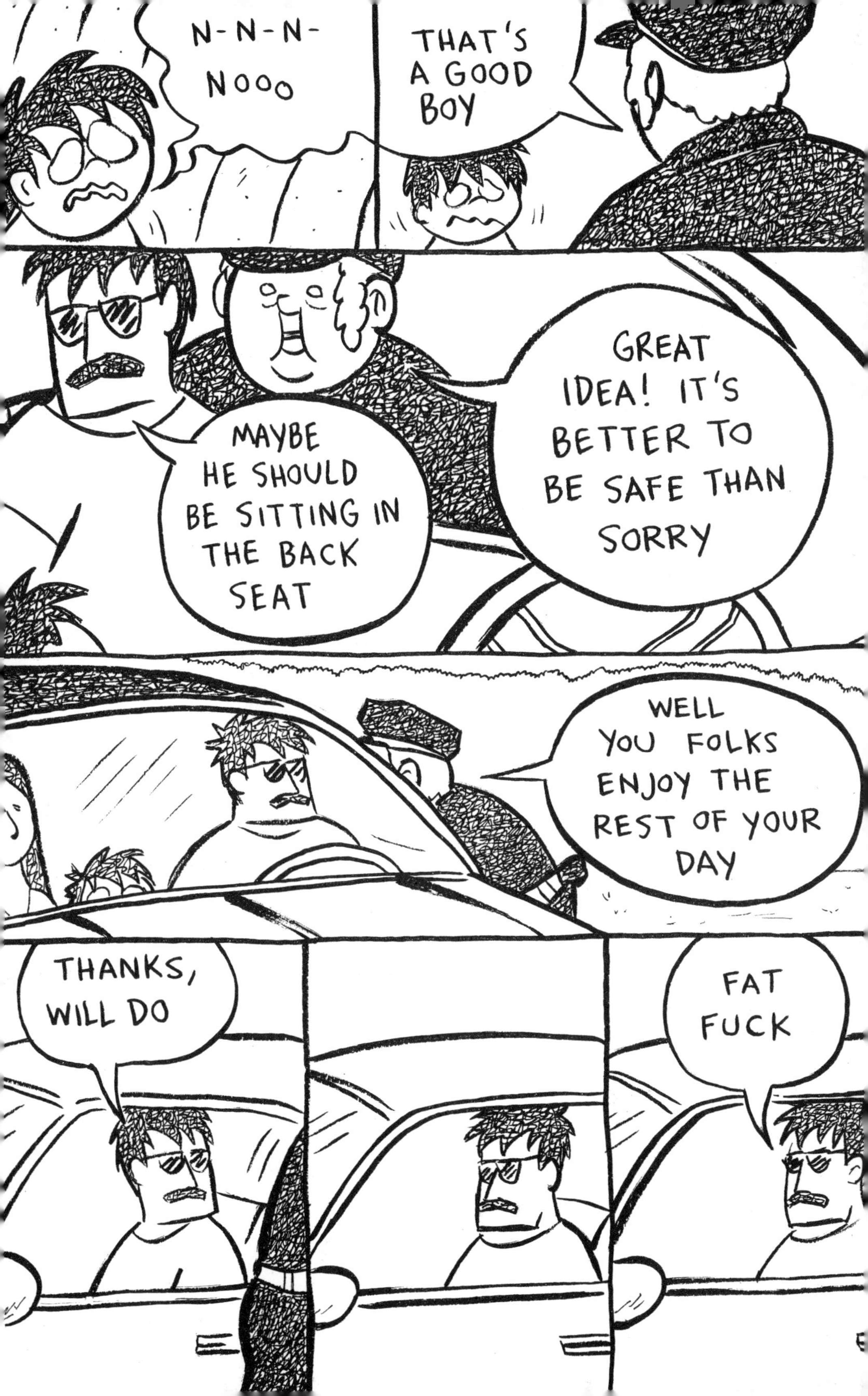
N-N-N-
NOOO
THAT'S A GOOD BOY
MAYBE HE SHOULD BE SITTING IN THE BACK SEAT
GREAT IDEA! IT'S BETTER TO BE SAFE THAN SORRY
WELL YOU FOLKS ENJOY THE REST OF YOUR DAY
THANKS, WILL DO
FAT FUCK

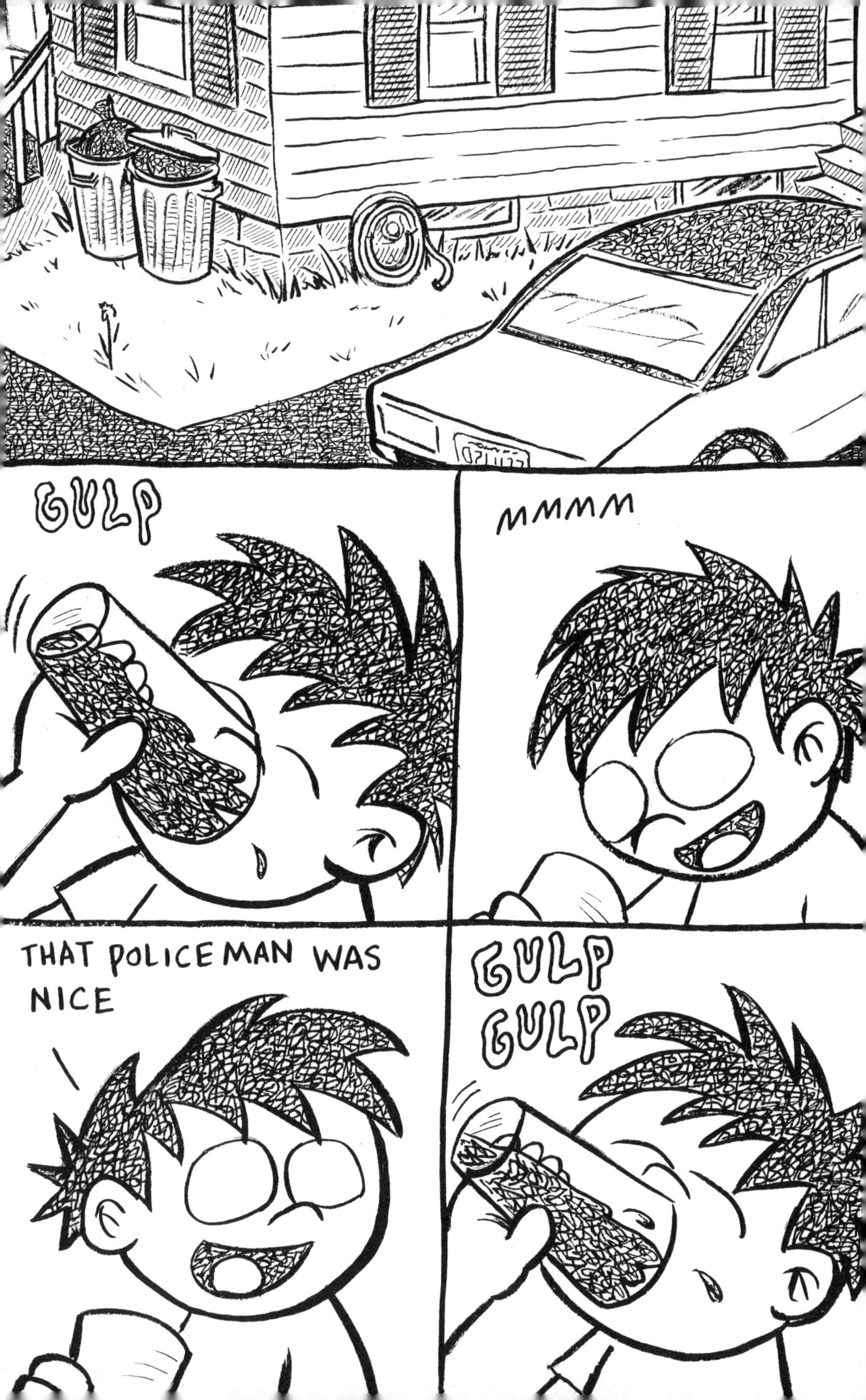
GULP
MMMM
THAT POLICEMAN WAS NICE
GULP
GULP

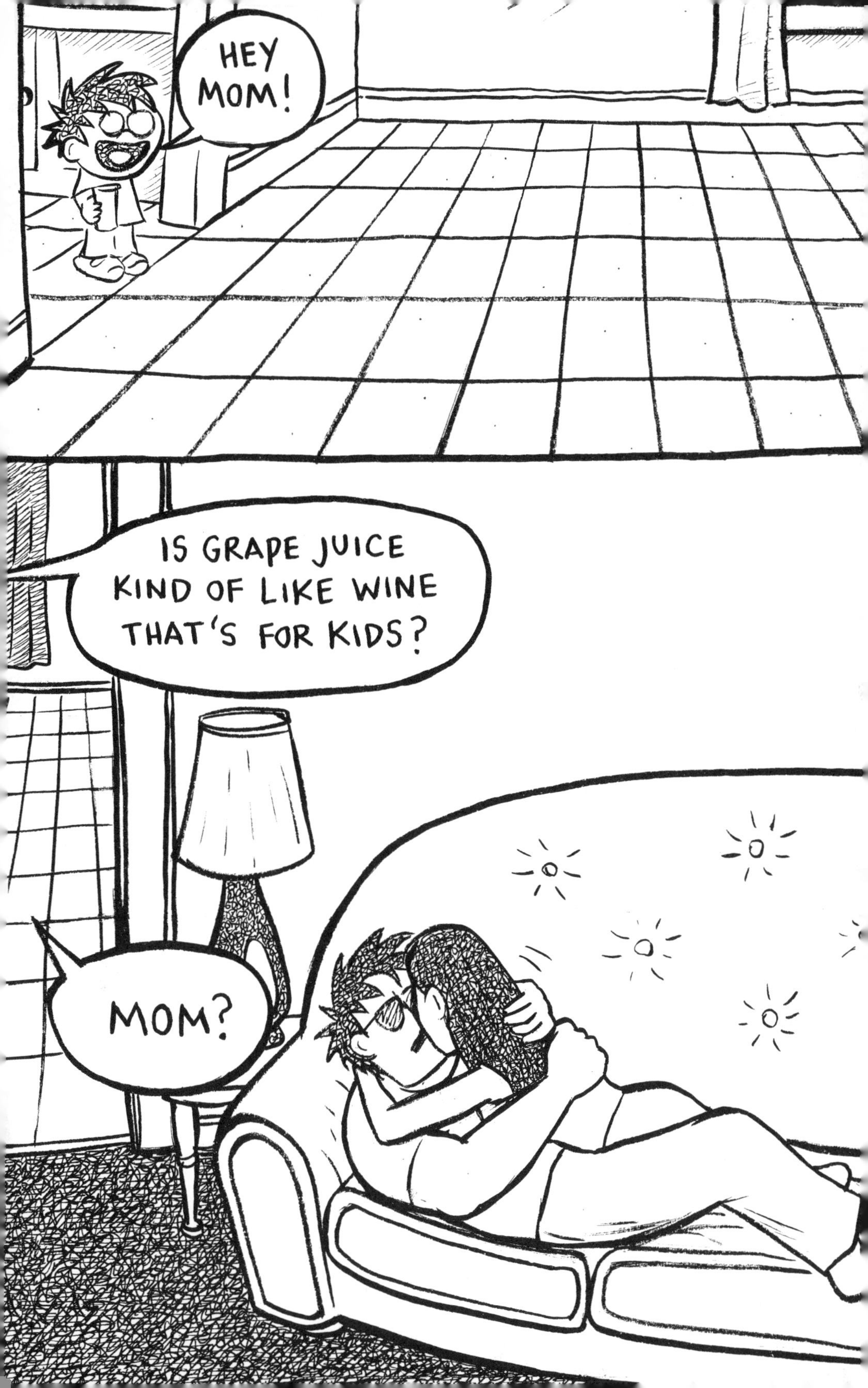
HEY MOM!
IS GRAPE JUICE KIND OF LIKE WINE THAT'S FOR KIDS?
MOM?

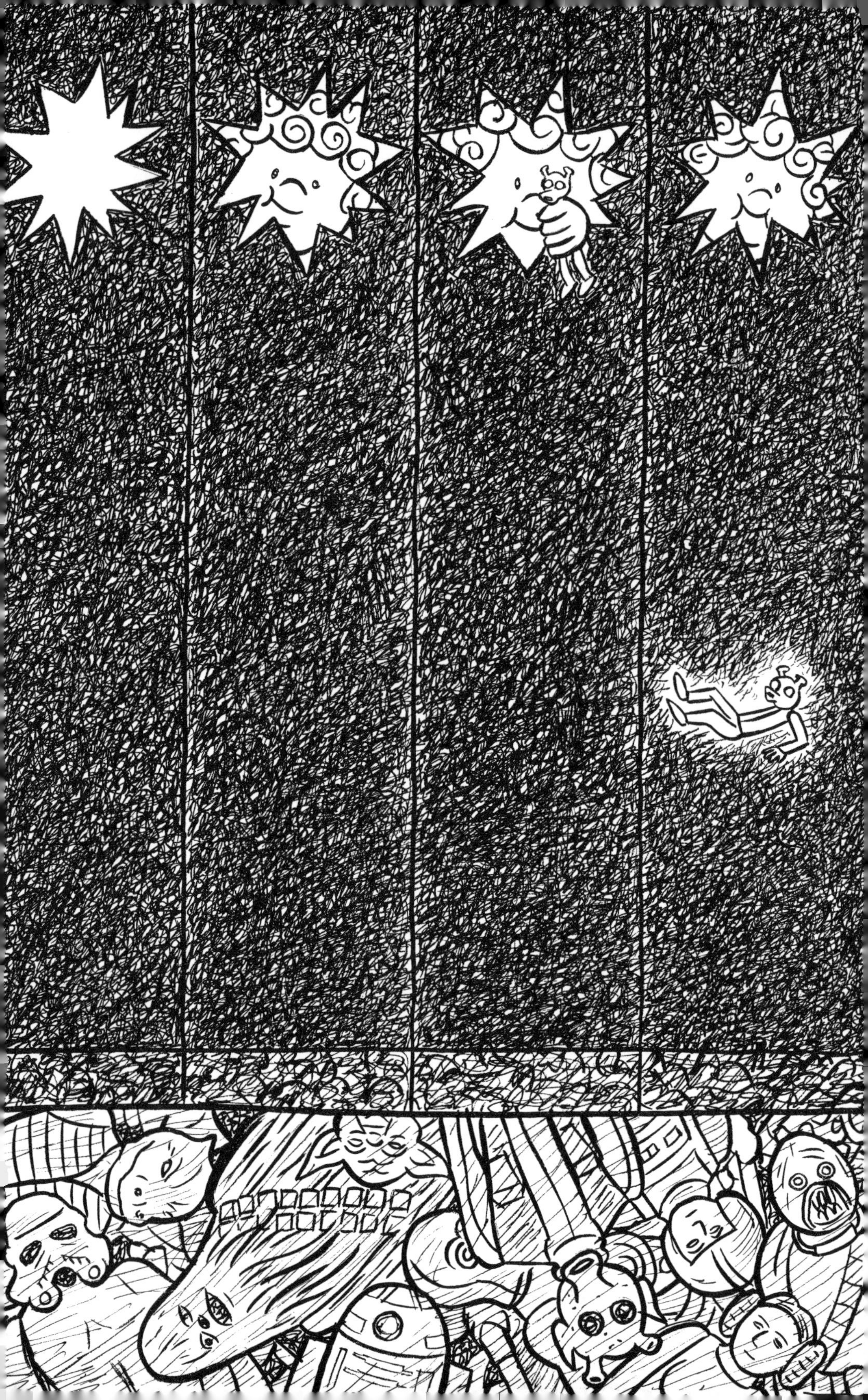

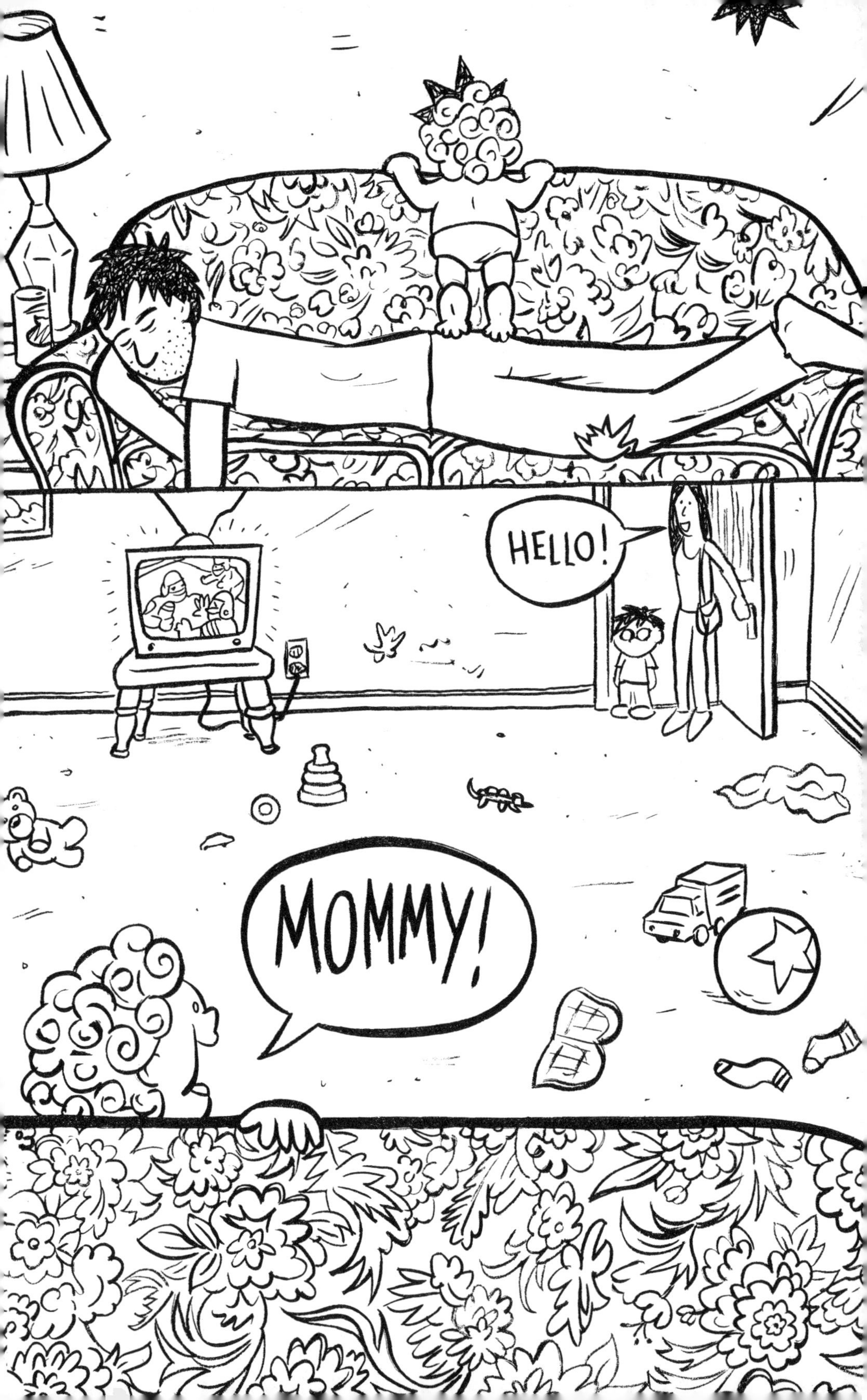
HELLO!
MOMMY!

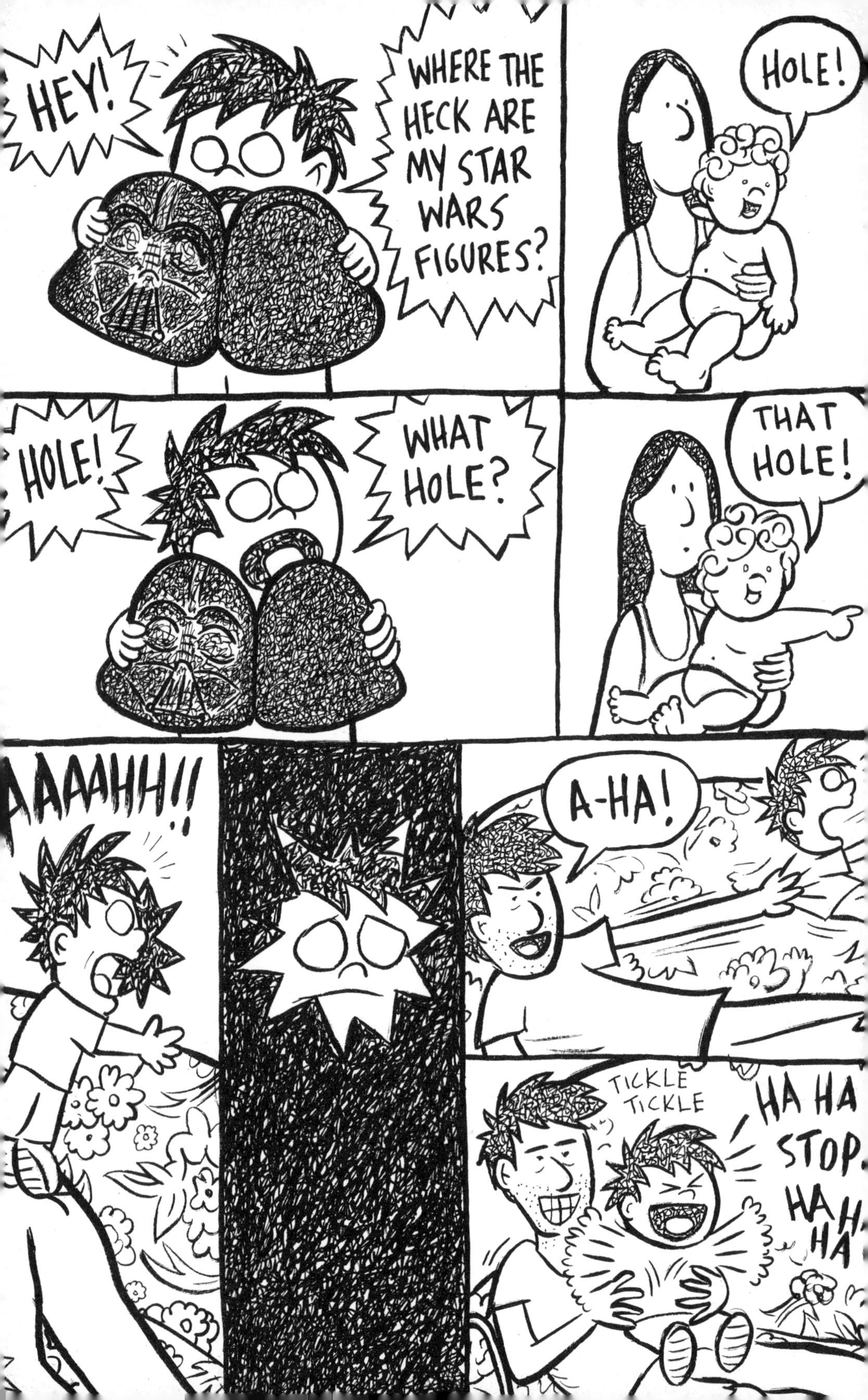
HEY!
WHERE THE HECK ARE MY STAR WARS FIGURES?
HOLE!
HOLE!
WHAT HOLE?
THAT HOLE!
AAAAHH!!
A-HA!
TICKLE TICKLE
HA HA STOP. HA HA HA

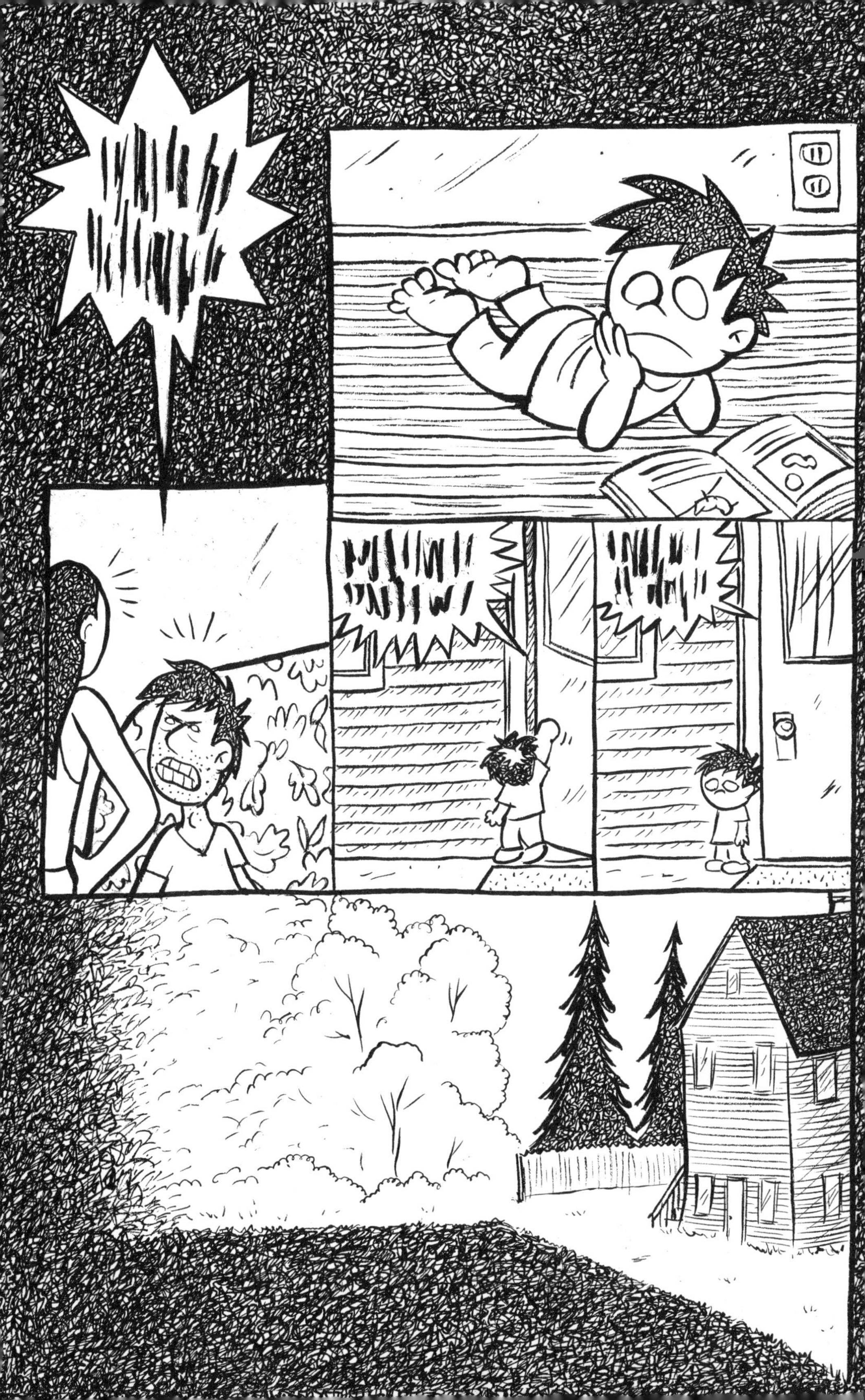

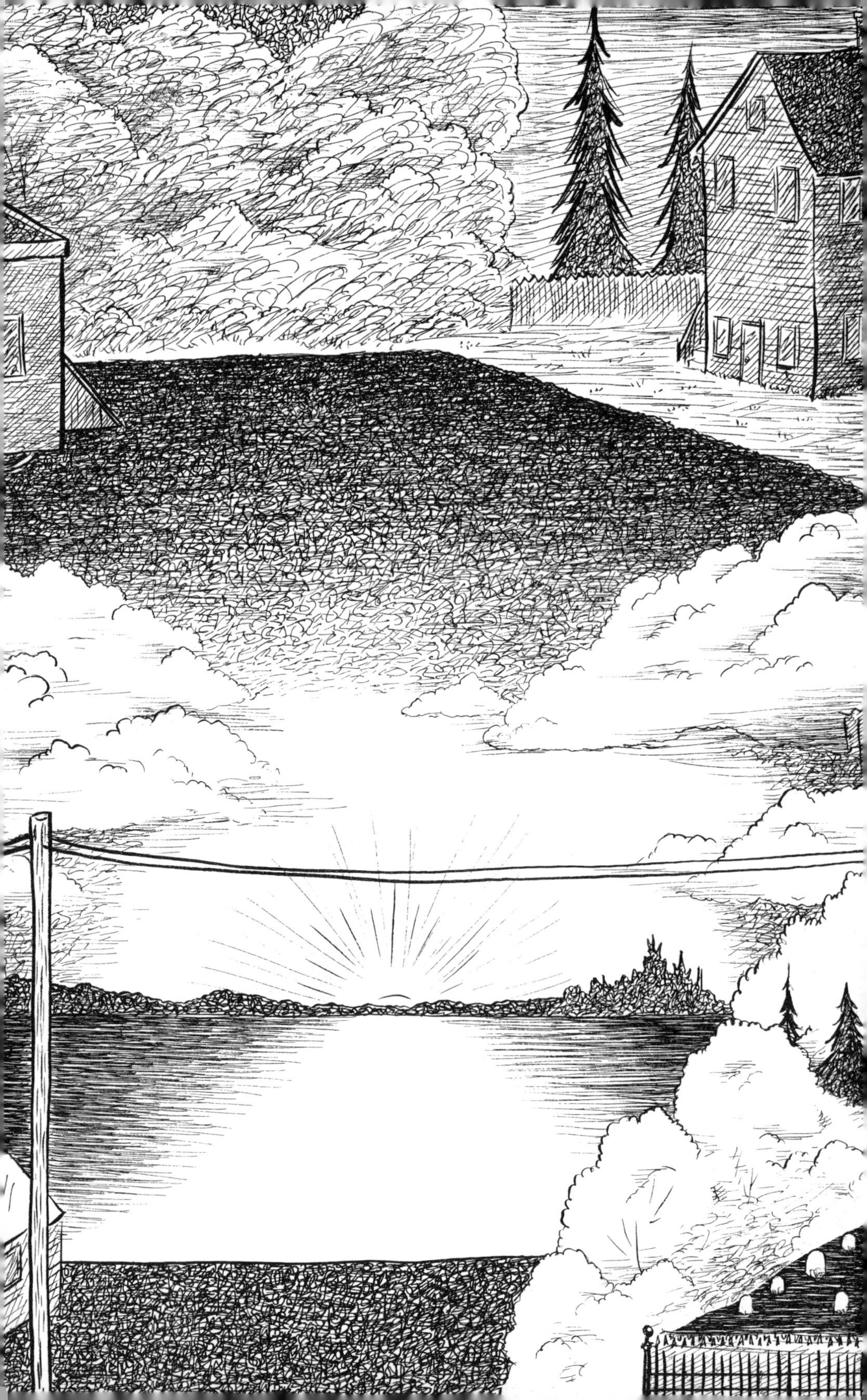

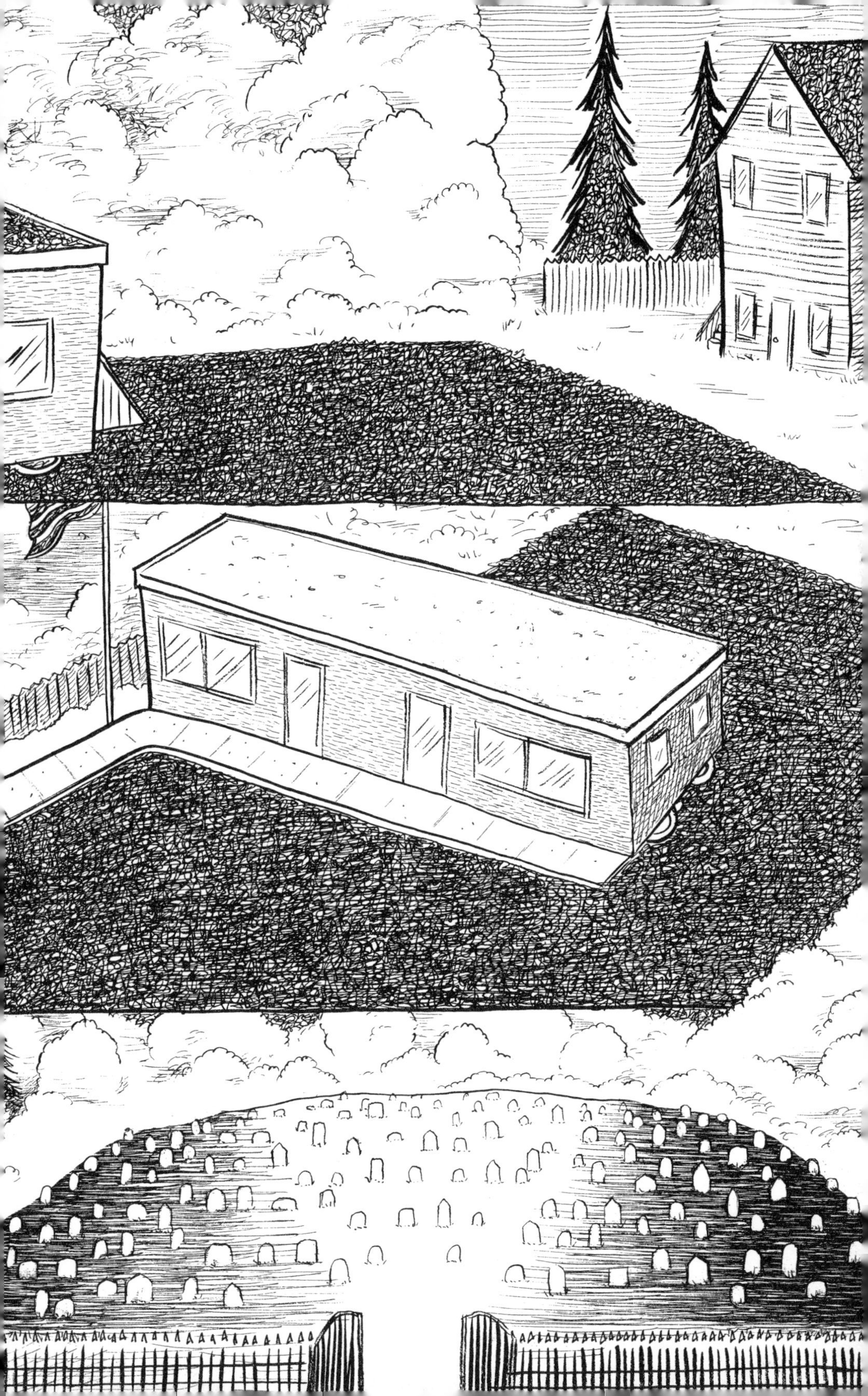

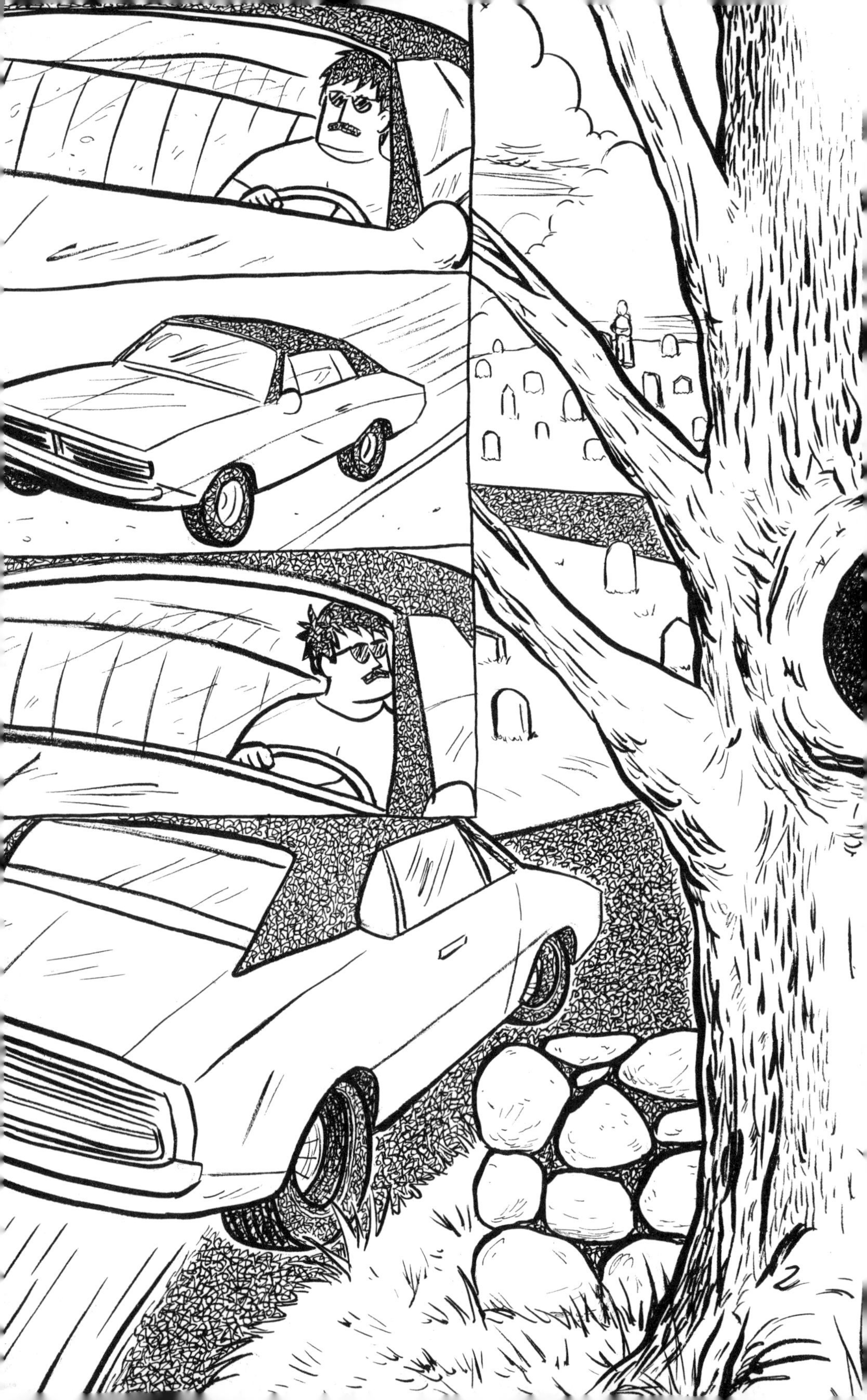

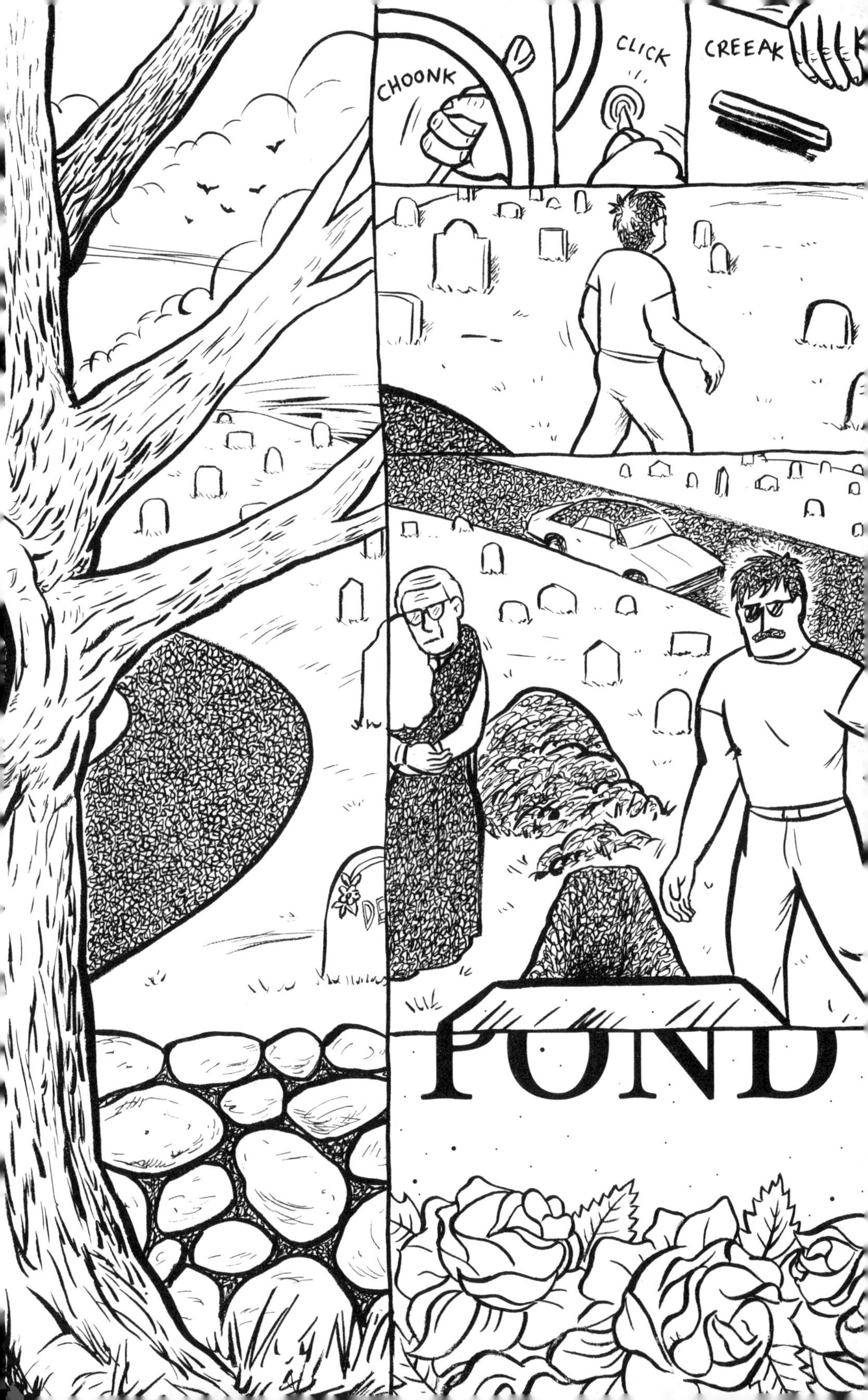
CHOONK
CLICK
CREEAK
POND

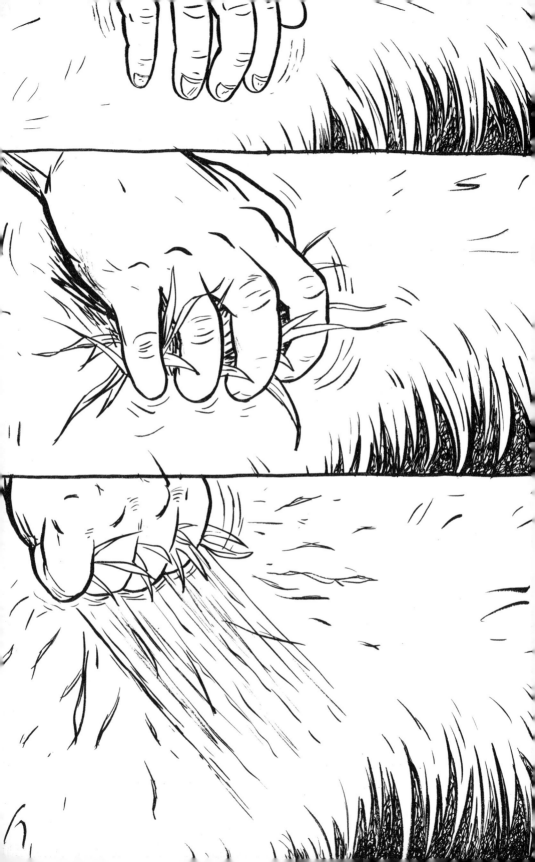

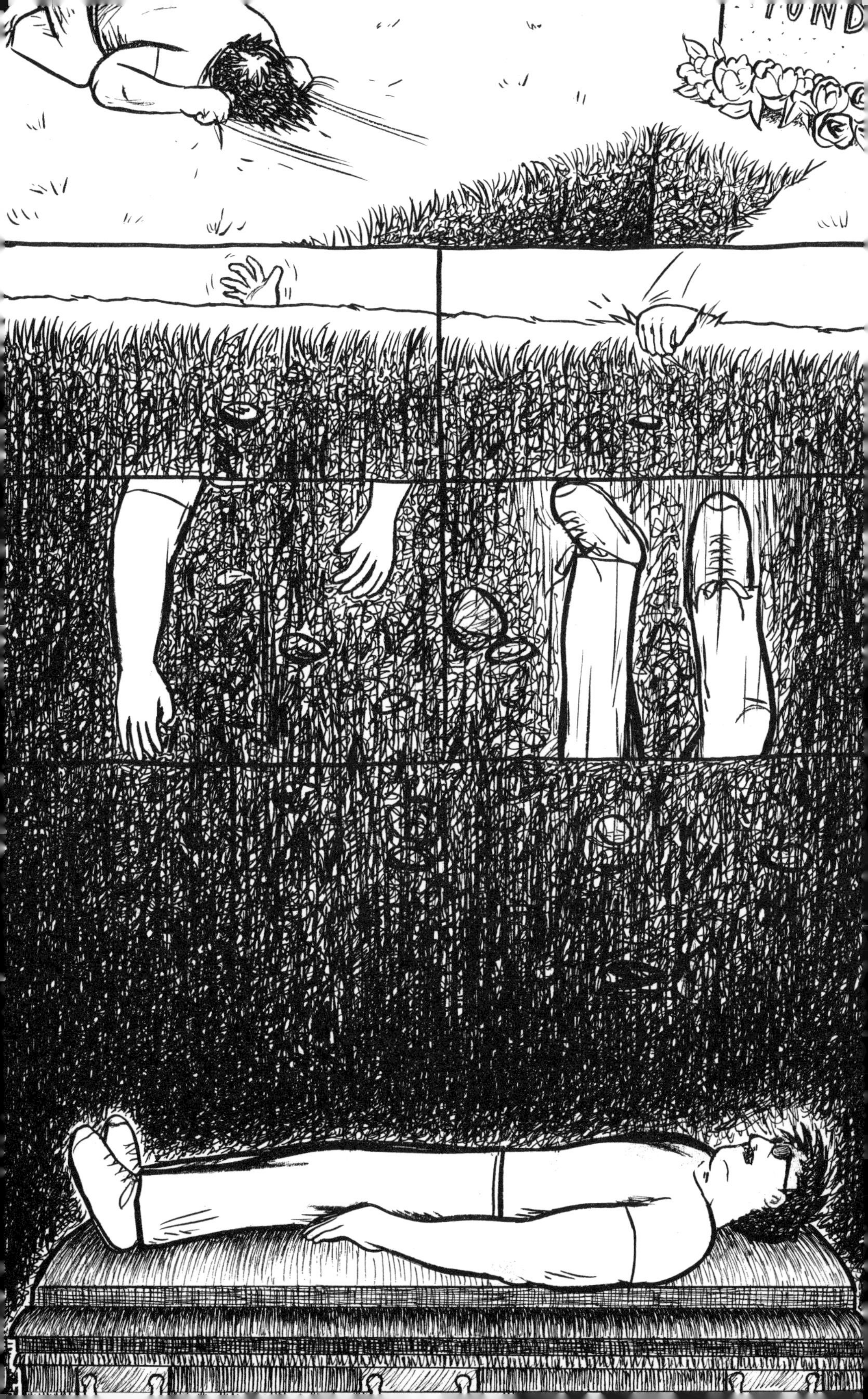

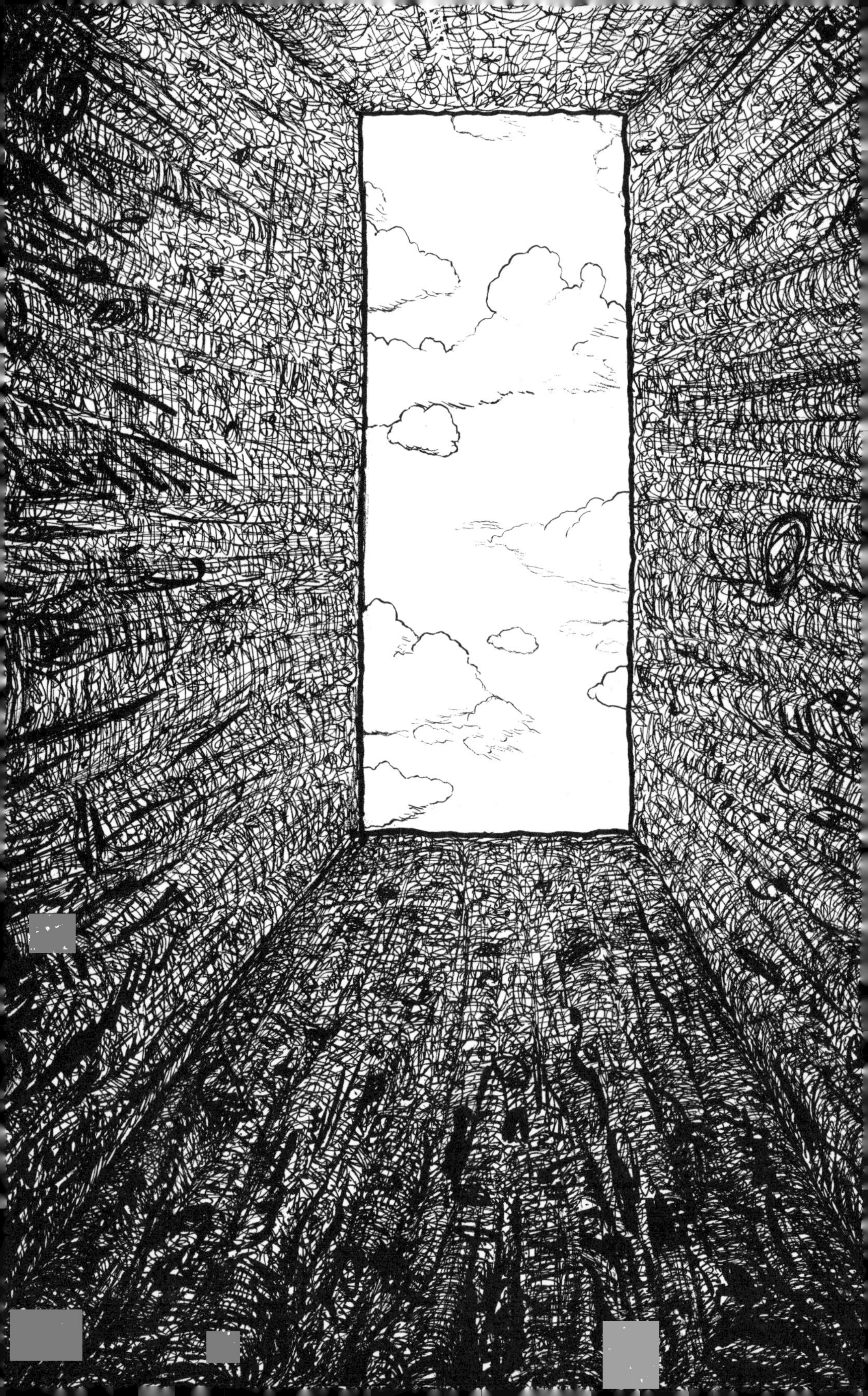

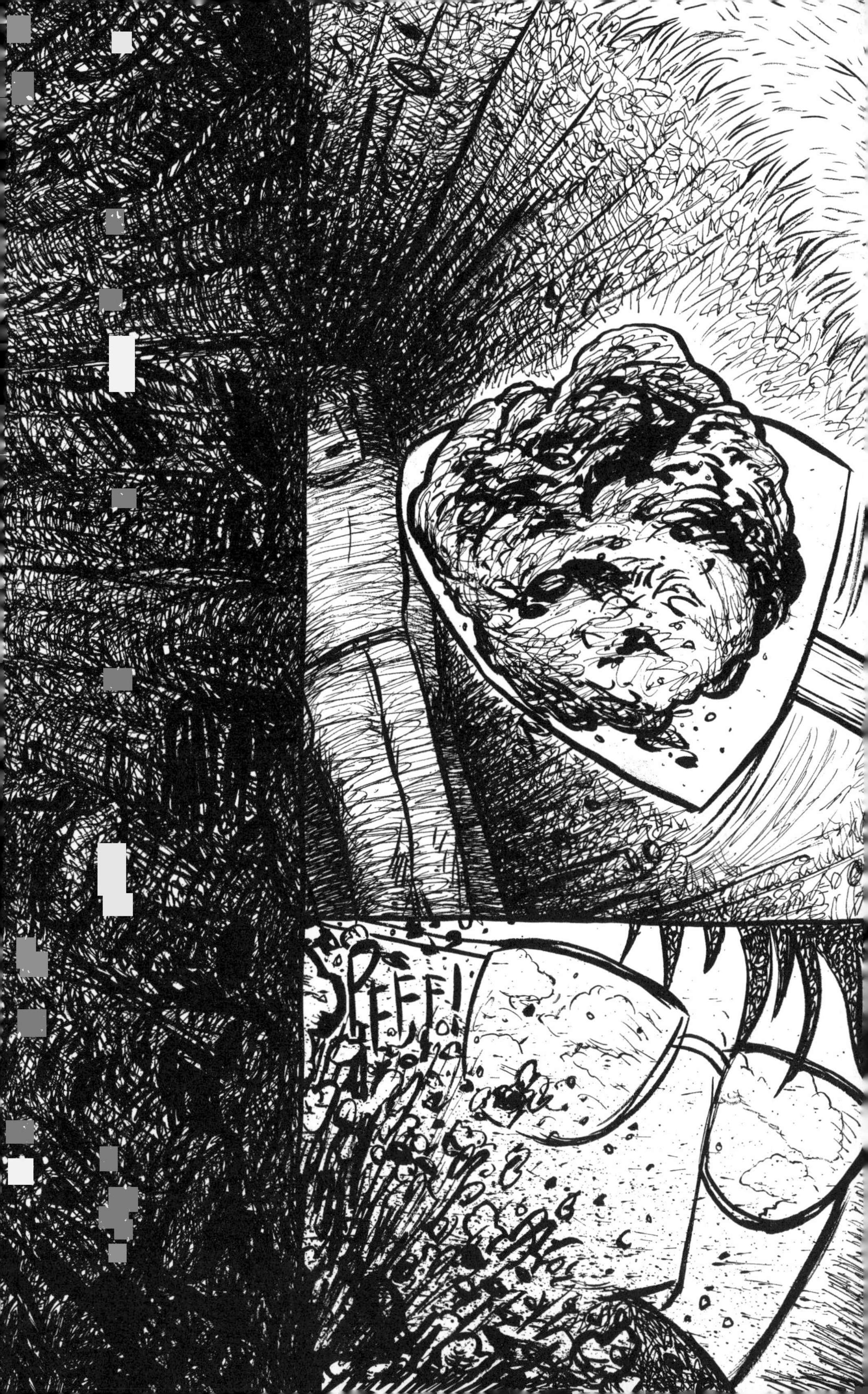
SPEEF!

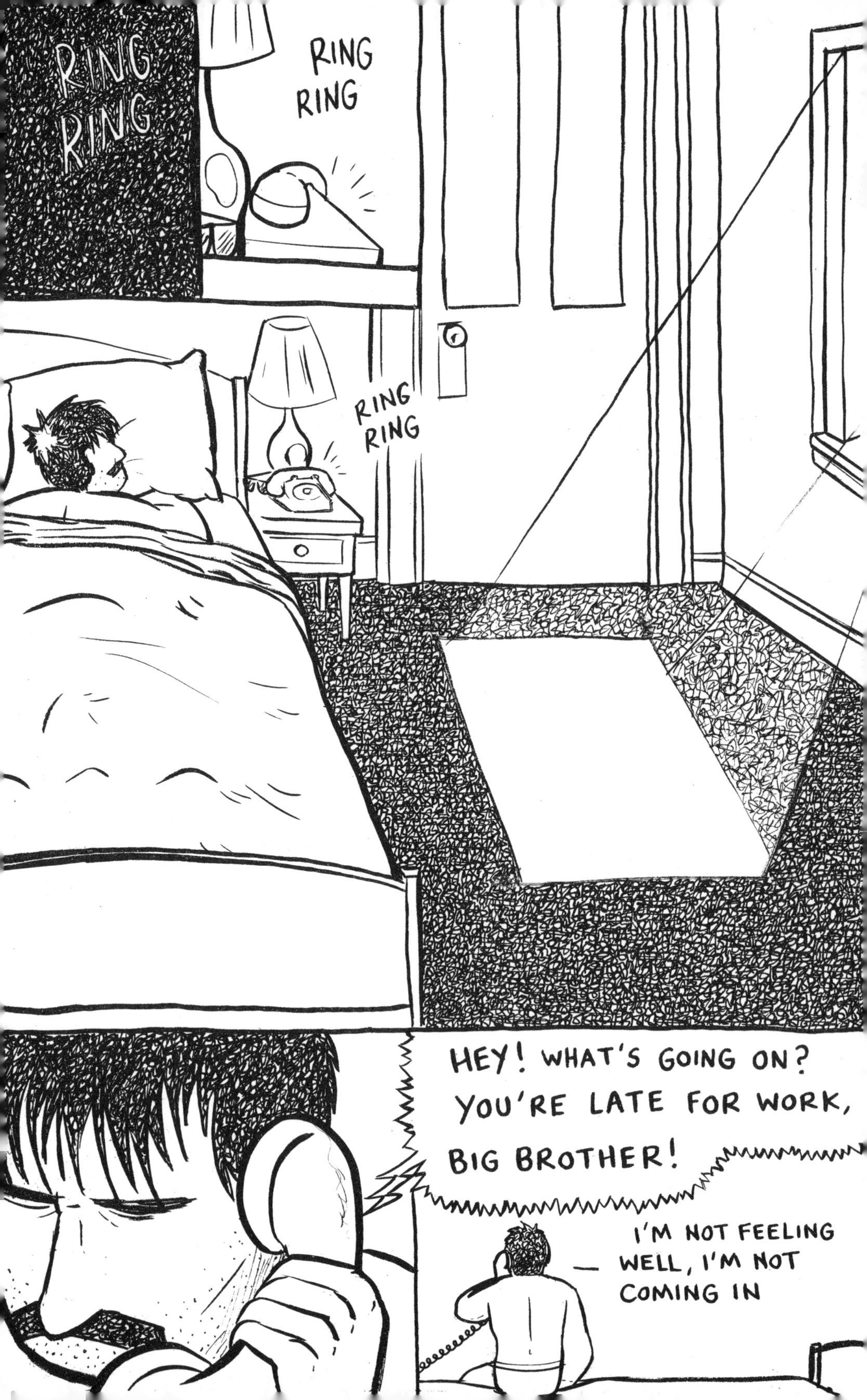
RING
RING
RING
RING
RING
RING
HEY! WHAT'S GOING ON? YOU'RE LATE FOR WORK, BIG BROTHER!
— I'M NOT FEELING WELL, I'M NOT COMING IN

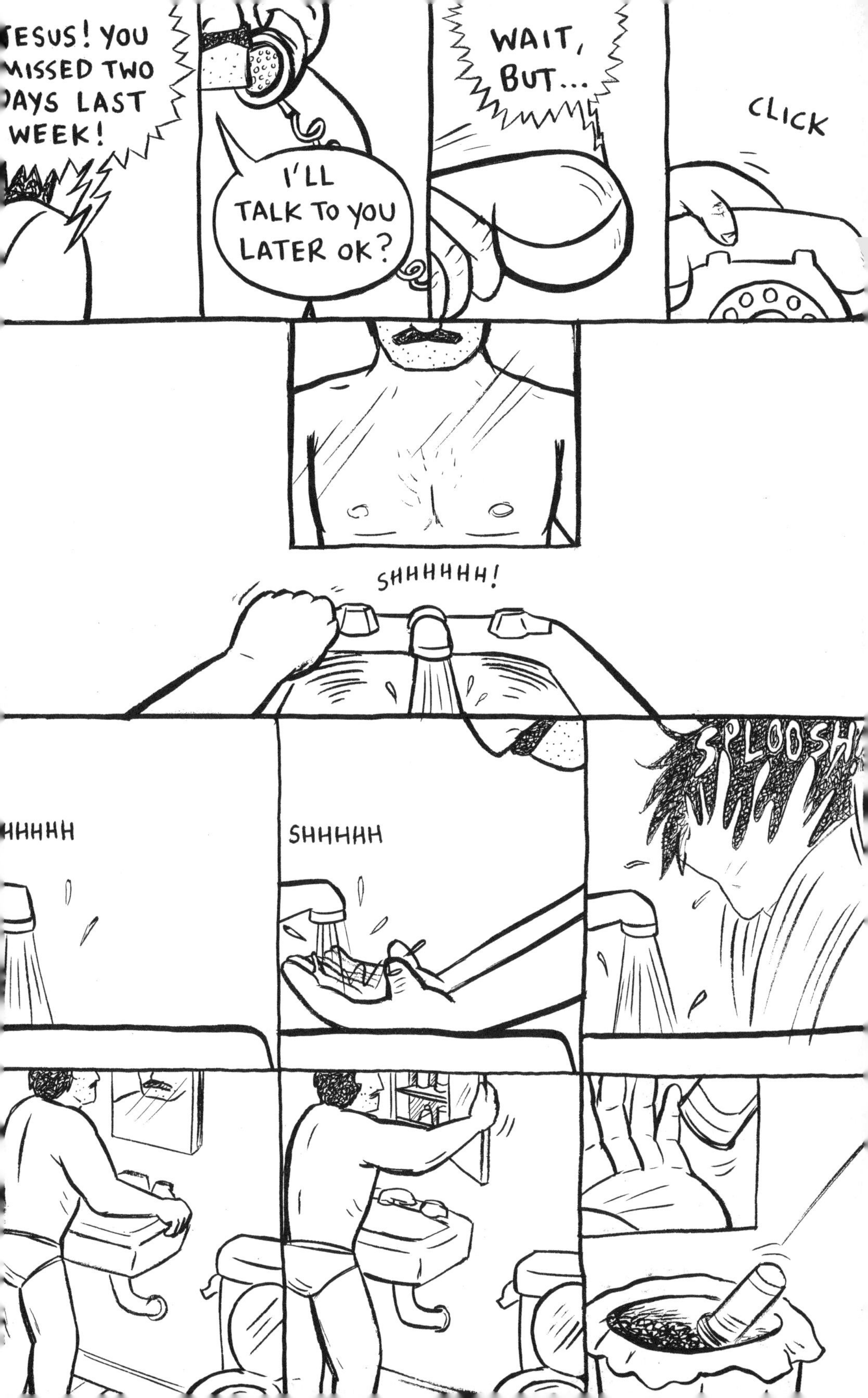
JESUS! YOU MISSED TWO DAYS LAST WEEK!
I'LL TALK TO YOU LATER OK?
WAIT, BUT...
CLICK
SHHHHHH!
HHHHH
SHHHHH
SPLOOSH!

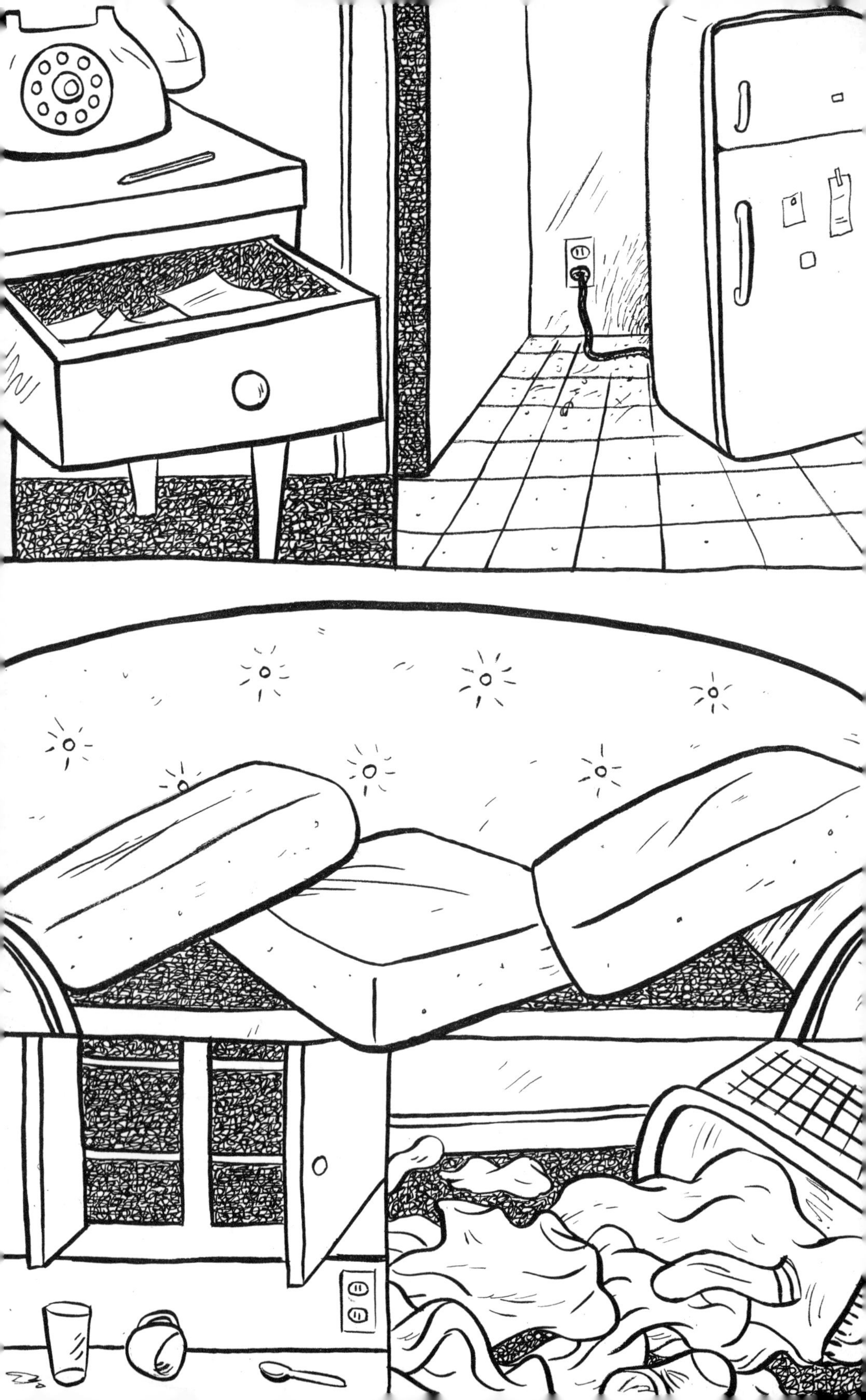

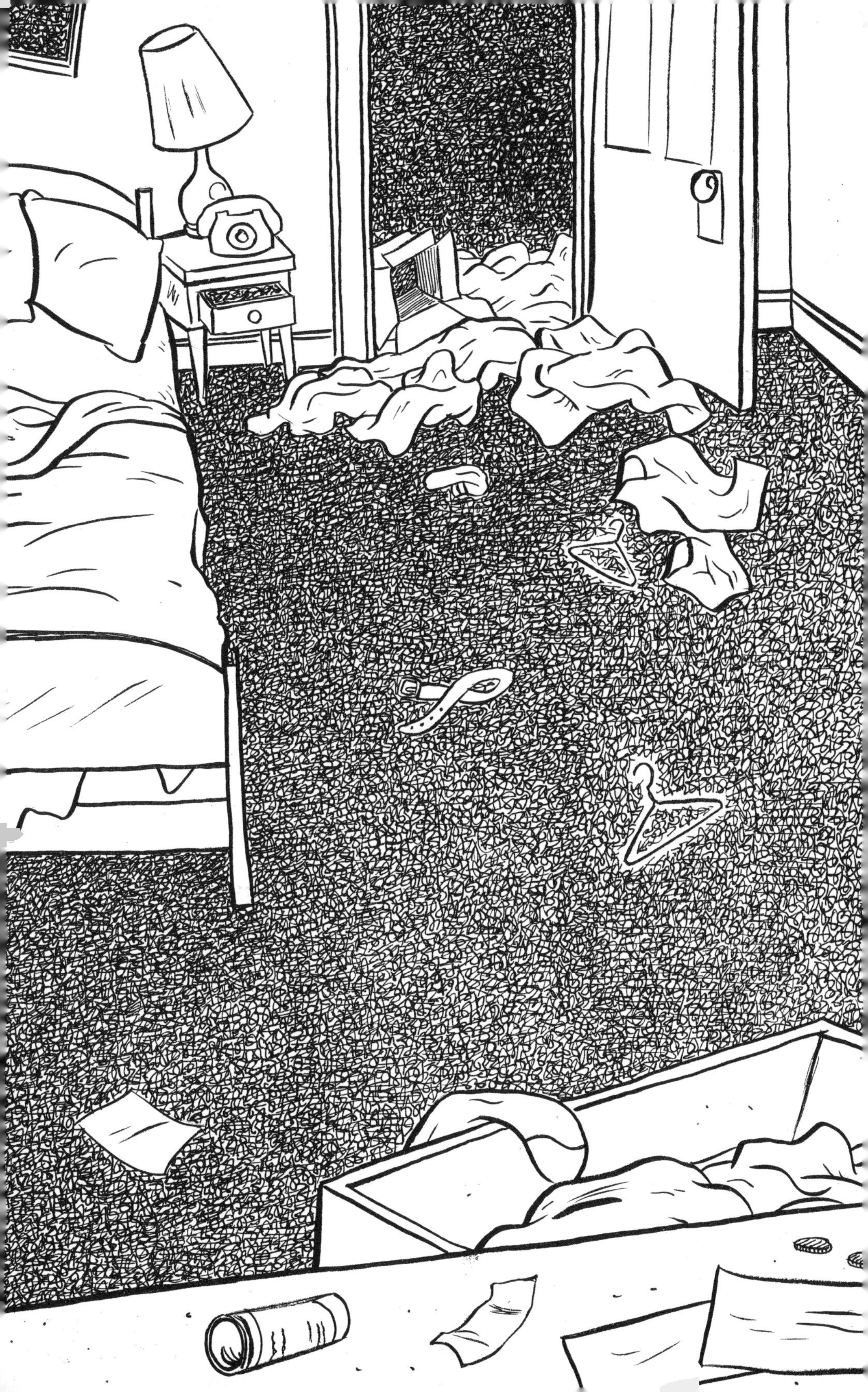

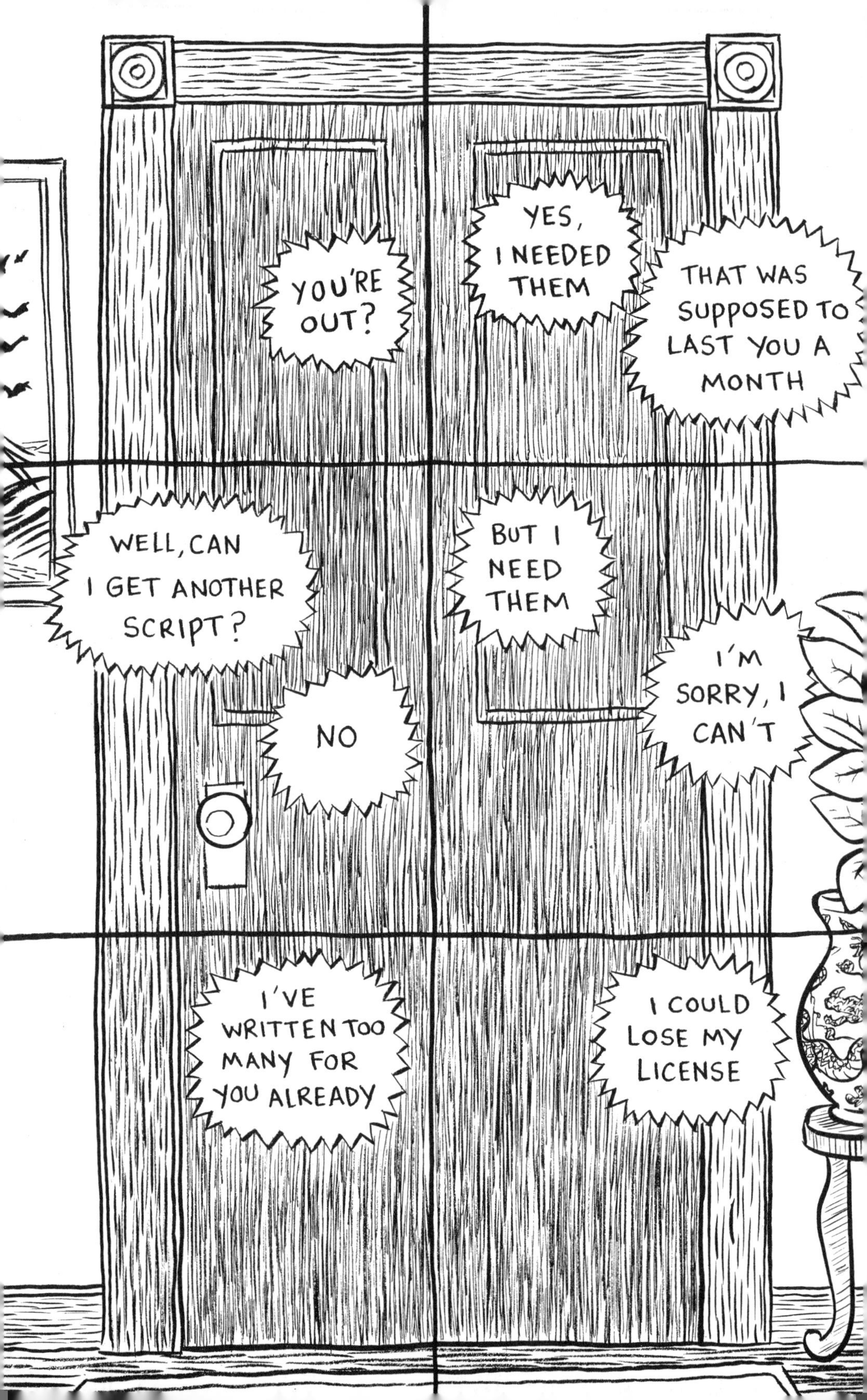
YOU'RE OUT?
YES, I NEEDED THEM
THAT WAS SUPPOSED TO LAST YOU A MONTH
WELL, CAN I GET ANOTHER SCRIPT?
BUT I NEED THEM
NO
I'M SORRY, I CAN'T
I'VE WRITTEN TOO MANY FOR YOU ALREADY
I COULD LOSE MY LICENSE

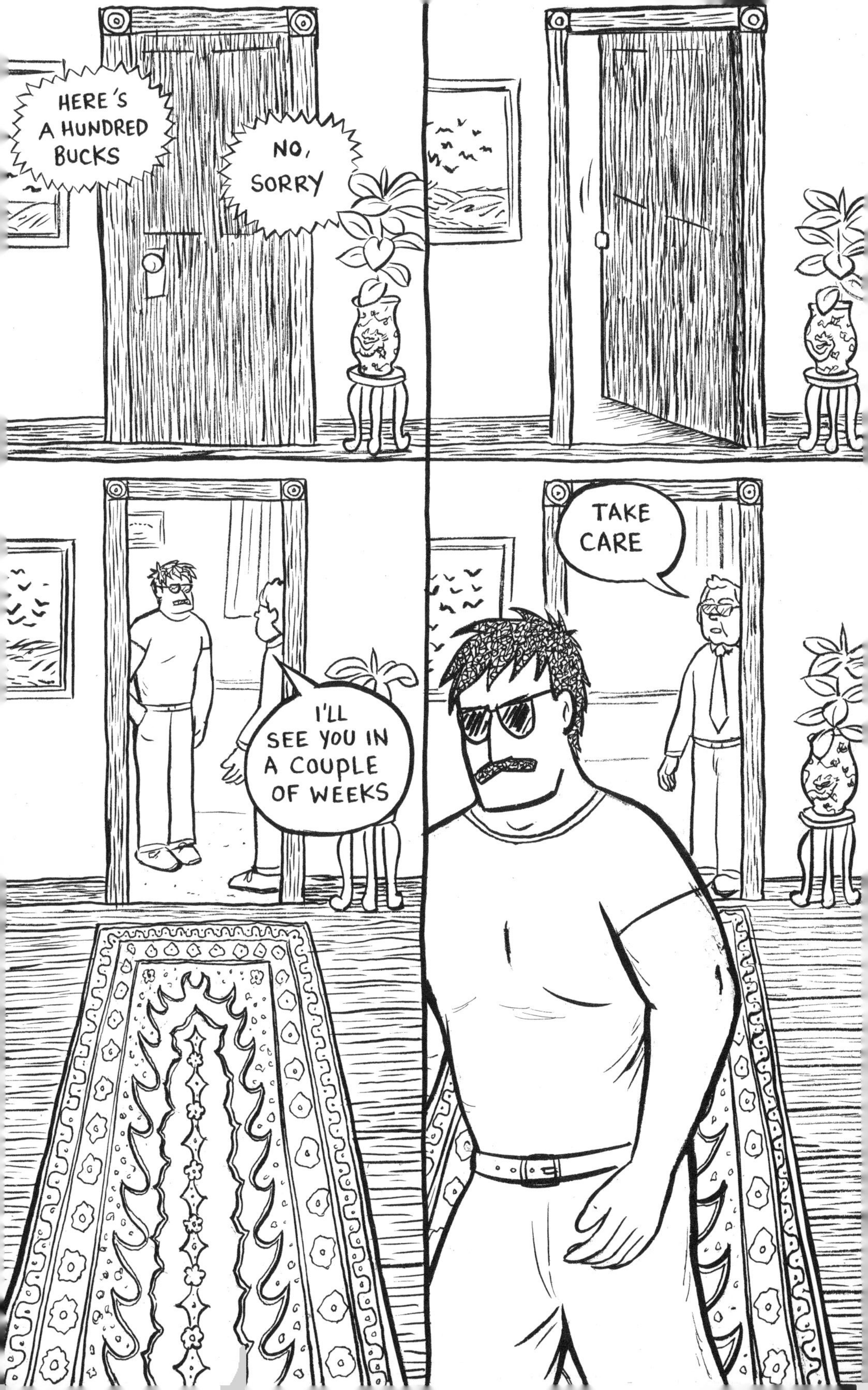
HERE'S A HUNDRED BUCKS
NO, SORRY
I'LL SEE YOU IN A COUPLE OF WEEKS
TAKE CARE

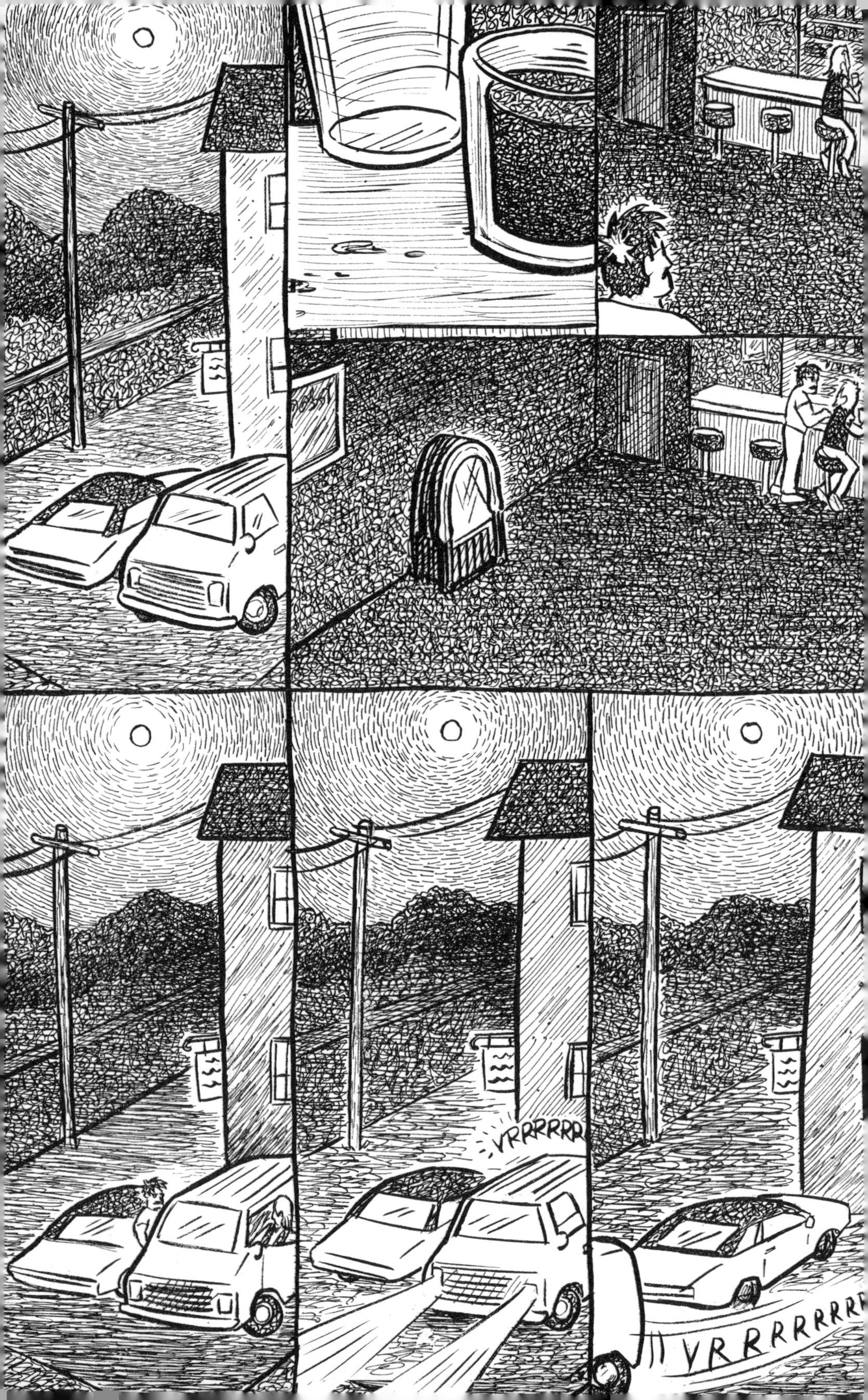
VRRRRRR
VRRRRRRRR

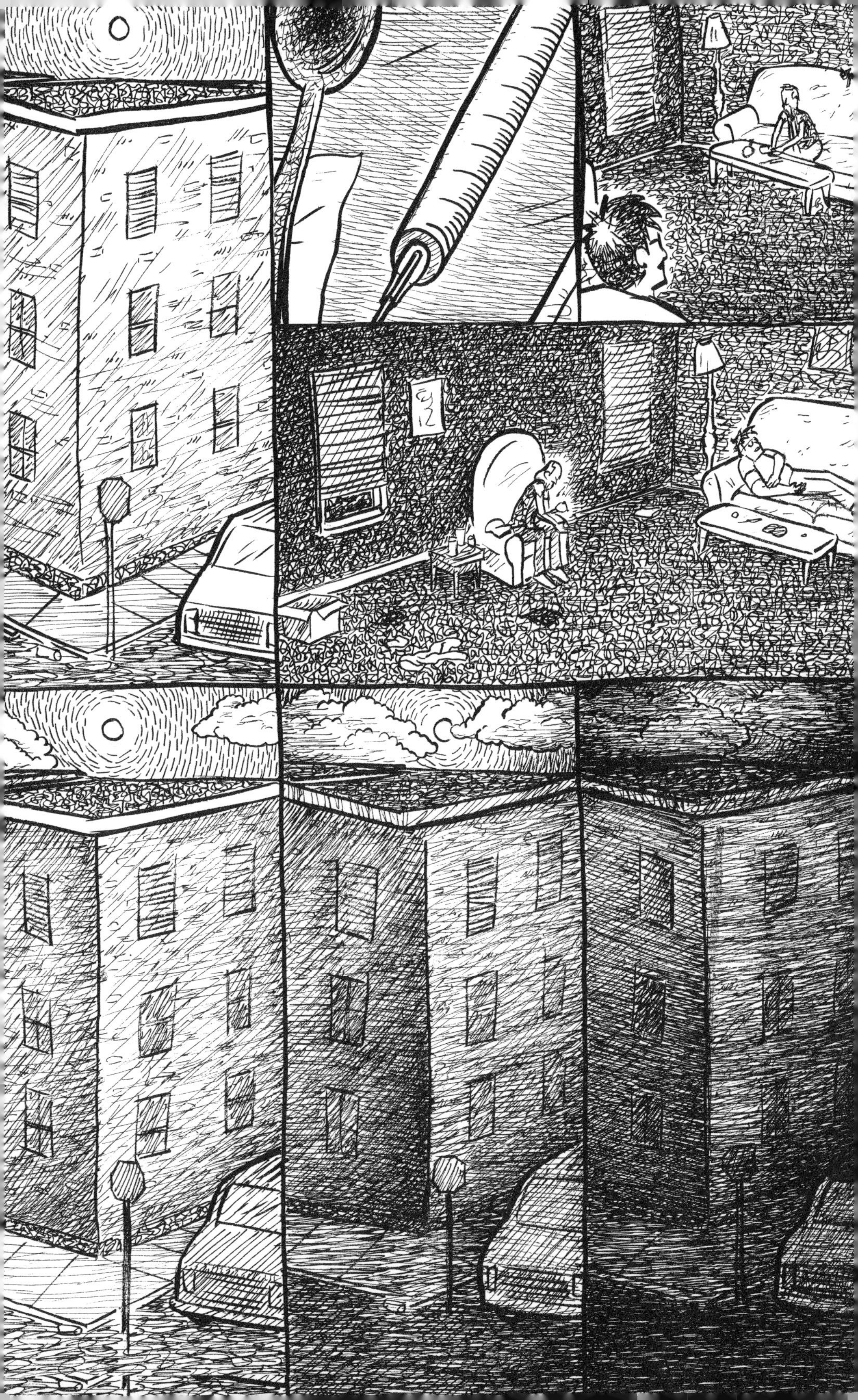

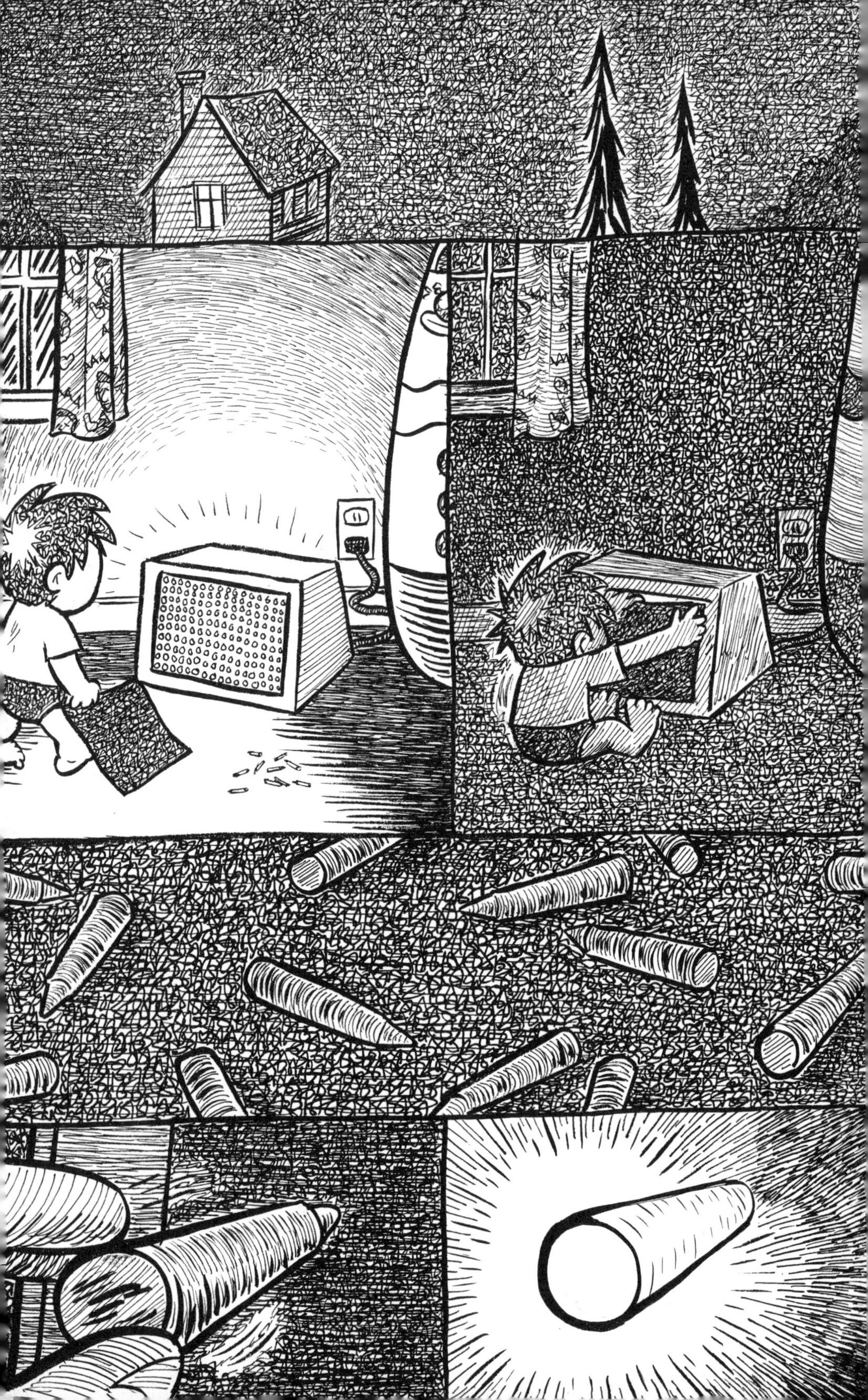

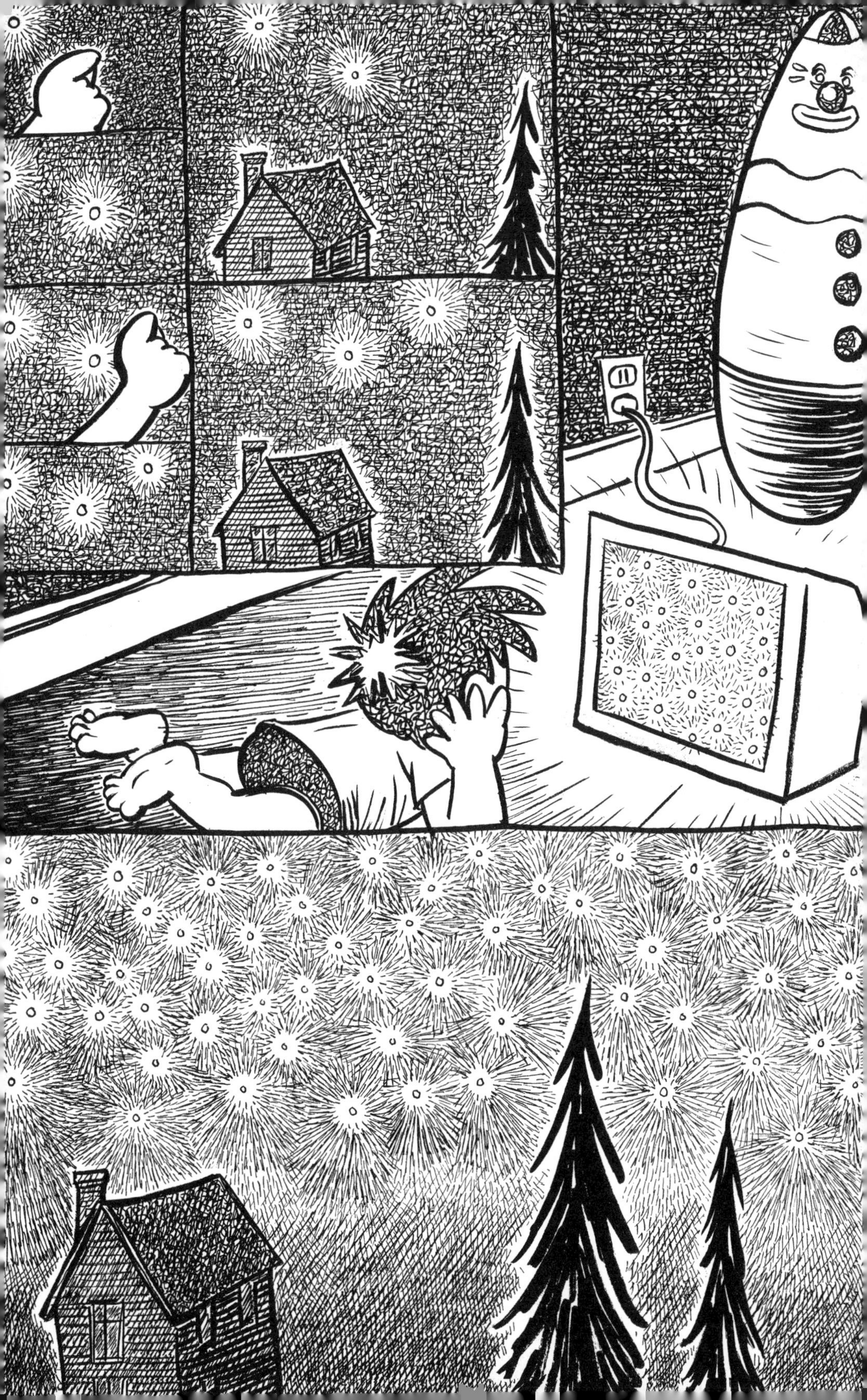

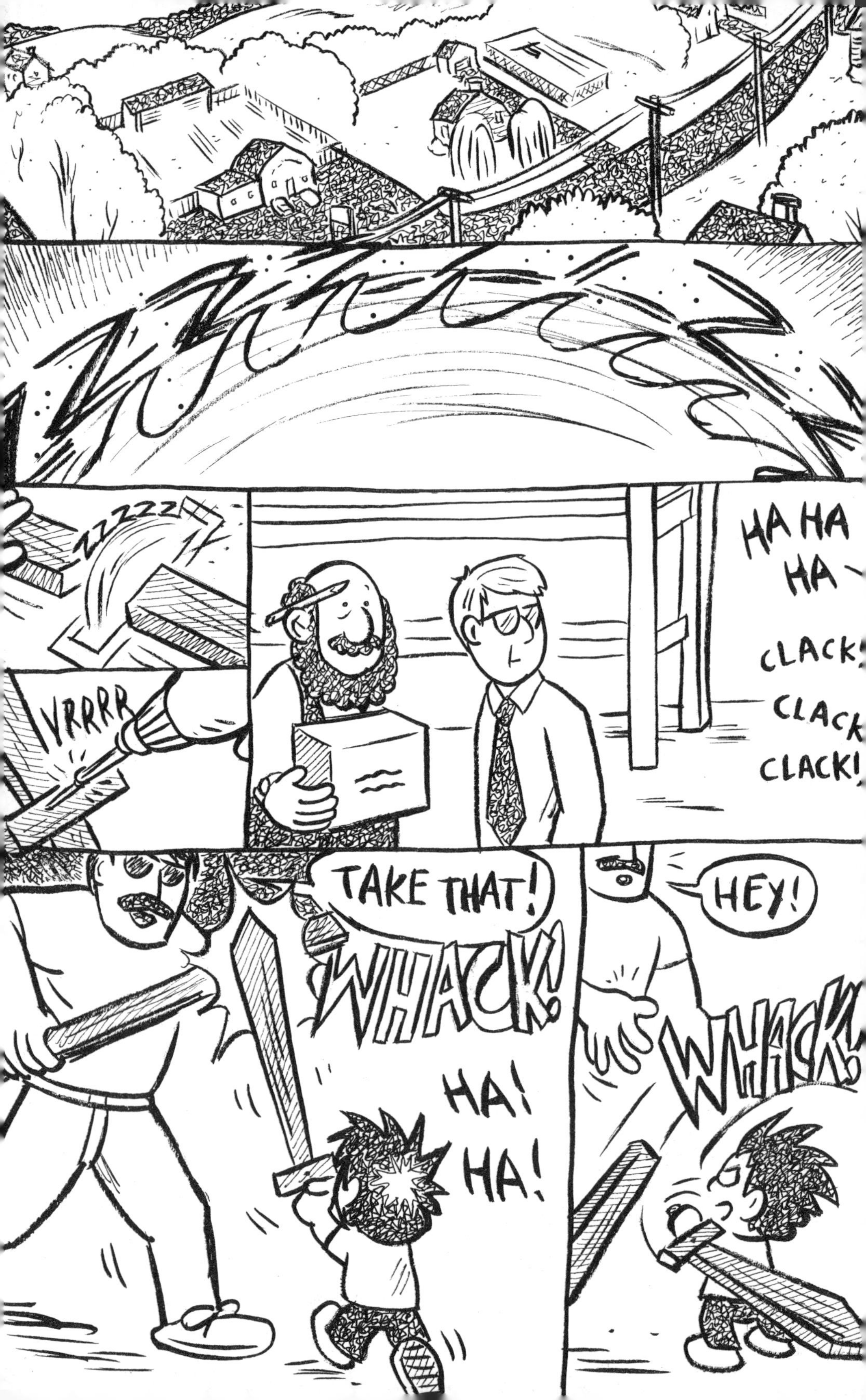
ZZZZZ
VRRRR
HA HA HA HA
CLACK!
CLACK
CLACK!
TAKE THAT!
WHACK!
HA! HA!
HEY!
WHACK!

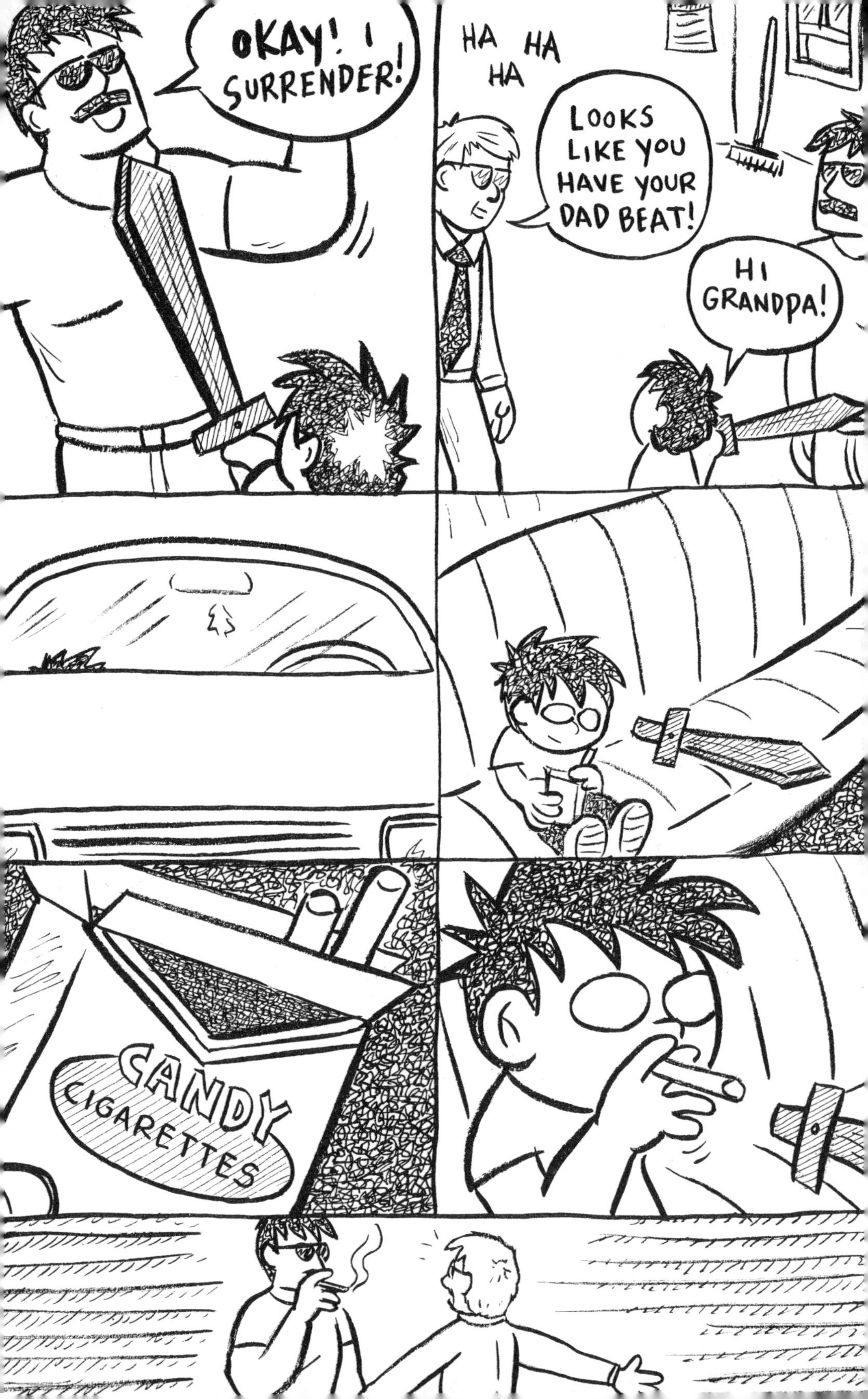
OKAY! I SURRENDER!
HA HA HA
LOOKS LIKE YOU HAVE YOUR DAD BEAT!
HI GRANDPA!
CANDY CIGARETTES

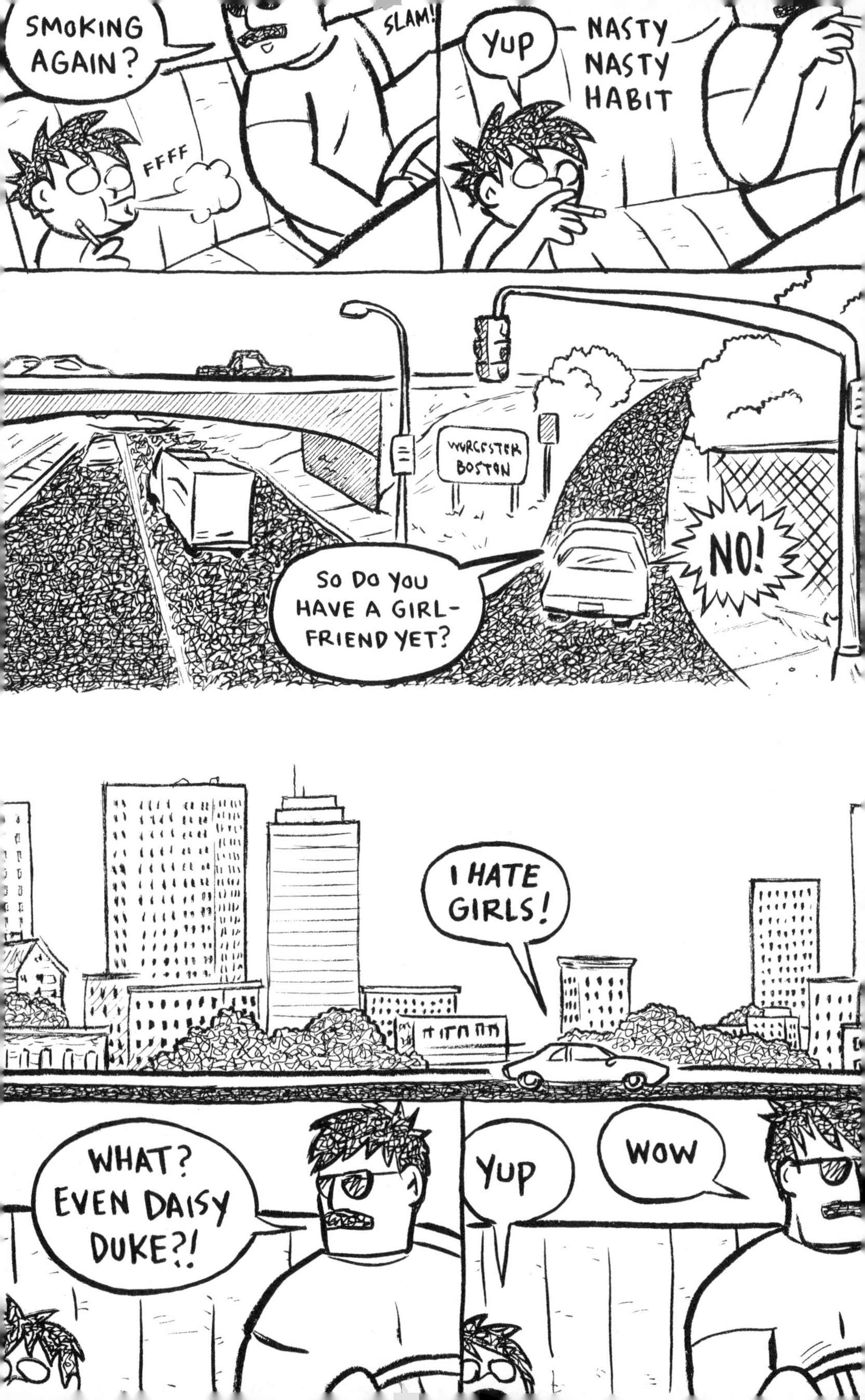
SMOKING AGAIN?
SLAM!
FFFF
YUP
NASTY NASTY HABIT
WORCESTER
BOSTON
SO DO YOU HAVE A GIRL-FRIEND YET?
NO!
I HATE GIRLS!
WHAT? EVEN DAISY DUKE?!
YUP
WOW

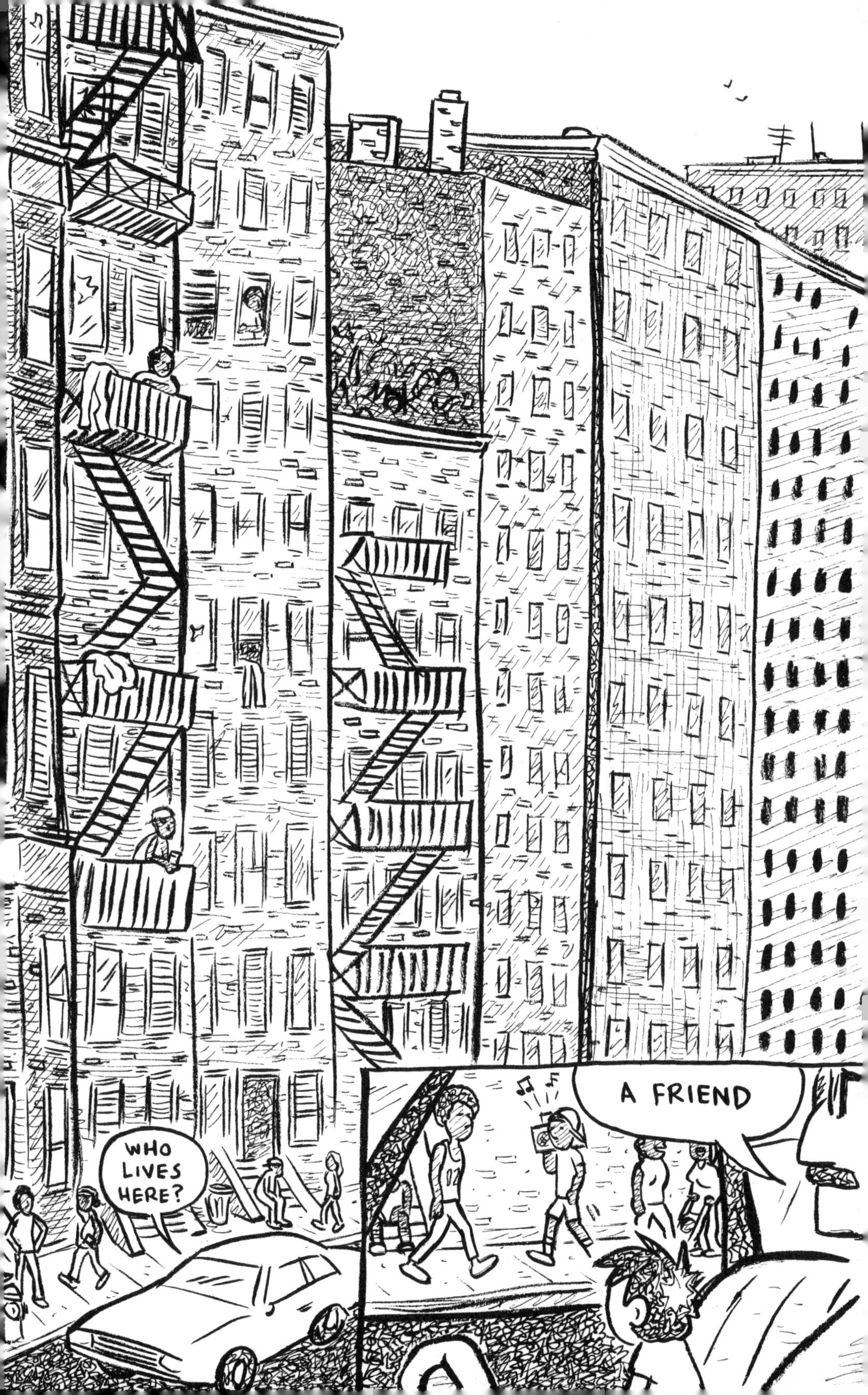
WHO LIVES HERE?
A FRIEND

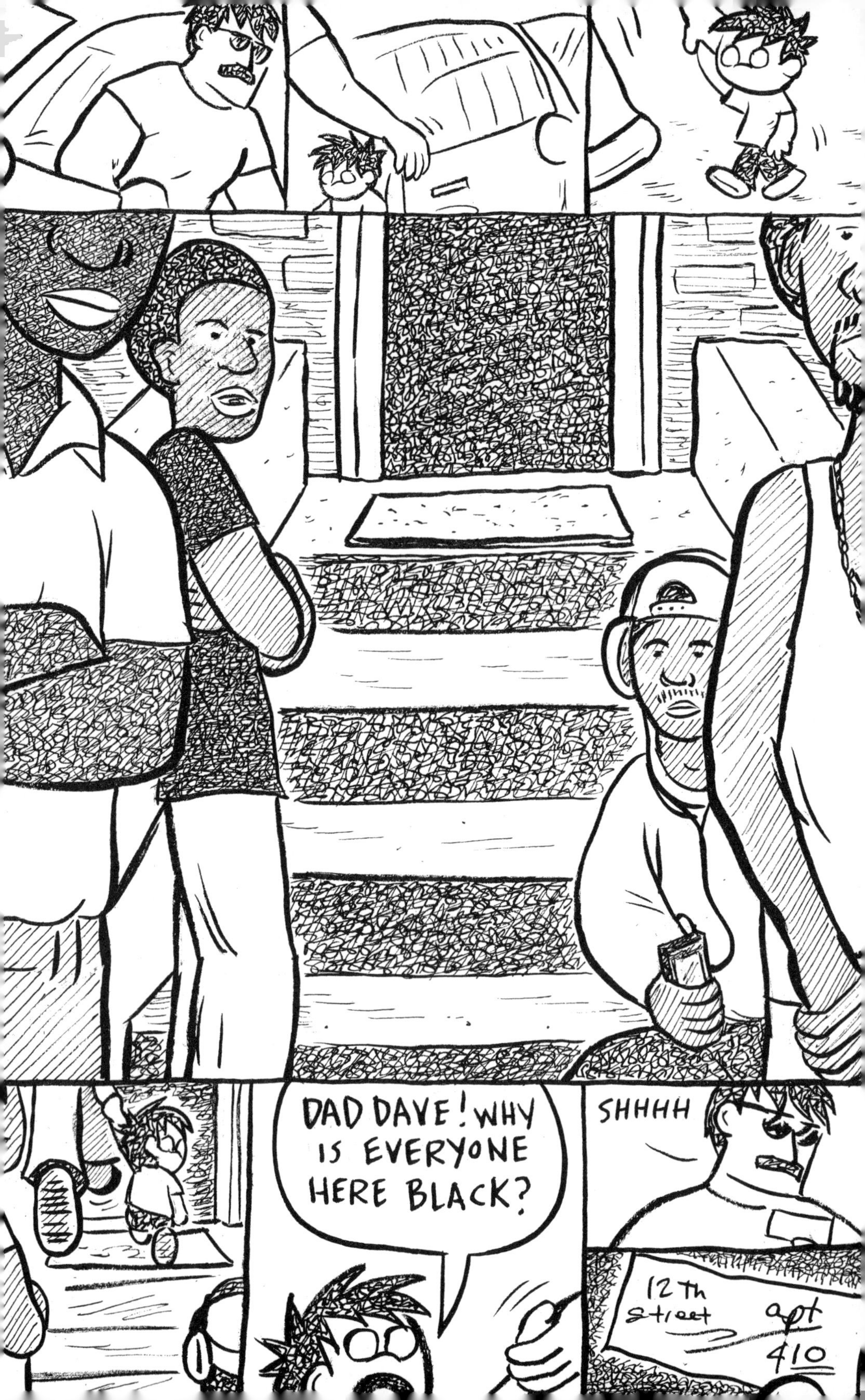
DAD DAVE! WHY IS EVERYONE HERE BLACK?
SHHHH
12th street apt 410

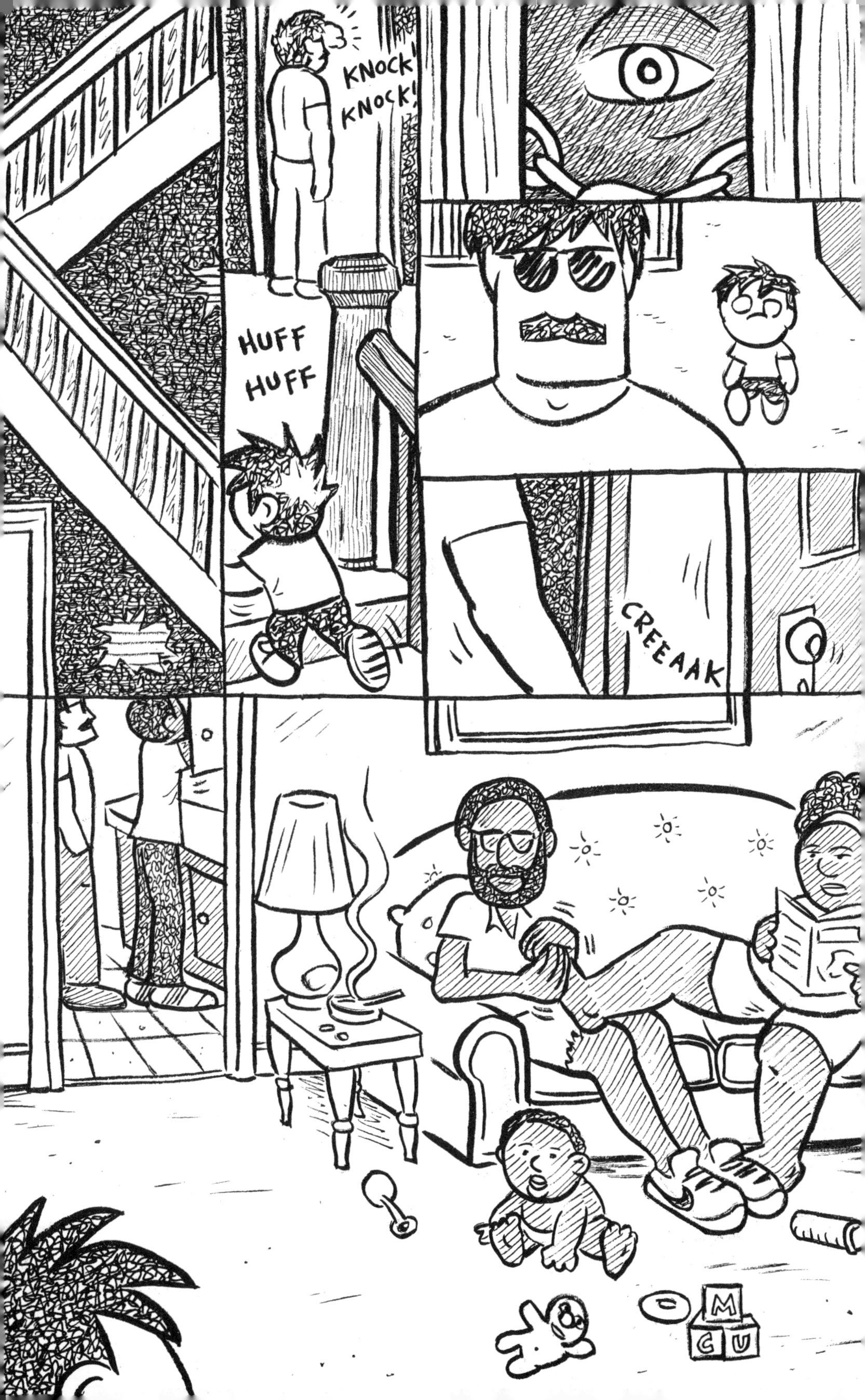
KNOCK
KNOCK!
HUFF
HUFF
CREEAAK
M
C U

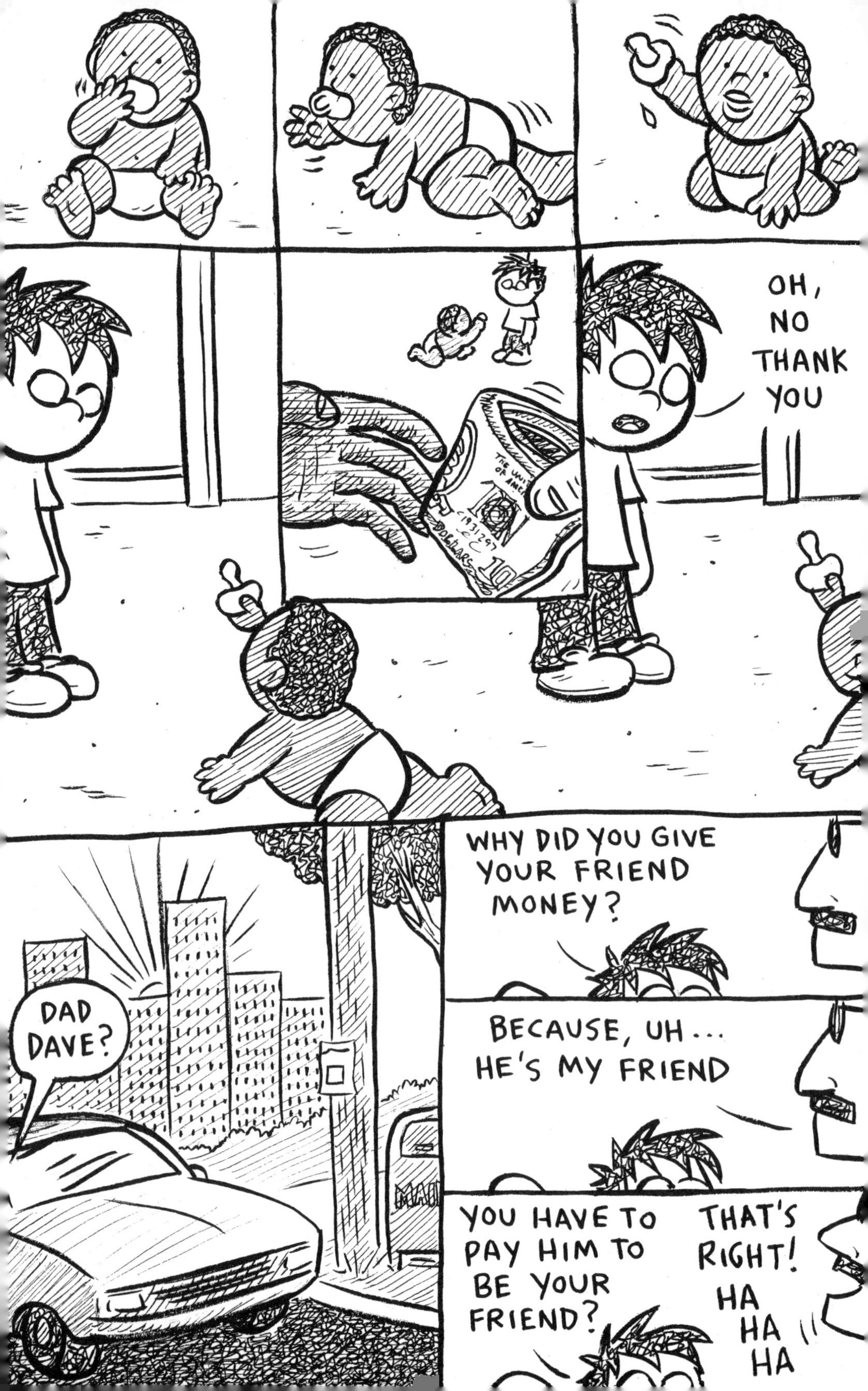
OH, NO THANK YOU
DAD DAVE?
WHY DID YOU GIVE YOUR FRIEND MONEY?
BECAUSE, UH... HE'S MY FRIEND
YOU HAVE TO PAY HIM TO BE YOUR FRIEND?
THAT'S RIGHT! HA HA HA

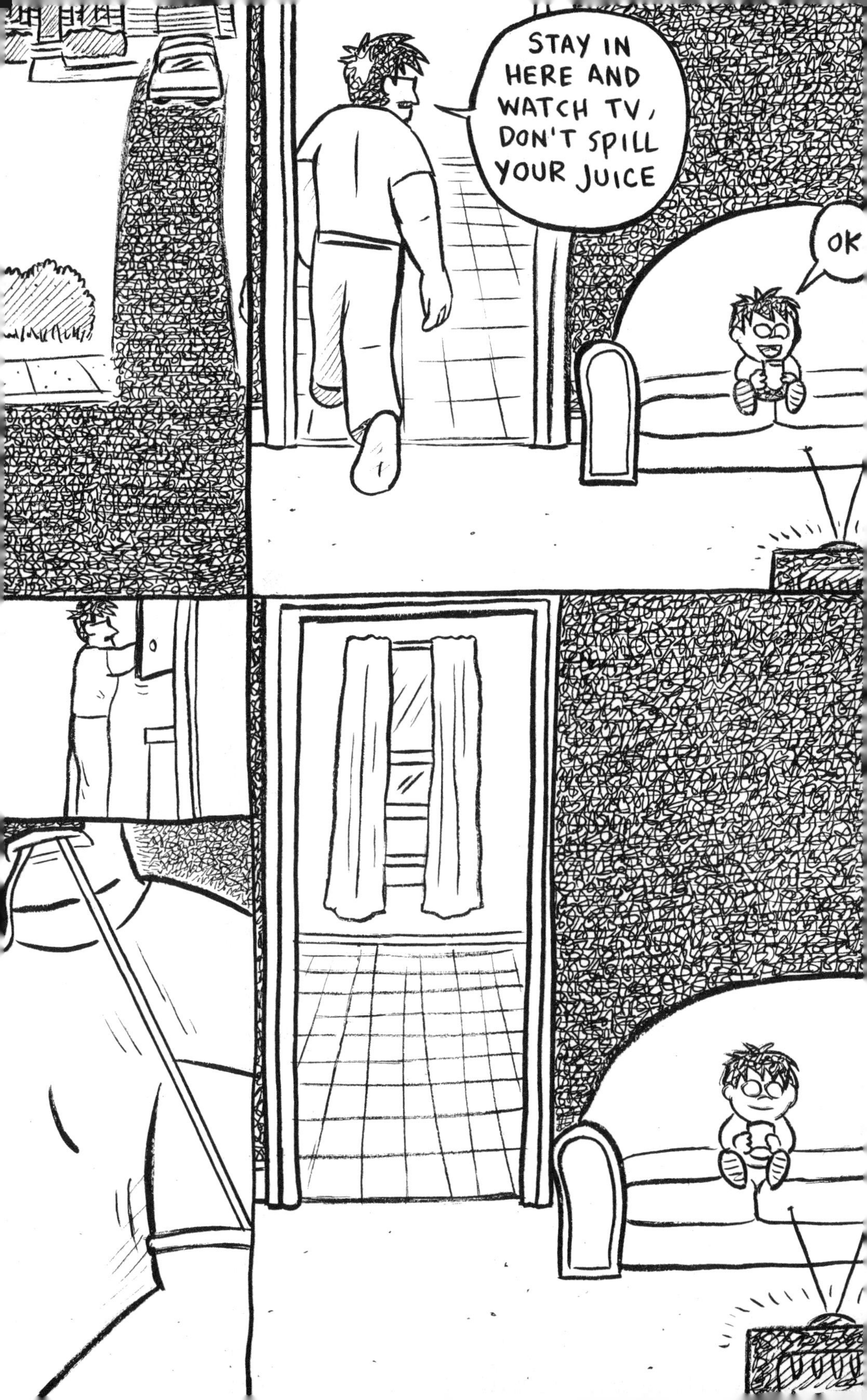
STAY IN HERE AND WATCH TV, DON'T SPILL YOUR JUICE
OK

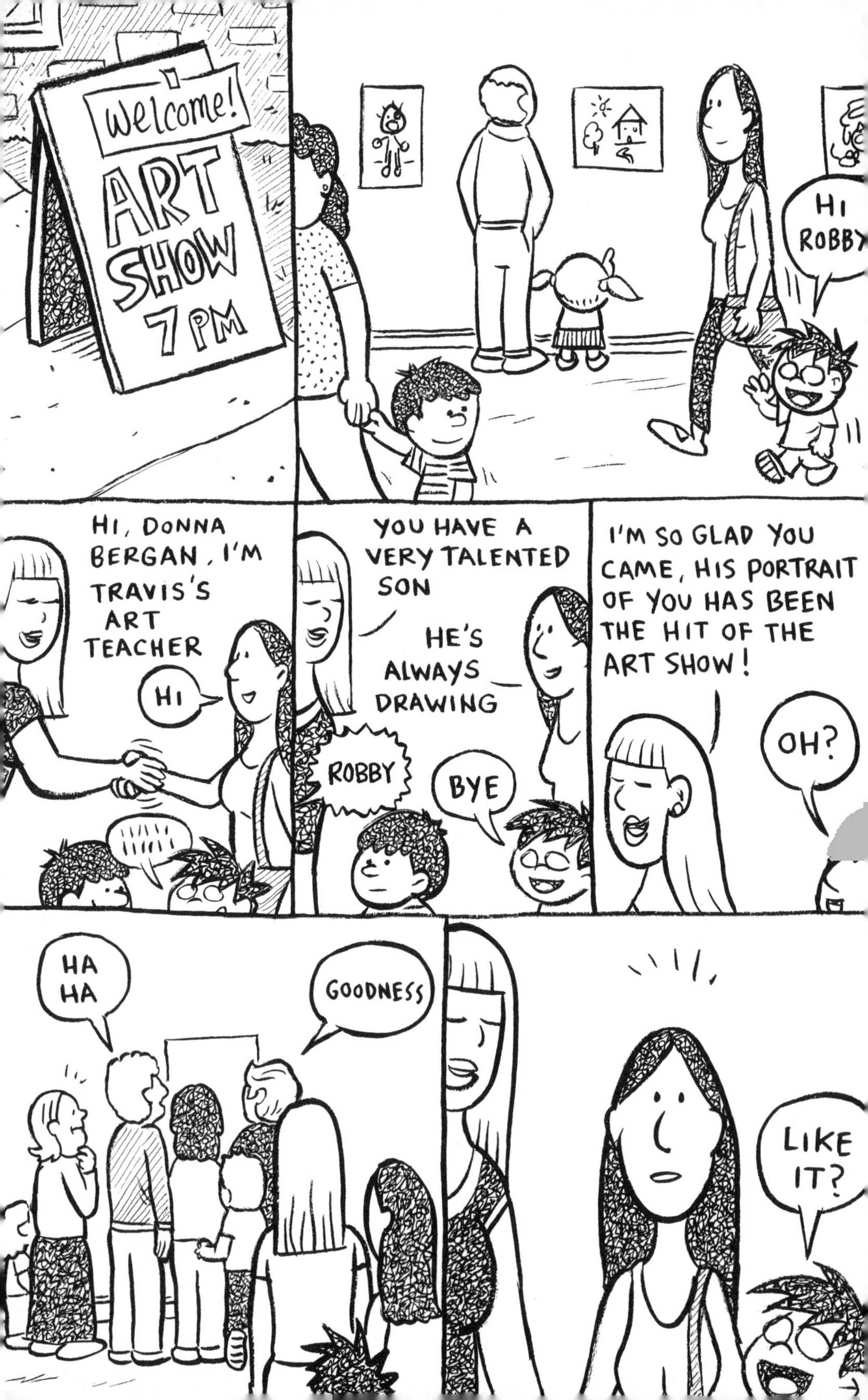

Welcome!
ART SHOW
7 PM
HI ROBBY
HI, DONNA BERGAN, I'M TRAVIS'S ART TEACHER
HI
YOU HAVE A VERY TALENTED SON
HE'S ALWAYS DRAWING
ROBBY
BYE
I'M SO GLAD YOU CAME, HIS PORTRAIT OF YOU HAS BEEN THE HIT OF THE ART SHOW!
OH?
HA HA
GOODNESS
LIKE IT?

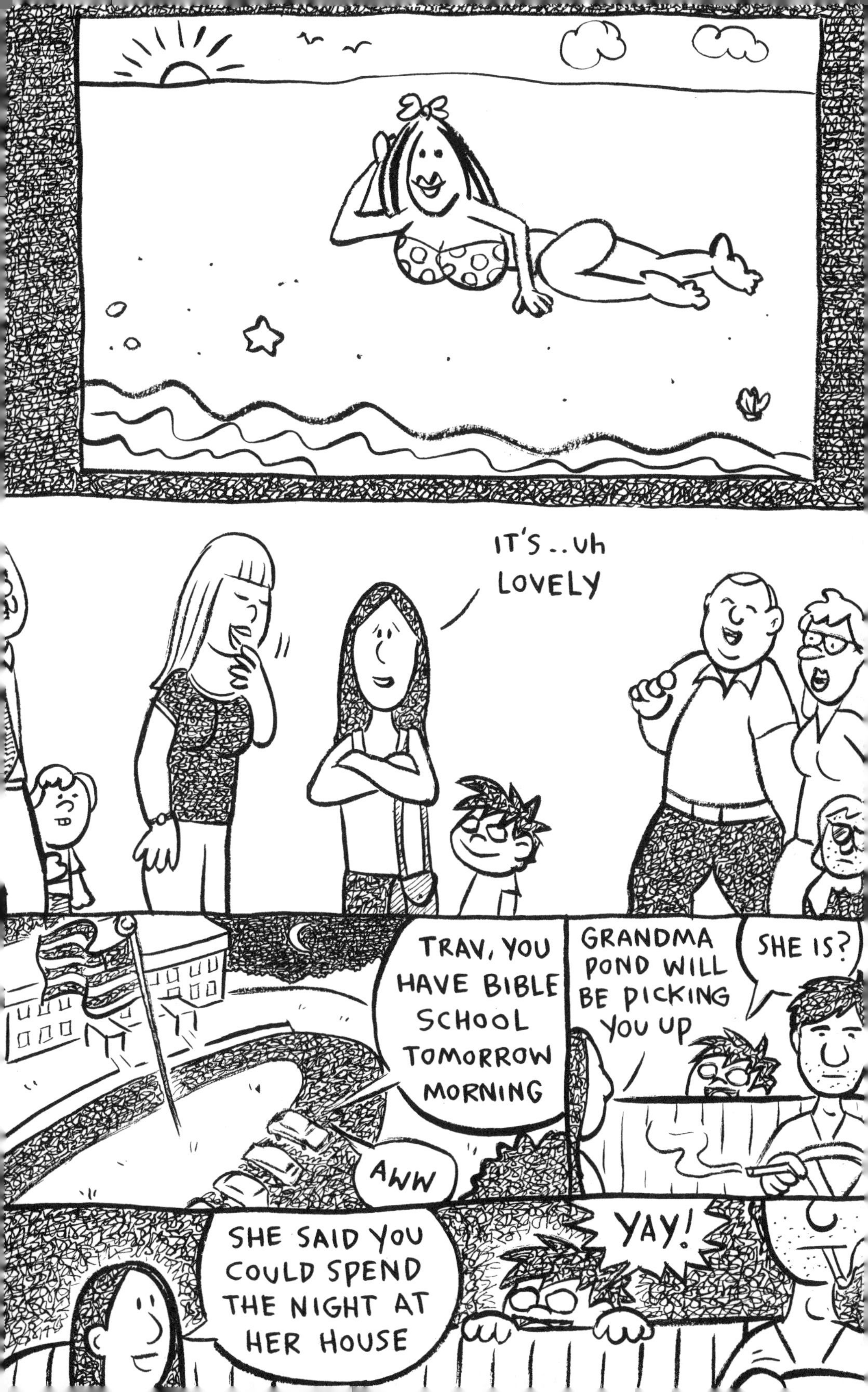
IT'S..uh LOVELY
TRAV, YOU HAVE BIBLE SCHOOL TOMORROW MORNING
AWW
GRANDMA POND WILL BE PICKING YOU UP
SHE IS?
SHE SAID YOU COULD SPEND THE NIGHT AT HER HOUSE
YAY!

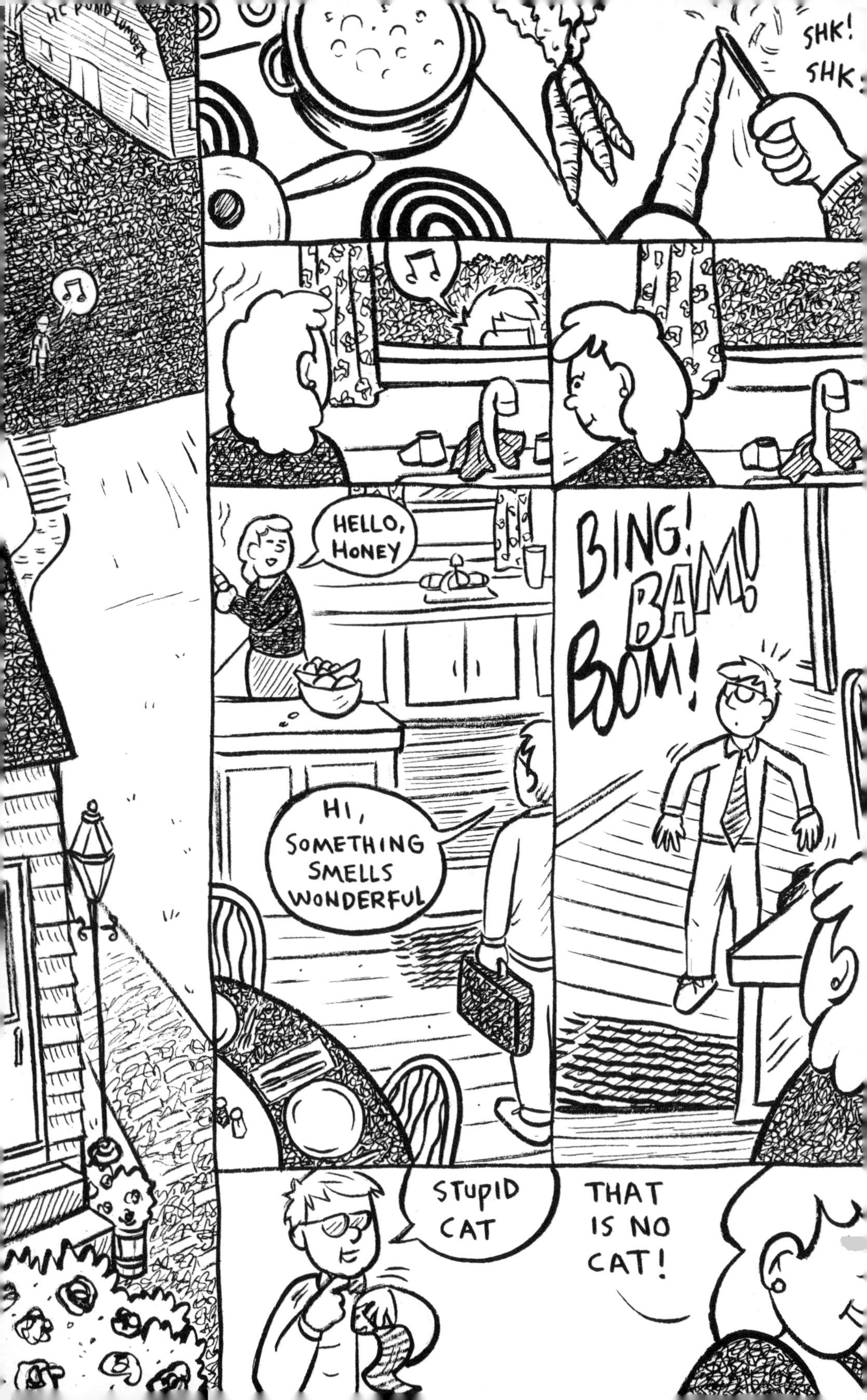
HC POND LUMBER
SHK! SHK!
HELLO, HONEY
HI, SOMETHING SMELLS WONDERFUL
BING! BAM! BOOM!
STUPID CAT
THAT IS NO CAT!

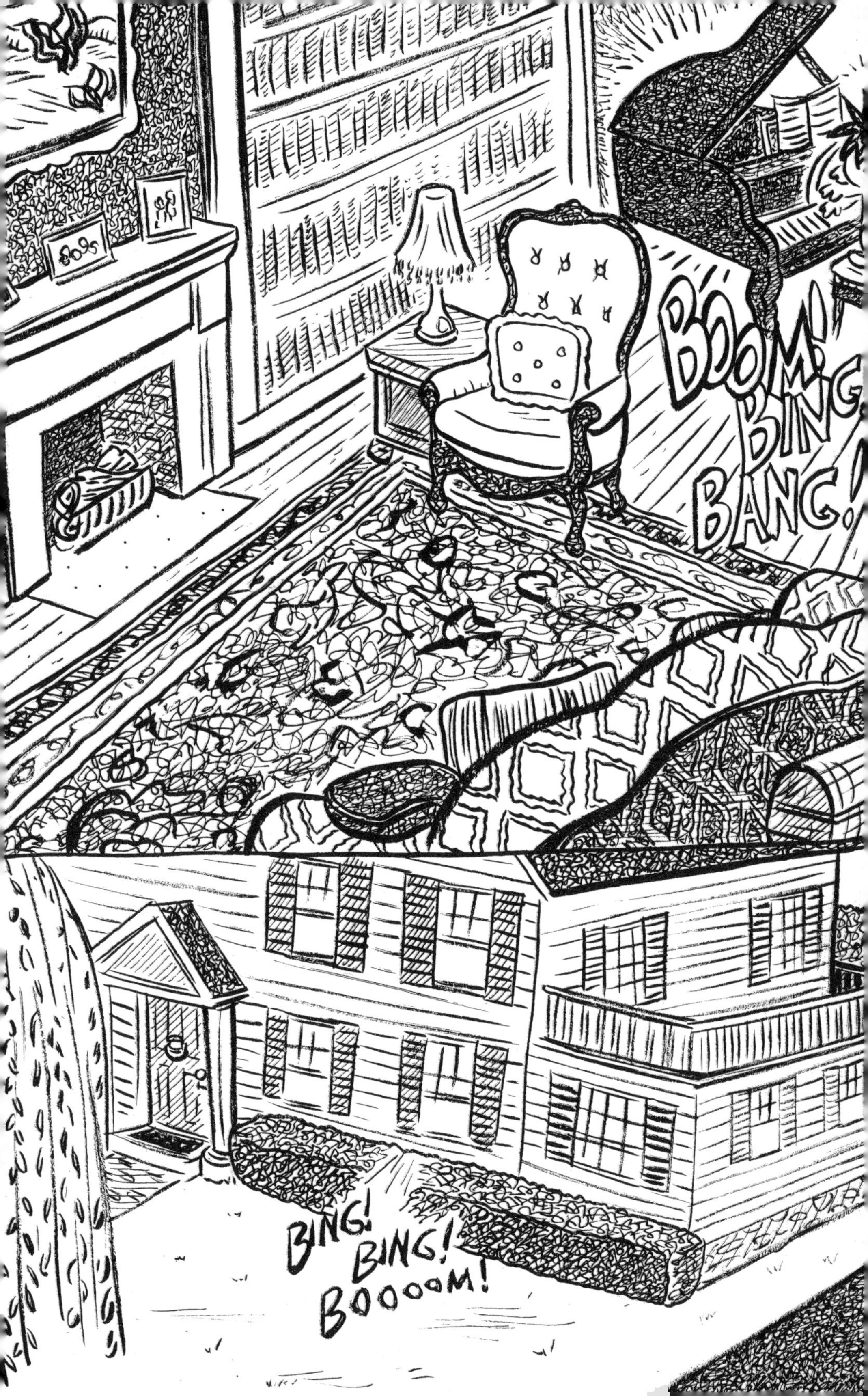
BOOM! BING BANG!
BING! BING! BOOOOOM!

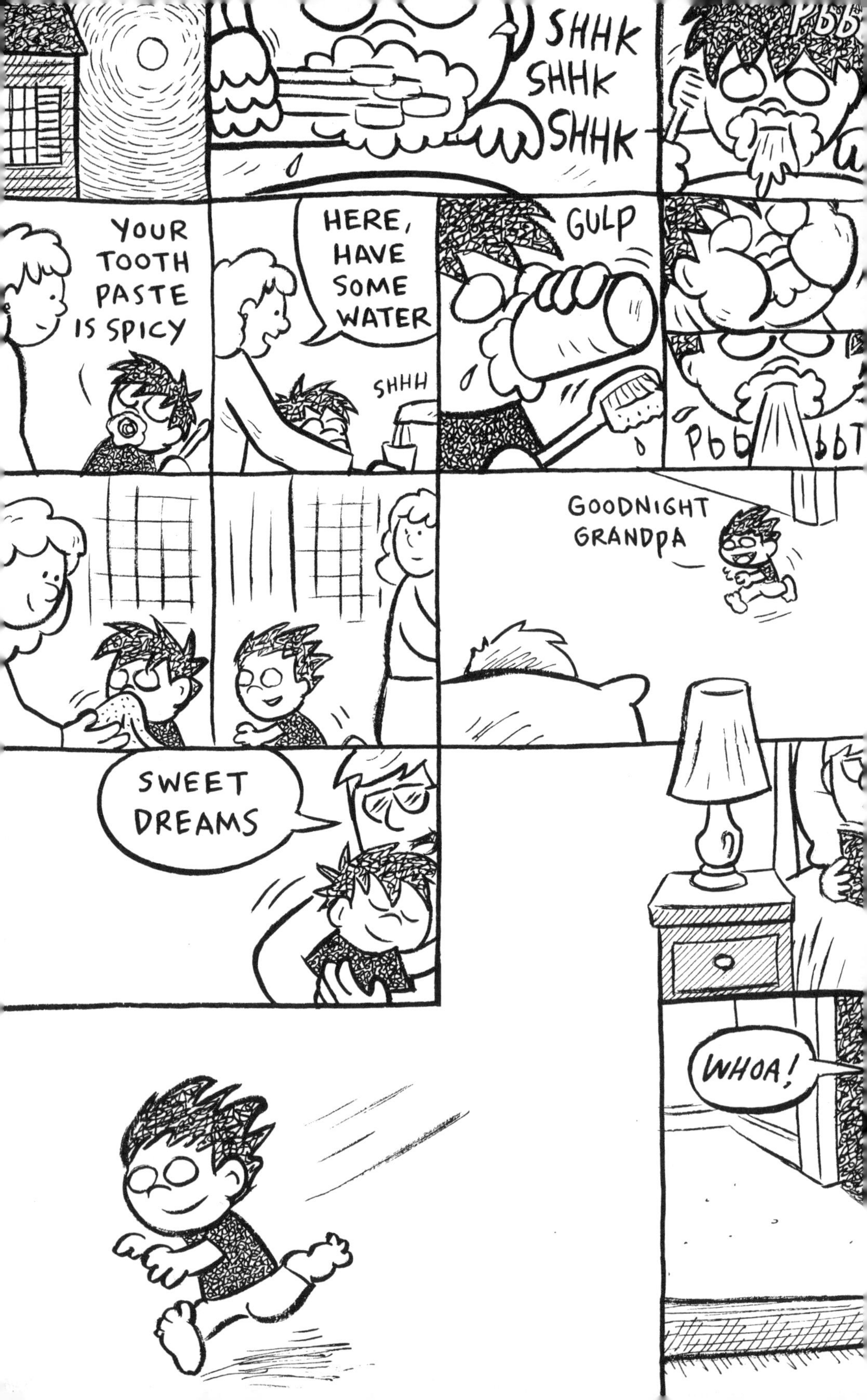
SHHK
SHHK
SHHK
PBB
YOUR TOOTH PASTE IS SPICY
HERE, HAVE SOME WATER
SHHH
GULP
PBB
BBT
GOODNIGHT GRANDPA
SWEET DREAMS
WHOA!

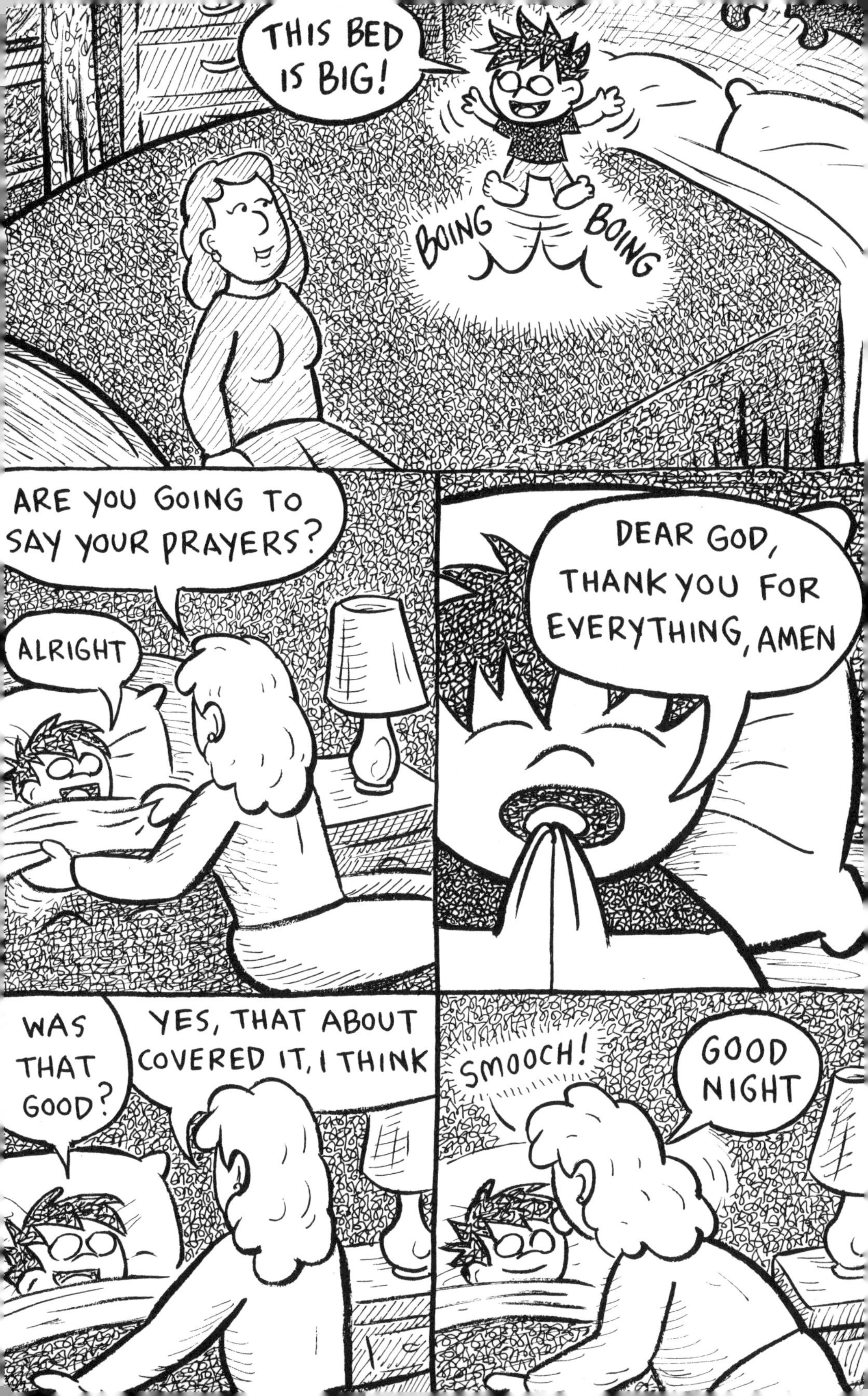
THIS BED IS BIG!
BOING BOING
ARE YOU GOING TO SAY YOUR PRAYERS?
ALRIGHT
DEAR GOD, THANK YOU FOR EVERYTHING, AMEN
WAS THAT GOOD?
YES, THAT ABOUT COVERED IT, I THINK
SMOOCH!
GOOD NIGHT

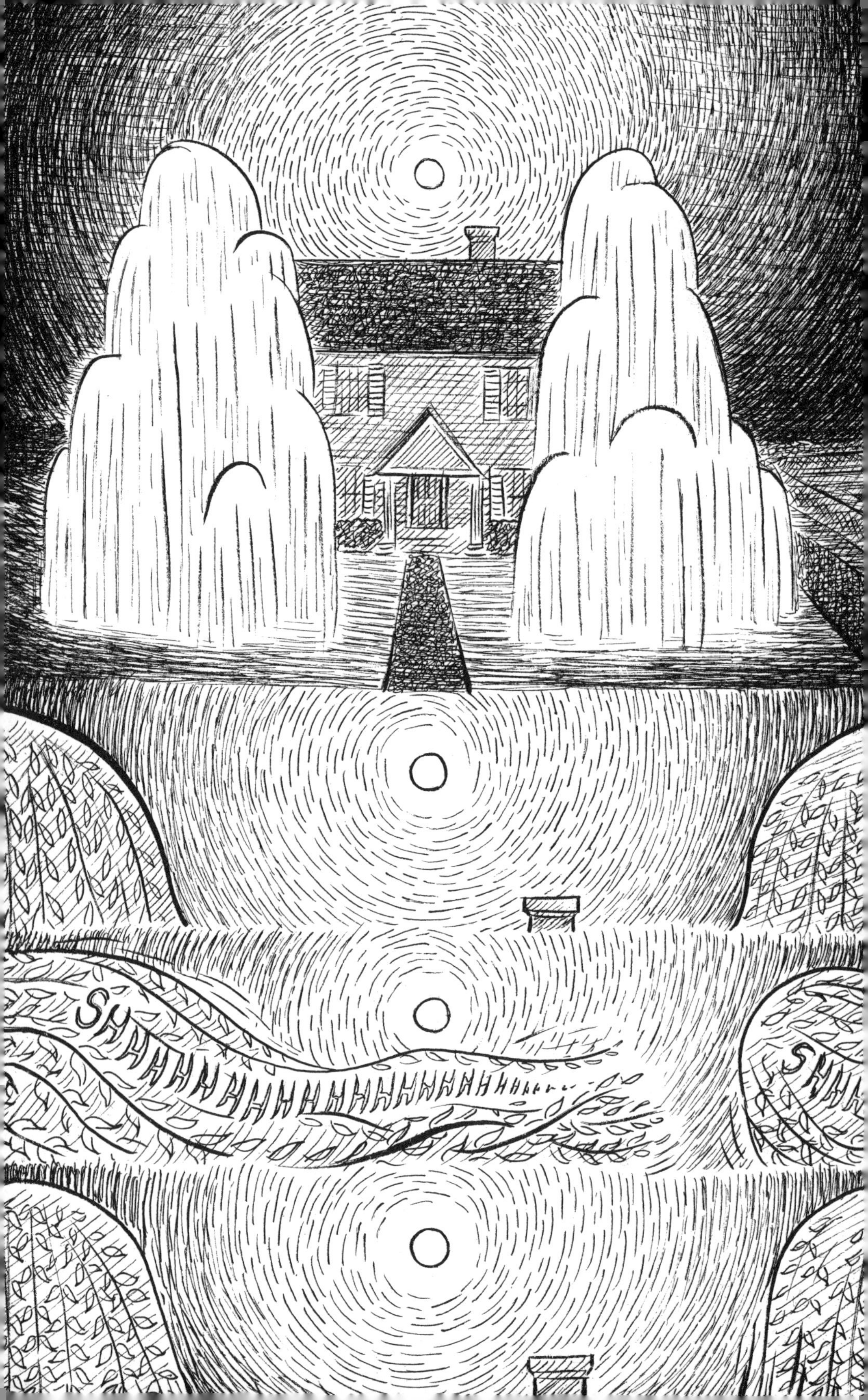
SHHHHHHHHHHHHHHHHHHHHHHHhhhh.....
SHH

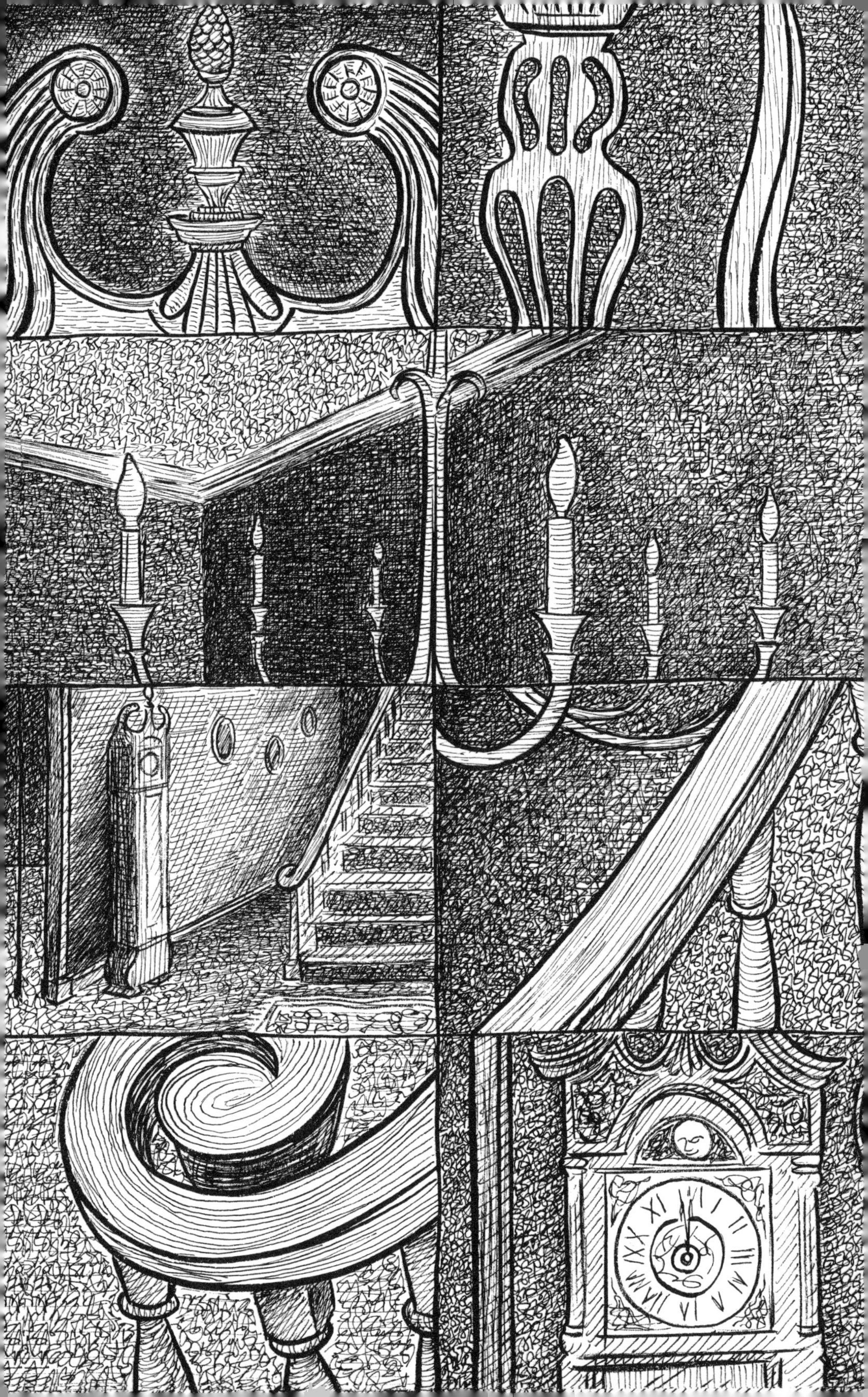

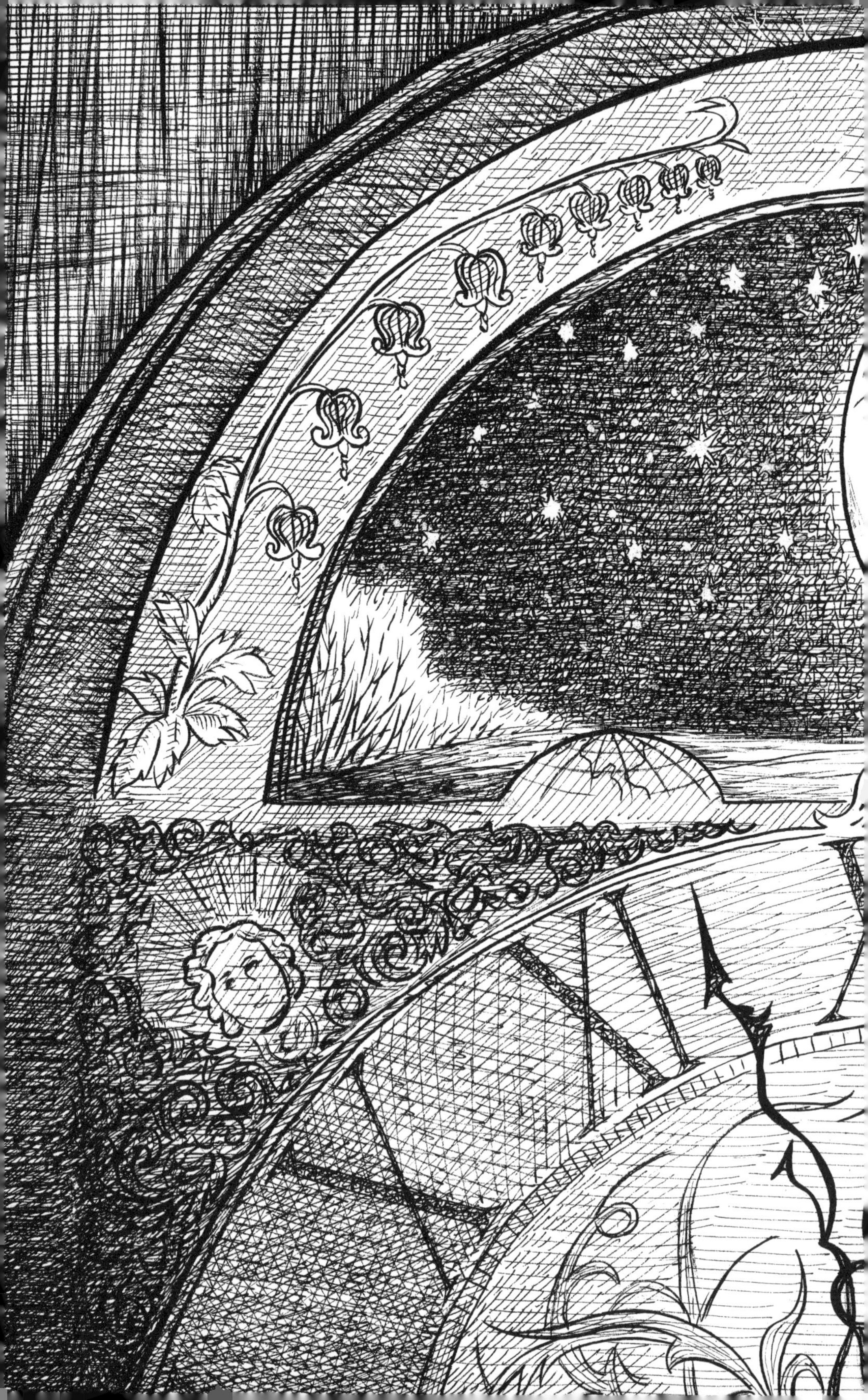

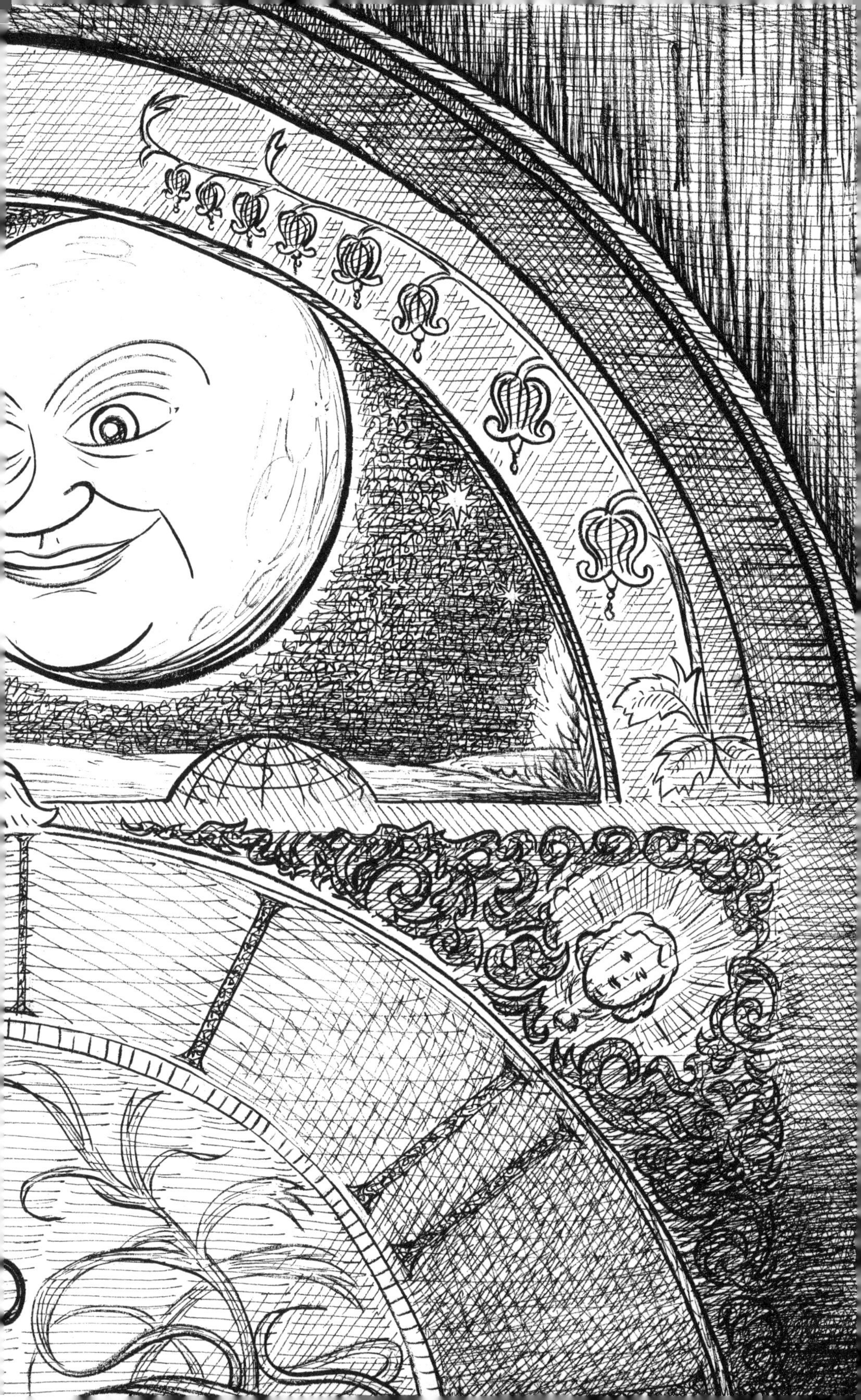

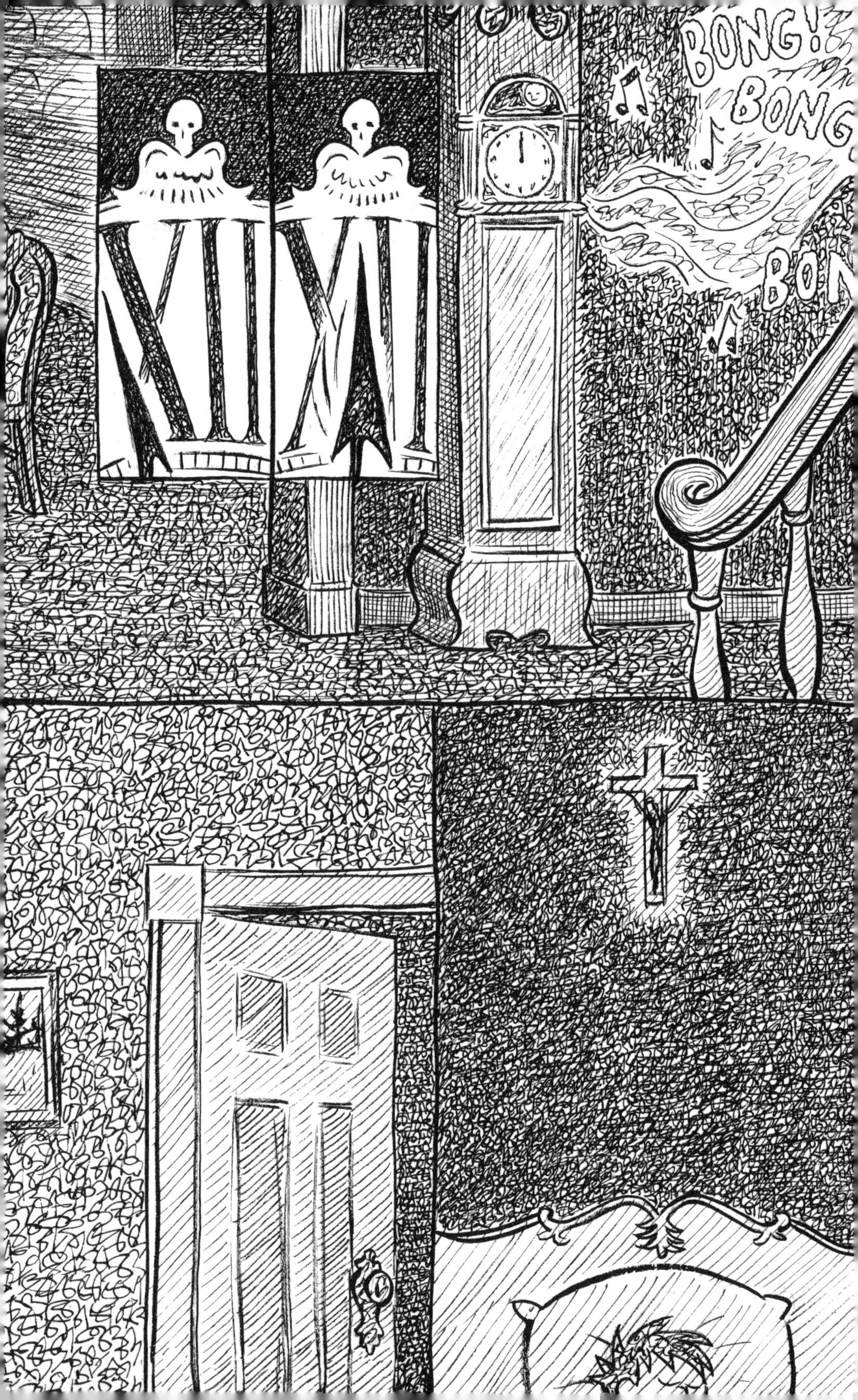
BONG!
BONG

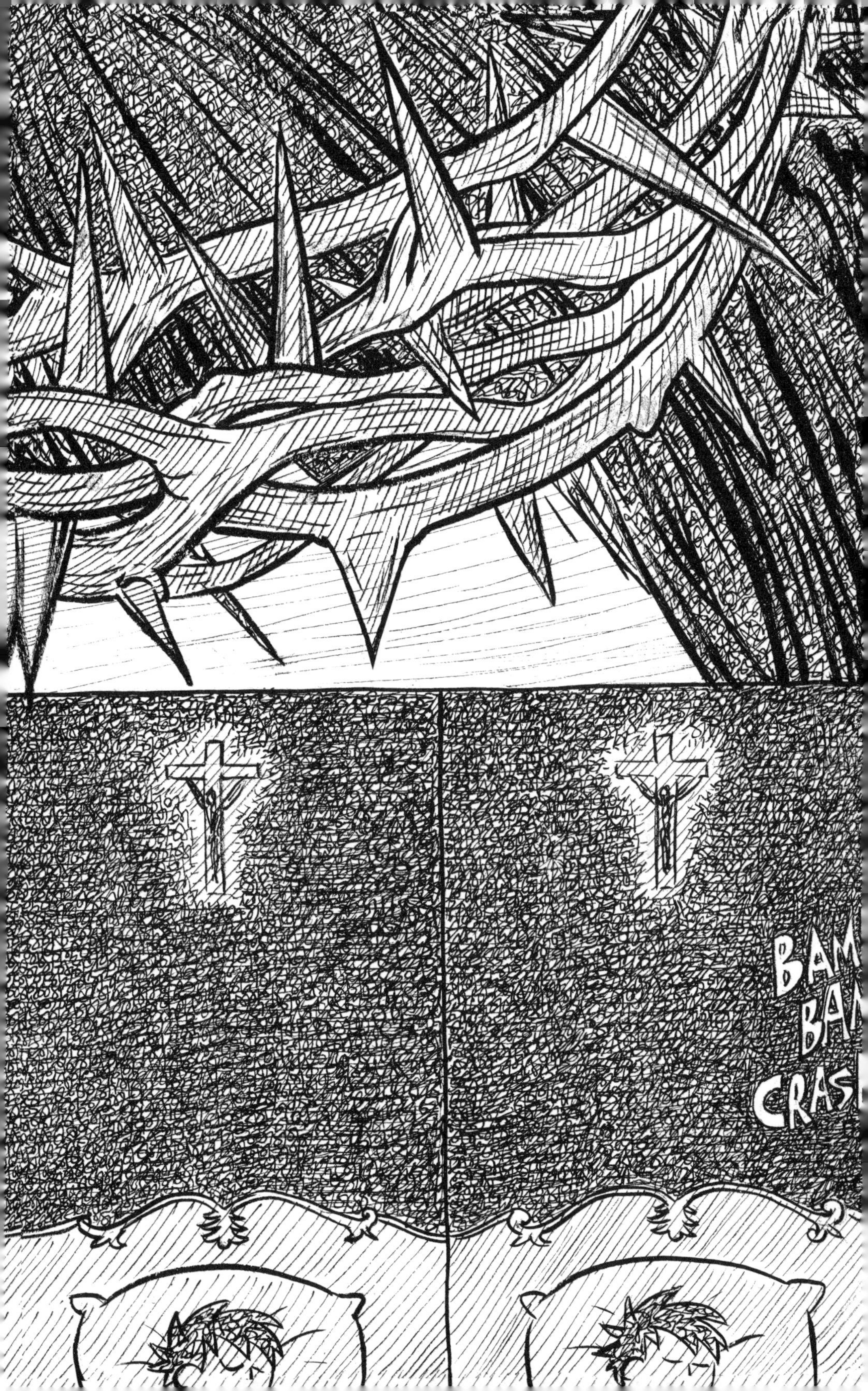
BAM

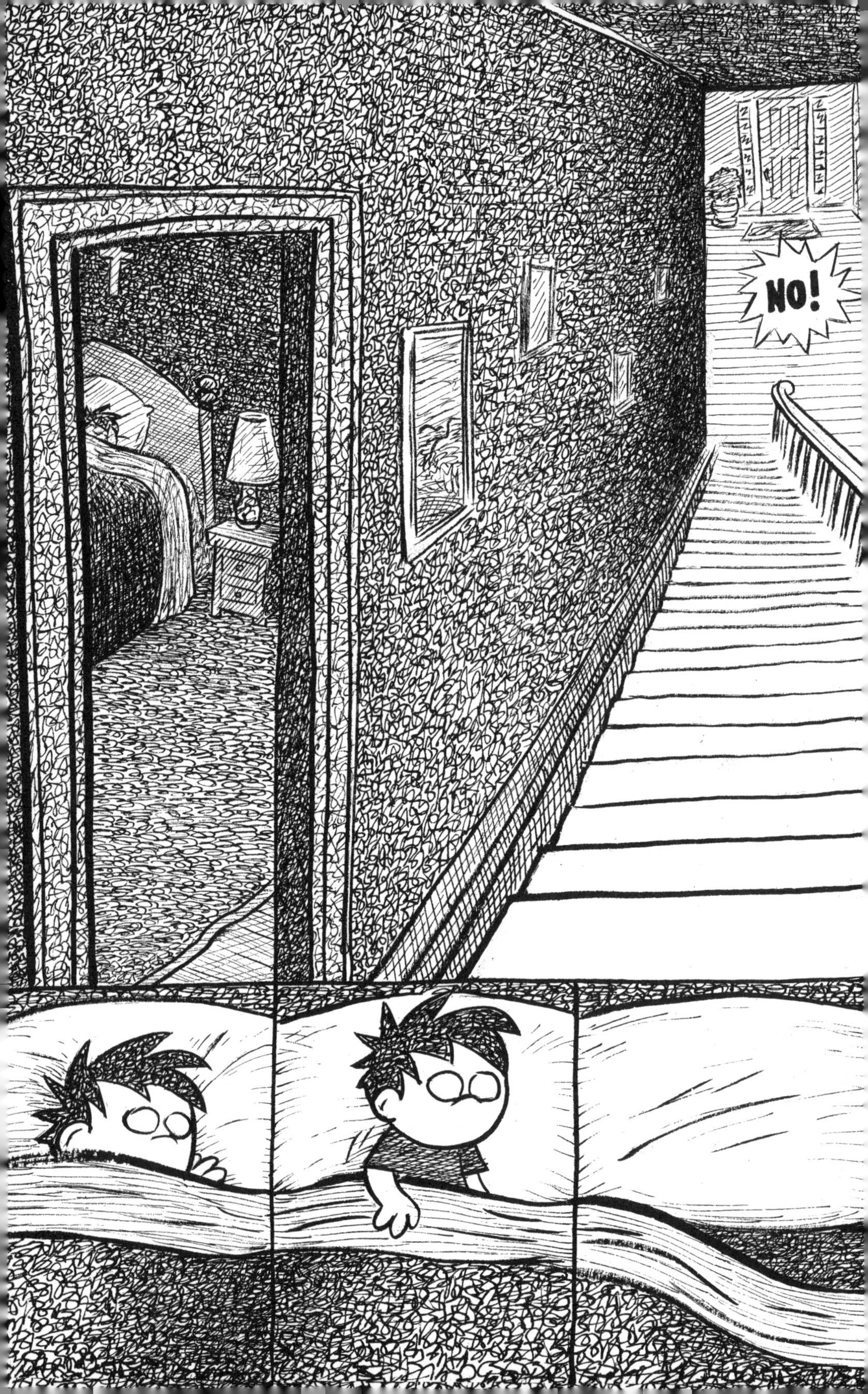
NO!

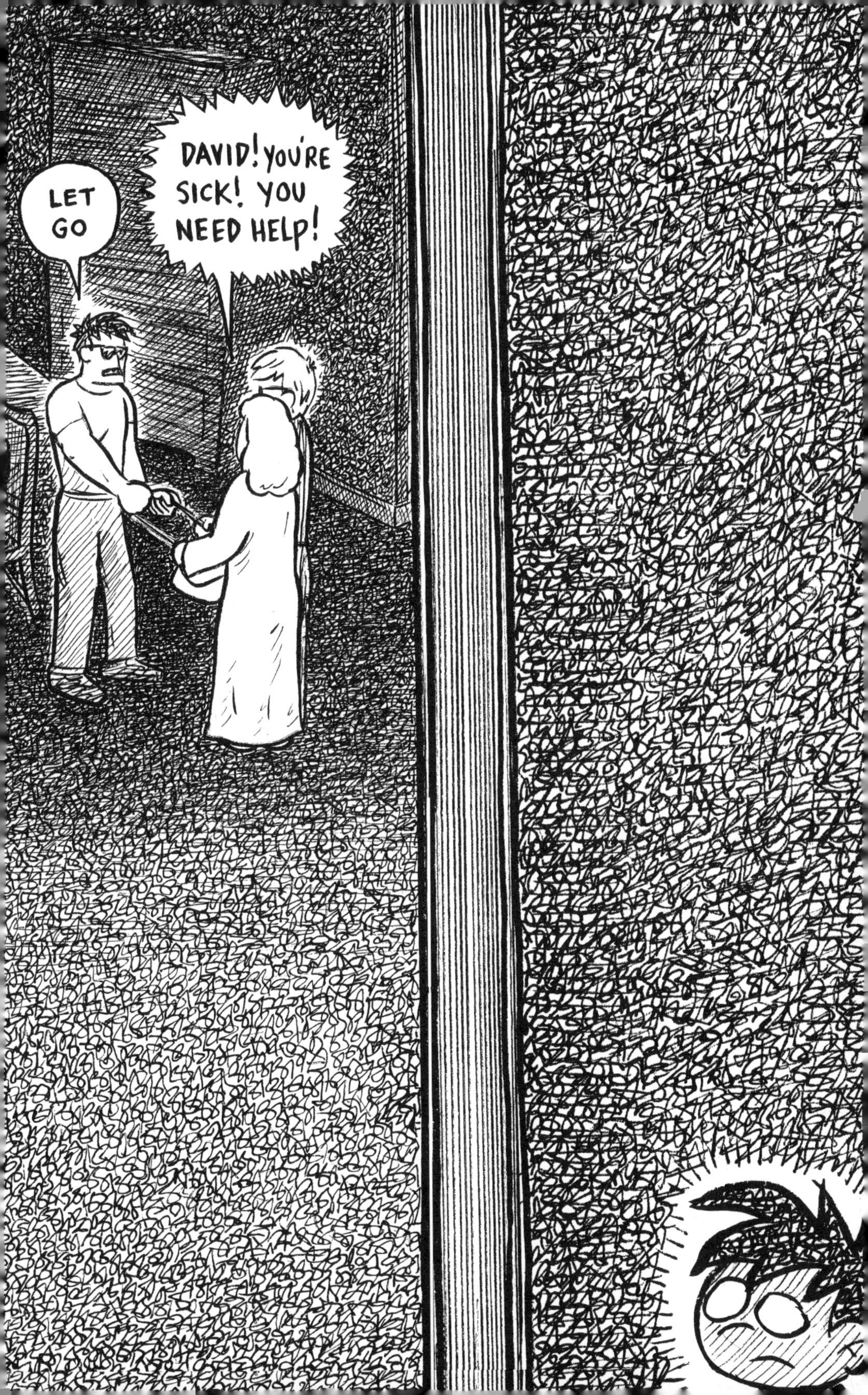
LET GO
DAVID! YOU'RE SICK! YOU NEED HELP!

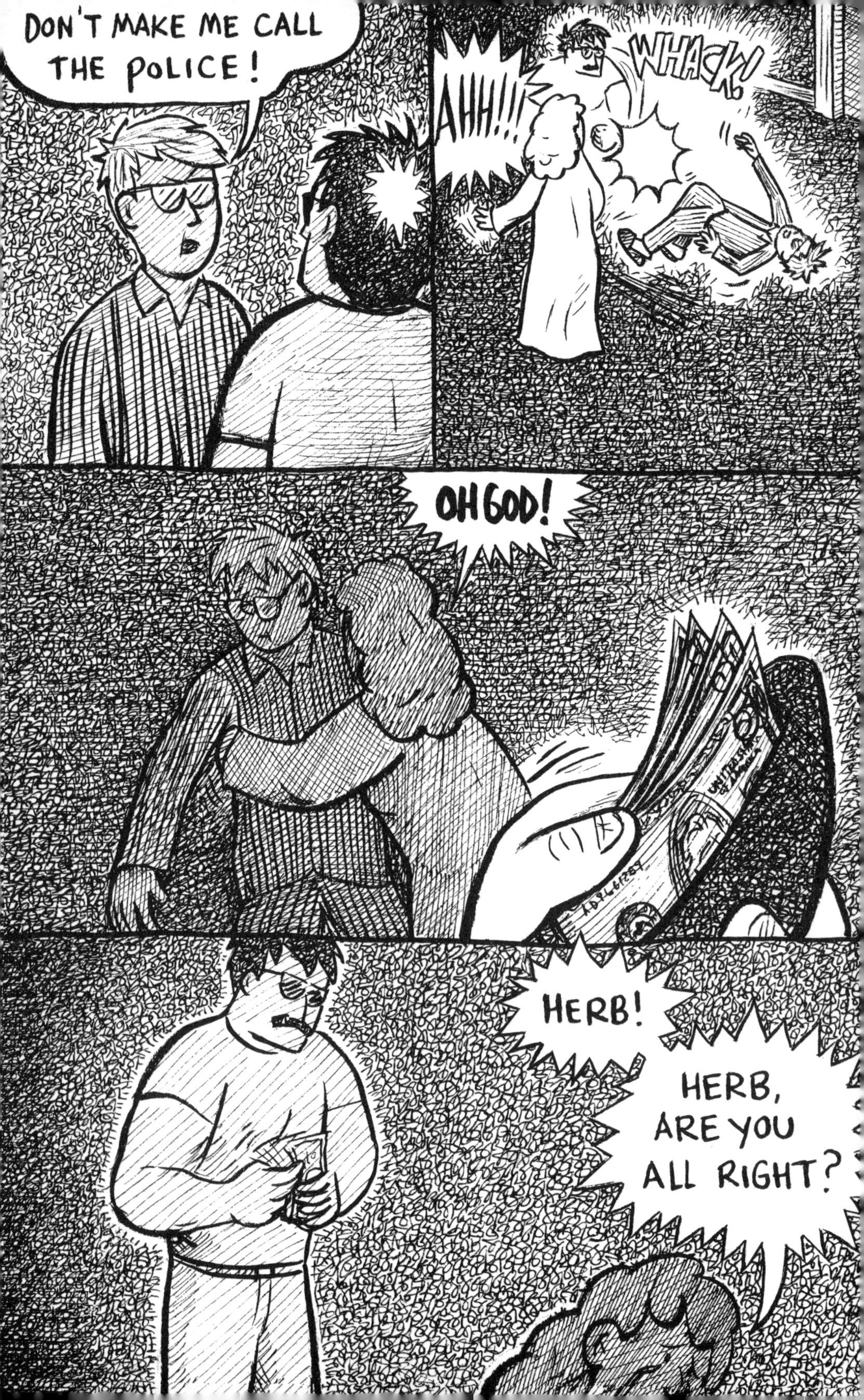
DON'T MAKE ME CALL THE POLICE!
AHH!!!
WHACK!
OH GOD!
HERB!
HERB, ARE YOU ALL RIGHT?

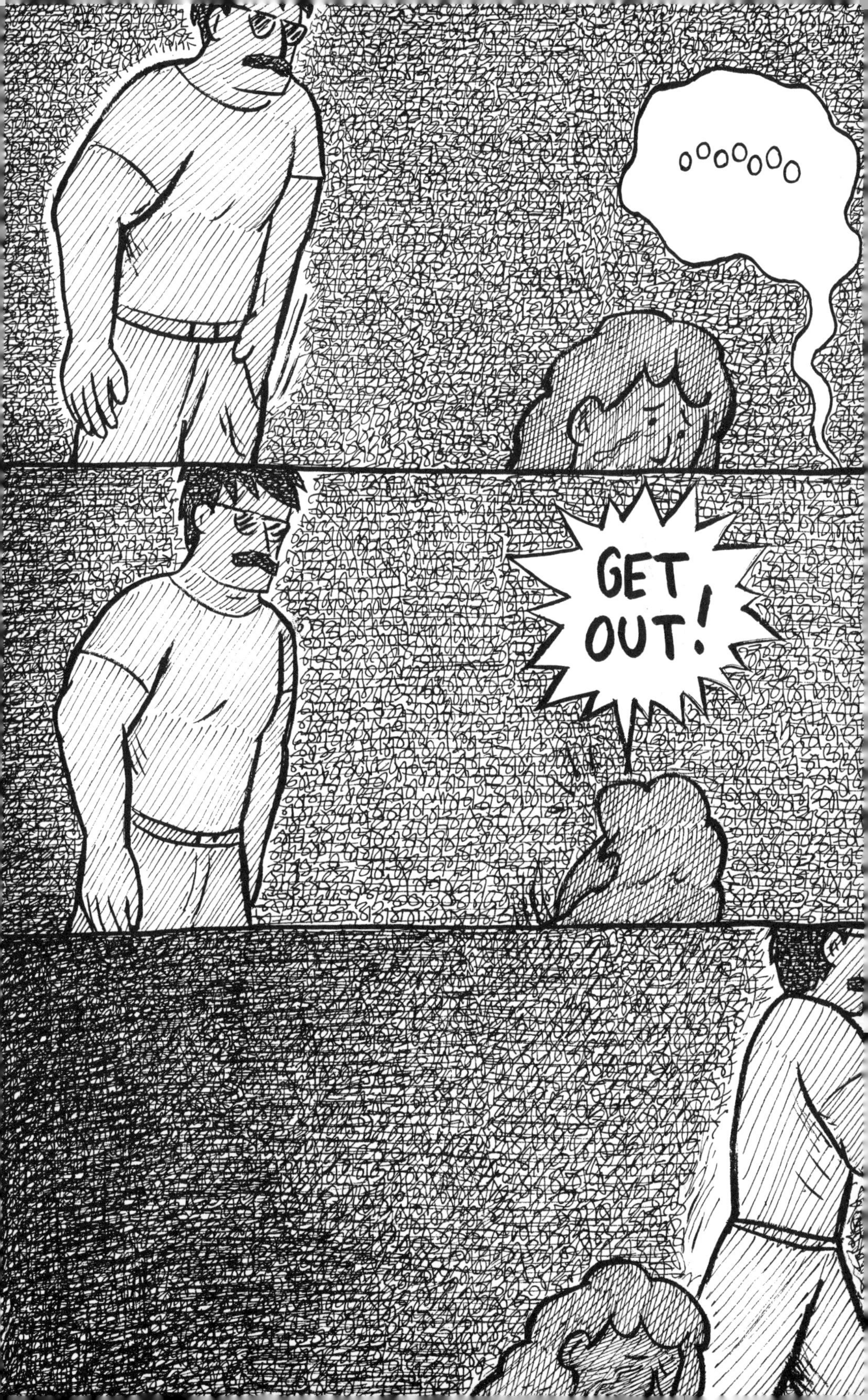
oooOooo
GET OUT!

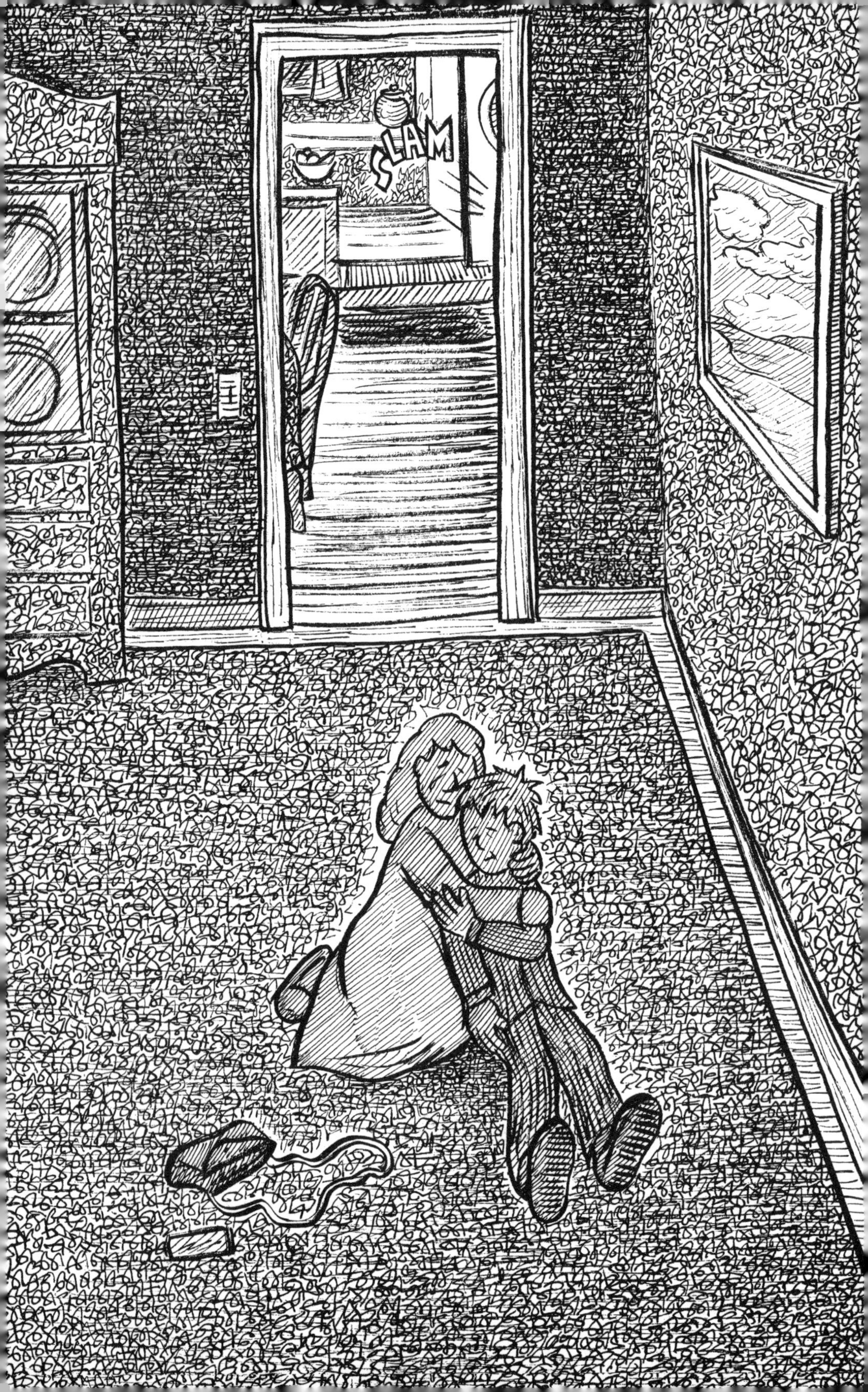
SLAM

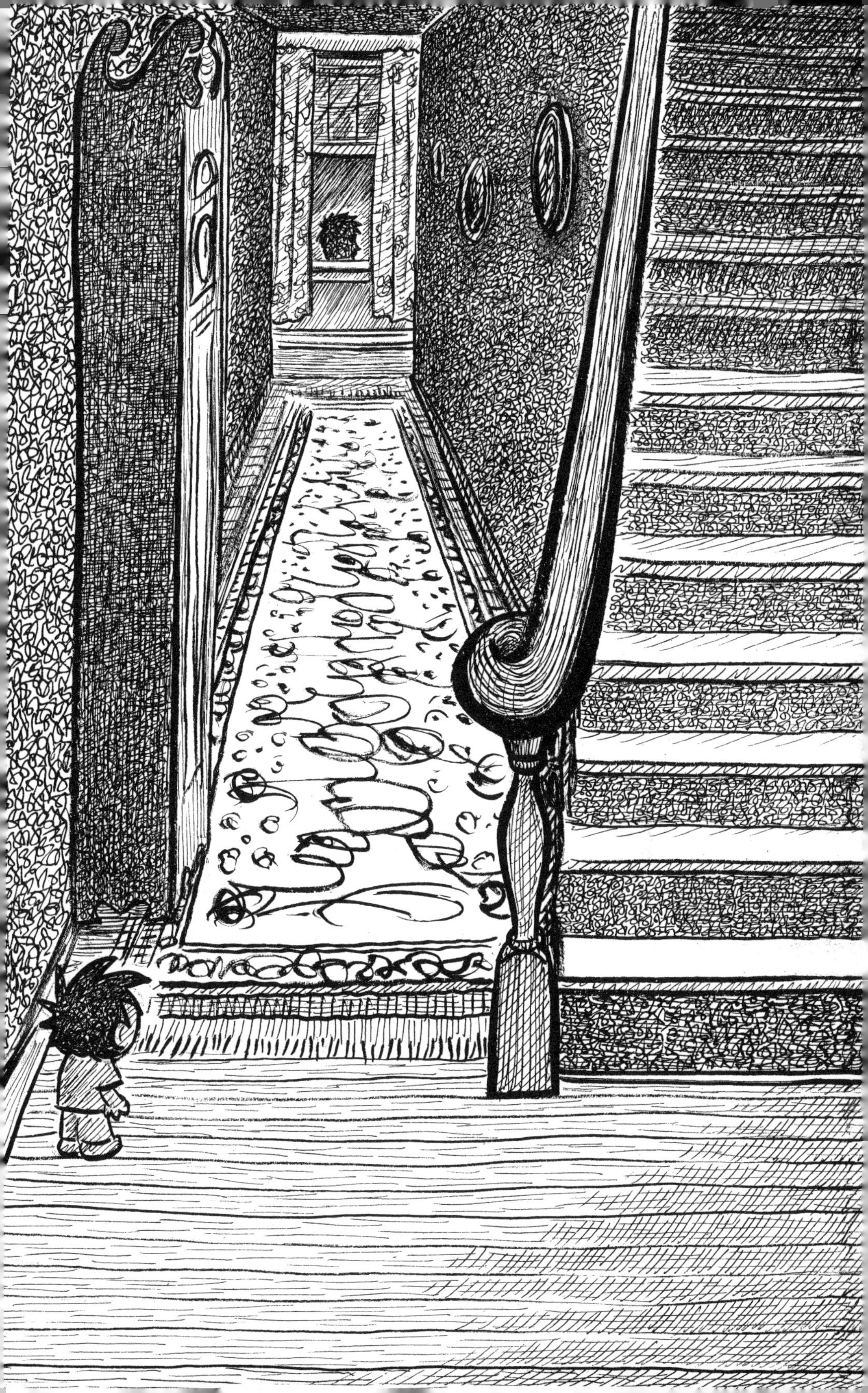

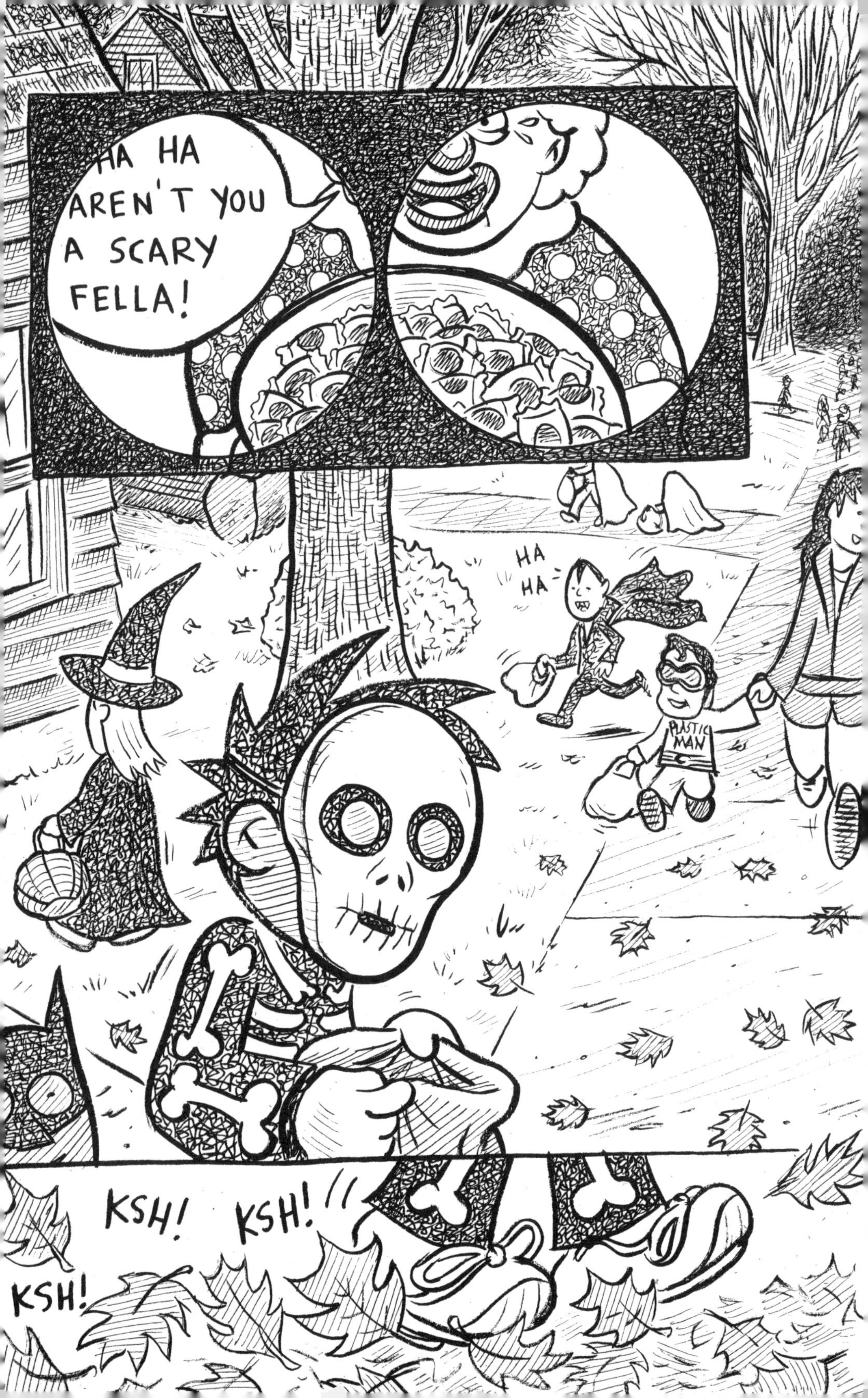
HA HA AREN'T YOU A SCARY FELLA!
HA HA
PLASTIC MAN
KSH! KSH!
KSH!

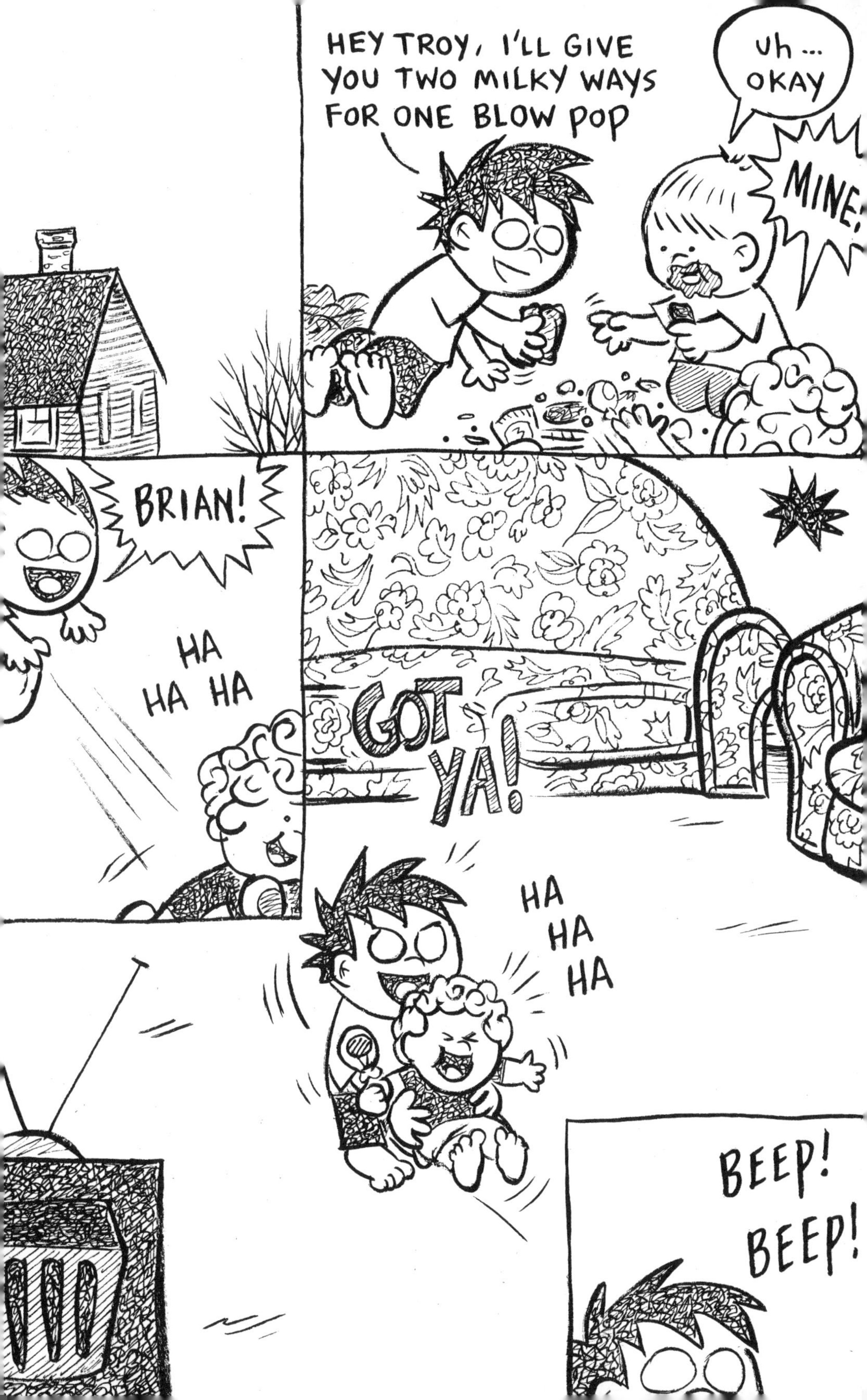
HEY TROY, I'LL GIVE YOU TWO MILKY WAYS FOR ONE BLOW POP
uh ... OKAY
MINE!
BRIAN!
HA HA HA
GOT YA!
HA HA HA
BEEP! BEEP!

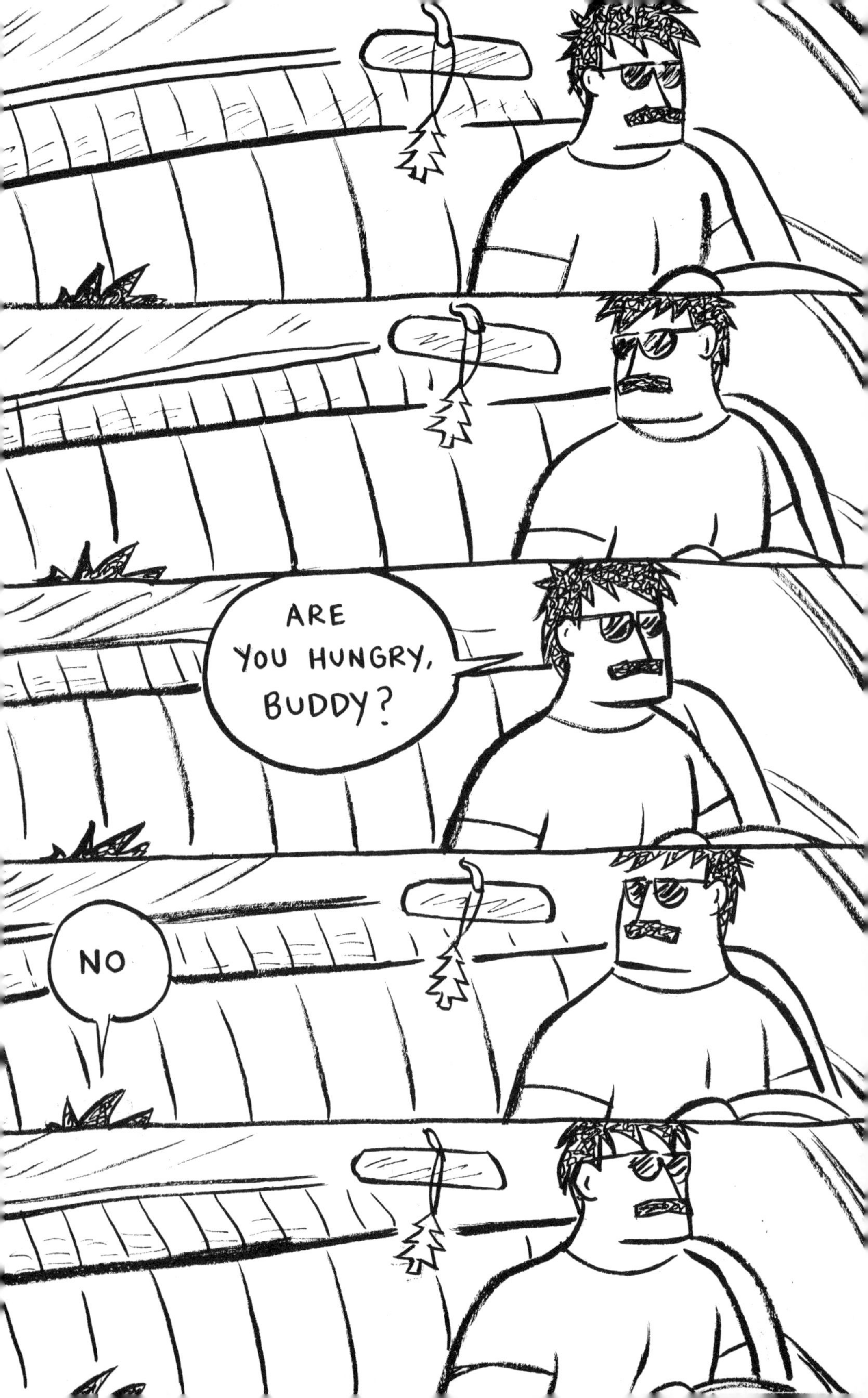
ARE YOU HUNGRY, BUDDY?
NO

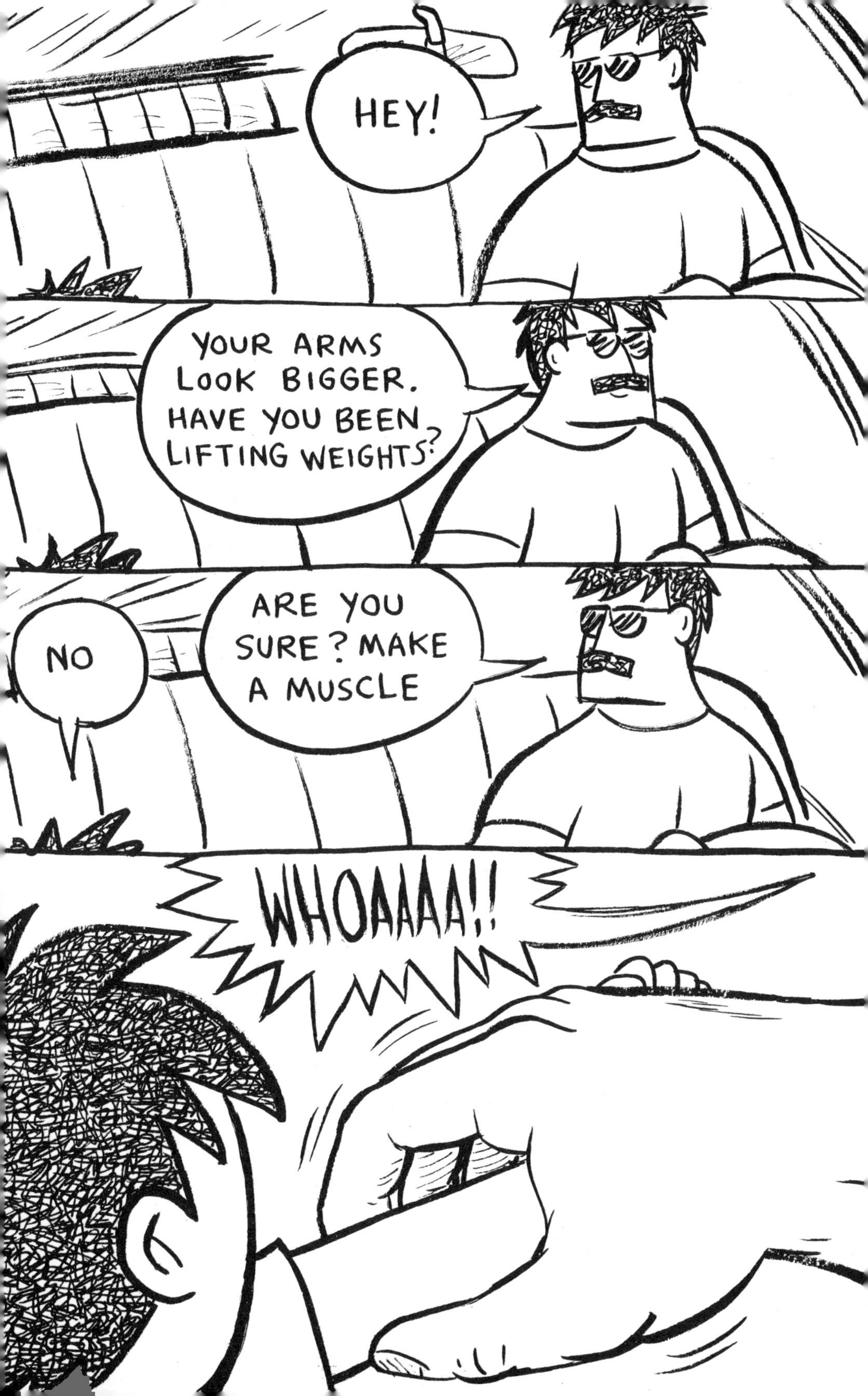
HEY!
YOUR ARMS LOOK BIGGER. HAVE YOU BEEN LIFTING WEIGHTS?
NO
ARE YOU SURE? MAKE A MUSCLE
WHOAAAA!!

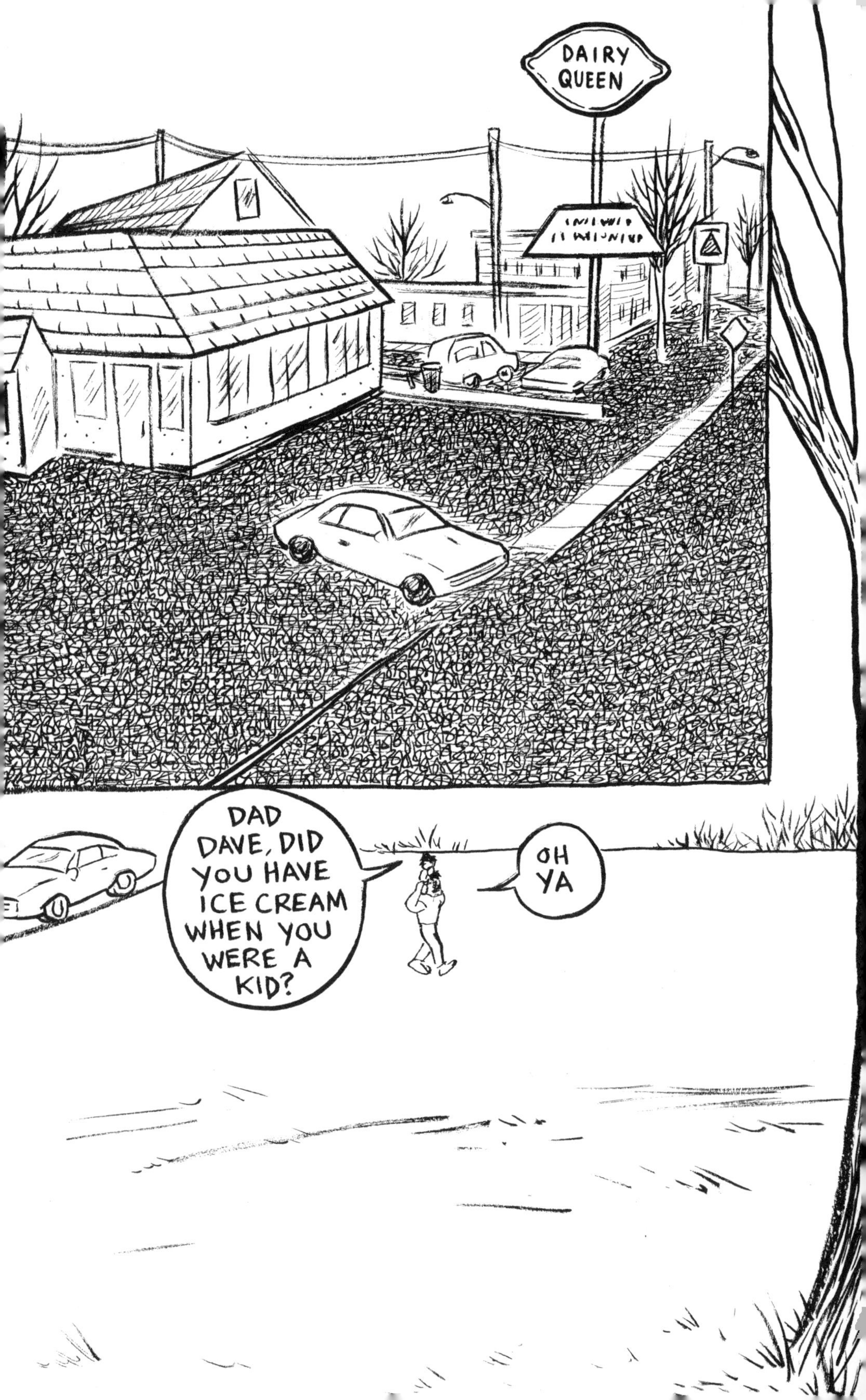
DAIRY QUEEN
DAD DAVE, DID YOU HAVE ICE CREAM WHEN YOU WERE A KID?
OH YA

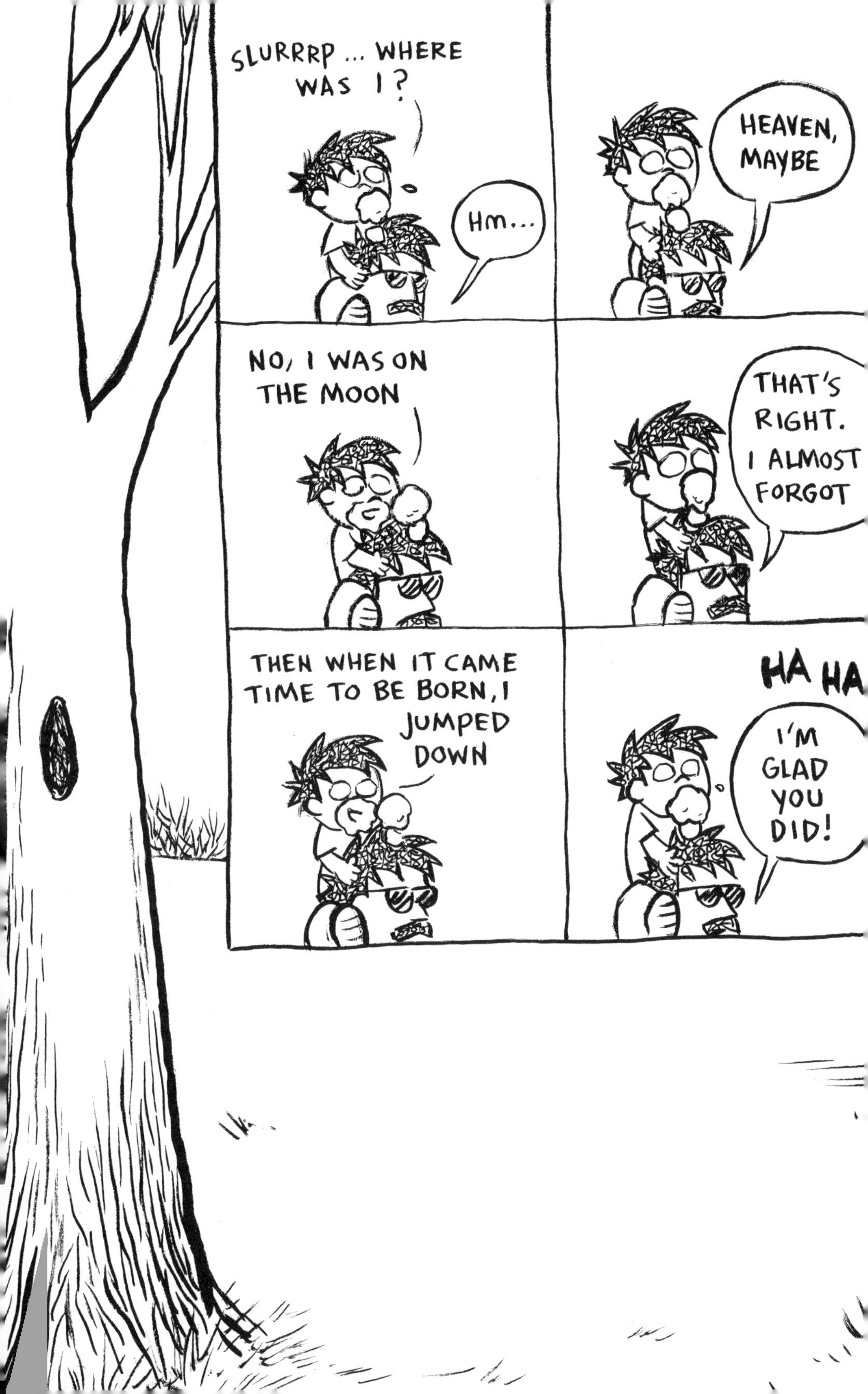
SLURRRP ... WHERE WAS I?
Hm...
HEAVEN, MAYBE
NO, I WAS ON THE MOON
THAT'S RIGHT. I ALMOST FORGOT
THEN WHEN IT CAME TIME TO BE BORN, I JUMPED DOWN
HA HA
I'M GLAD YOU DID!

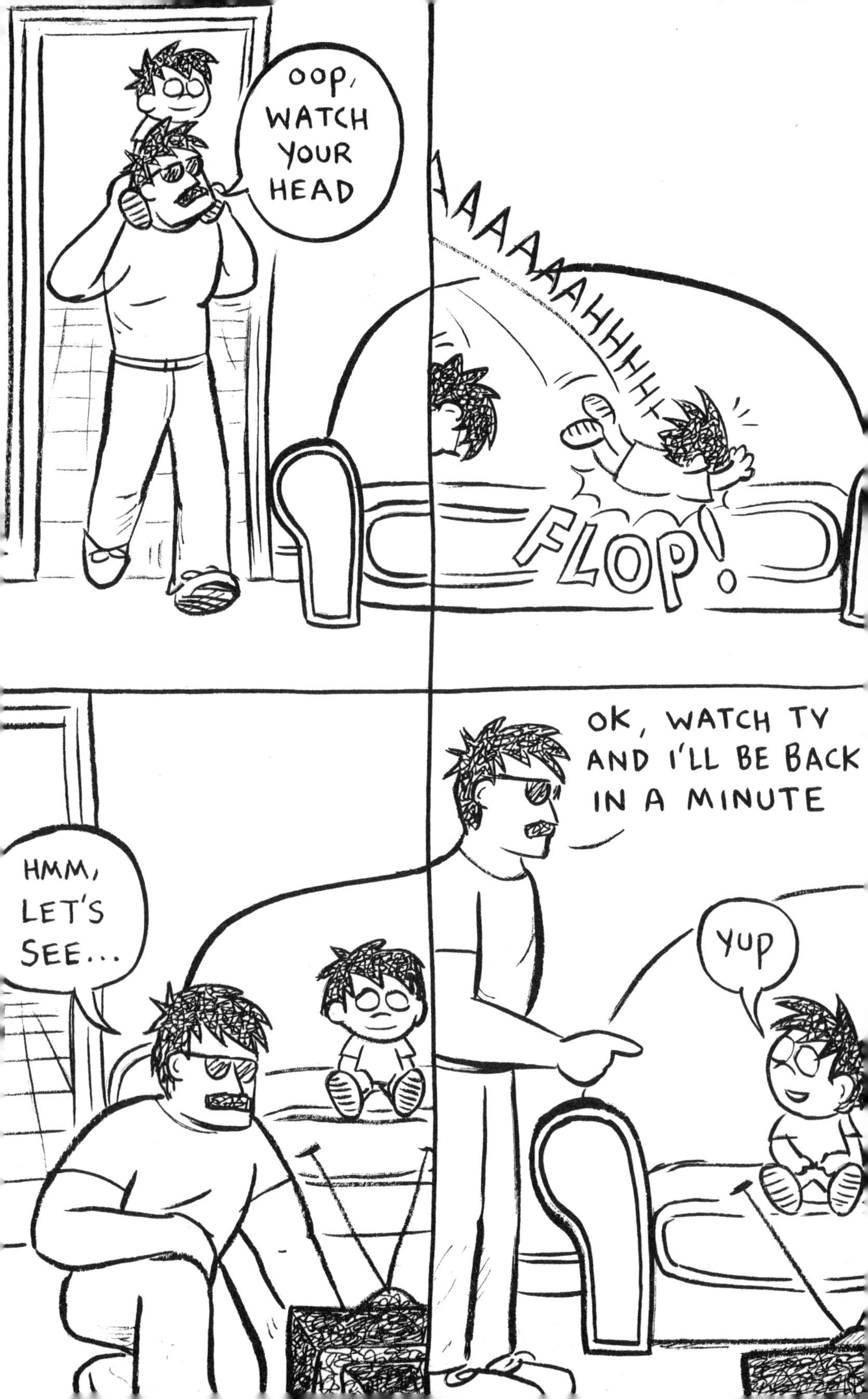
OOP, WATCH YOUR HEAD
AAAAAAAHHHHH
FLOP!
HMM, LET'S SEE...
OK, WATCH TV AND I'LL BE BACK IN A MINUTE
YUP

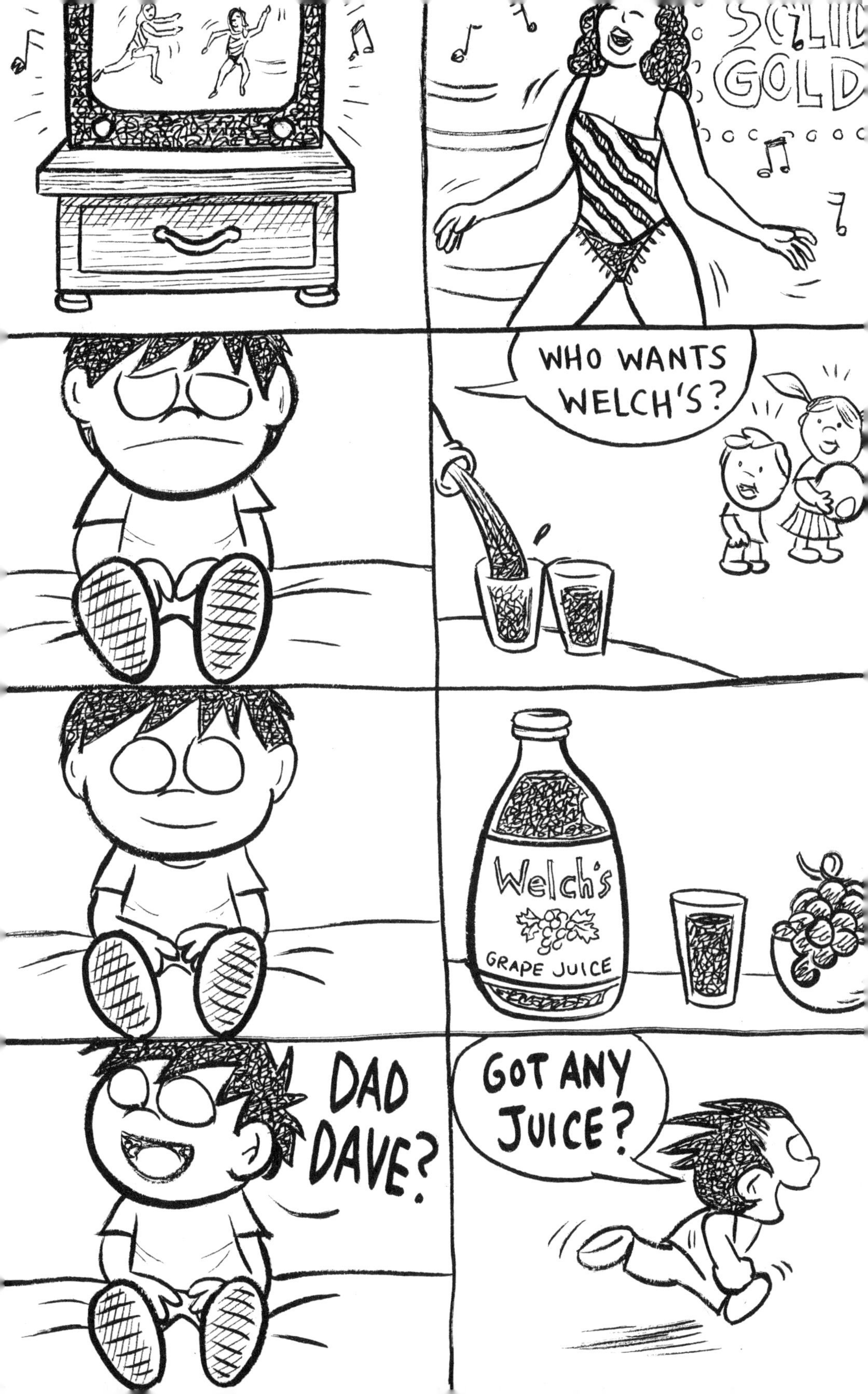
SOLID GOLD
WHO WANTS WELCH'S?
Welch's
GRAPE JUICE
DAD DAVE?
GOT ANY JUICE?

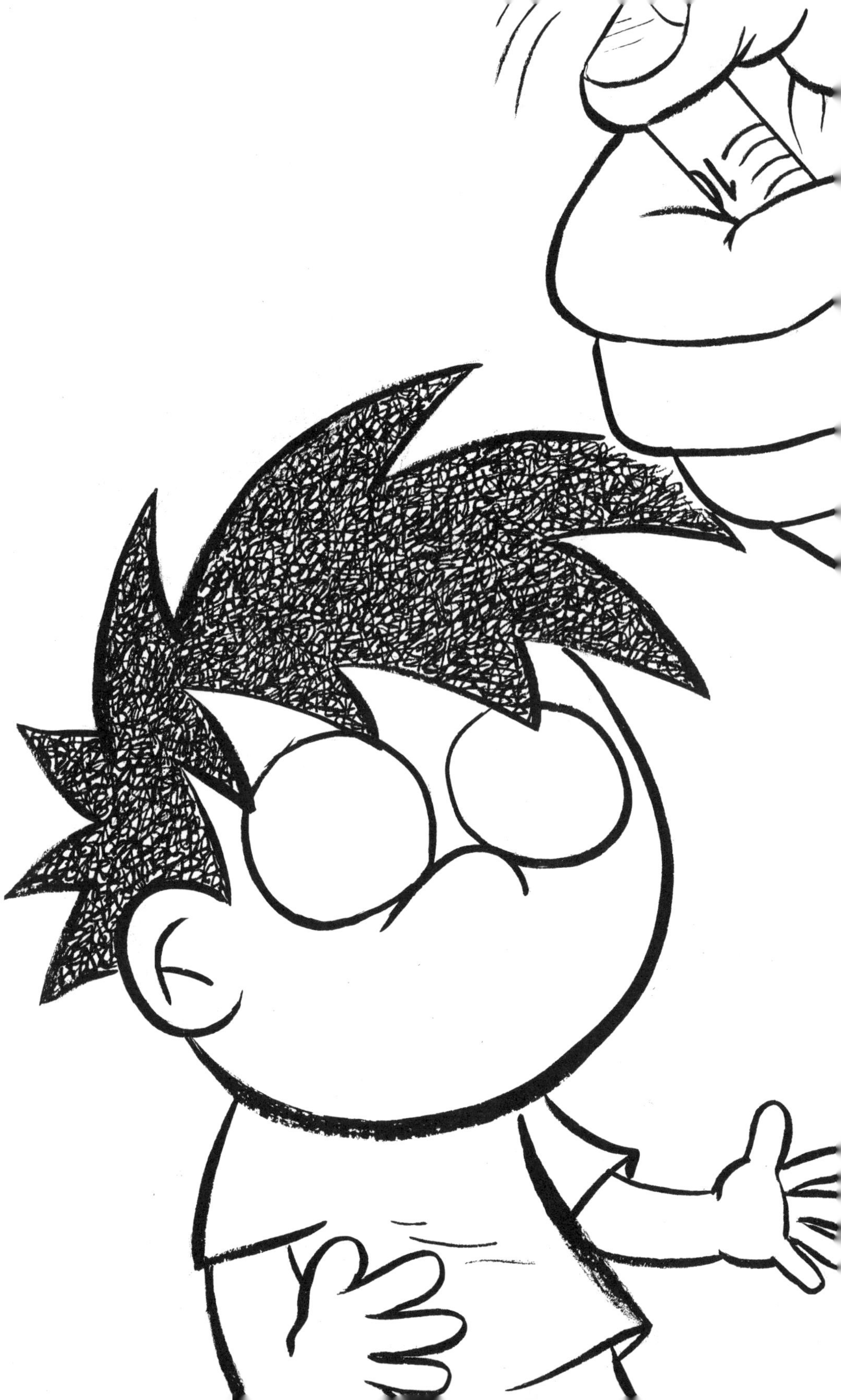

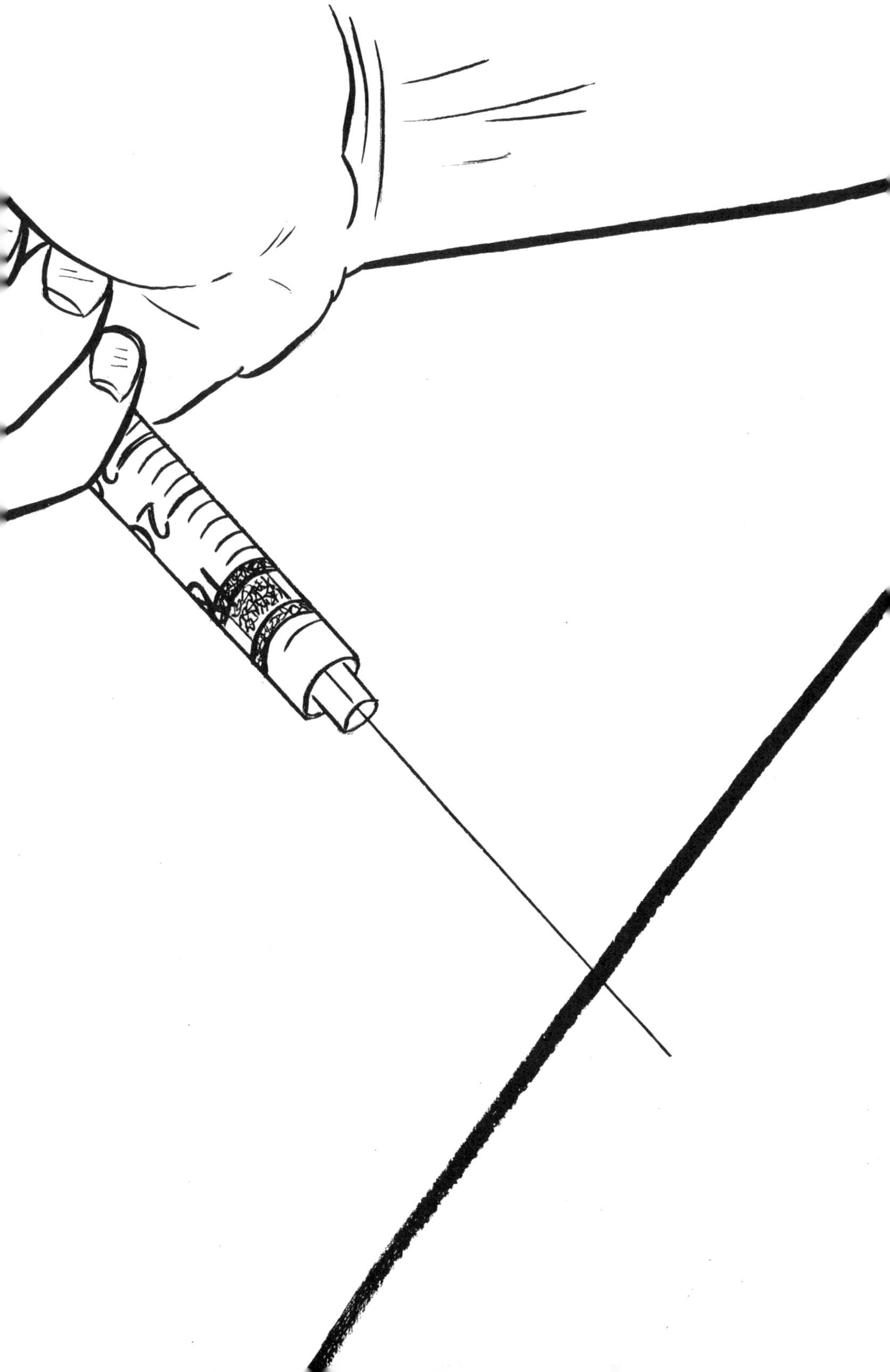

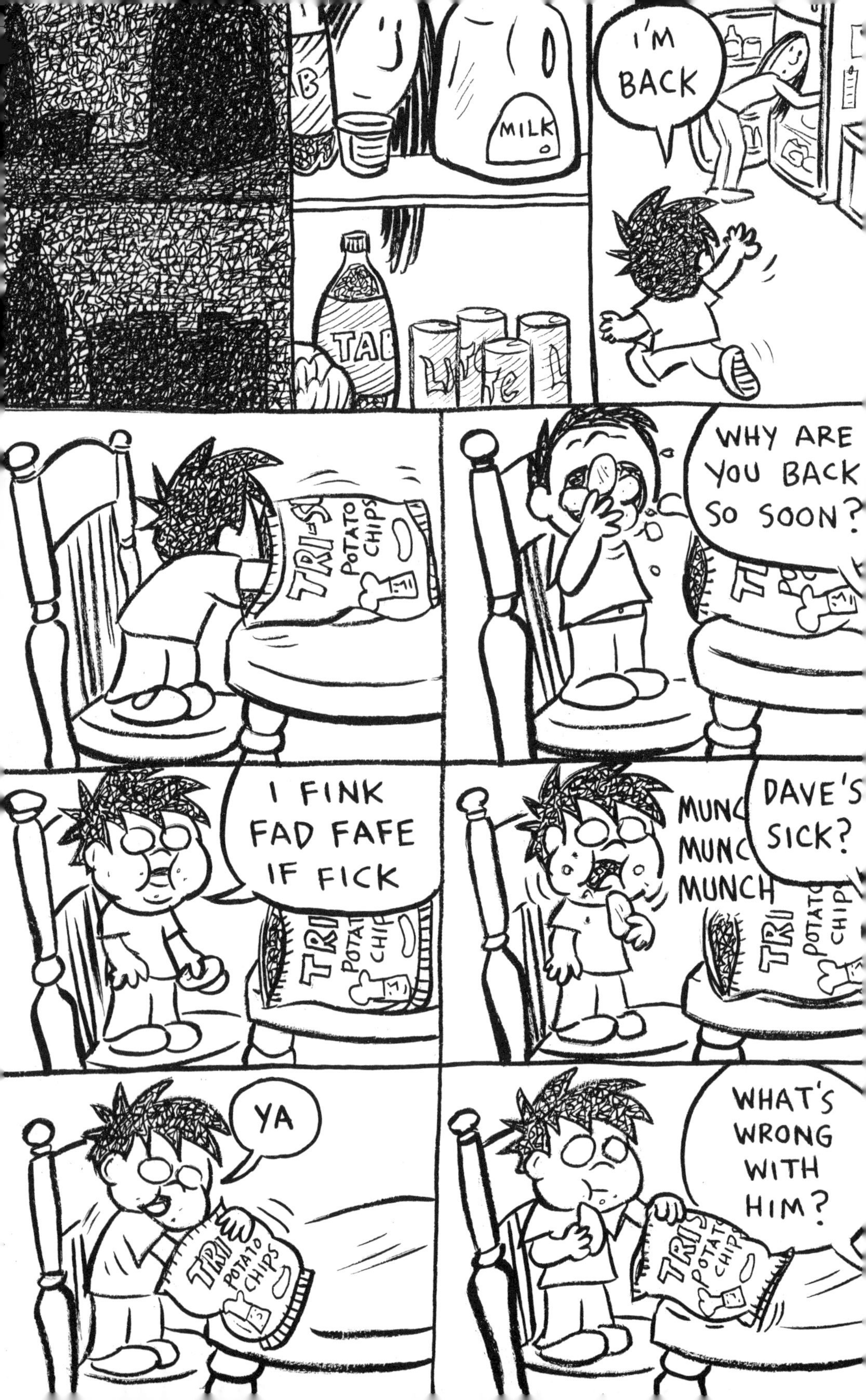
MILK
I'M BACK
TAB
WHY ARE YOU BACK SO SOON?
TRI-S POTATO CHIPS
I FINK FAD FAFE IF FICK
MUNCH MUNCH MUNCH
DAVE'S SICK?
YA
WHAT'S WRONG WITH HIM?

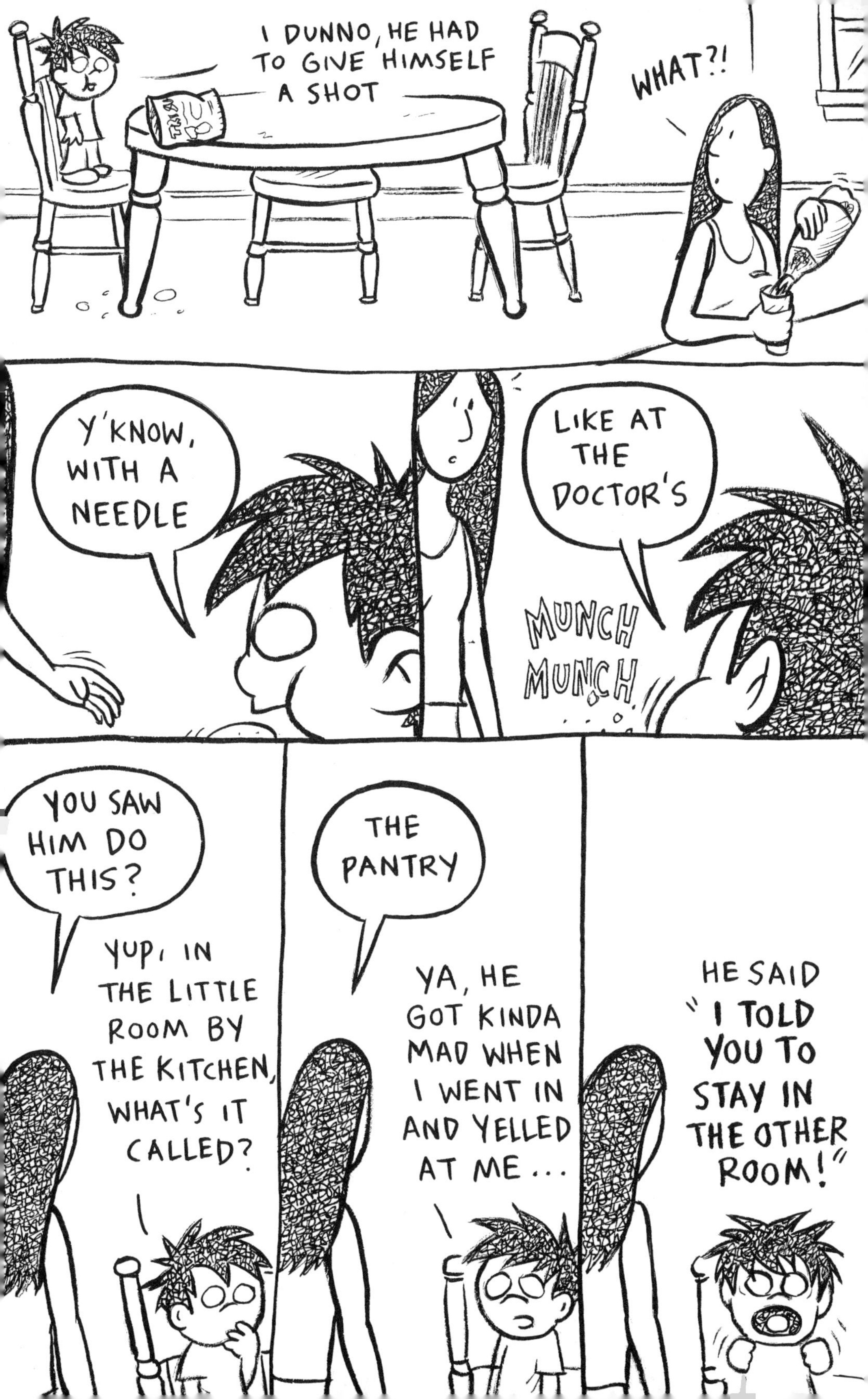
I DUNNO, HE HAD TO GIVE HIMSELF A SHOT
WHAT?!
Y'KNOW, WITH A NEEDLE
LIKE AT THE DOCTOR'S
MUNCH MUNCH
YOU SAW HIM DO THIS?
YUP, IN THE LITTLE ROOM BY THE KITCHEN, WHAT'S IT CALLED?
THE PANTRY
YA, HE GOT KINDA MAD WHEN I WENT IN AND YELLED AT ME...
HE SAID "I TOLD YOU TO STAY IN THE OTHER ROOM!"

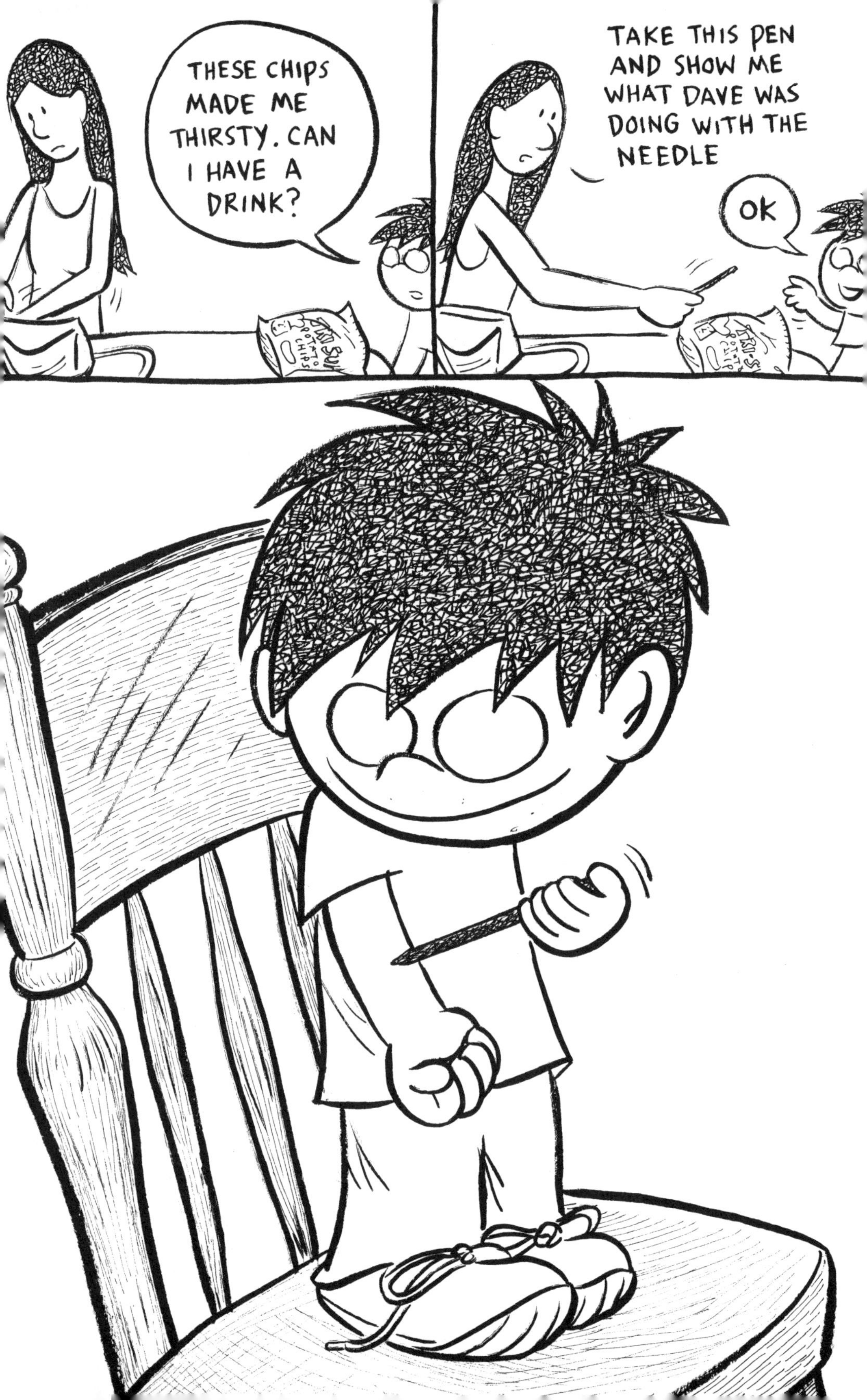
THESE CHIPS MADE ME THIRSTY. CAN I HAVE A DRINK?
TAKE THIS PEN AND SHOW ME WHAT DAVE WAS DOING WITH THE NEEDLE
OK

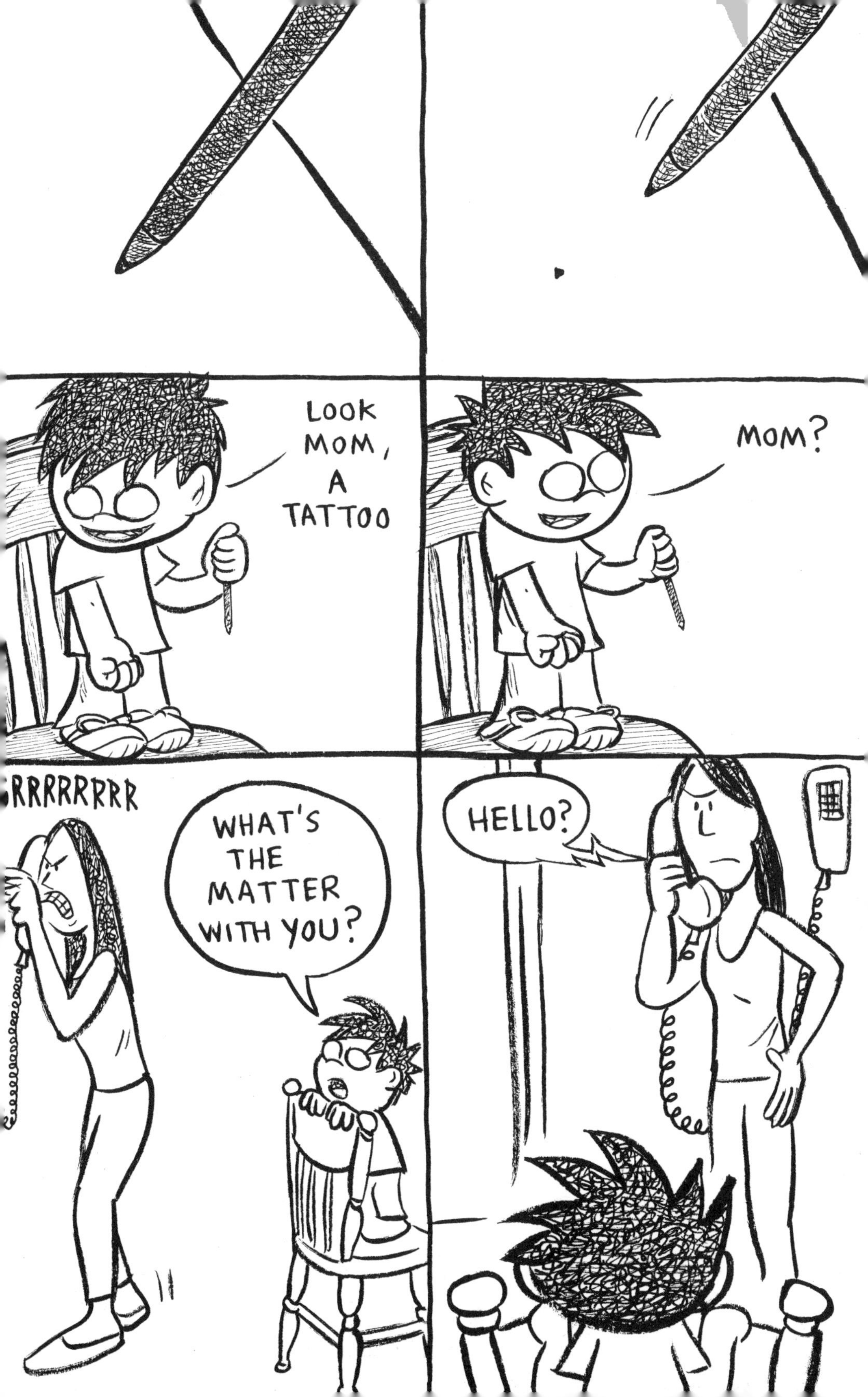
LOOK MOM, A TATTOO
MOM?
RRRRRRRR
WHAT'S THE MATTER WITH YOU?
HELLO?

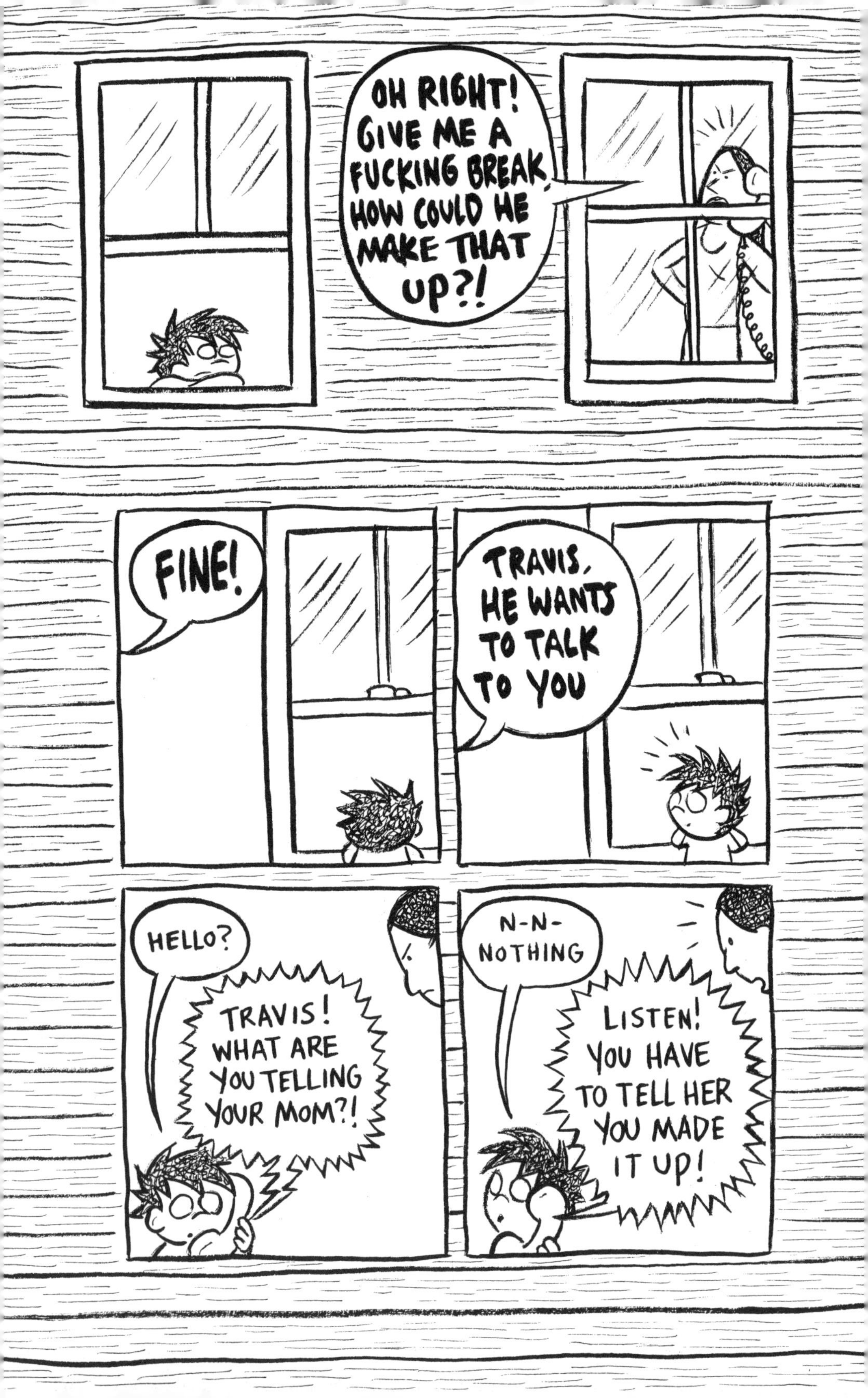
OH RIGHT! GIVE ME A FUCKING BREAK. HOW COULD HE MAKE THAT UP?!
FINE!
TRAVIS, HE WANTS TO TALK TO YOU
HELLO?
TRAVIS! WHAT ARE YOU TELLING YOUR MOM?!
N-N-NOTHING
LISTEN! YOU HAVE TO TELL HER YOU MADE IT UP!

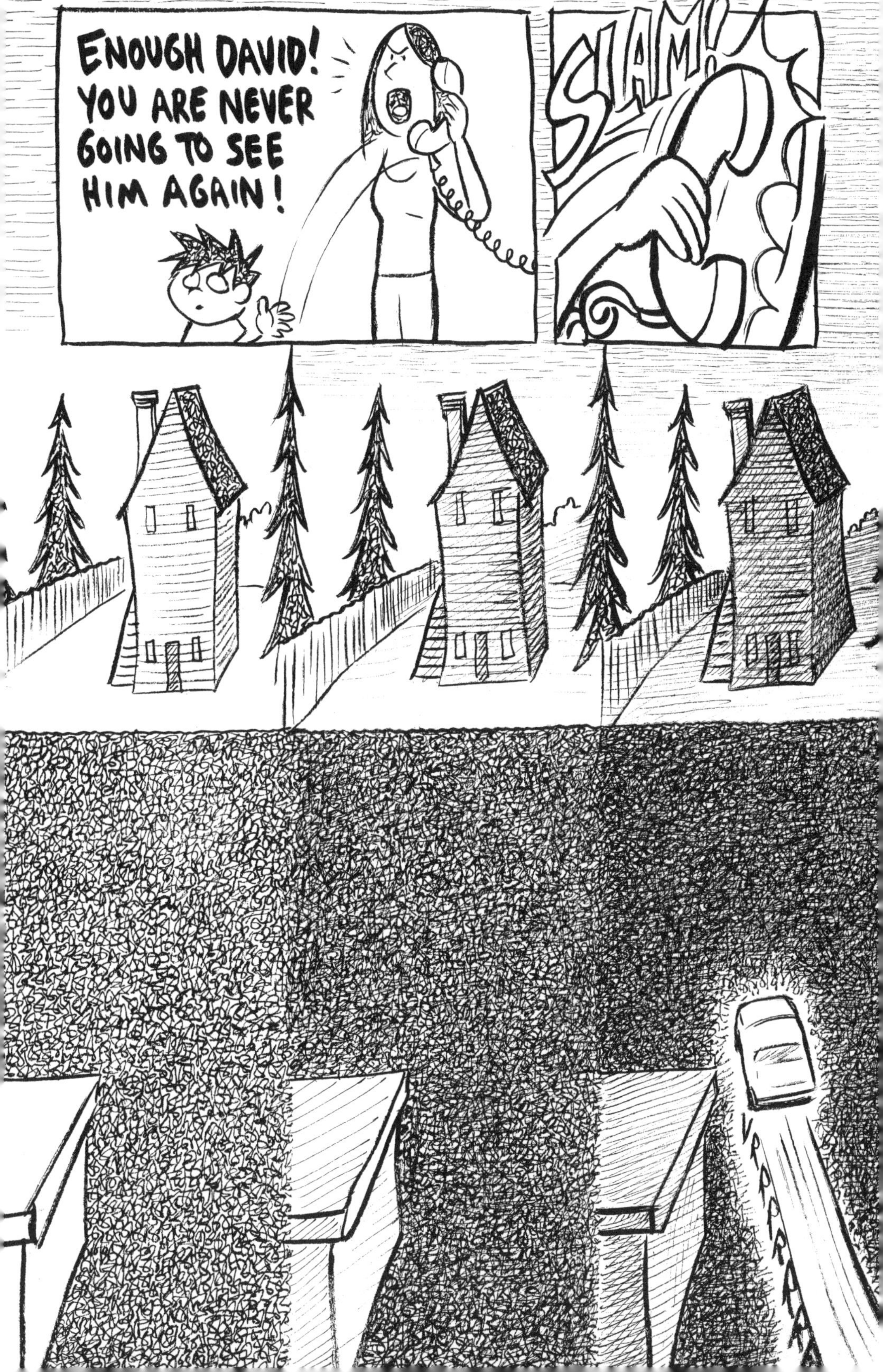
ENOUGH DAVID! YOU ARE NEVER GOING TO SEE HIM AGAIN!
SLAM!
VRRRRRR

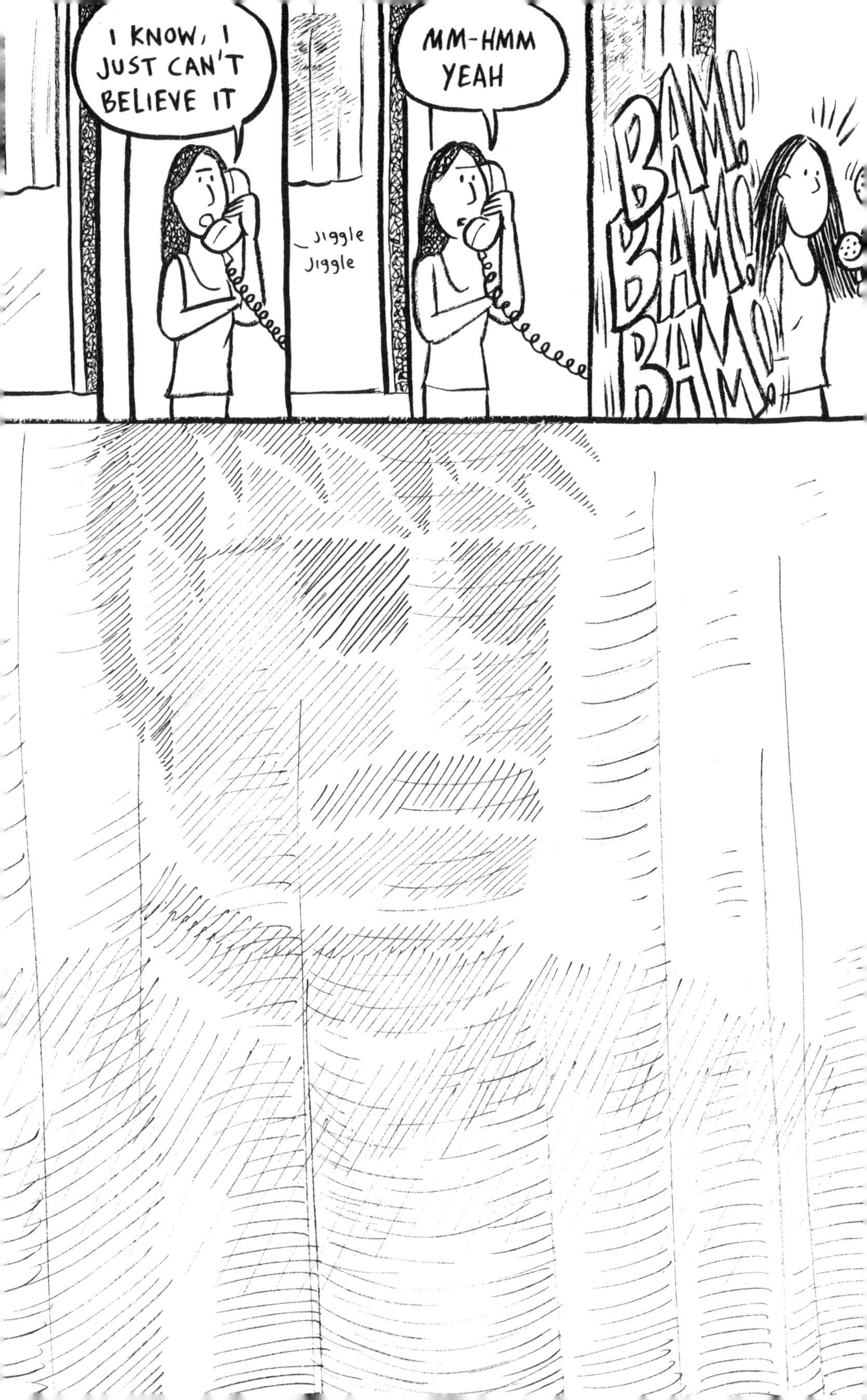
I KNOW, I JUST CAN'T BELIEVE IT
JIGGLE JIGGLE
MM-HMM YEAH
BAM! BAM! BAM!

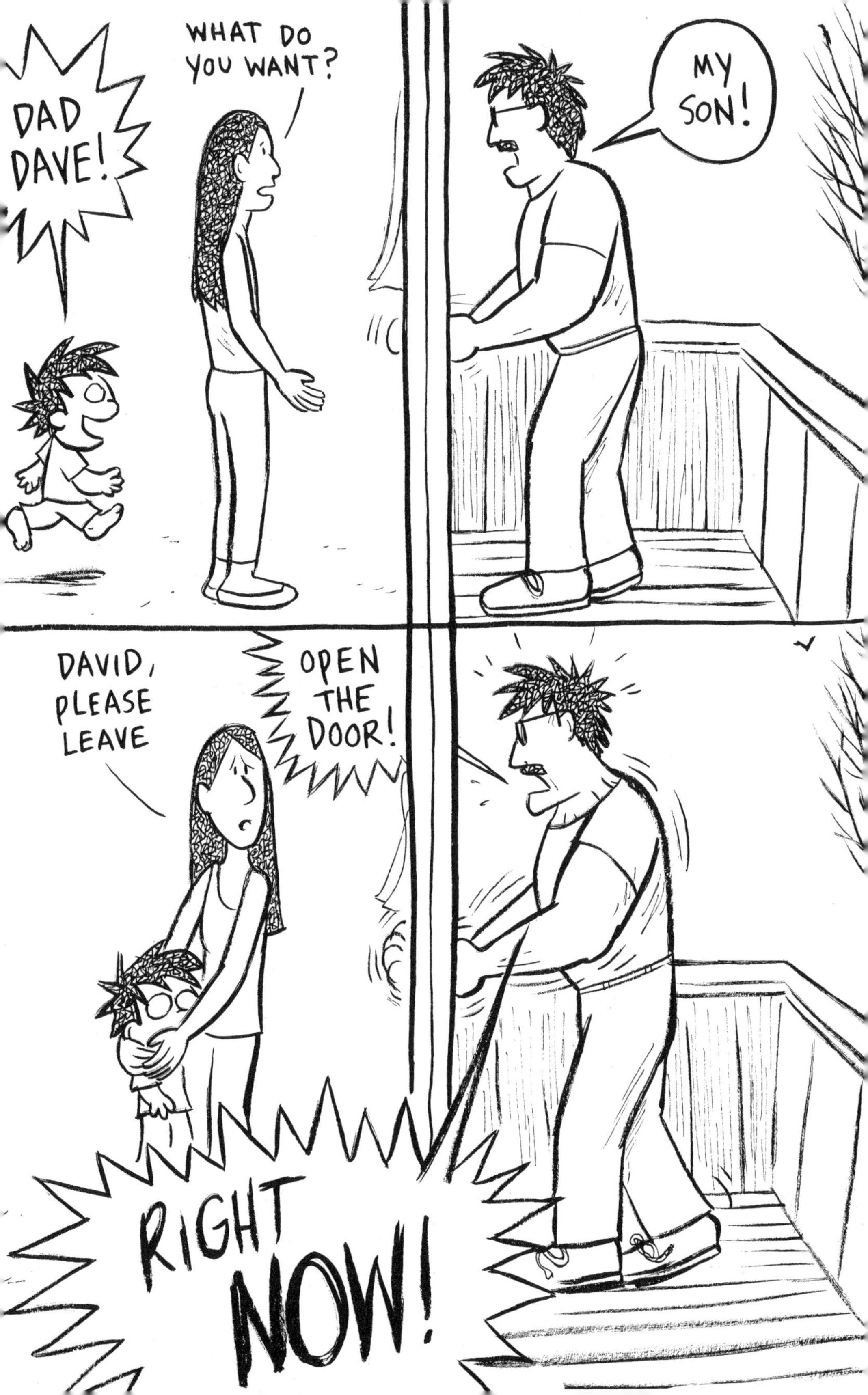
DAD DAVE!
WHAT DO YOU WANT?
MY SON!
DAVID, PLEASE LEAVE
OPEN THE DOOR!
RIGHT NOW!

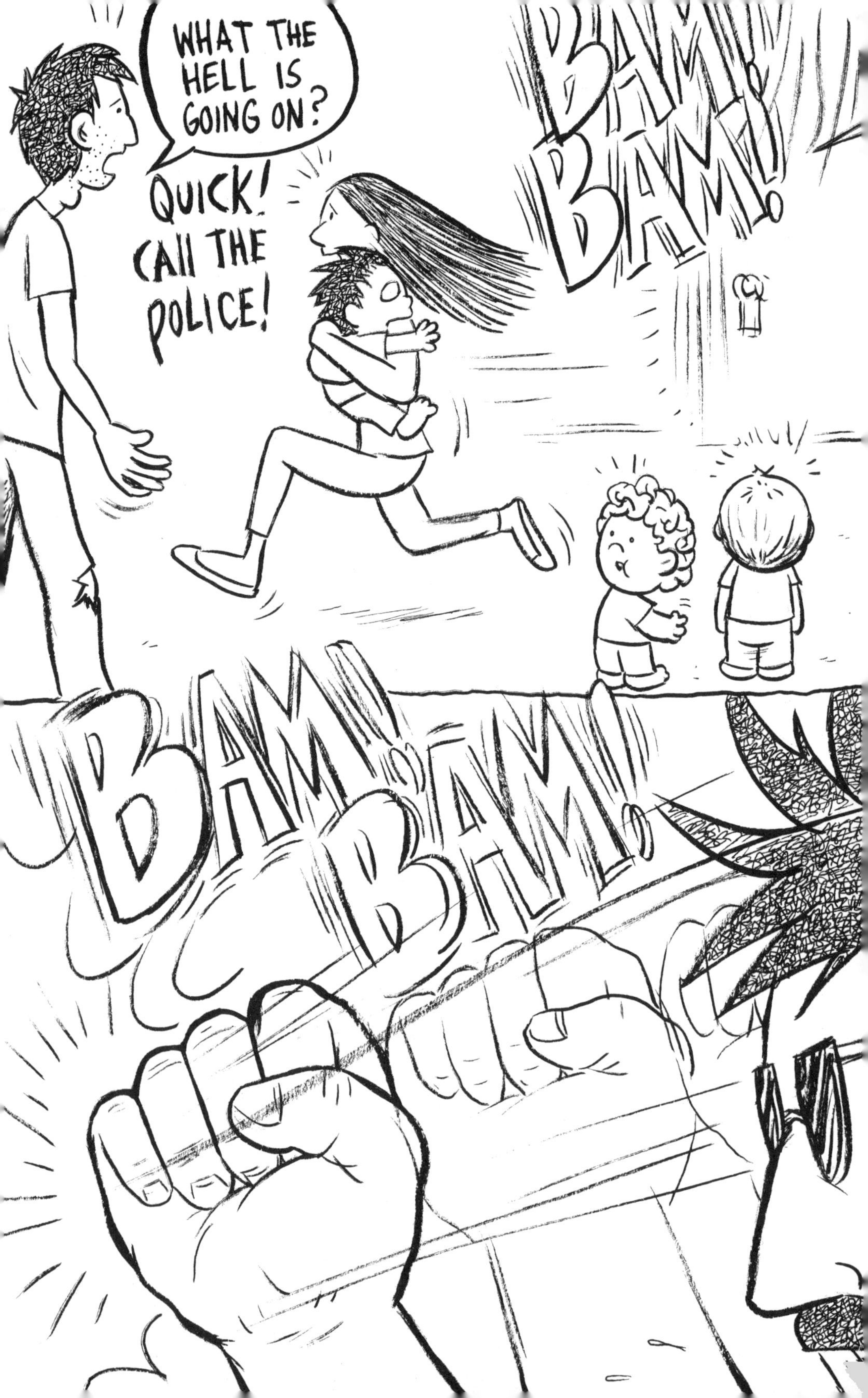
WHAT THE HELL IS GOING ON?
QUICK! CALL THE POLICE!
BAM! BAM!
BAM! BAM!

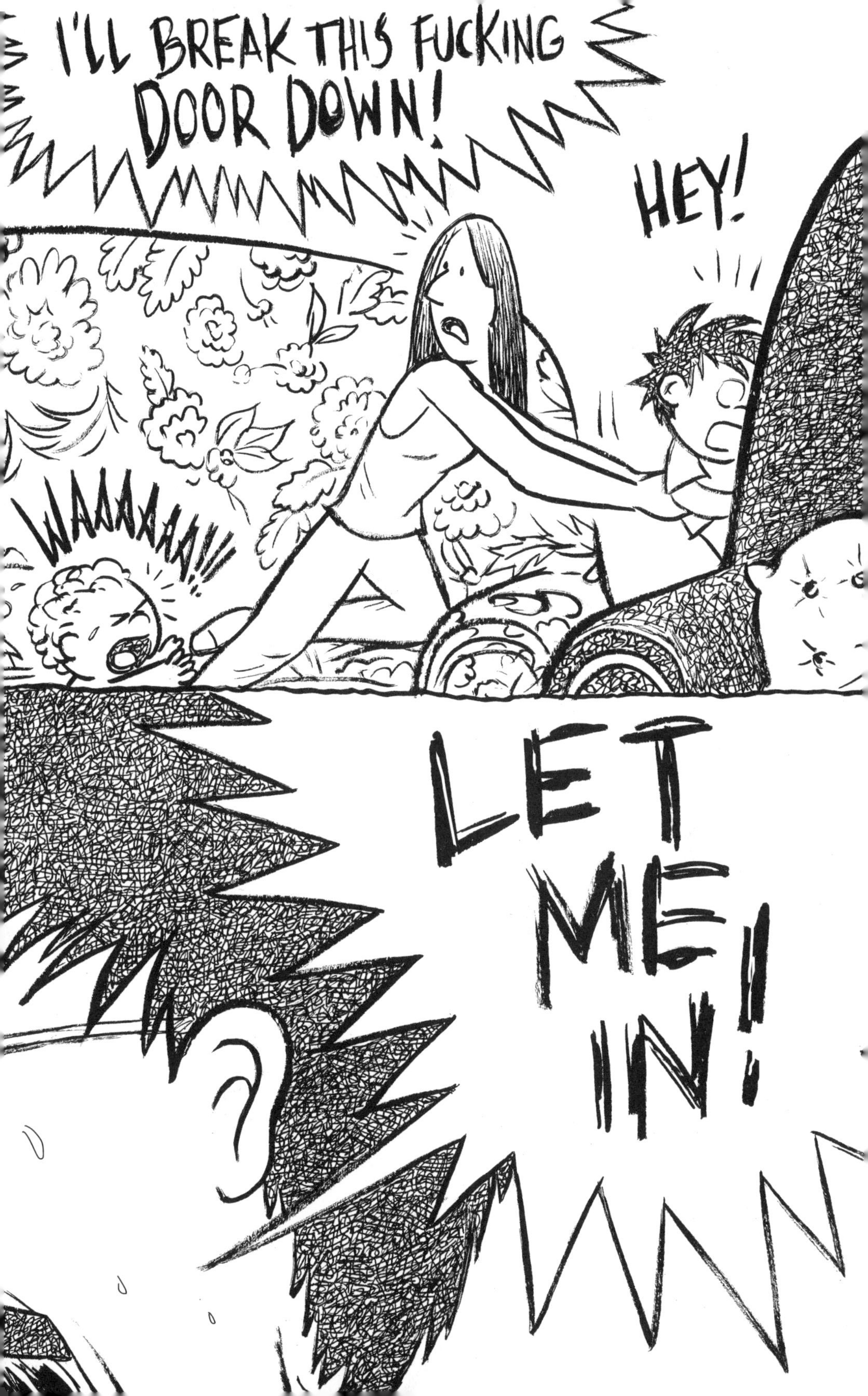
I'LL BREAK THIS FUCKING DOOR DOWN!
HEY!
WAAAAAA!!!
LET ME IN!

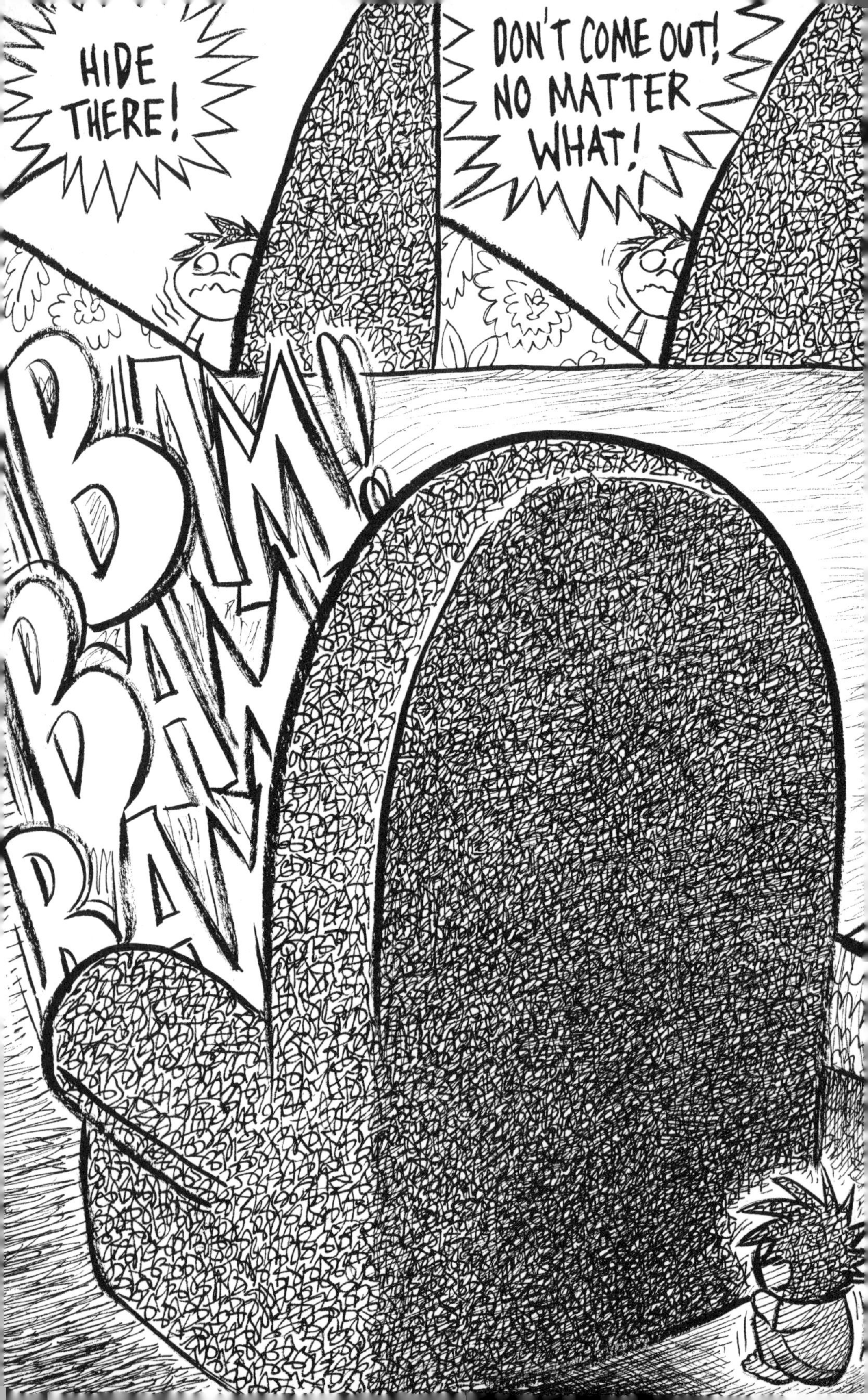
HIDE THERE!
DON'T COME OUT! NO MATTER WHAT!
BAM! BAM! BAM!

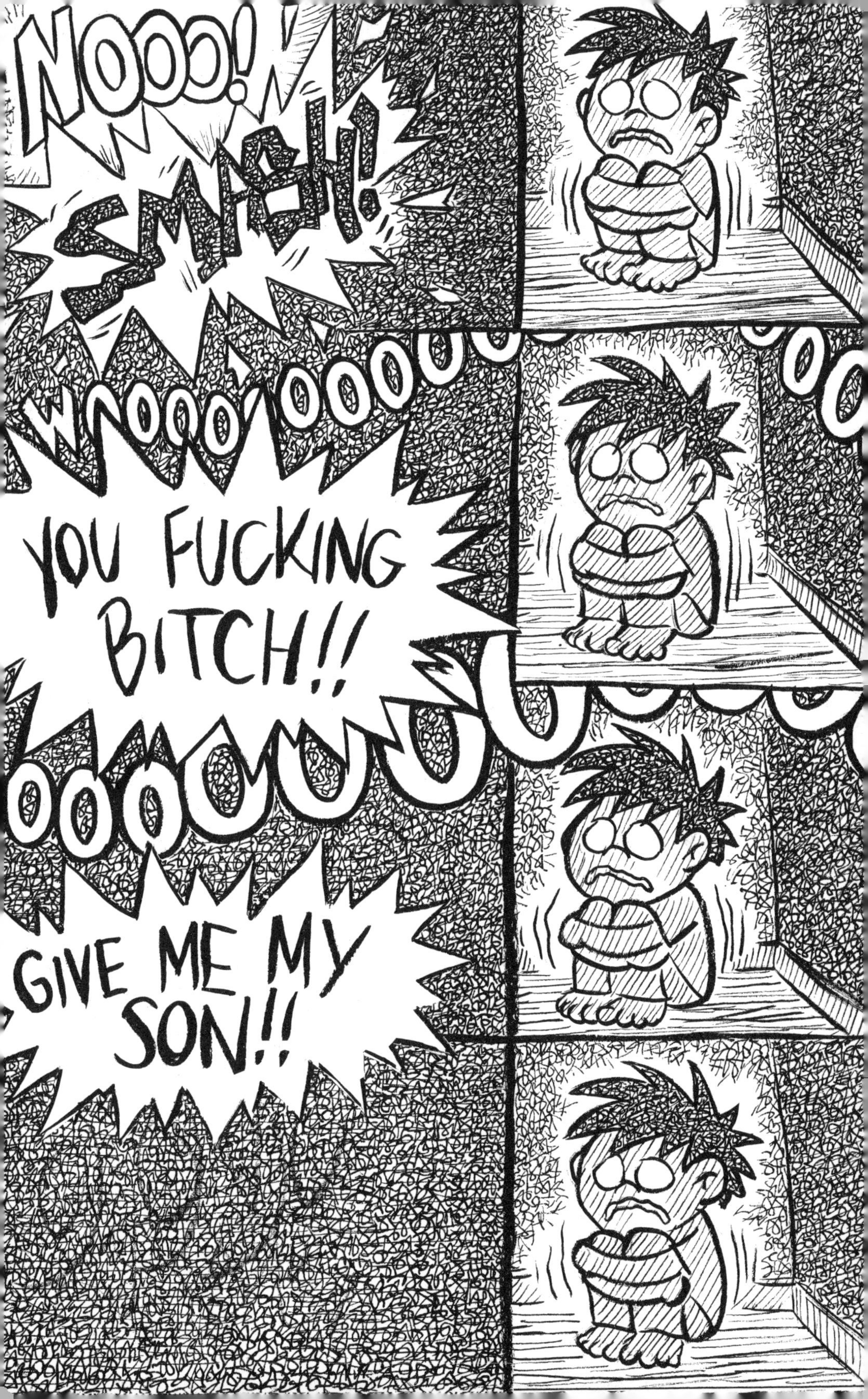
NOOO!
SMASH!
WROOOOOOOOOOOOOOOOOOUUUUUUUUU
YOU FUCKING BITCH!!
GIVE ME MY SON!!

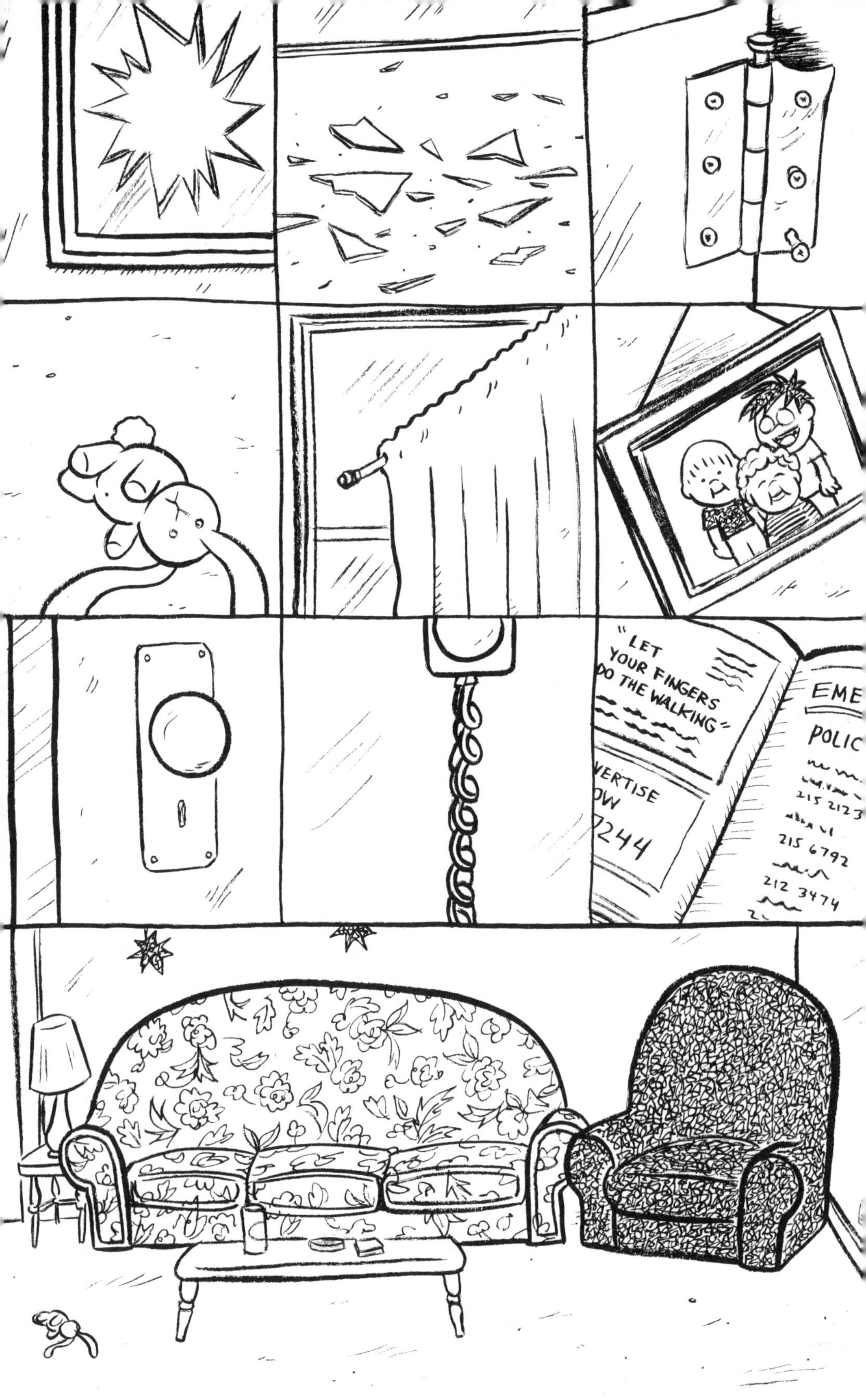
"LET YOUR FINGERS DO THE WALKING"
VERTISE
OW
7244
EME
POLIC
215 2123
215 6792
212 3474

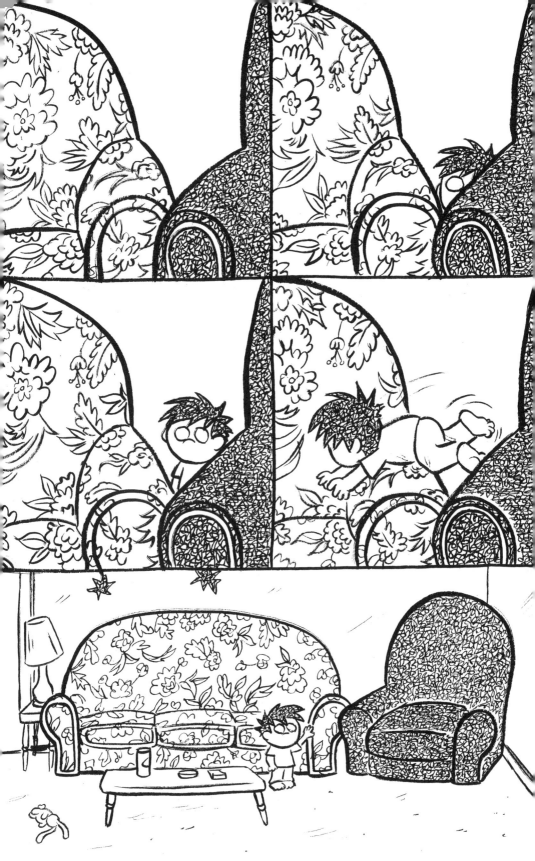

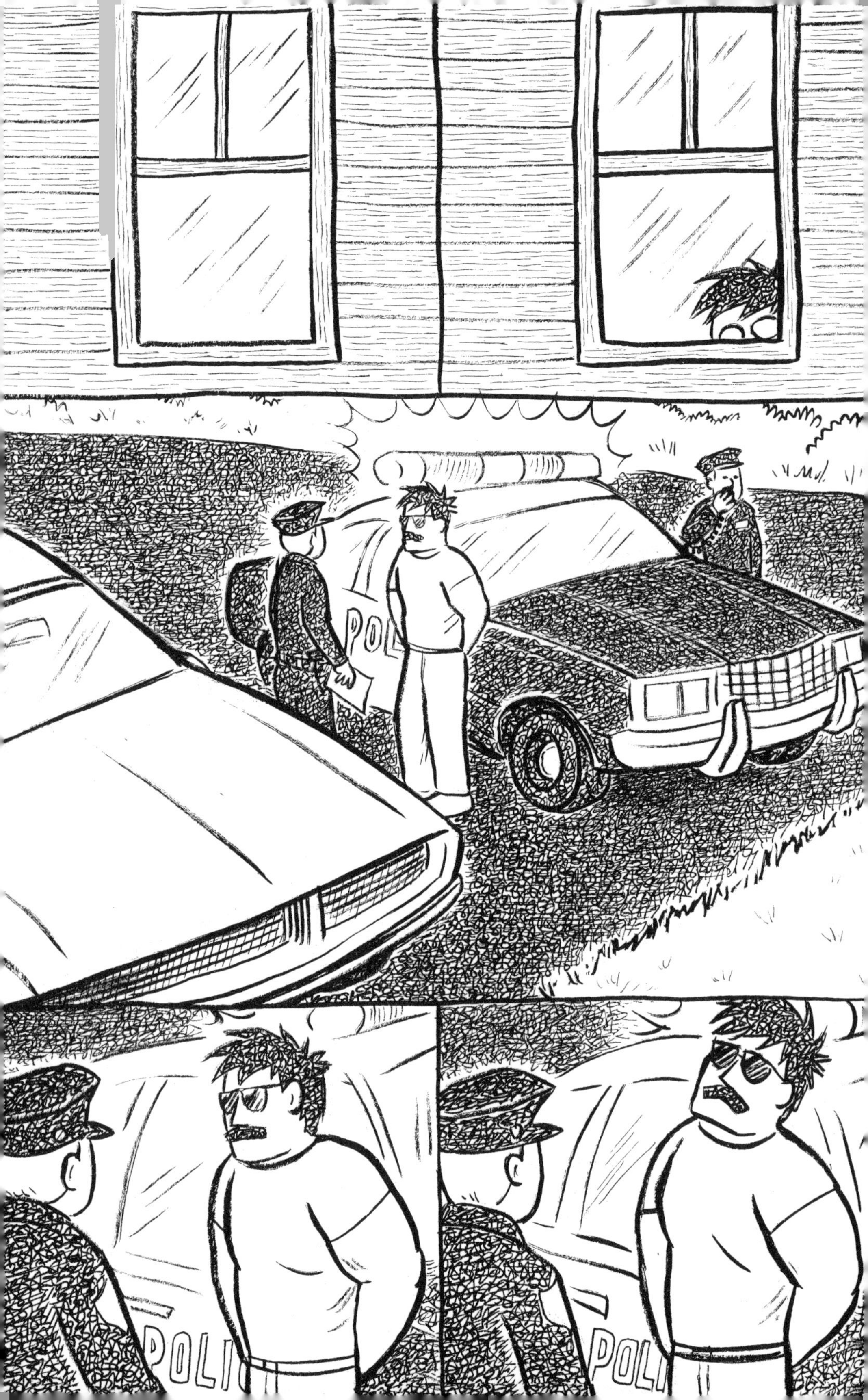
POL
POLI
POLI

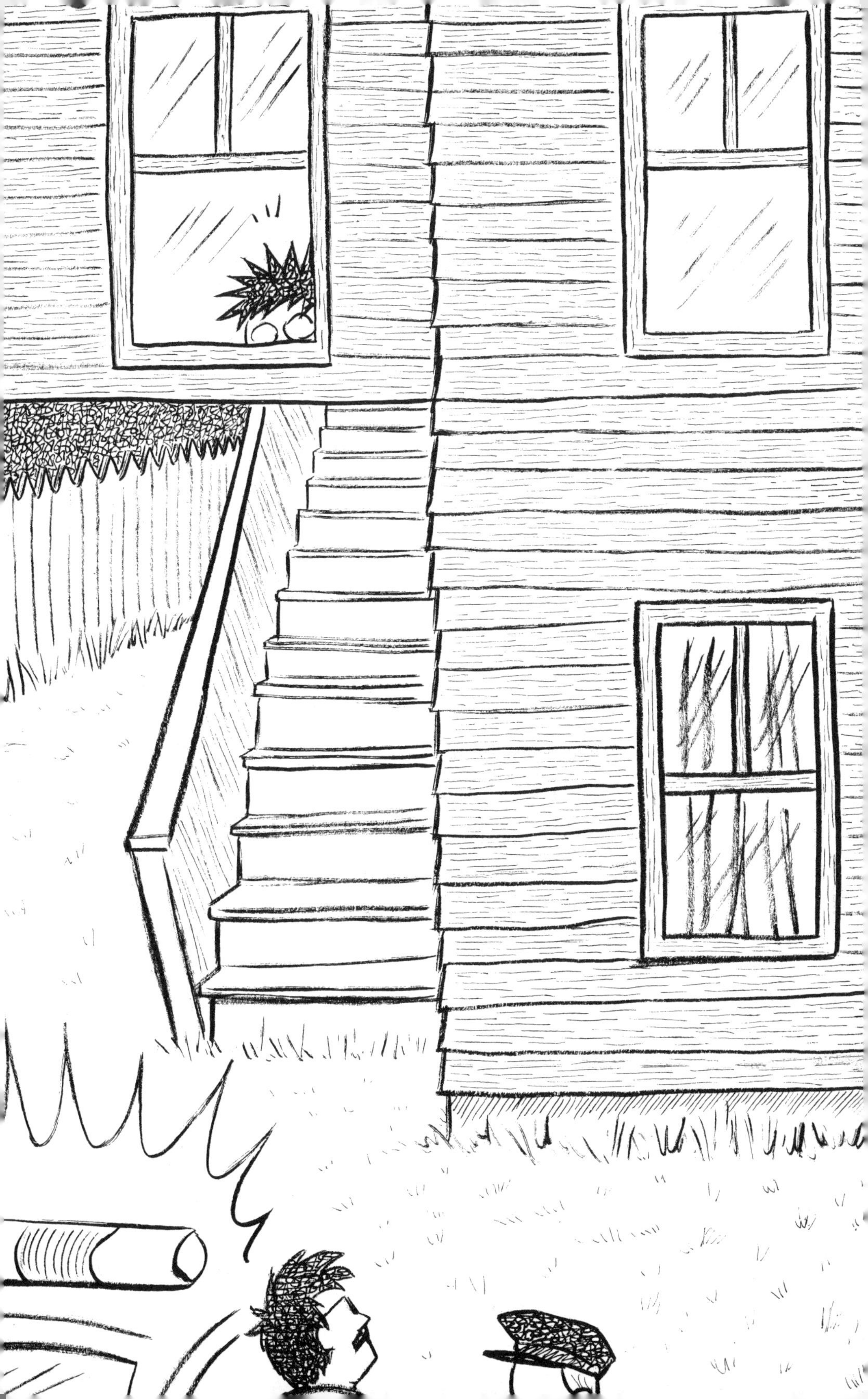

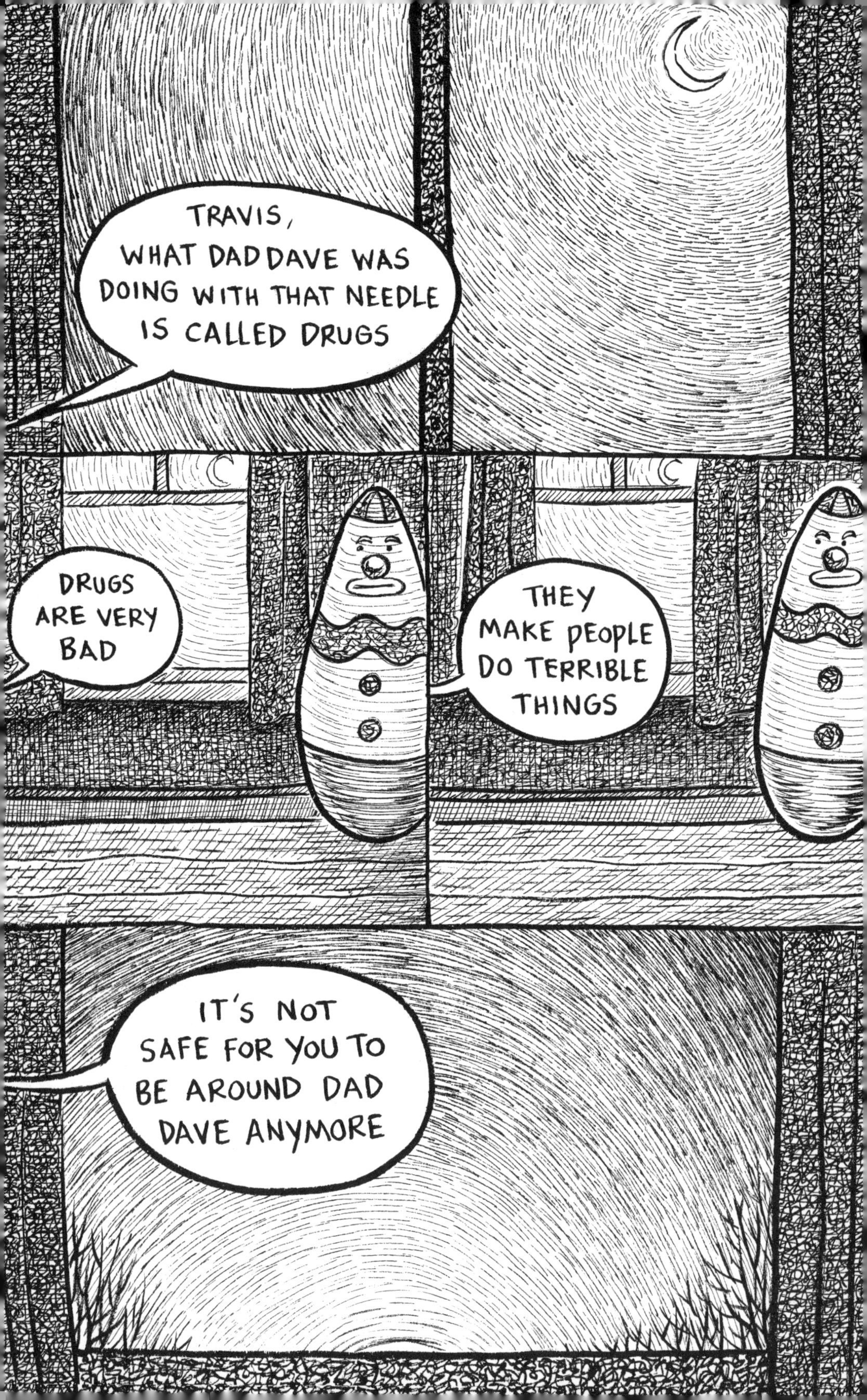
TRAVIS, WHAT DAD DAVE WAS DOING WITH THAT NEEDLE IS CALLED DRUGS
DRUGS ARE VERY BAD
THEY MAKE PEOPLE DO TERRIBLE THINGS
IT'S NOT SAFE FOR YOU TO BE AROUND DAD DAVE ANYMORE

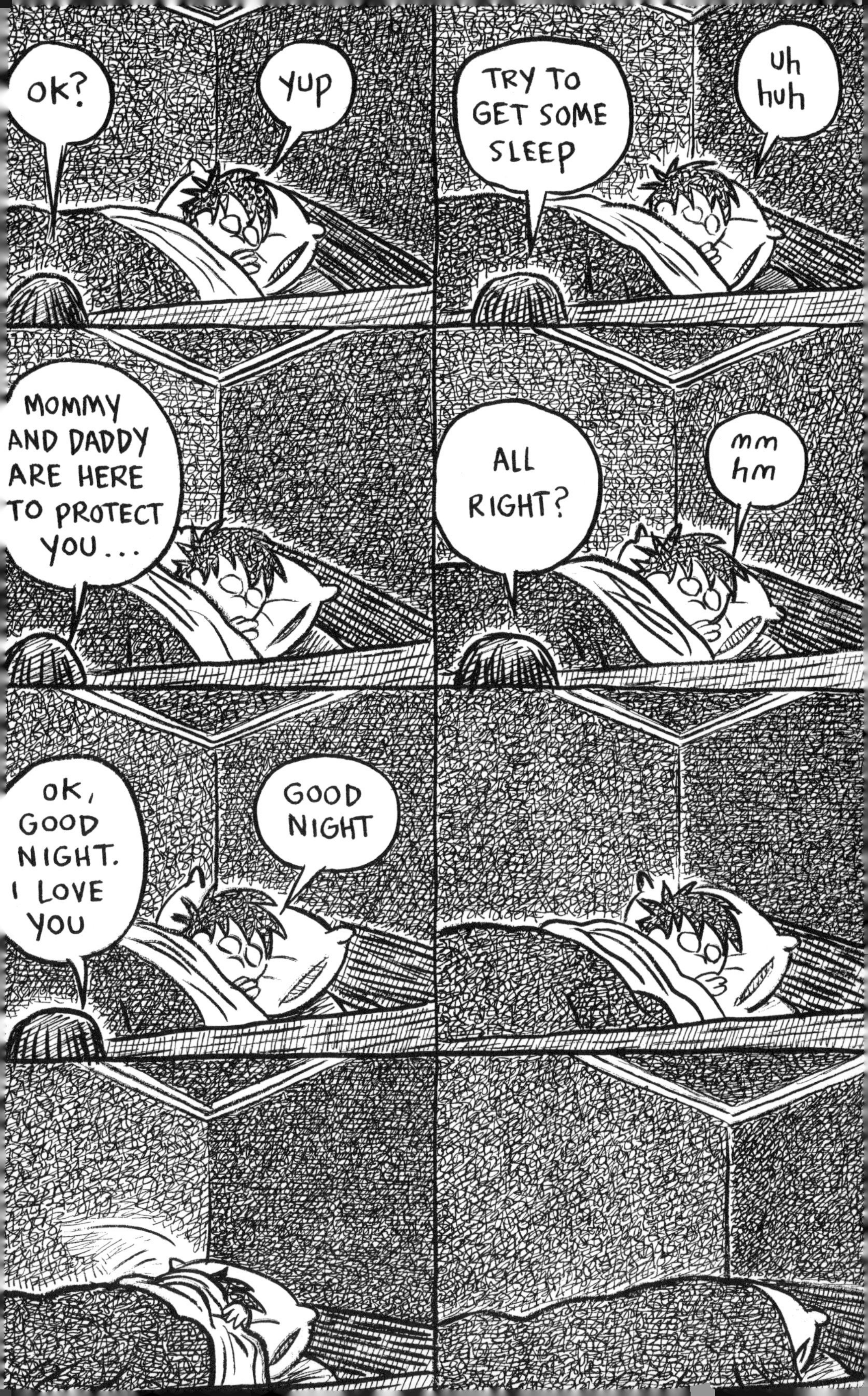
OK?
yup
TRY TO GET SOME SLEEP
uh huh
MOMMY AND DADDY ARE HERE TO PROTECT YOU...
ALL RIGHT?
mm hm
OK, GOOD NIGHT. I LOVE YOU
GOOD NIGHT

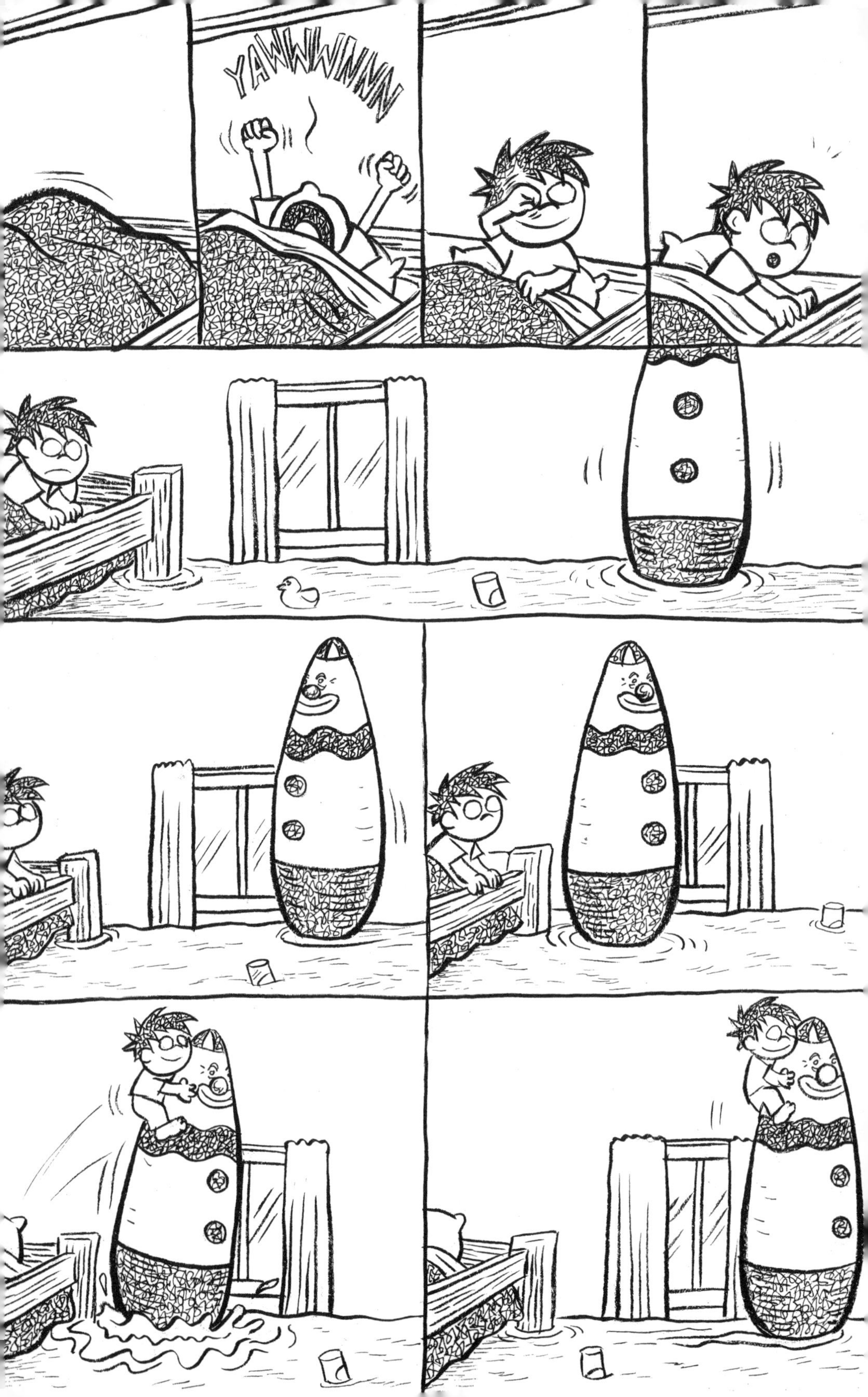
YAWWWNNN

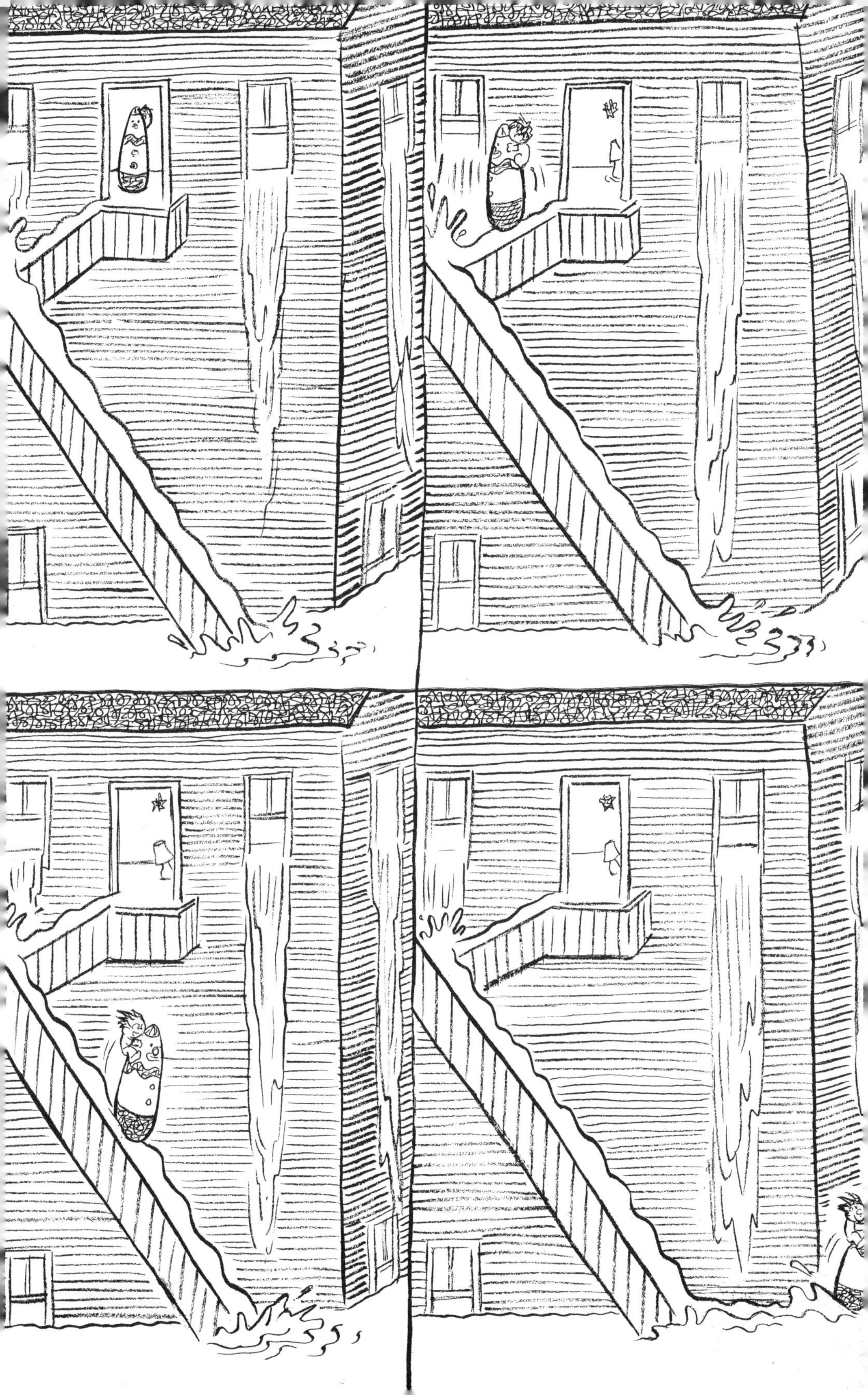

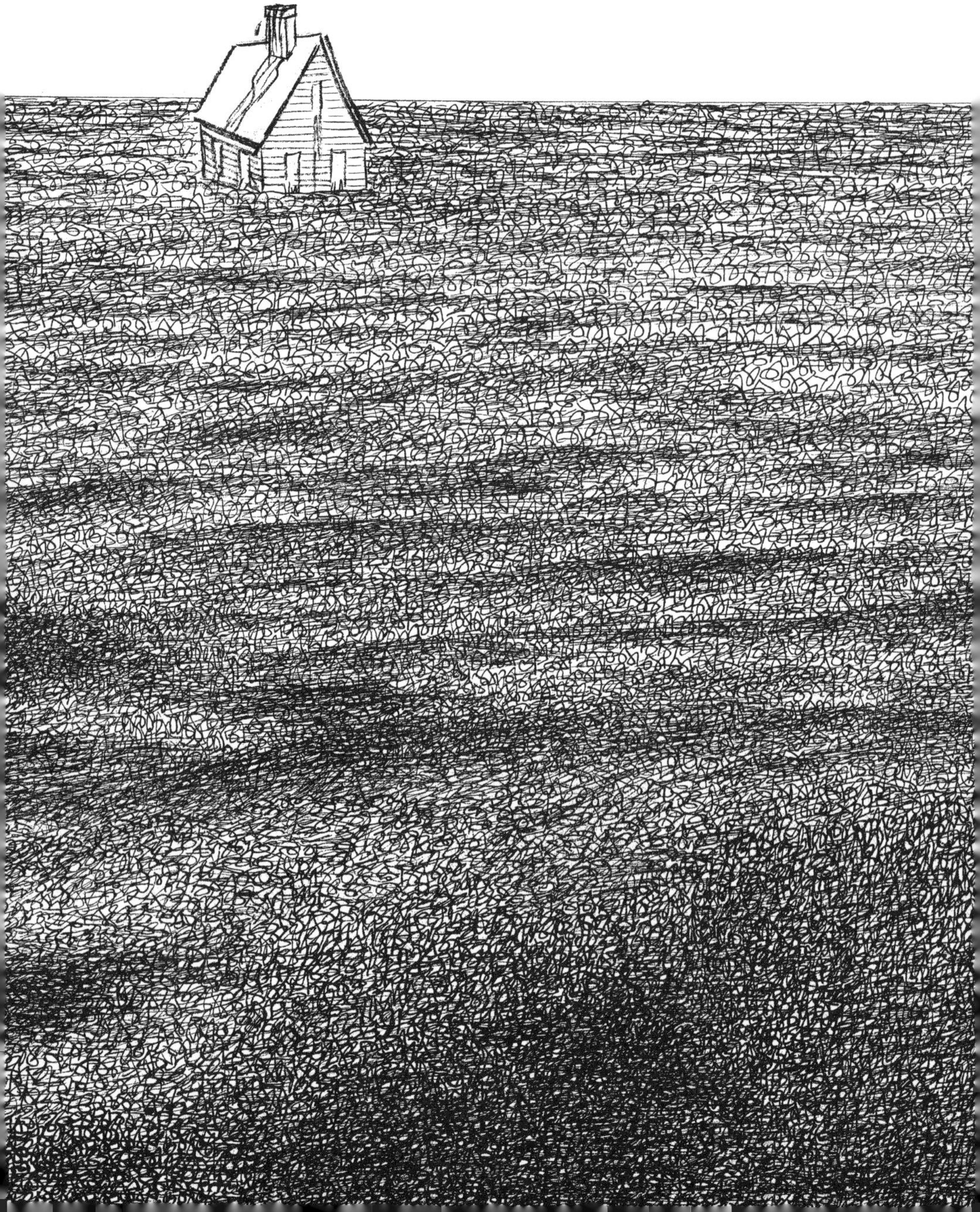

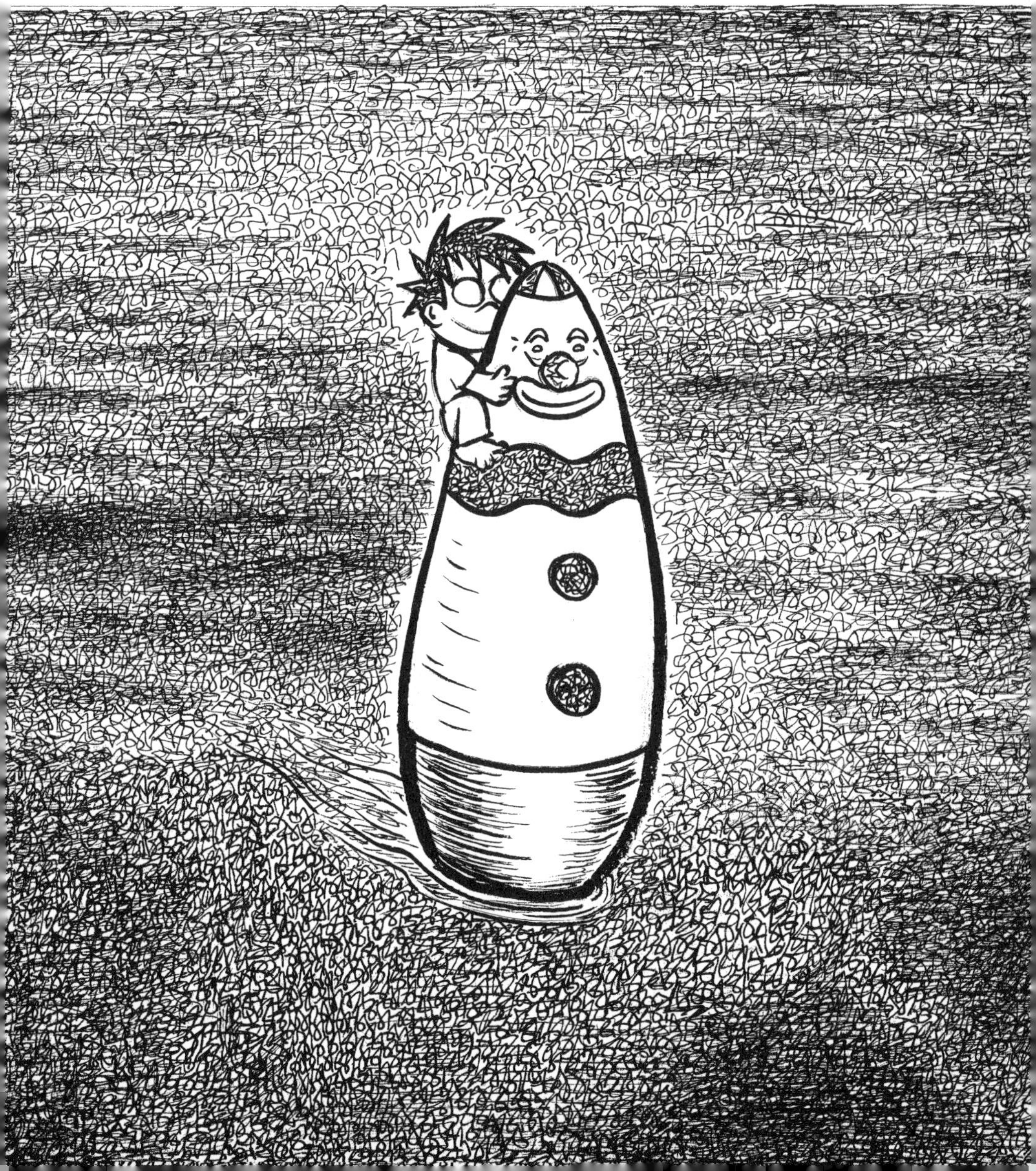

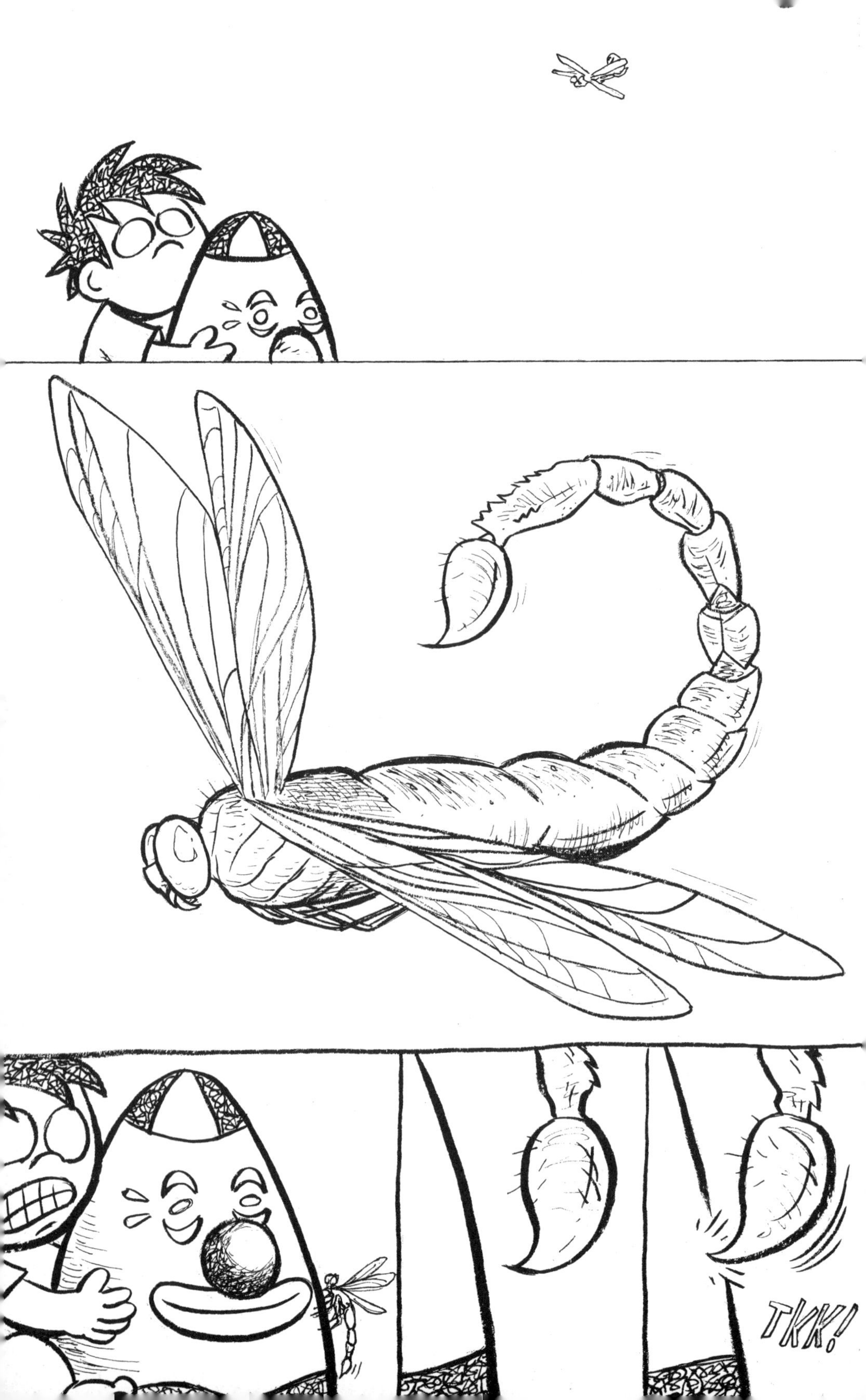
TKK!

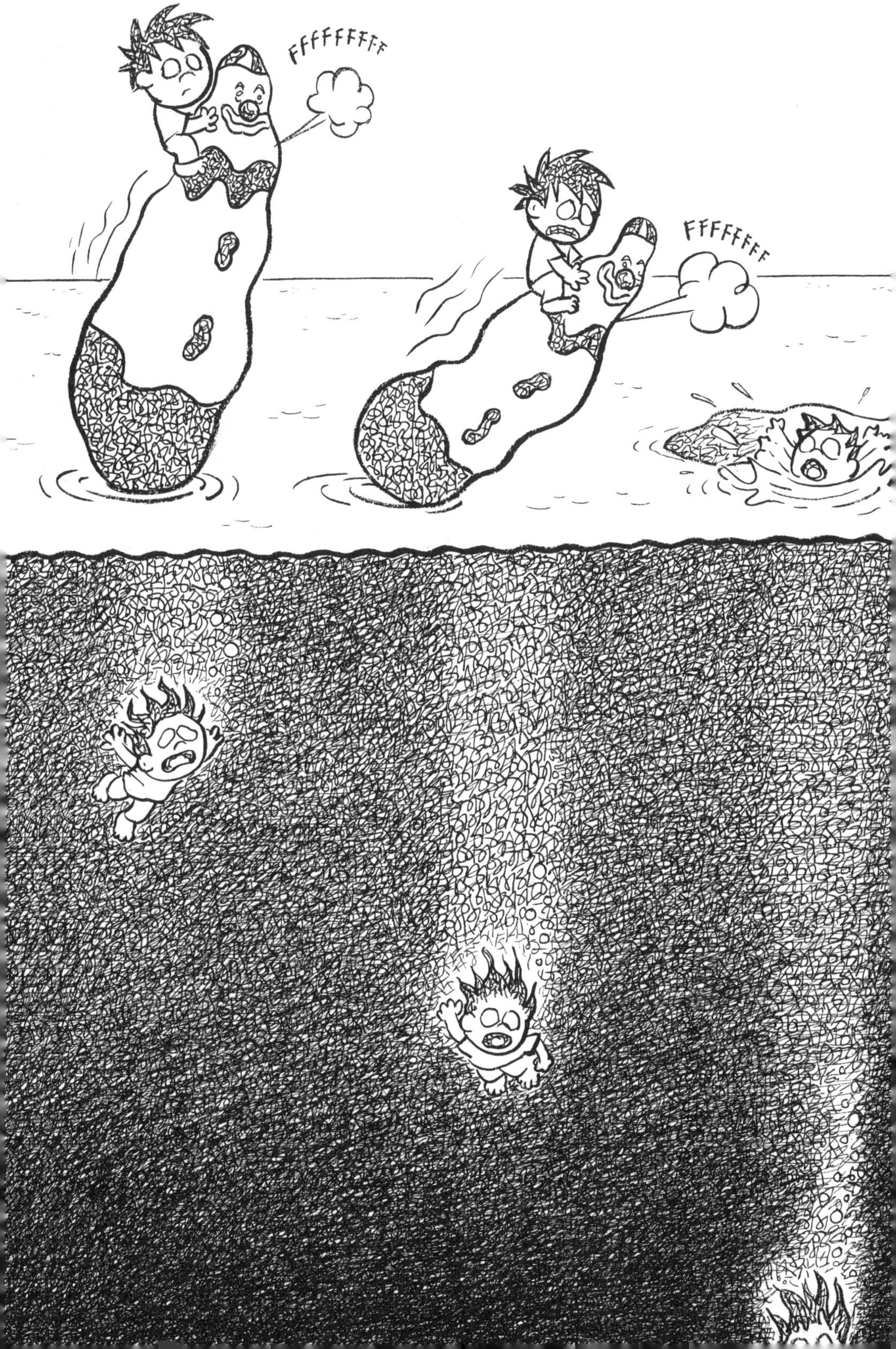
FFFFFFFFF
FFFFFFFF

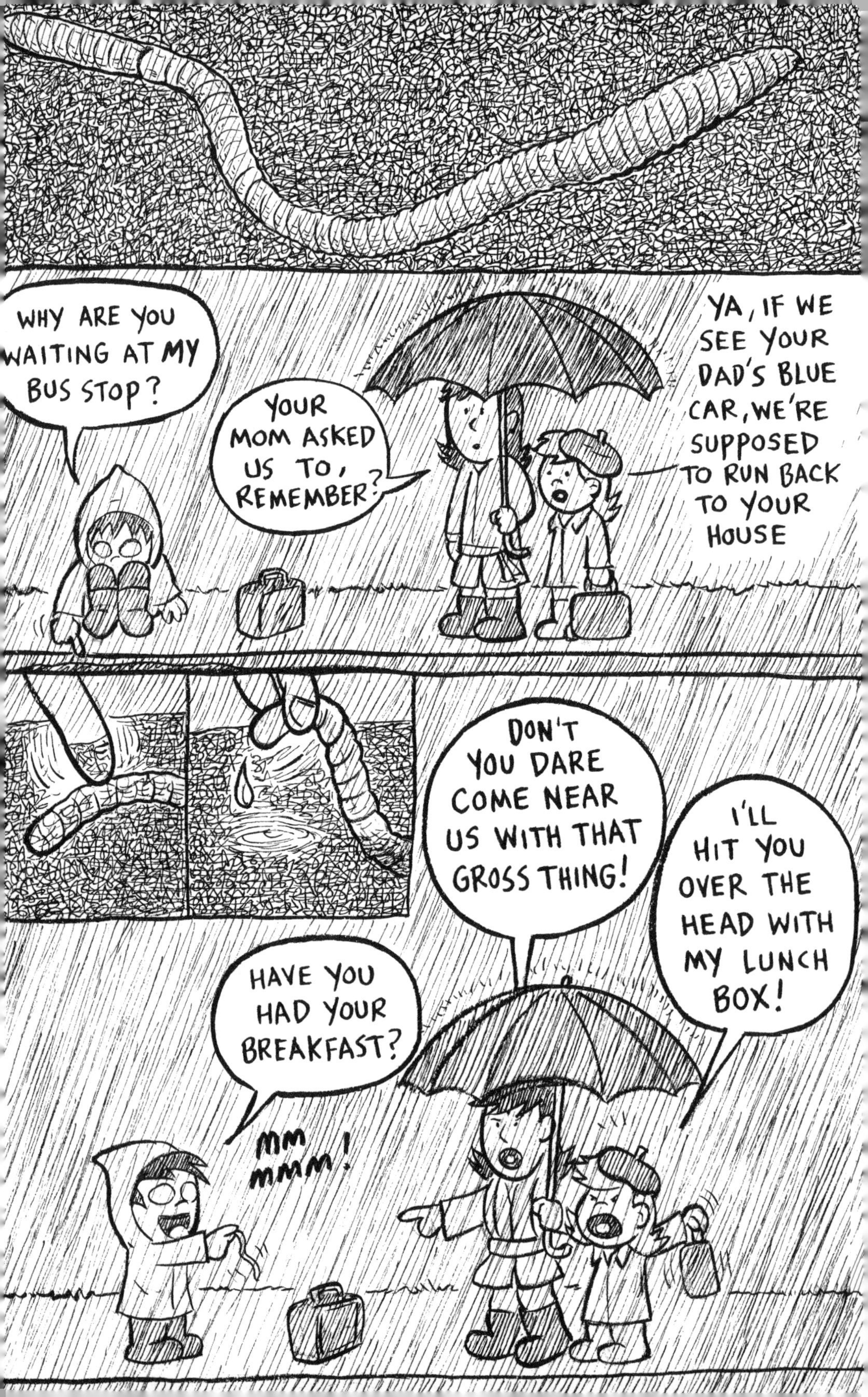
WHY ARE YOU WAITING AT MY BUS STOP?
YOUR MOM ASKED US TO, REMEMBER?
YA, IF WE SEE YOUR DAD'S BLUE CAR, WE'RE SUPPOSED TO RUN BACK TO YOUR HOUSE
HAVE YOU HAD YOUR BREAKFAST?
MM MMM!
DON'T YOU DARE COME NEAR US WITH THAT GROSS THING!
I'LL HIT YOU OVER THE HEAD WITH MY LUNCH BOX!

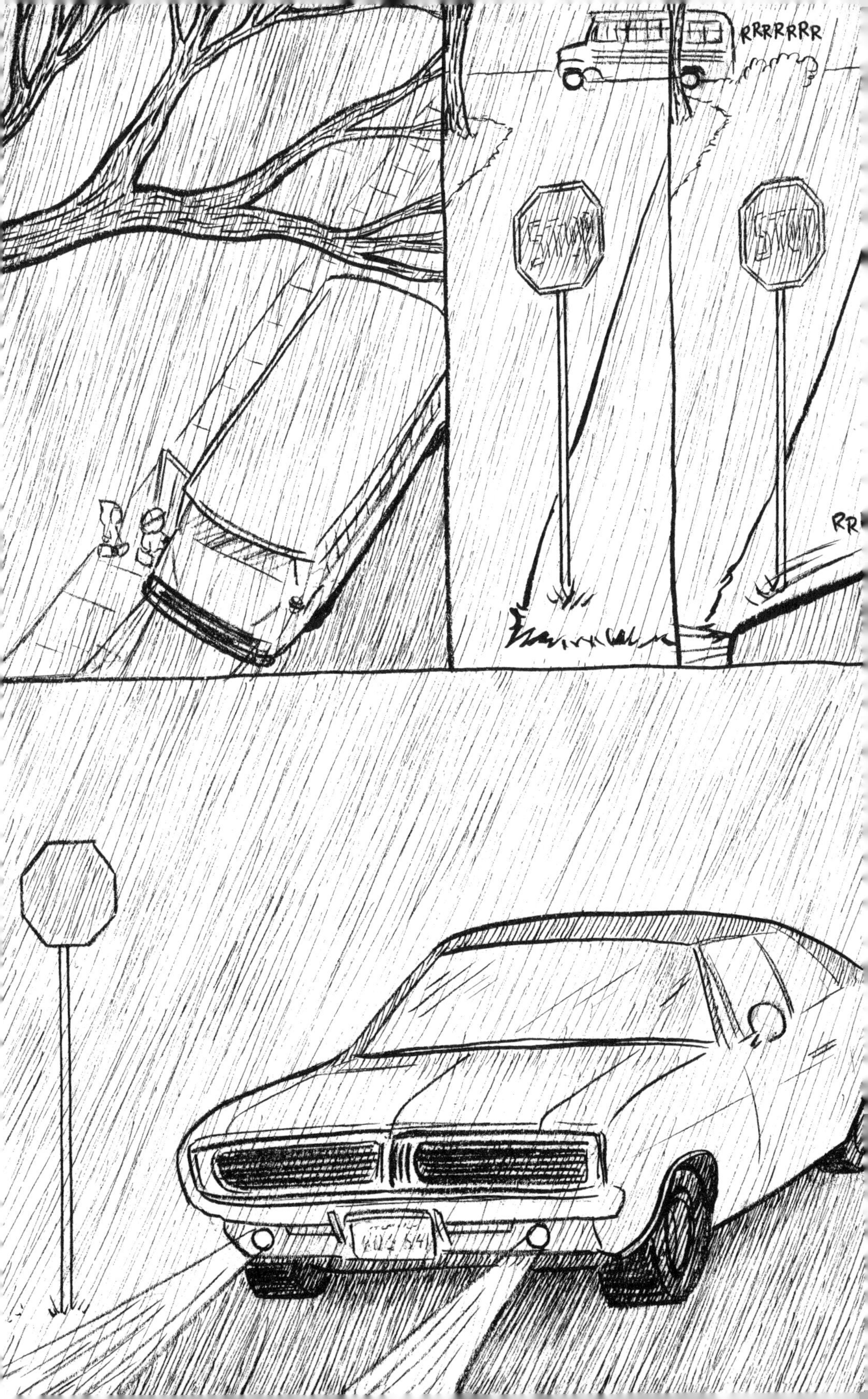
RRRRRRR
RR

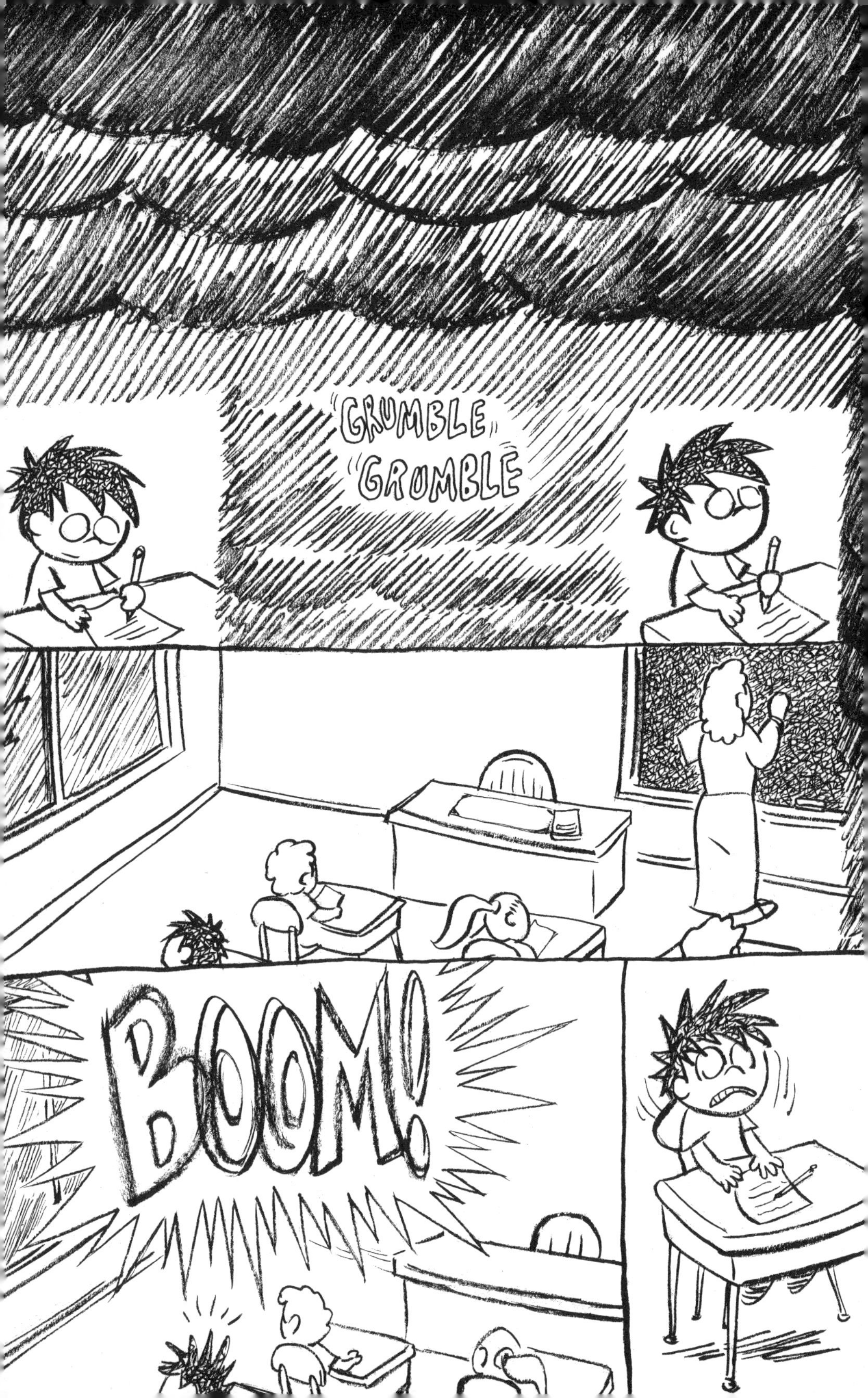
GRUMBLE
GRUMBLE
BOOM!

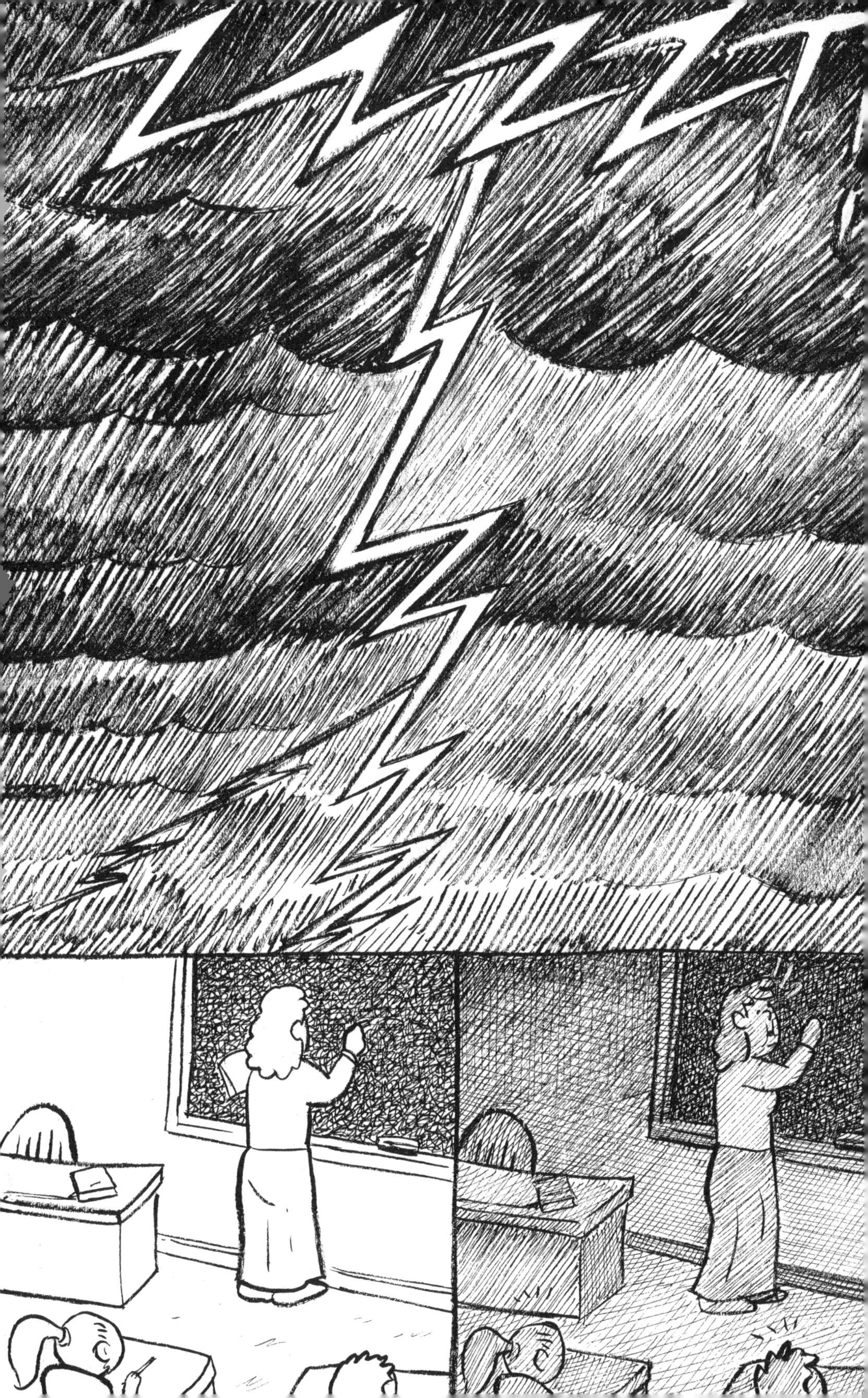

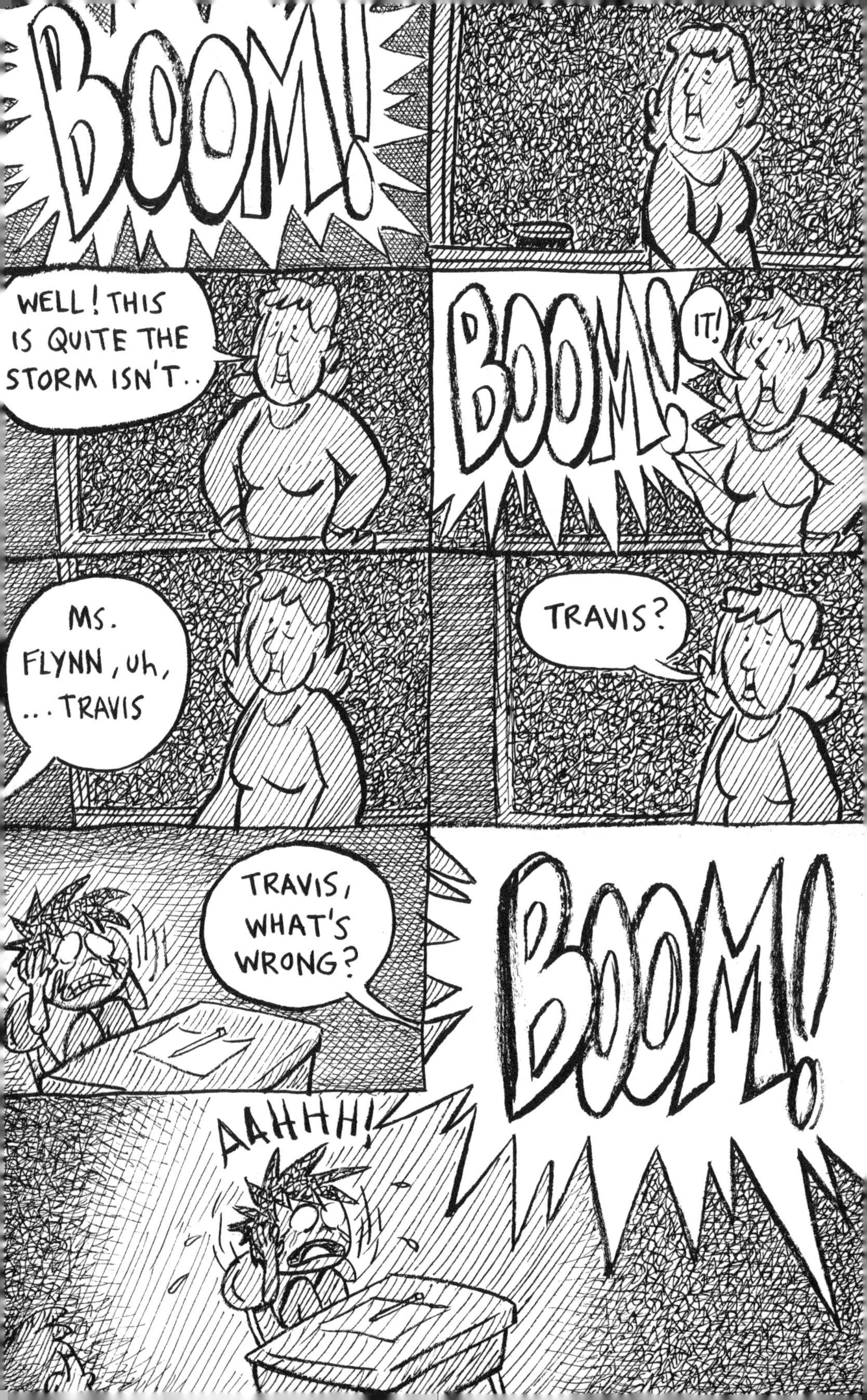
BOOM!
WELL! THIS IS QUITE THE STORM ISN'T..
BOOM!
IT!
MS. FLYNN, uh, ...TRAVIS
TRAVIS?
TRAVIS, WHAT'S WRONG?
BOOM!
AAHHH!

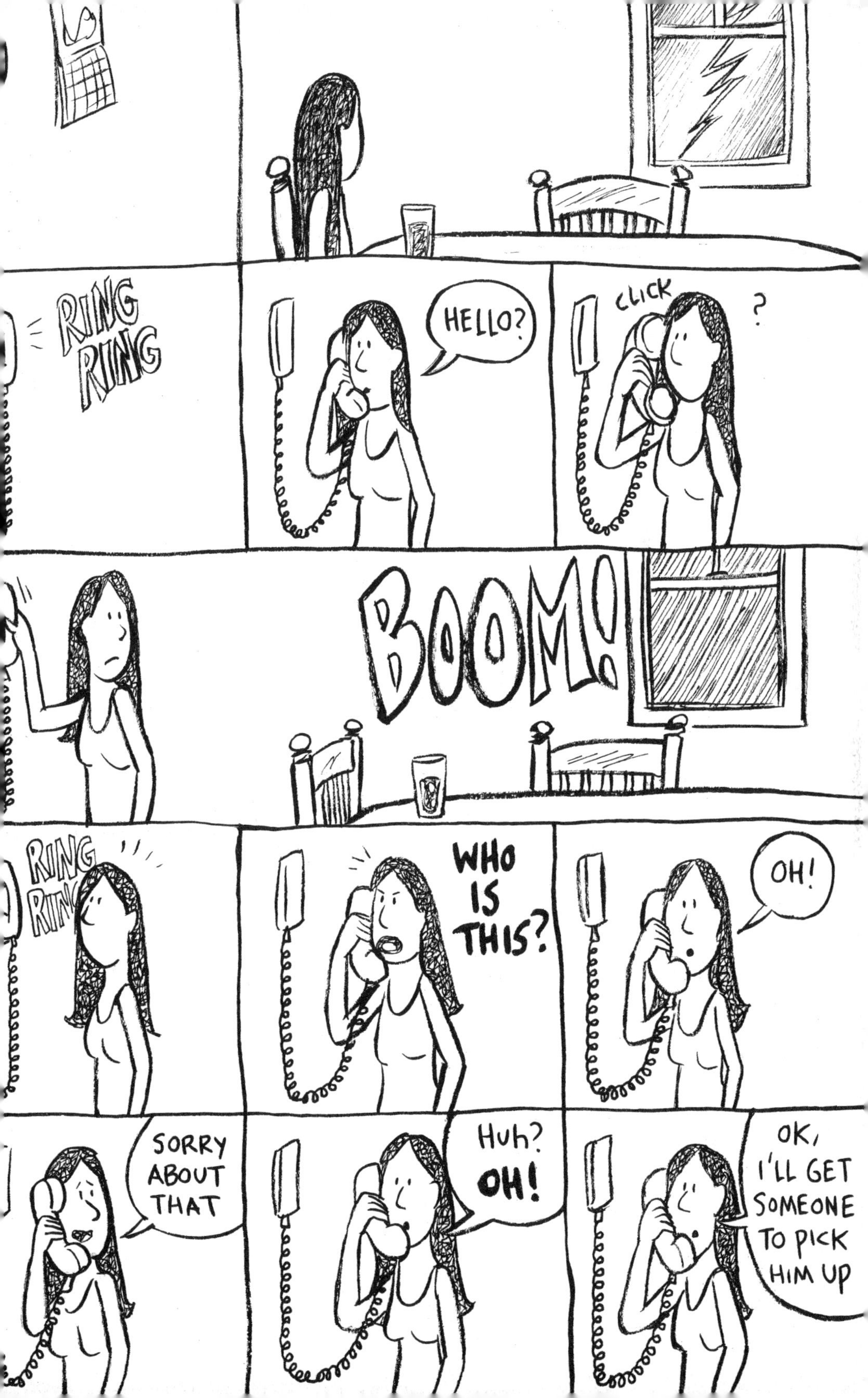
RING
RING
HELLO?
CLICK
?
BOOM!
RING
RING
WHO IS THIS?
OH!
SORRY ABOUT THAT
Huh?
OH!
OK, I'LL GET SOMEONE TO PICK HIM UP

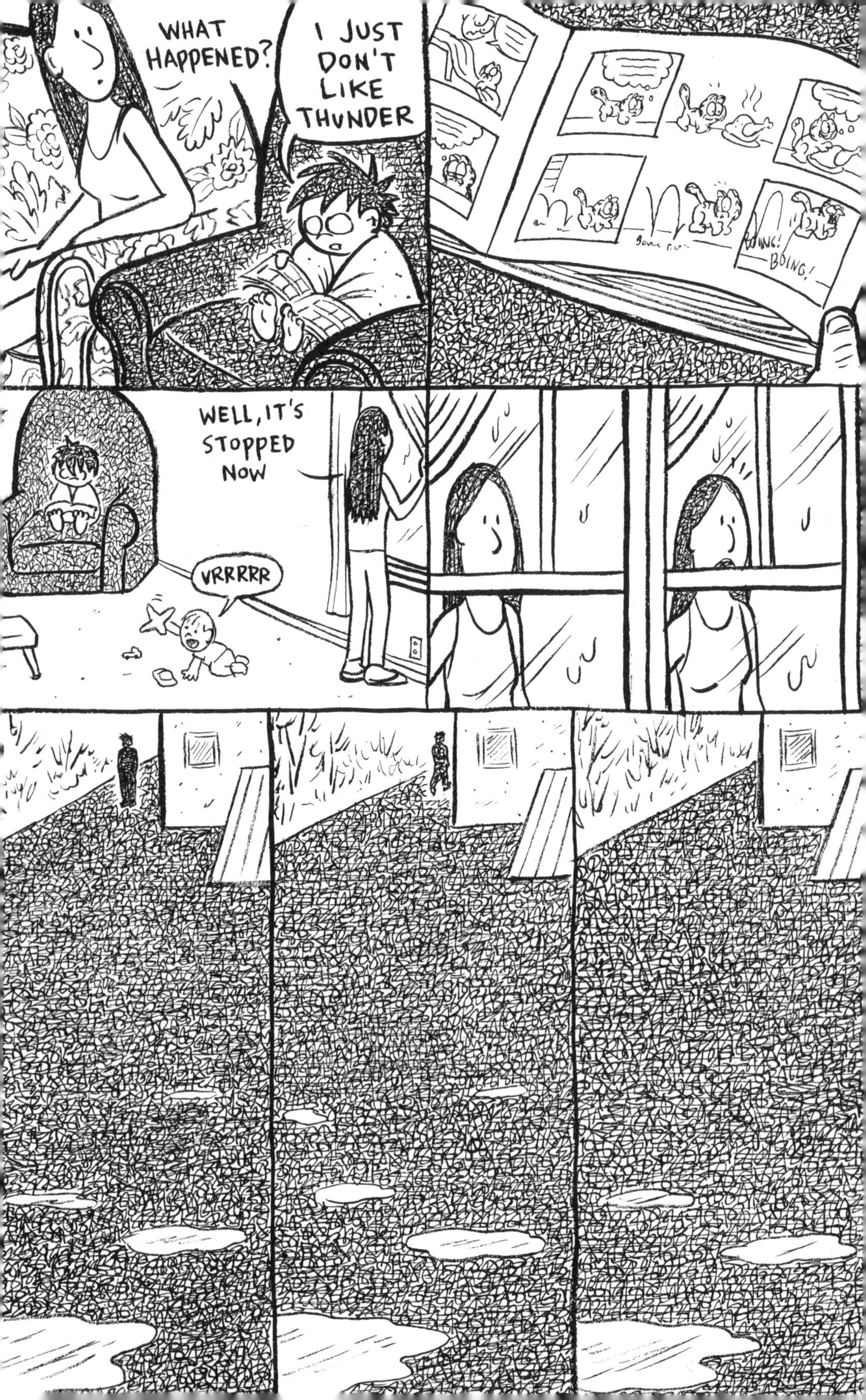
WHAT HAPPENED?
I JUST DON'T LIKE THUNDER
BOING!
BOING!
WELL, IT'S STOPPED NOW
VRRRRR

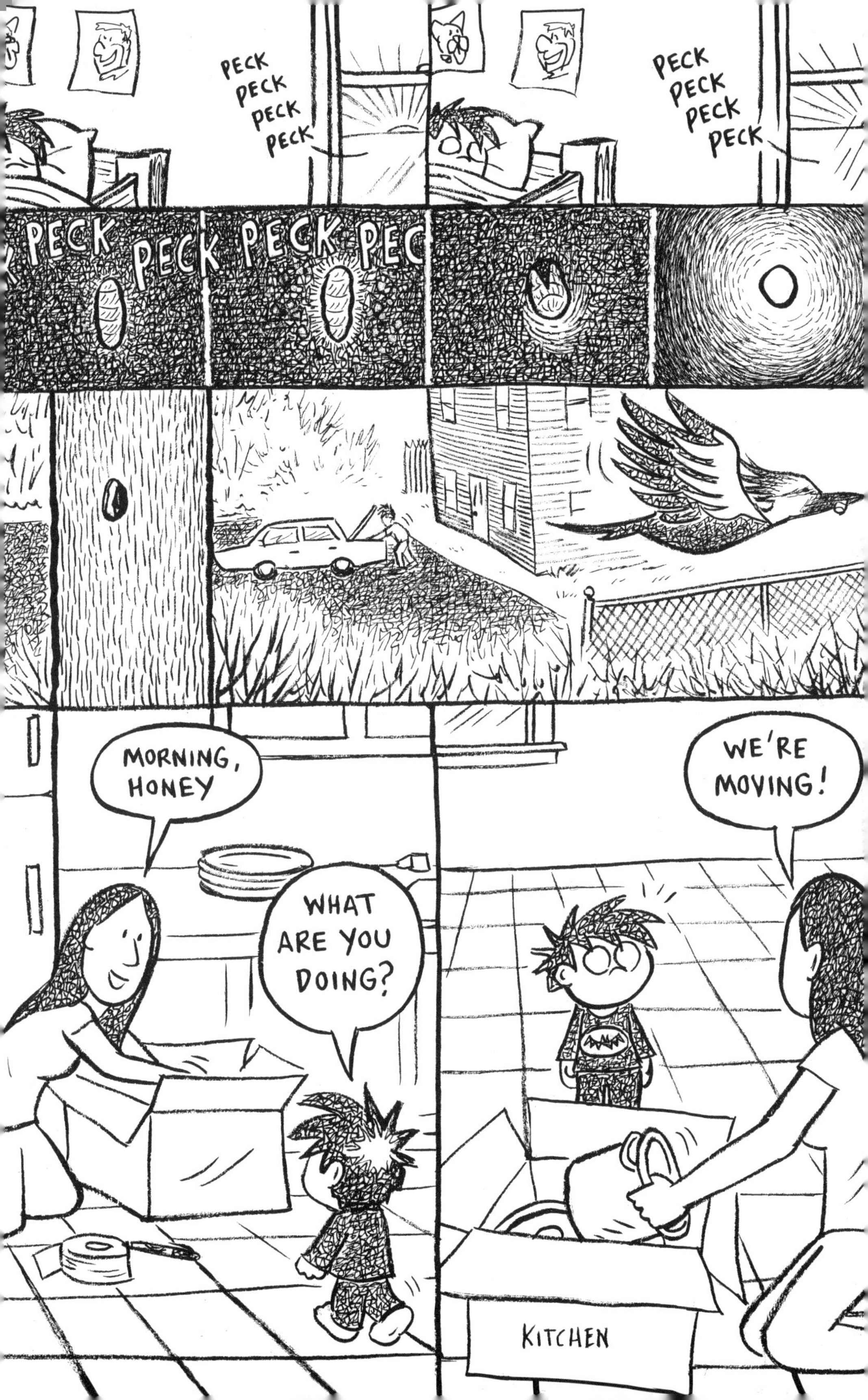
PECK
PECK
PECK
PECK
PECK
PECK
PECK
PECK
PECK
PECK PECK PECK PEC
MORNING, HONEY
WHAT ARE YOU DOING?
WE'RE MOVING!
KITCHEN

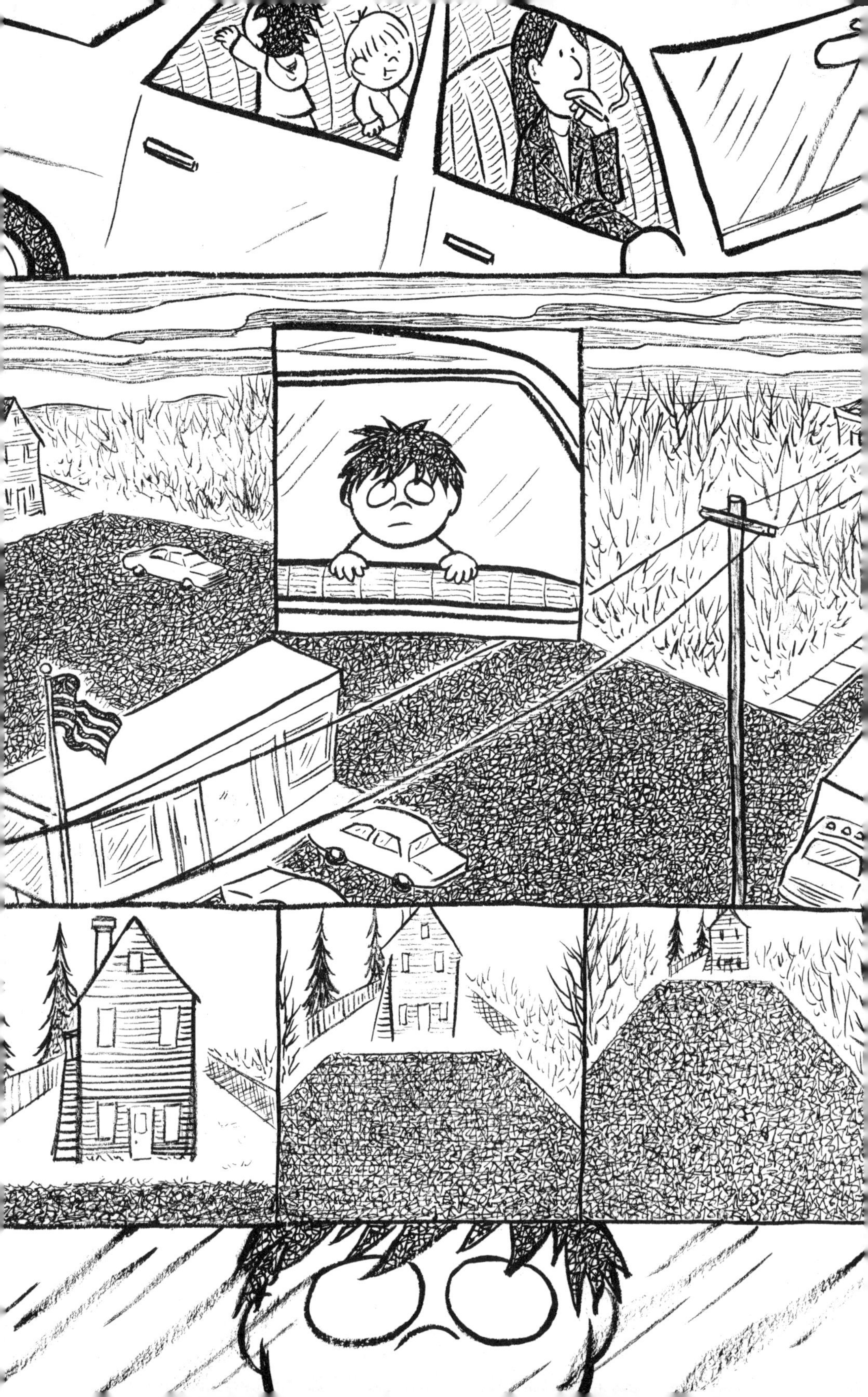

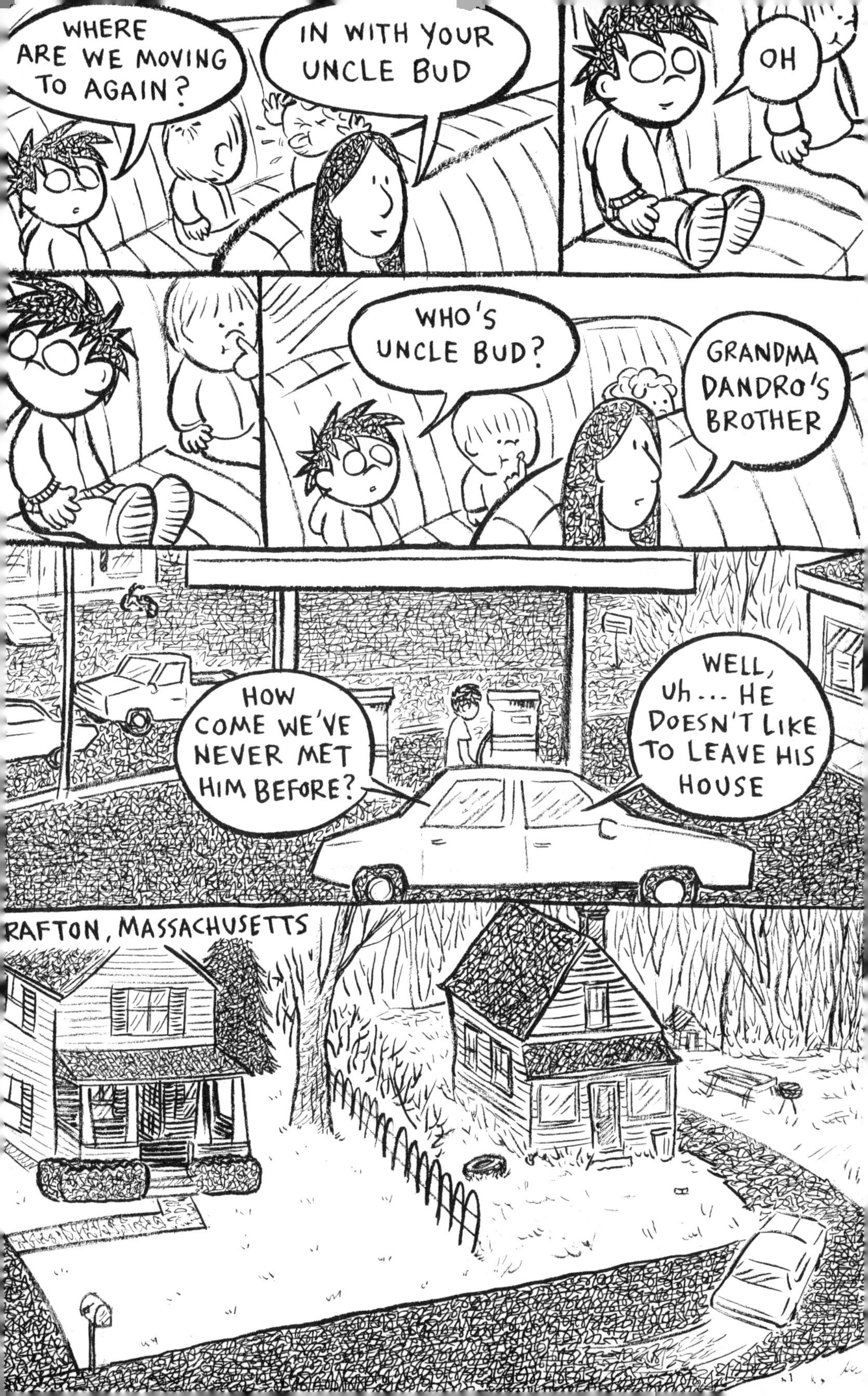
WHERE ARE WE MOVING TO AGAIN?
IN WITH YOUR UNCLE BUD
OH
WHO'S UNCLE BUD?
GRANDMA DANDRO'S BROTHER
HOW COME WE'VE NEVER MET HIM BEFORE?
WELL, Uh... HE DOESN'T LIKE TO LEAVE HIS HOUSE
RAFTON, MASSACHUSETTS

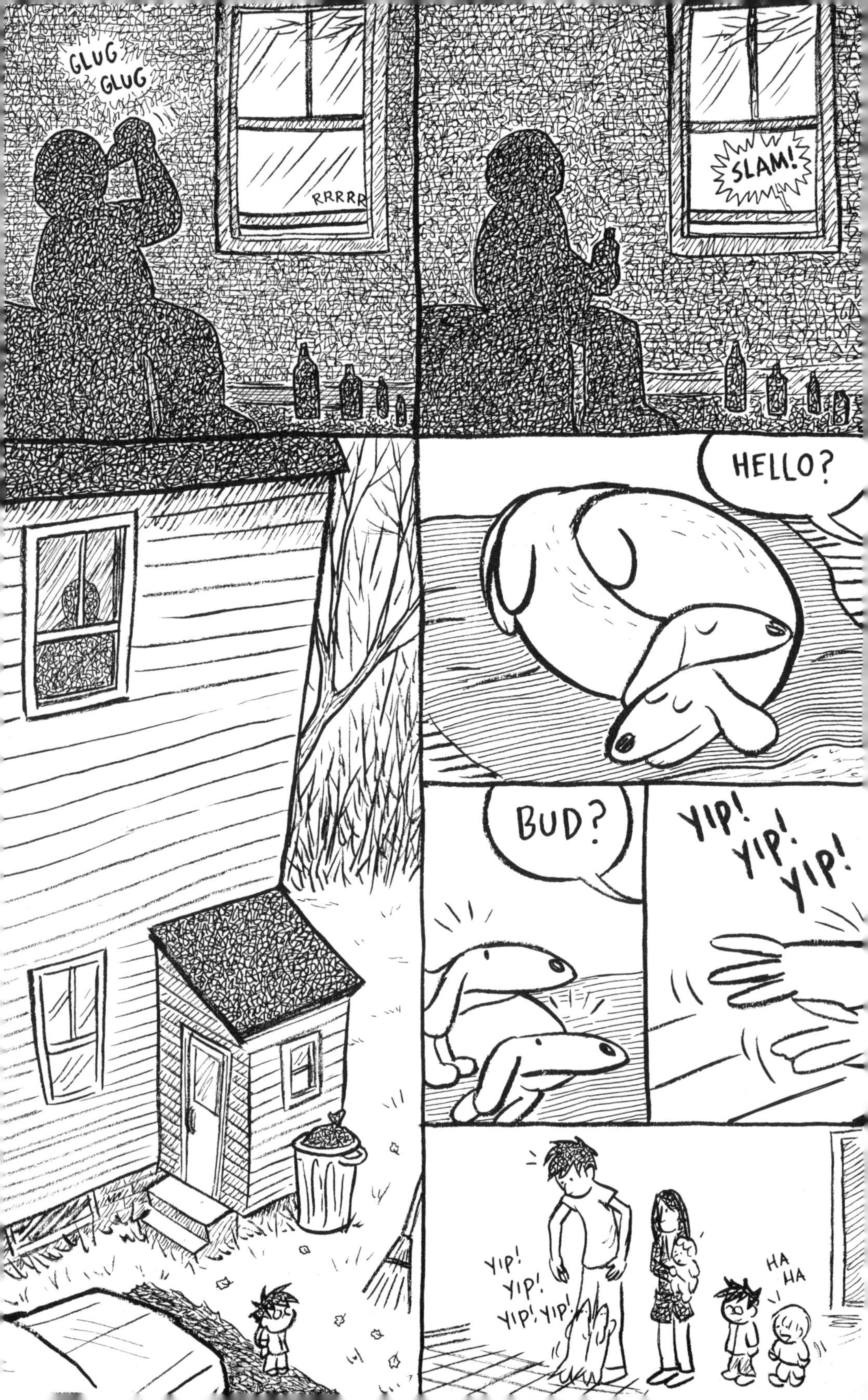
GLUG GLUG
RRRRR
SLAM!
HELLO?
BUD?
YIP! YIP! YIP!
YIP! YIP! YIP! YIP!
HA HA

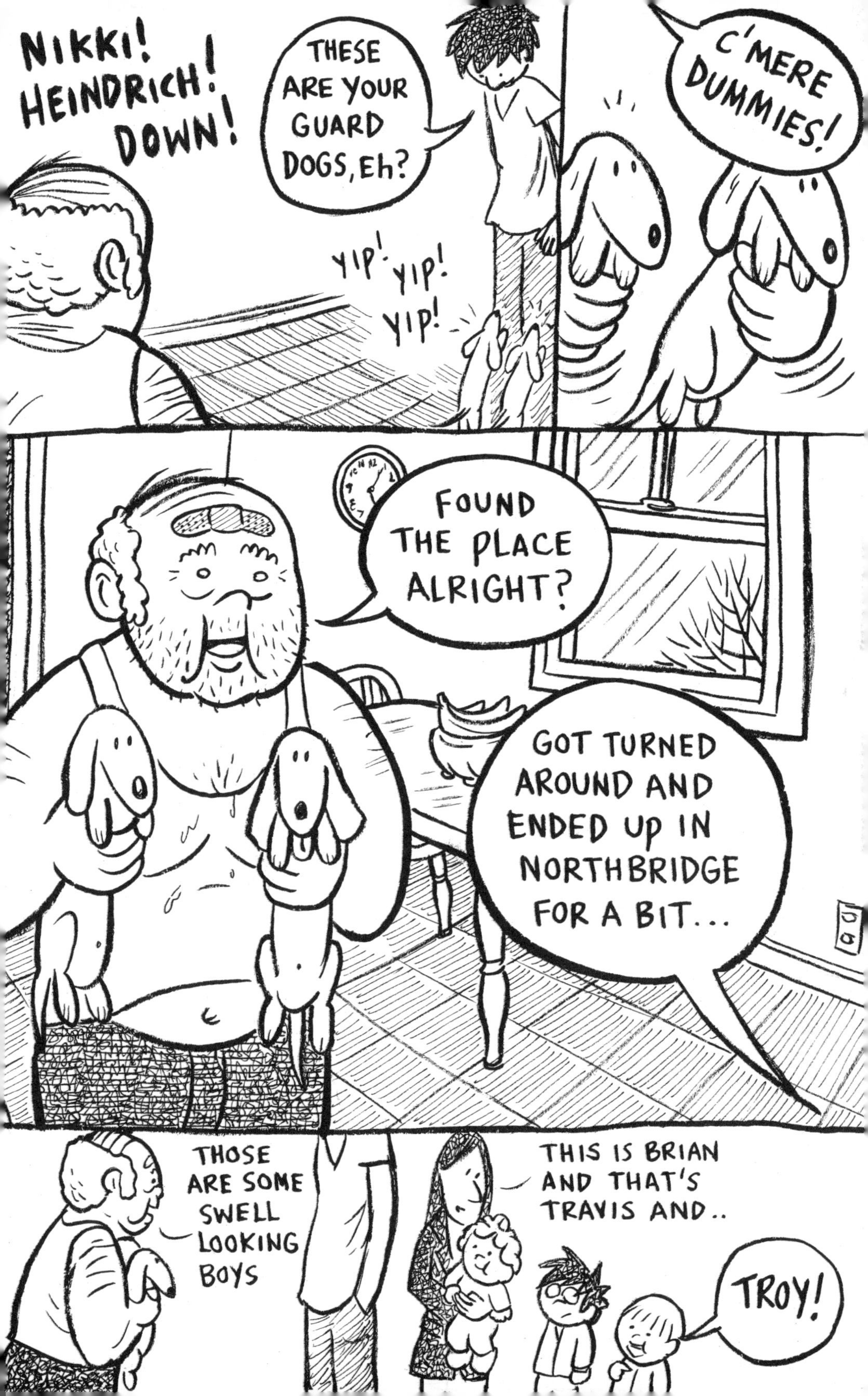
NIKKI! HEINDRICH! DOWN!
THESE ARE YOUR GUARD DOGS, Eh?
YIP! YIP! YIP!
C'MERE DUMMIES!
FOUND THE PLACE ALRIGHT?
GOT TURNED AROUND AND ENDED UP IN NORTHBRIDGE FOR A BIT...
THOSE ARE SOME SWELL LOOKING BOYS
THIS IS BRIAN AND THAT'S TRAVIS AND..
TROY!

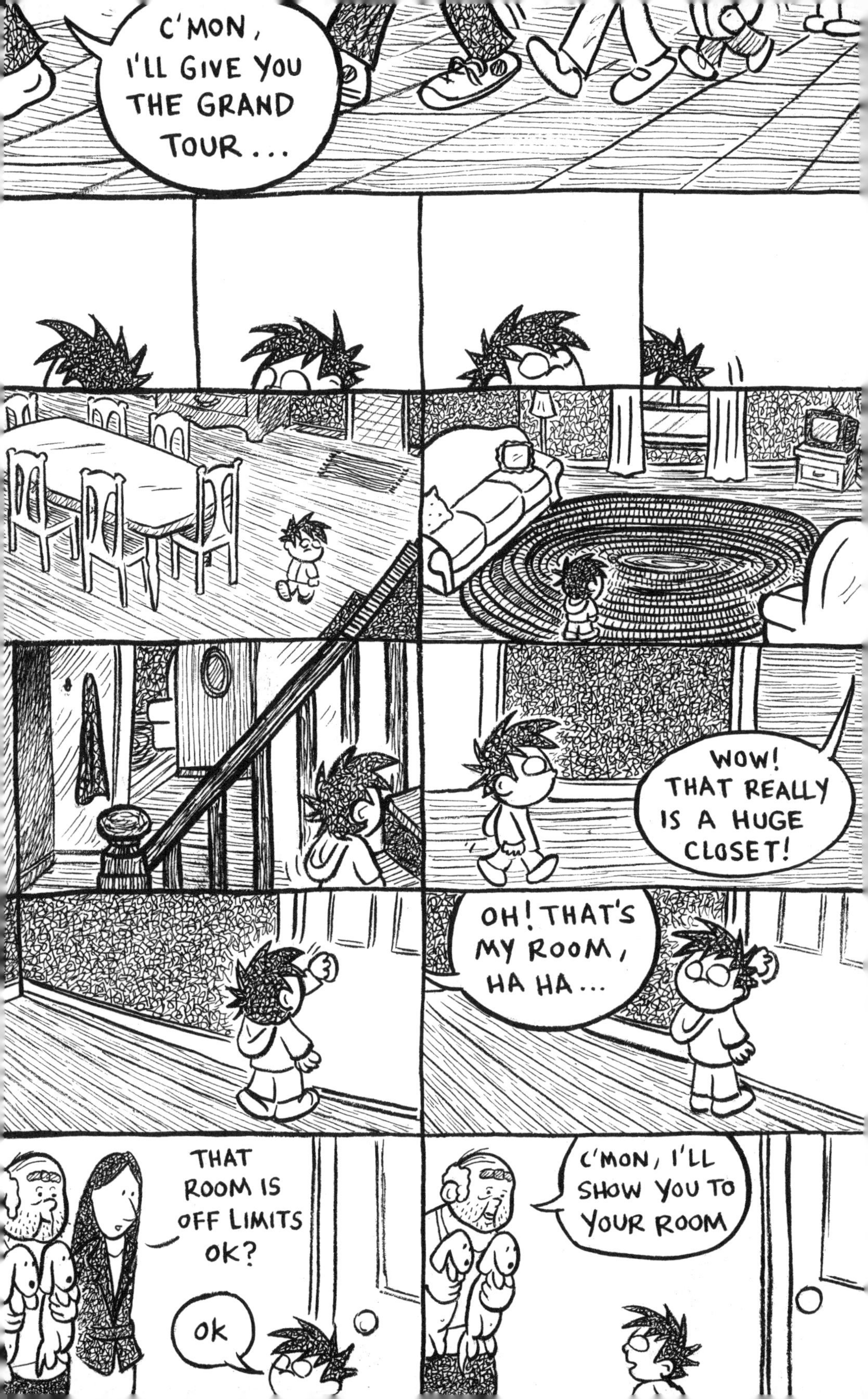
C'MON, I'LL GIVE YOU THE GRAND TOUR...
WOW! THAT REALLY IS A HUGE CLOSET!
OH! THAT'S MY ROOM, HA HA...
THAT ROOM IS OFF LIMITS OK?
OK
C'MON, I'LL SHOW YOU TO YOUR ROOM

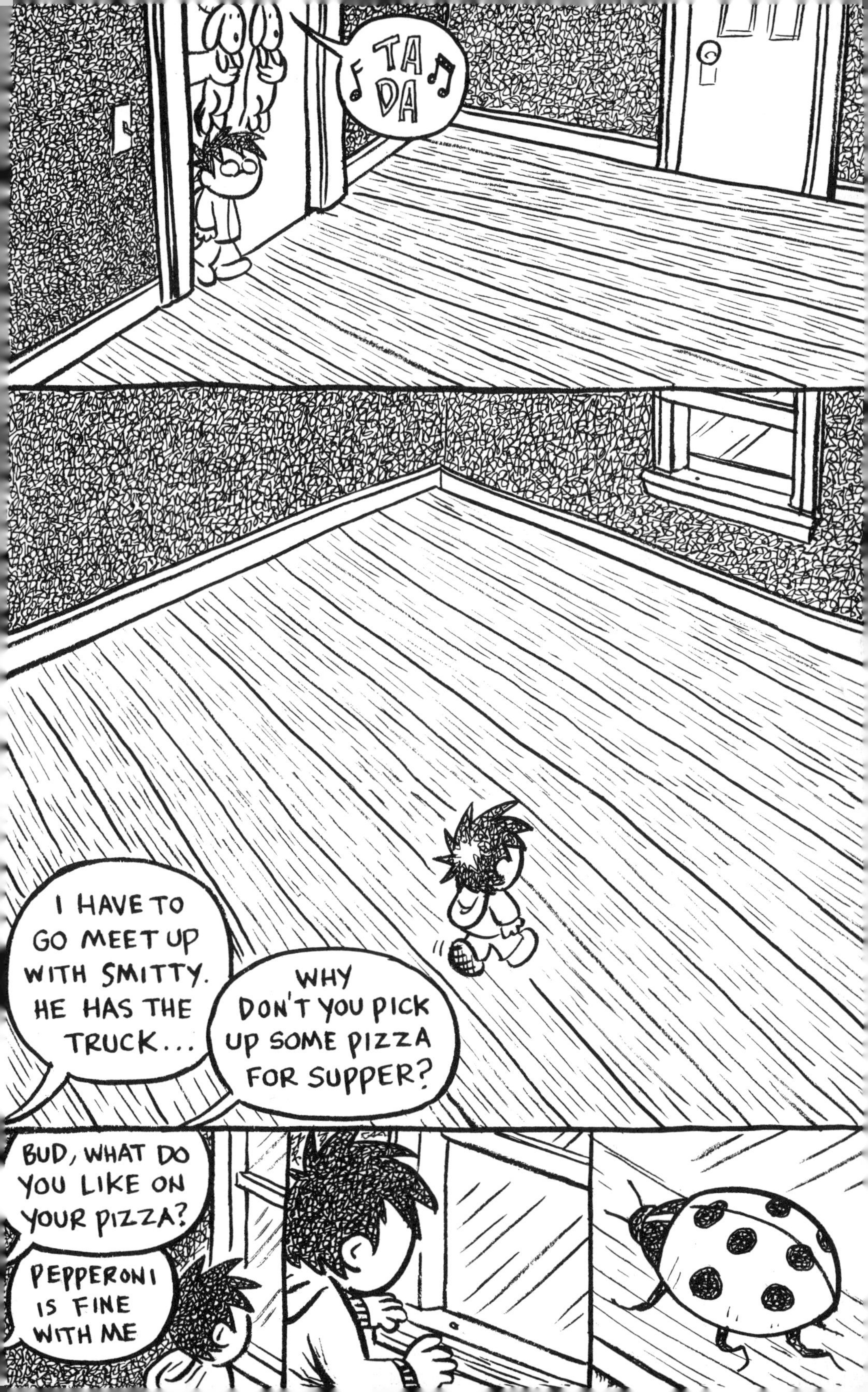
TA DA
I HAVE TO GO MEET UP WITH SMITTY. HE HAS THE TRUCK...
WHY DON'T YOU PICK UP SOME PIZZA FOR SUPPER?
BUD, WHAT DO YOU LIKE ON YOUR PIZZA?
PEPPERONI IS FINE WITH ME

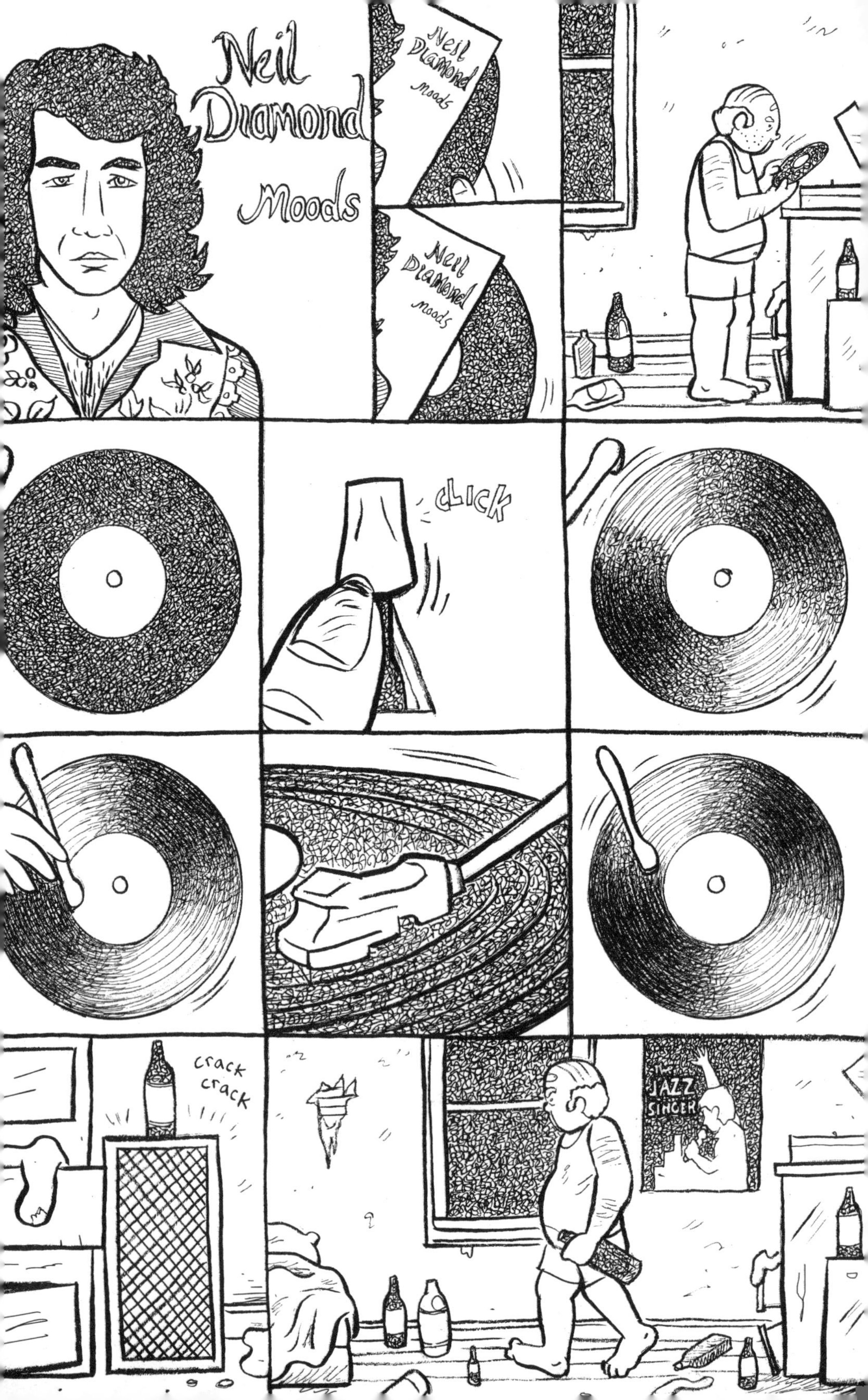
Neil Diamond
Moods
Neil Diamond
Moods
Neil Diamond
Moods
CLICK
crack
crack
The JAZZ SINGER

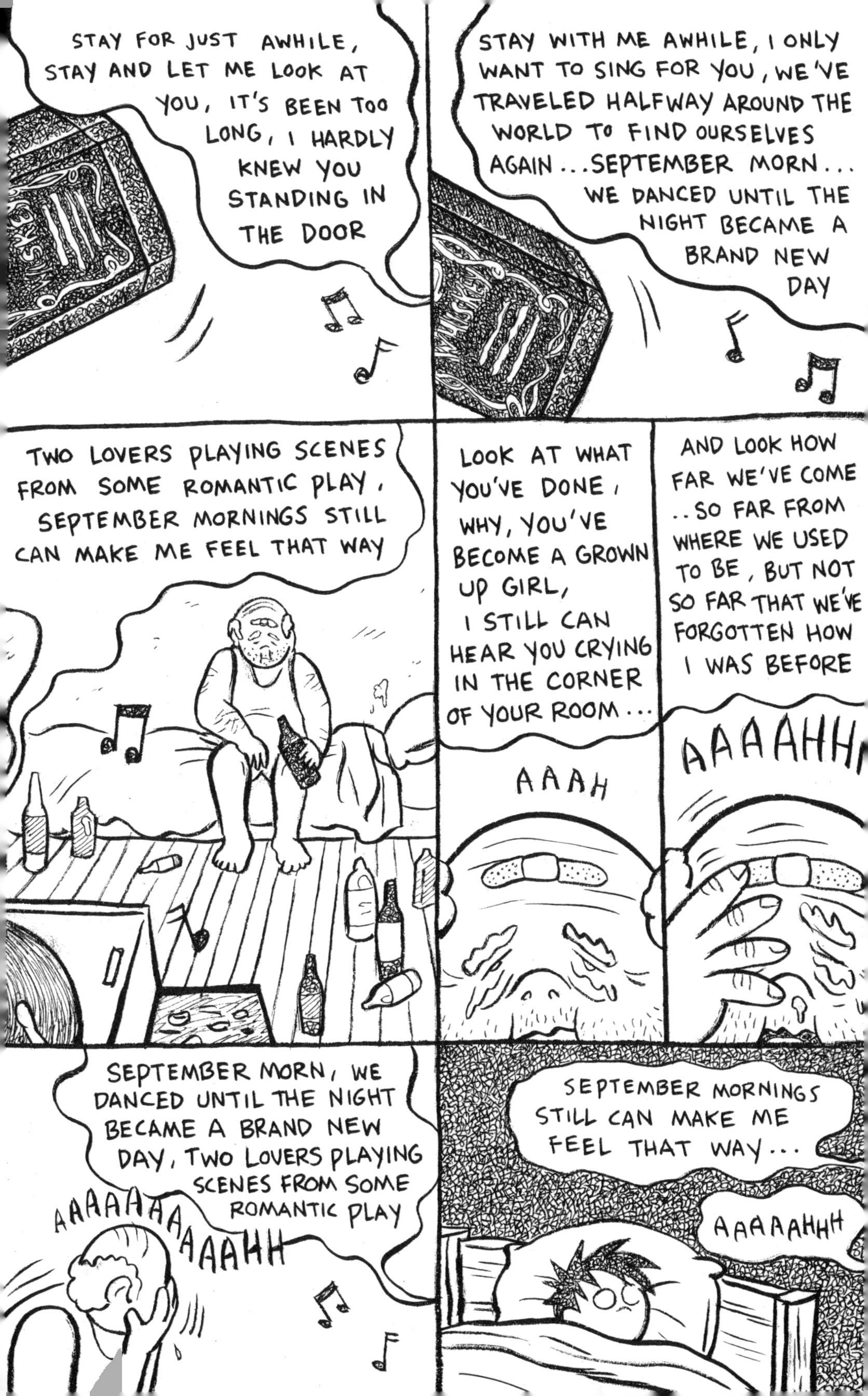

STAY FOR JUST AWHILE, STAY AND LET ME LOOK AT YOU, IT'S BEEN TOO LONG, I HARDLY KNEW YOU STANDING IN THE DOOR
STAY WITH ME AWHILE, I ONLY WANT TO SING FOR YOU, WE'VE TRAVELED HALFWAY AROUND THE WORLD TO FIND OURSELVES AGAIN ... SEPTEMBER MORN ... WE DANCED UNTIL THE NIGHT BECAME A BRAND NEW DAY
TWO LOVERS PLAYING SCENES FROM SOME ROMANTIC PLAY, SEPTEMBER MORNINGS STILL CAN MAKE ME FEEL THAT WAY
LOOK AT WHAT YOU'VE DONE, WHY, YOU'VE BECOME A GROWN UP GIRL, I STILL CAN HEAR YOU CRYING IN THE CORNER OF YOUR ROOM ...
AAAH
AND LOOK HOW FAR WE'VE COME .. SO FAR FROM WHERE WE USED TO BE, BUT NOT SO FAR THAT WE'VE FORGOTTEN HOW I WAS BEFORE
AAAAHH
SEPTEMBER MORN, WE DANCED UNTIL THE NIGHT BECAME A BRAND NEW DAY, TWO LOVERS PLAYING SCENES FROM SOME ROMANTIC PLAY
AAAAAAAAAAAHH
SEPTEMBER MORNINGS STILL CAN MAKE ME FEEL THAT WAY ...
AAAAAHHH

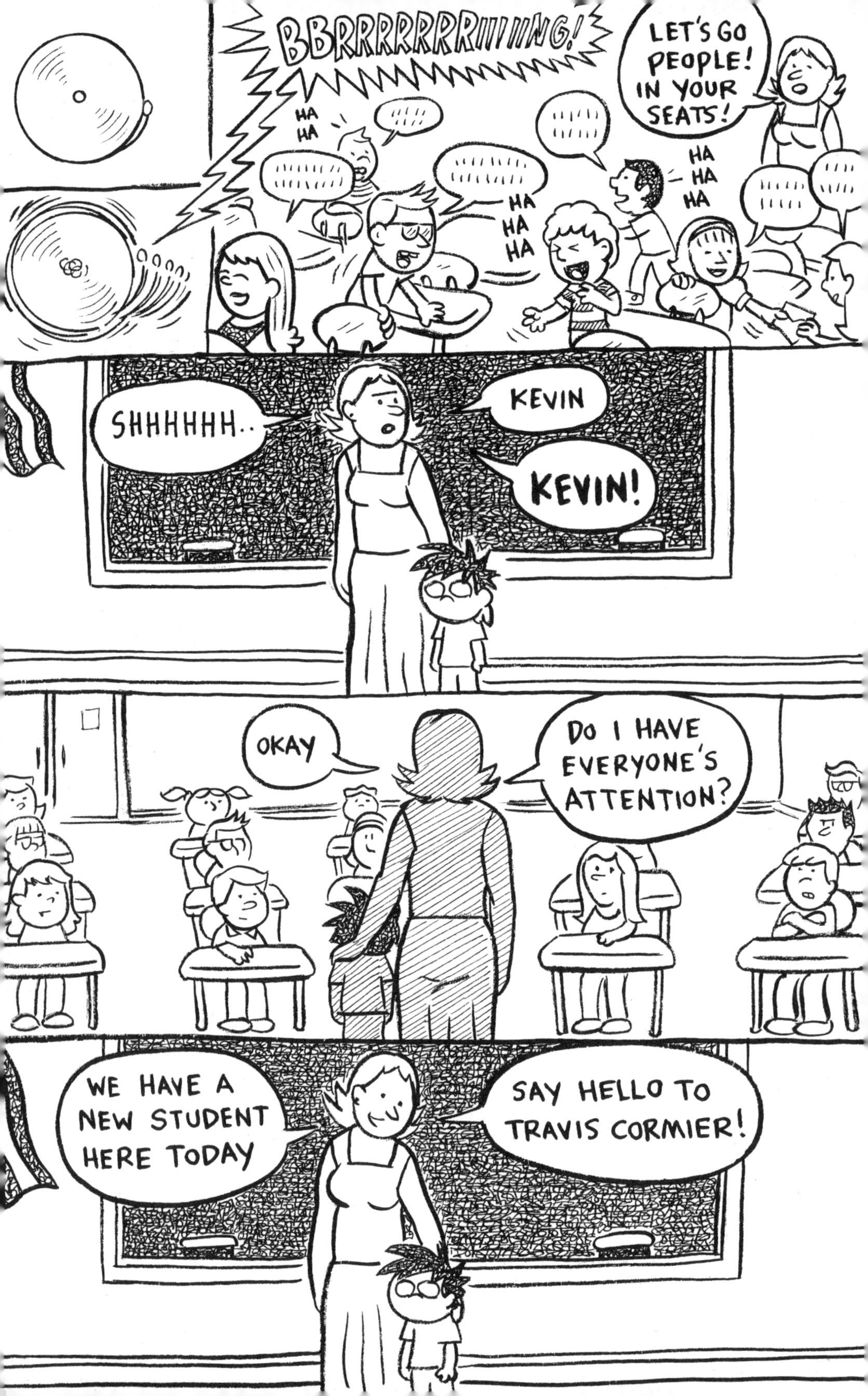
BBRRRRRRRIIIIING!
LET'S GO PEOPLE! IN YOUR SEATS!
HA HA
HA HA HA
HA HA HA
SHHHHHH..
KEVIN
KEVIN!
OKAY
Do I HAVE EVERYONE'S ATTENTION?
WE HAVE A NEW STUDENT HERE TODAY
SAY HELLO TO TRAVIS CORMIER!

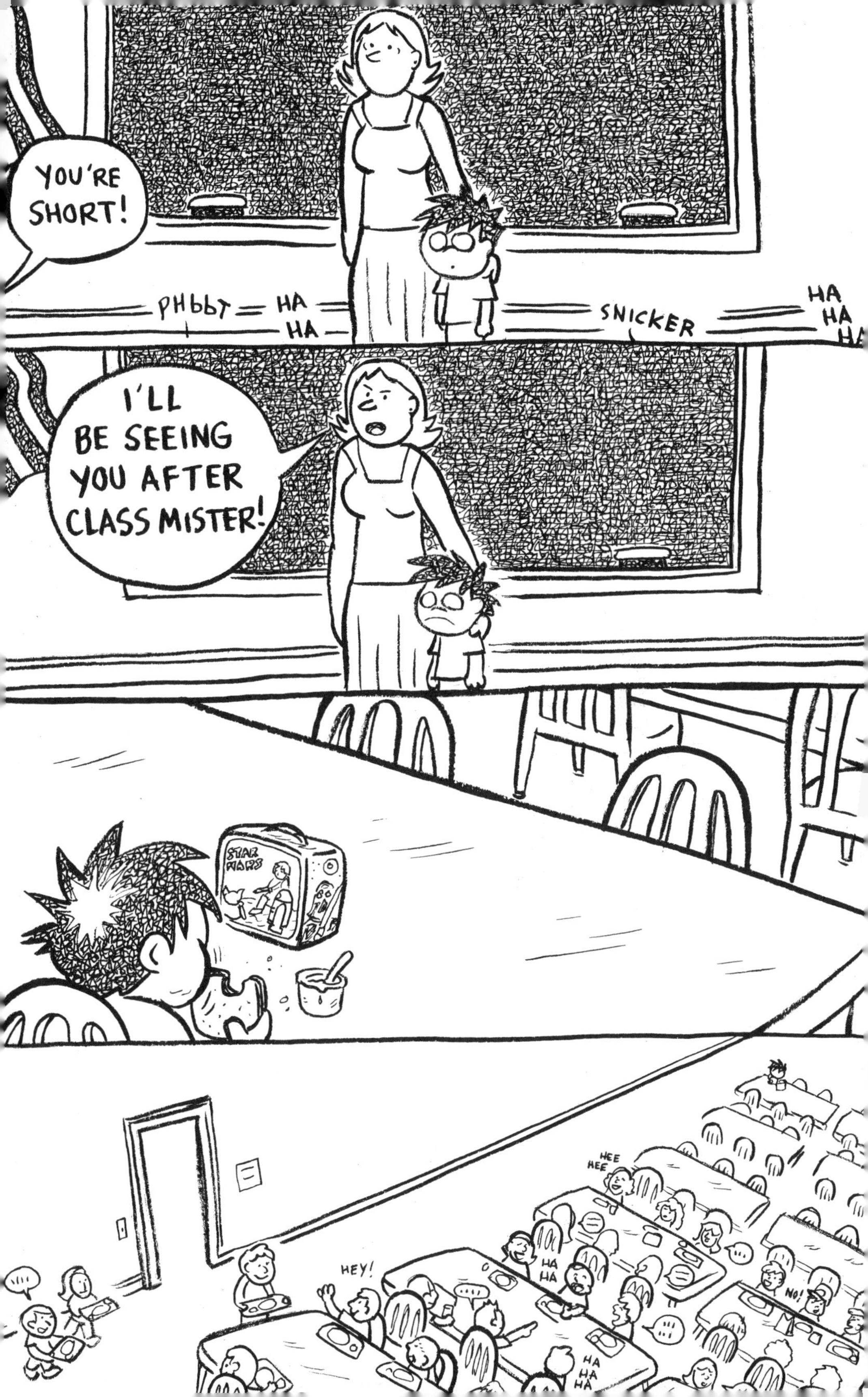

YOU'RE SHORT!
PHBBT
HA HA
SNICKER
HA HA HA
I'LL BE SEEING YOU AFTER CLASS MISTER!
STAR WARS
HEE HEE
HEY!
HA HA
NO!
HA HA HA

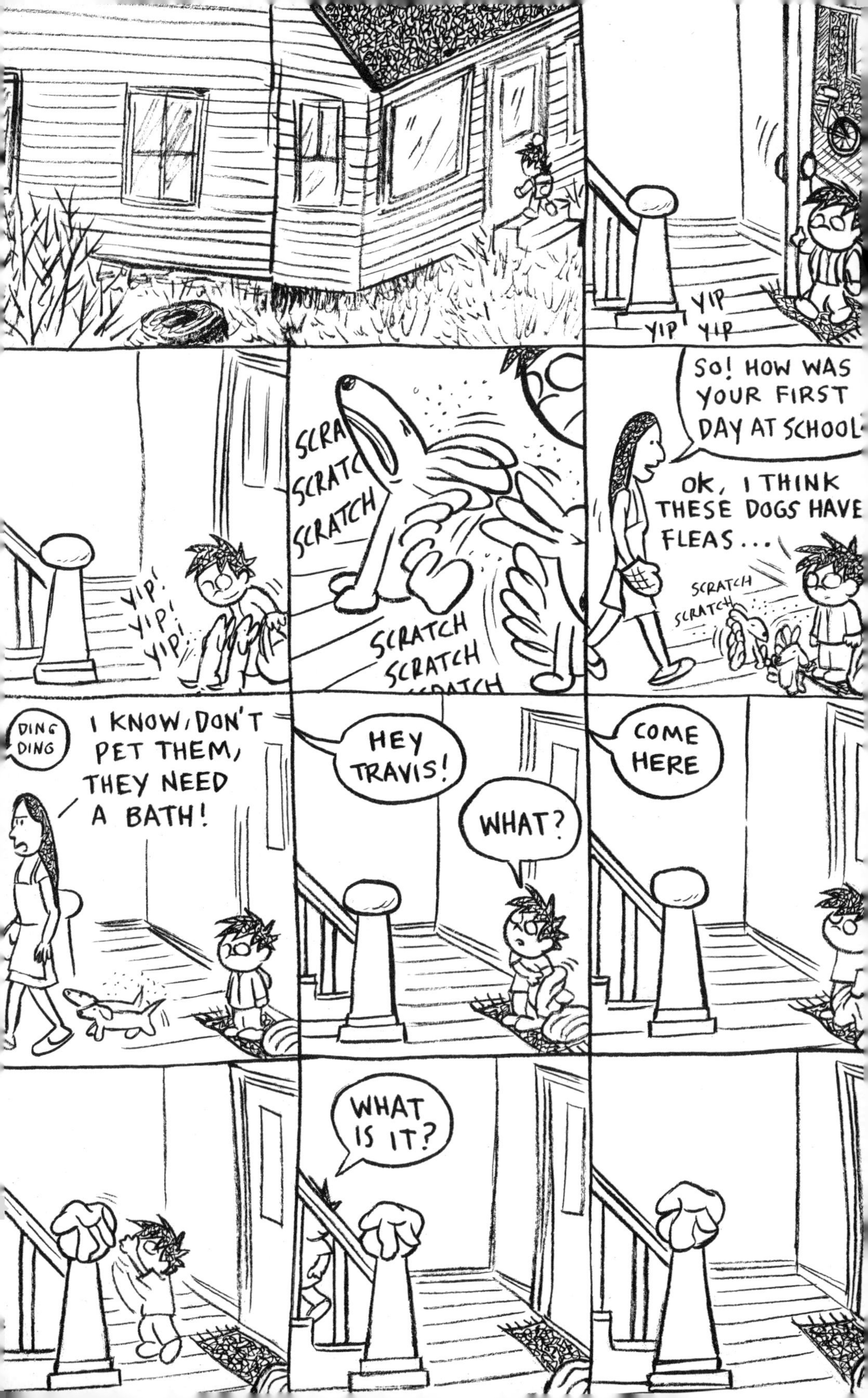
YIP
YIP
YIP
YIP! YIP! YIP!
SCRA
SCRATC
SCRATCH
SCRATCH
SCRATCH
SO! HOW WAS YOUR FIRST DAY AT SCHOOL
OK, I THINK THESE DOGS HAVE FLEAS...
SCRATCH
SCRATCH
DING DING
I KNOW, DON'T PET THEM, THEY NEED A BATH!
HEY TRAVIS!
WHAT?
COME HERE
WHAT IS IT?

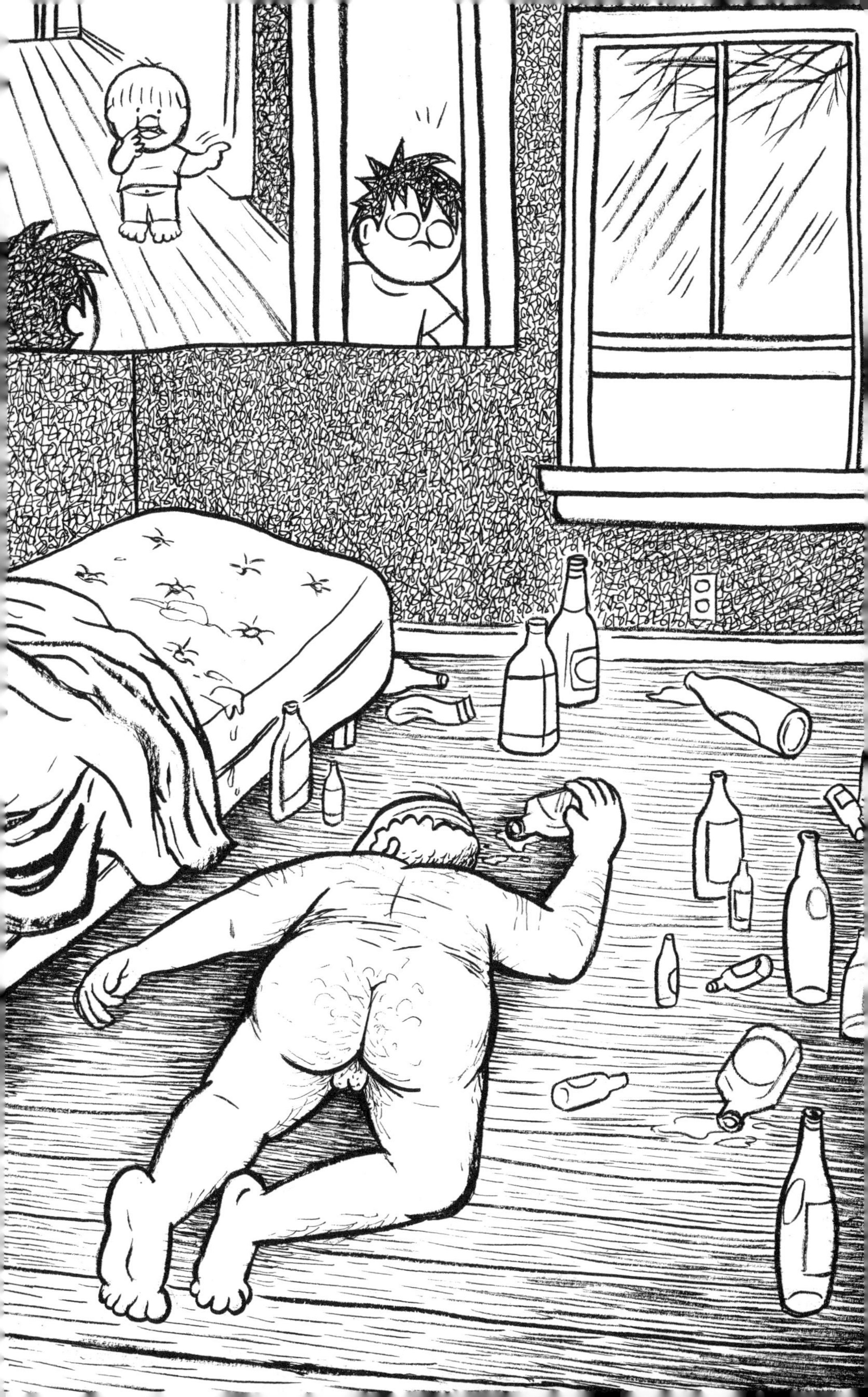

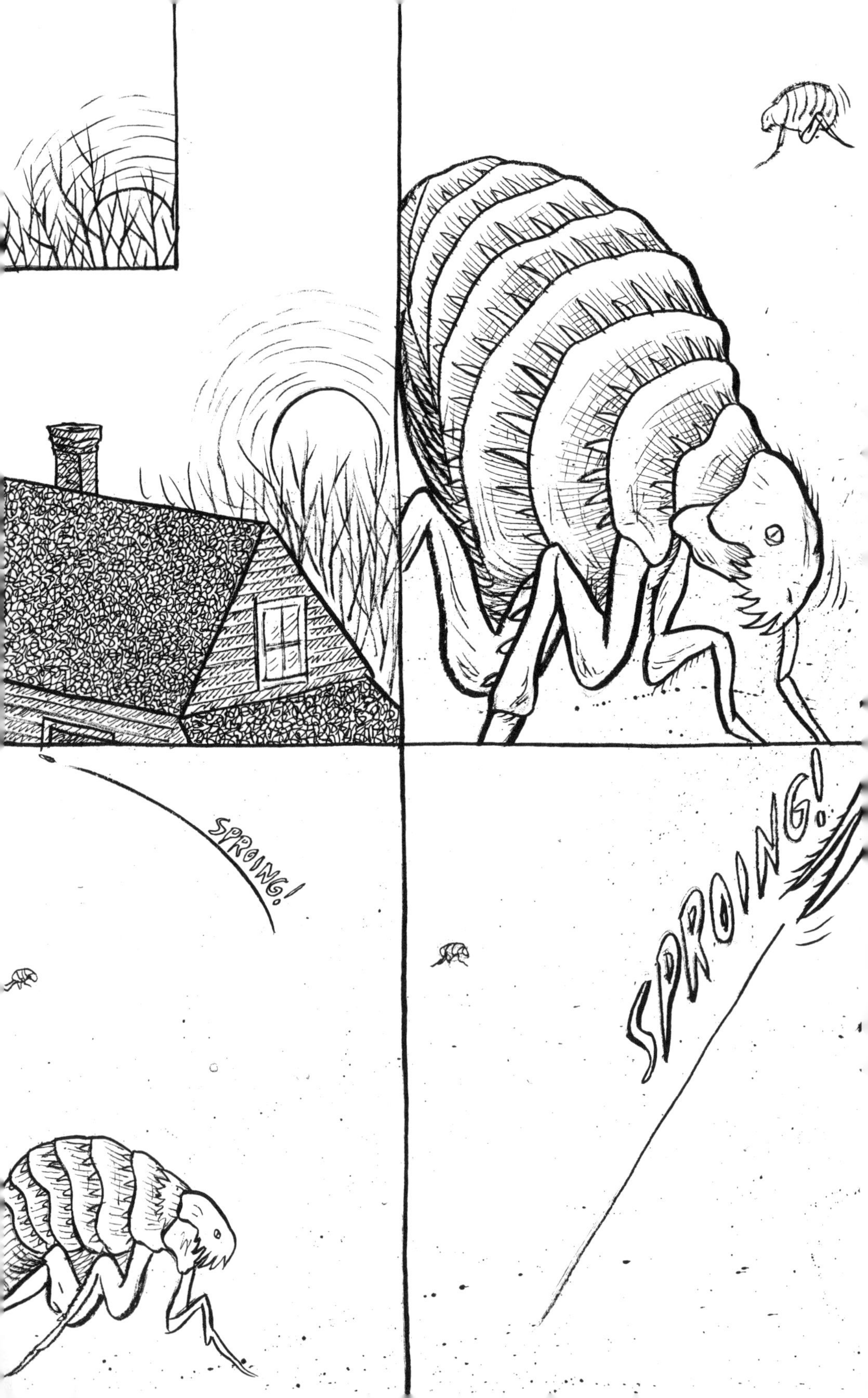
SPROING!
SPROING!

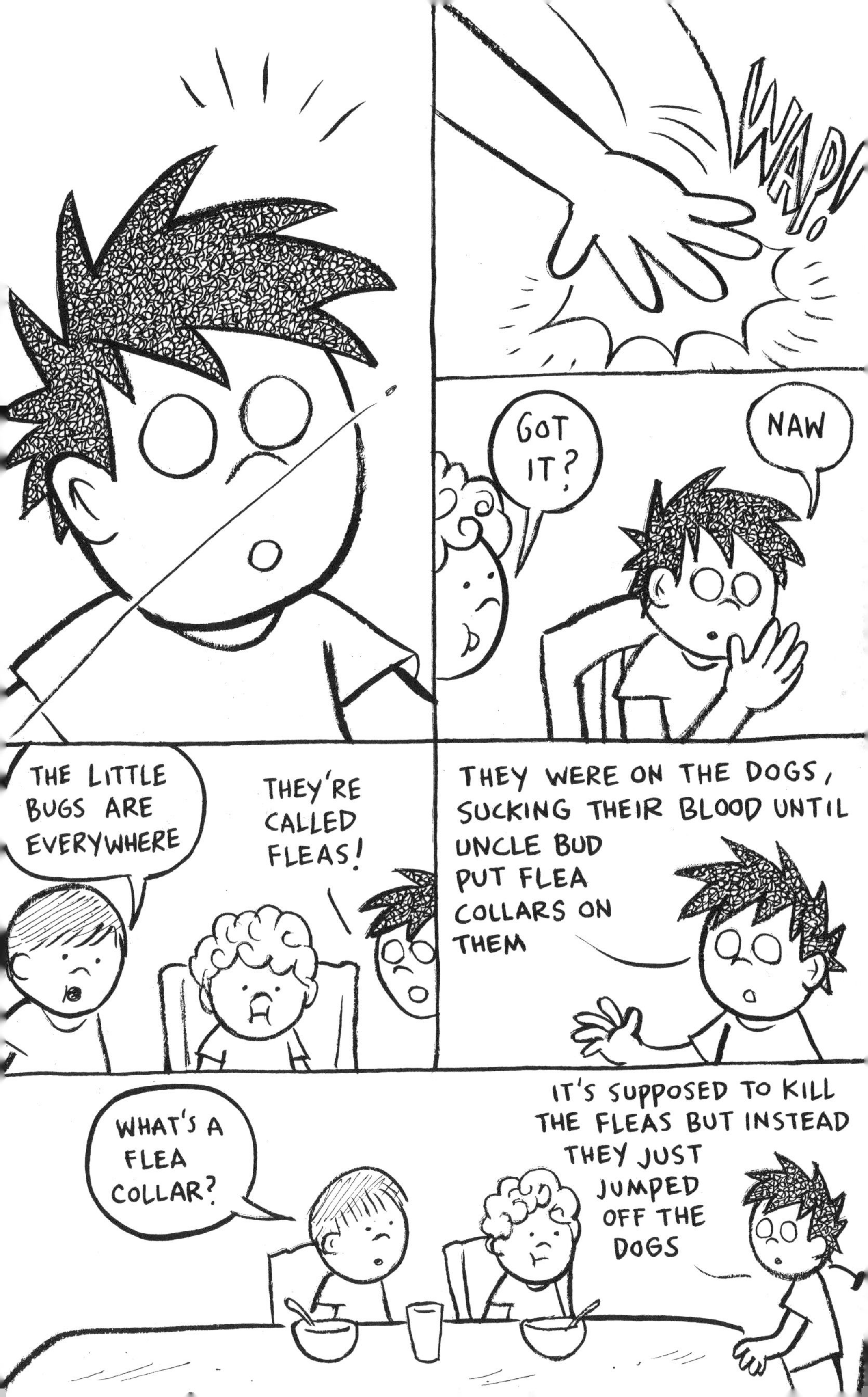
WAP!
GOT IT?
NAW
THE LITTLE BUGS ARE EVERYWHERE
THEY'RE CALLED FLEAS!
THEY WERE ON THE DOGS, SUCKING THEIR BLOOD UNTIL UNCLE BUD PUT FLEA COLLARS ON THEM
WHAT'S A FLEA COLLAR?
IT'S SUPPOSED TO KILL THE FLEAS BUT INSTEAD THEY JUST JUMPED OFF THE DOGS

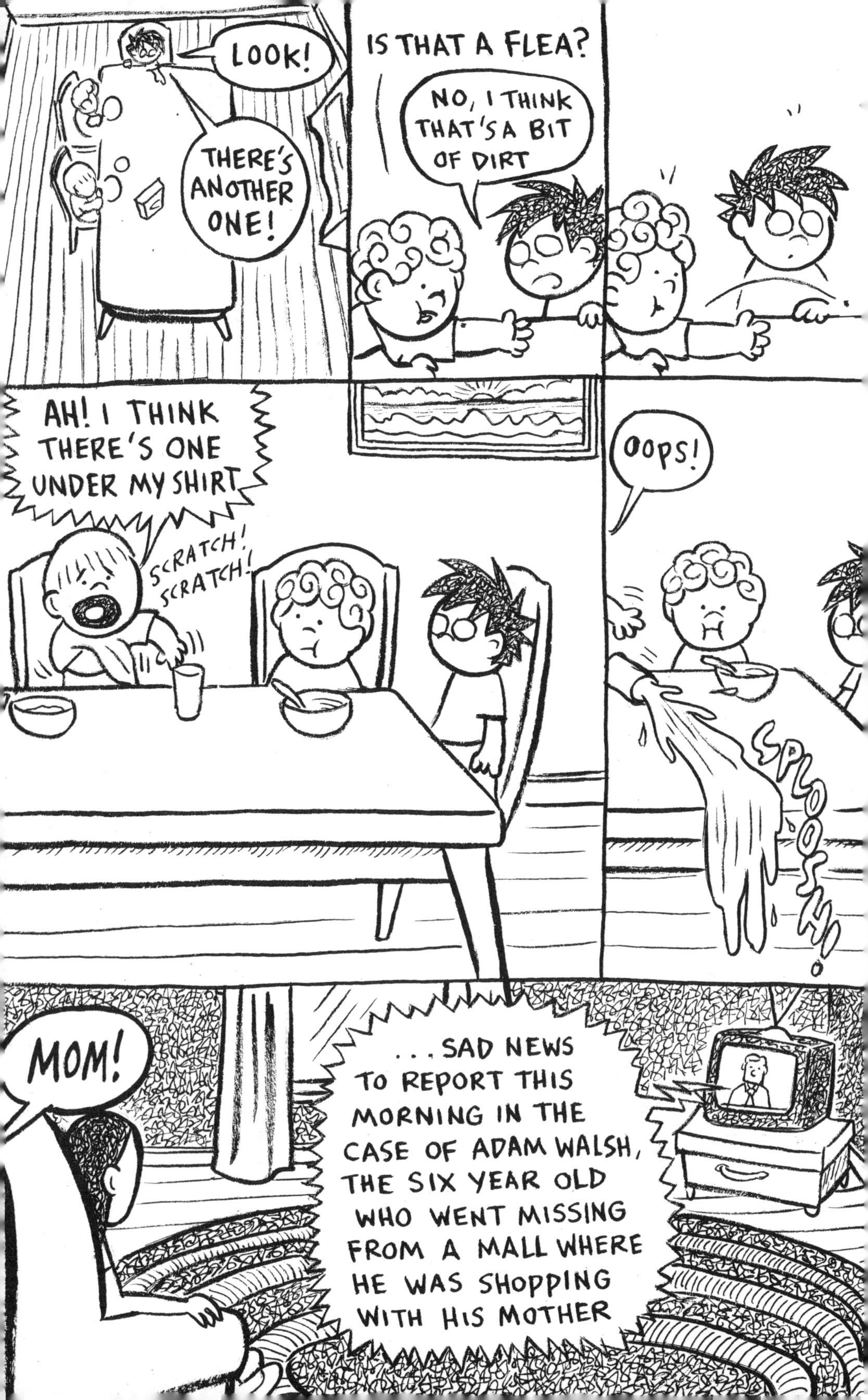
LOOK!
THERE'S ANOTHER ONE!
IS THAT A FLEA?
NO, I THINK THAT'S A BIT OF DIRT
AH! I THINK THERE'S ONE UNDER MY SHIRT
SCRATCH! SCRATCH!
OOPS!
SPLOOSH!
MOM!
. . . SAD NEWS TO REPORT THIS MORNING IN THE CASE OF ADAM WALSH, THE SIX YEAR OLD WHO WENT MISSING FROM A MALL WHERE HE WAS SHOPPING WITH HIS MOTHER

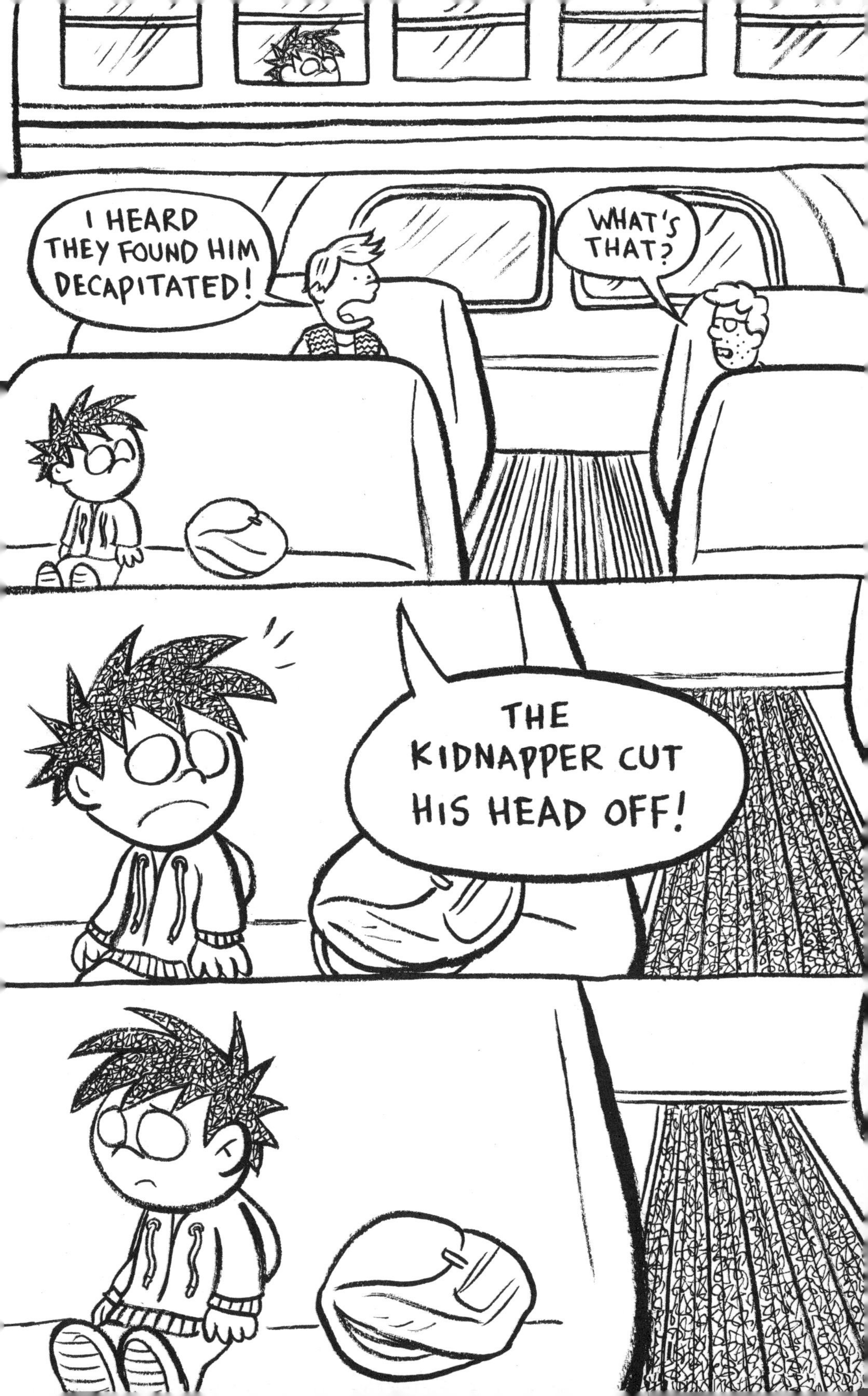
I HEARD THEY FOUND HIM DECAPITATED!
WHAT'S THAT?
THE KIDNAPPER CUT HIS HEAD OFF!

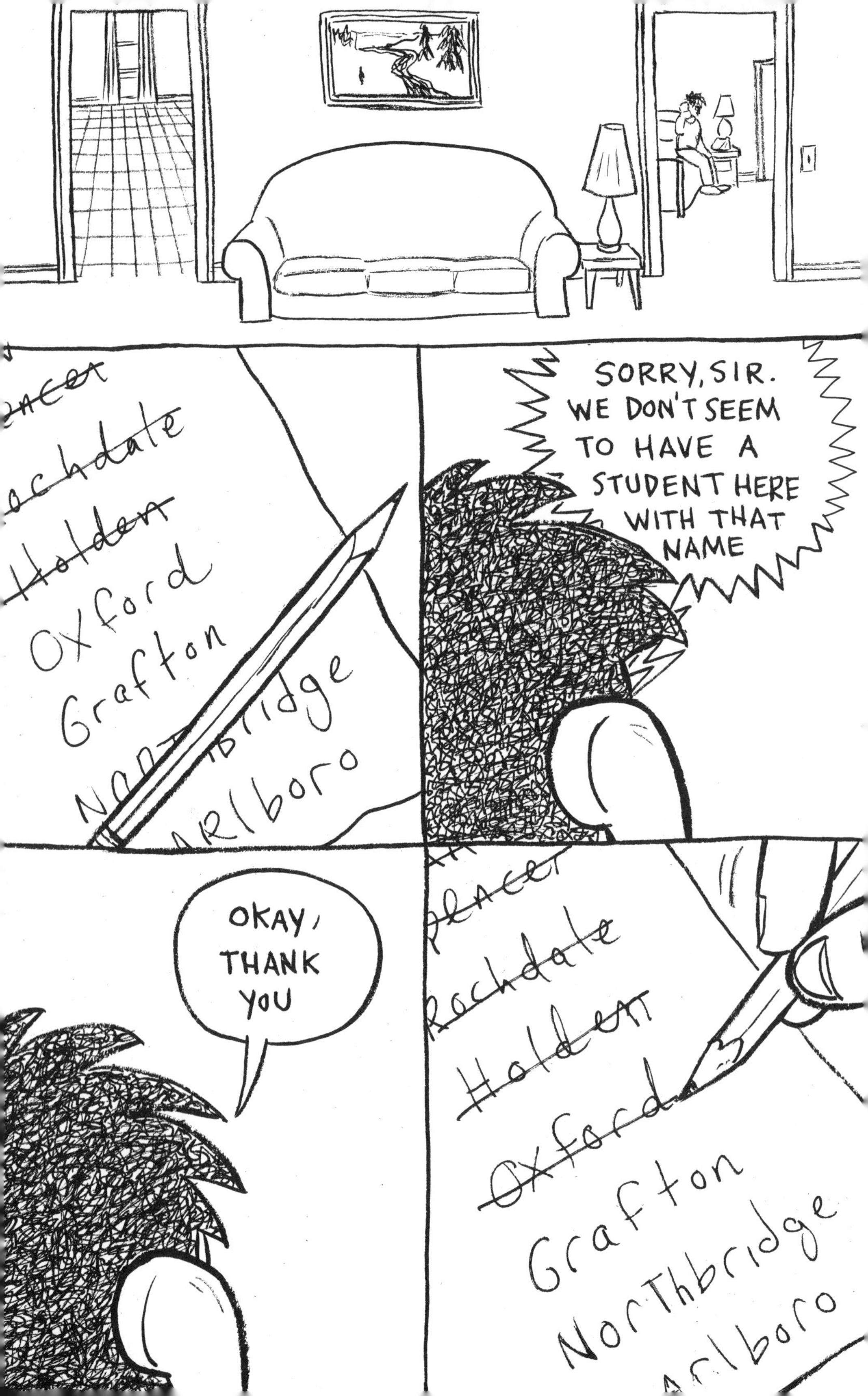
Holden
Oxford
Grafton
SORRY, SIR. WE DON'T SEEM TO HAVE A STUDENT HERE WITH THAT NAME
OKAY, THANK YOU
Rochdale
Holden
Oxford
Grafton
Northbridge

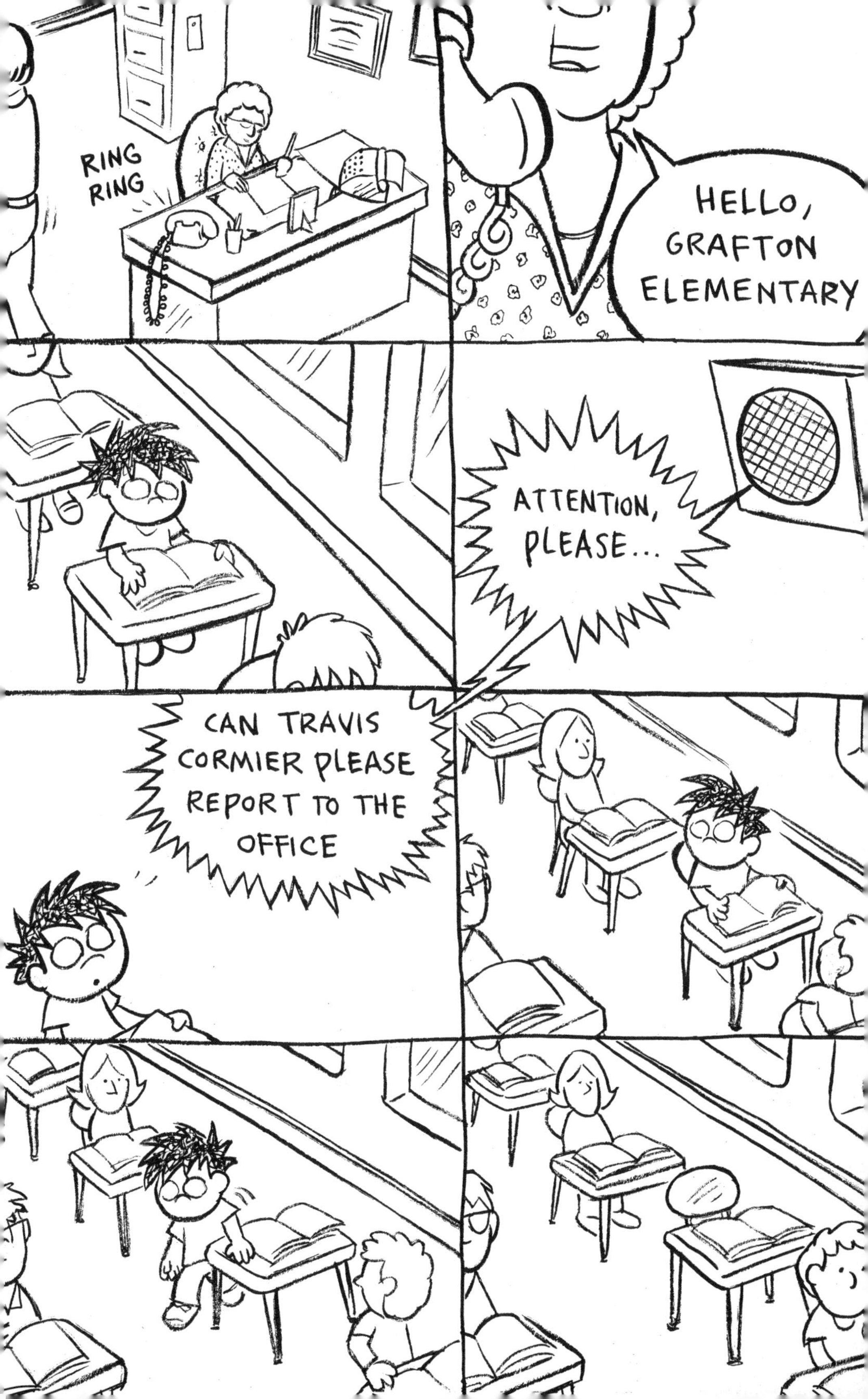
RING RING
HELLO, GRAFTON ELEMENTARY
ATTENTION, PLEASE...
CAN TRAVIS CORMIER PLEASE REPORT TO THE OFFICE

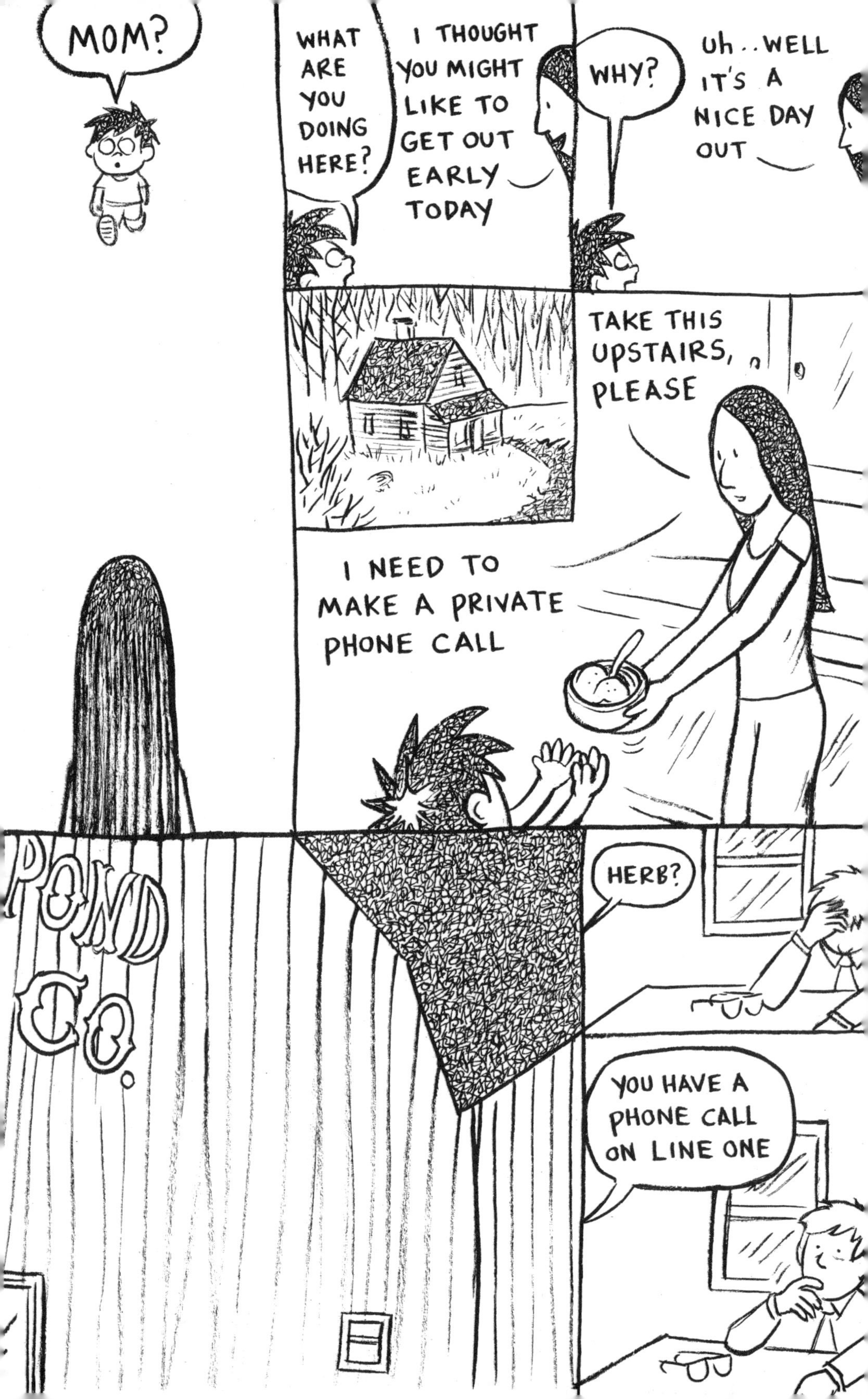
MOM?
WHAT ARE YOU DOING HERE?
I THOUGHT YOU MIGHT LIKE TO GET OUT EARLY TODAY
WHY?
Uh..WELL IT'S A NICE DAY OUT
TAKE THIS UPSTAIRS, PLEASE
I NEED TO MAKE A PRIVATE PHONE CALL
POND CO.
HERB?
YOU HAVE A PHONE CALL ON LINE ONE

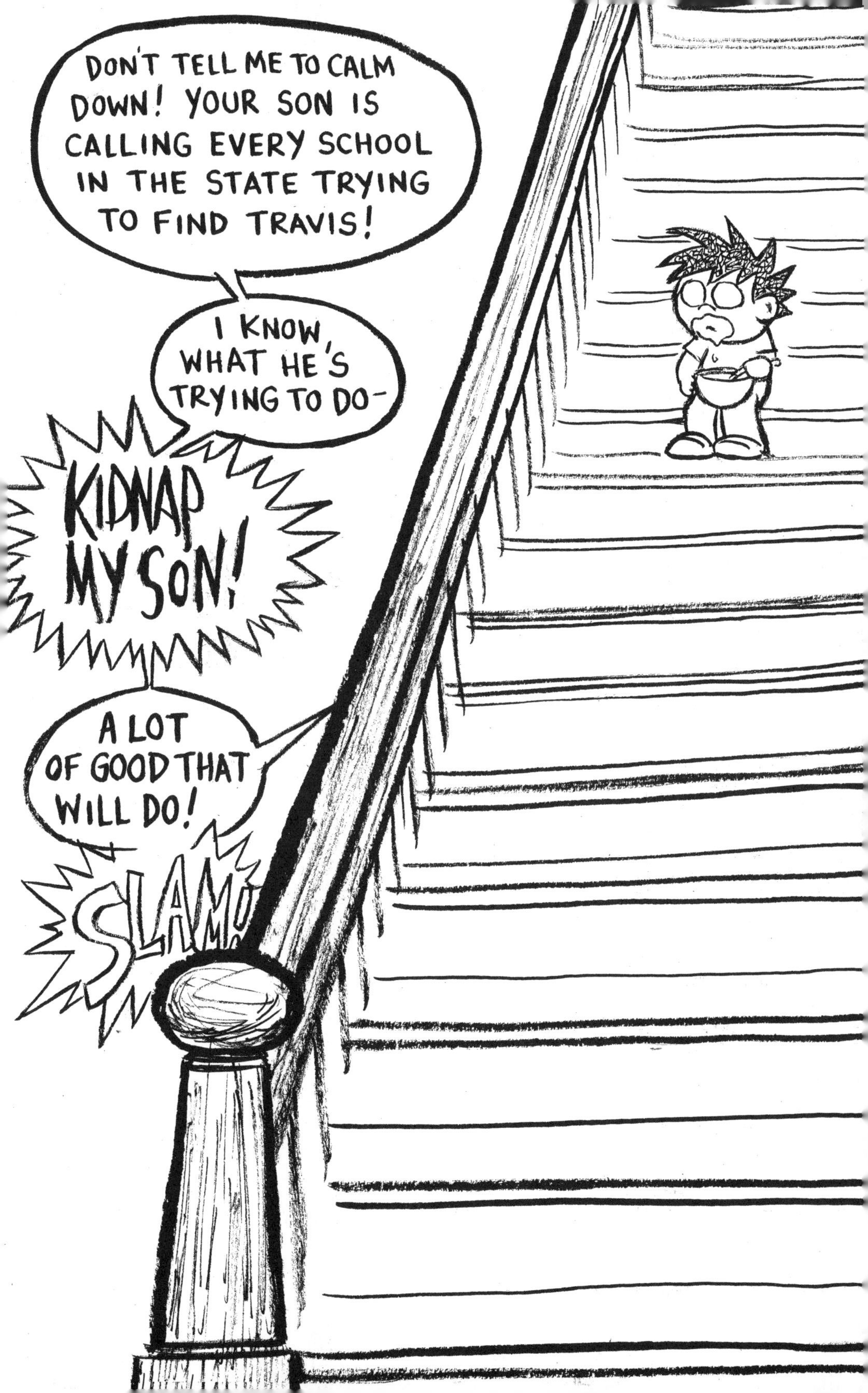
DON'T TELL ME TO CALM DOWN! YOUR SON IS CALLING EVERY SCHOOL IN THE STATE TRYING TO FIND TRAVIS!
I KNOW, WHAT HE'S TRYING TO DO-
KIDNAP MY SON!
A LOT OF GOOD THAT WILL DO!
SLAM!

VRRRRRRRRRR

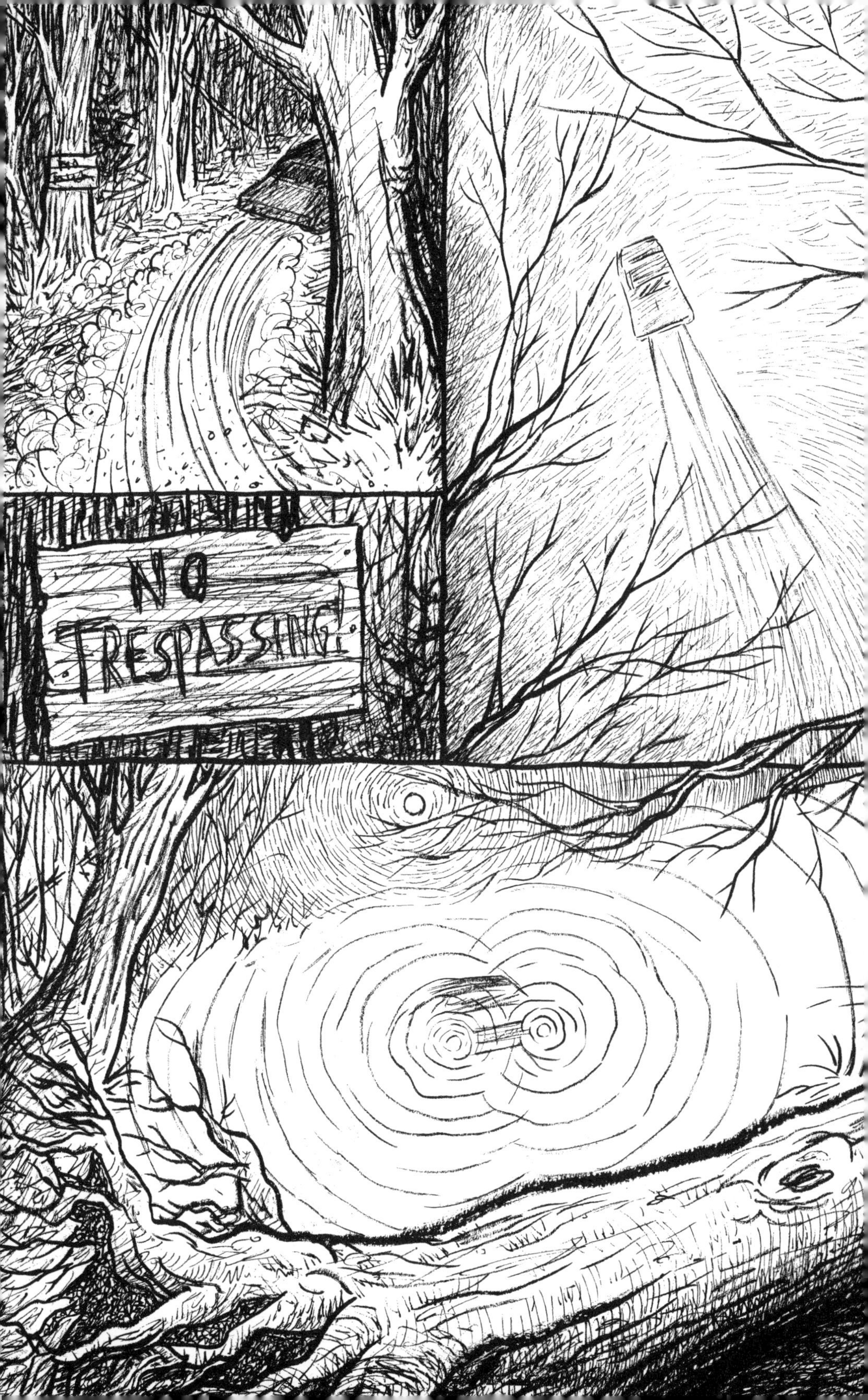
NO TRESPASSING!

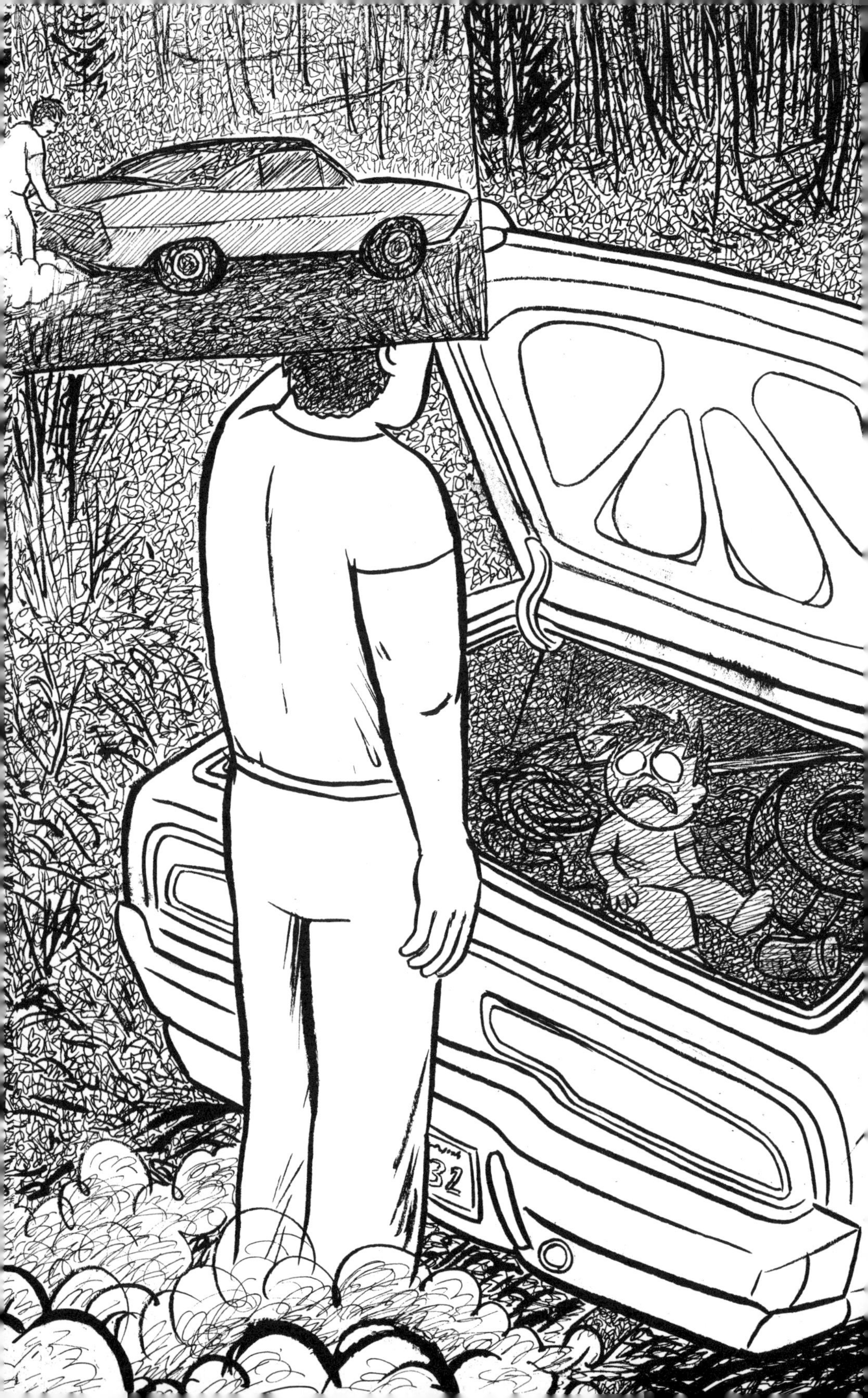
32

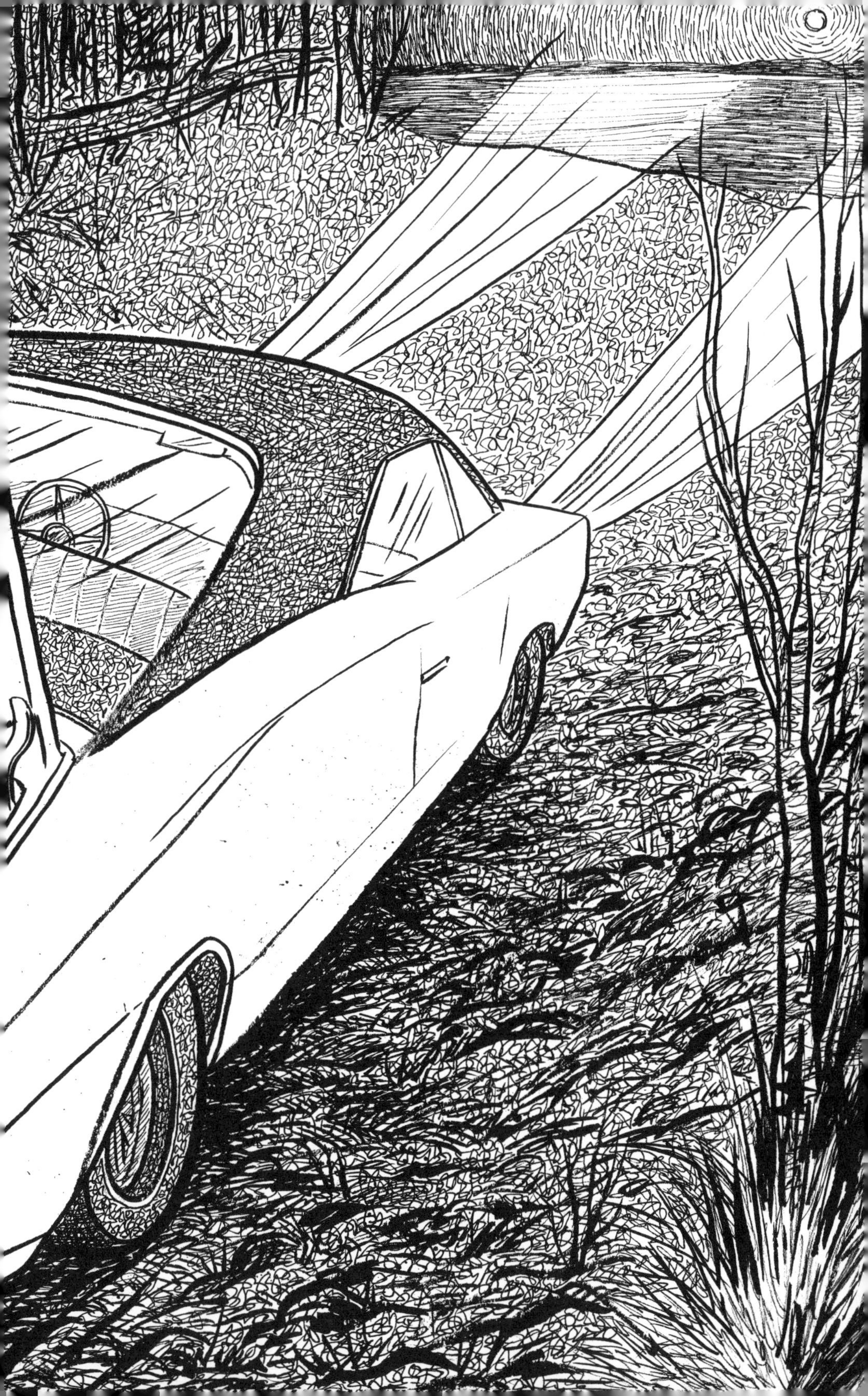

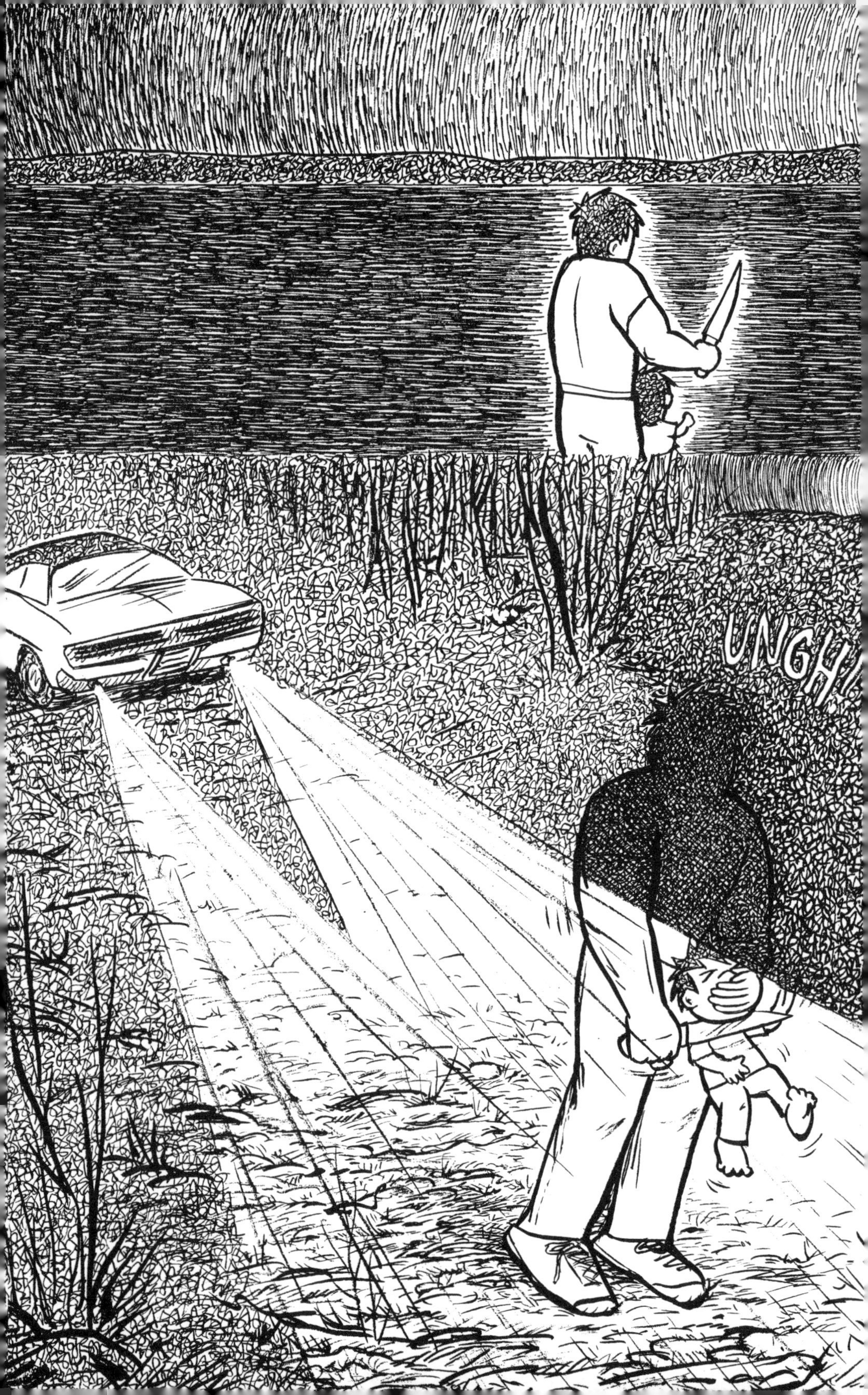
UNGH!

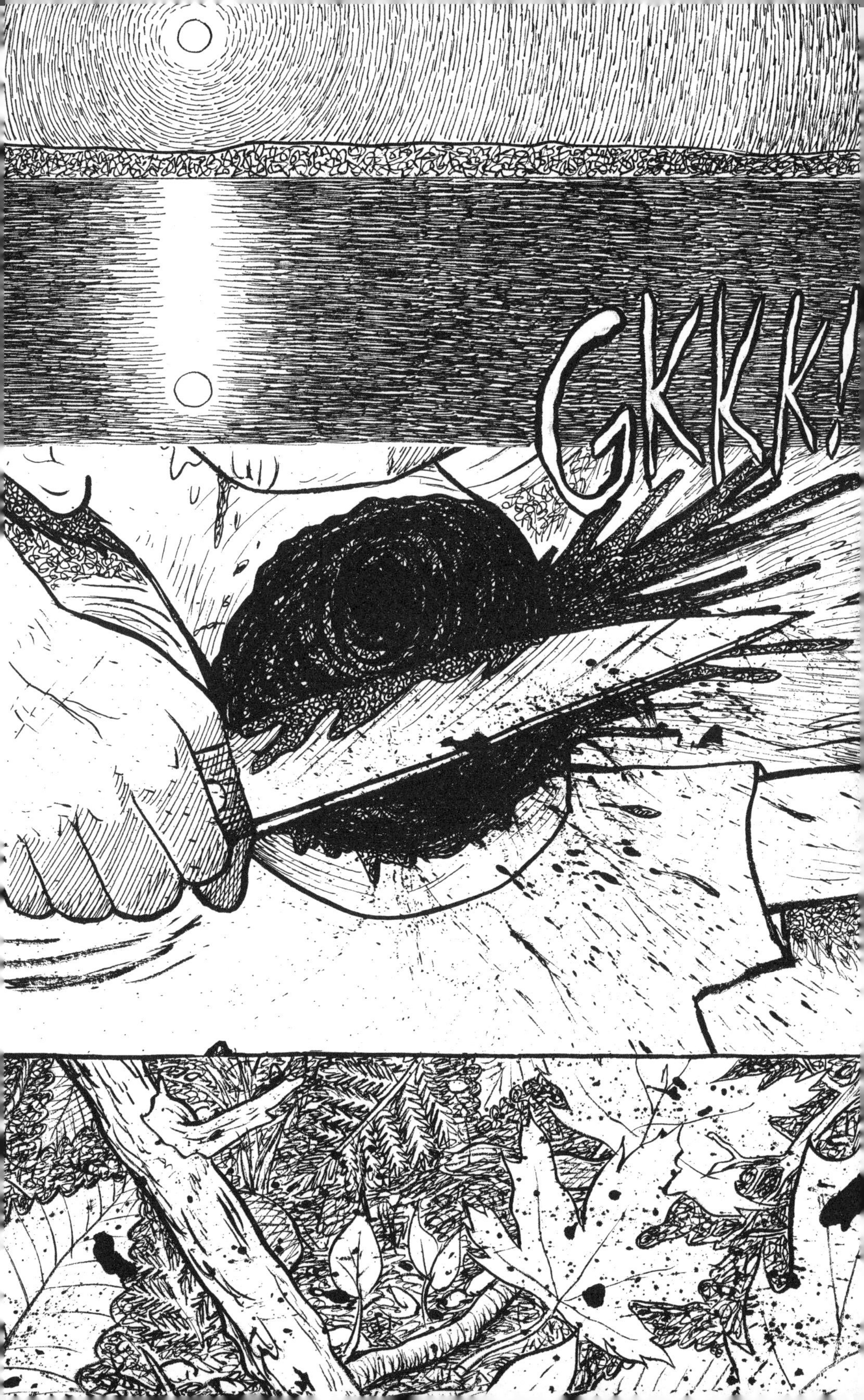
GKKK!

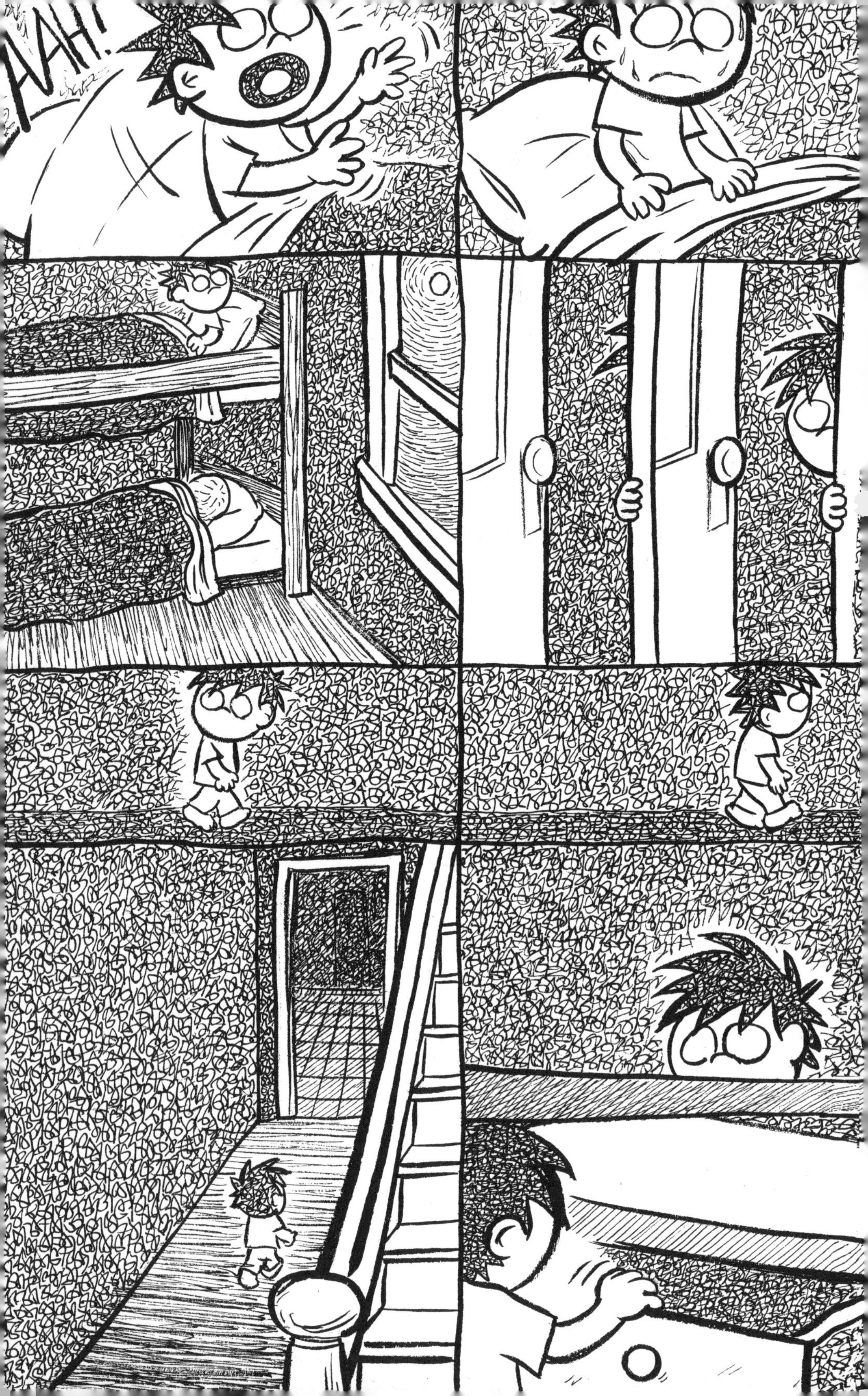
AAH!

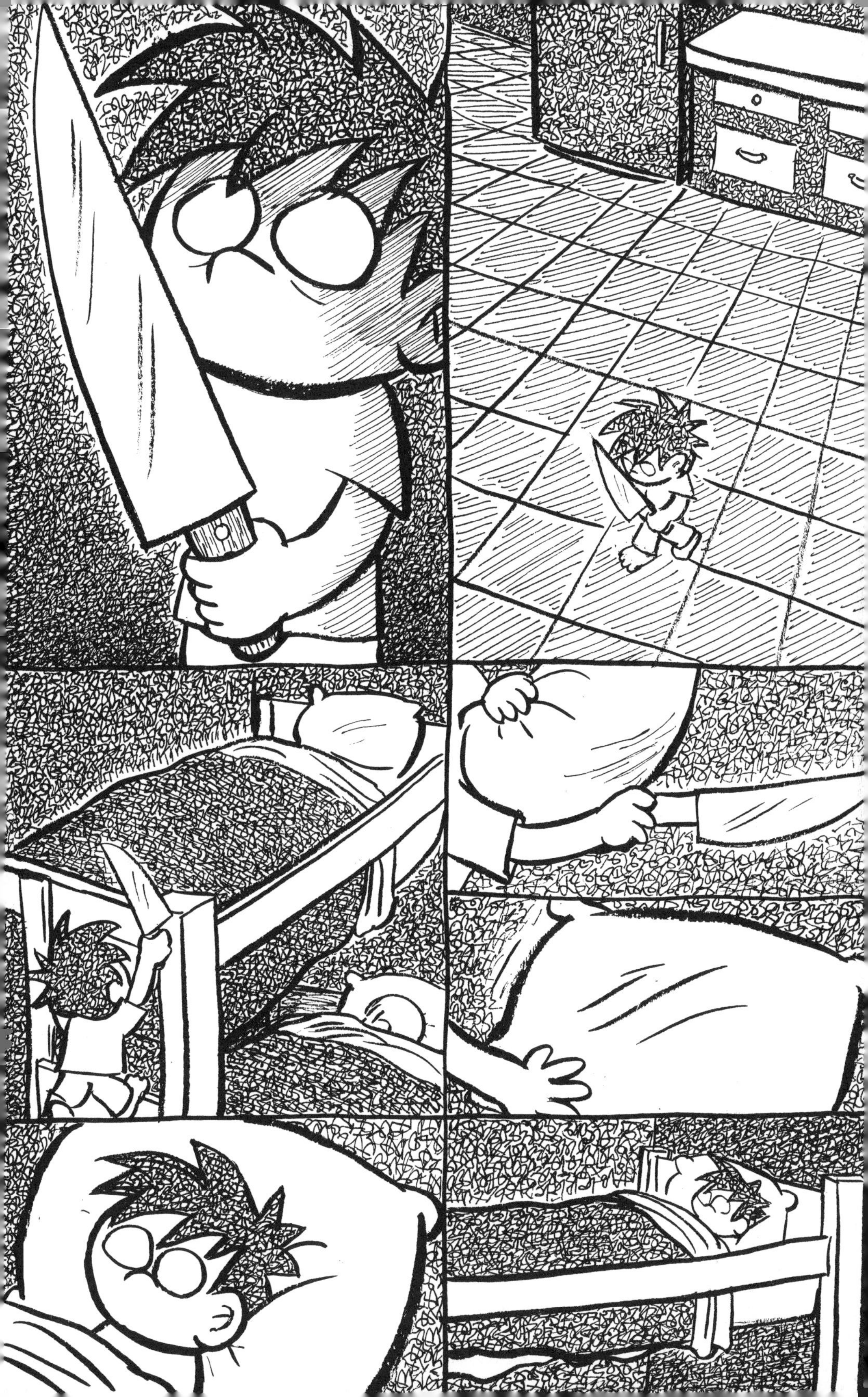

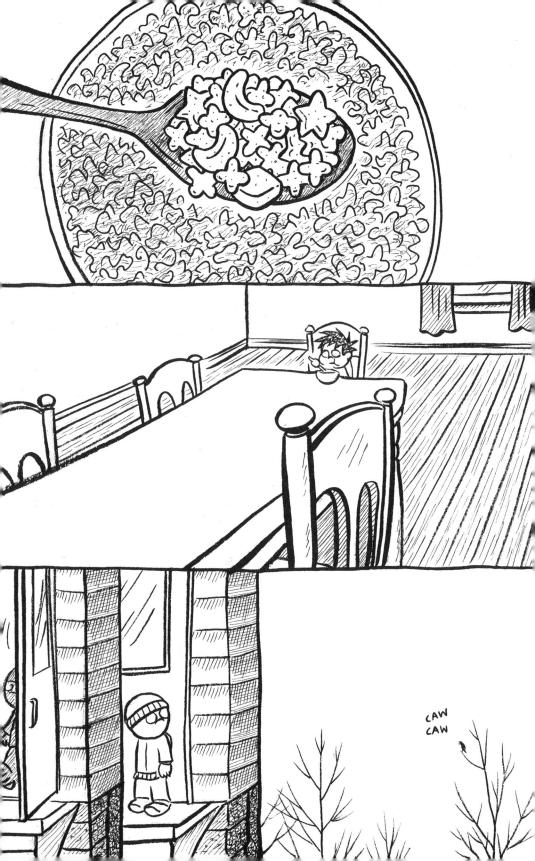

CAW
CAW

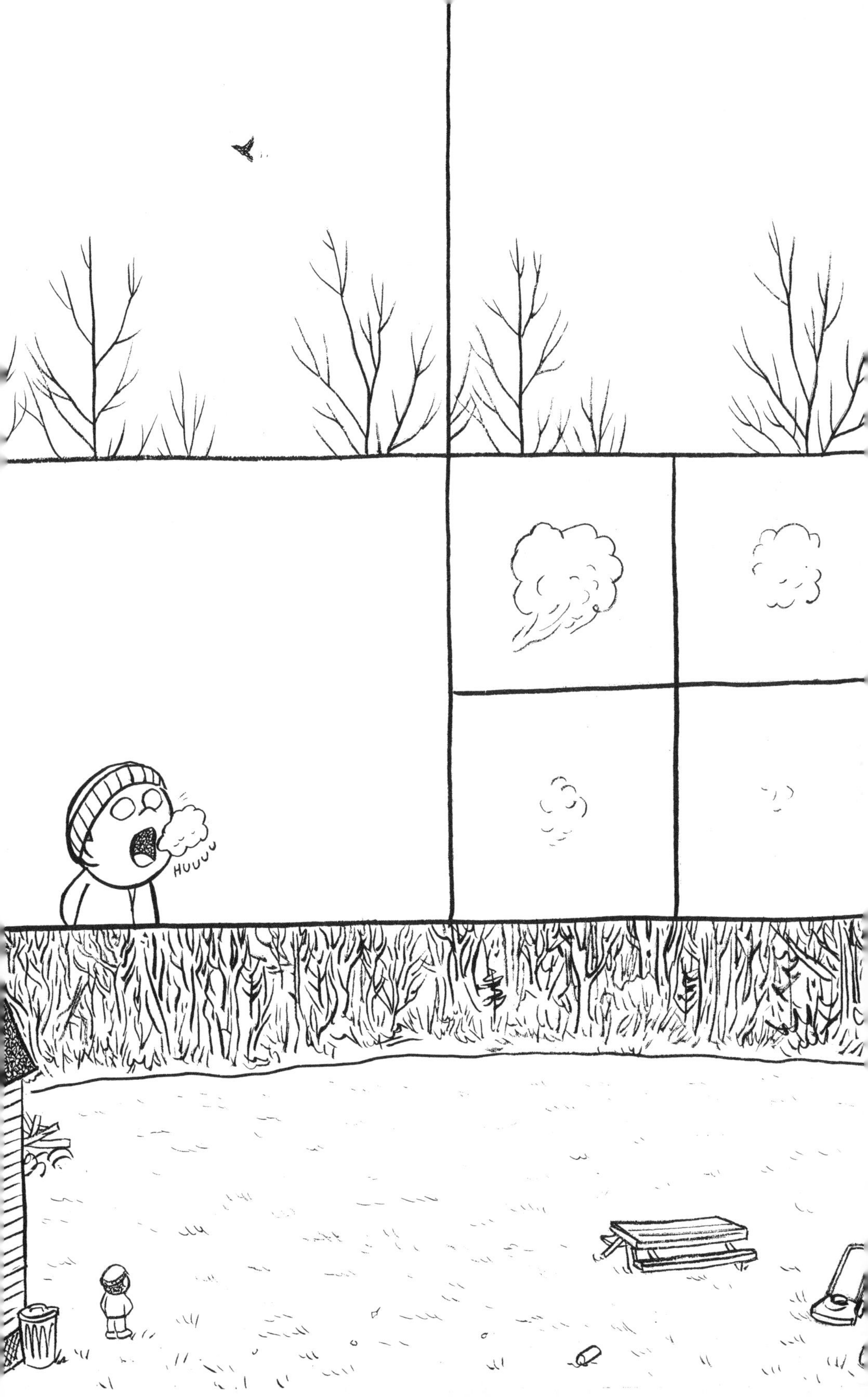
HUUUU

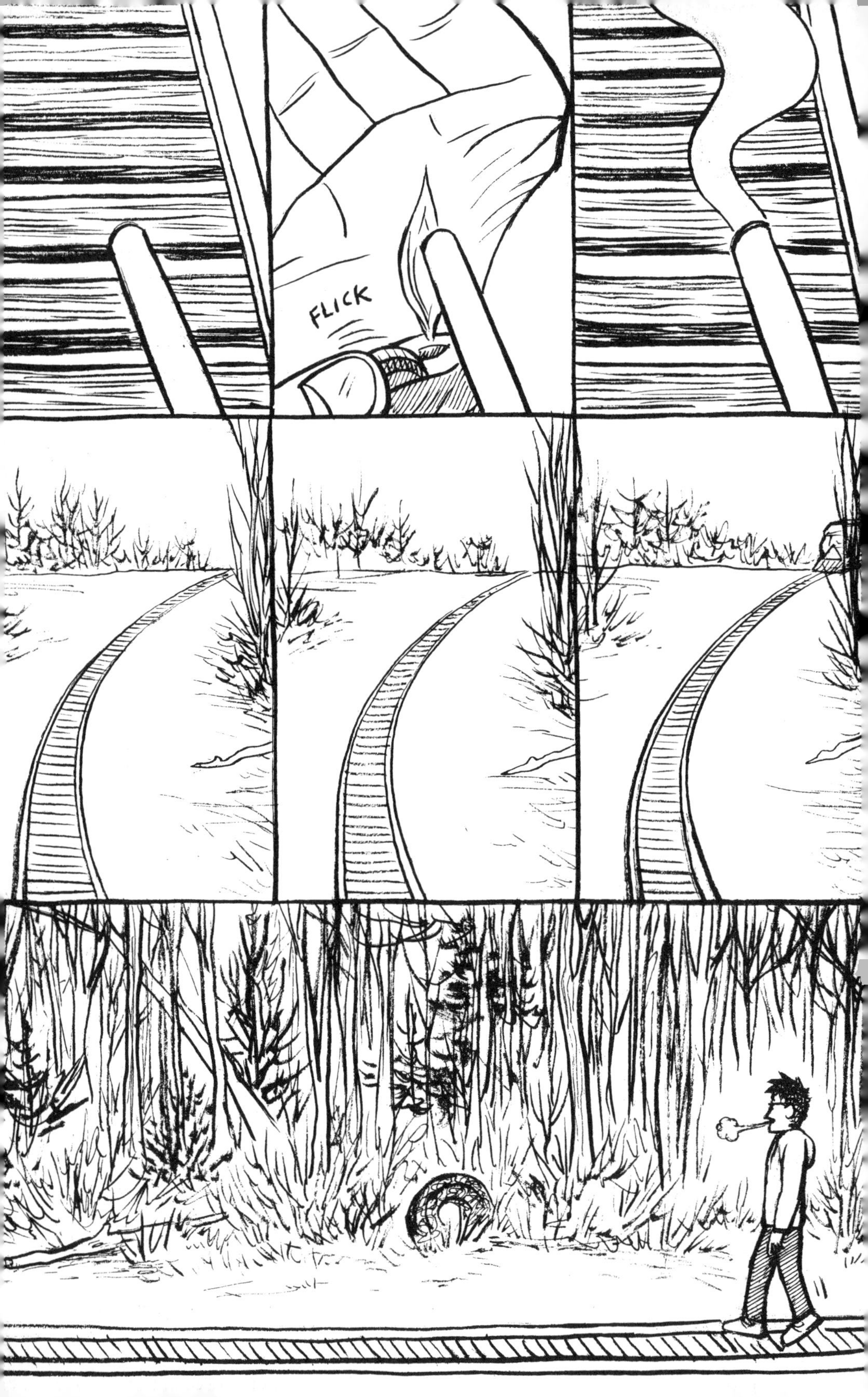
FLICK

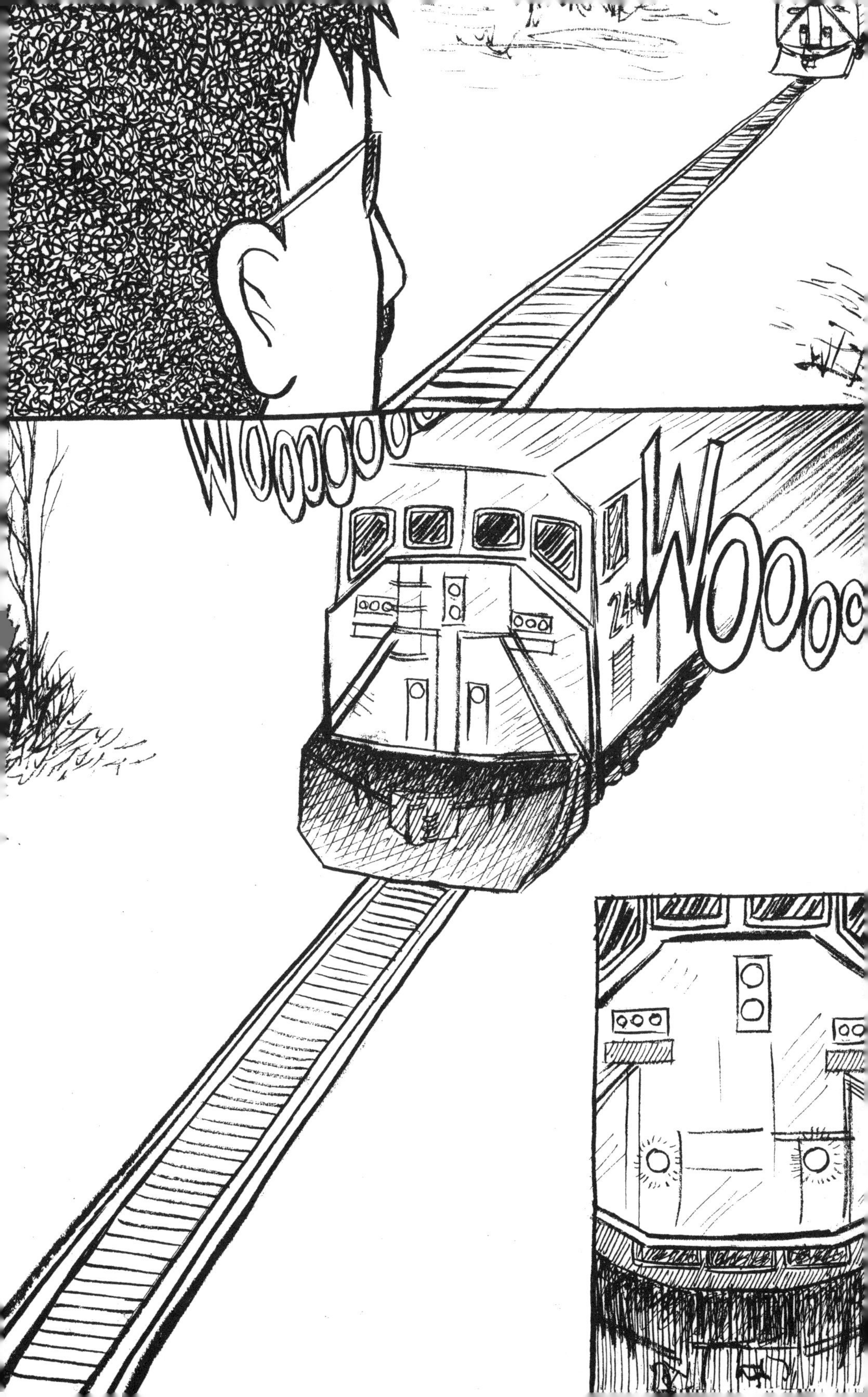
WOOOOOOO
WOOOO

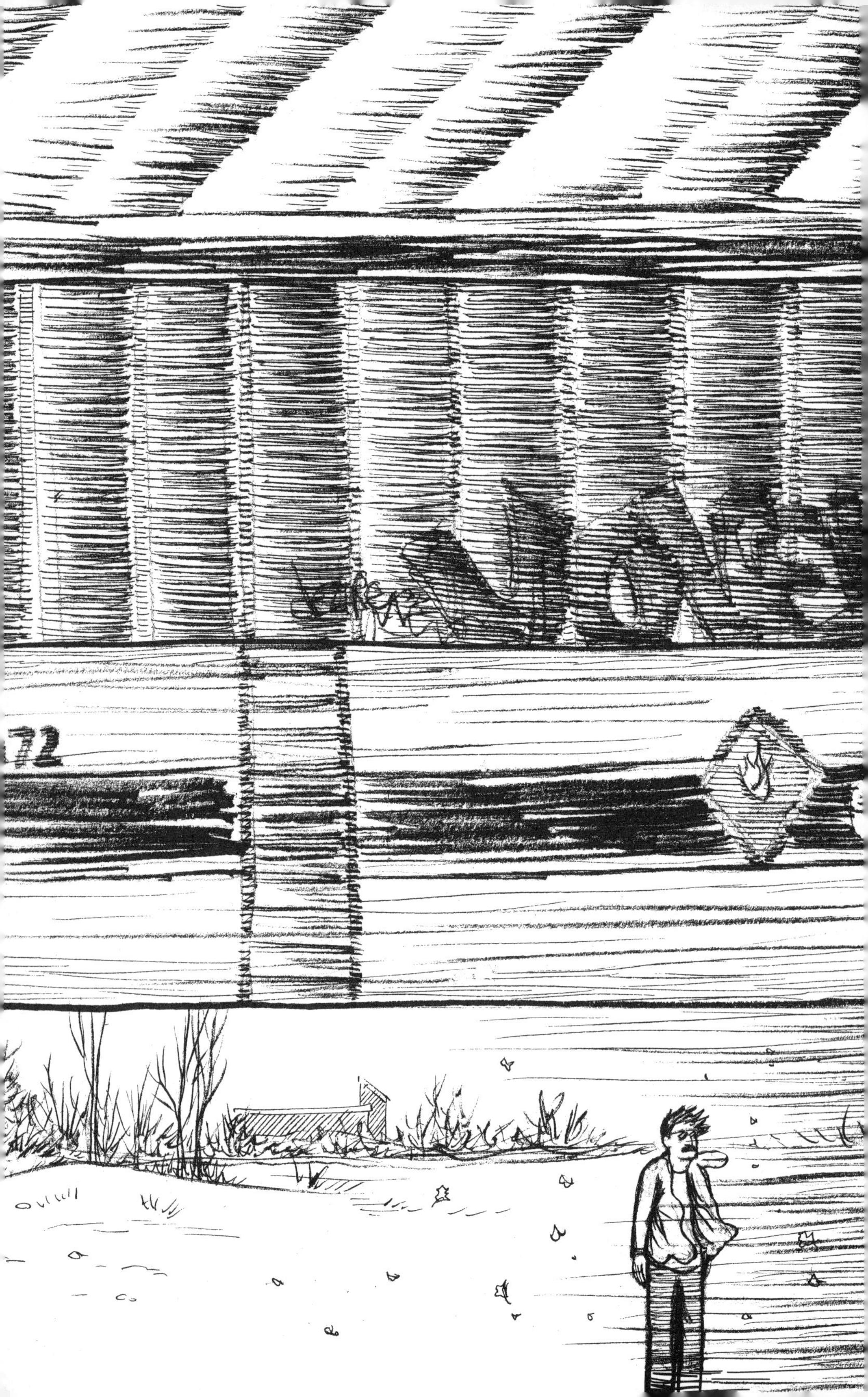
72

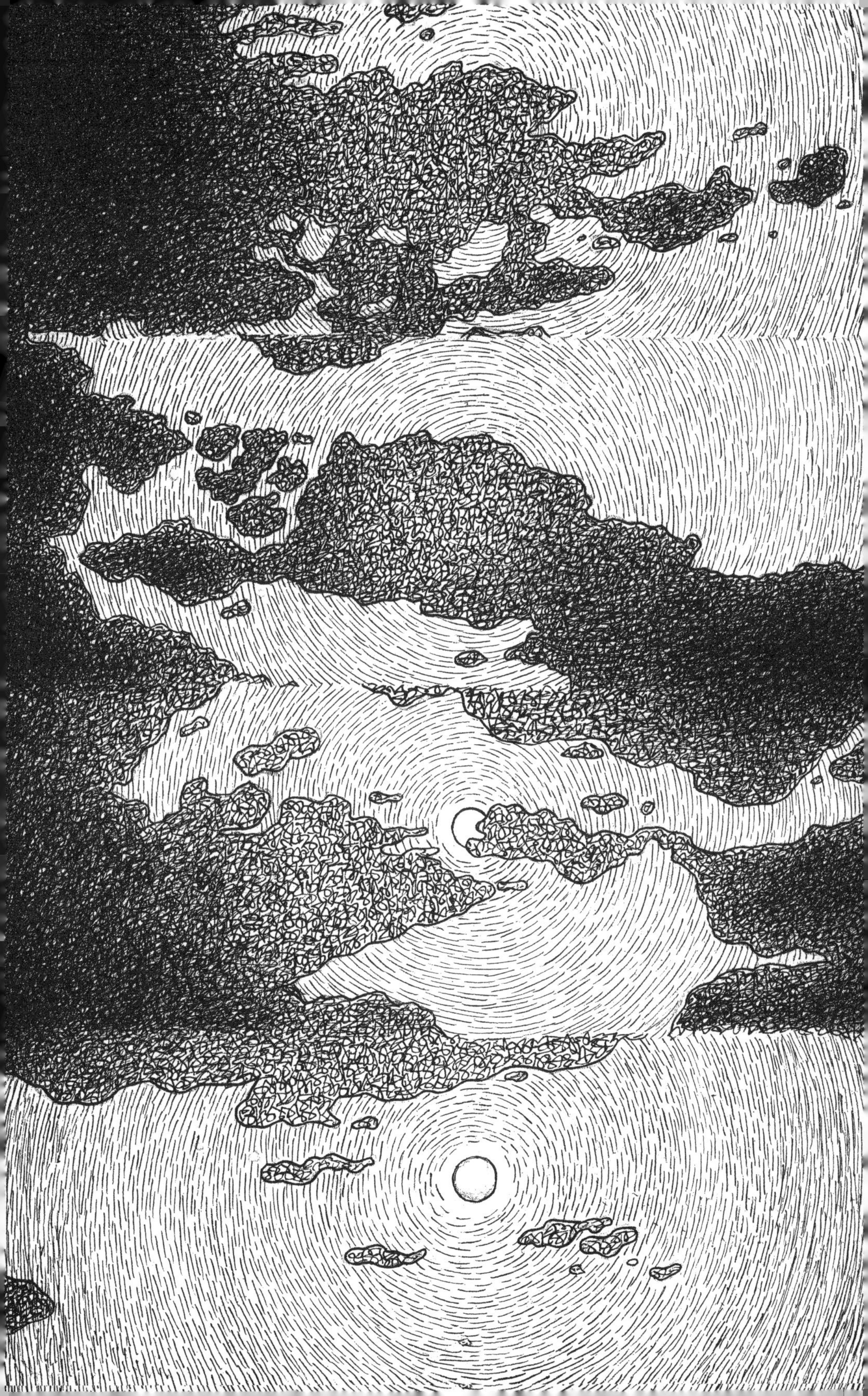

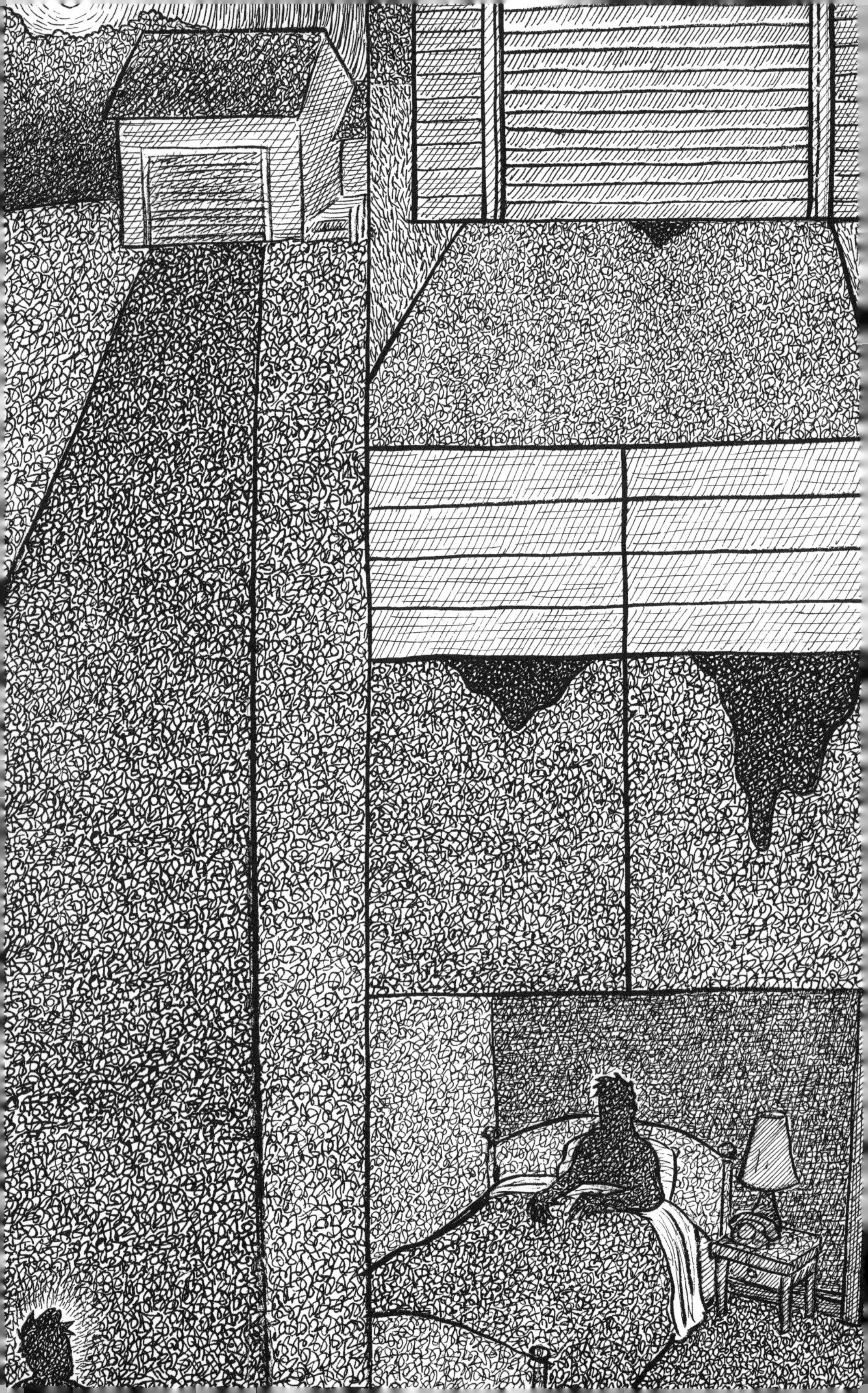

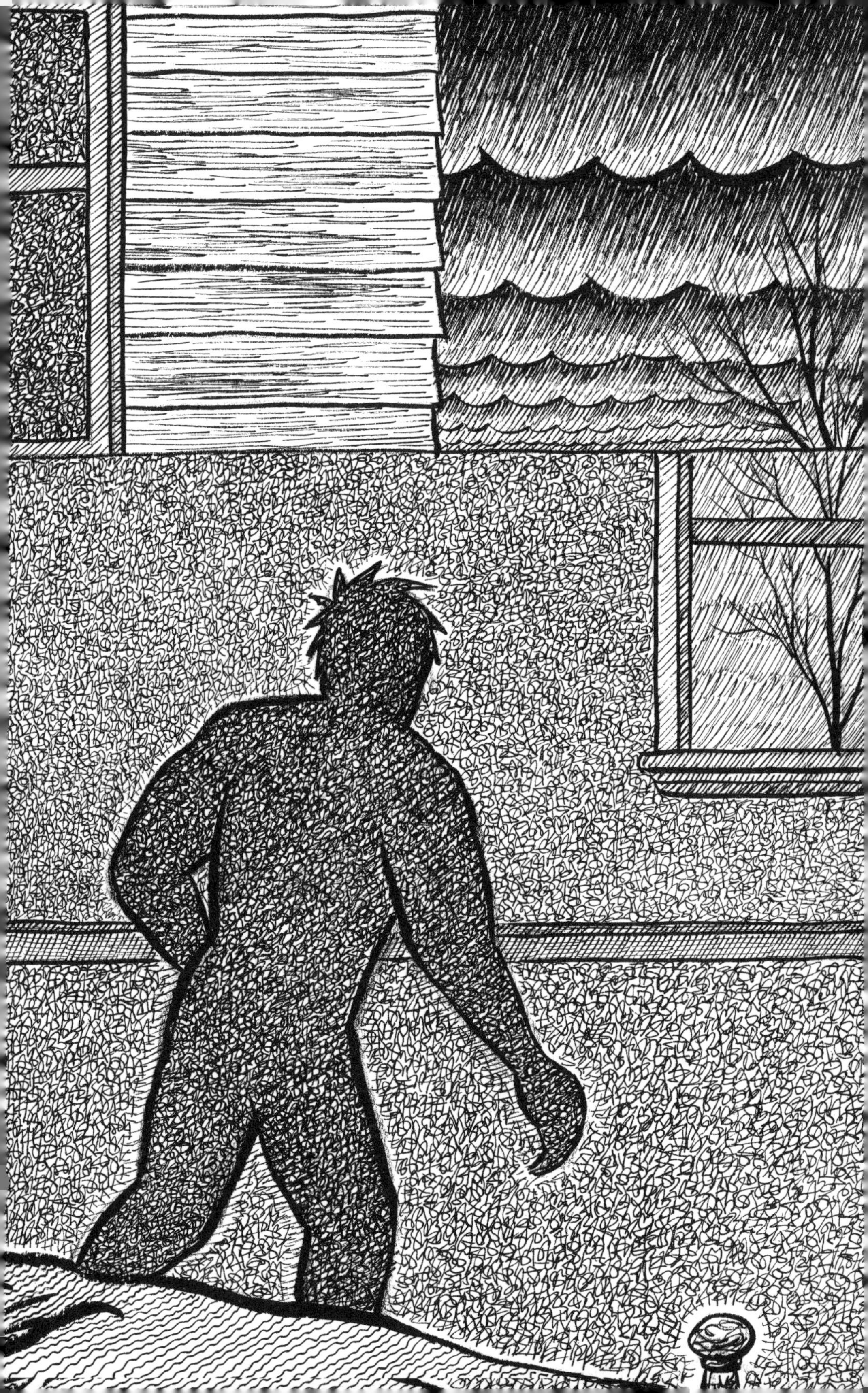

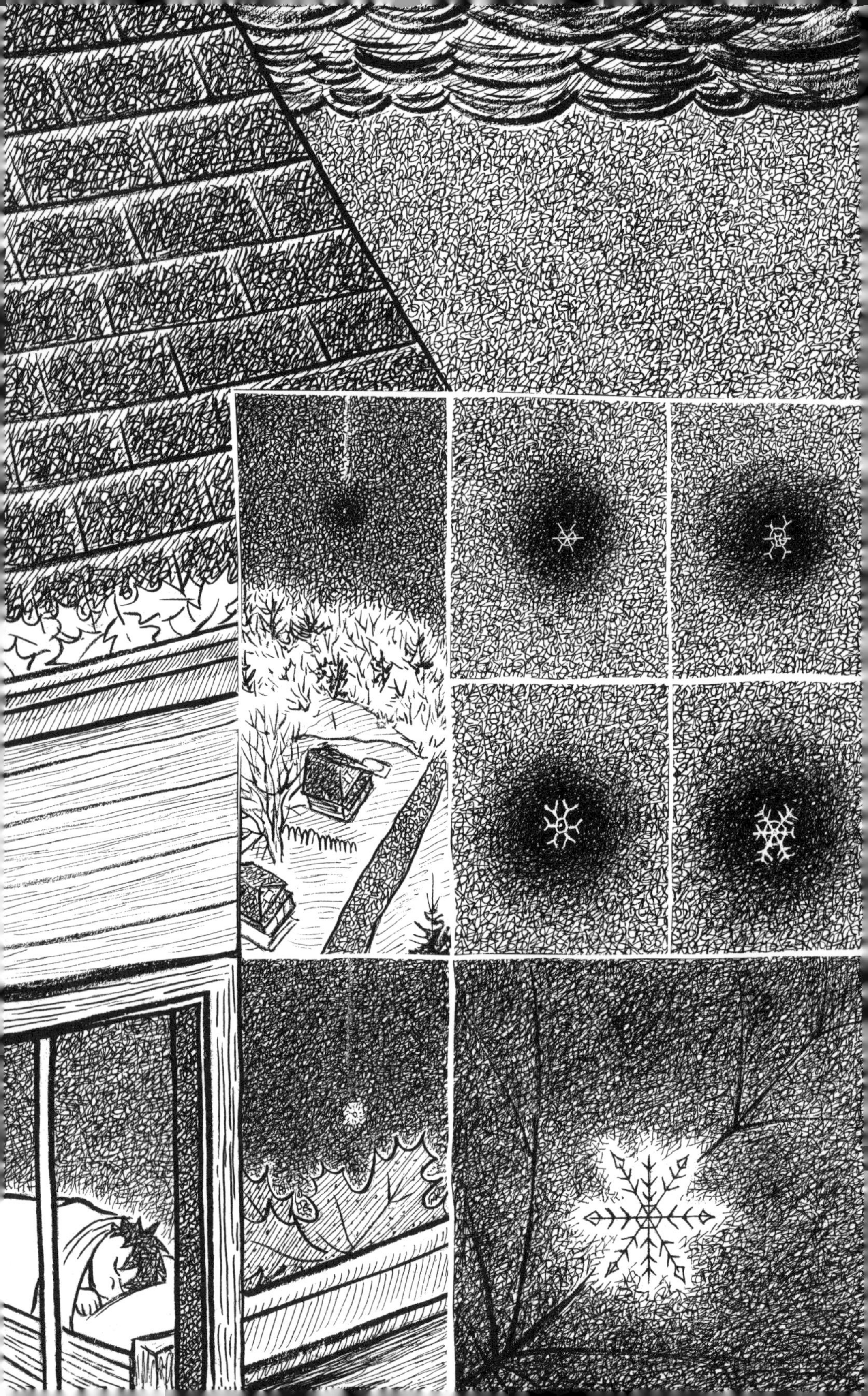

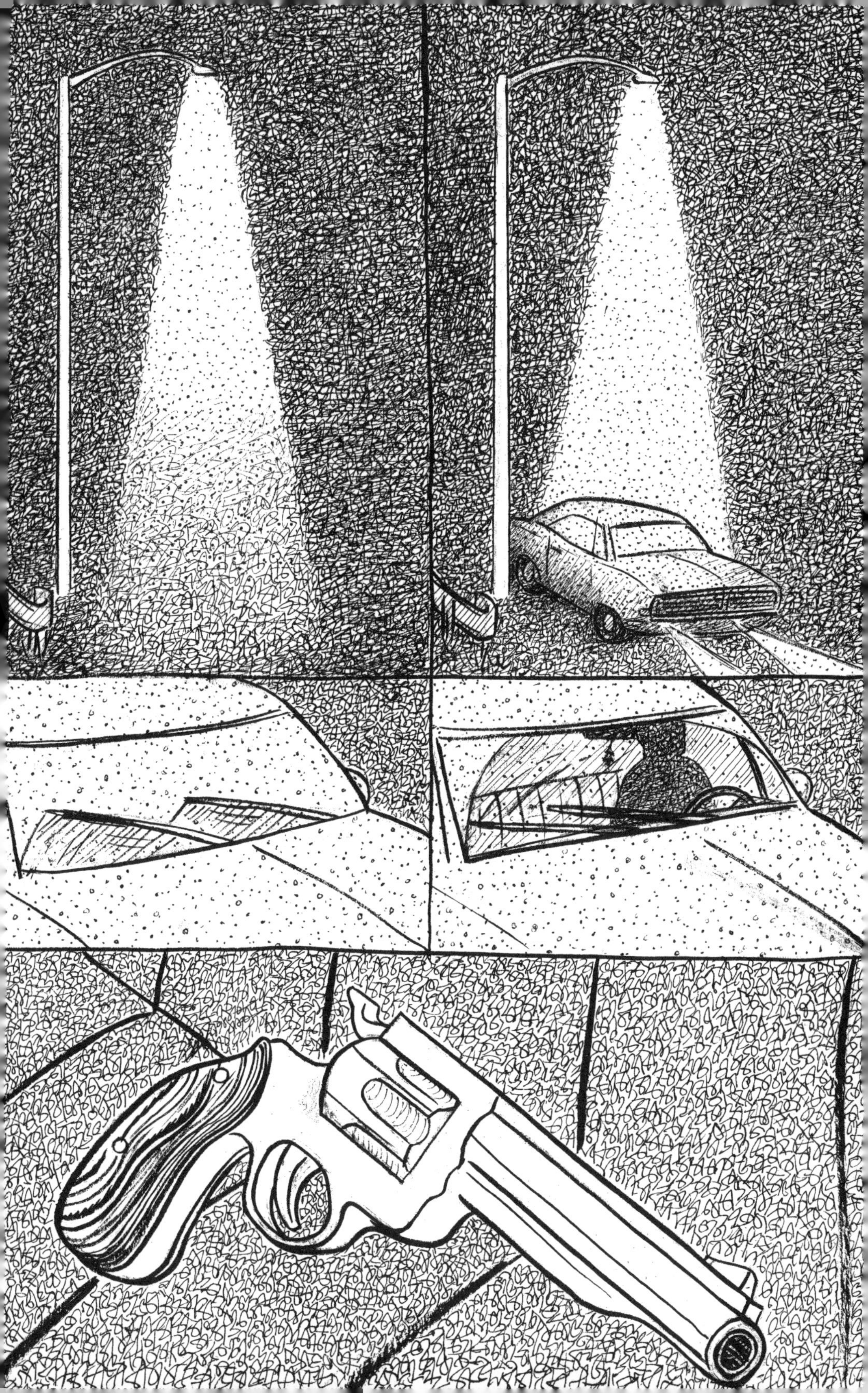

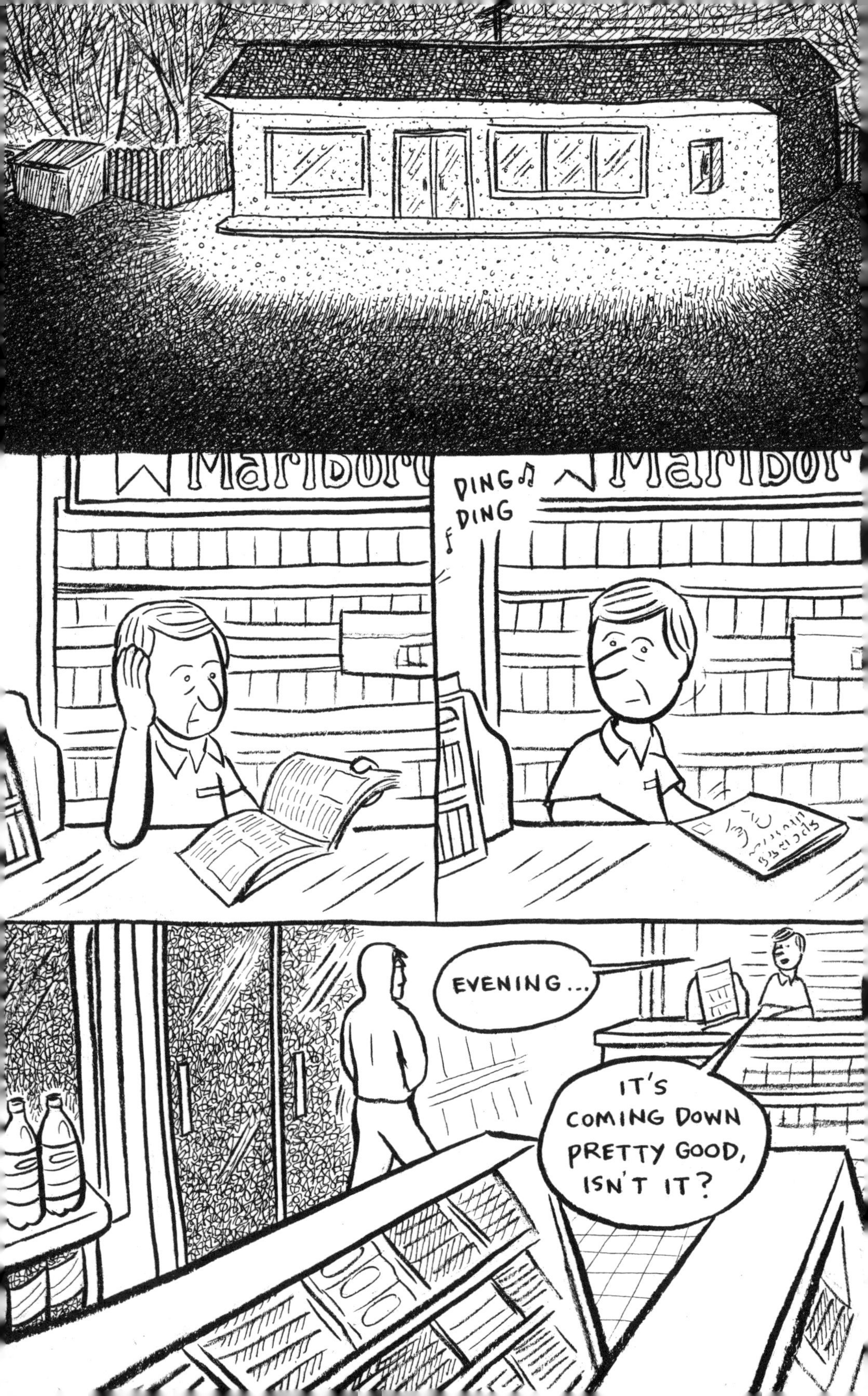
Marlboro
DING♫ DING
EVENING...
IT'S COMING DOWN PRETTY GOOD, ISN'T IT?

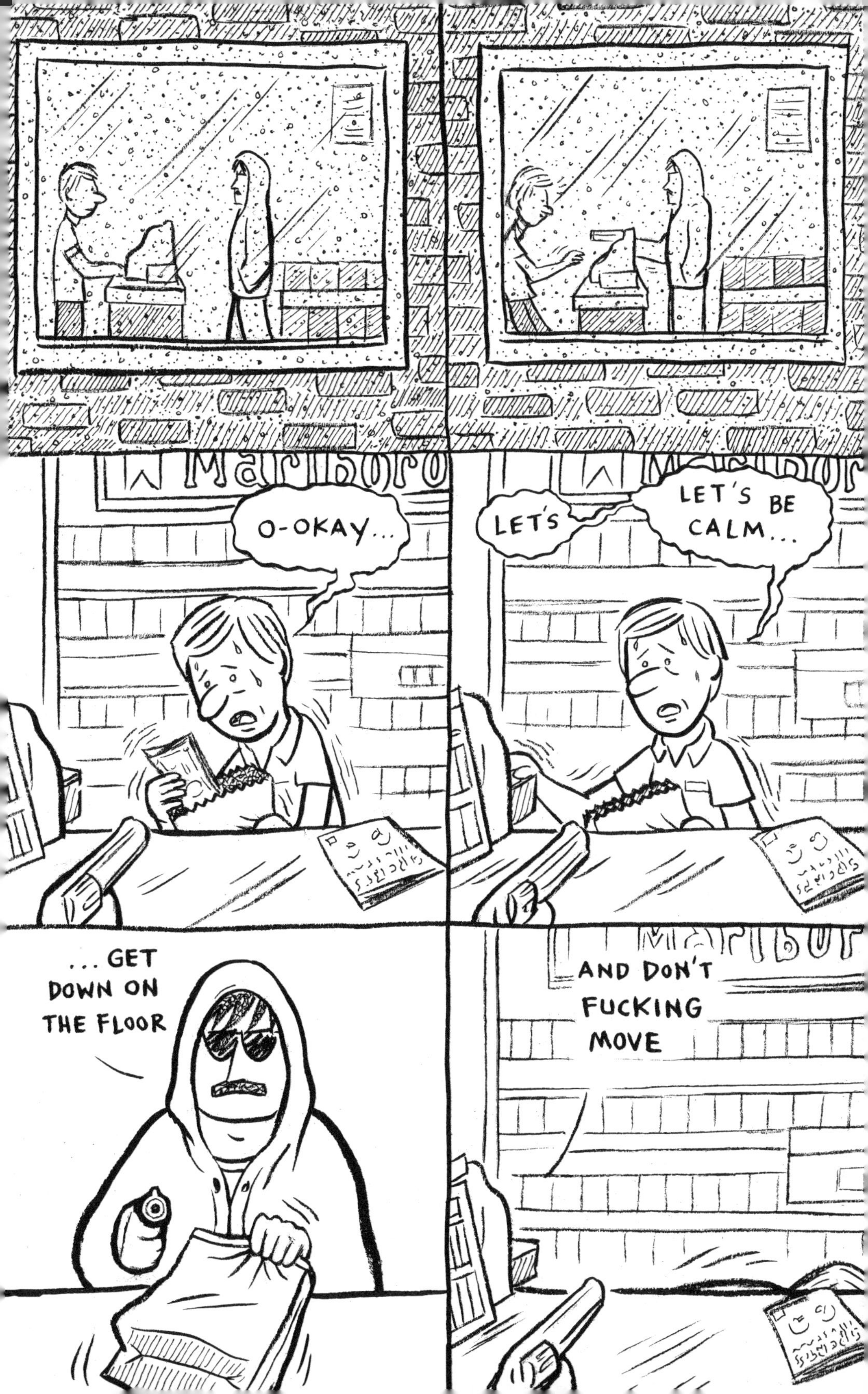
O-OKAY...
LET'S
LET'S BE CALM...
...GET DOWN ON THE FLOOR
AND DON'T FUCKING MOVE

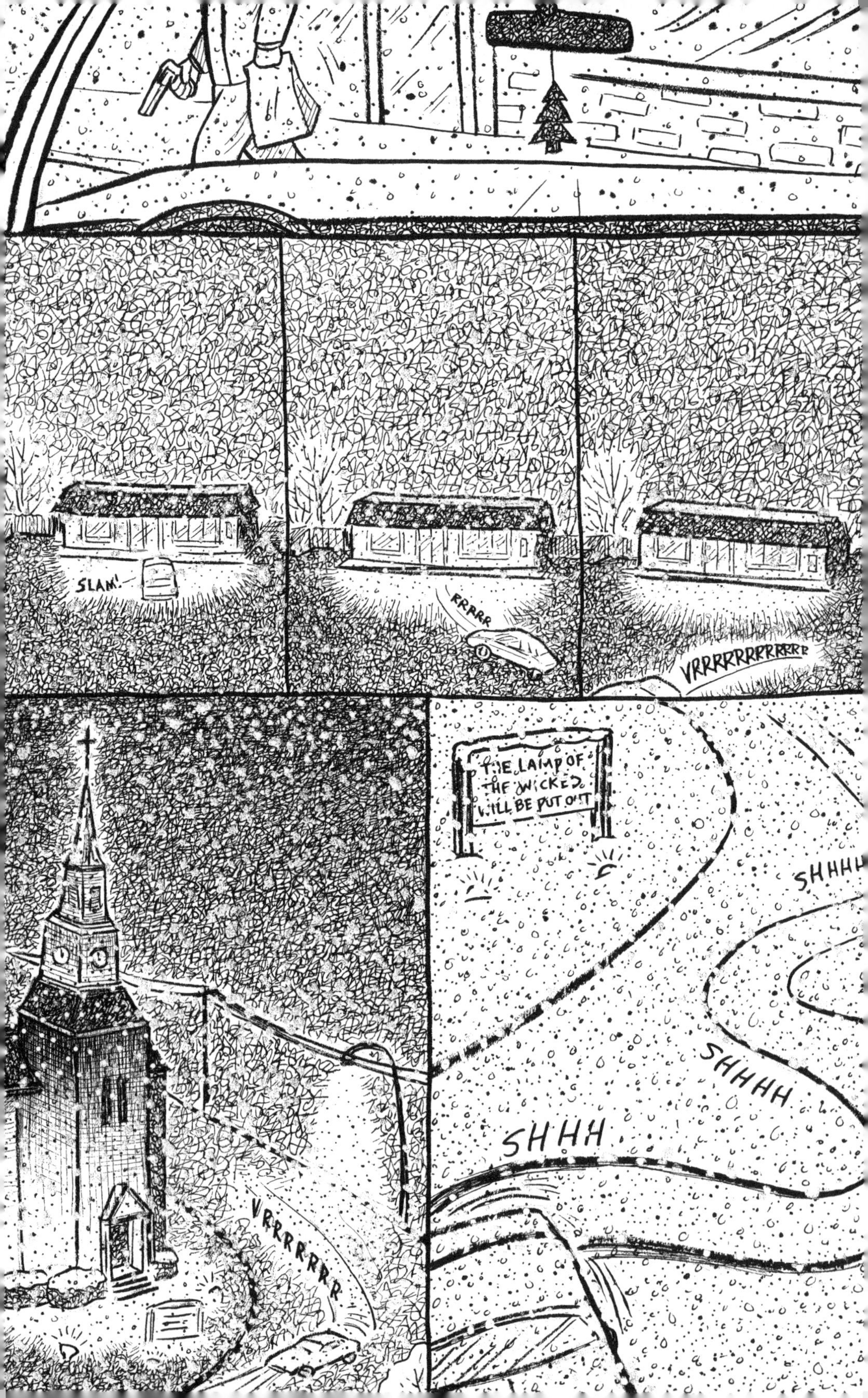
SLAM!
RRRRR
VRRRRRRRRRRR
VRRRRRRRR
THE LAMP OF THE WICKED WILL BE PUT OUT
SHHHH
SHHHH
SHHH

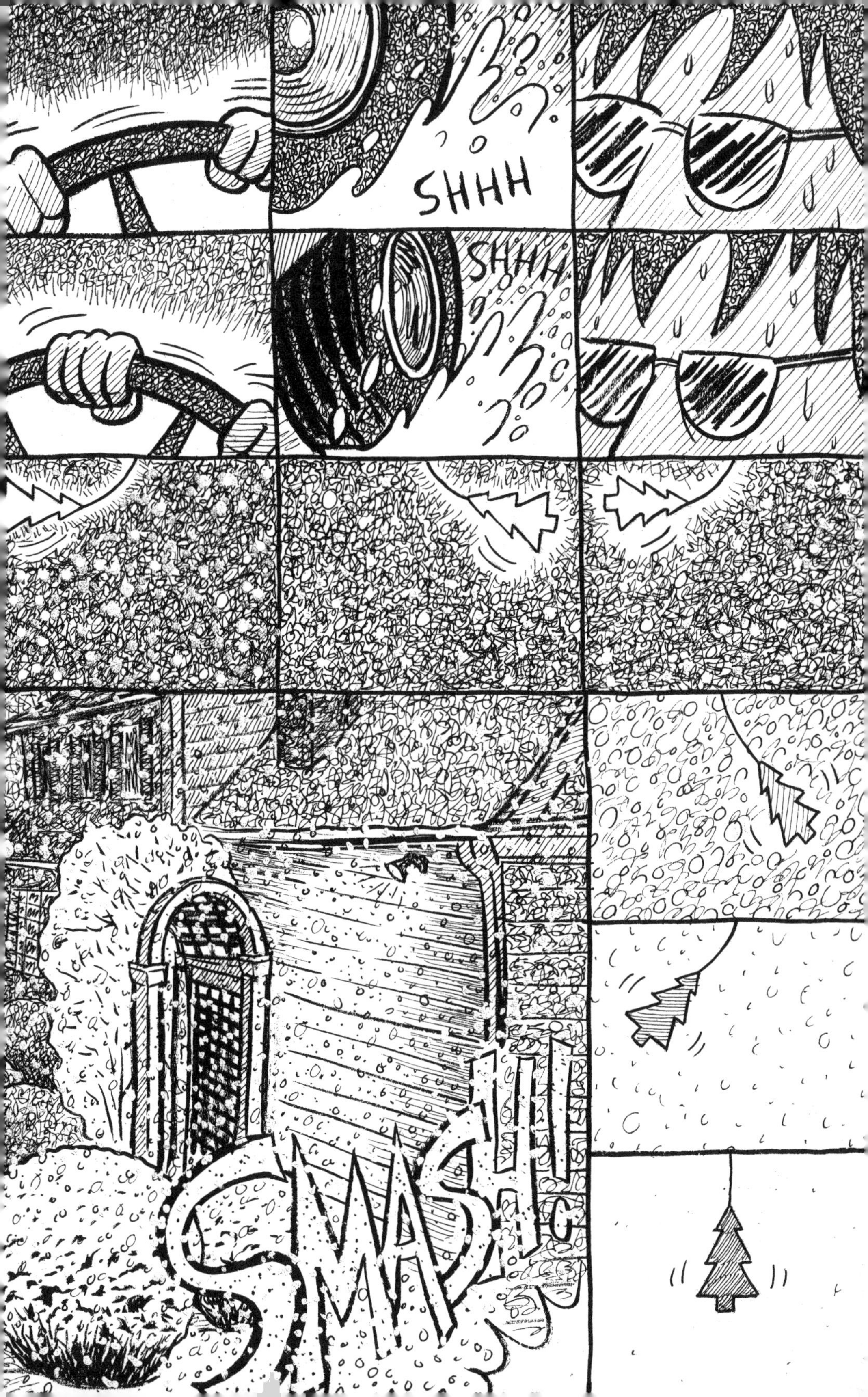
SHHH
SHHH
SMASH

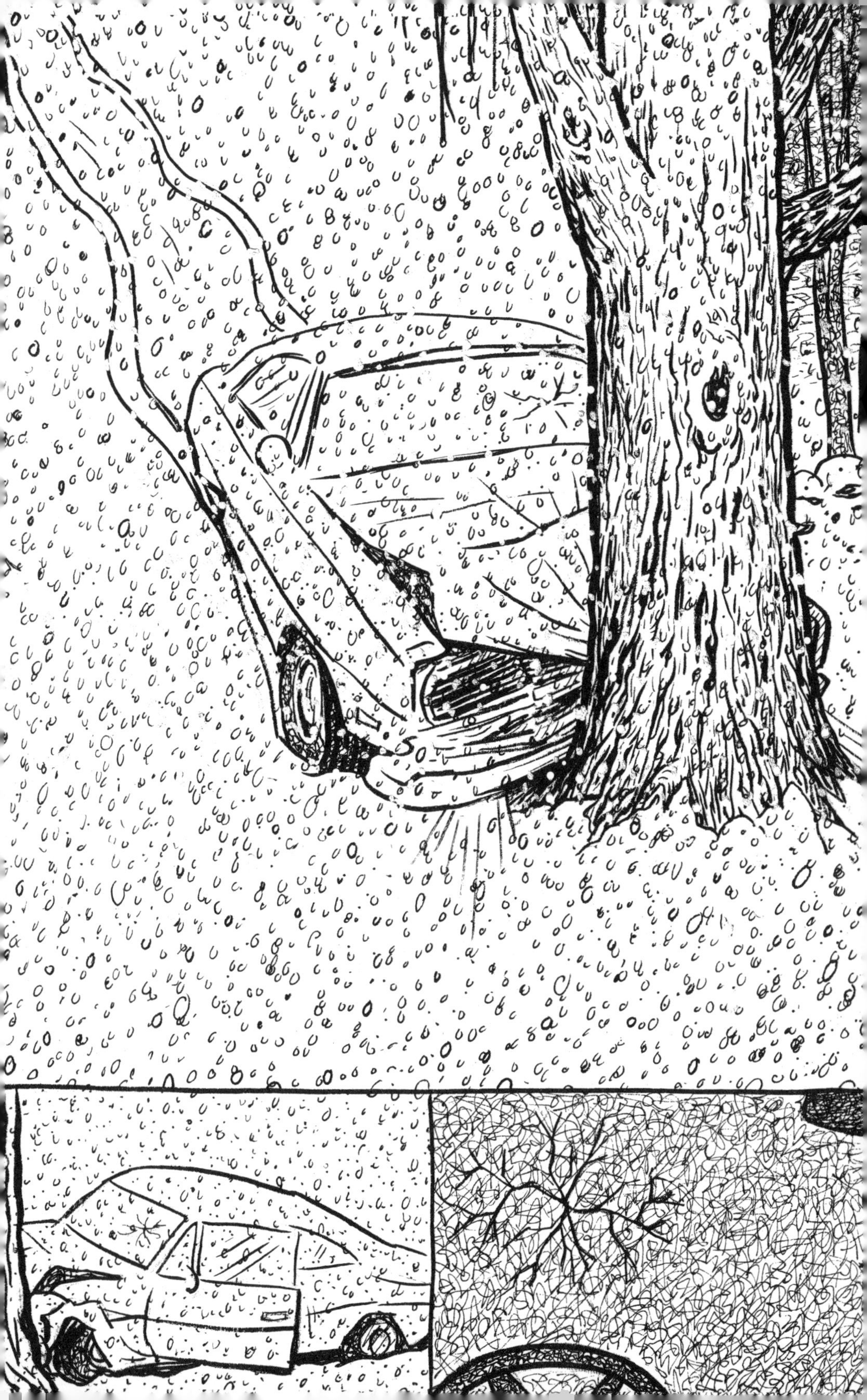

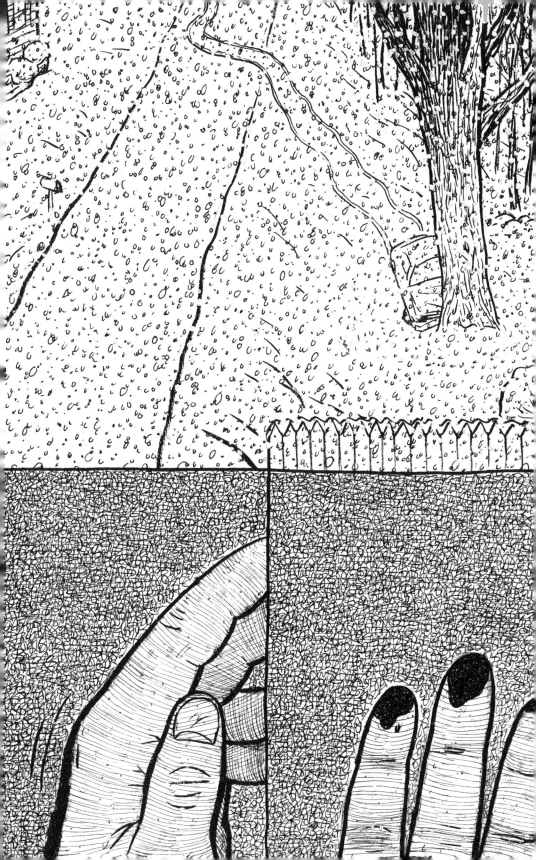

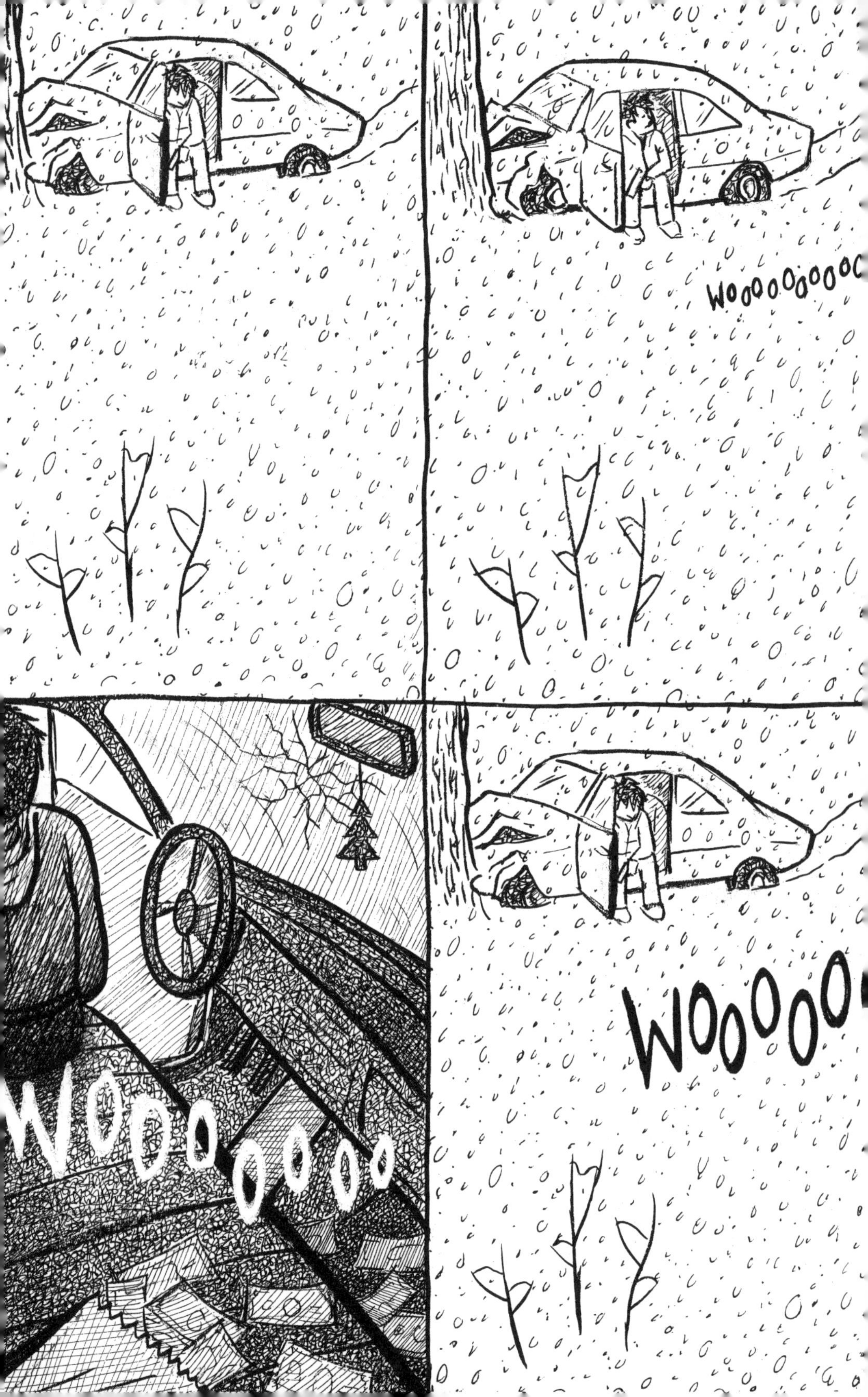
WOOOOOOOOO
WOOOOOOOOO
WOOOOO

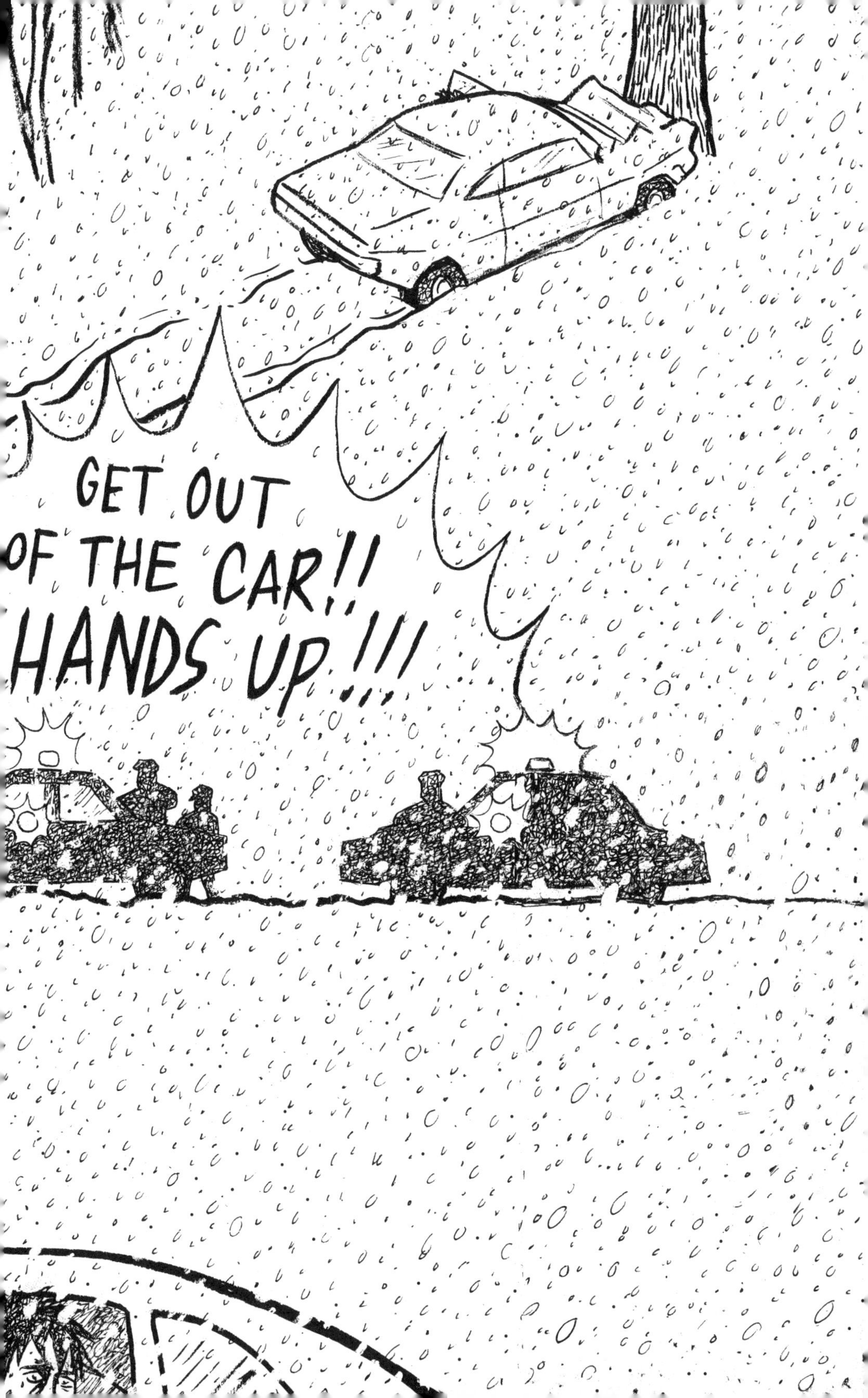
GET OUT OF THE CAR!! HANDS UP!!!

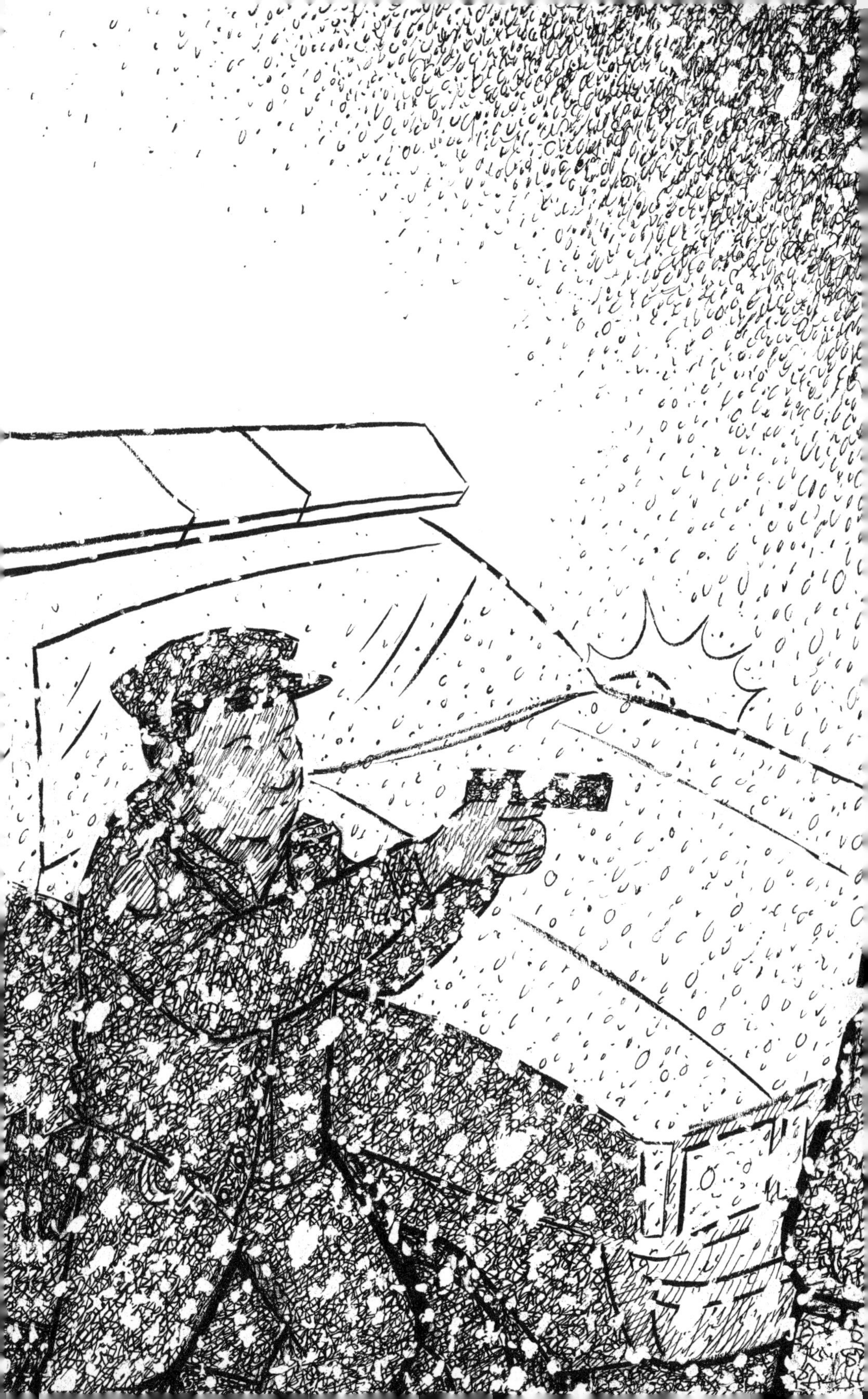

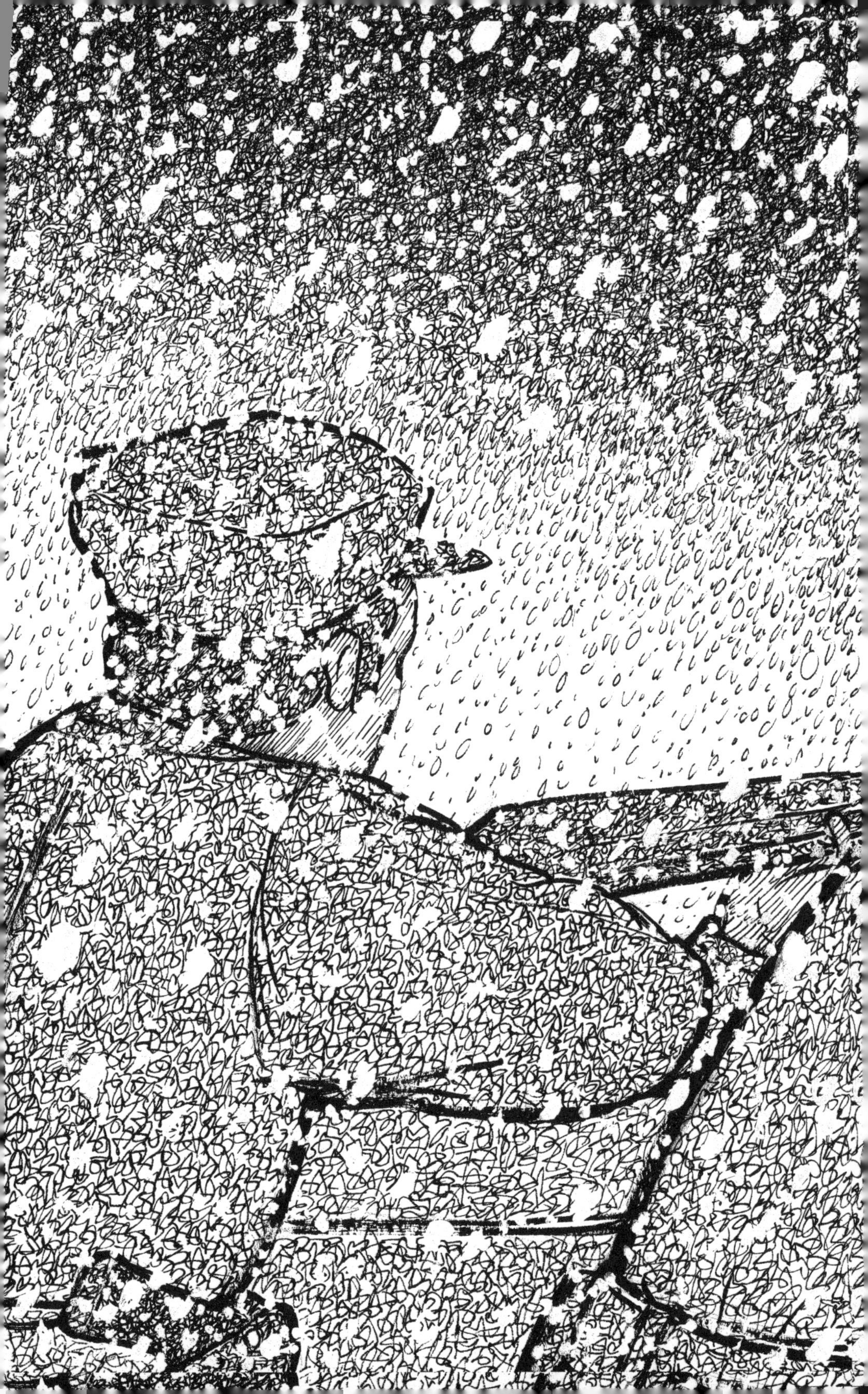

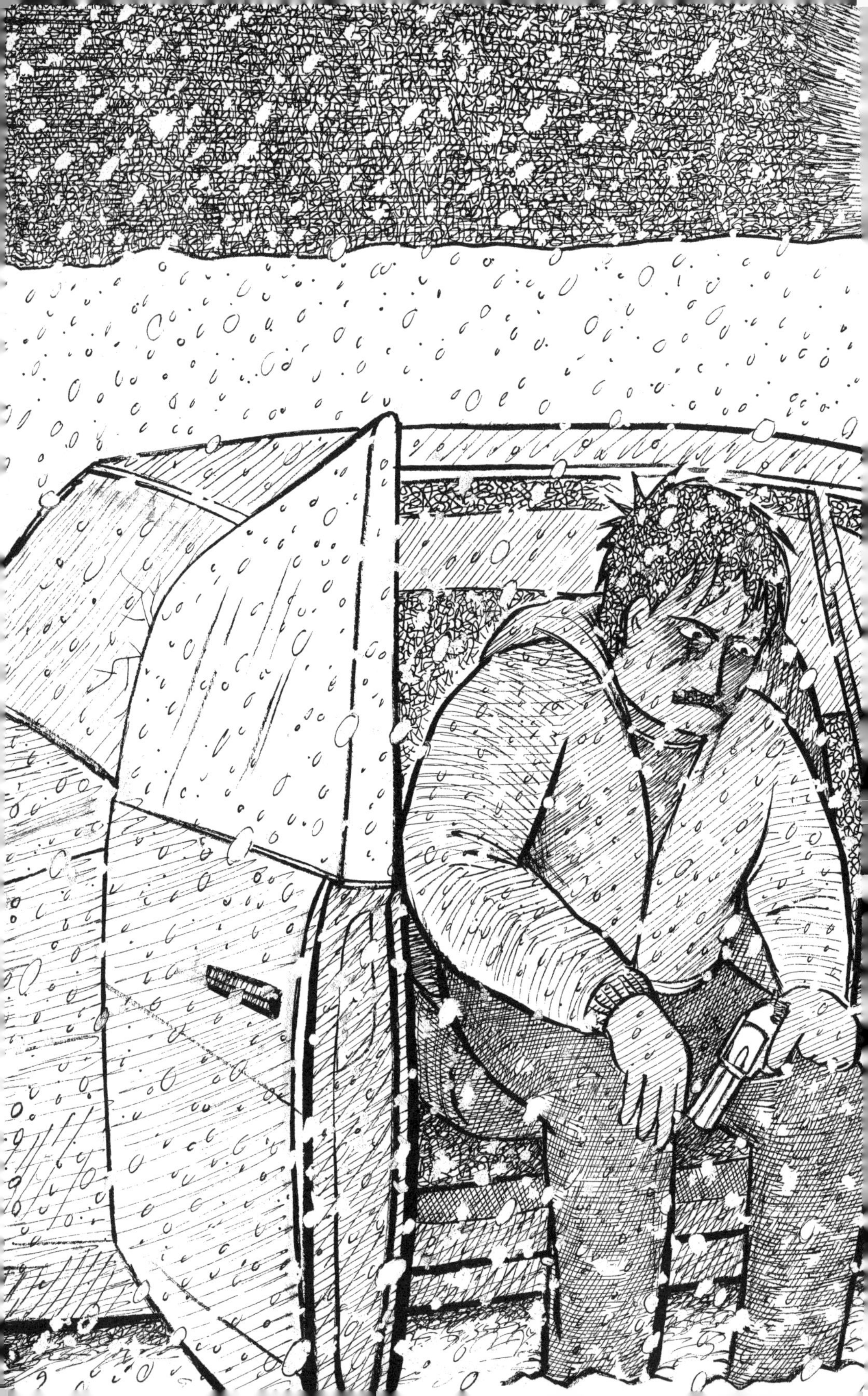

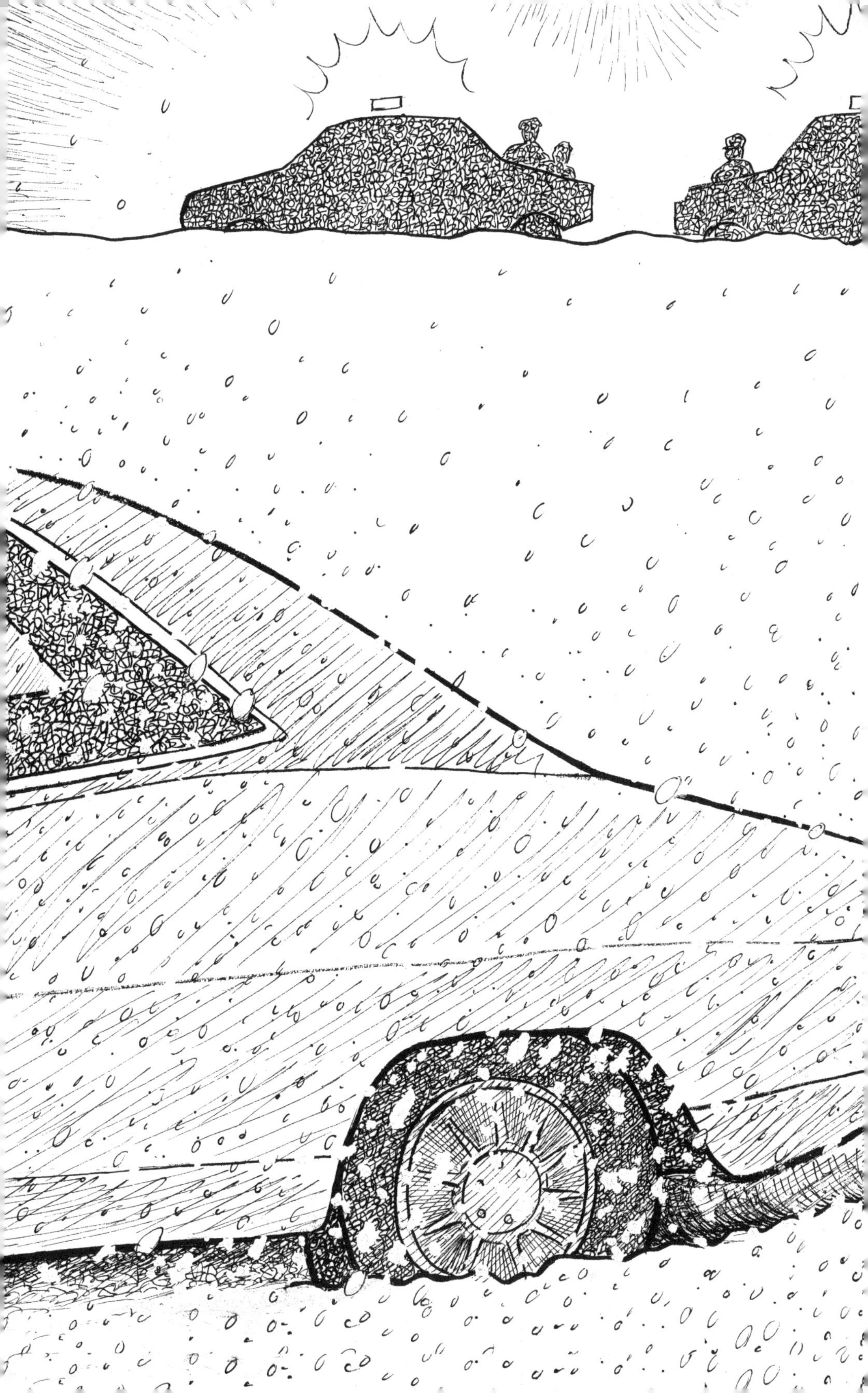

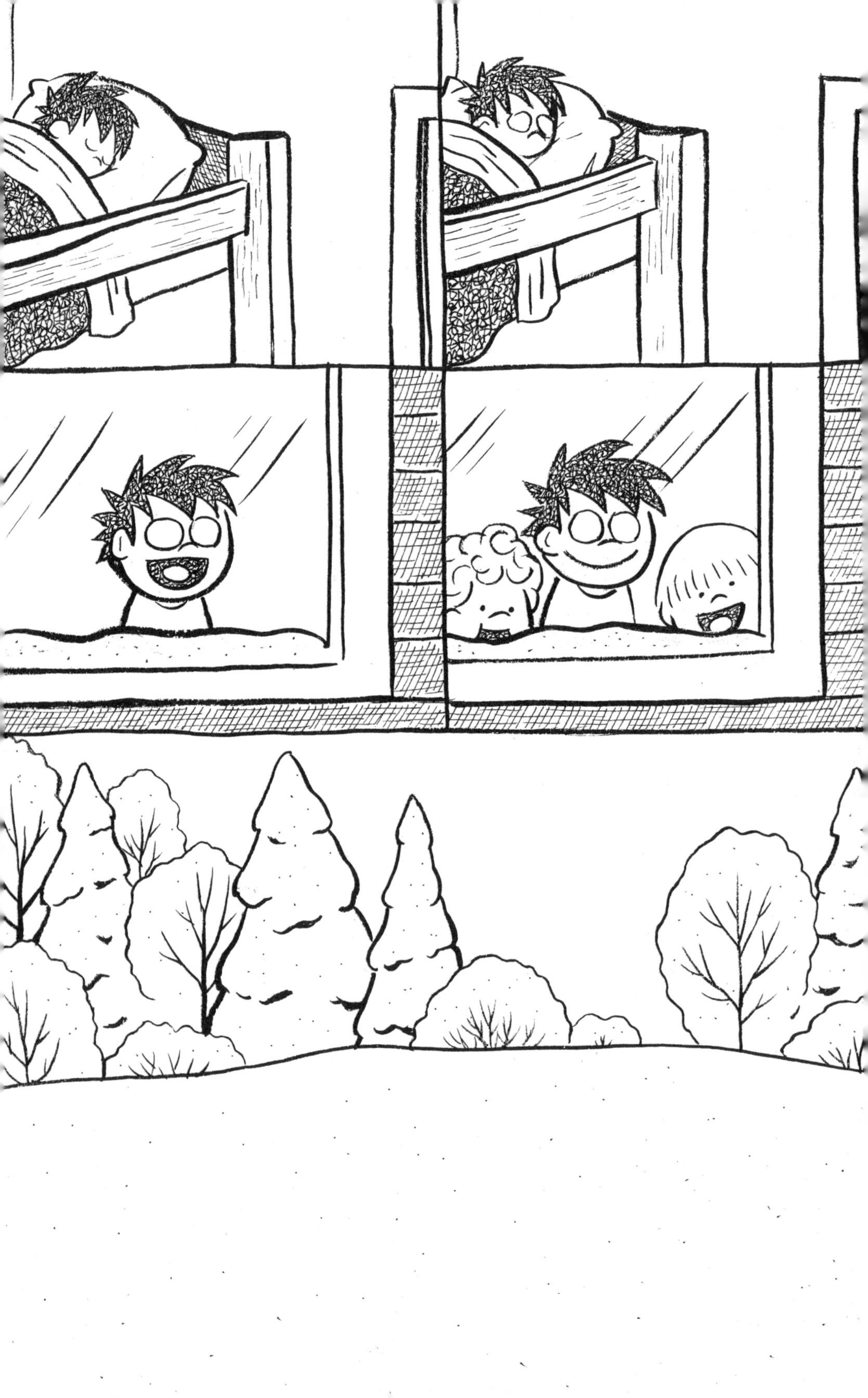

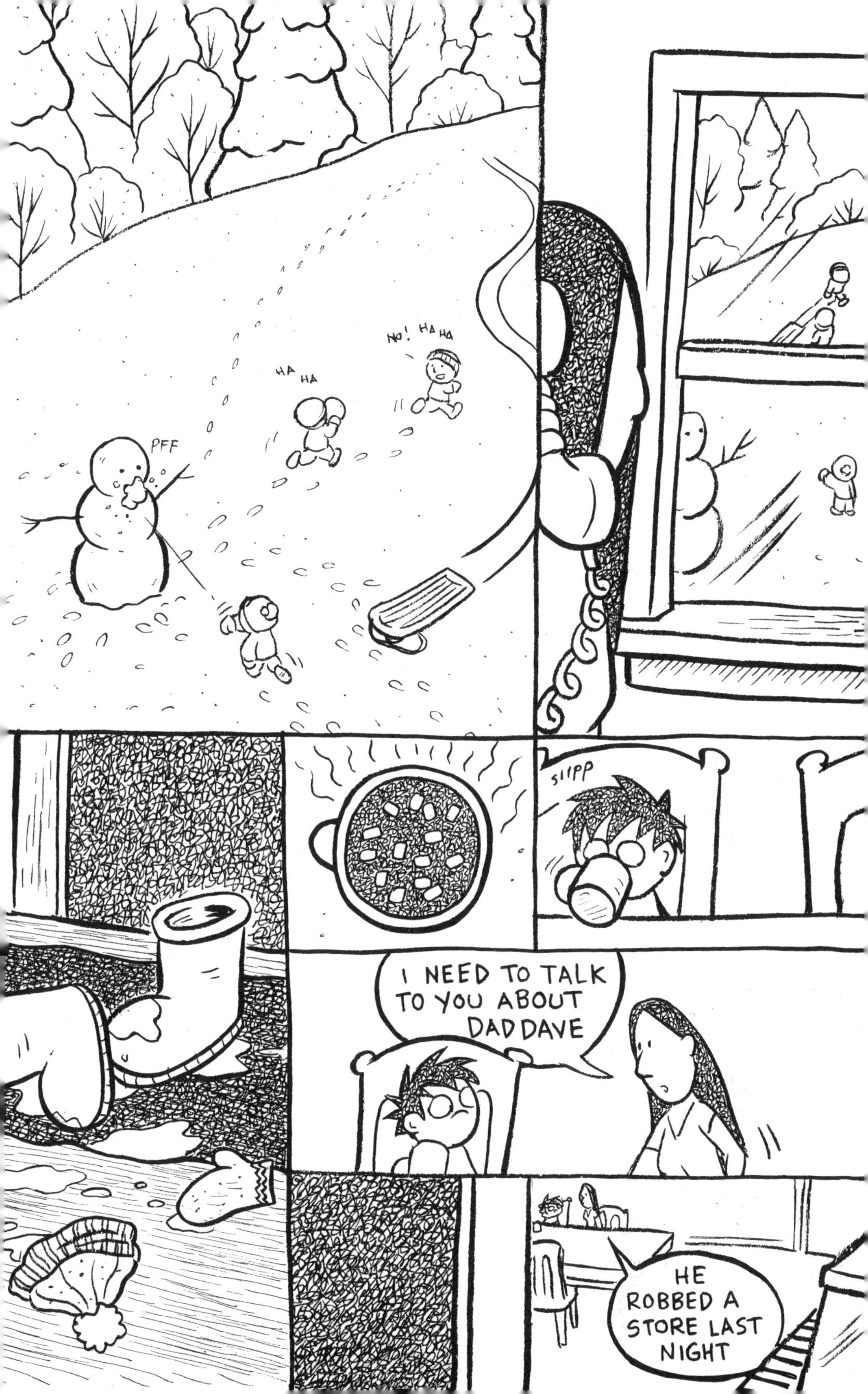
NO! HA HA
HA HA
PFF
SLIPP
I NEED TO TALK TO YOU ABOUT DAD DAVE
HE ROBBED A STORE LAST NIGHT

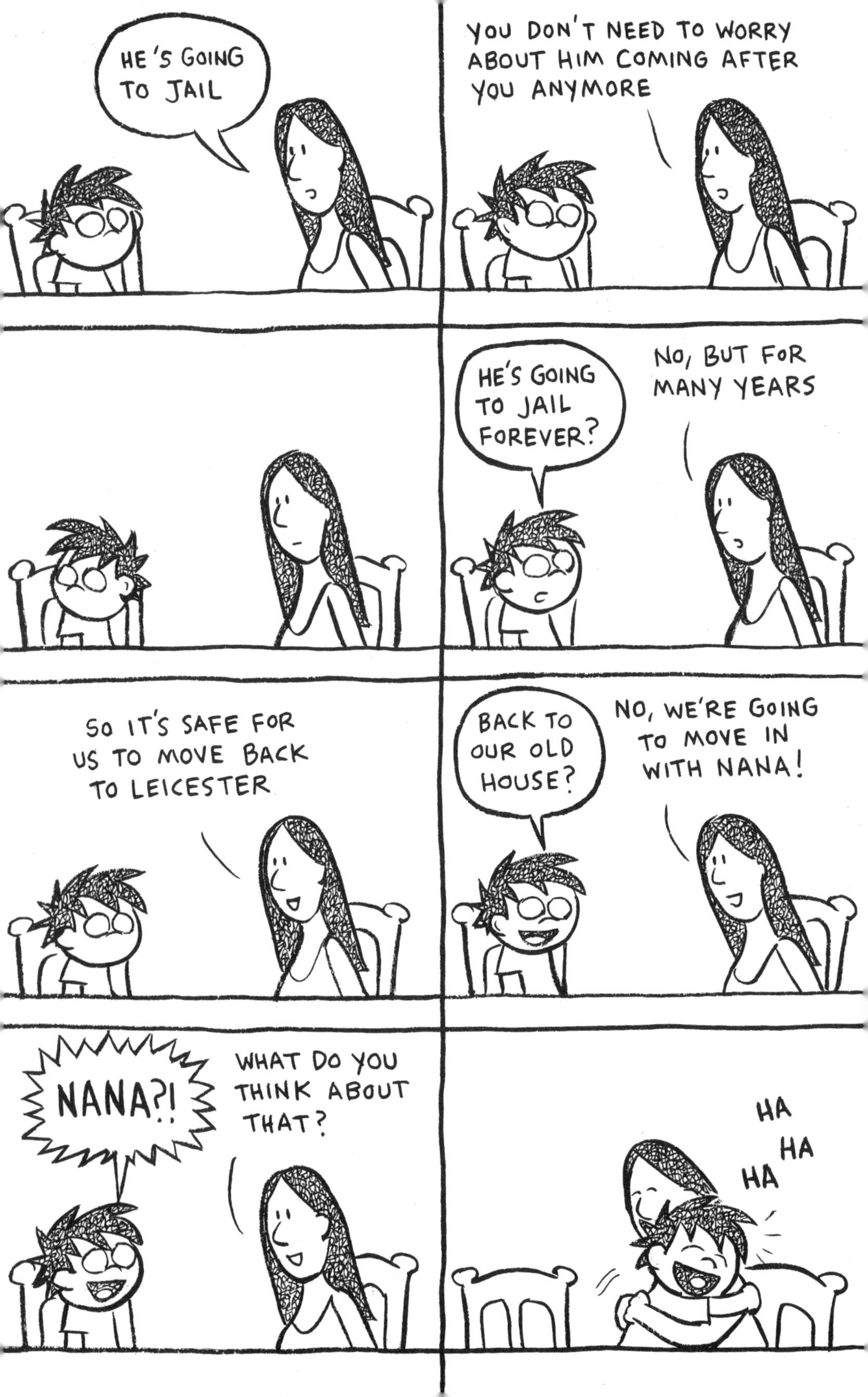
HE'S GOING TO JAIL
YOU DON'T NEED TO WORRY ABOUT HIM COMING AFTER YOU ANYMORE
HE'S GOING TO JAIL FOREVER?
NO, BUT FOR MANY YEARS
SO IT'S SAFE FOR US TO MOVE BACK TO LEICESTER
BACK TO OUR OLD HOUSE?
NO, WE'RE GOING TO MOVE IN WITH NANA!
NANA?!
WHAT DO YOU THINK ABOUT THAT?
HA
HA
HA

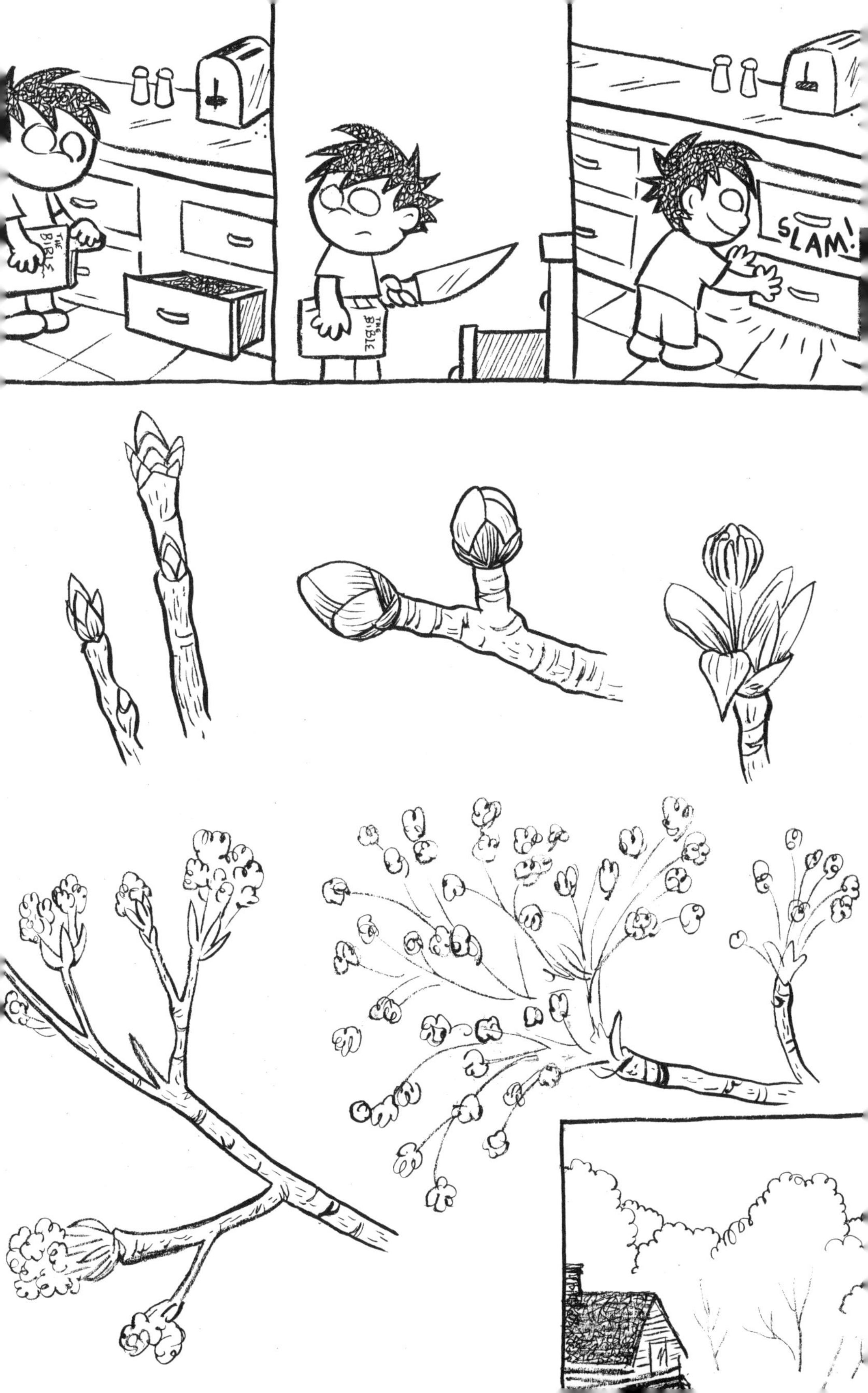
THE BIBLE
THE BIBLE
SLAM!

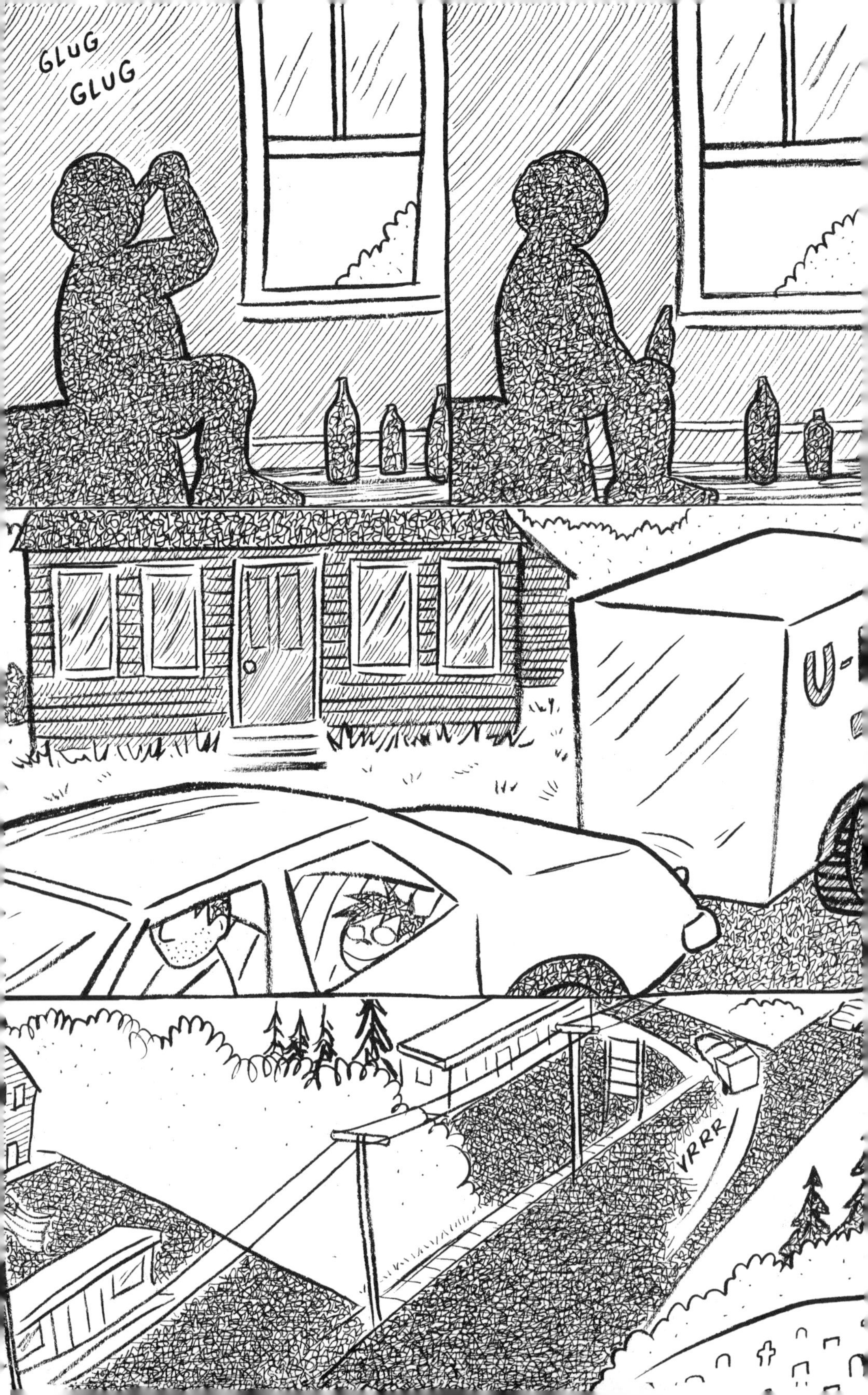
GLUG
GLUG
VRRR

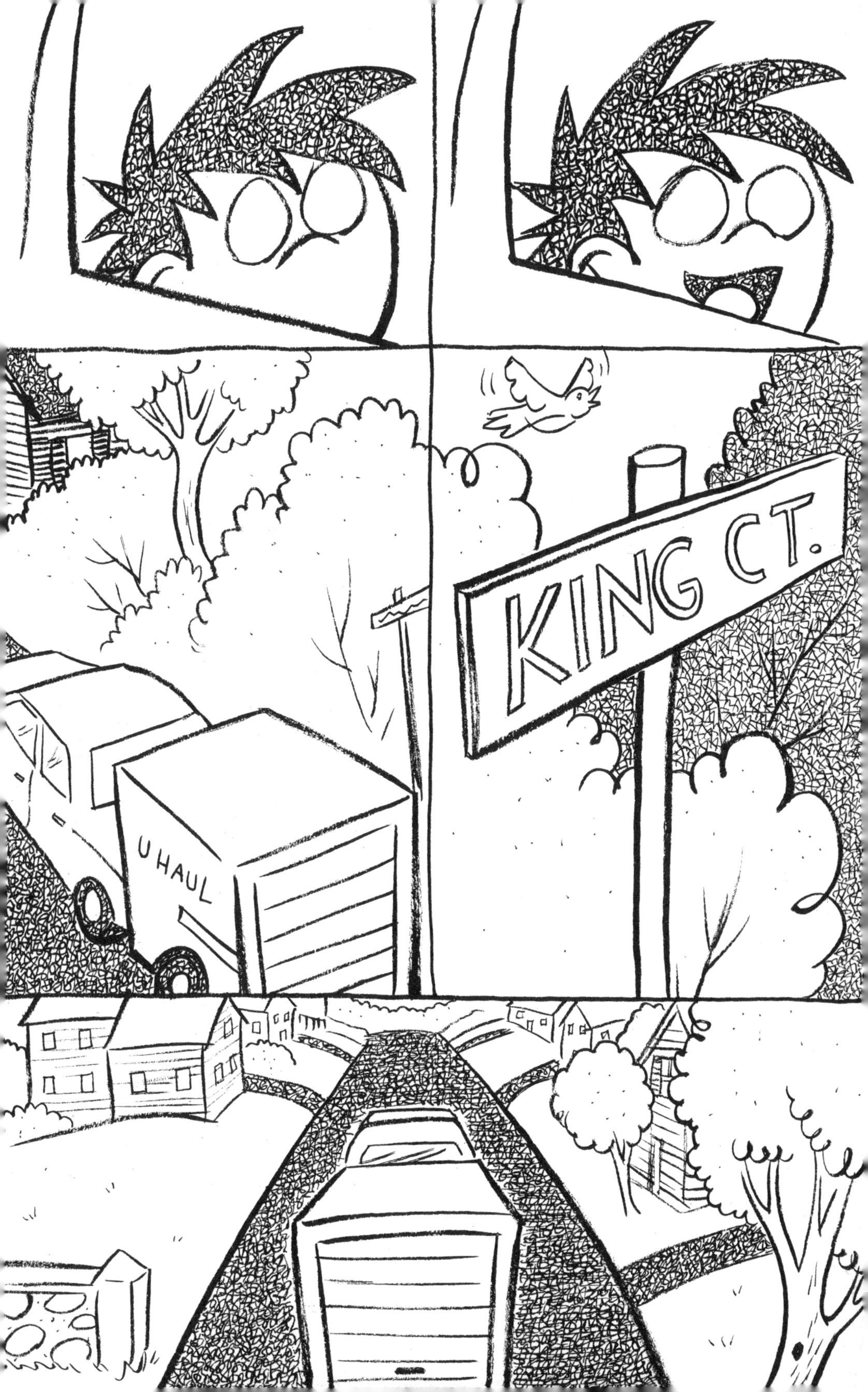
KING CT.
UHAUL

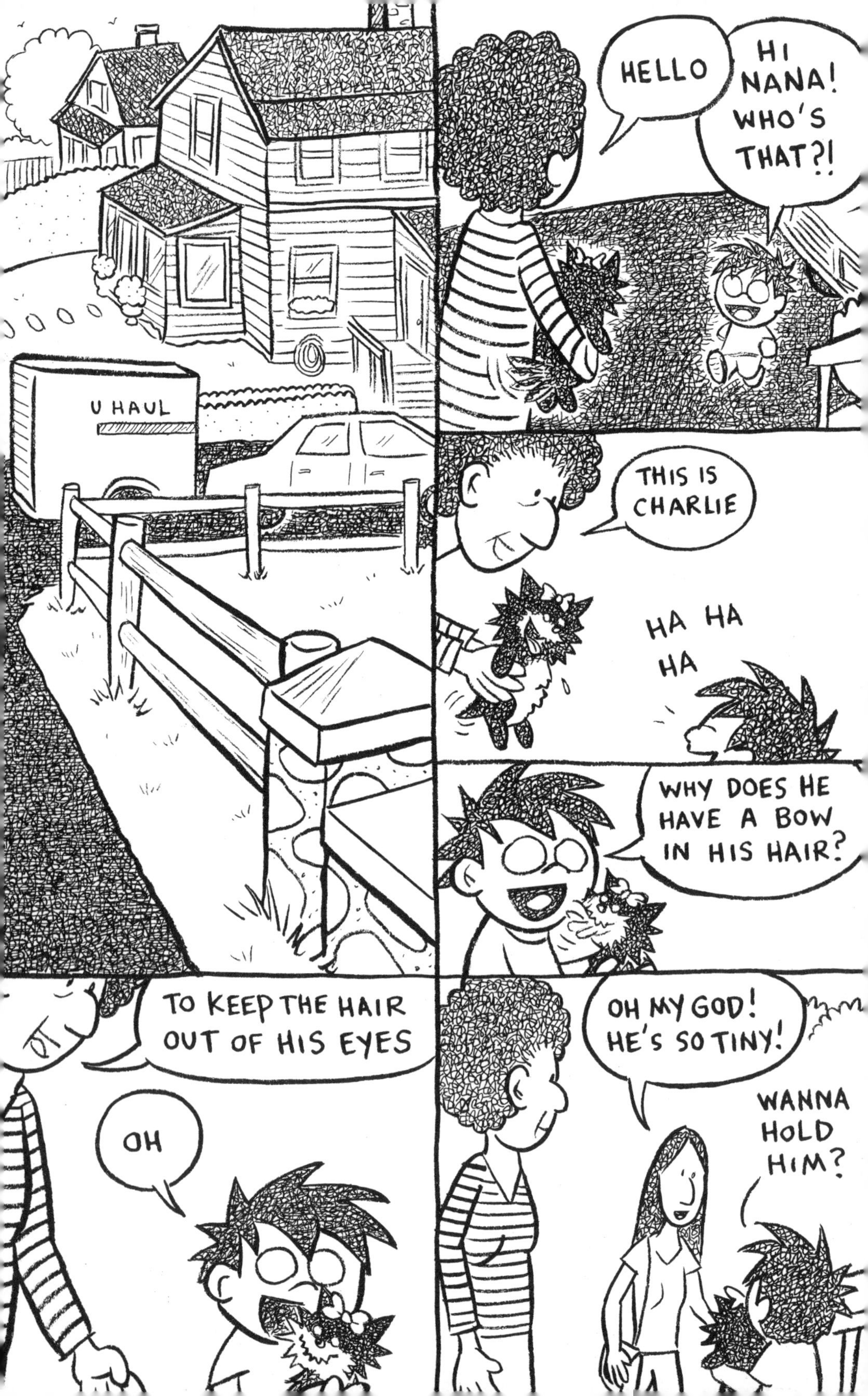
U HAUL
HELLO
HI NANA! WHO'S THAT?!
THIS IS CHARLIE
HA HA HA
WHY DOES HE HAVE A BOW IN HIS HAIR?
TO KEEP THE HAIR OUT OF HIS EYES
OH
OH MY GOD! HE'S SO TINY!
WANNA HOLD HIM?

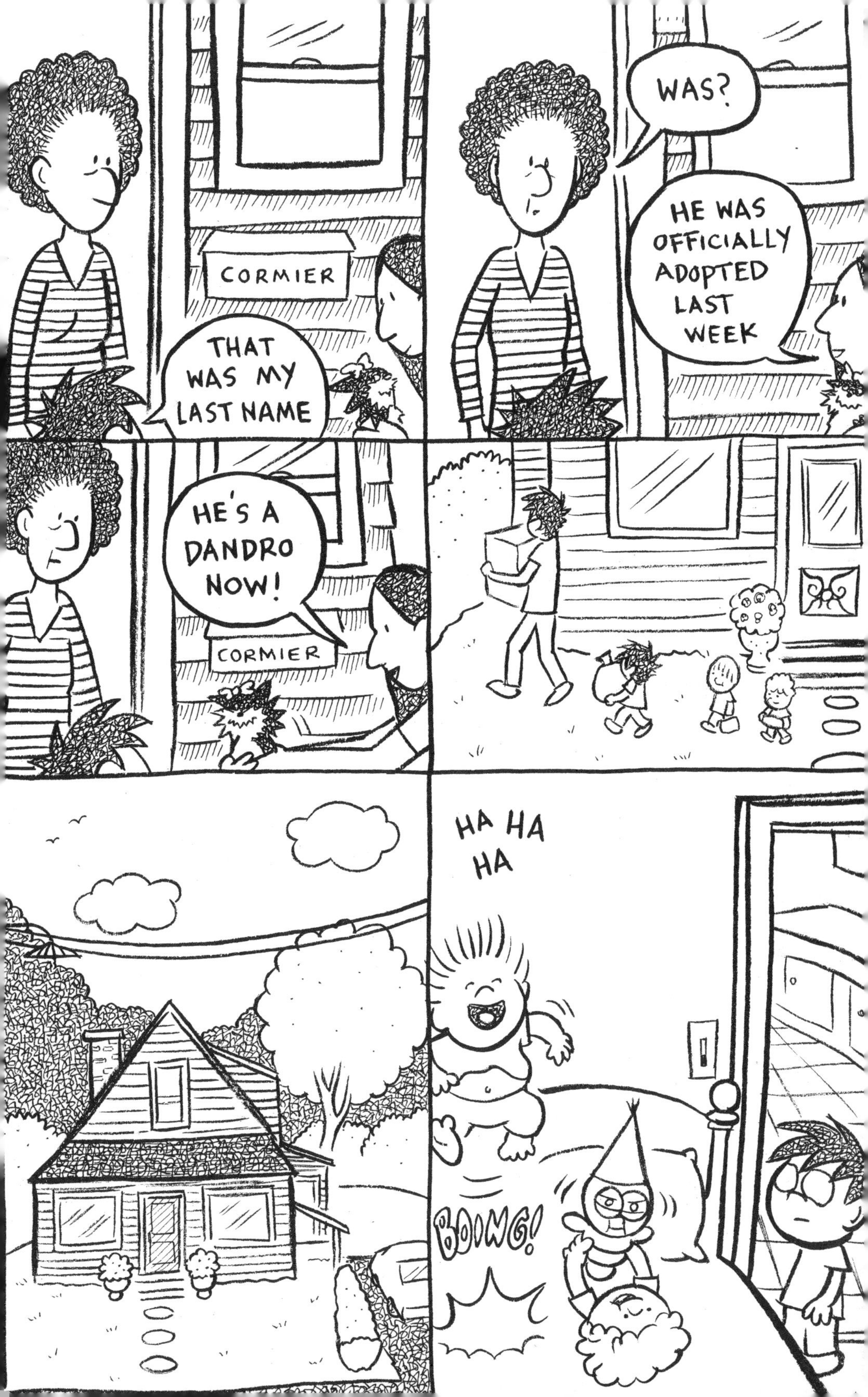
CORMIER
THAT WAS MY LAST NAME
WAS?
HE WAS OFFICIALLY ADOPTED LAST WEEK
HE'S A DANDRO NOW!
CORMIER
HA HA HA
BOING!

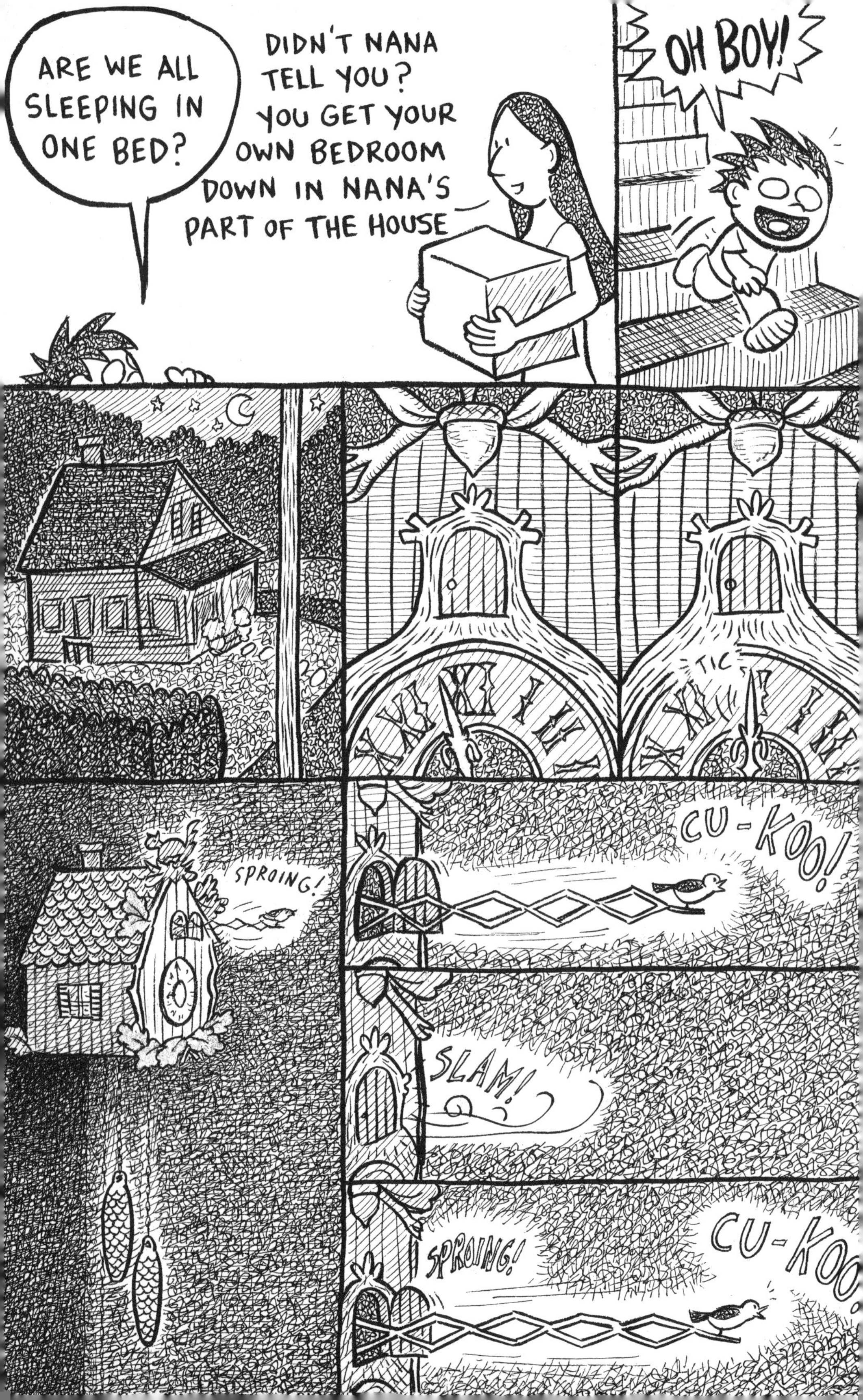
ARE WE ALL SLEEPING IN ONE BED?
DIDN'T NANA TELL YOU? YOU GET YOUR OWN BEDROOM DOWN IN NANA'S PART OF THE HOUSE
OH BOY!
TIC
SPROING!
CU-KOO!
SLAM!
SPROING!
CU-KOO

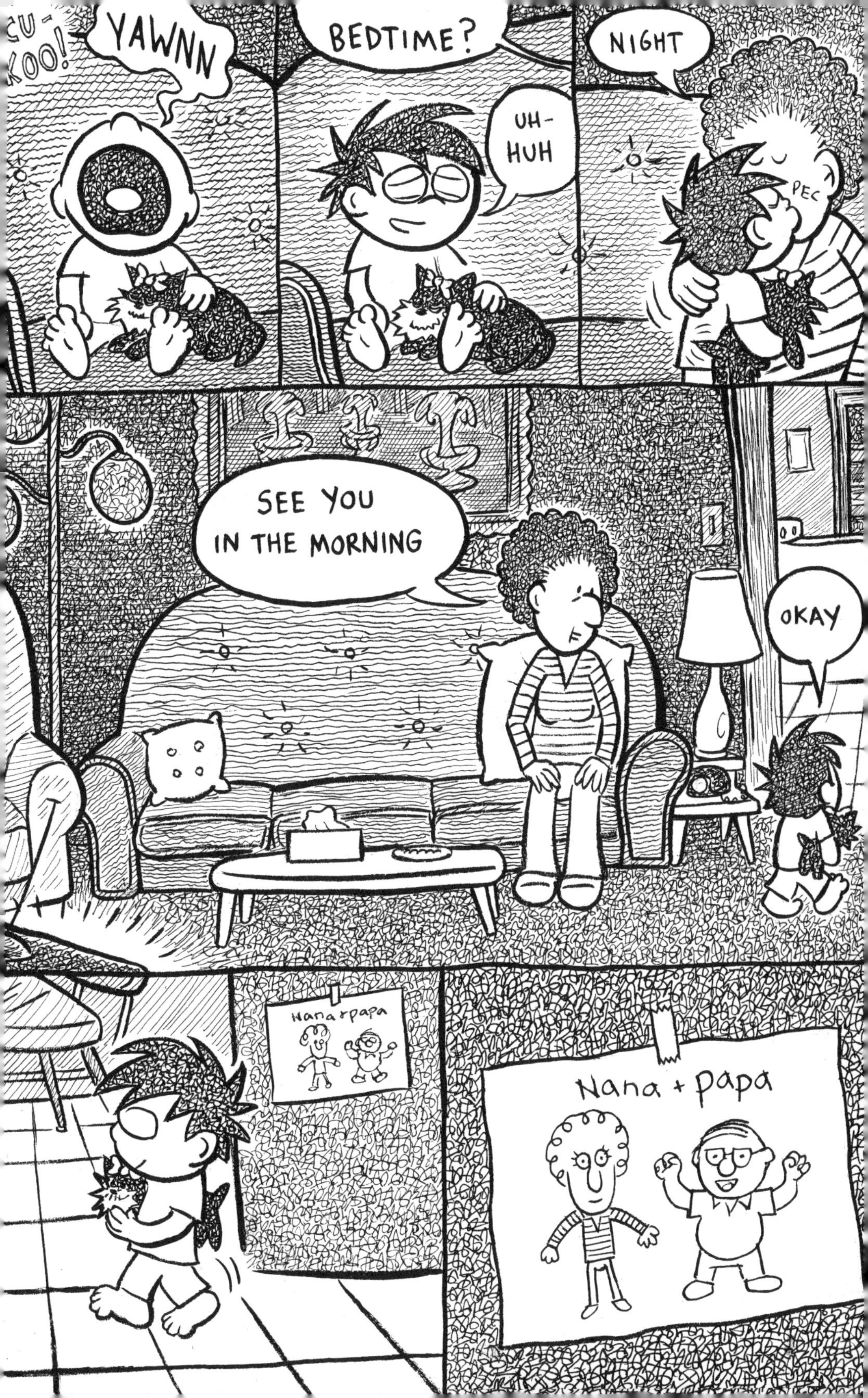
CU-KOO!
YAWNN
BEDTIME?
UH-HUH
NIGHT
PEC
SEE YOU IN THE MORNING
OKAY
Nana + papa
Nana + papa

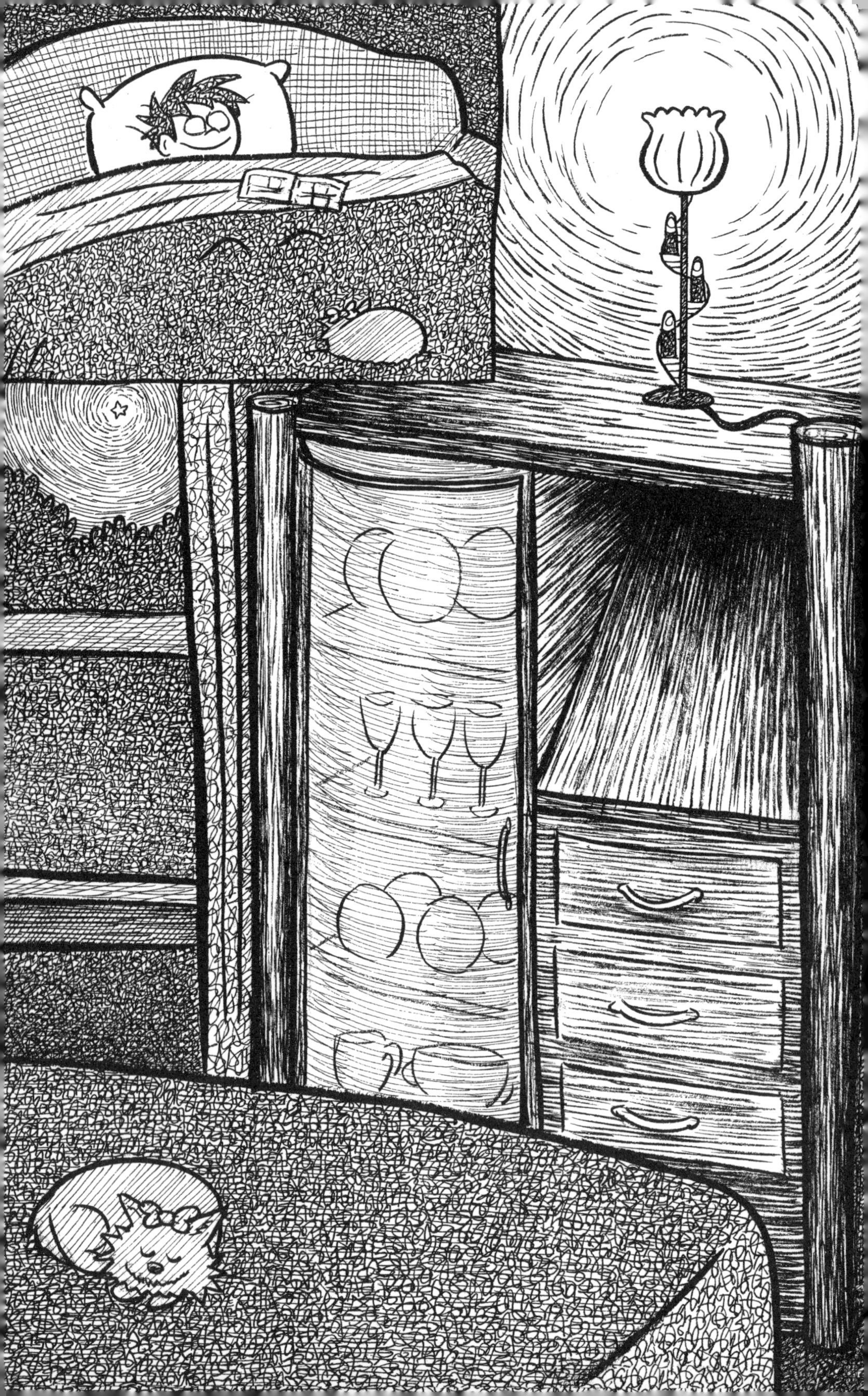

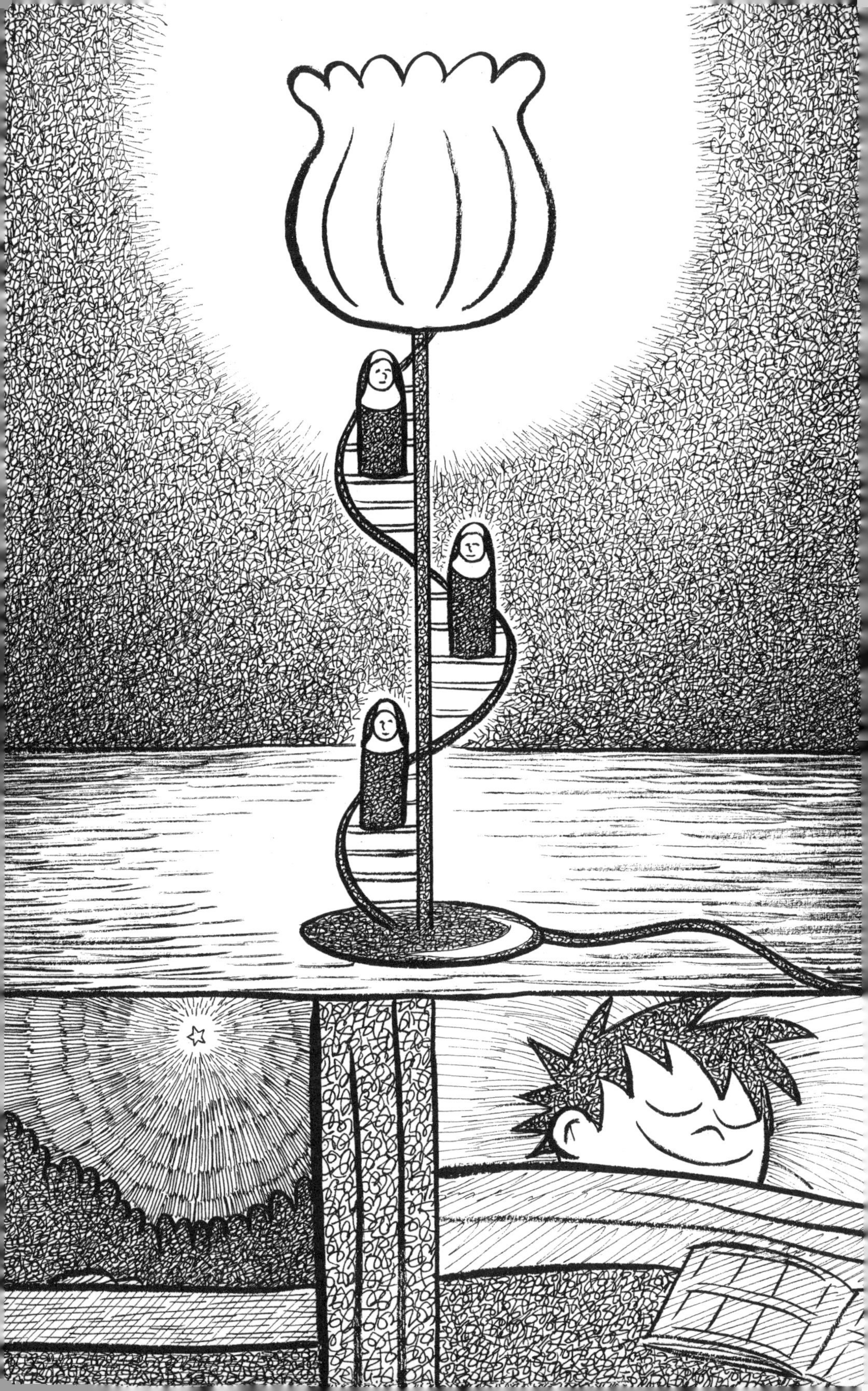

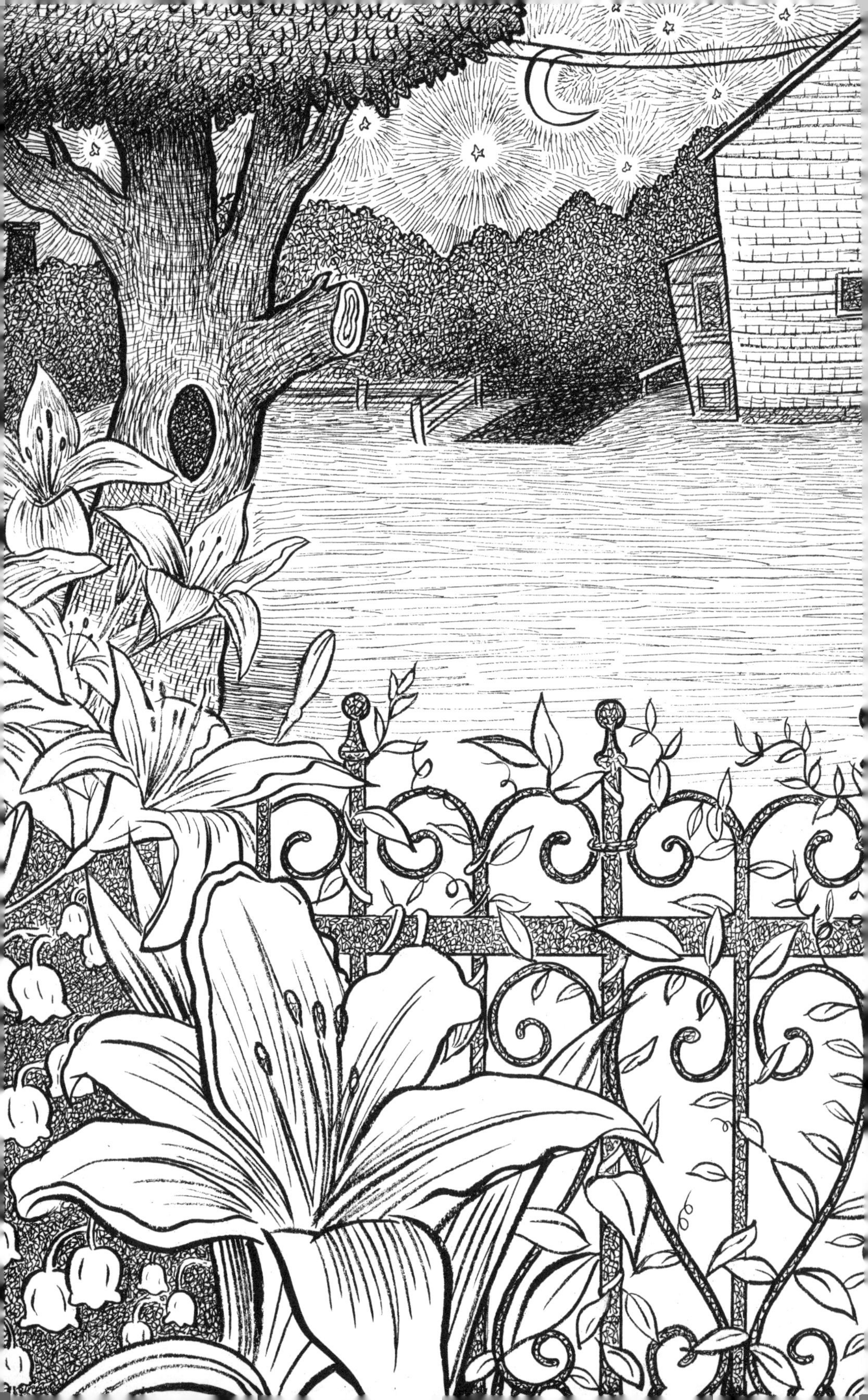

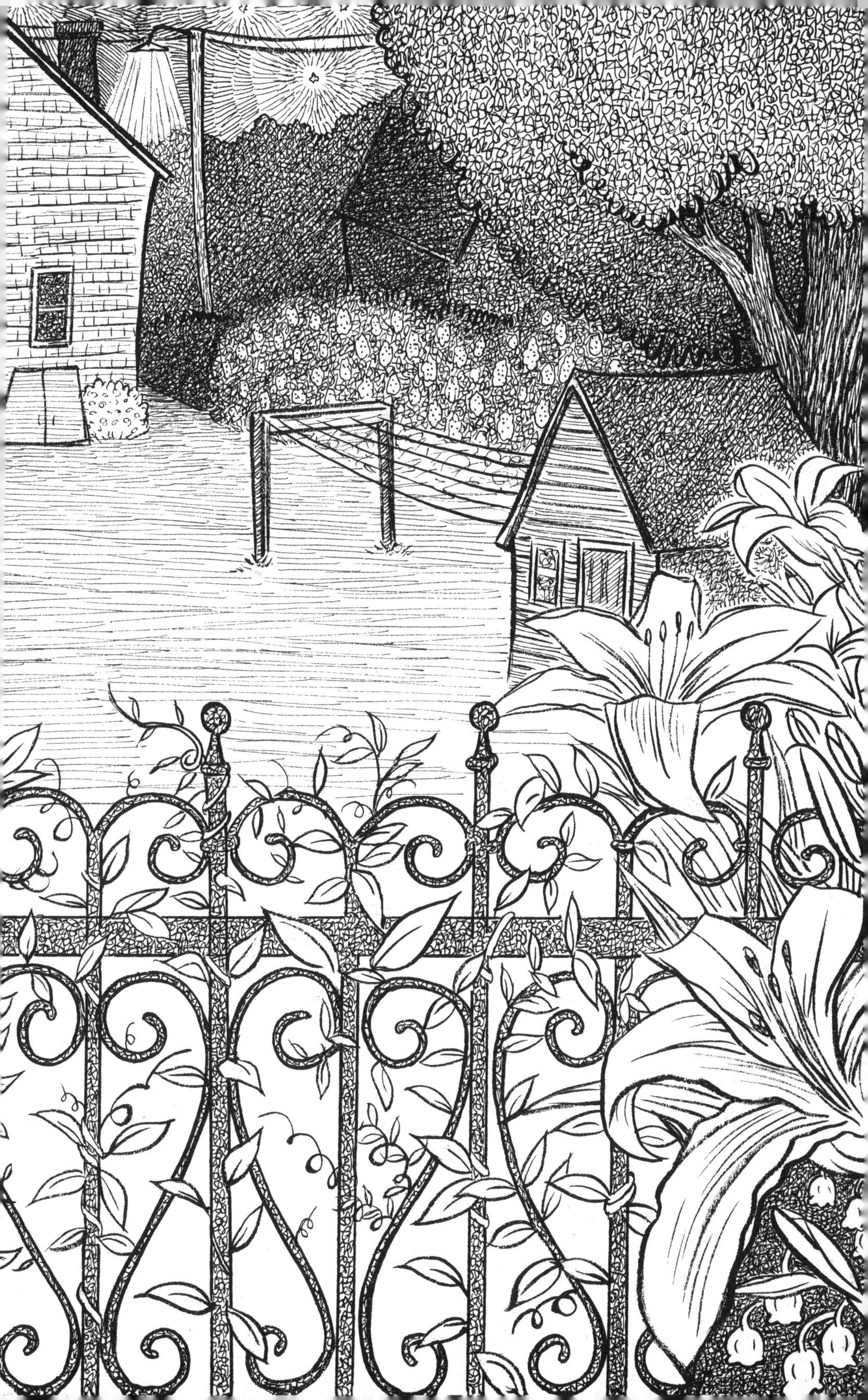

Eight Years Later

(1990)

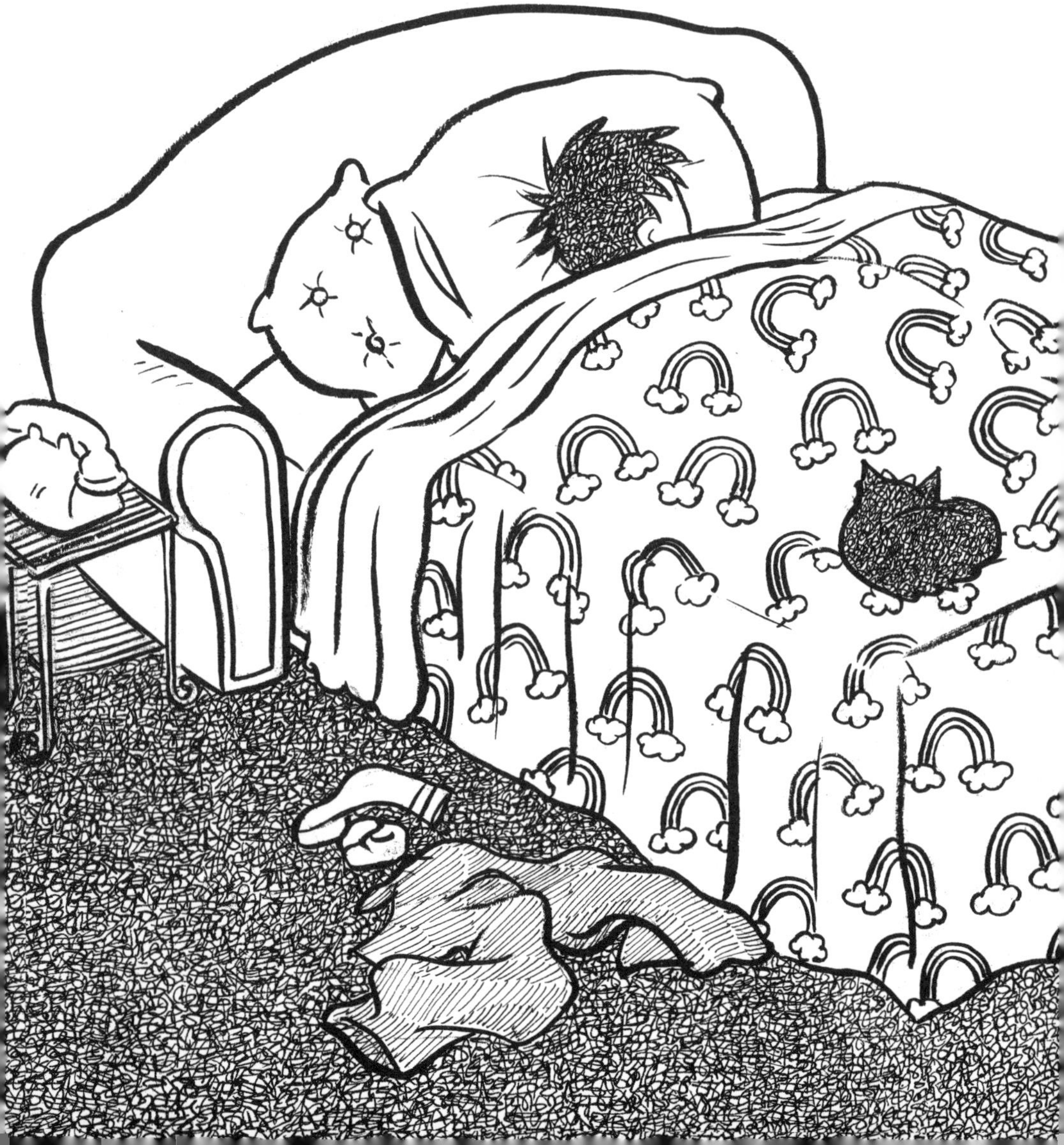

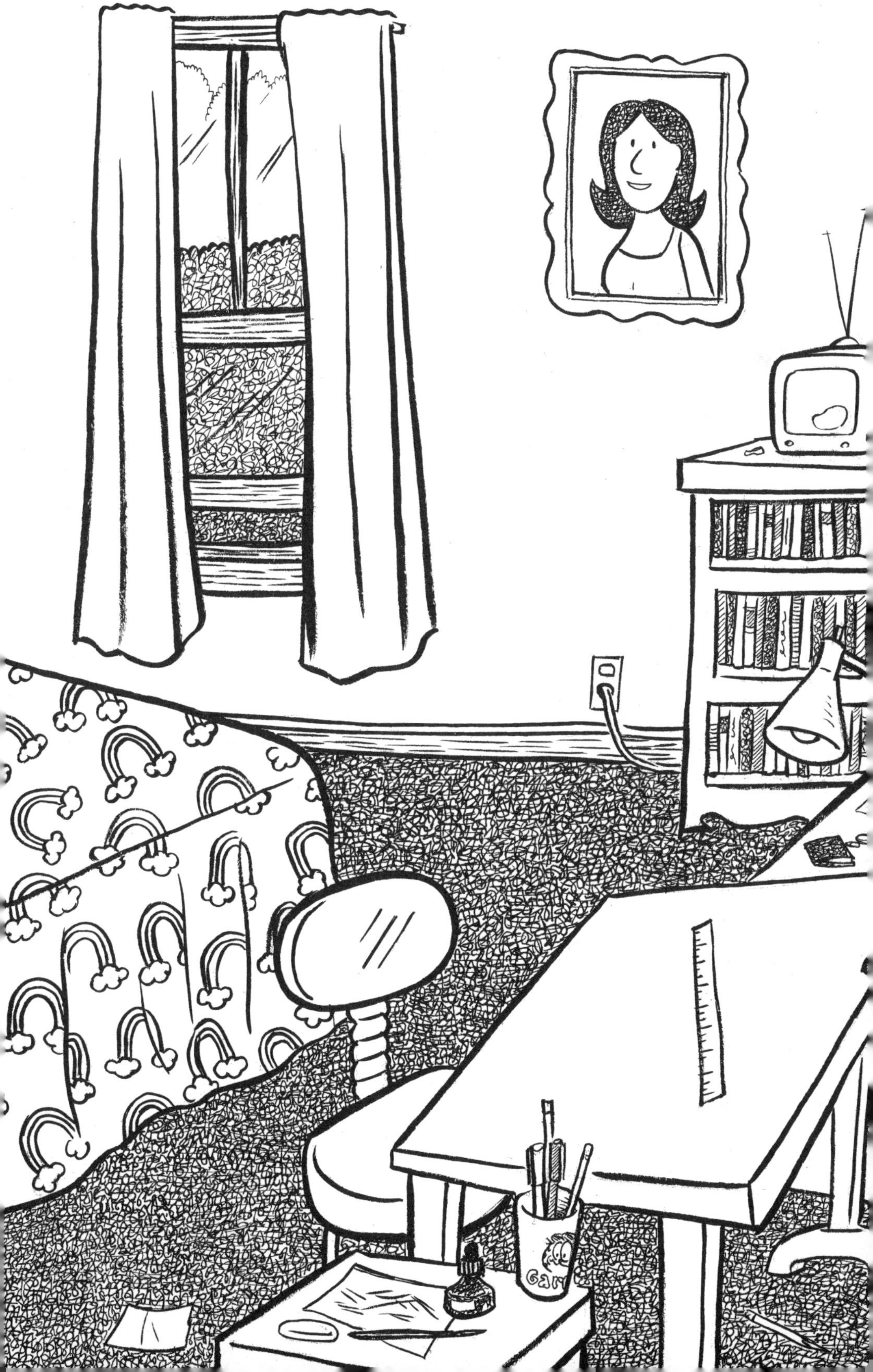

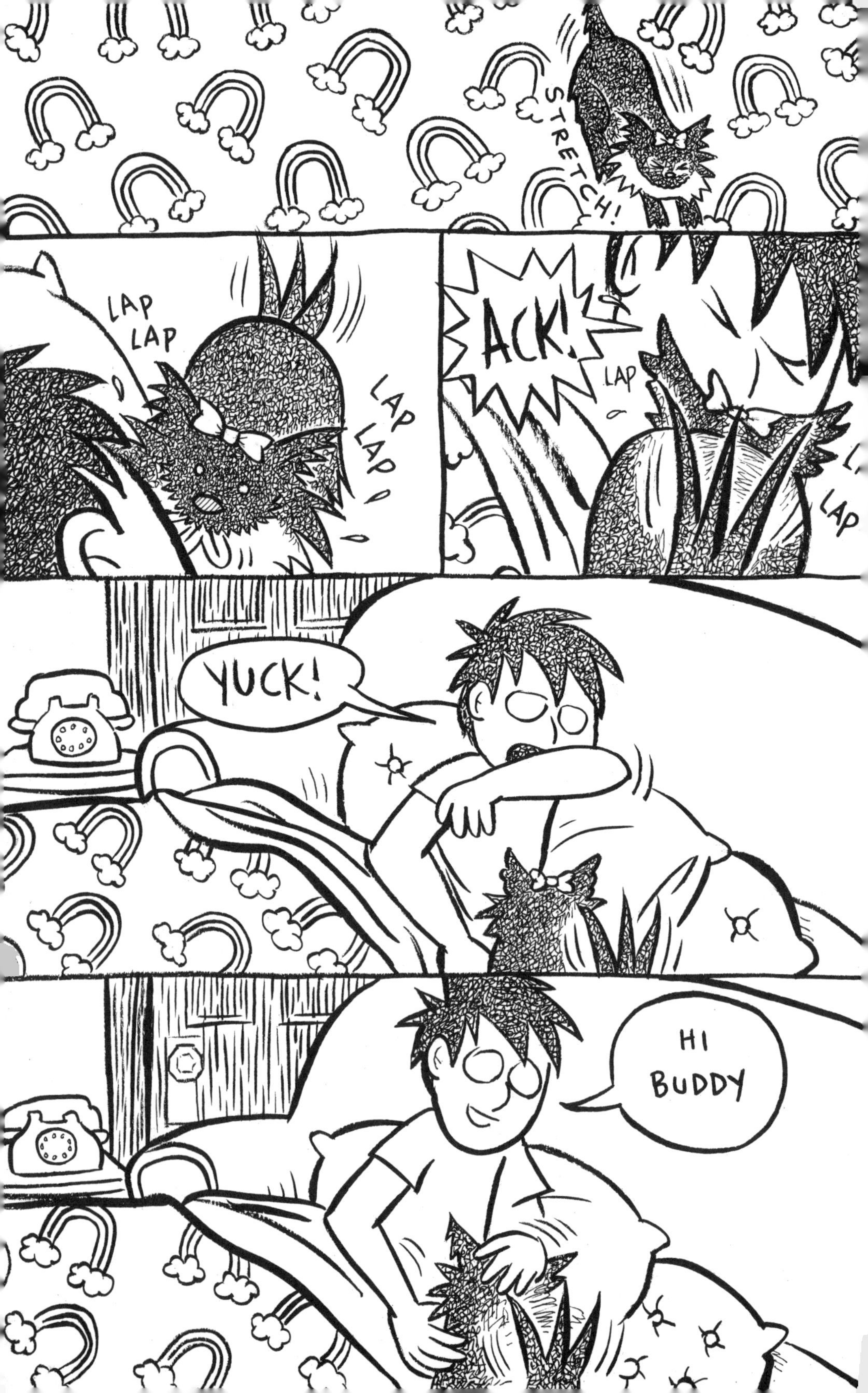
STRETCH!
LAP LAP
LAP LAP
ACK!
LAP
LAP
YUCK!
HI BUDDY

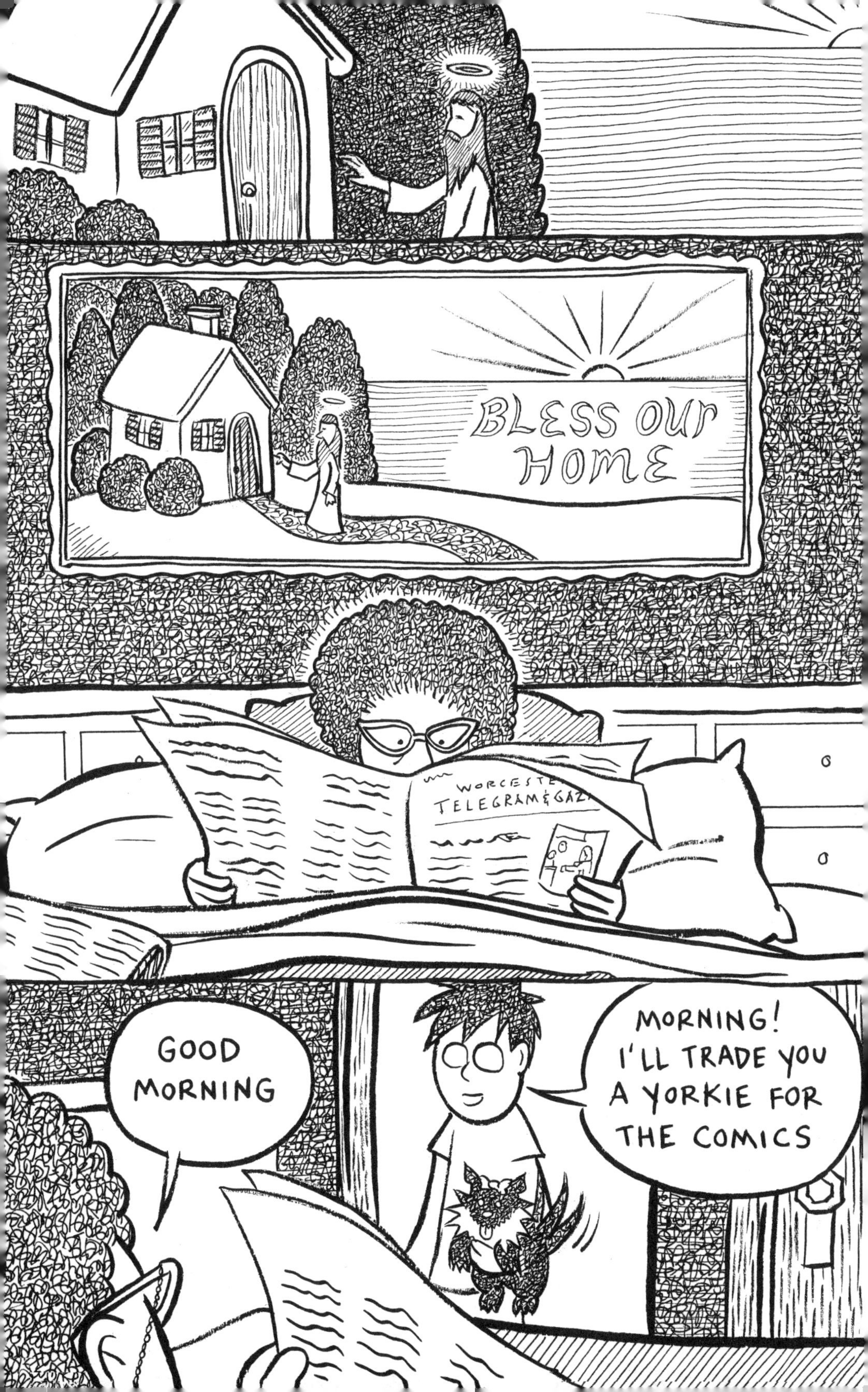
BLESS OUR HOME
WORCESTER
TELEGRAM & GAZ
GOOD MORNING
MORNING! I'LL TRADE YOU A YORKIE FOR THE COMICS

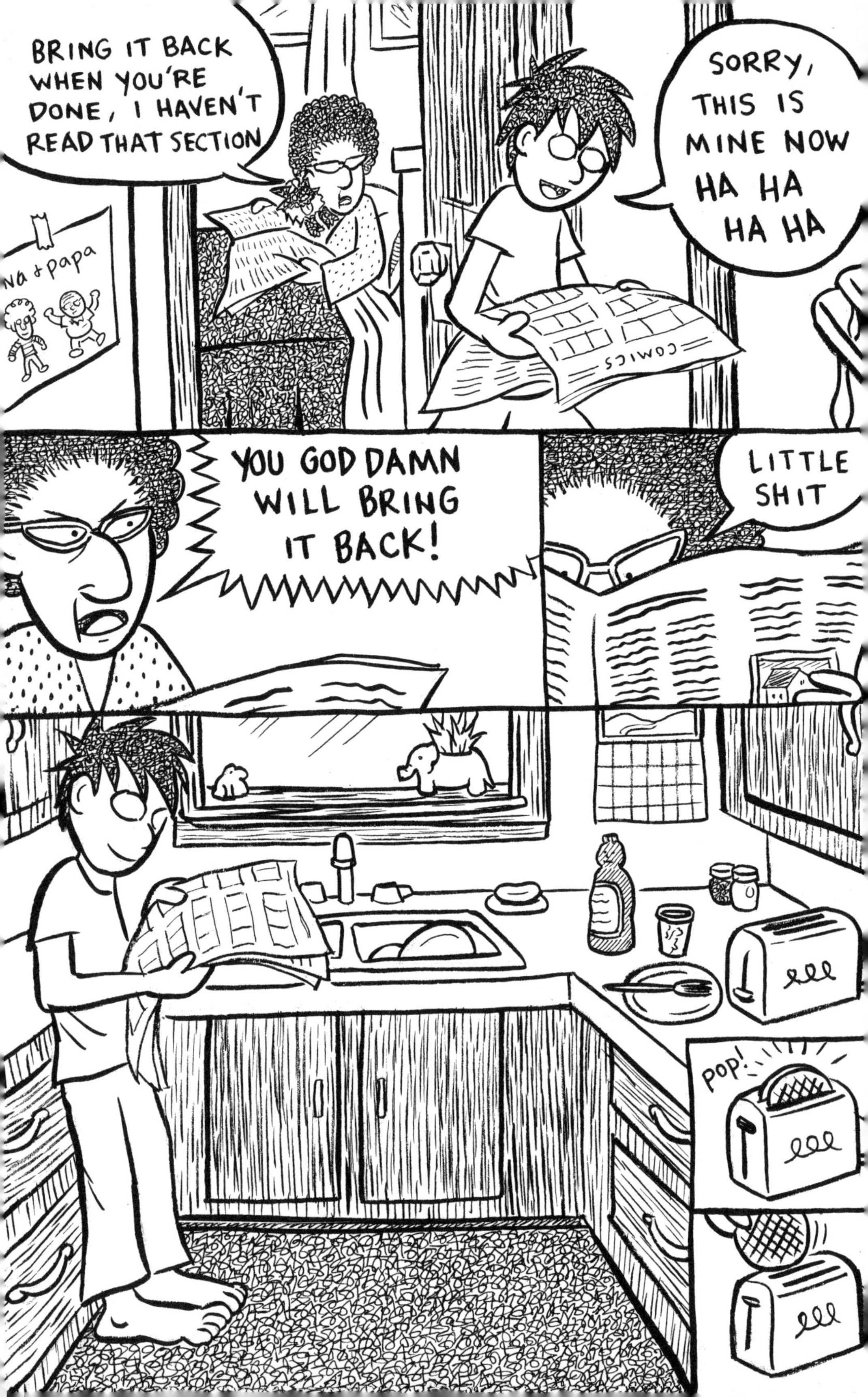
BRING IT BACK WHEN YOU'RE DONE, I HAVEN'T READ THAT SECTION
SORRY, THIS IS MINE NOW HA HA HA HA
Na & papa
COMICS
YOU GOD DAMN WILL BRING IT BACK!
LITTLE SHIT
POP!

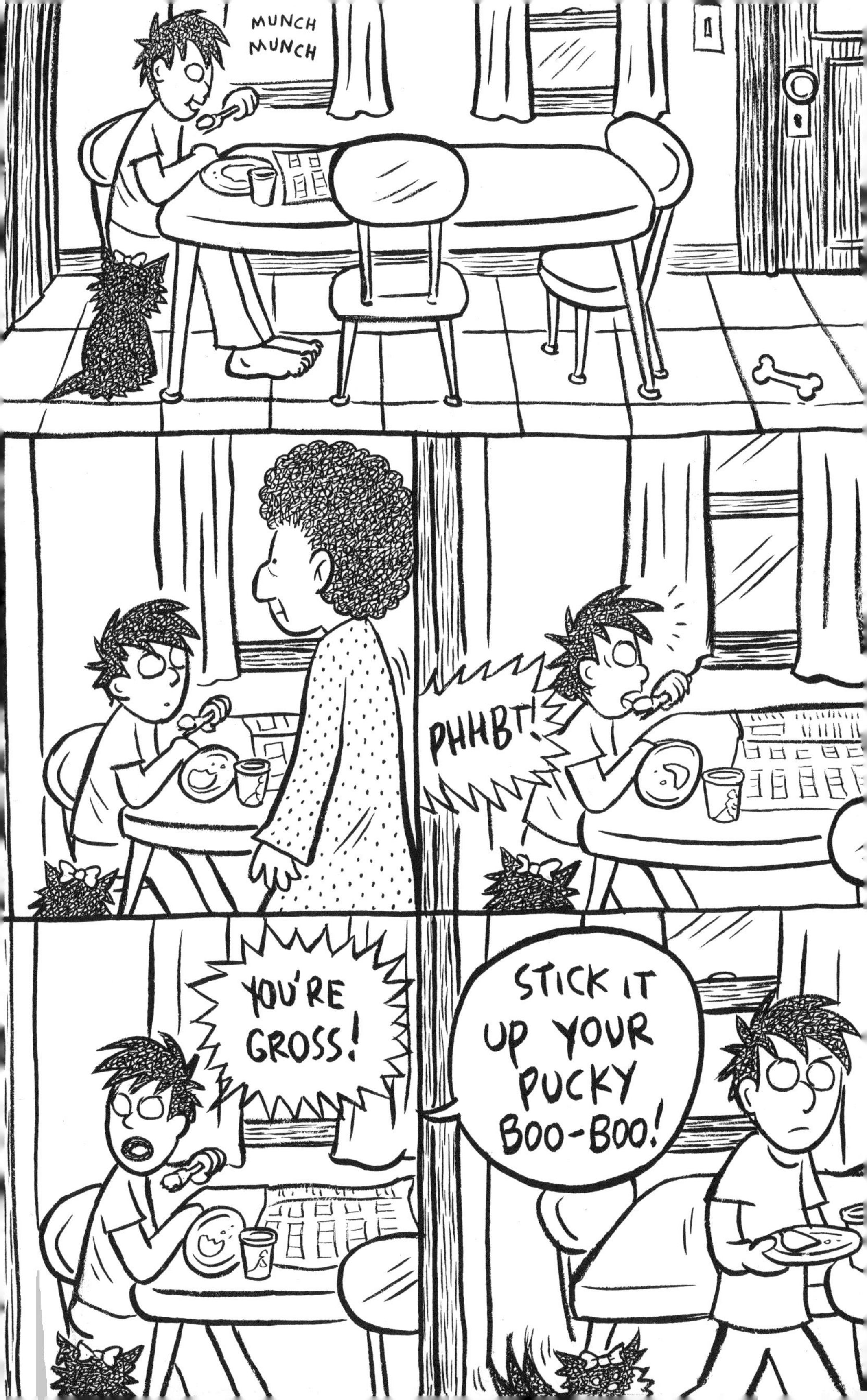
MUNCH
MUNCH
PHHBT!
YOU'RE GROSS!
STICK IT UP YOUR PUCKY BOO-BOO!

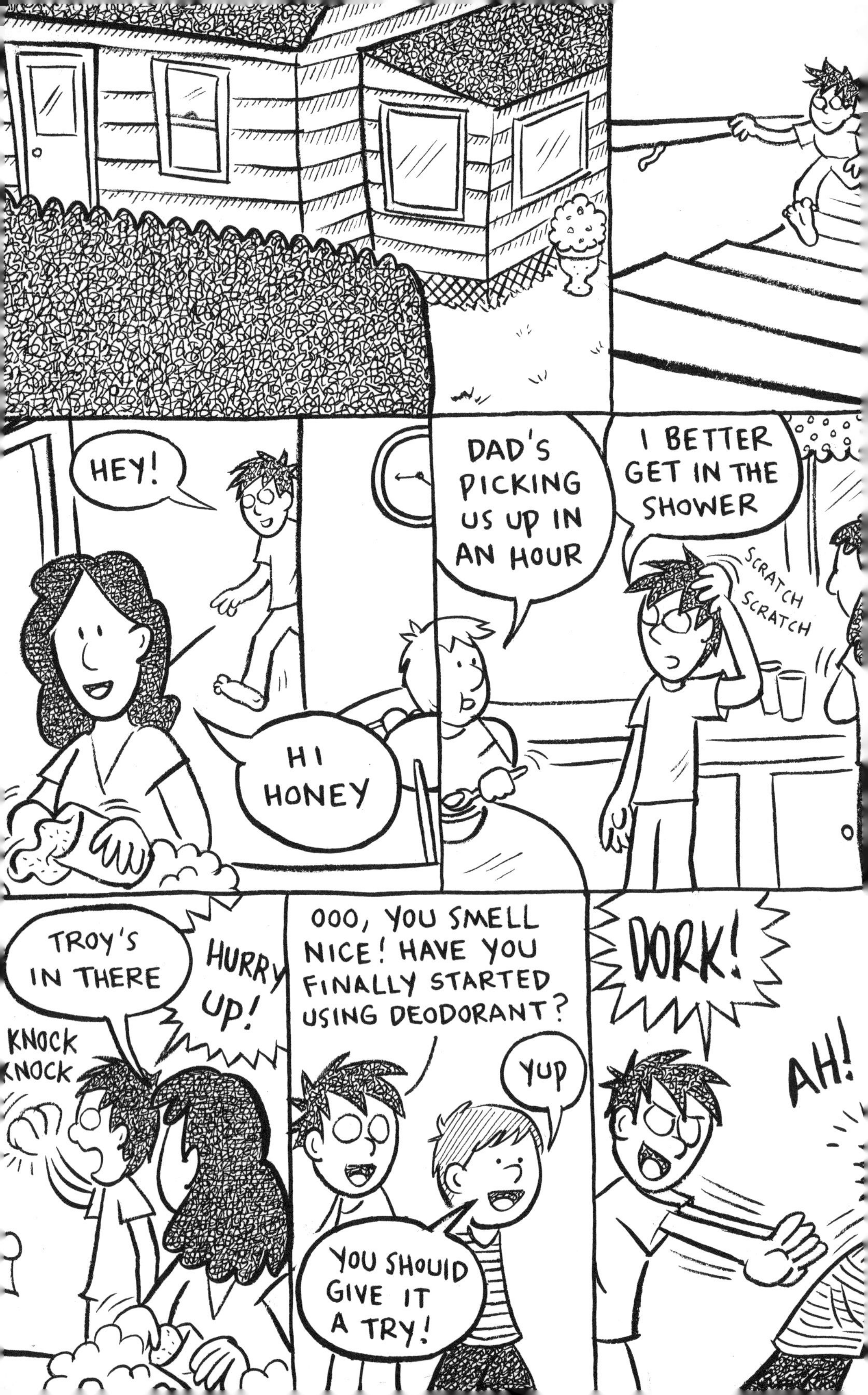
HEY!
HI HONEY
DAD'S PICKING US UP IN AN HOUR
I BETTER GET IN THE SHOWER
SCRATCH SCRATCH
TROY'S IN THERE
HURRY UP!
KNOCK KNOCK
OOO, YOU SMELL NICE! HAVE YOU FINALLY STARTED USING DEODORANT?
YUP
YOU SHOUID GIVE IT A TRY!
DORK!
AH!

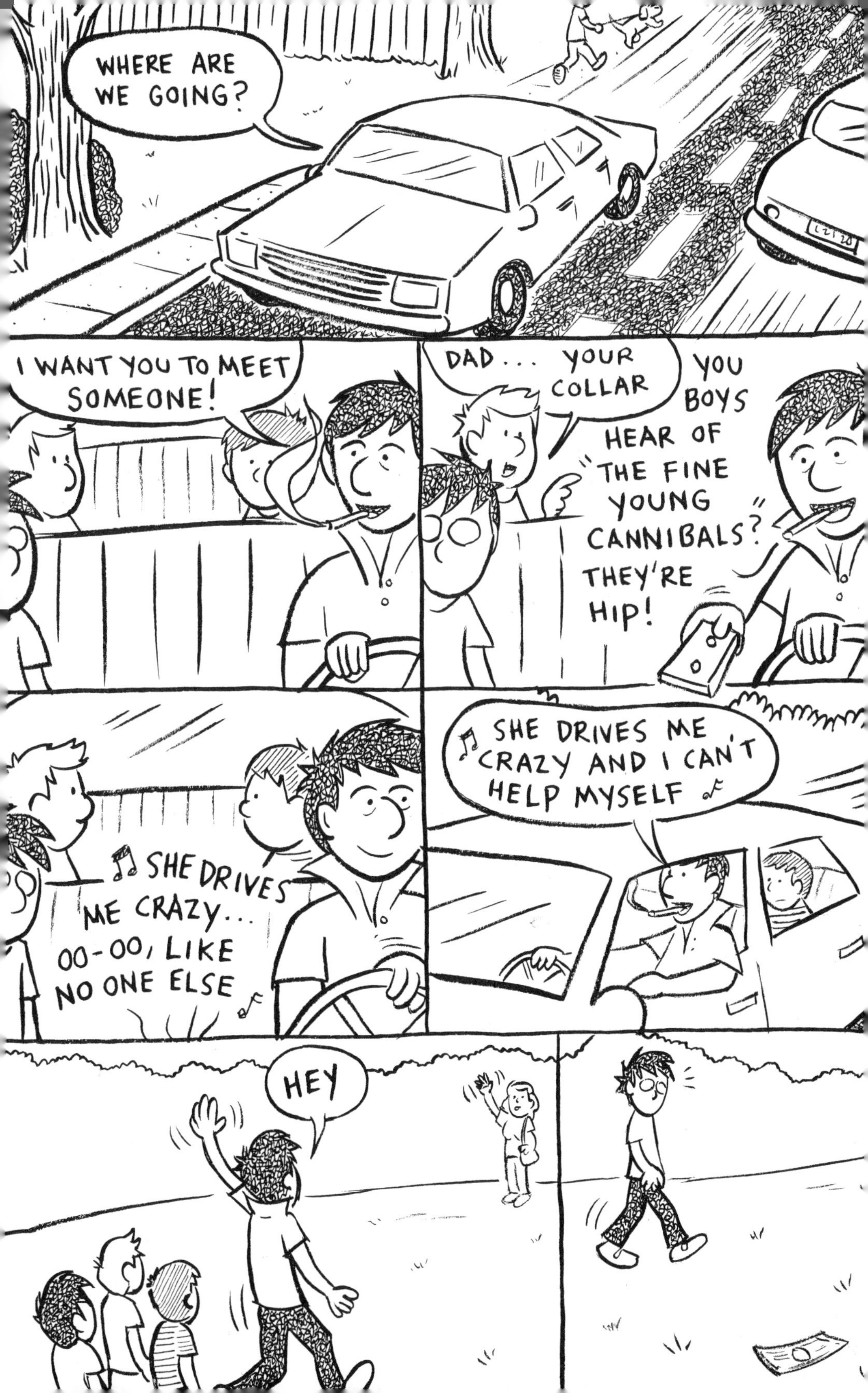
WHERE ARE WE GOING?
I WANT YOU TO MEET SOMEONE!
DAD... YOUR COLLAR
YOU BOYS HEAR OF THE FINE YOUNG CANNIBALS? THEY'RE HIP!
♫ SHE DRIVES ME CRAZY... OO-OO, LIKE NO ONE ELSE ♫
♫ SHE DRIVES ME CRAZY AND I CAN'T HELP MYSELF ♫
HEY

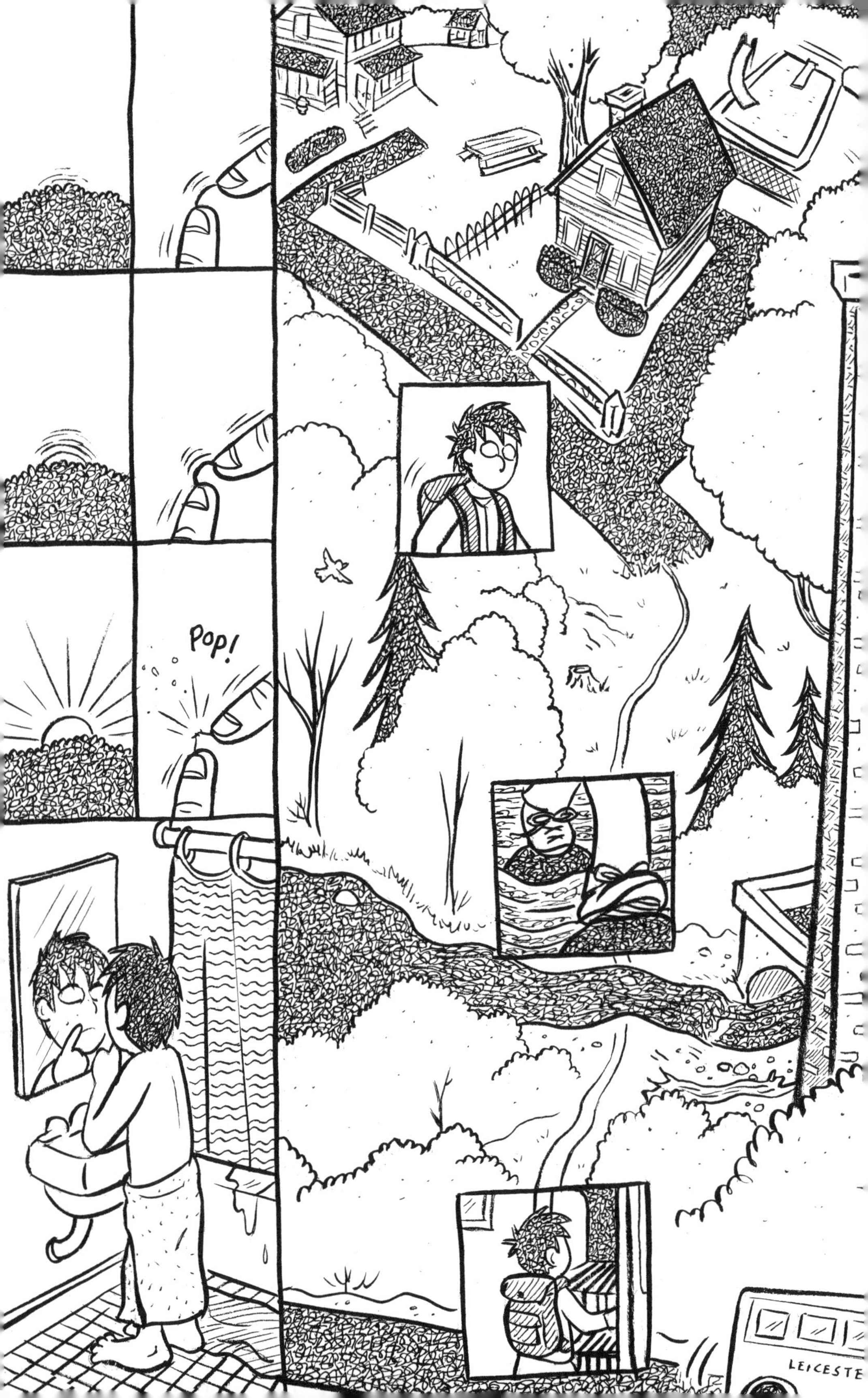
Pop!
LEICESTE

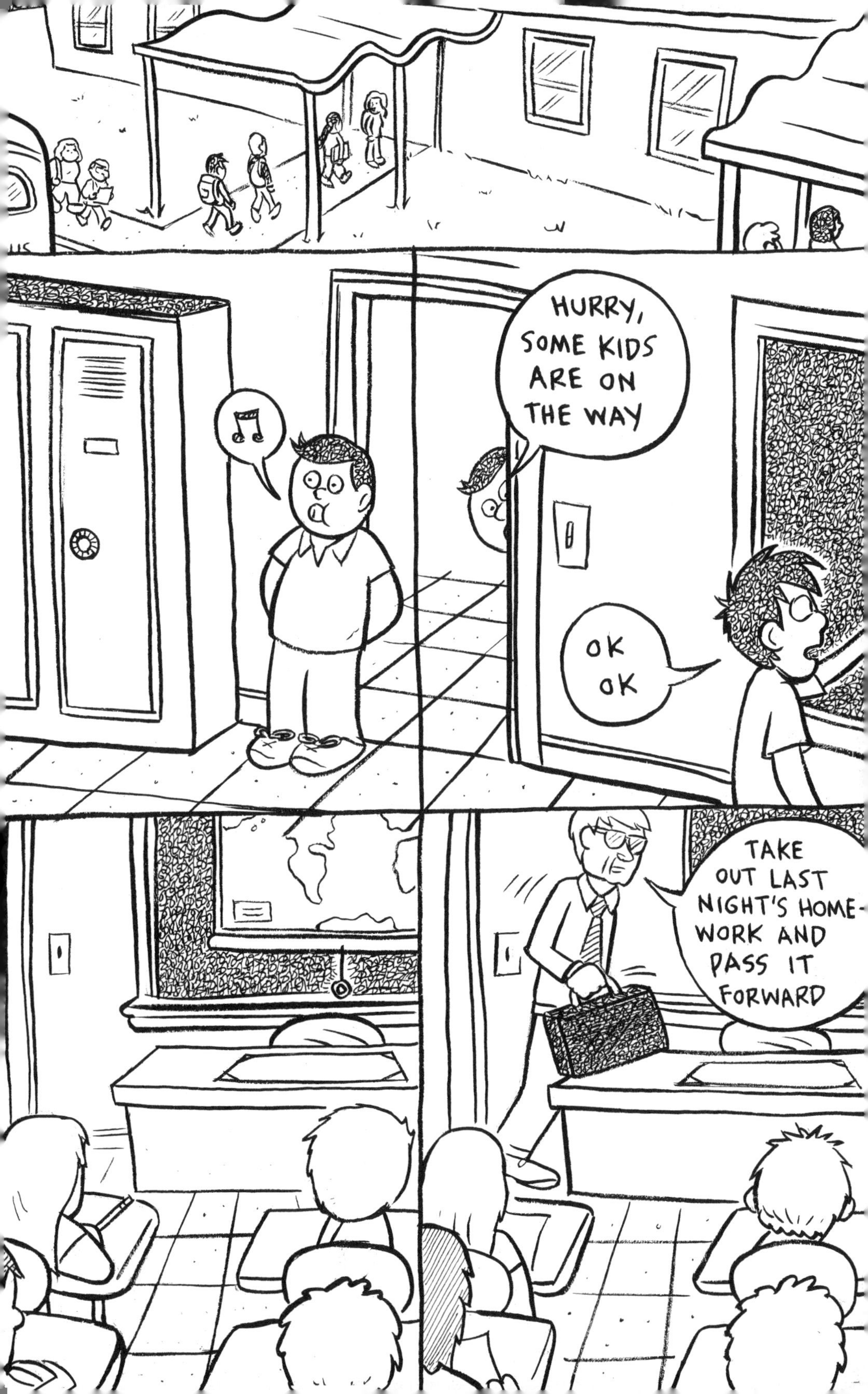
HURRY, SOME KIDS ARE ON THE WAY
OK OK
TAKE OUT LAST NIGHT'S HOME-WORK AND PASS IT FORWARD

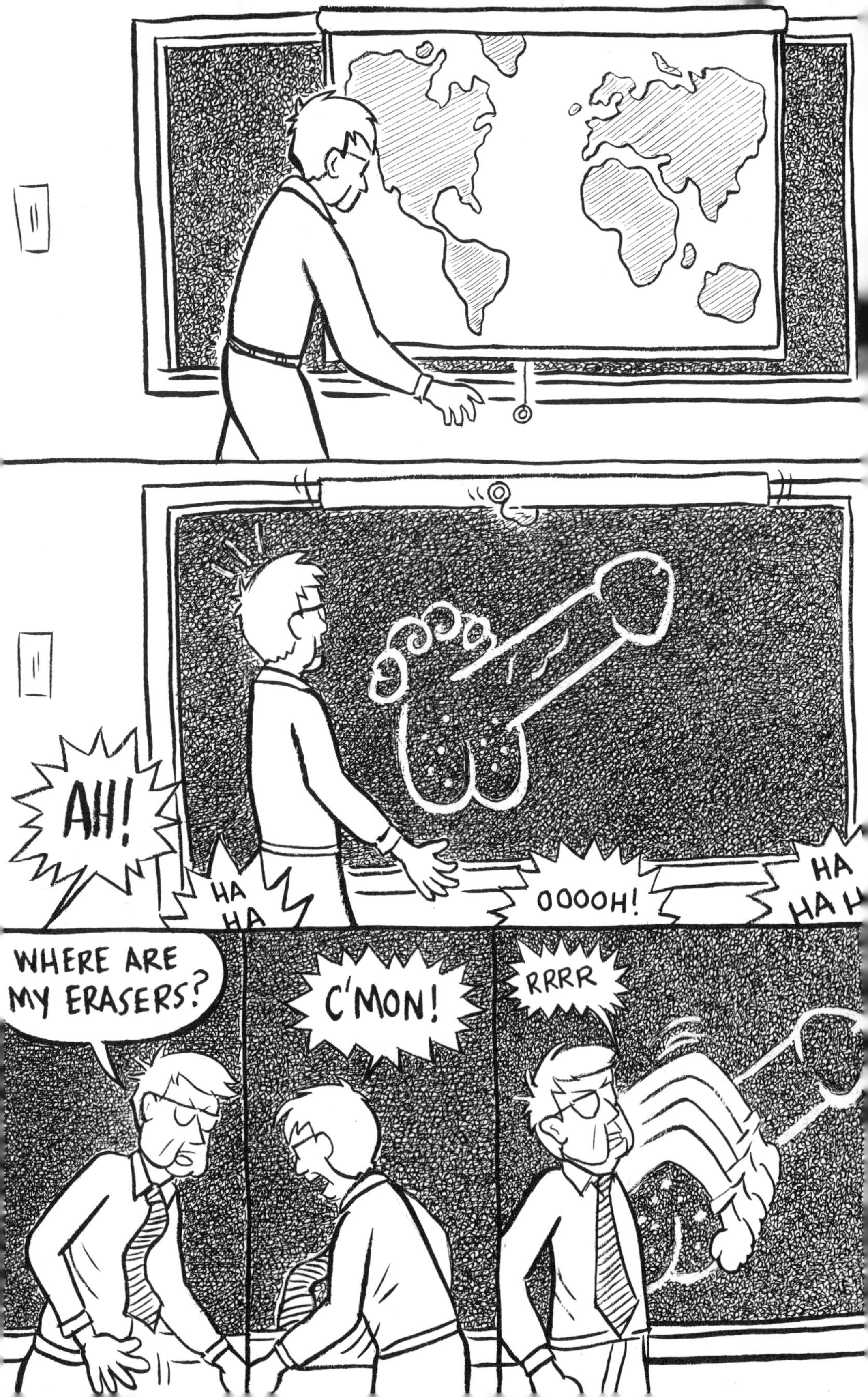
AH!
HA HA
OOOOH!
HA HA HA
WHERE ARE MY ERASERS?
C'MON!
RRRR

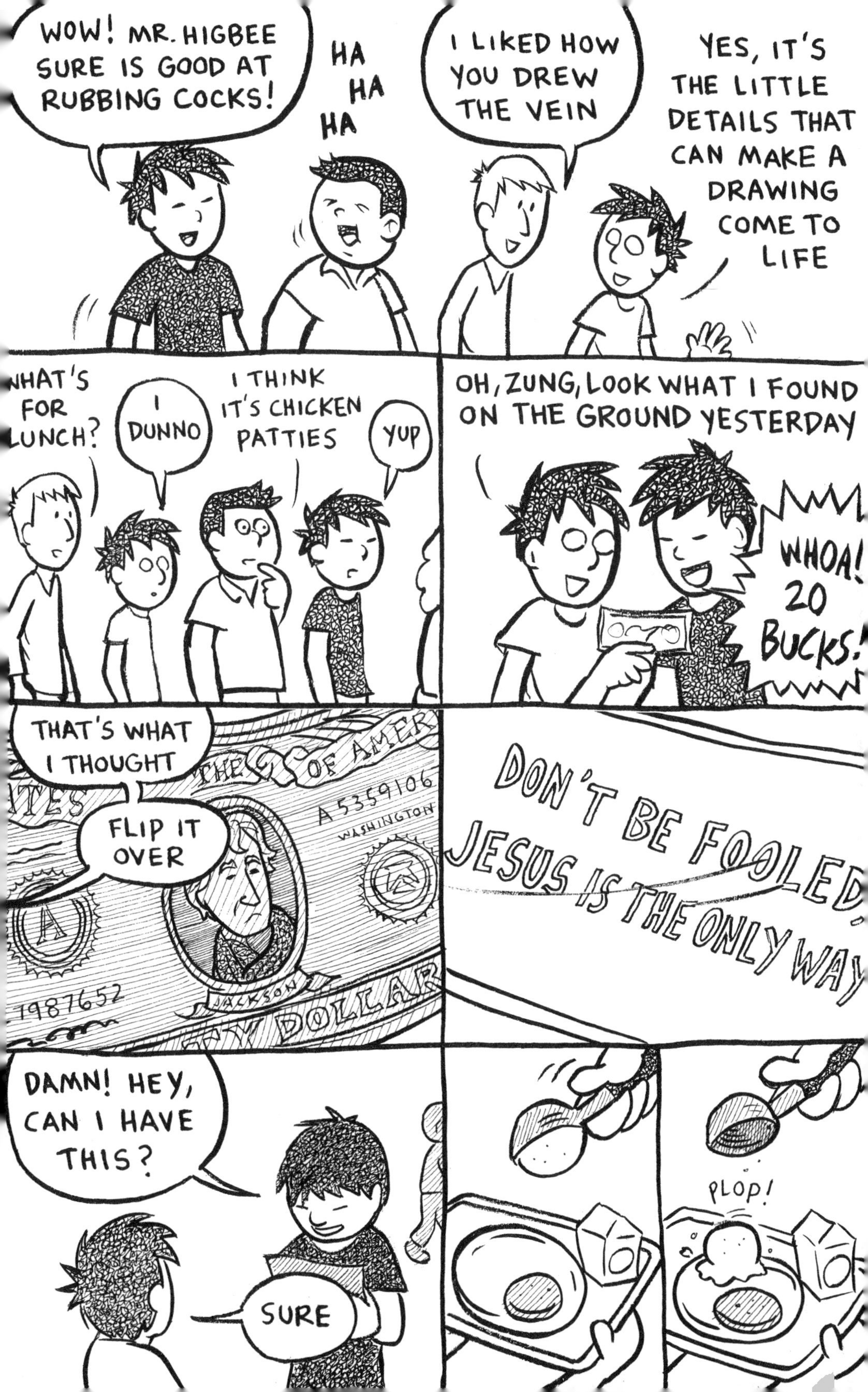
WOW! MR. HIGBEE SURE IS GOOD AT RUBBING COCKS!
HA HA HA
I LIKED HOW YOU DREW THE VEIN
YES, IT'S THE LITTLE DETAILS THAT CAN MAKE A DRAWING COME TO LIFE
WHAT'S FOR LUNCH?
I DUNNO
I THINK IT'S CHICKEN PATTIES
YUP
OH, ZUNG, LOOK WHAT I FOUND ON THE GROUND YESTERDAY
WHOA! 20 BUCKS!
THAT'S WHAT I THOUGHT
FLIP IT OVER
DON'T BE FOOLED, JESUS IS THE ONLY WAY
DAMN! HEY, CAN I HAVE THIS?
SURE
PLOP!

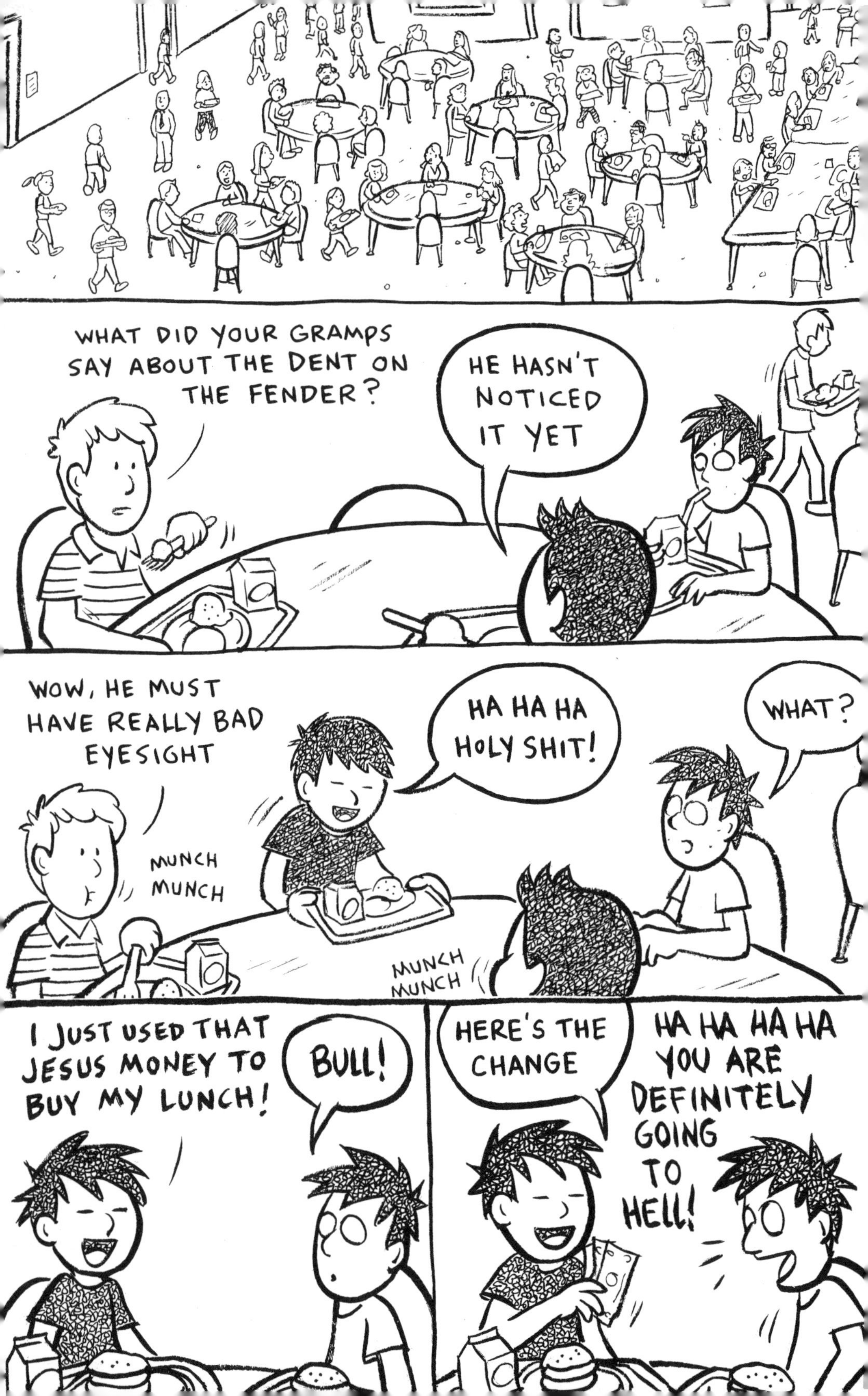
WHAT DID YOUR GRAMPS SAY ABOUT THE DENT ON THE FENDER?
HE HASN'T NOTICED IT YET
WOW, HE MUST HAVE REALLY BAD EYESIGHT
MUNCH MUNCH
HA HA HA HOLY SHIT!
WHAT?
MUNCH MUNCH
I JUST USED THAT JESUS MONEY TO BUY MY LUNCH!
BULL!
HERE'S THE CHANGE
HA HA HA HA YOU ARE DEFINITELY GOING TO HELL!

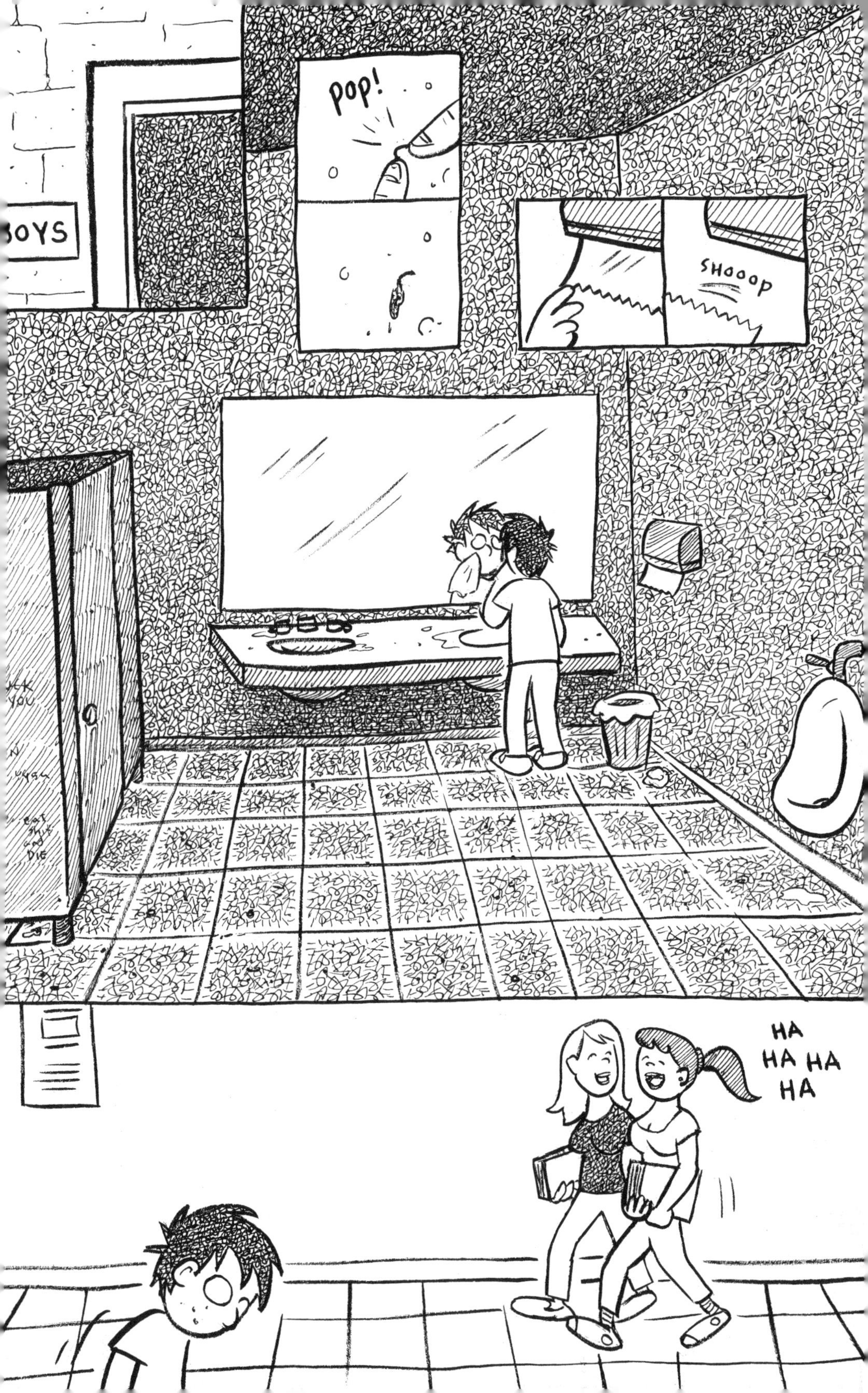
BOYS
pop!
SHOOOP
eat shit and DIE
HA HA HA HA

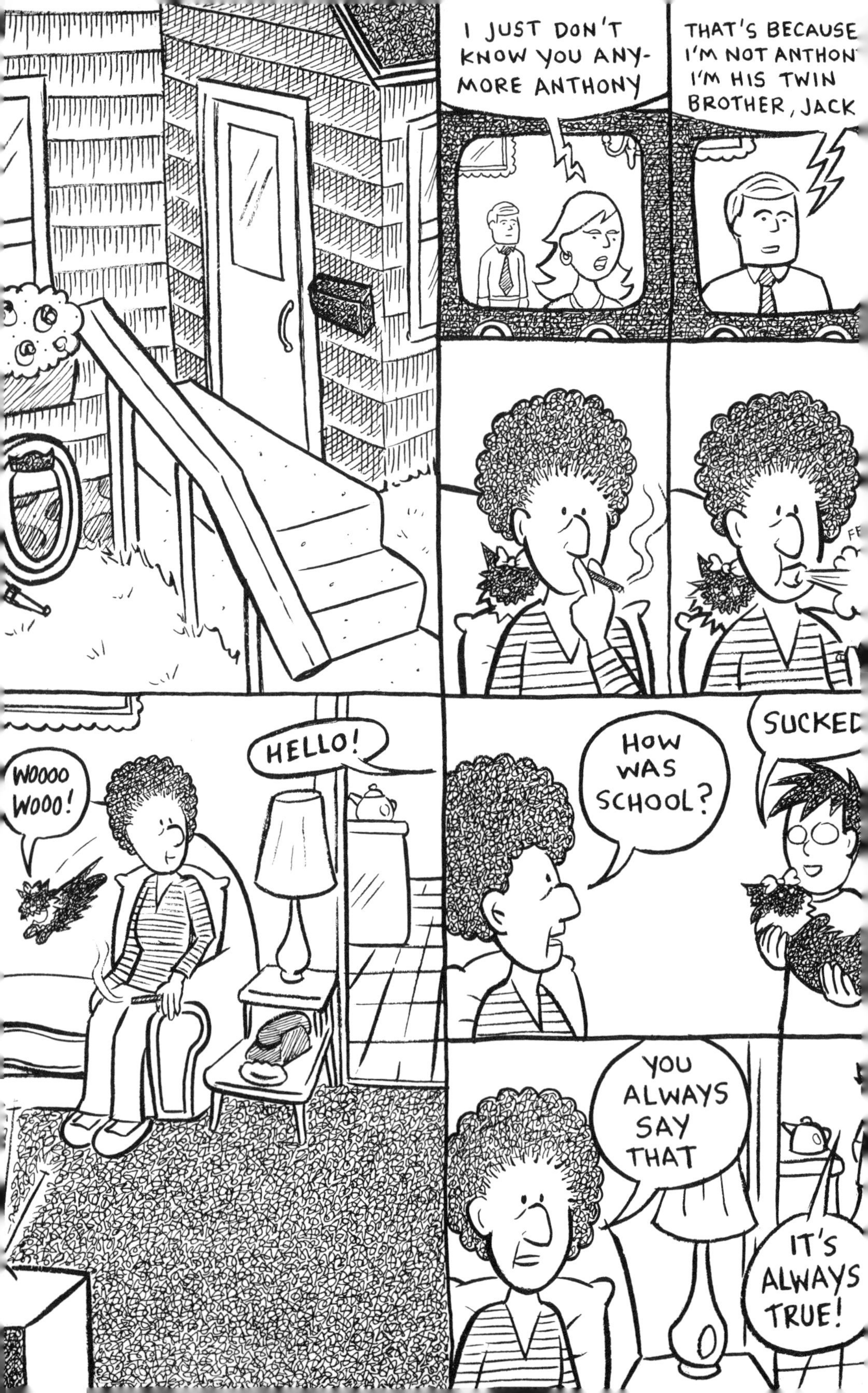
I JUST DON'T KNOW YOU ANY-MORE ANTHONY
THAT'S BECAUSE I'M NOT ANTHON I'M HIS TWIN BROTHER, JACK
WOOOO WOOO!
HELLO!
HOW WAS SCHOOL?
SUCKED
YOU ALWAYS SAY THAT
IT'S ALWAYS TRUE!

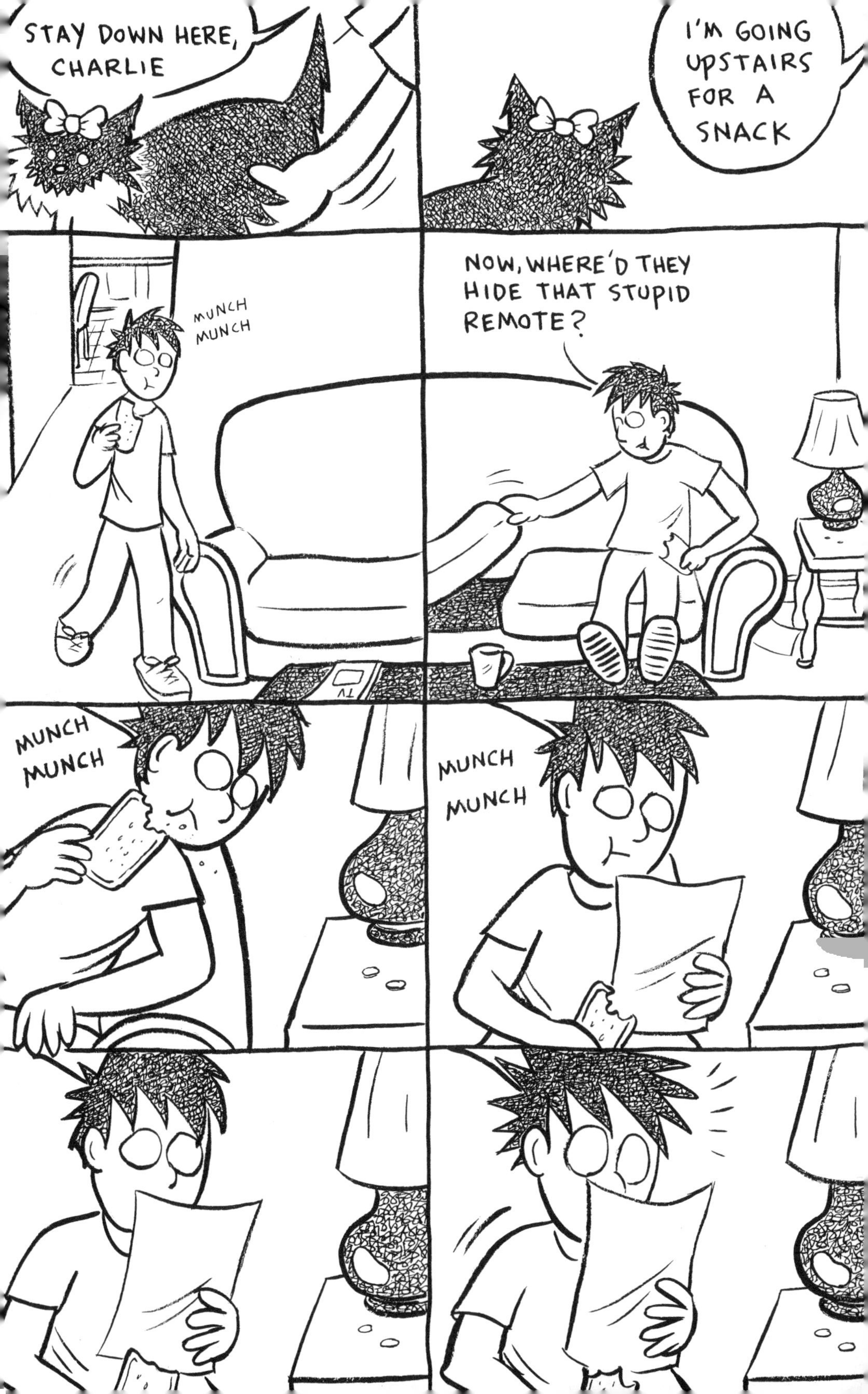
STAY DOWN HERE, CHARLIE
I'M GOING UPSTAIRS FOR A SNACK
MUNCH MUNCH
NOW, WHERE'D THEY HIDE THAT STUPID REMOTE?
TV
MUNCH MUNCH
MUNCH MUNCH

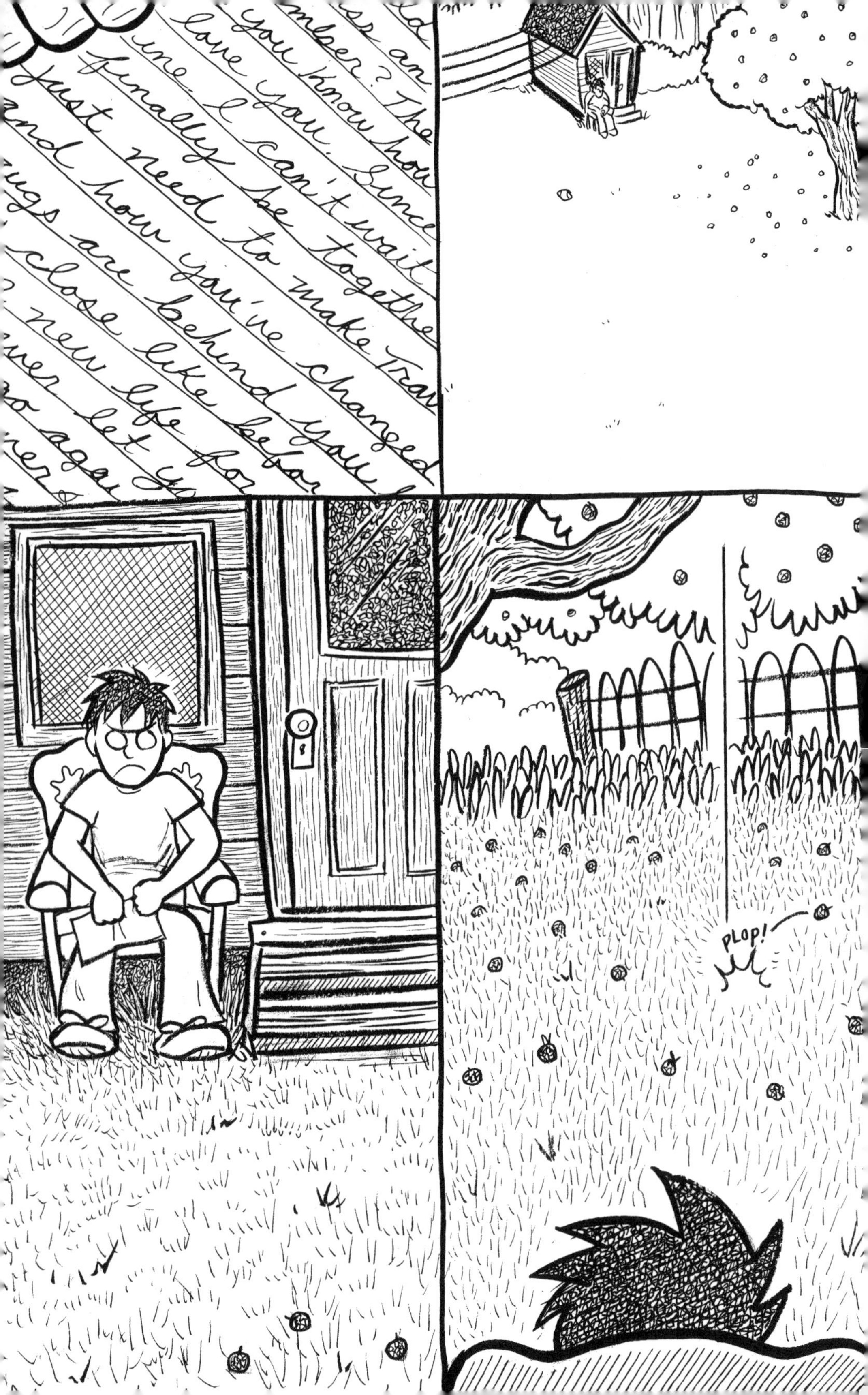
PLOP!

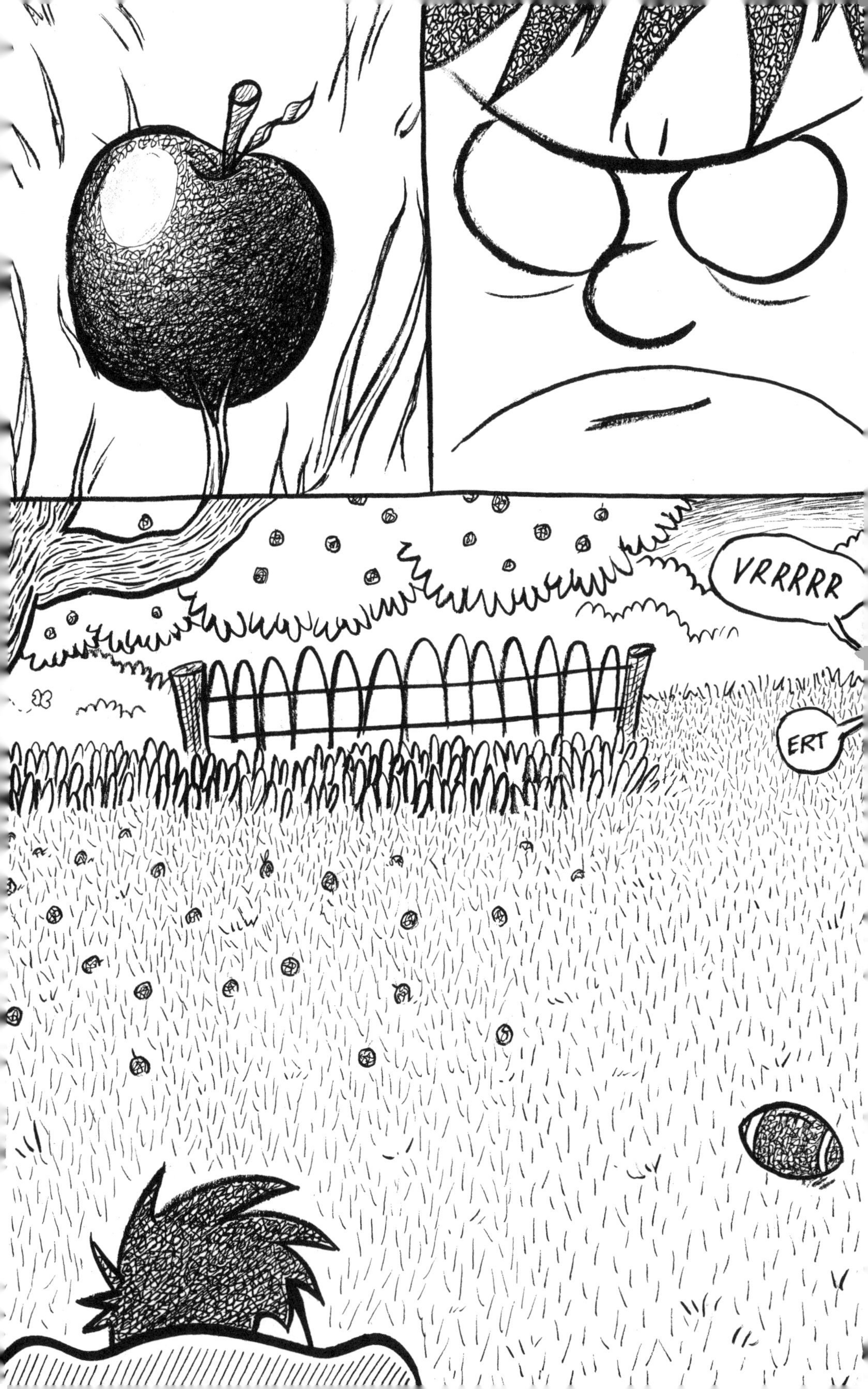
VRRRRR
ERT

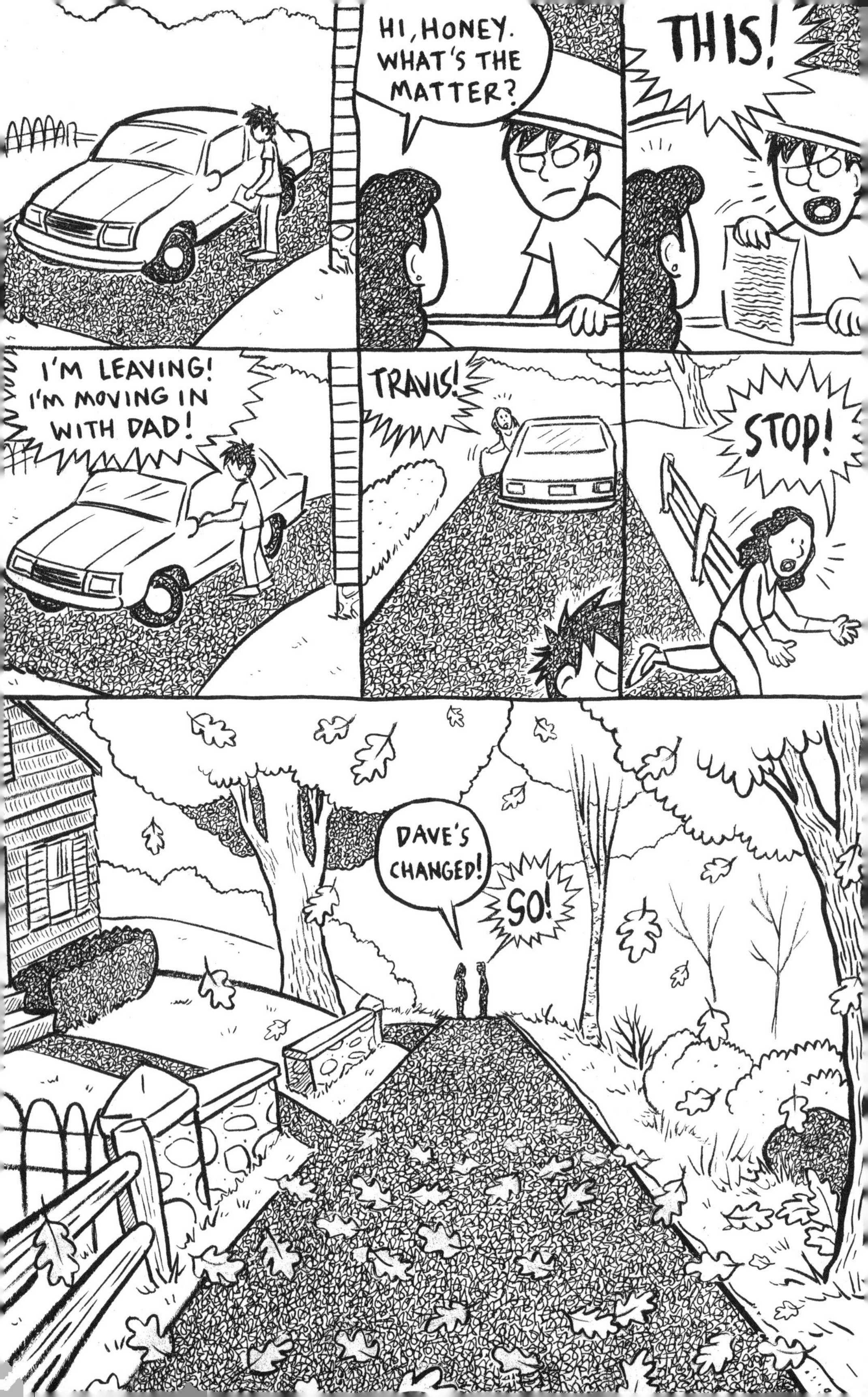
HI, HONEY. WHAT'S THE MATTER?
THIS!
I'M LEAVING! I'M MOVING IN WITH DAD!
TRAVIS!
STOP!
DAVE'S CHANGED!
SO!

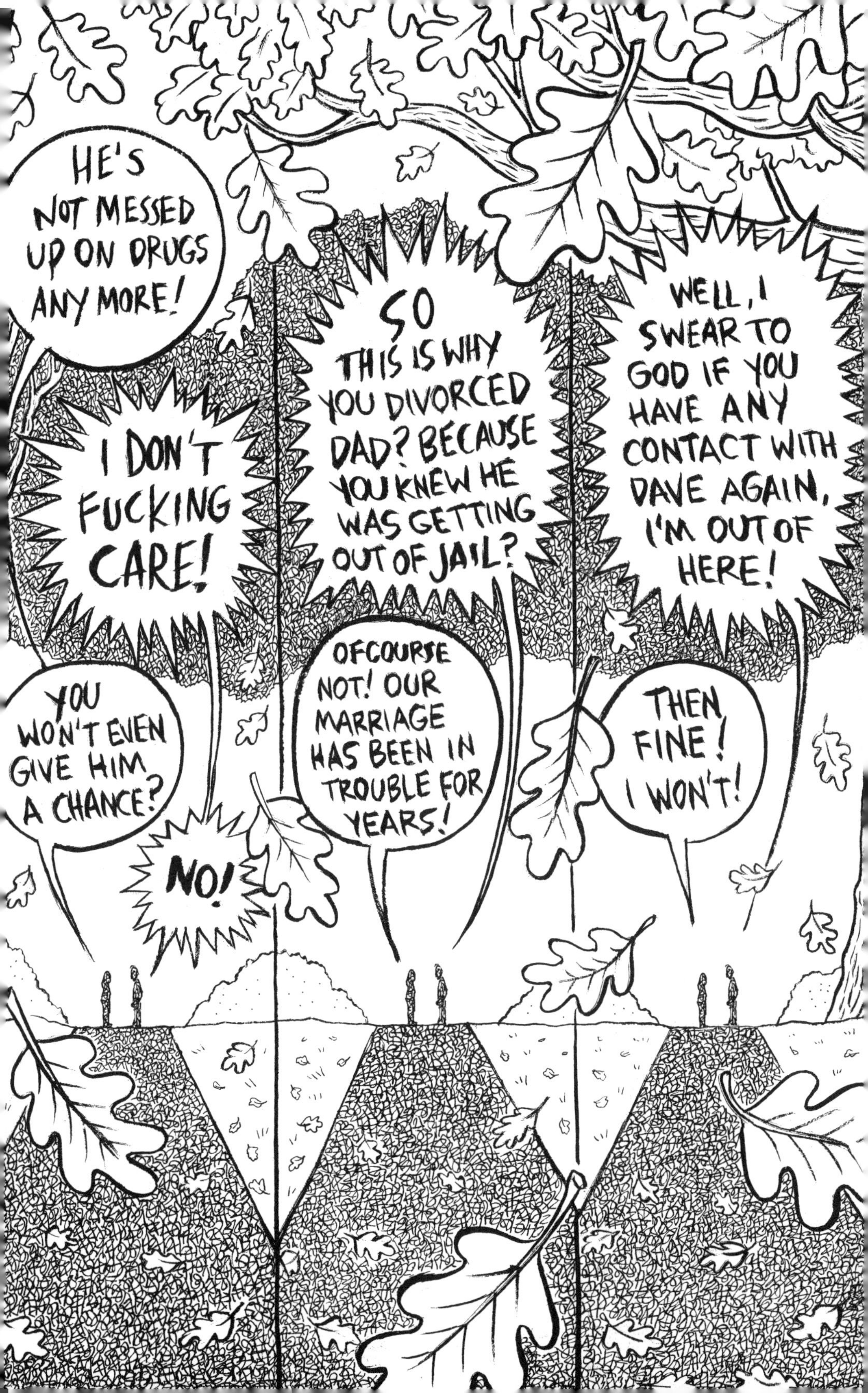
HE'S NOT MESSED UP ON DRUGS ANY MORE!
I DON'T FUCKING CARE!
YOU WON'T EVEN GIVE HIM A CHANCE?
NO!
SO THIS IS WHY YOU DIVORCED DAD? BECAUSE YOU KNEW HE WAS GETTING OUT OF JAIL?
OF COURSE NOT! OUR MARRIAGE HAS BEEN IN TROUBLE FOR YEARS!
WELL, I SWEAR TO GOD IF YOU HAVE ANY CONTACT WITH DAVE AGAIN, I'M OUT OF HERE!
THEN FINE! I WON'T!

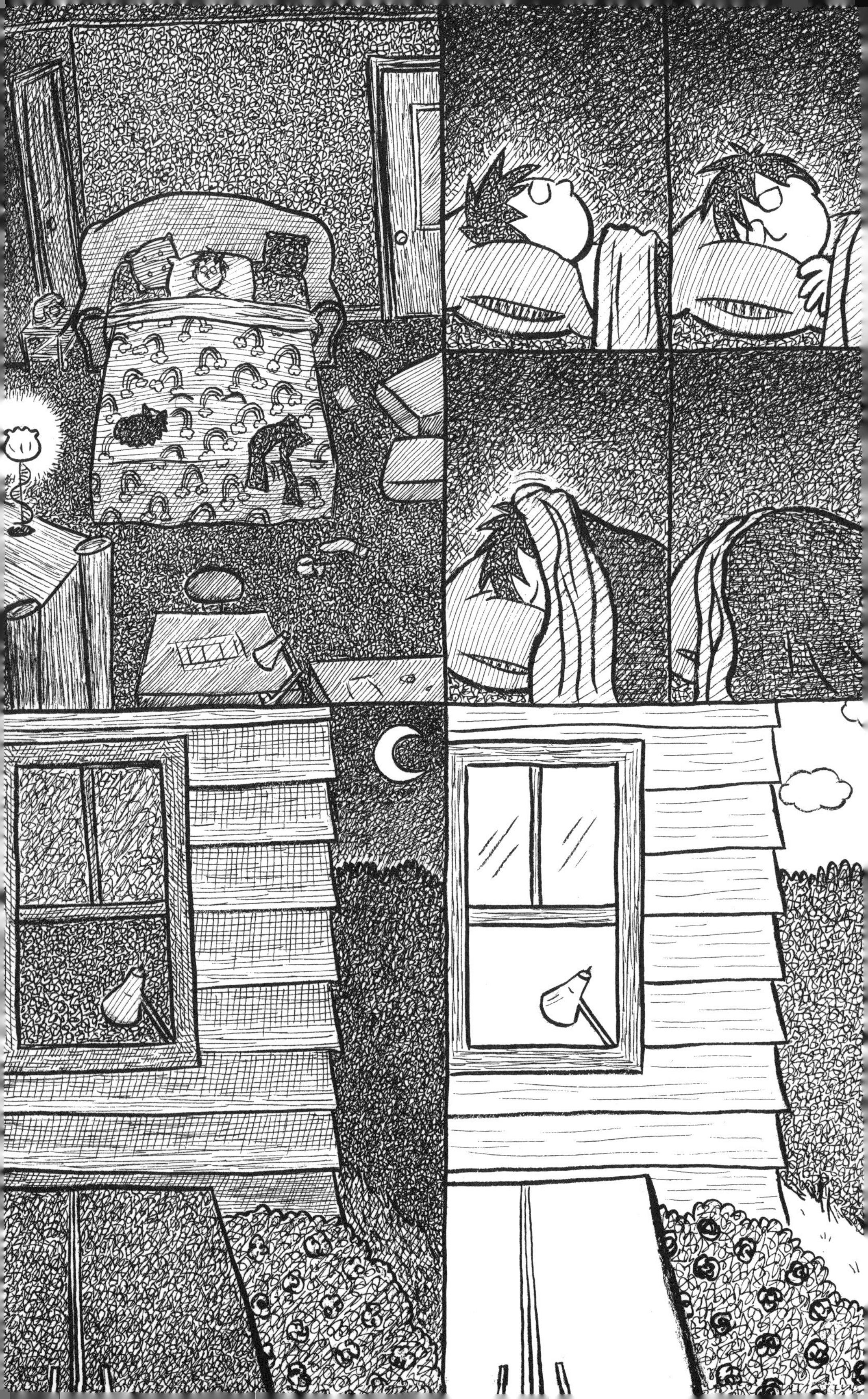

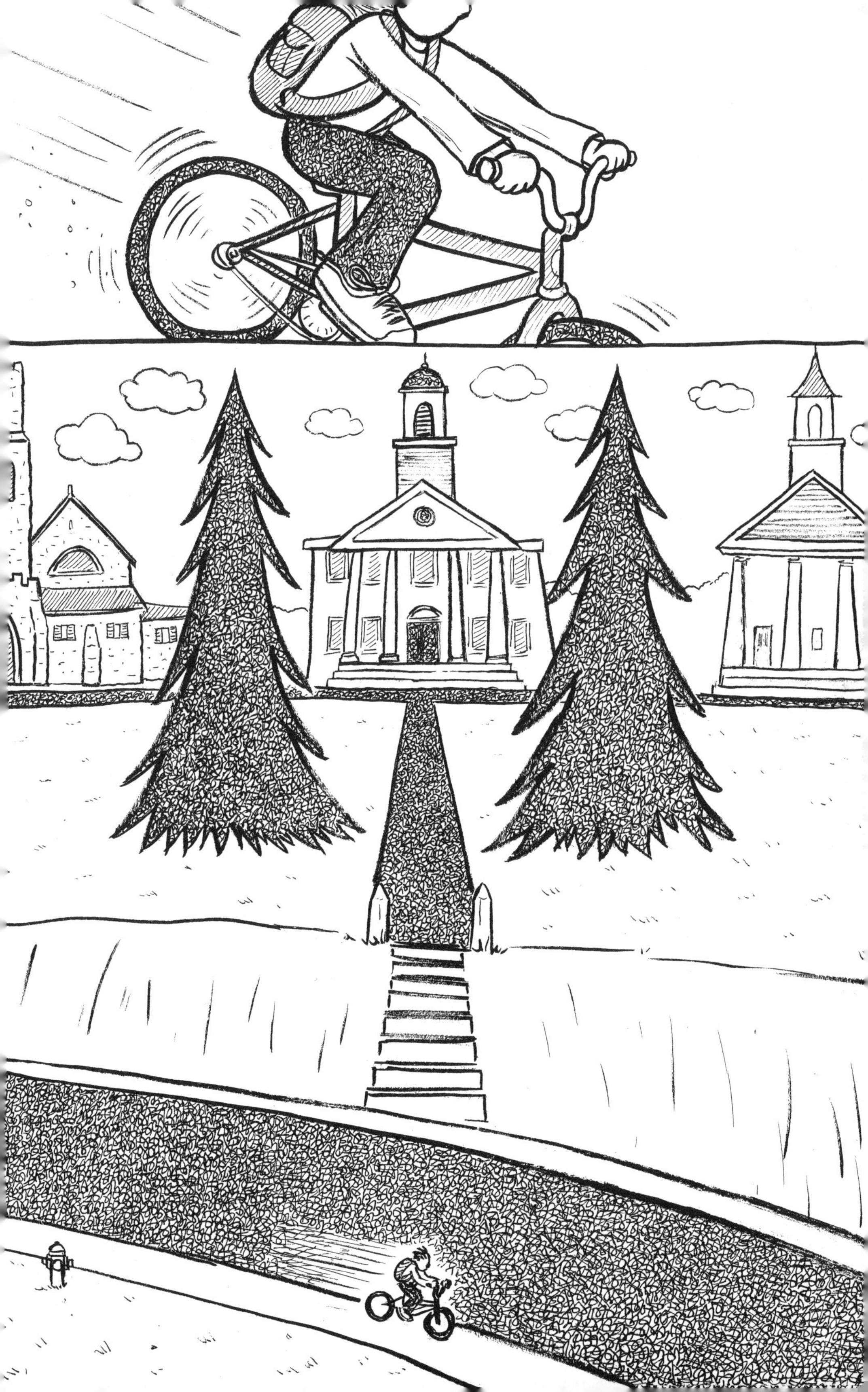

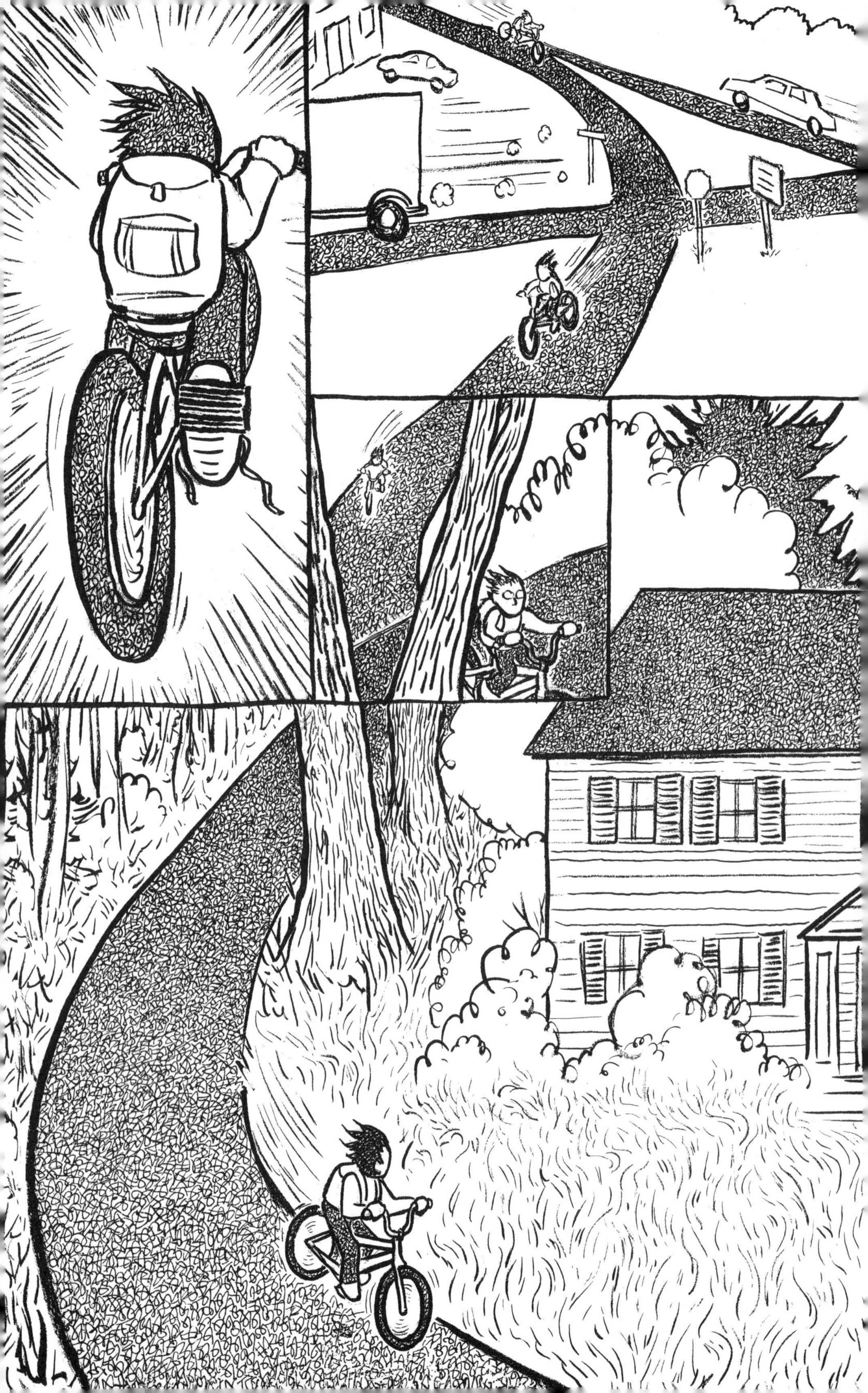

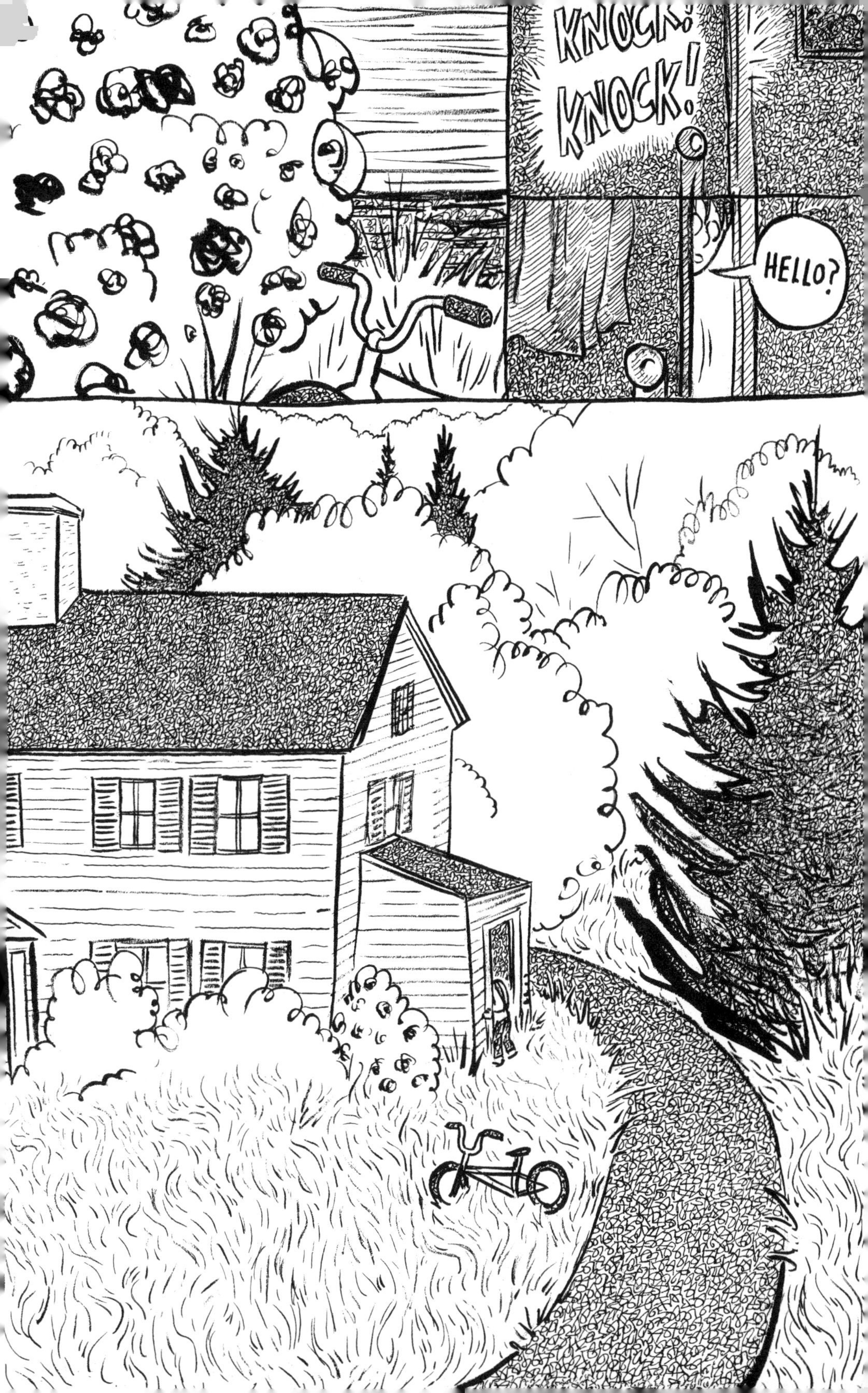
KNOCK! KNOCK!
HELLO?

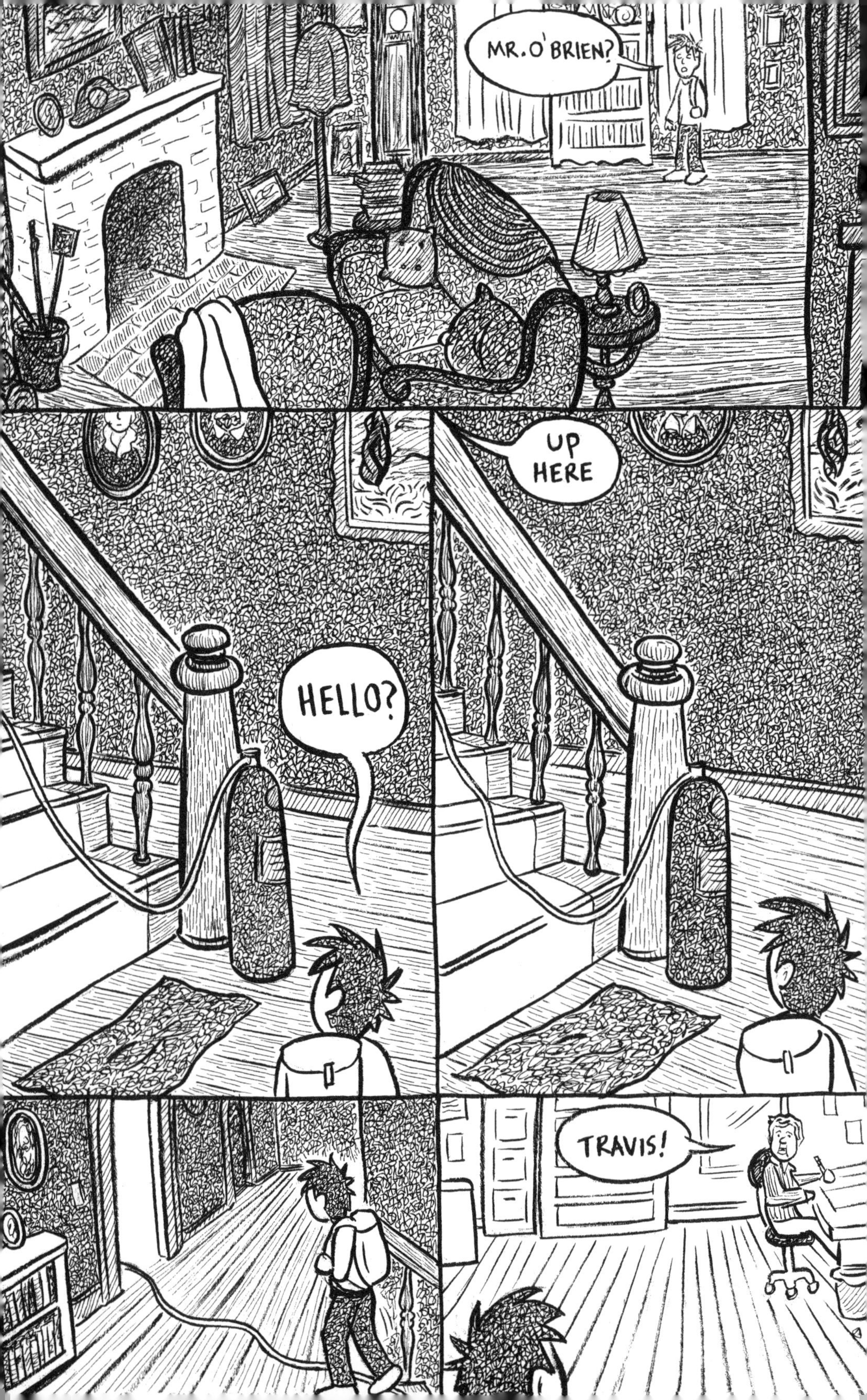
MR. O'BRIEN?
HELLO?
UP HERE
TRAVIS!

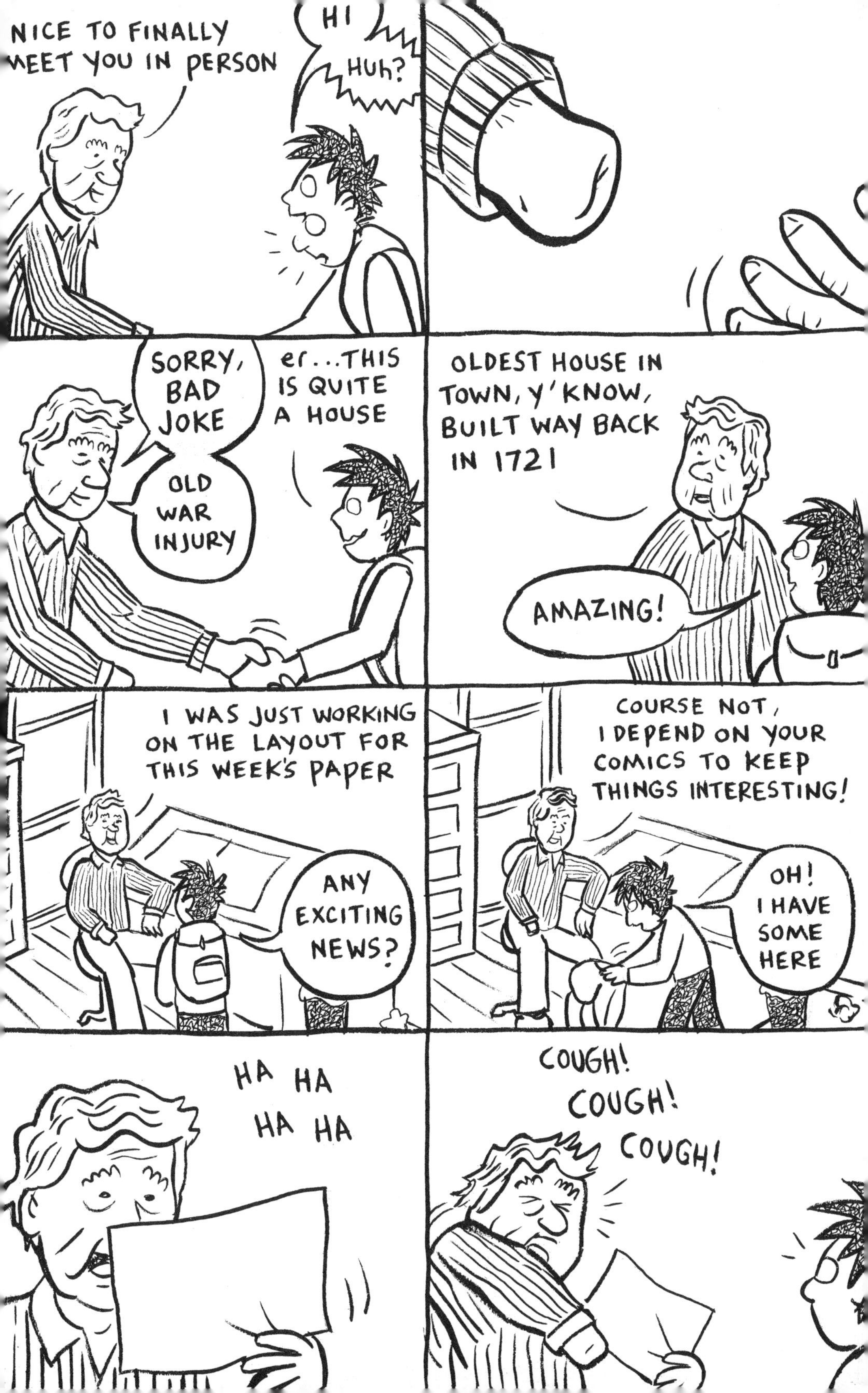
NICE TO FINALLY MEET YOU IN PERSON
HI
HUH?
SORRY, BAD JOKE
OLD WAR INJURY
er...THIS IS QUITE A HOUSE
OLDEST HOUSE IN TOWN, Y'KNOW, BUILT WAY BACK IN 1721
AMAZING!
I WAS JUST WORKING ON THE LAYOUT FOR THIS WEEK'S PAPER
ANY EXCITING NEWS?
COURSE NOT, I DEPEND ON YOUR COMICS TO KEEP THINGS INTERESTING!
OH! I HAVE SOME HERE
HA HA
HA HA
COUGH!
COUGH!
COUGH!

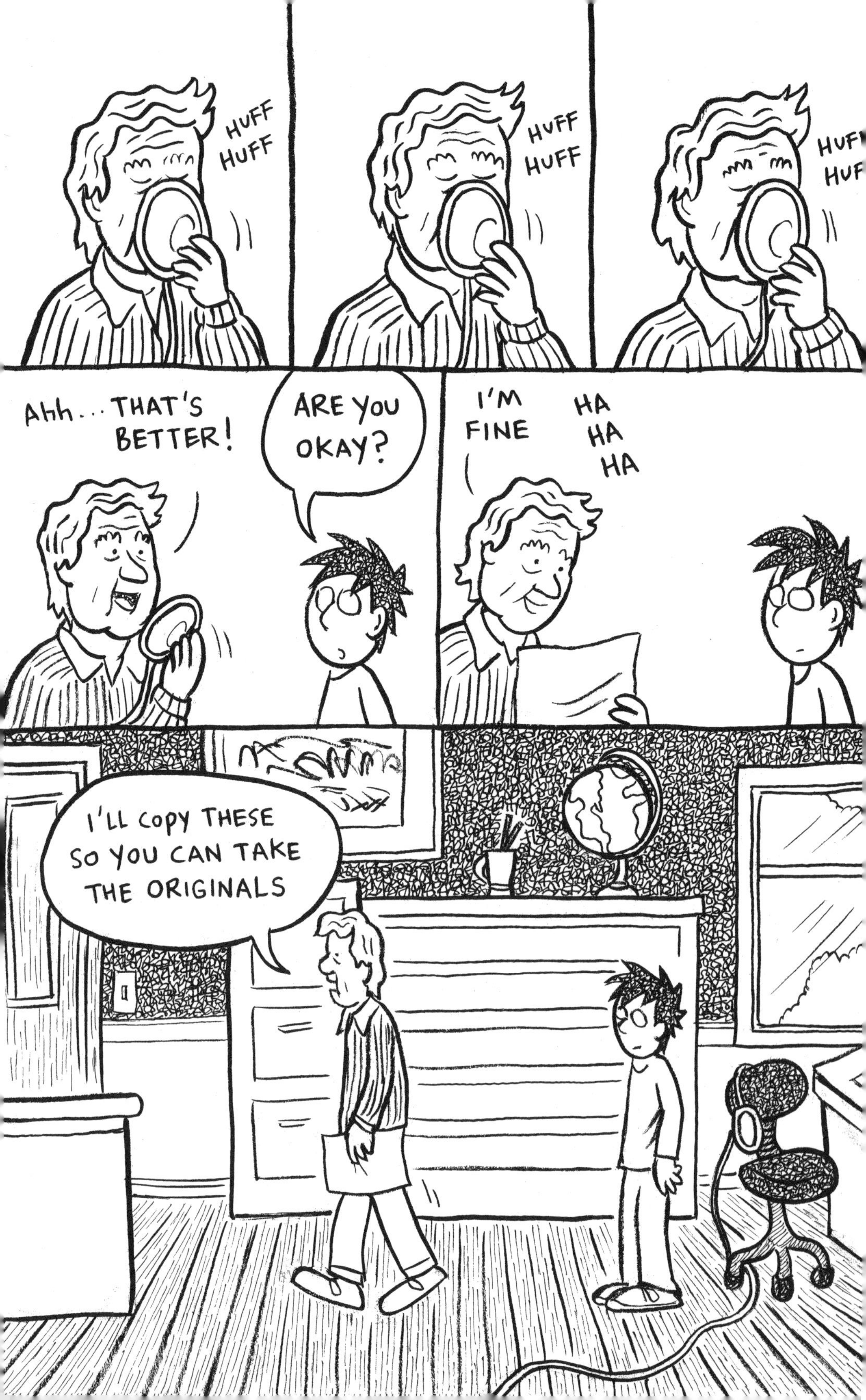
HUFF
HUFF
HUFF
HUFF
HUFF
HUFF
Ahh... THAT'S BETTER!
ARE YOU OKAY?
I'M FINE
HA
HA
HA
I'LL COPY THESE SO YOU CAN TAKE THE ORIGINALS

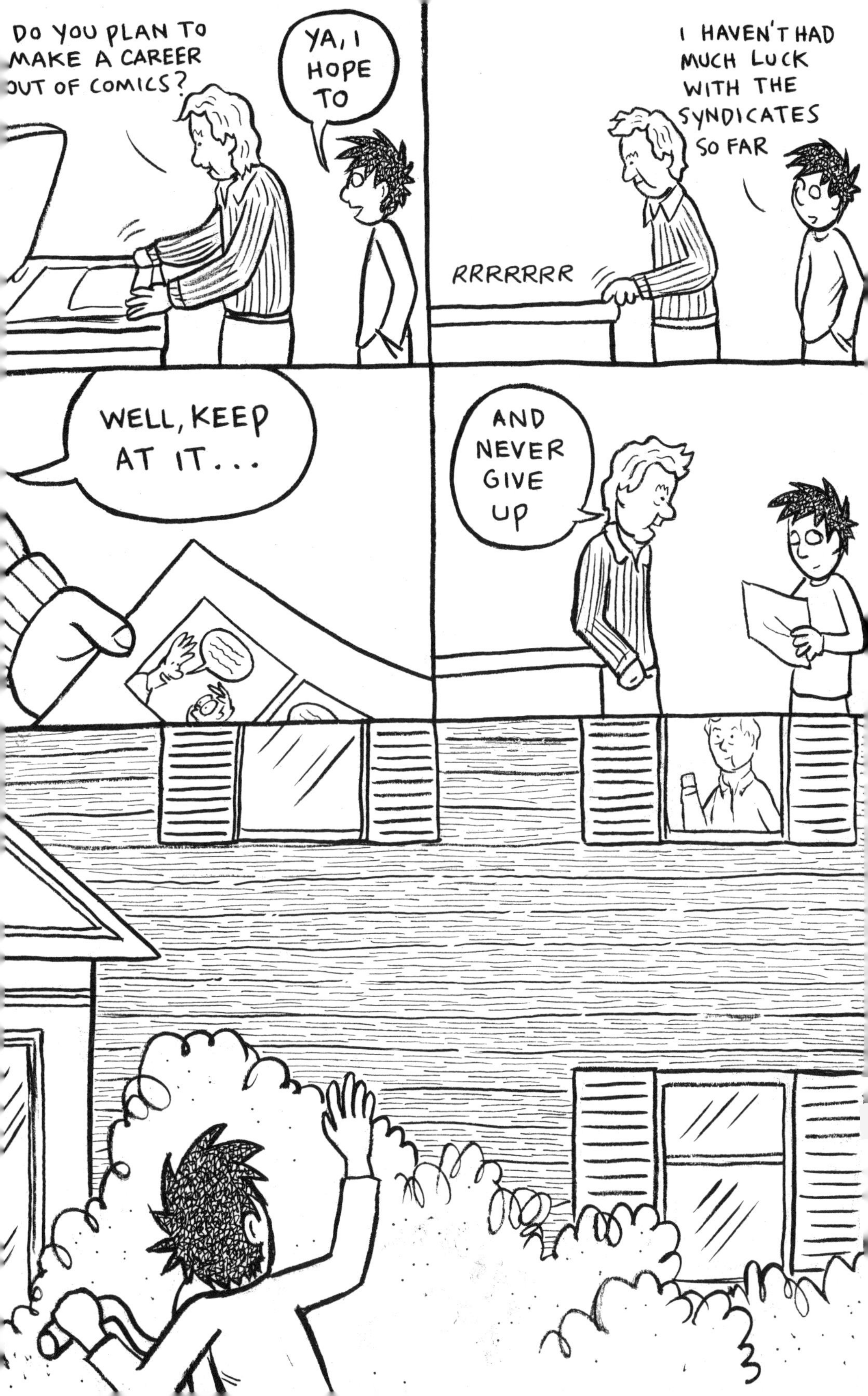
DO YOU PLAN TO MAKE A CAREER OUT OF COMICS?
YA, I HOPE TO
I HAVEN'T HAD MUCH LUCK WITH THE SYNDICATES SO FAR
RRRRRRR
WELL, KEEP AT IT...
AND NEVER GIVE UP

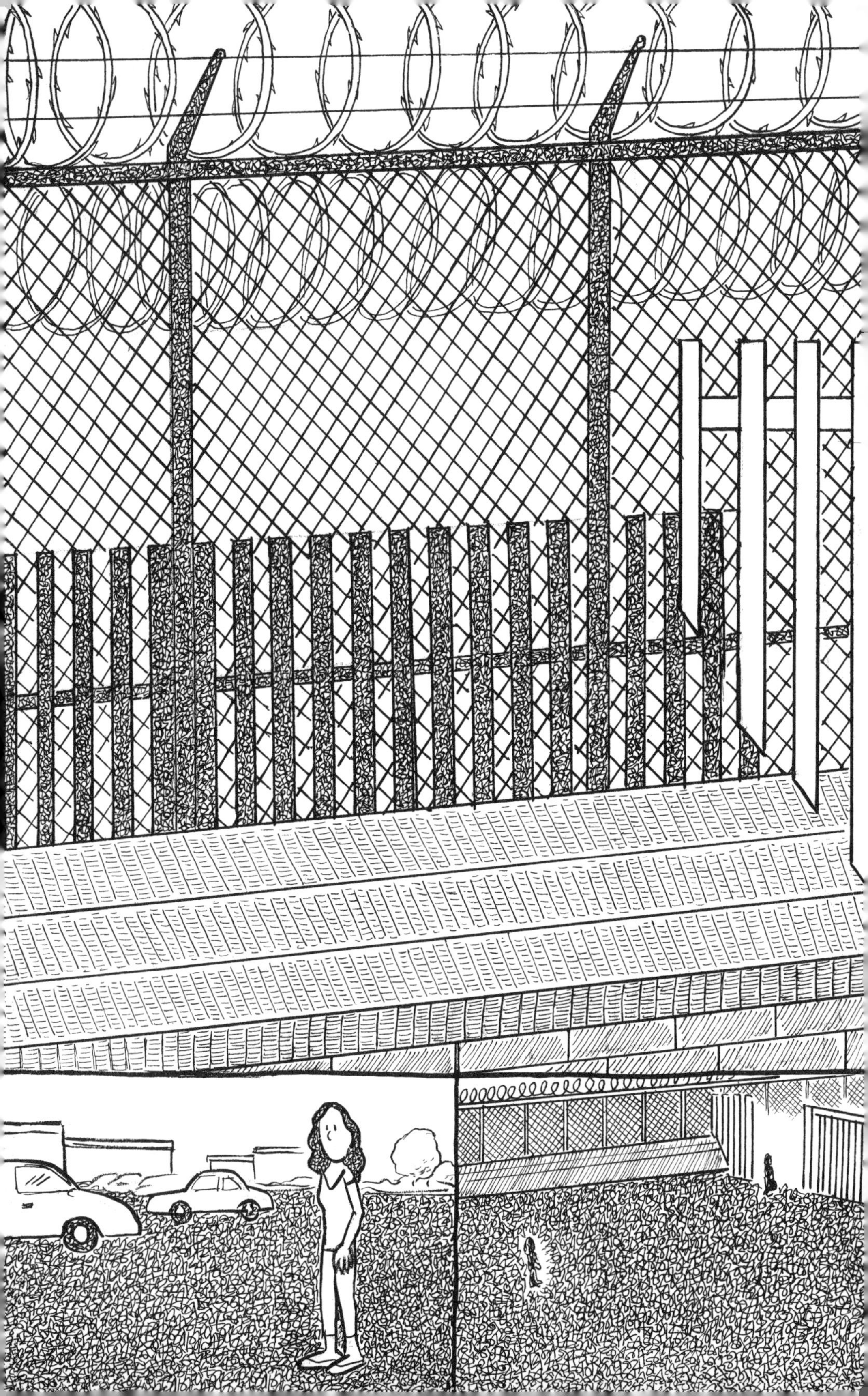

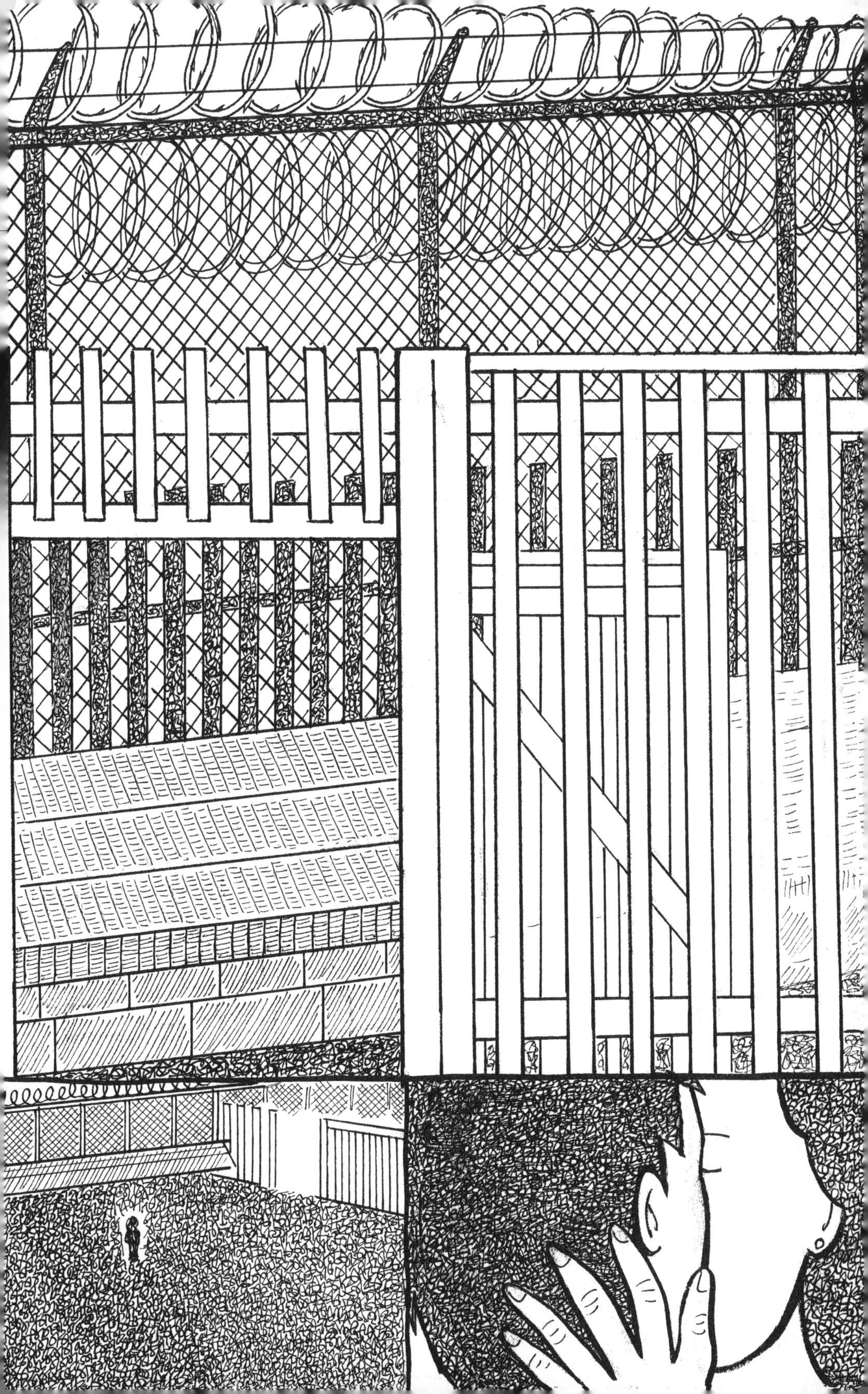

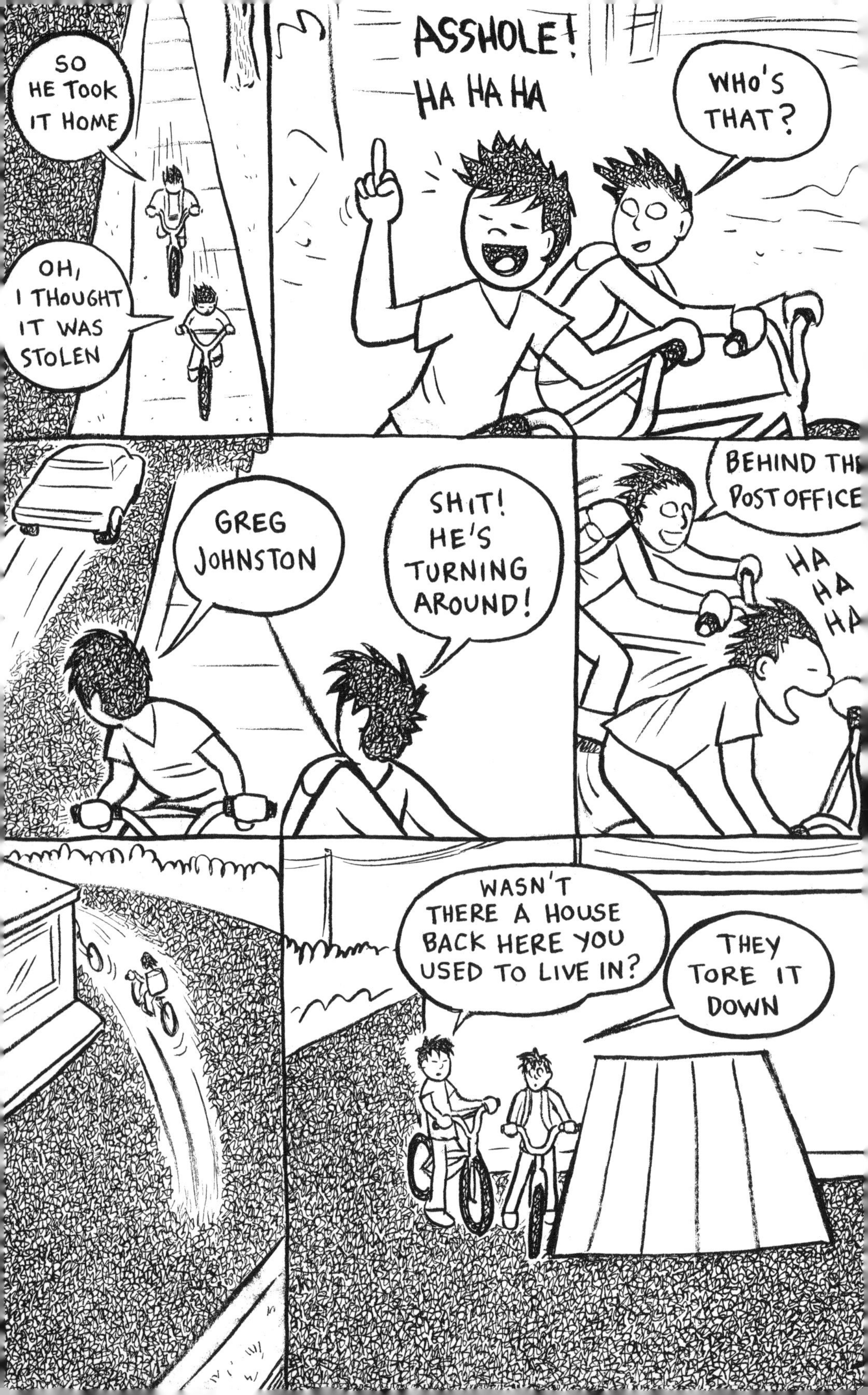
SO HE TOOK IT HOME
OH, I THOUGHT IT WAS STOLEN
ASSHOLE!
HA HA HA
WHO'S THAT?
GREG JOHNSTON
SHIT! HE'S TURNING AROUND!
BEHIND TH POST OFFICE
HA HA HA
WASN'T THERE A HOUSE BACK HERE YOU USED TO LIVE IN?
THEY TORE IT DOWN

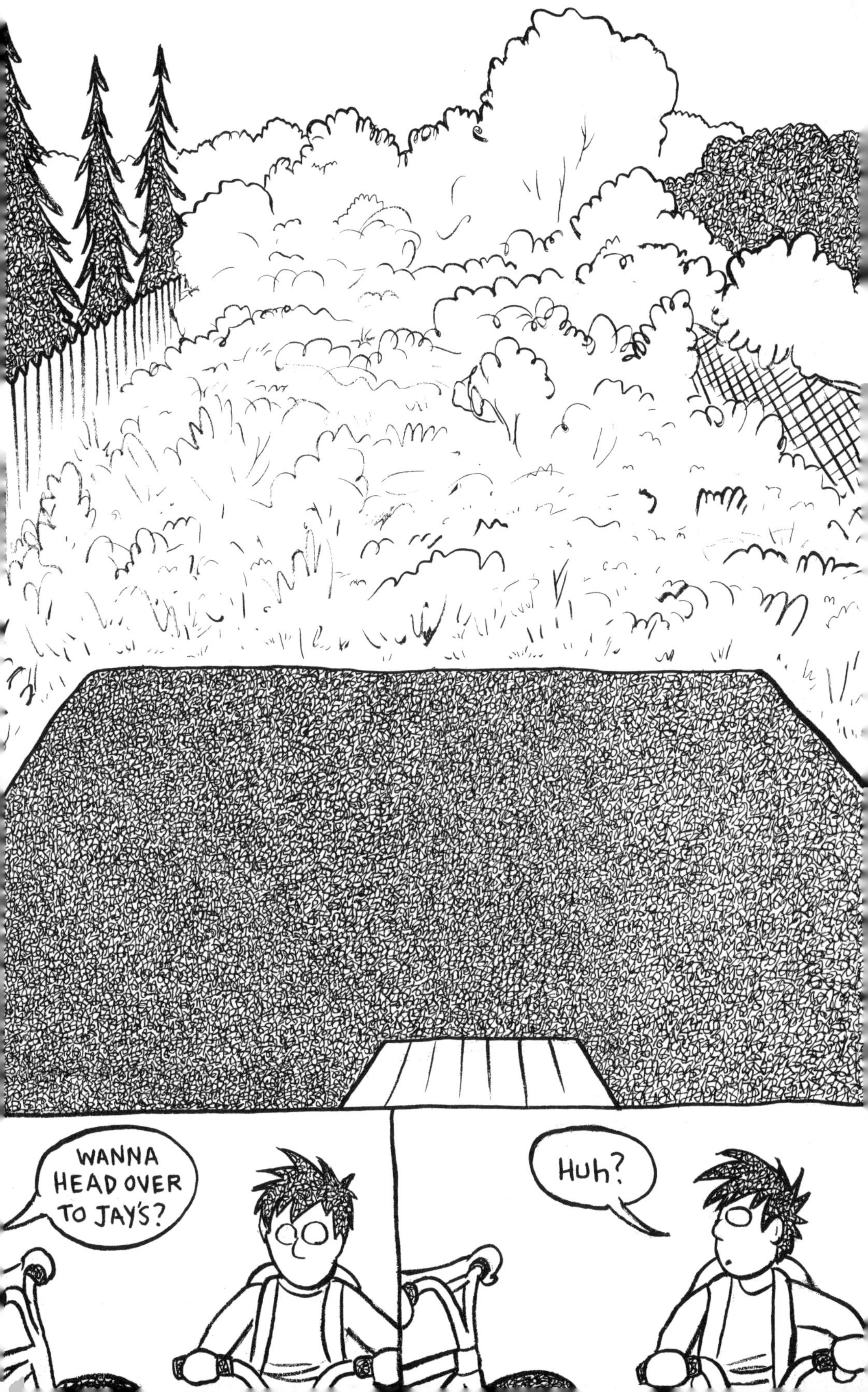
WANNA HEAD OVER TO JAY'S?
Huh?

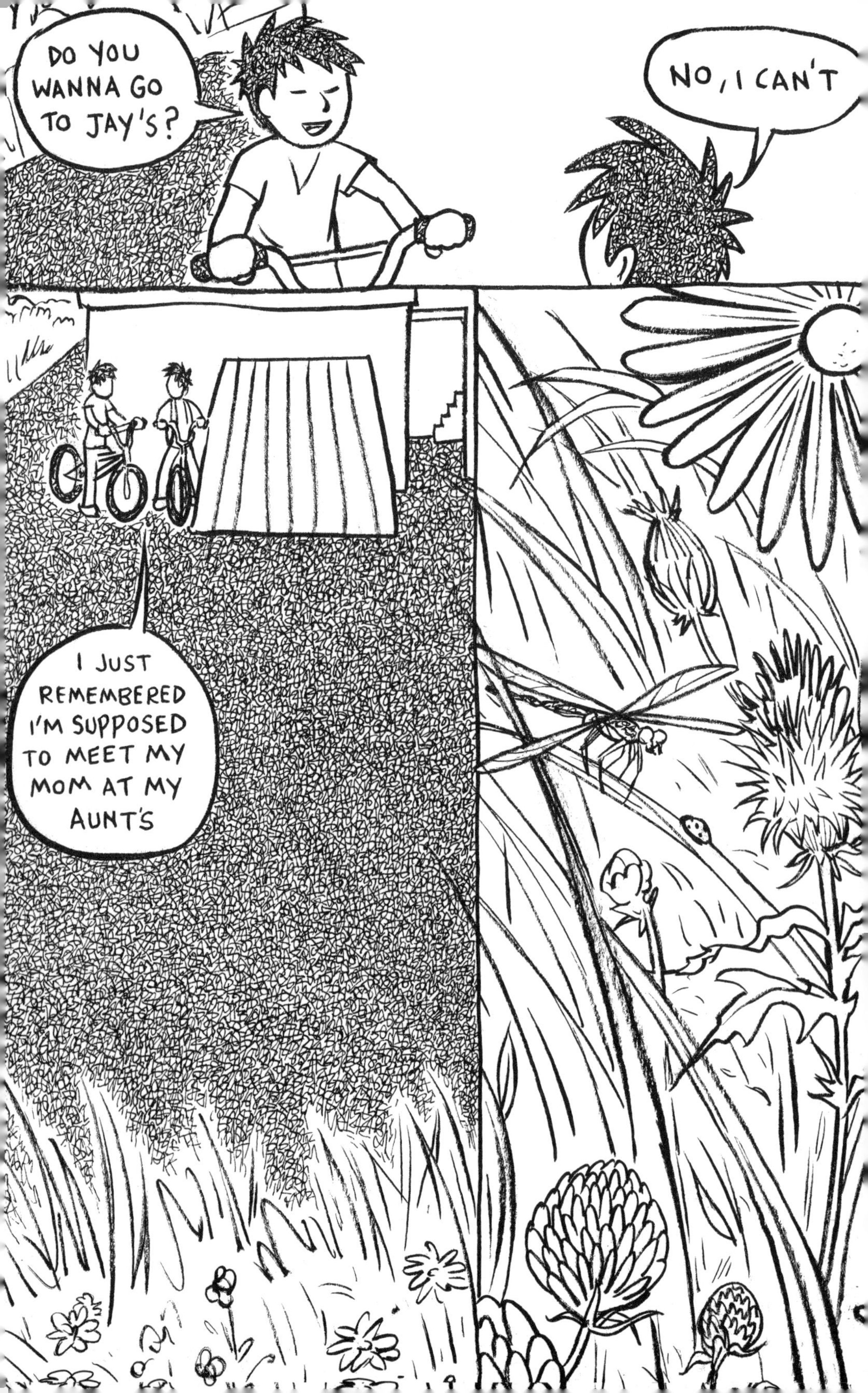
DO YOU WANNA GO TO JAY'S?
NO, I CAN'T
I JUST REMEMBERED I'M SUPPOSED TO MEET MY MOM AT MY AUNT'S

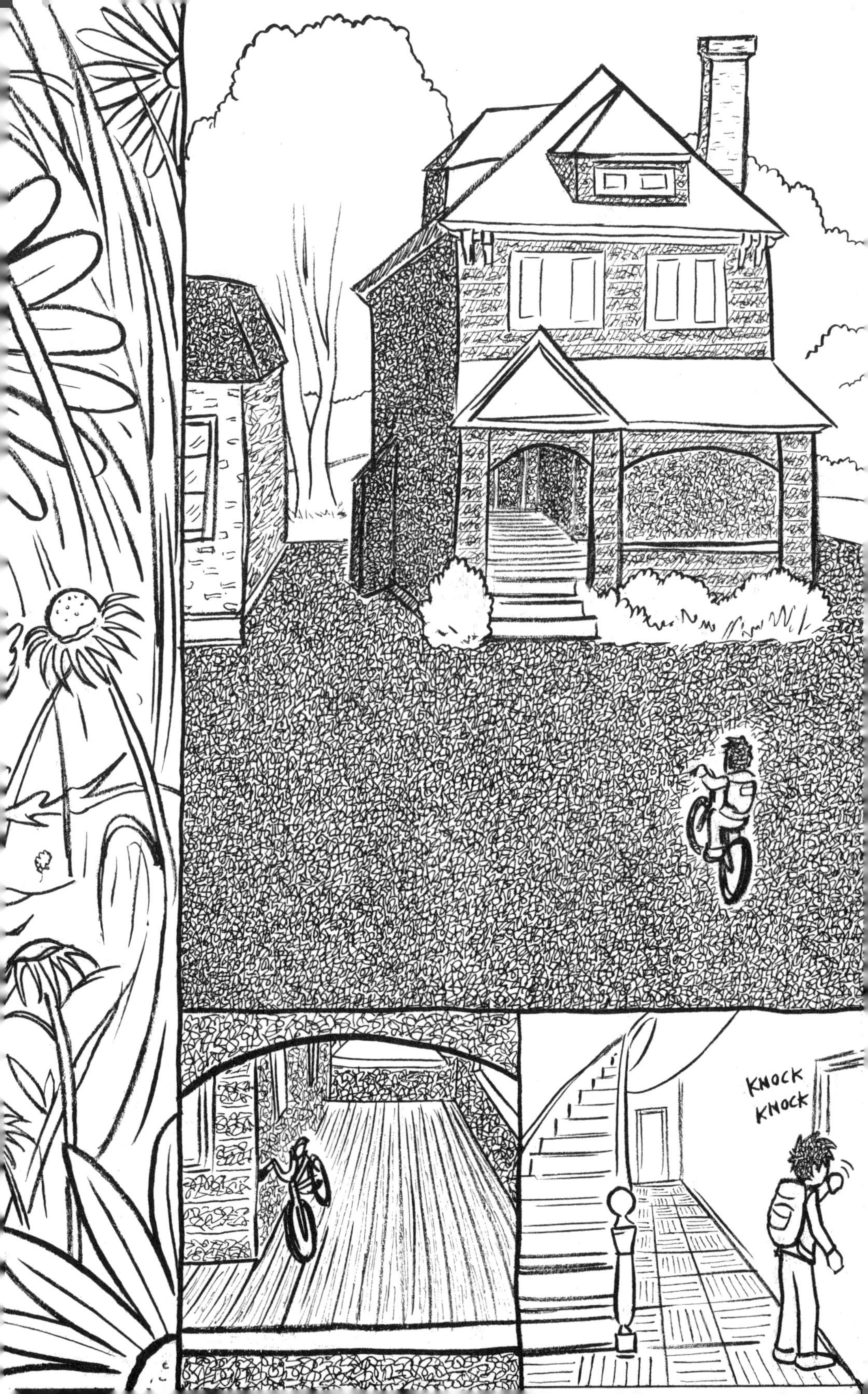
KNOCK
KNOCK

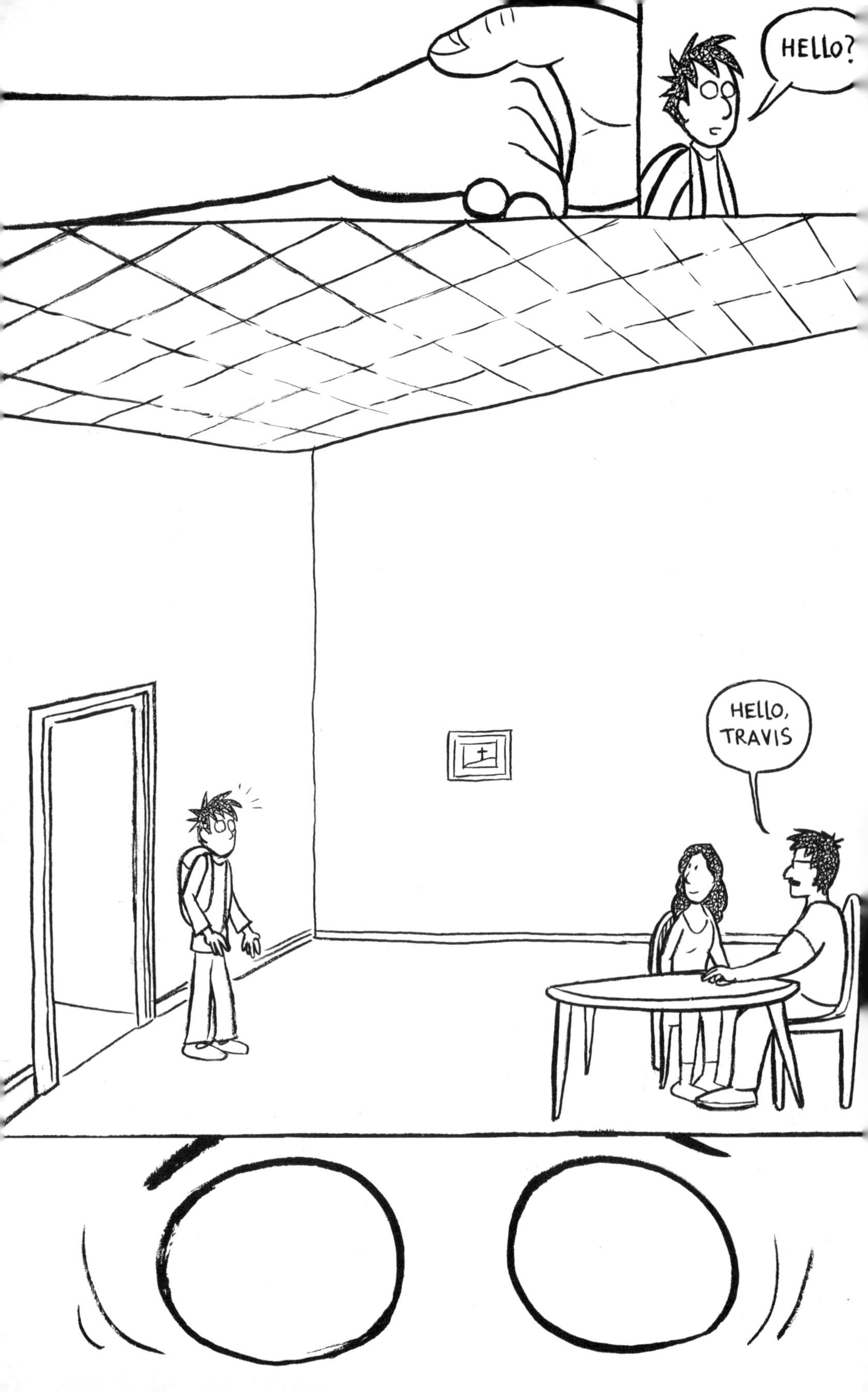
HELLO?
HELLO, TRAVIS

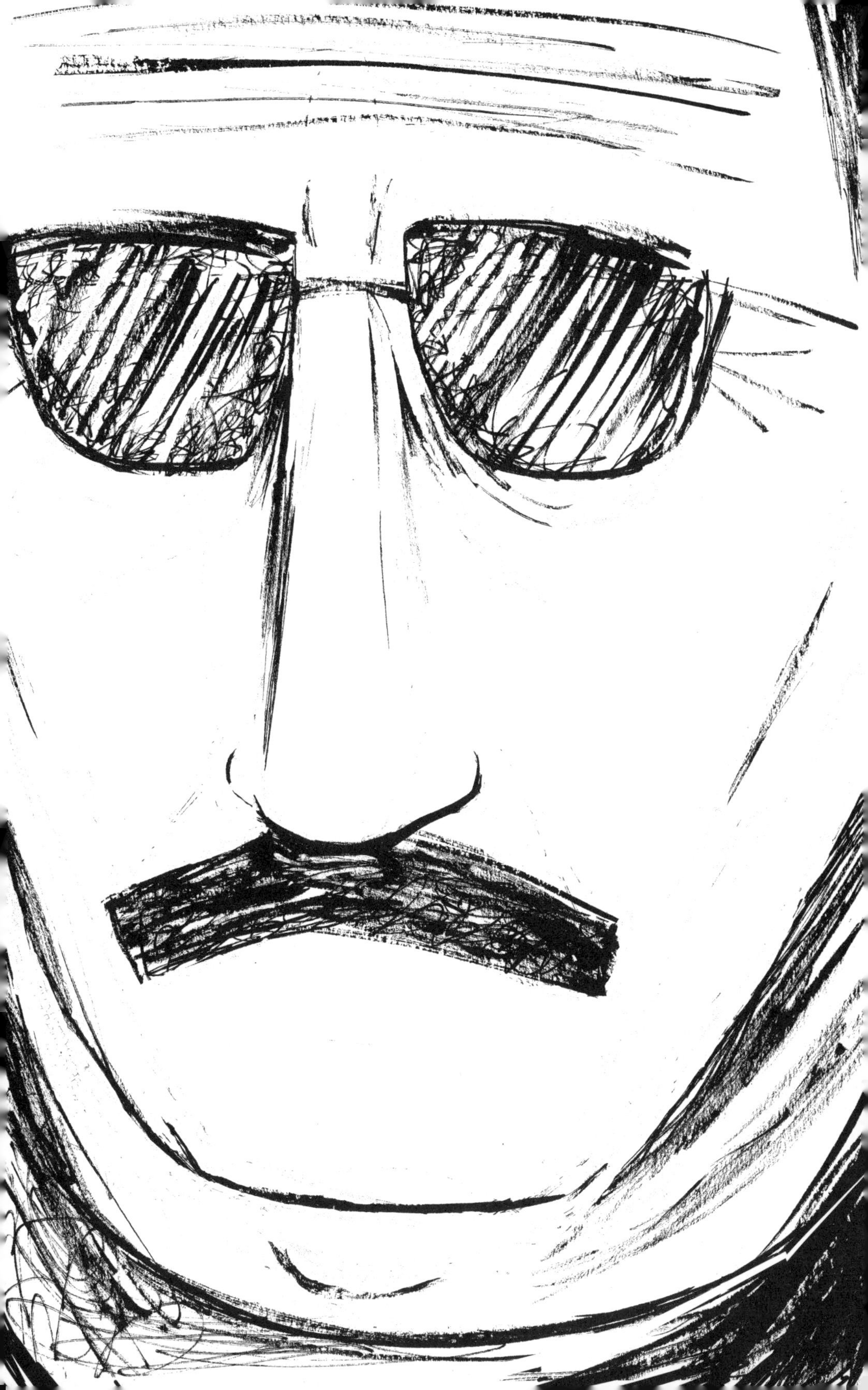

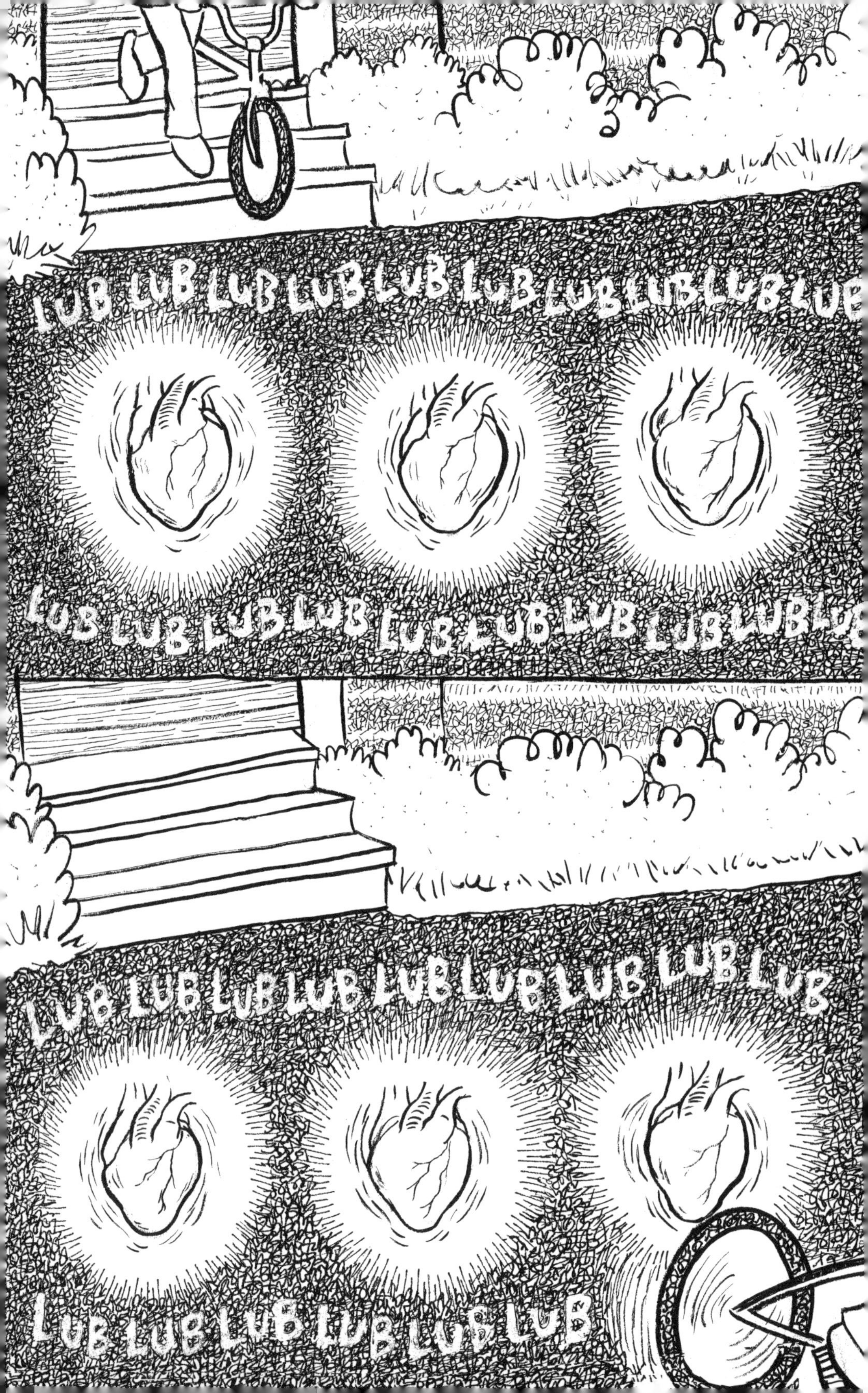
LUB LUB LUB LUB LUB LUB LUB LUB LUB LUB
LUB LUB LUB LUB LUB LUB LUB LUB LUB
LUB LUB LUB LUB LUB LUB LUB LUB LUB
LUB LUB LUB LUB LUB LUB LUB

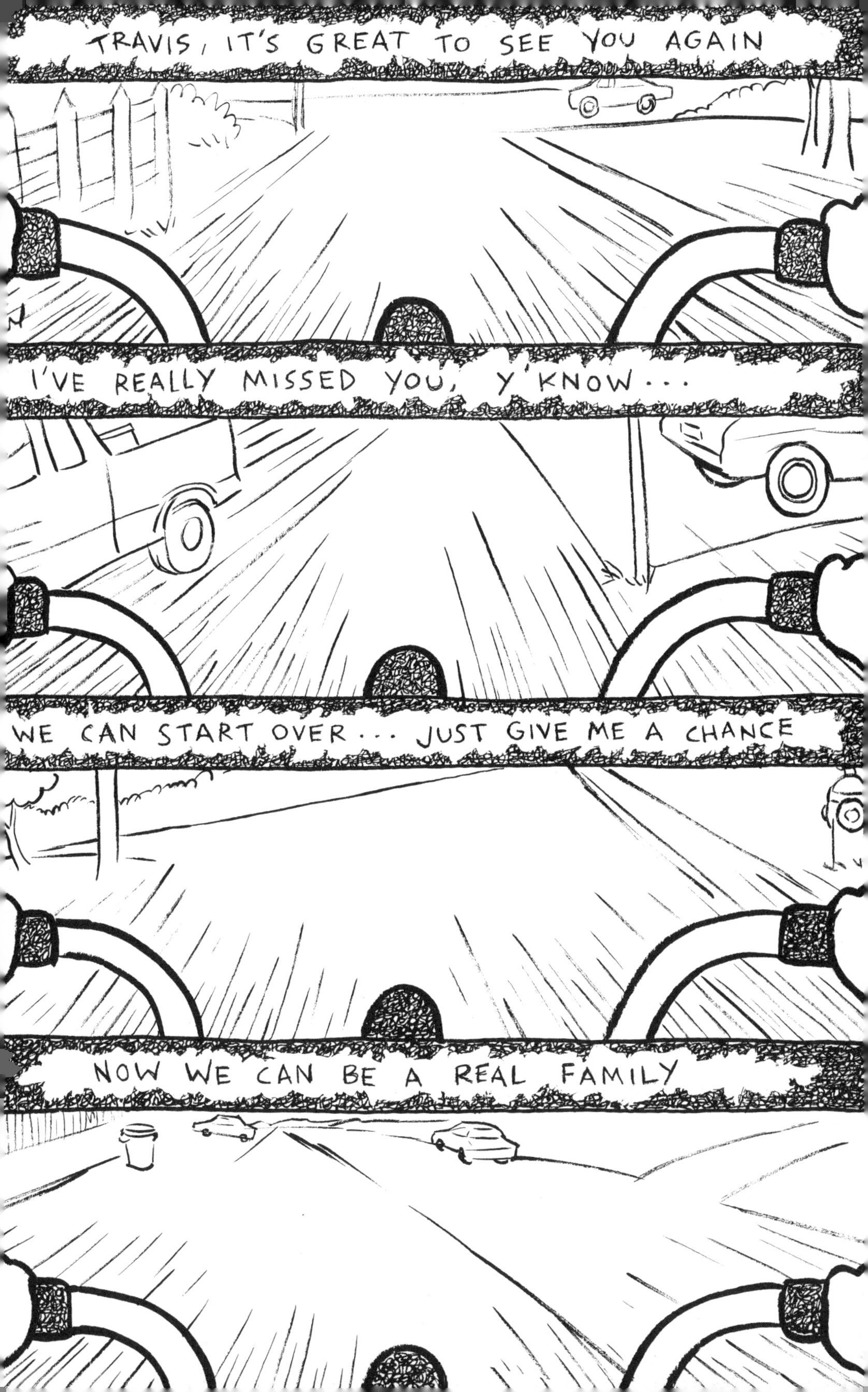
TRAVIS, IT'S GREAT TO SEE YOU AGAIN
I'VE REALLY MISSED YOU, Y'KNOW...
WE CAN START OVER... JUST GIVE ME A CHANCE
NOW WE CAN BE A REAL FAMILY

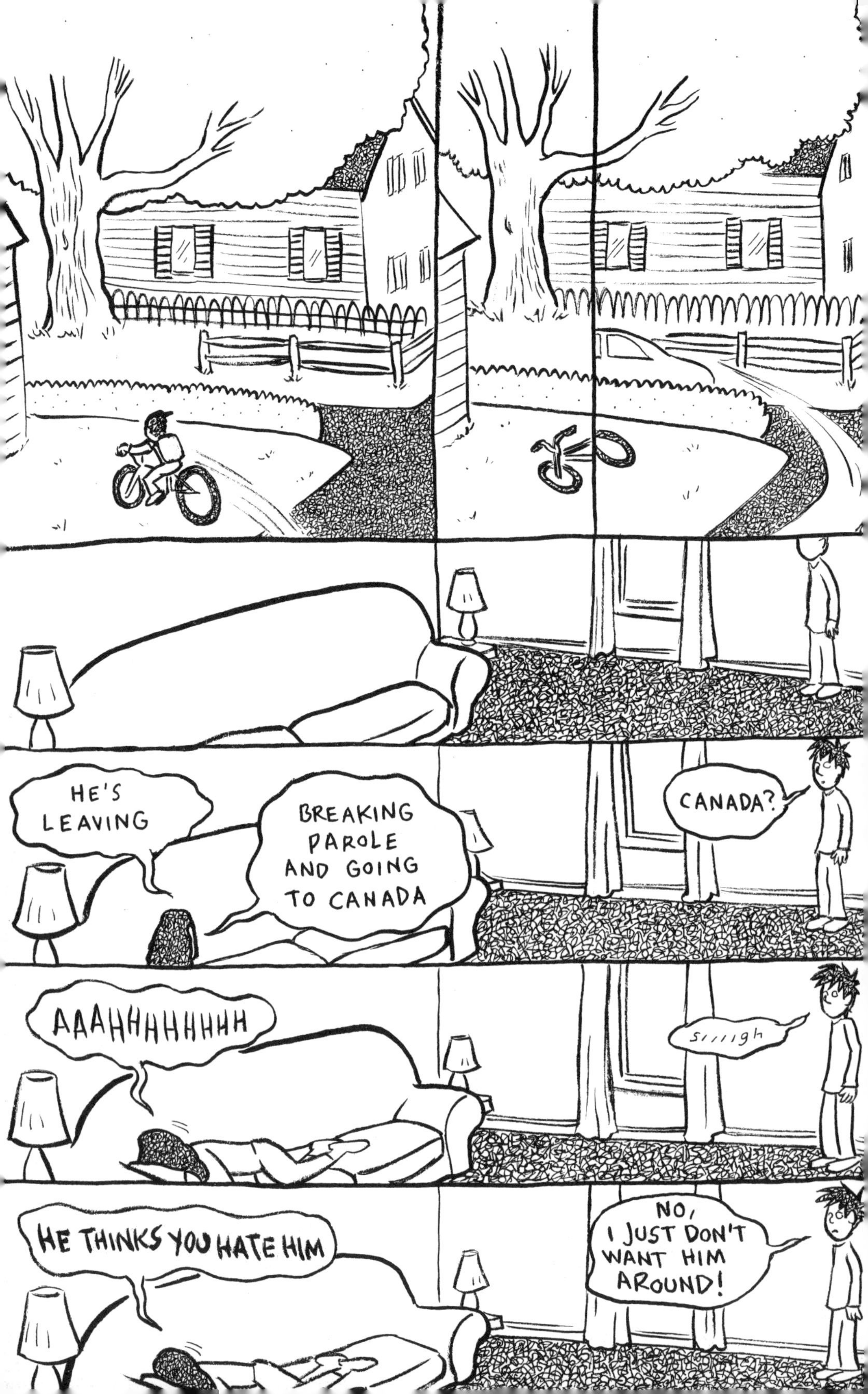
HE'S LEAVING
BREAKING PAROLE AND GOING TO CANADA
CANADA?
AAAHHHHHHHH
sighhh
HE THINKS YOU HATE HIM
NO, I JUST DON'T WANT HIM AROUND!

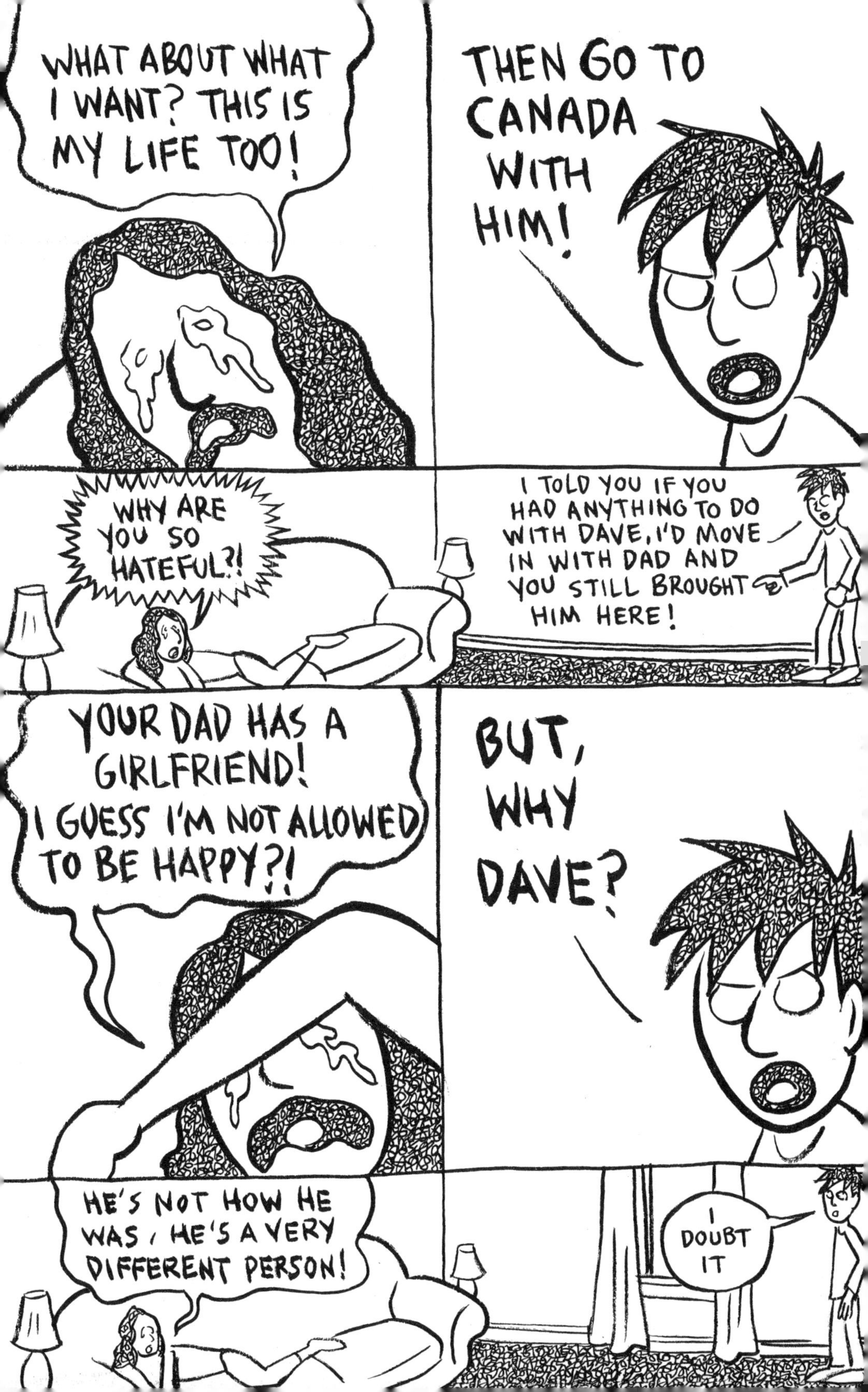
WHAT ABOUT WHAT I WANT? THIS IS MY LIFE TOO!
THEN GO TO CANADA WITH HIM!
WHY ARE YOU SO HATEFUL?!
I TOLD YOU IF YOU HAD ANYTHING TO DO WITH DAVE, I'D MOVE IN WITH DAD AND YOU STILL BROUGHT HIM HERE!
YOUR DAD HAS A GIRLFRIEND! I GUESS I'M NOT ALLOWED TO BE HAPPY?!
BUT, WHY DAVE?
HE'S NOT HOW HE WAS, HE'S A VERY DIFFERENT PERSON!
I DOUBT IT

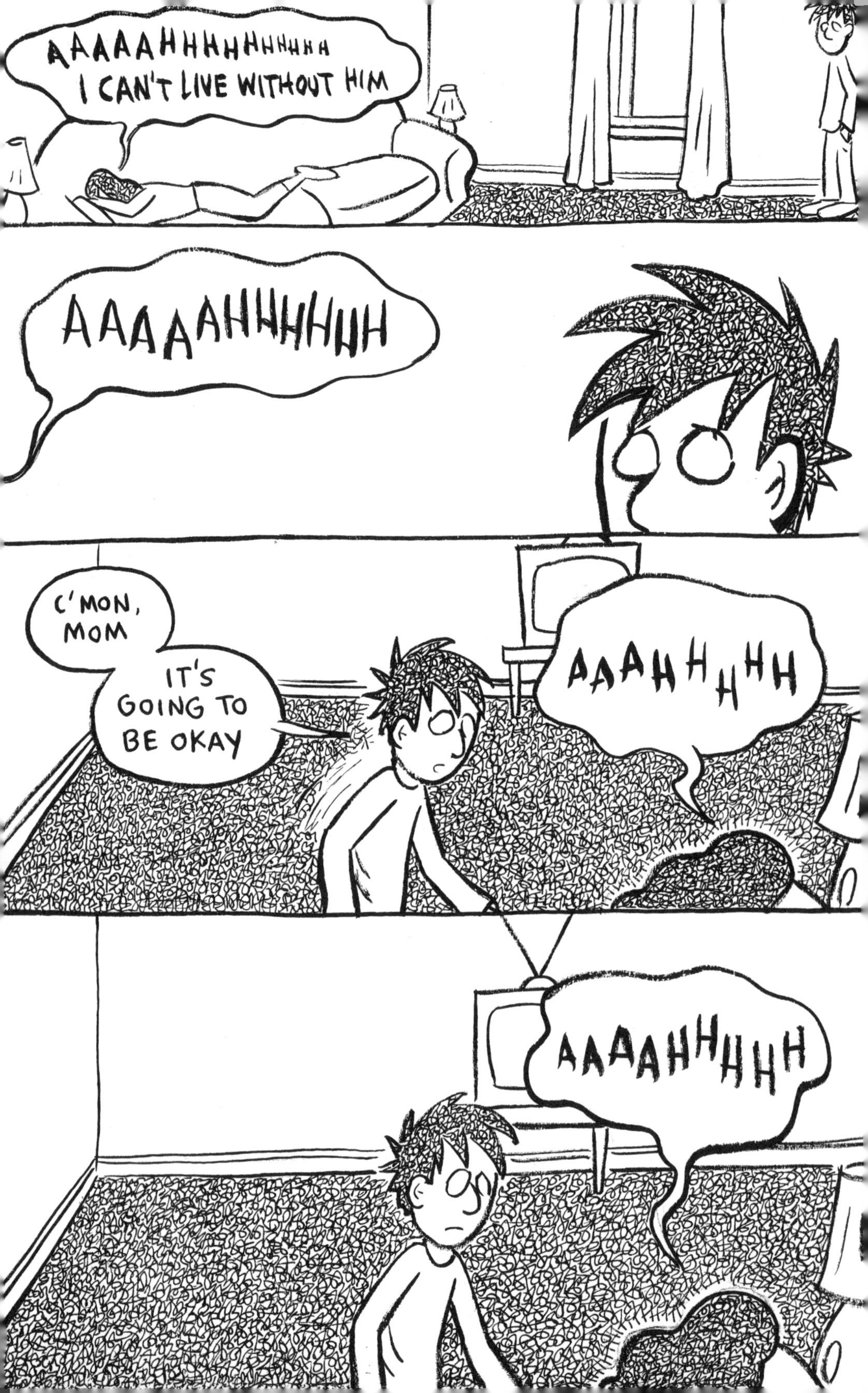
AAAAAHHHHHHHHH
I CAN'T LIVE WITHOUT HIM
AAAAAHHHHHHH
C'MON, MOM
IT'S GOING TO BE OKAY
AAAHHHHH
AAAAHHHHHH

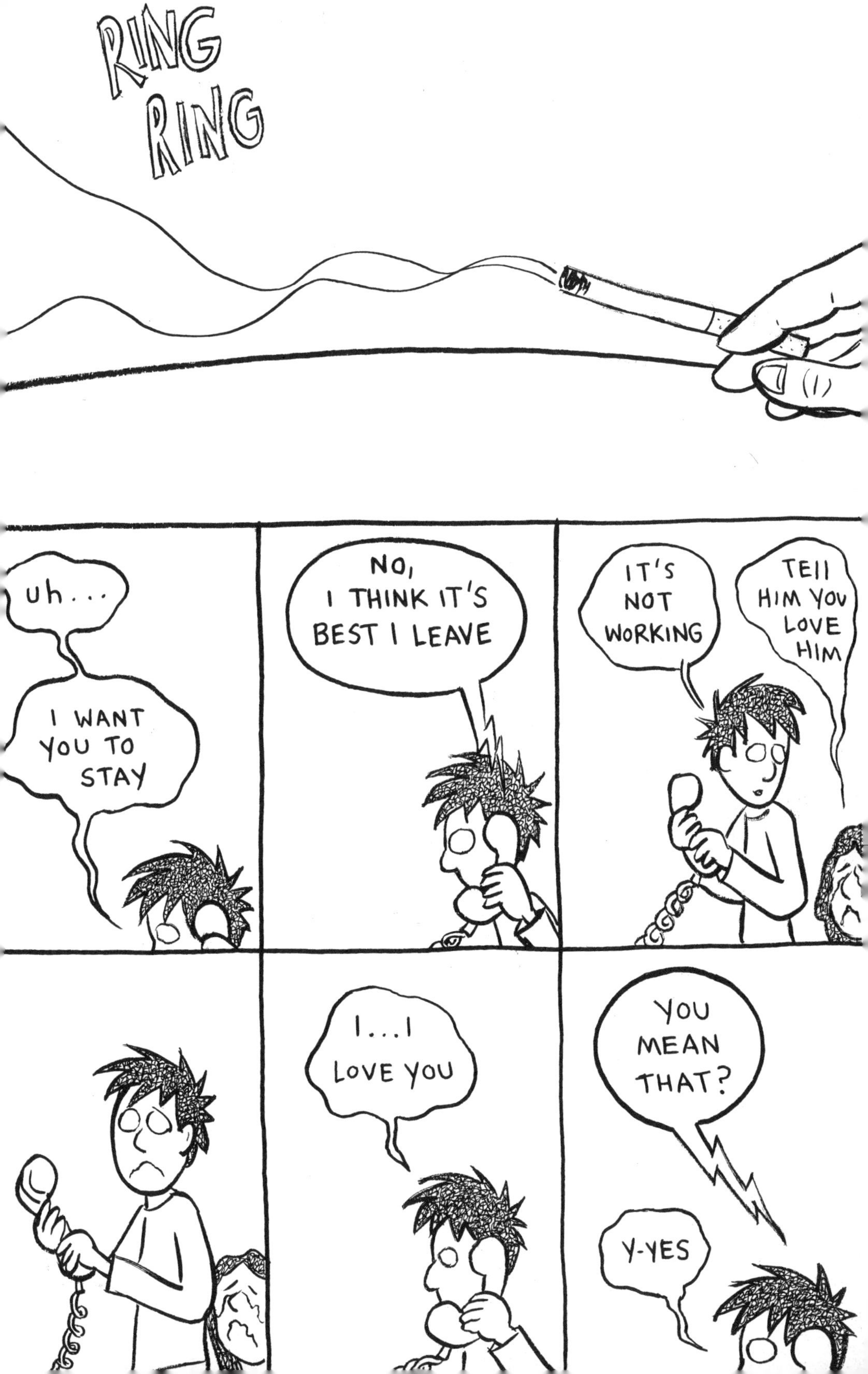
RING
RING
uh...
I WANT YOU TO STAY
NO, I THINK IT'S BEST I LEAVE
IT'S NOT WORKING
TEll HIM YOU LOVE HIM
I...I LOVE YOU
YOU MEAN THAT?
Y-YES

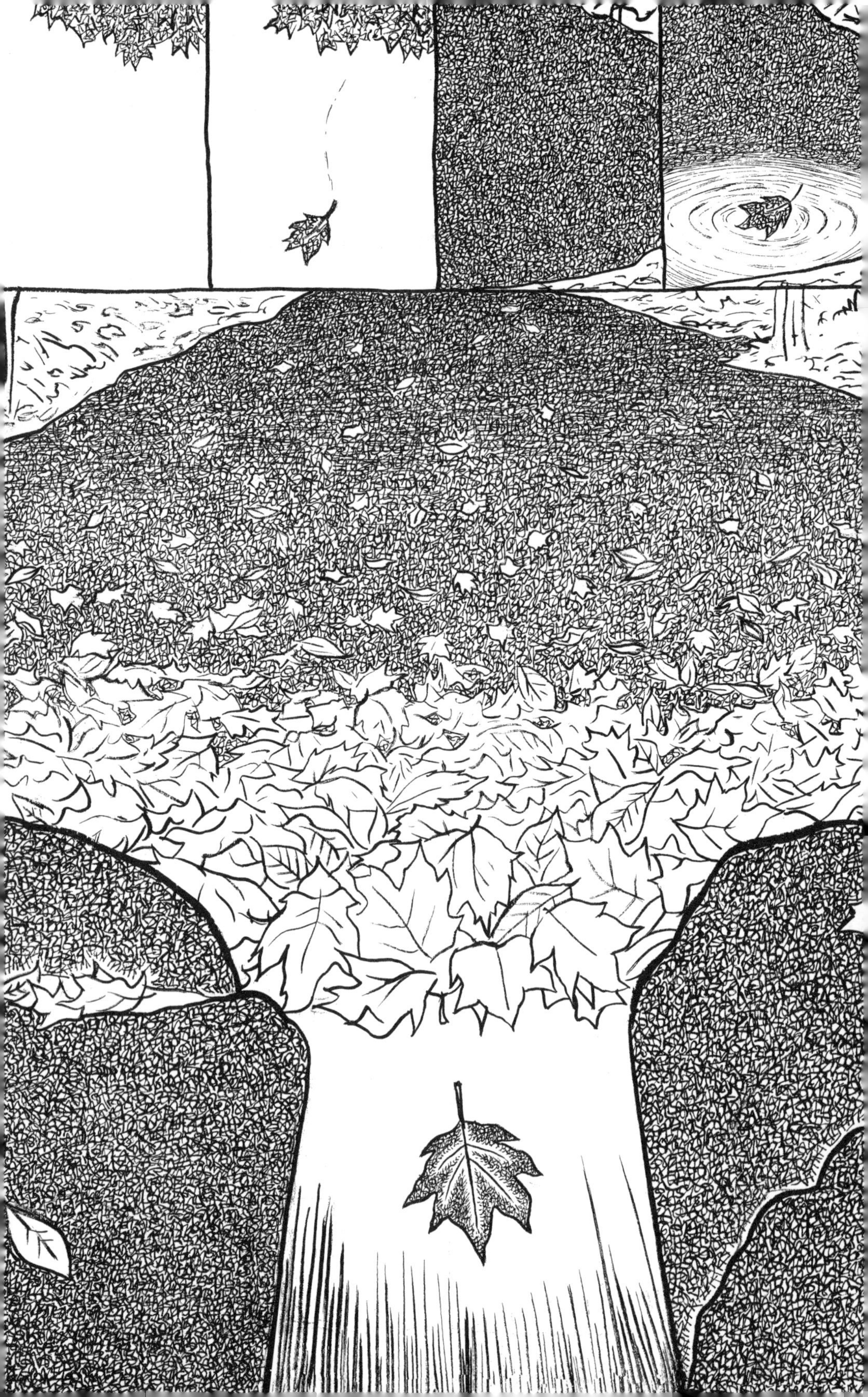

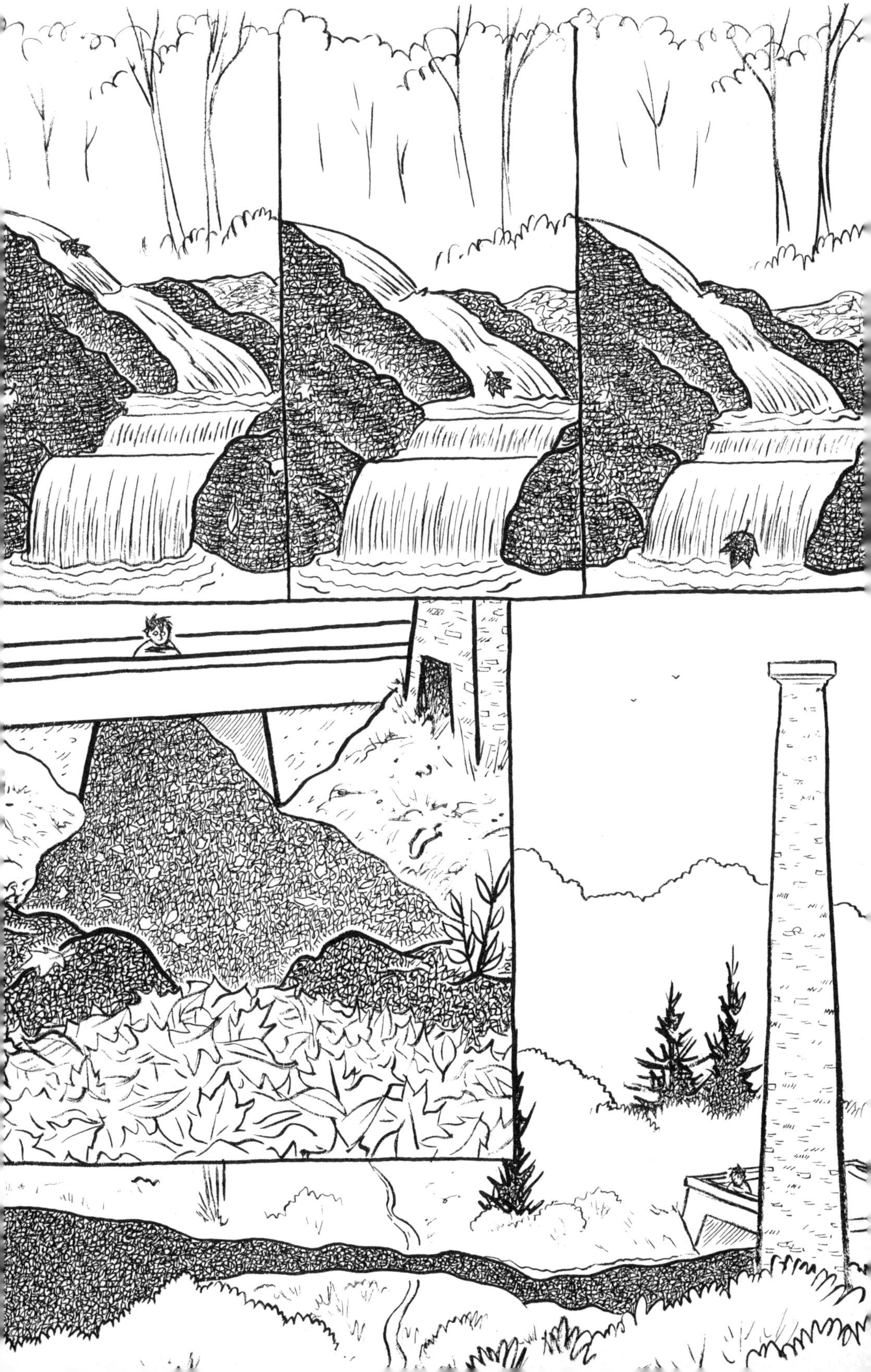

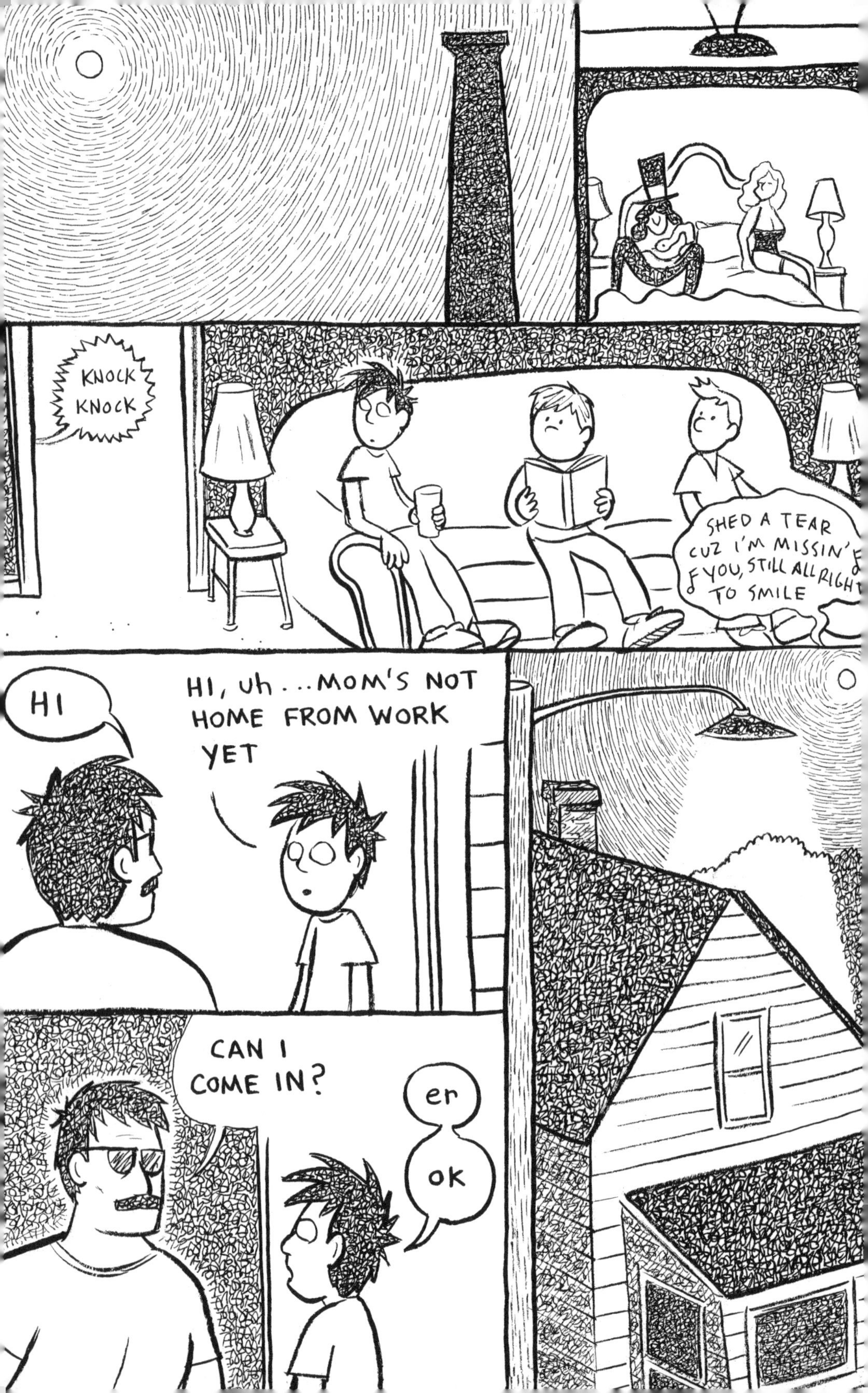
KNOCK KNOCK
SHED A TEAR CUZ I'M MISSIN' YOU, STILL ALL RIGHT TO SMILE
HI
HI, uh... MOM'S NOT HOME FROM WORK YET
CAN I COME IN?
er
ok

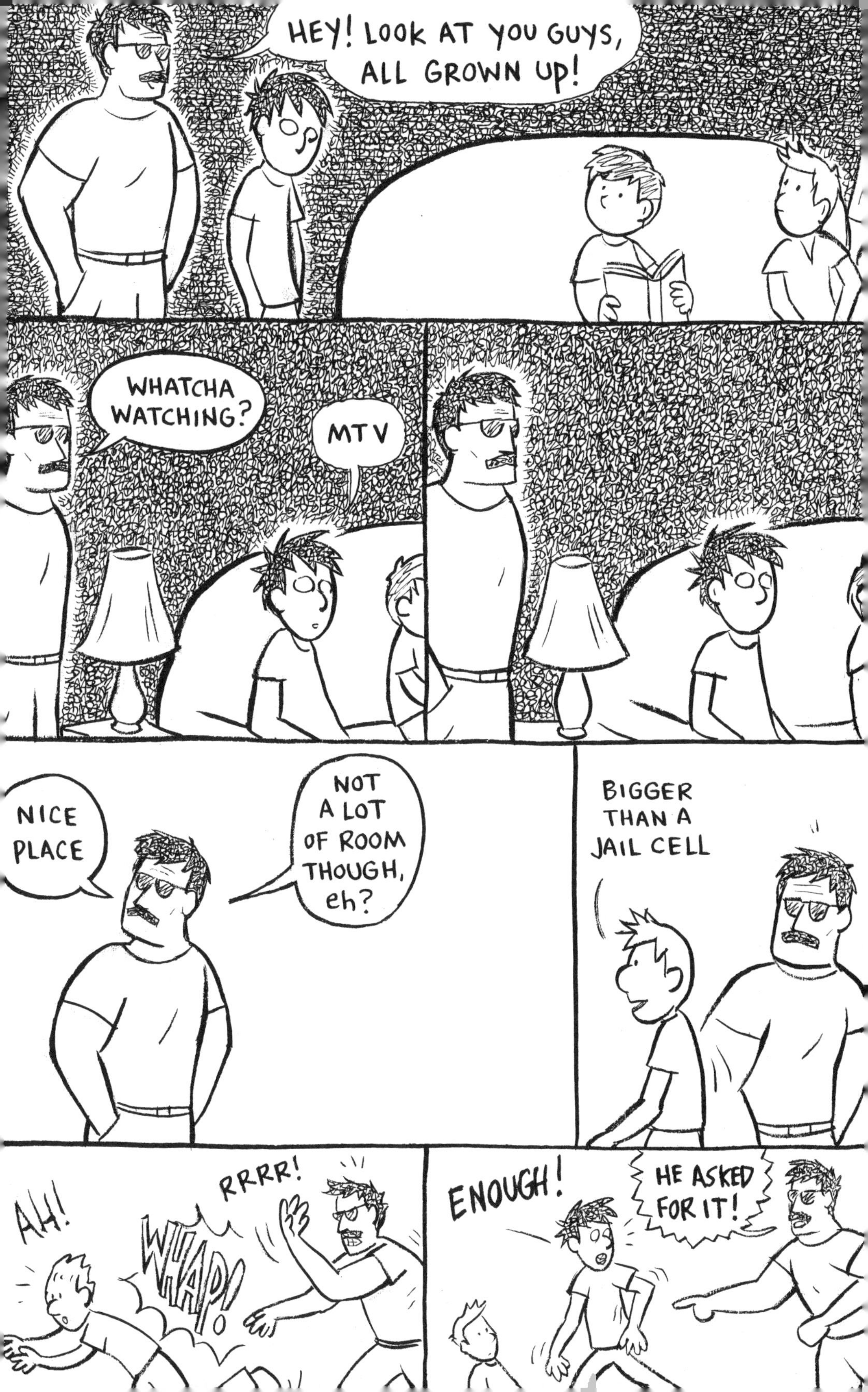
HEY! LOOK AT YOU GUYS, ALL GROWN UP!
WHATCHA WATCHING?
MTV
NICE PLACE
NOT A LOT OF ROOM THOUGH, eh?
BIGGER THAN A JAIL CELL
AH!
RRRR!
WHAP!
ENOUGH!
HE ASKED FOR IT!

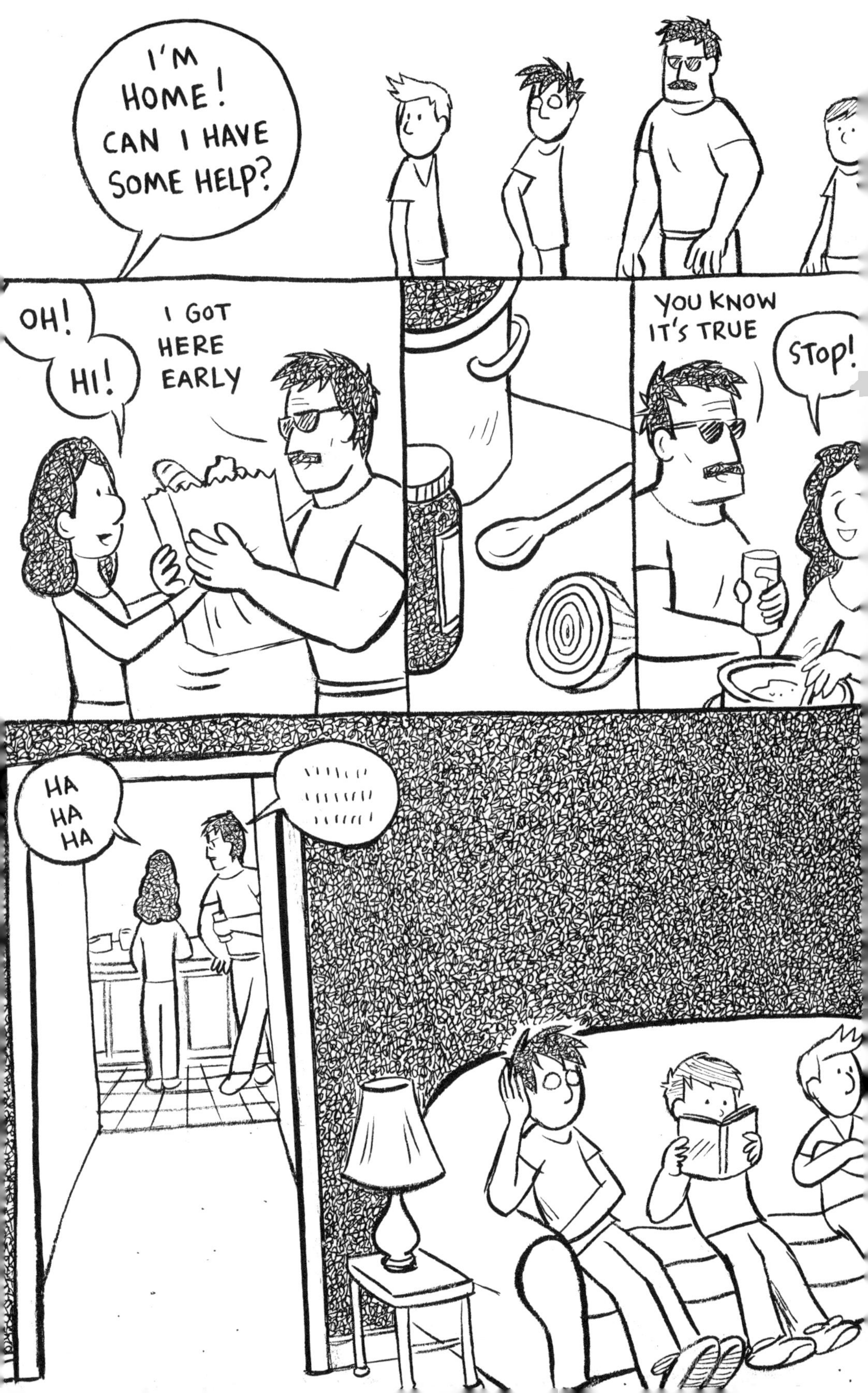
I'M HOME! CAN I HAVE SOME HELP?
OH!
HI!
I GOT HERE EARLY
YOU KNOW IT'S TRUE
STOP!
HA HA HA

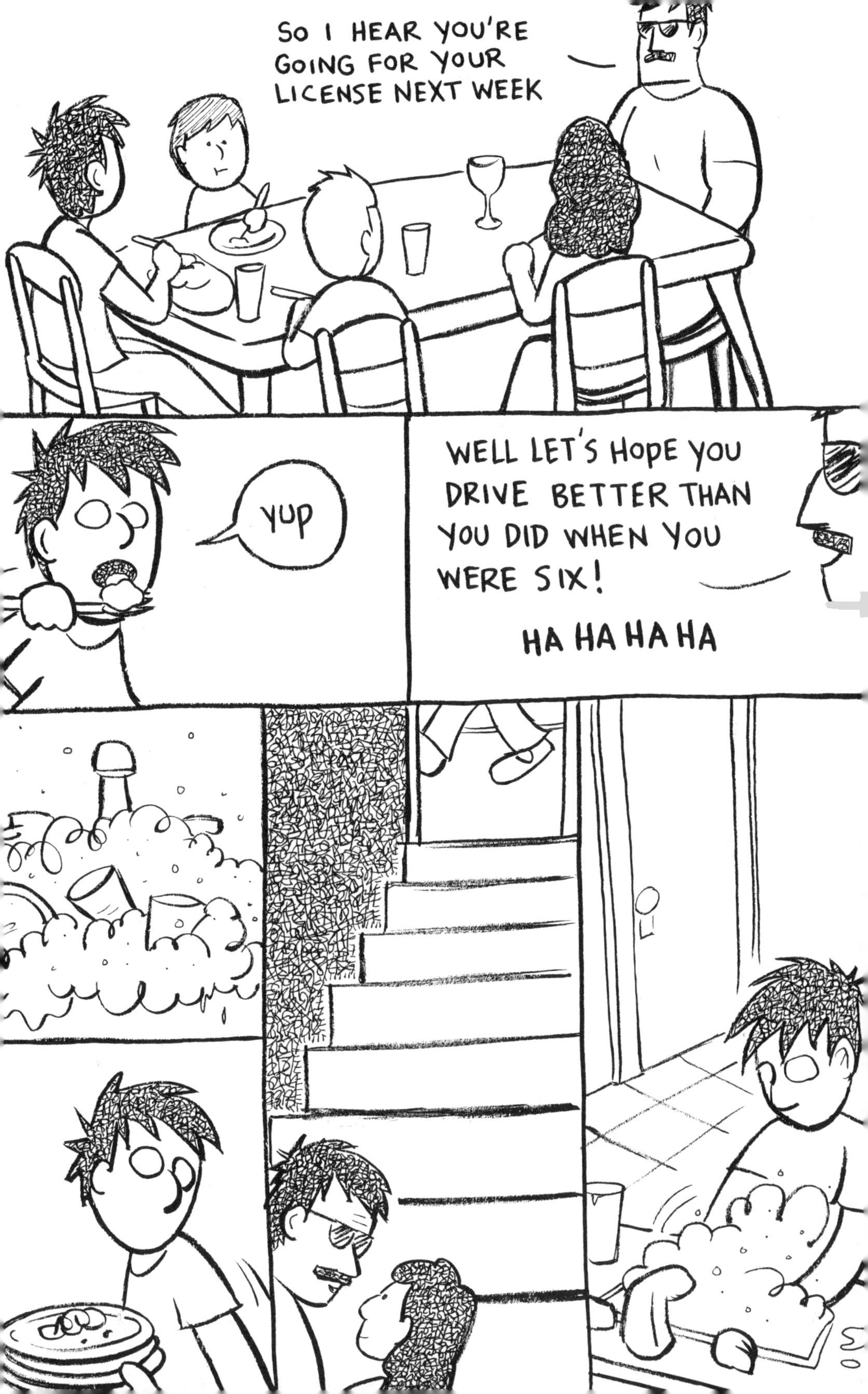
SO I HEAR YOU'RE GOING FOR YOUR LICENSE NEXT WEEK
YUP
WELL LET'S HOPE YOU DRIVE BETTER THAN YOU DID WHEN YOU WERE SIX!
HA HA HA HA

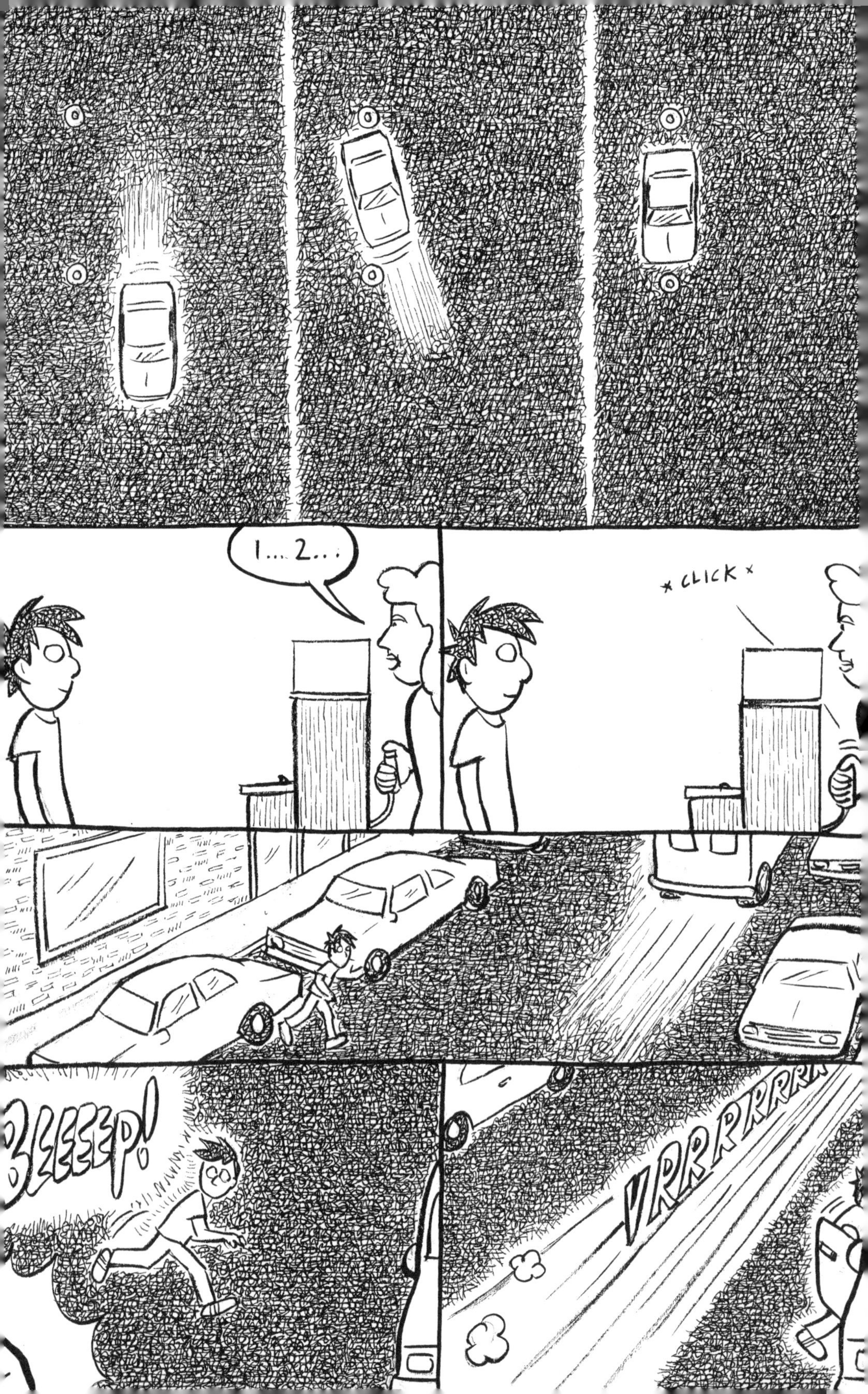
1... 2...
CLICK
BLEEEP!
VRRRRRRR

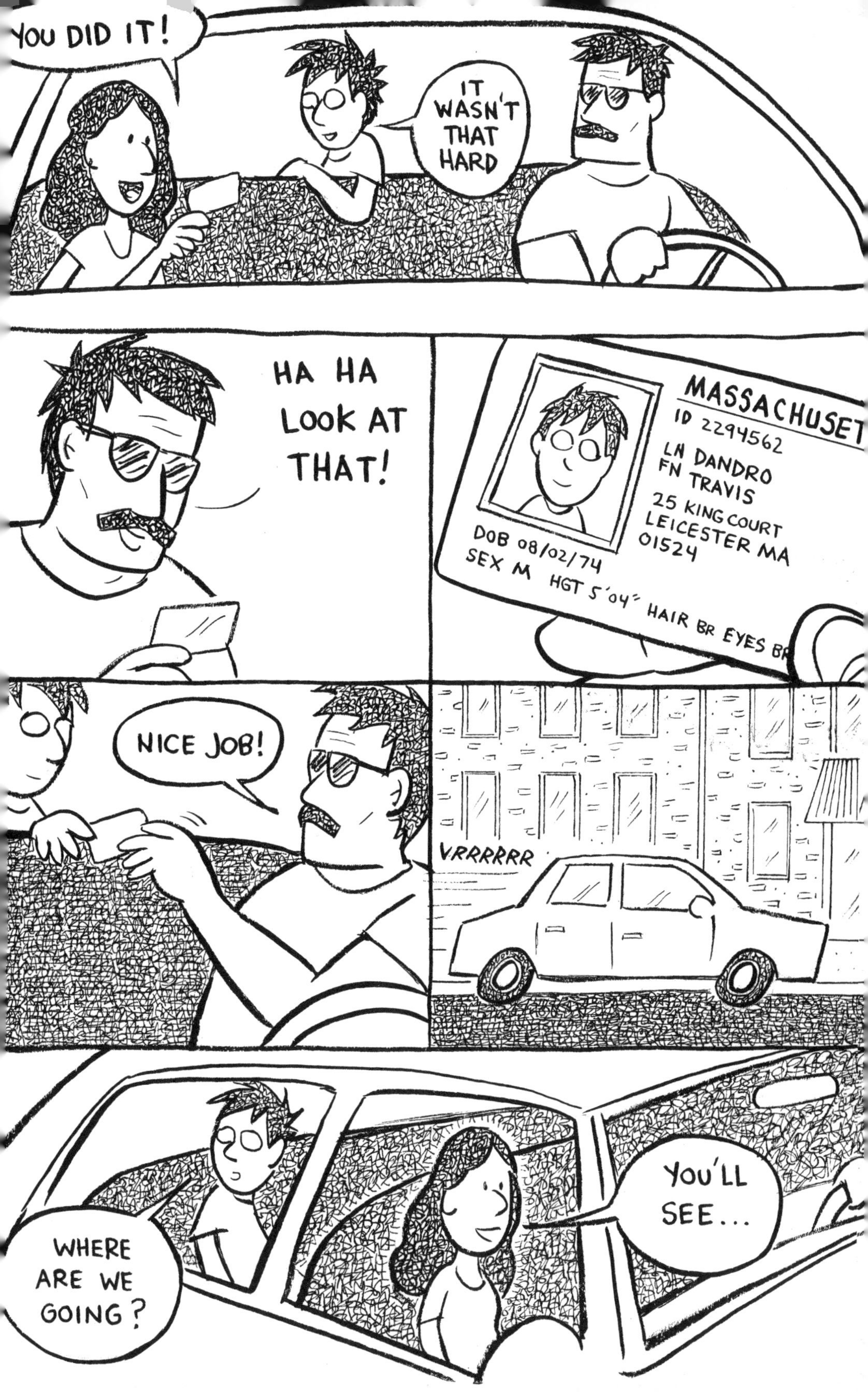
YOU DID IT!
IT WASN'T THAT HARD
HA HA LOOK AT THAT!
MASSACHUSET
ID 2294562
LN DANDRO
FN TRAVIS
25 KING COURT
LEICESTER MA
01524
DOB 08/02/74
SEX M HGT 5'04" HAIR BR EYES BR
NICE JOB!
VRRRRRR
WHERE ARE WE GOING?
YOU'LL SEE...

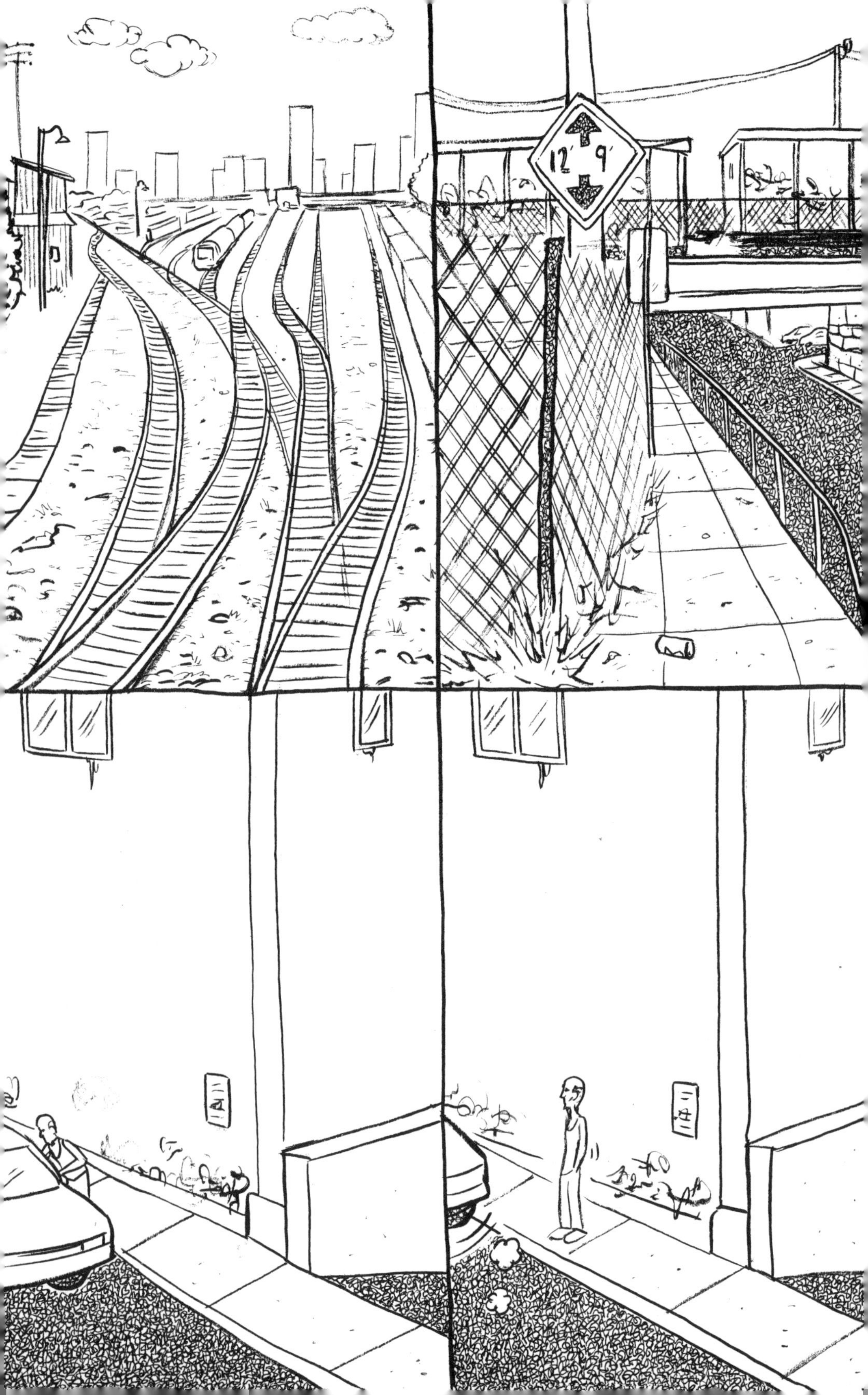
12' 9'

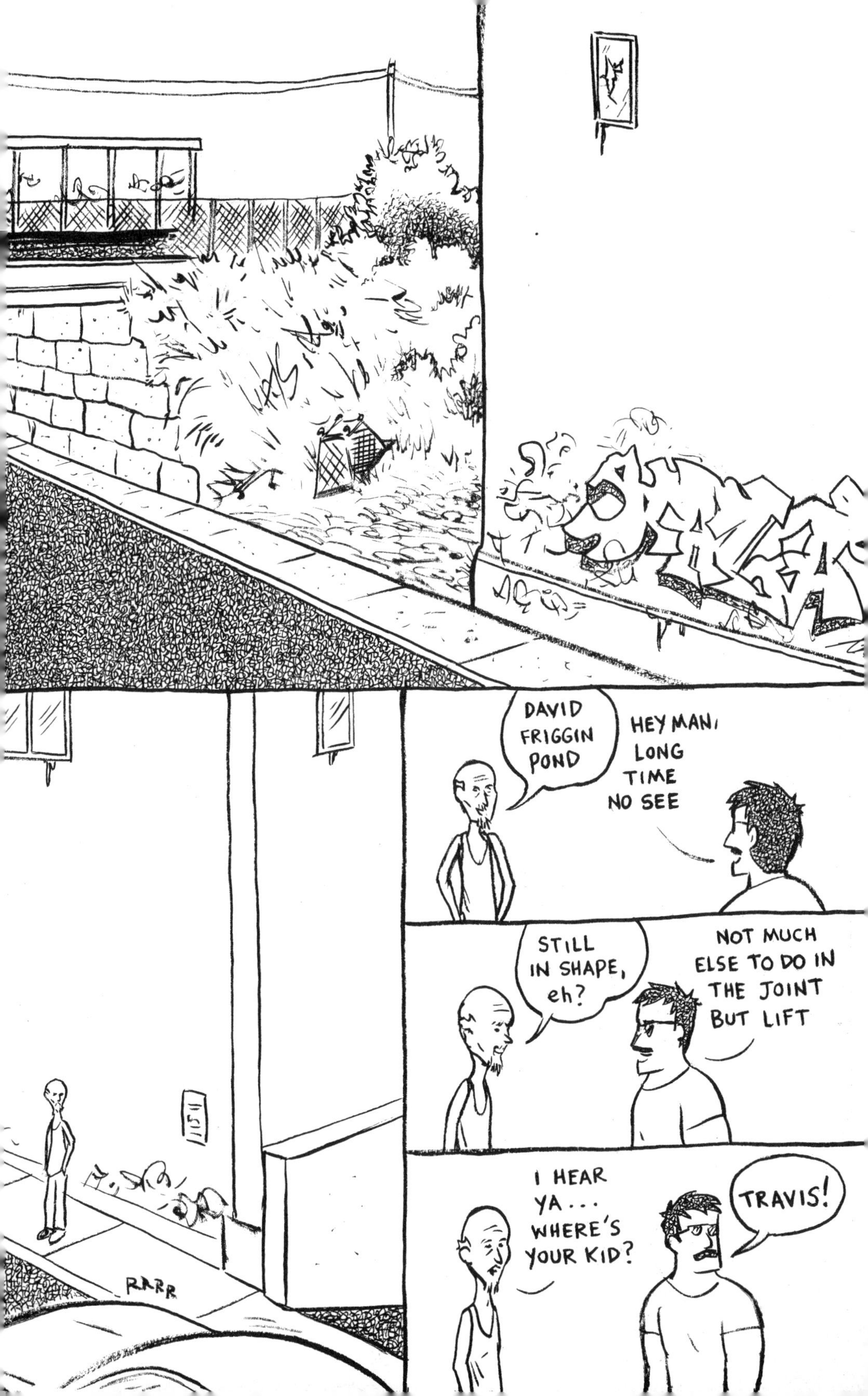
RRRR
DAVID FRIGGIN POND
HEY MAN, LONG TIME NO SEE
STILL IN SHAPE, eh?
NOT MUCH ELSE TO DO IN THE JOINT BUT LIFT
I HEAR YA... WHERE'S YOUR KID?
TRAVIS!

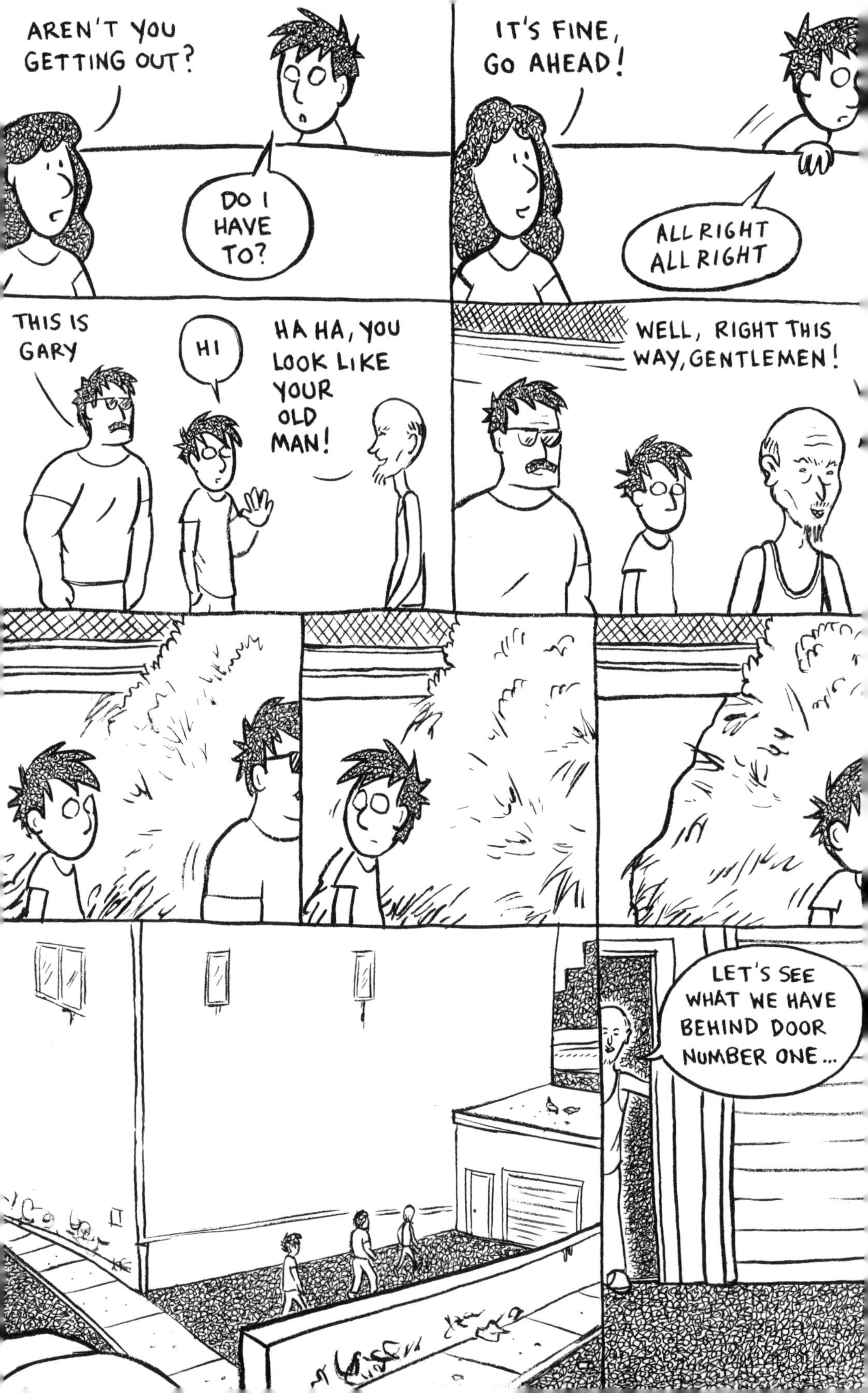
AREN'T YOU GETTING OUT?
DO I HAVE TO?
IT'S FINE, GO AHEAD!
ALL RIGHT ALL RIGHT
THIS IS GARY
HI
HA HA, YOU LOOK LIKE YOUR OLD MAN!
WELL, RIGHT THIS WAY, GENTLEMEN!
LET'S SEE WHAT WE HAVE BEHIND DOOR NUMBER ONE...

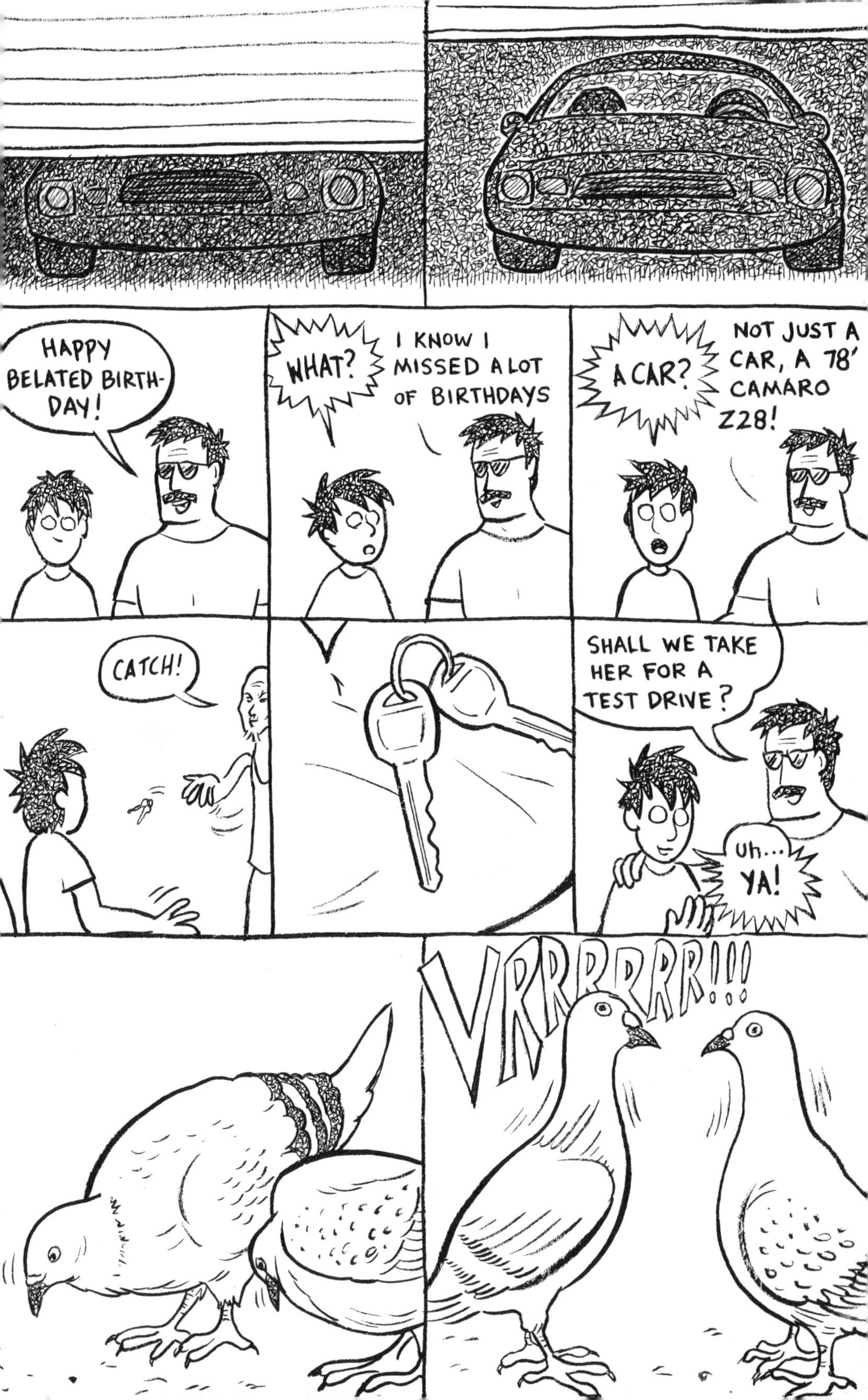
HAPPY BELATED BIRTH-DAY!
WHAT?
I KNOW I MISSED A LOT OF BIRTHDAYS
A CAR?
NOT JUST A CAR, A 78' CAMARO Z28!
CATCH!
SHALL WE TAKE HER FOR A TEST DRIVE?
Uh... YA!
VRRRRRR!!!

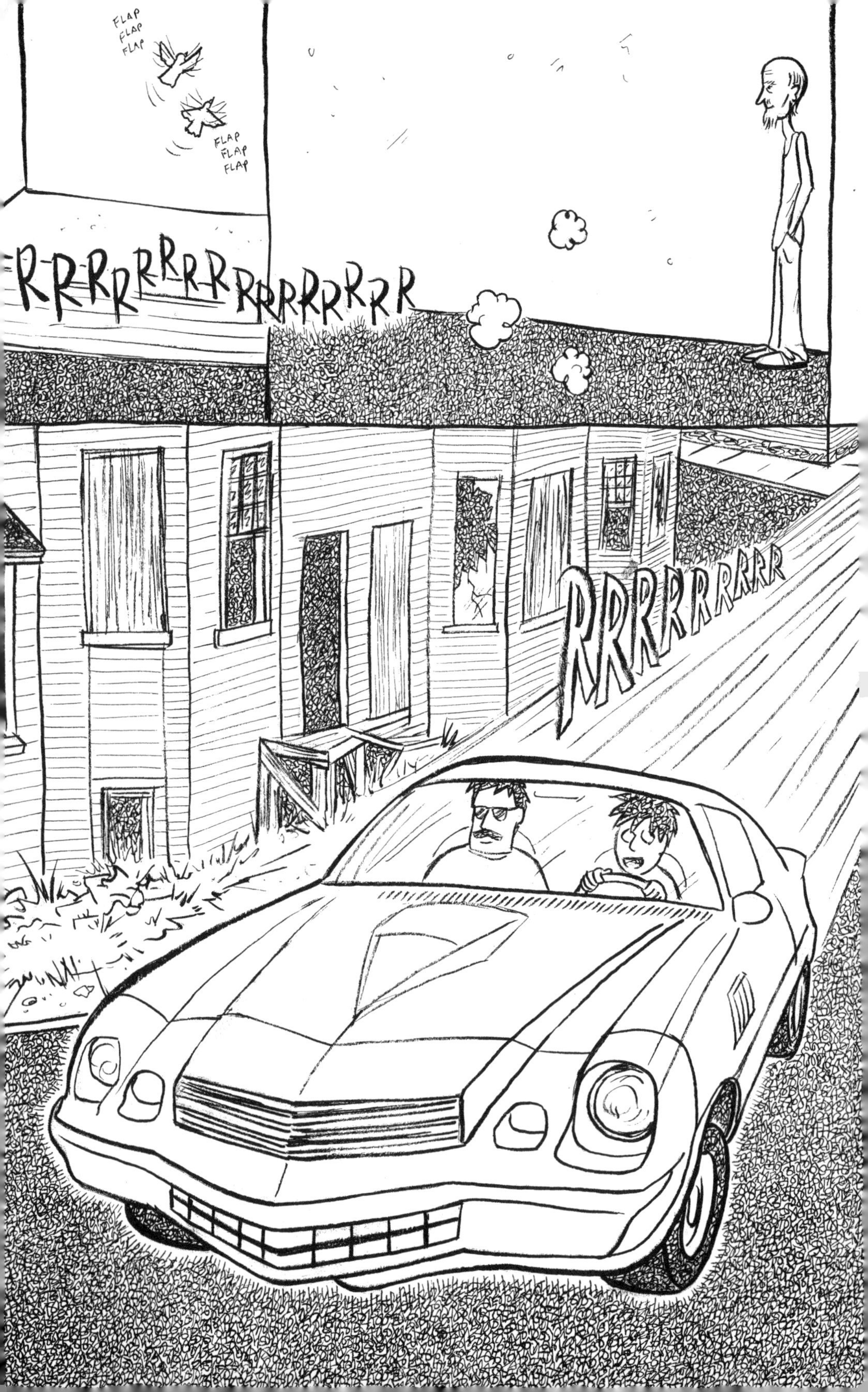
FLAP
FLAP
FLAP
FLAP
FLAP
FLAP
RRRRRRRRRRRRRRRRRRR
RRRRRRRRRR

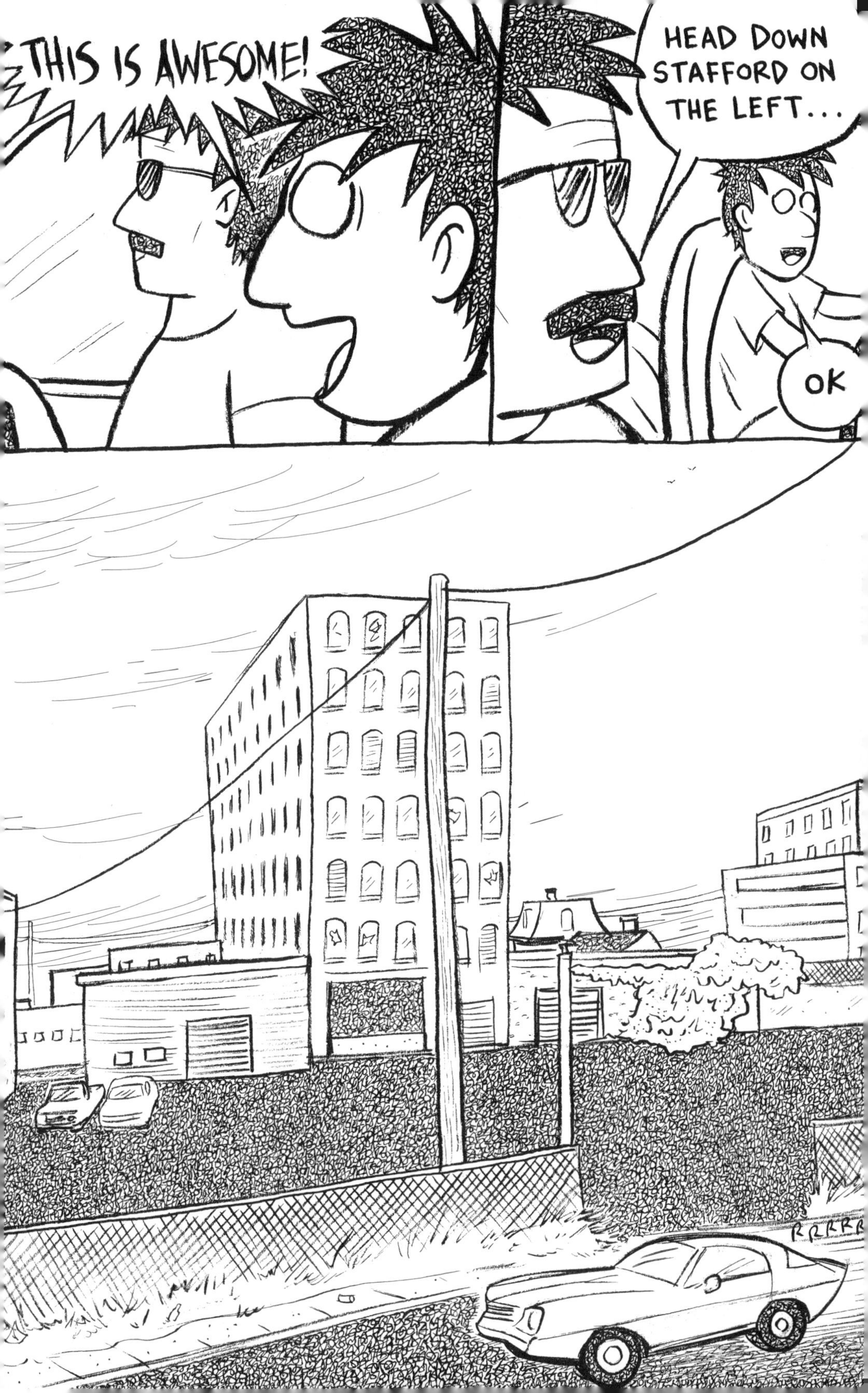
THIS IS AWESOME!
HEAD DOWN STAFFORD ON THE LEFT...
OK

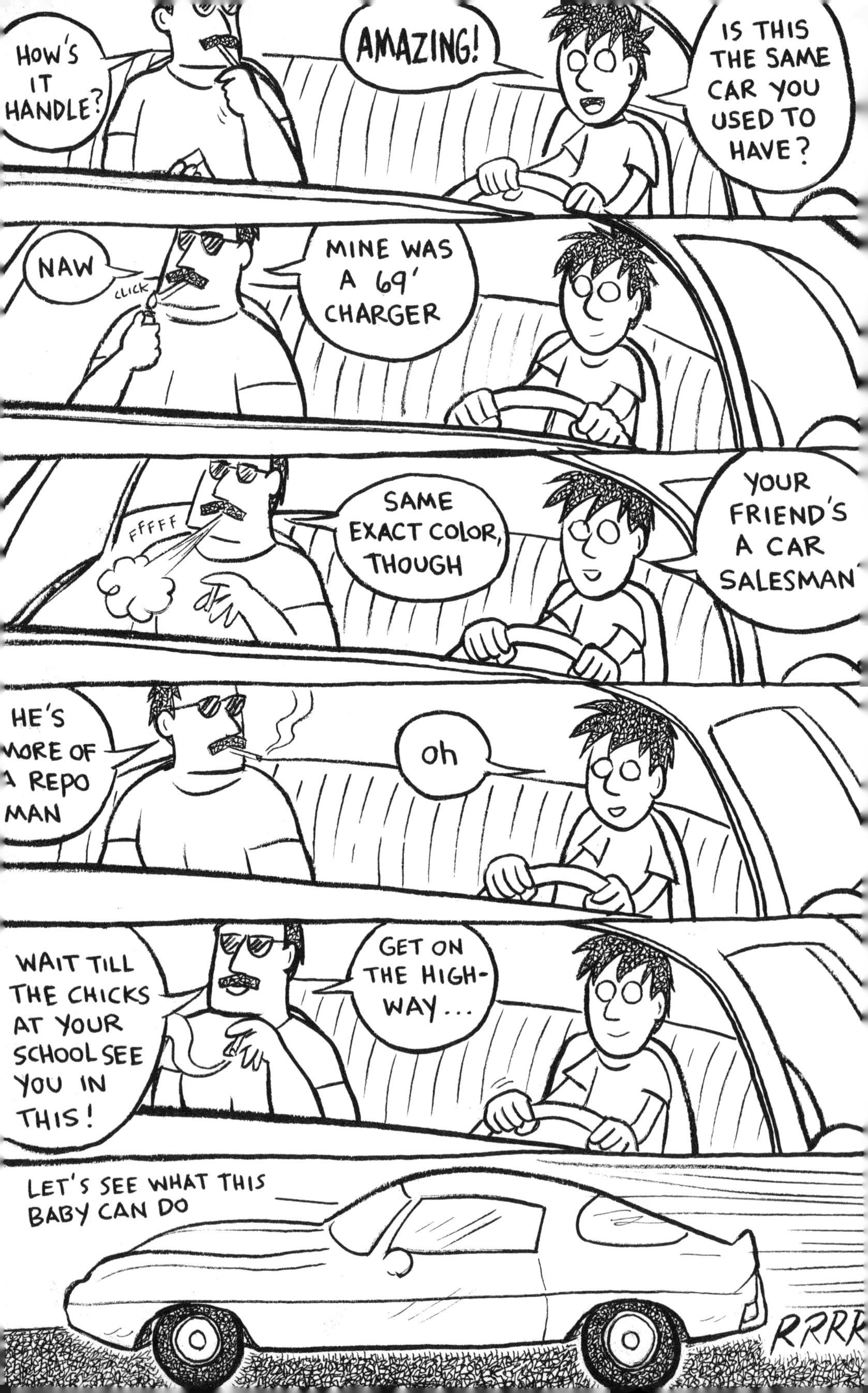
HOW'S IT HANDLE?
AMAZING!
IS THIS THE SAME CAR YOU USED TO HAVE?
NAW
CLICK
MINE WAS A 69' CHARGER
FFFFF
SAME EXACT COLOR, THOUGH
YOUR FRIEND'S A CAR SALESMAN
HE'S MORE OF A REPO MAN
oh
WAIT TILL THE CHICKS AT YOUR SCHOOL SEE YOU IN THIS!
GET ON THE HIGH-WAY...
LET'S SEE WHAT THIS BABY CAN DO
RRRR

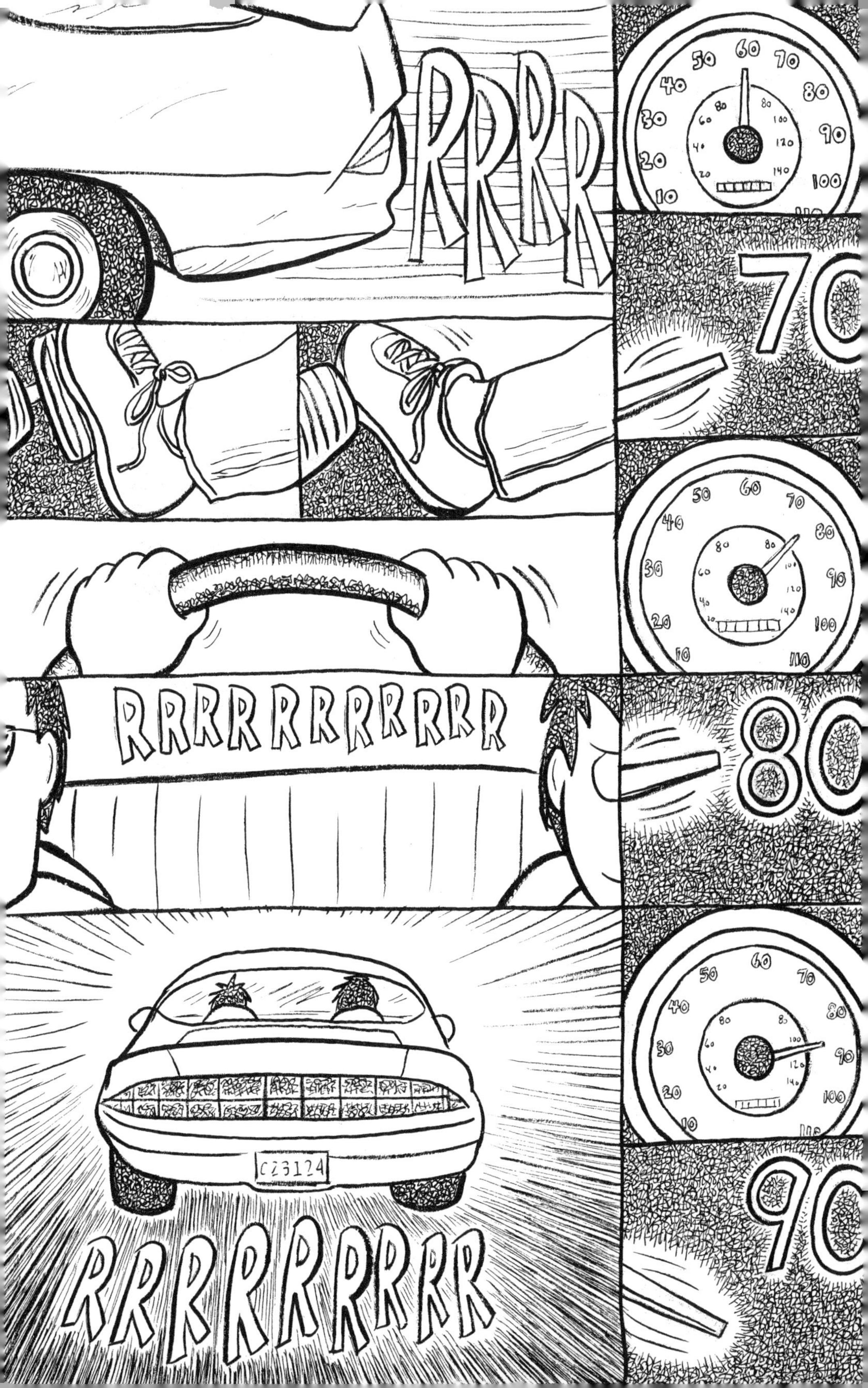
RRRRR
70
80
RRRRRRRRRRR
90
C23124
RRRRRRRRR

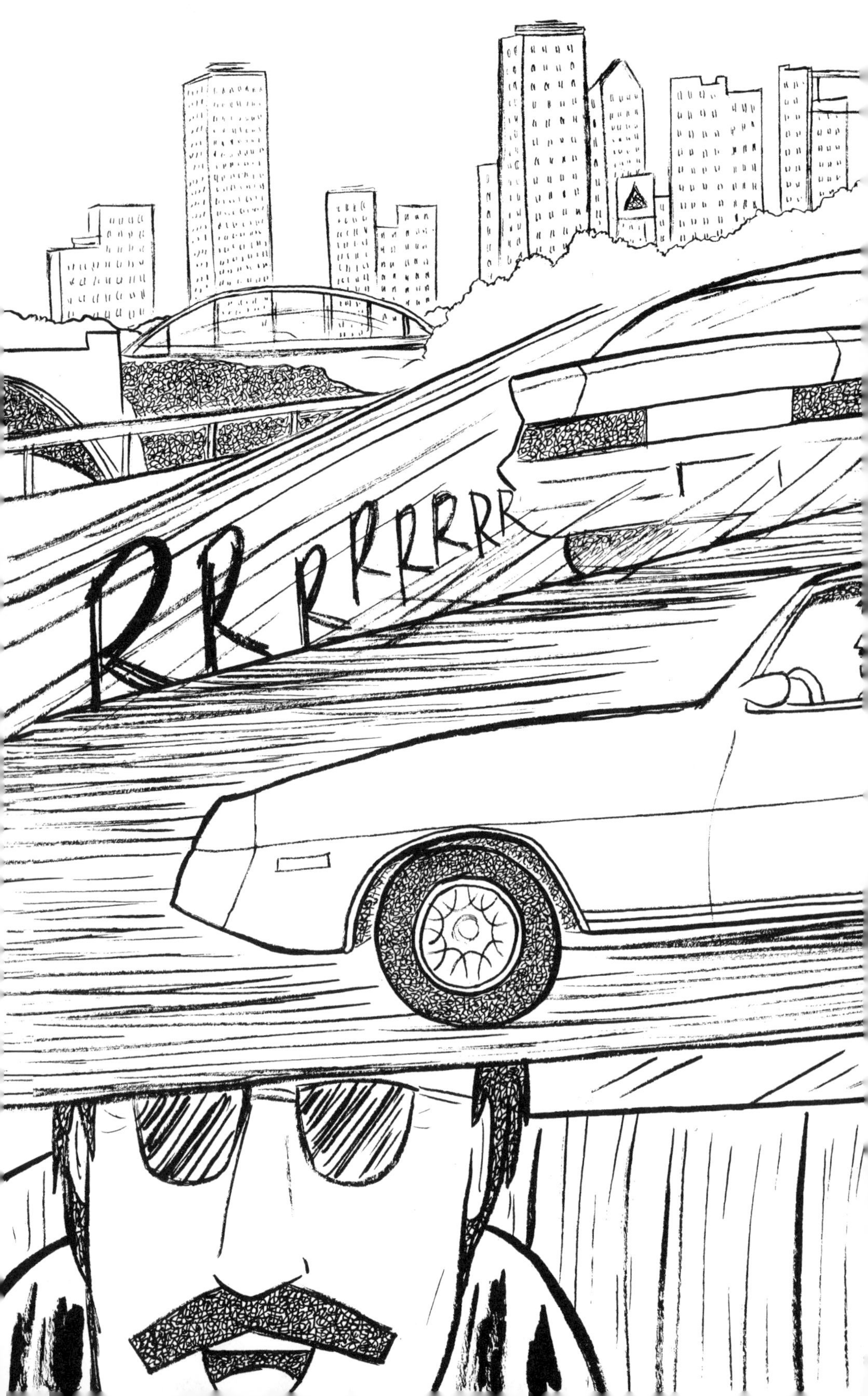
RRRRRRRR

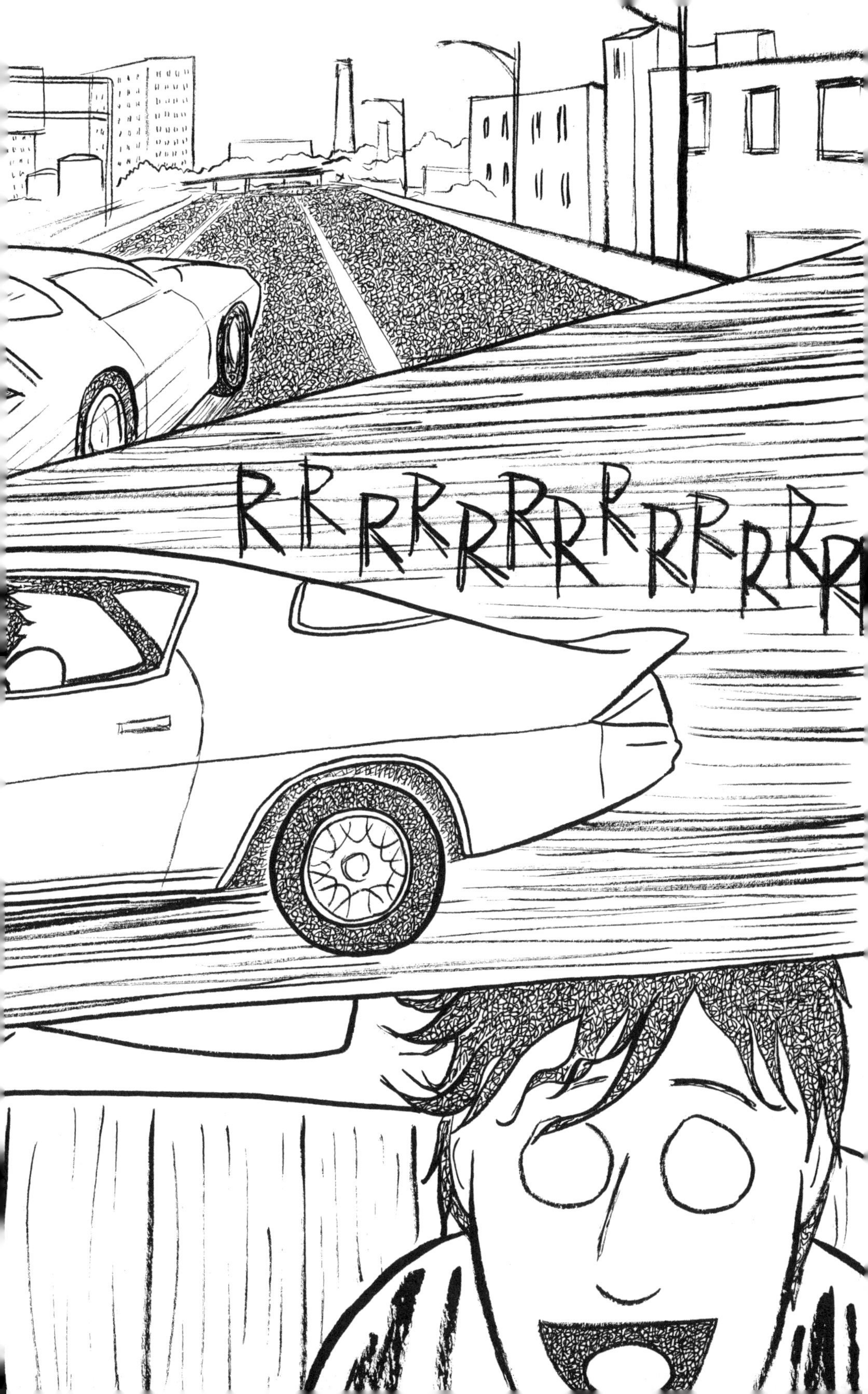
RRRRRRRRRRRRR

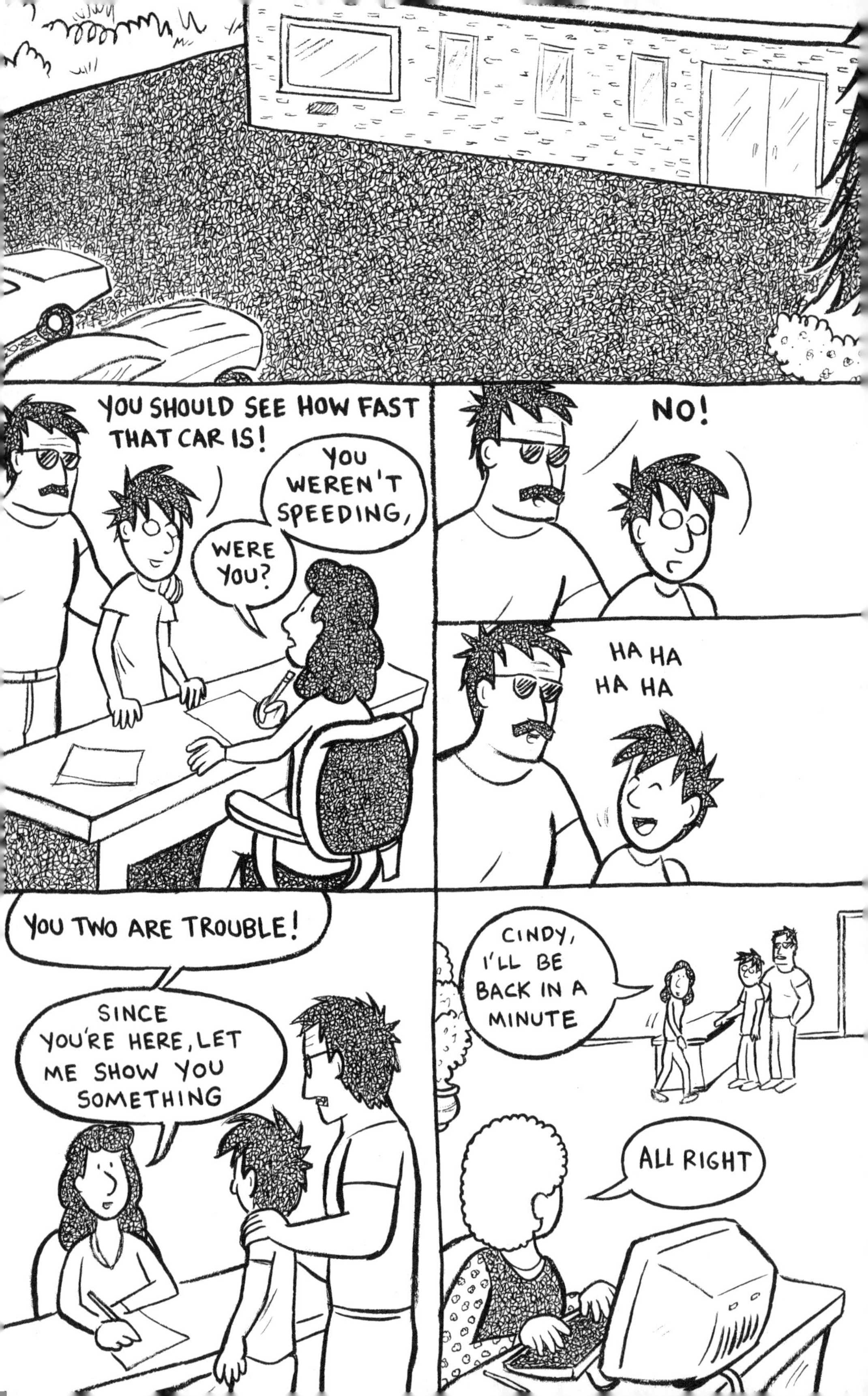
YOU SHOULD SEE HOW FAST THAT CAR IS!
YOU WEREN'T SPEEDING,
WERE YOU?
NO!
HA HA HA HA
YOU TWO ARE TROUBLE!
SINCE YOU'RE HERE, LET ME SHOW YOU SOMETHING
CINDY, I'LL BE BACK IN A MINUTE
ALL RIGHT

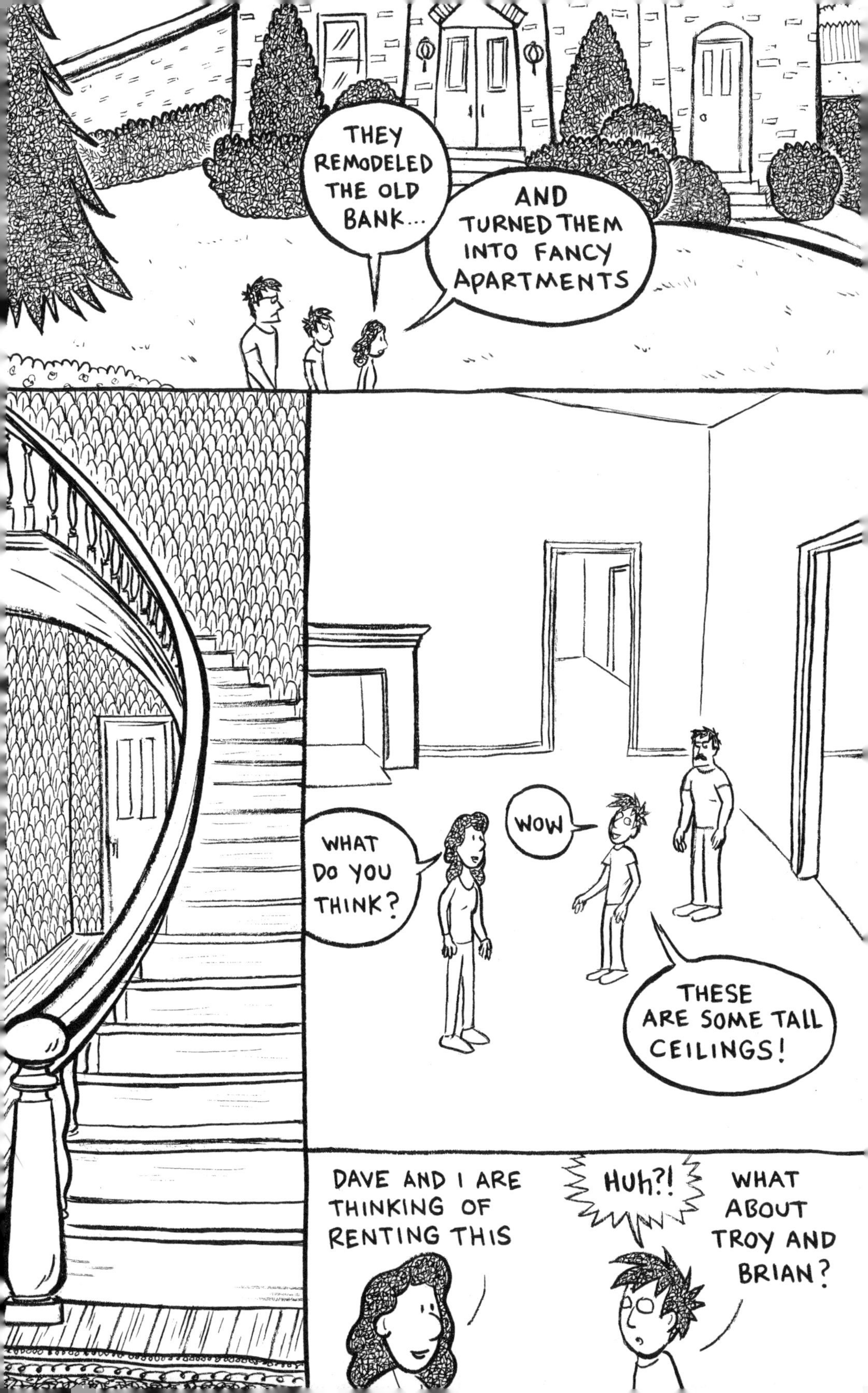
THEY REMODELED THE OLD BANK...
AND TURNED THEM INTO FANCY APARTMENTS
WHAT DO YOU THINK?
WOW
THESE ARE SOME TALL CEILINGS!
DAVE AND I ARE THINKING OF RENTING THIS
Huh?!
WHAT ABOUT TROY AND BRIAN?

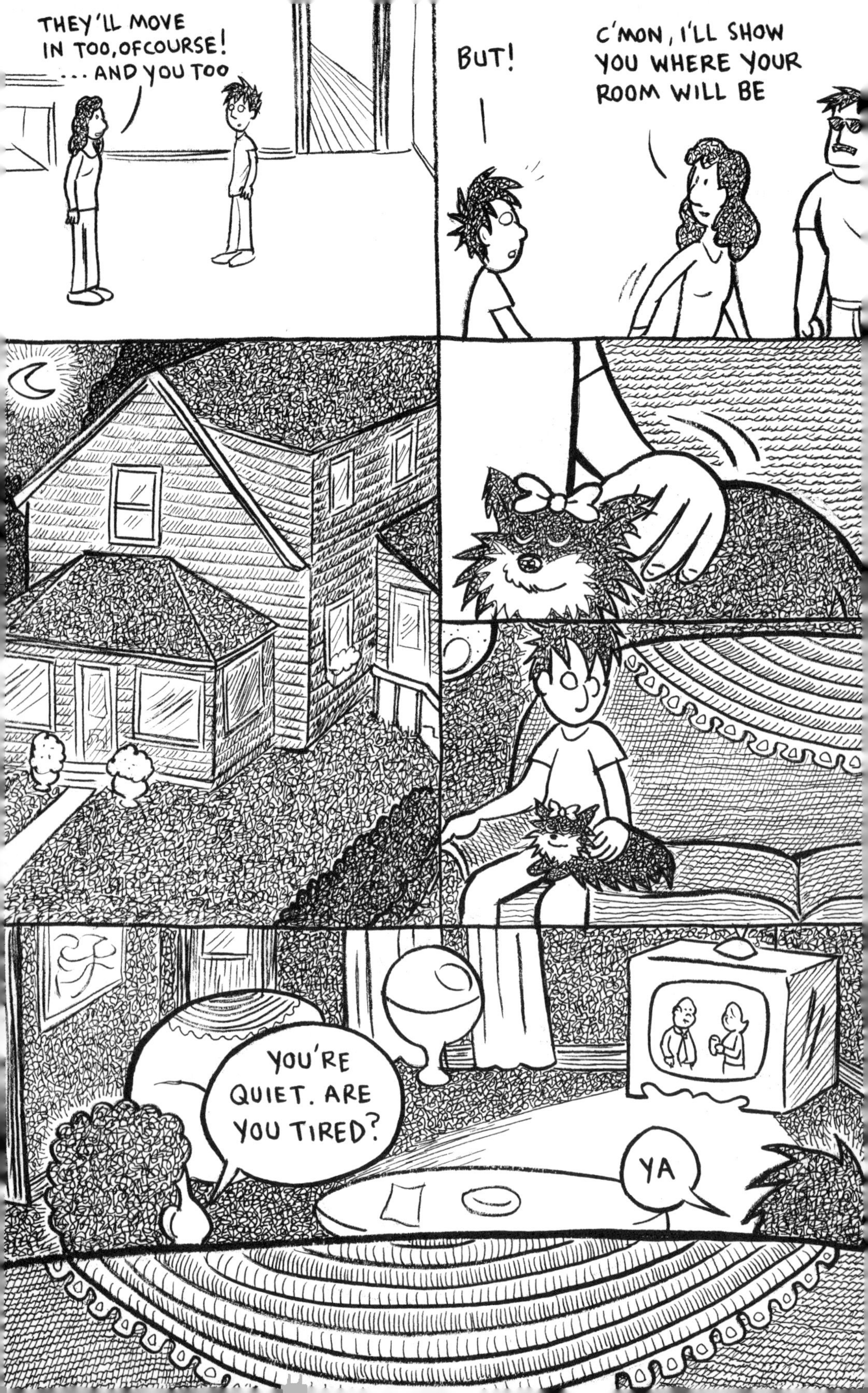
THEY'LL MOVE IN TOO, OFCOURSE! ... AND YOU TOO
BUT!
C'MON, I'LL SHOW YOU WHERE YOUR ROOM WILL BE
YOU'RE QUIET. ARE YOU TIRED?
YA

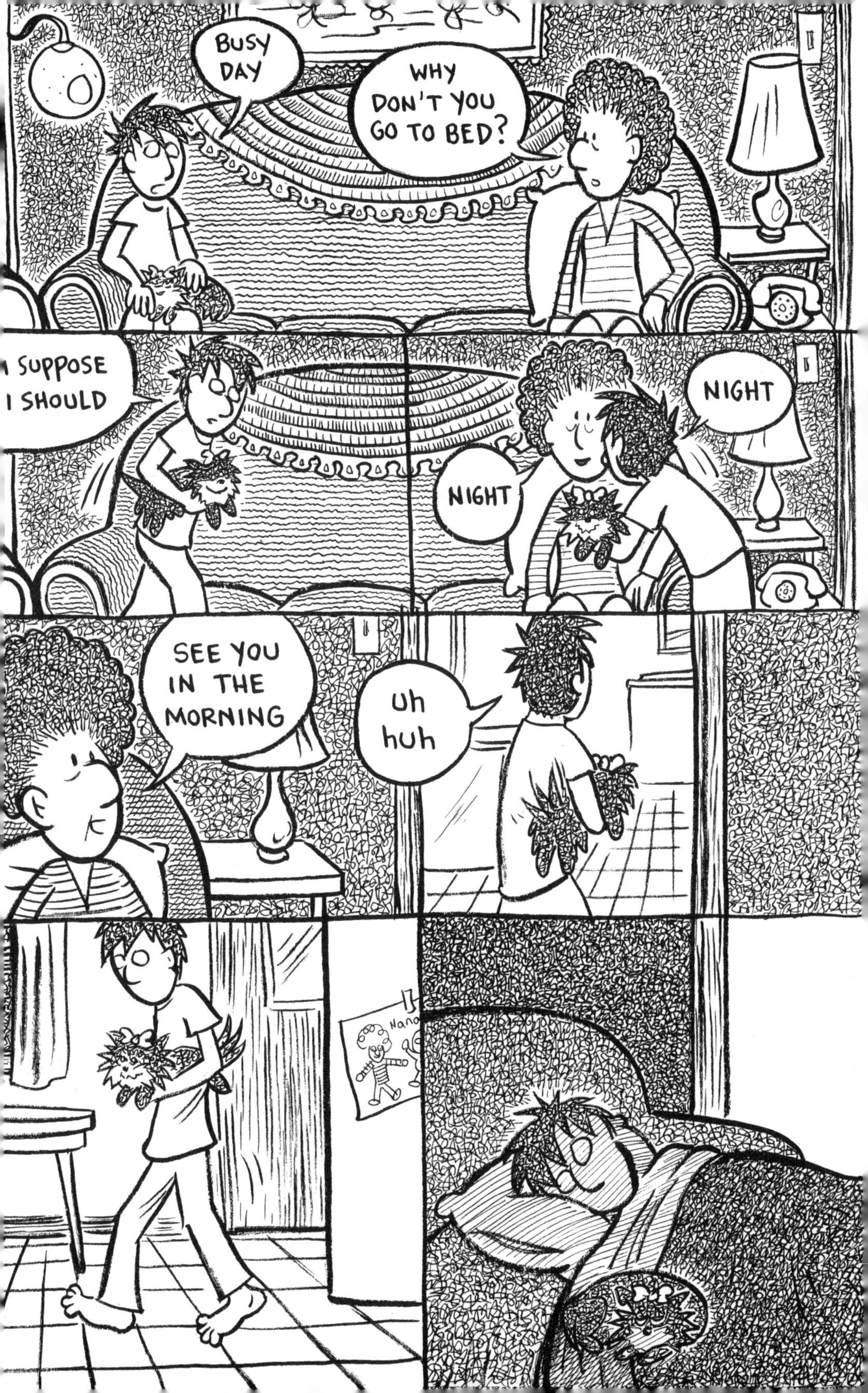
BUSY DAY
WHY DON'T YOU GO TO BED?
I SUPPOSE I SHOULD
NIGHT
NIGHT
SEE YOU IN THE MORNING
uh huh
Nana

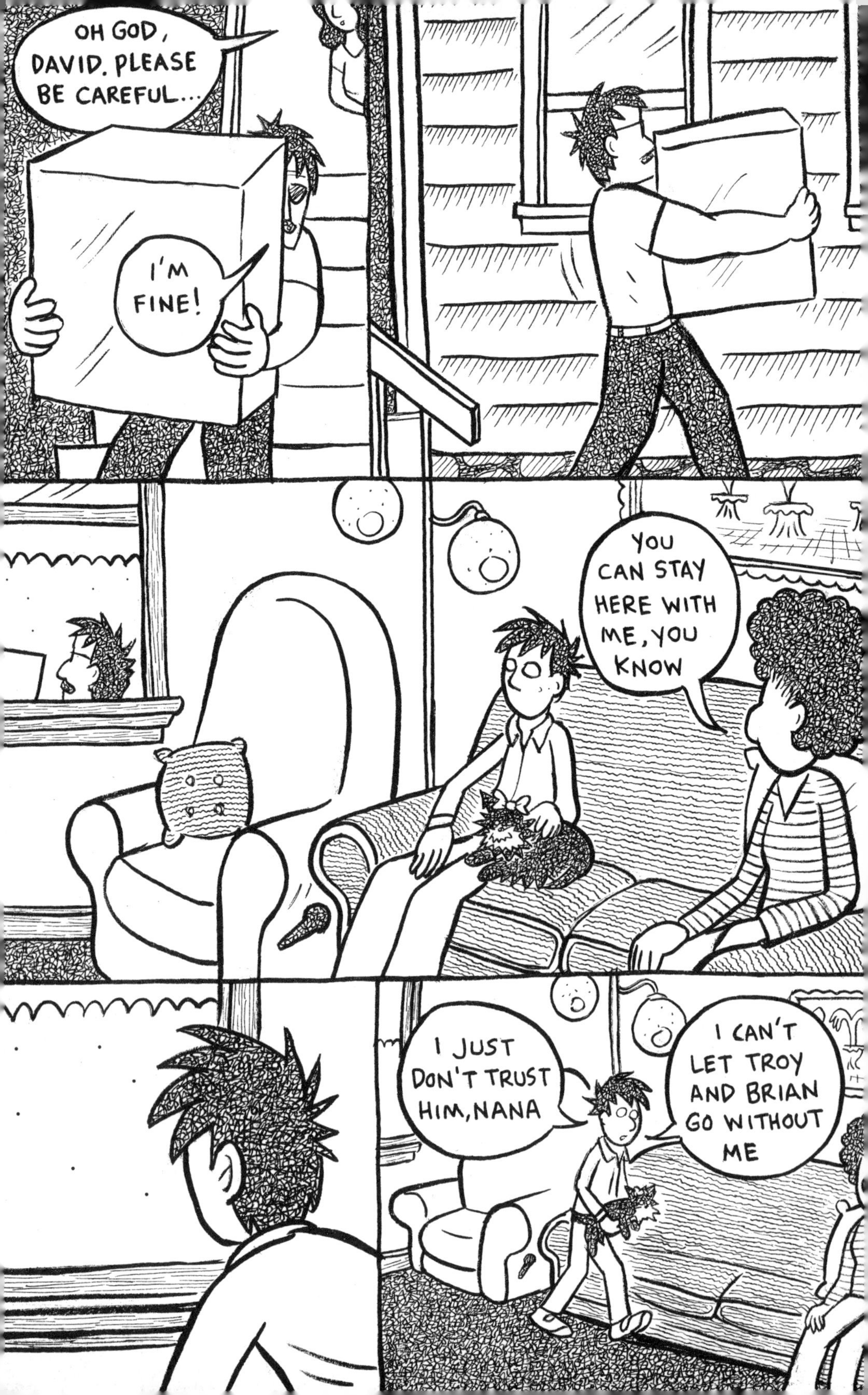
OH GOD, DAVID. PLEASE BE CAREFUL...
I'M FINE!
YOU CAN STAY HERE WITH ME, YOU KNOW
I JUST DON'T TRUST HIM, NANA
I CAN'T LET TROY AND BRIAN GO WITHOUT ME

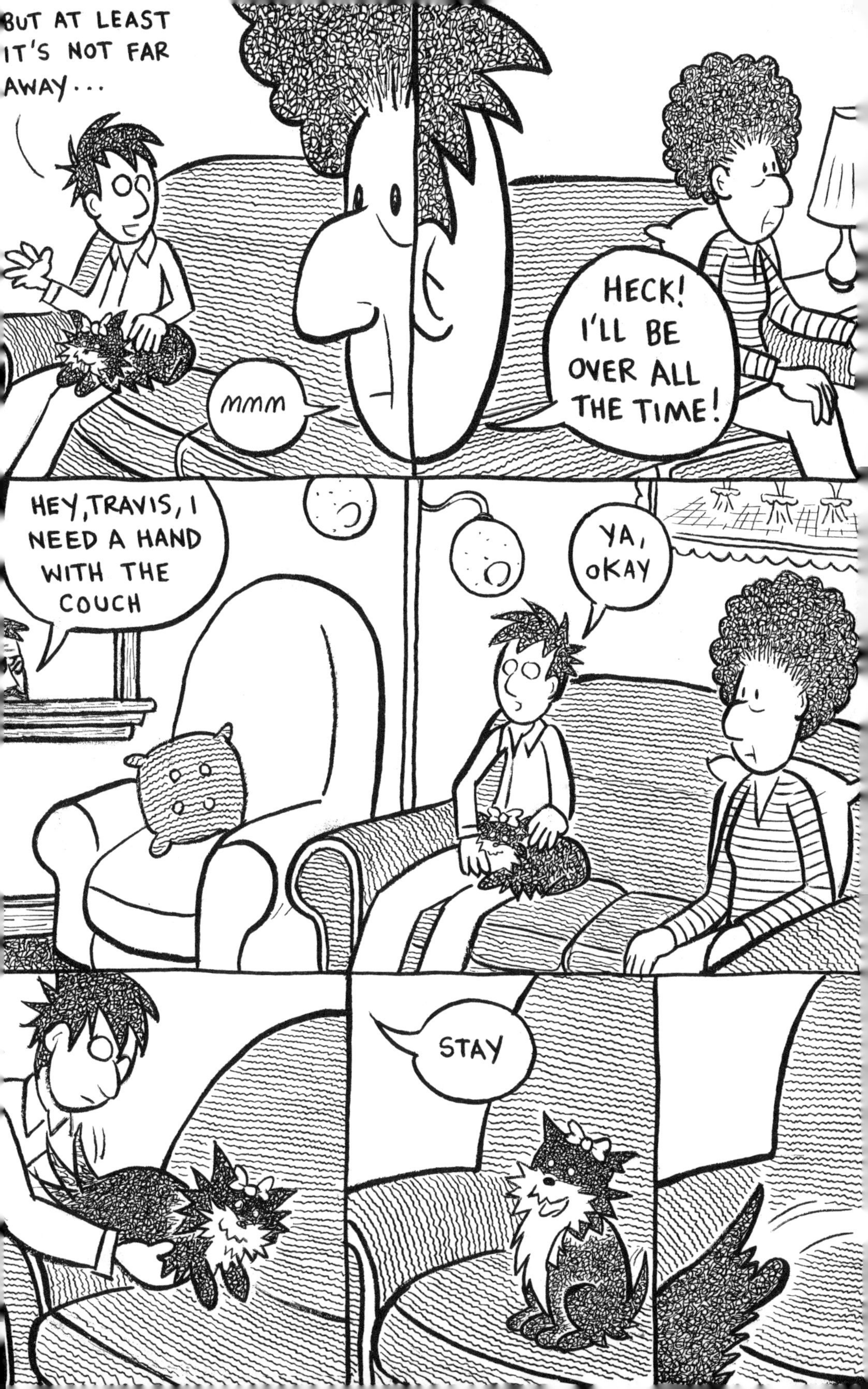
BUT AT LEAST IT'S NOT FAR AWAY...
MMM
HECK! I'LL BE OVER ALL THE TIME!
HEY, TRAVIS, I NEED A HAND WITH THE COUCH
YA, OKAY
STAY

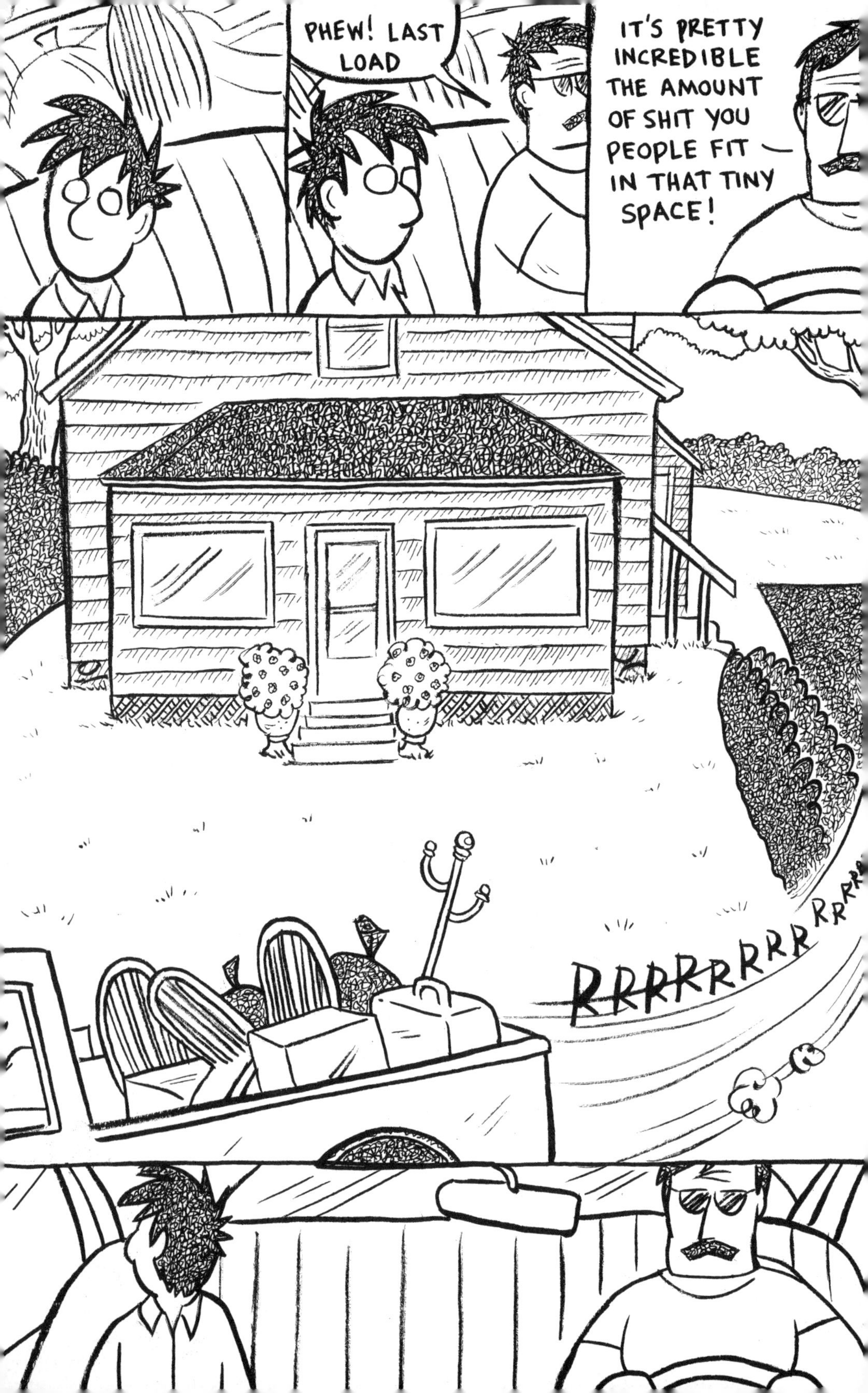
PHEW! LAST LOAD
IT'S PRETTY INCREDIBLE THE AMOUNT OF SHIT YOU PEOPLE FIT IN THAT TINY SPACE!
RRRRRRRRRRRRR

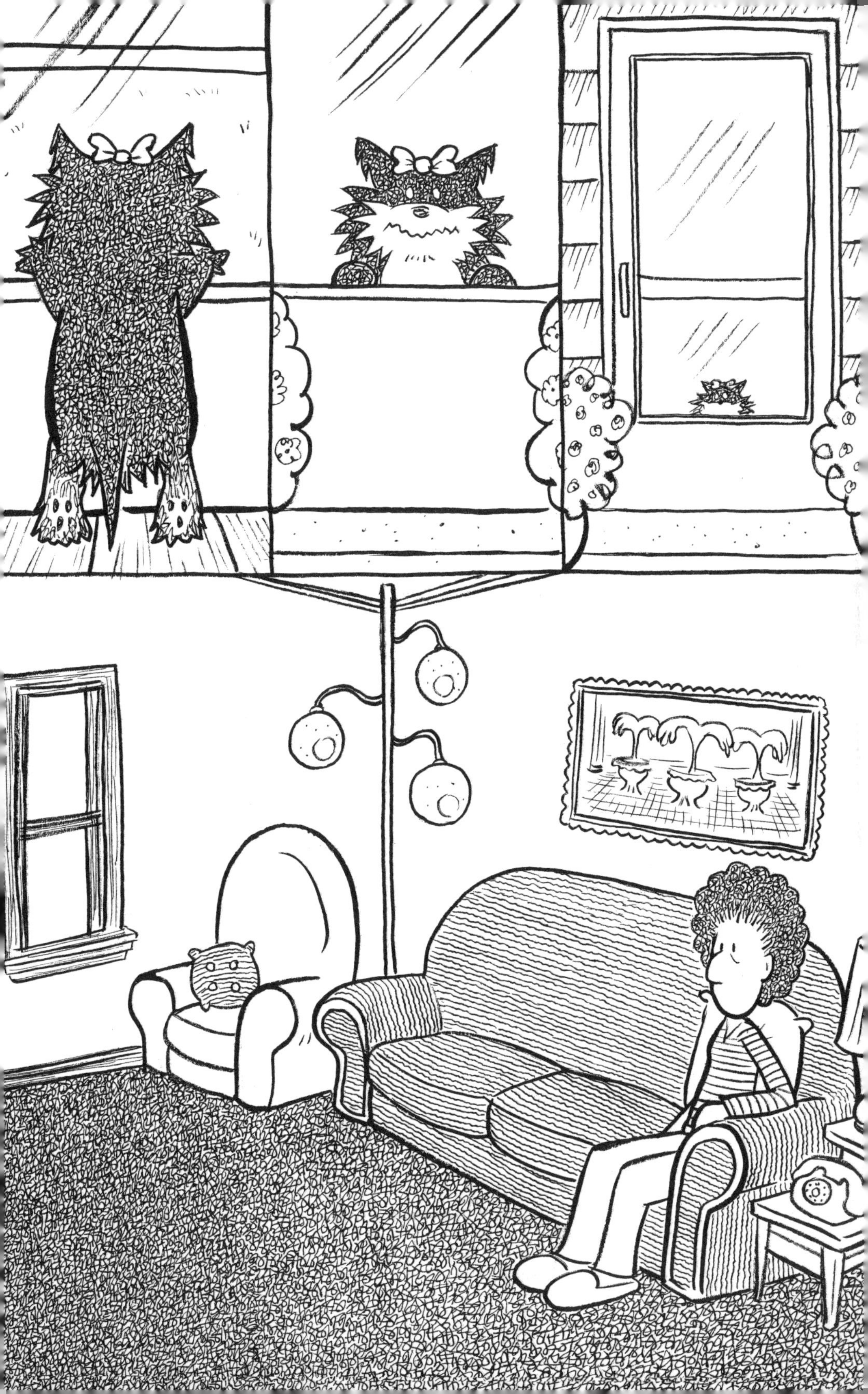

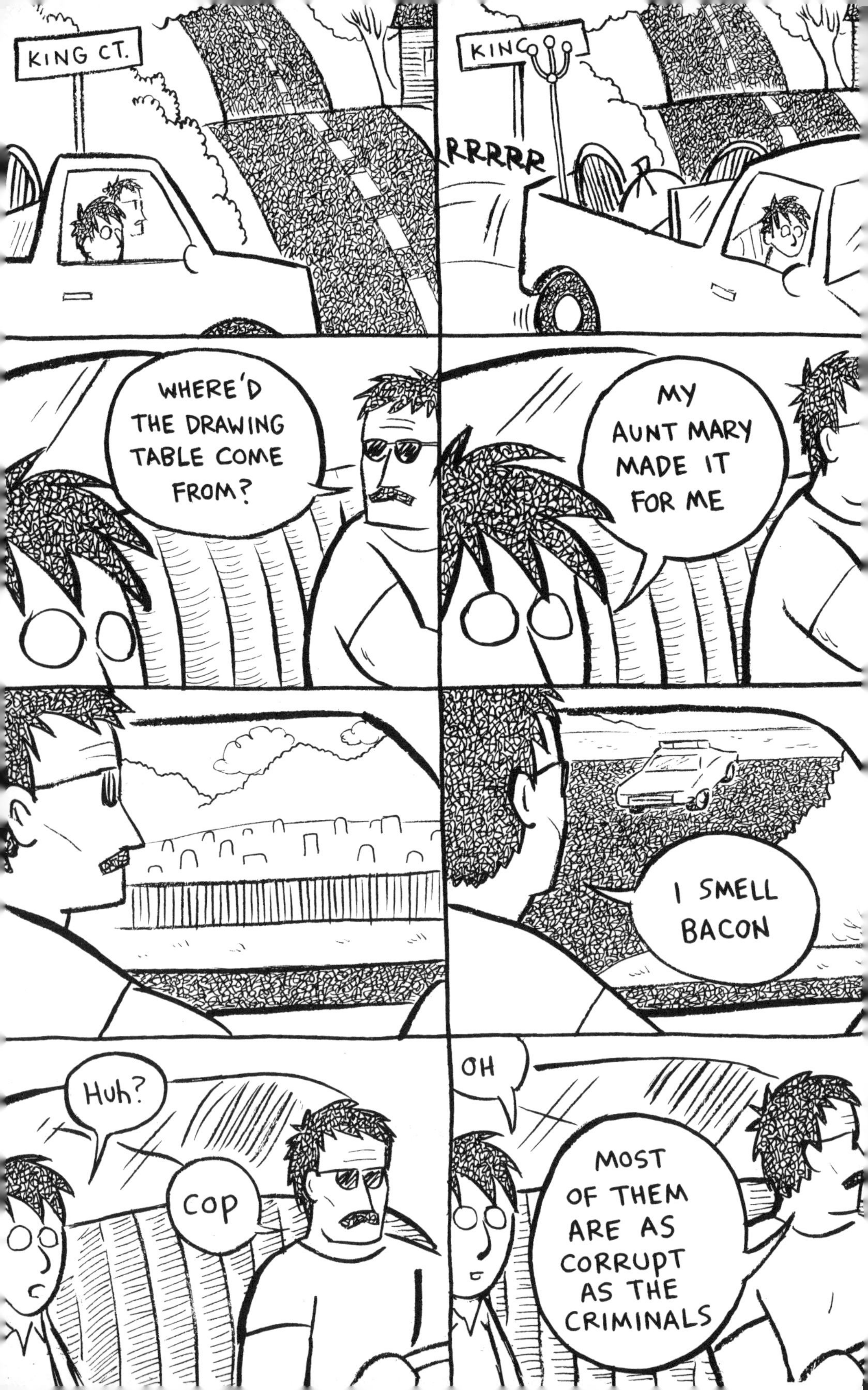
KING CT.
KING
RRRRR
WHERE'D THE DRAWING TABLE COME FROM?
MY AUNT MARY MADE IT FOR ME
I SMELL BACON
Huh?
Cop
OH
MOST OF THEM ARE AS CORRUPT AS THE CRIMINALS

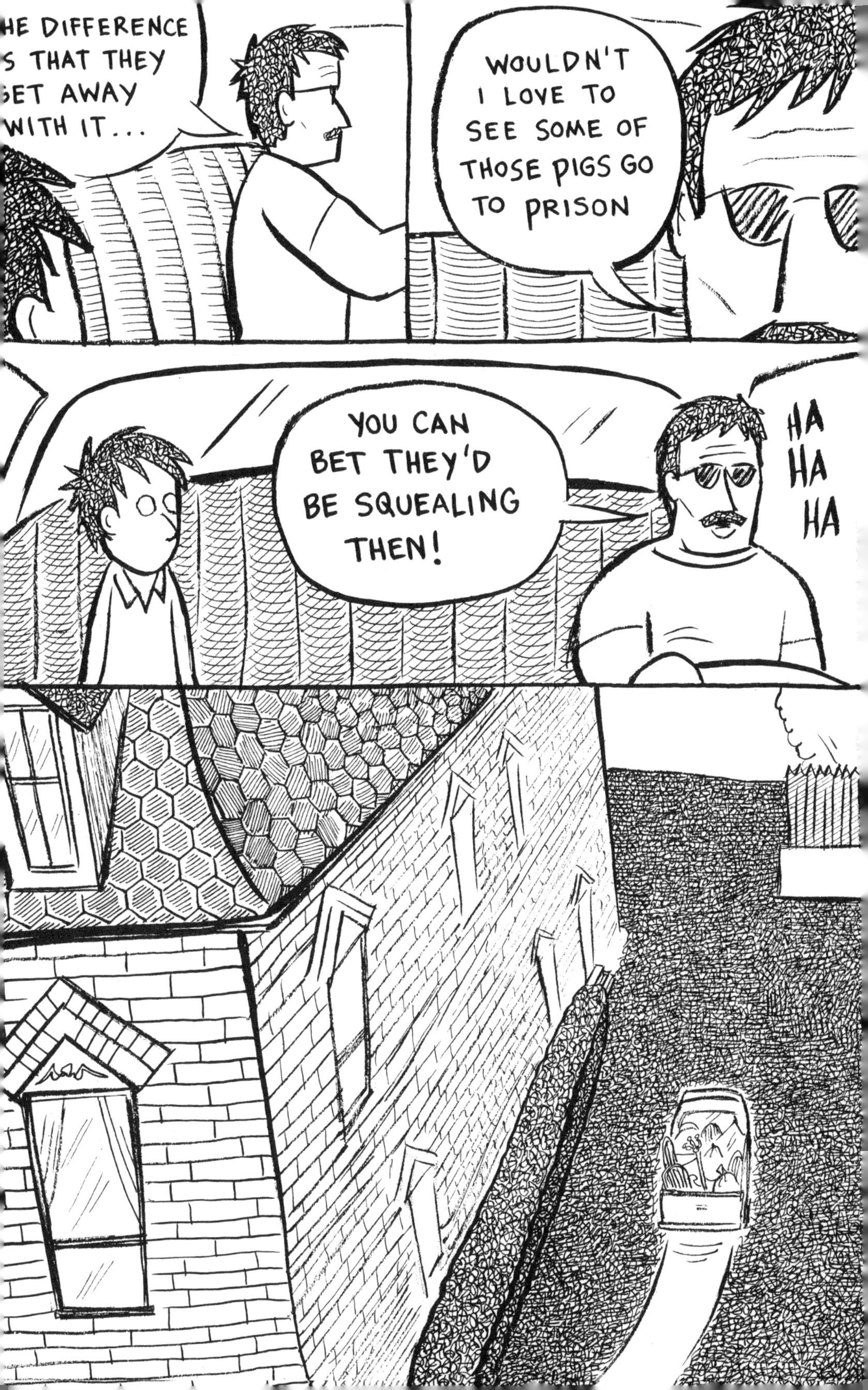
HE DIFFERENCE S THAT THEY ET AWAY WITH IT...
WOULDN'T I LOVE TO SEE SOME OF THOSE PIGS GO TO PRISON
YOU CAN BET THEY'D BE SQUEALING THEN!
HA HA HA

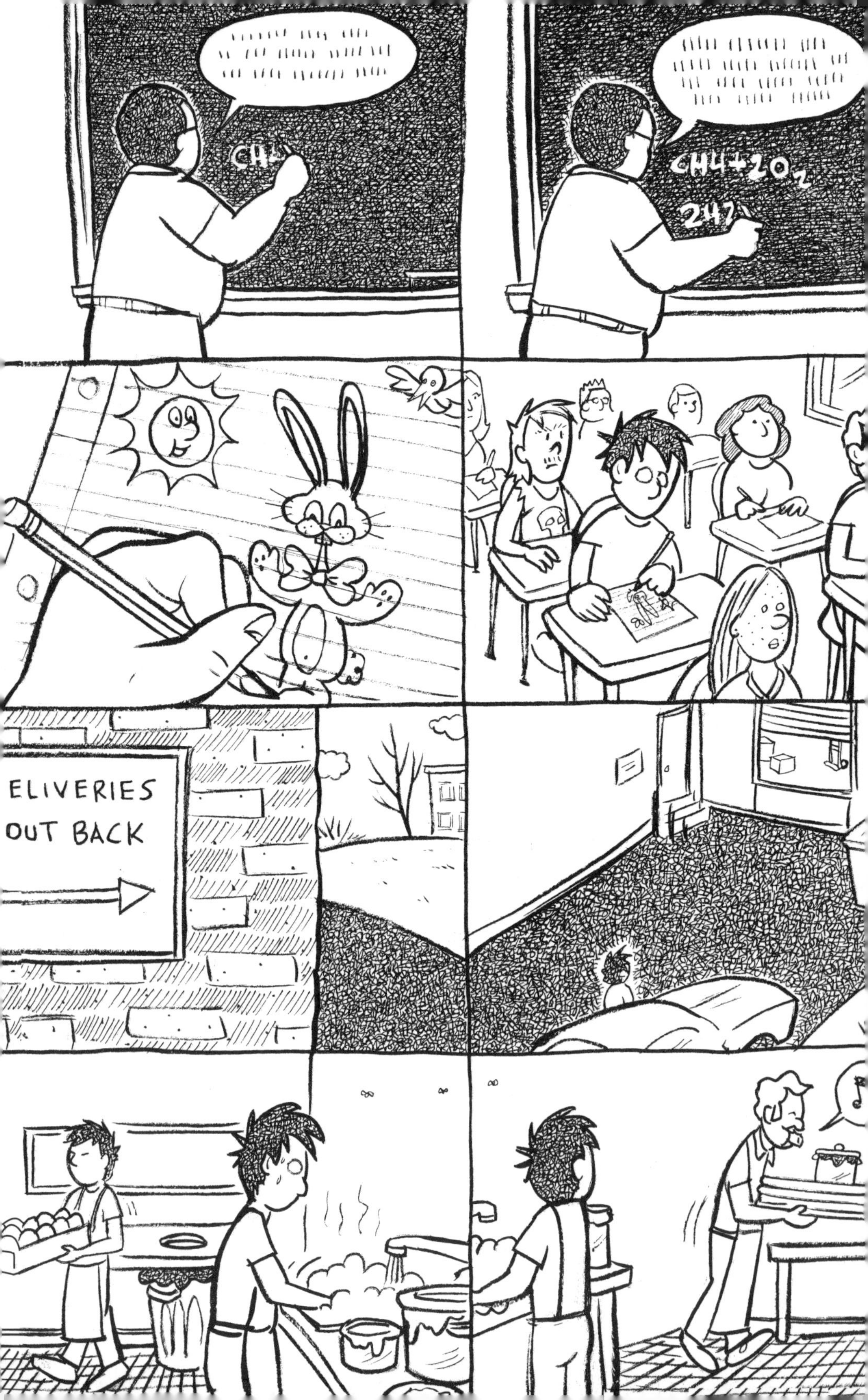
CH4+2O2
ELIVERIES
OUT BACK

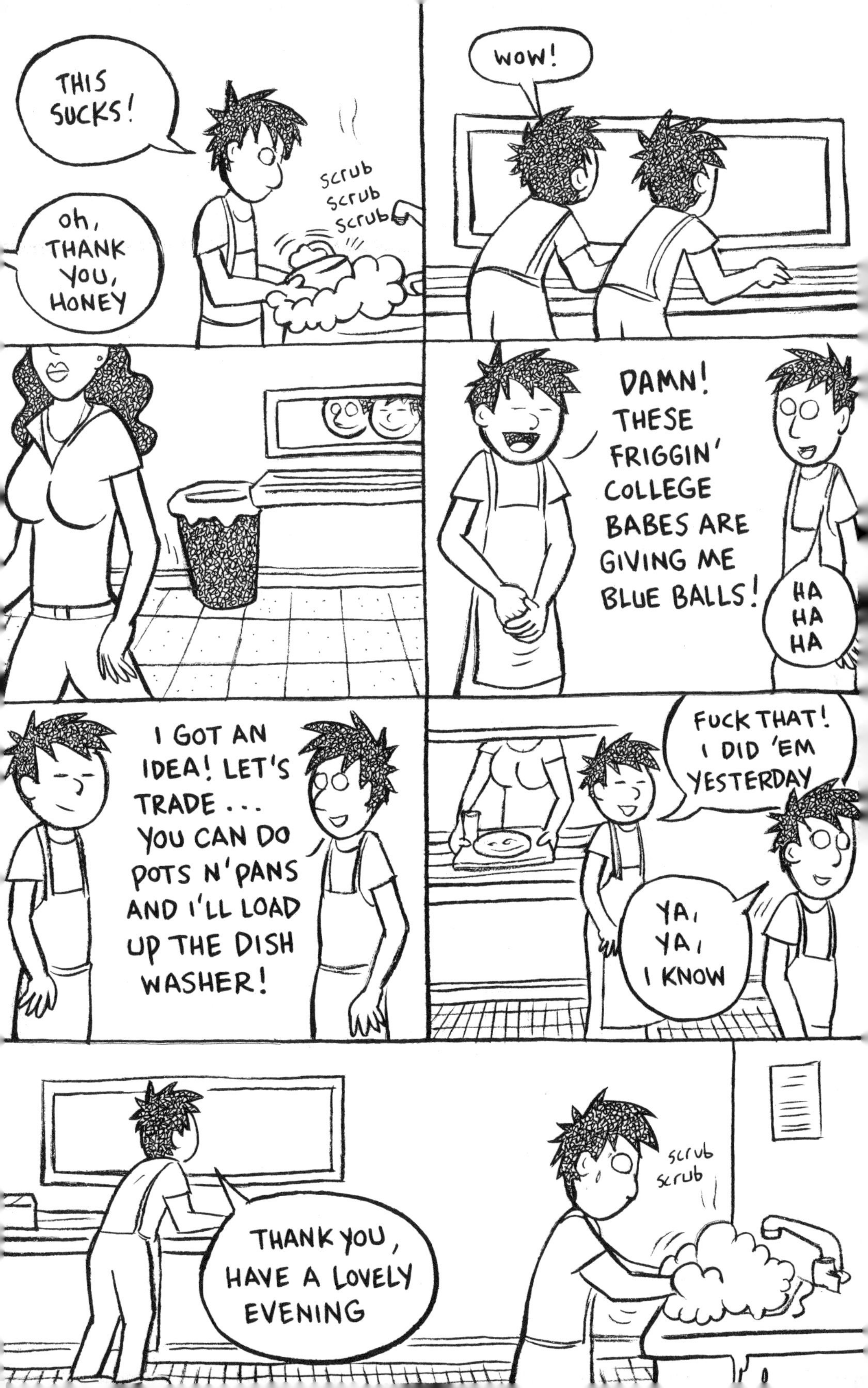
THIS SUCKS!
oh, THANK YOU, HONEY
scrub scrub scrub
WOW!
DAMN! THESE FRIGGIN' COLLEGE BABES ARE GIVING ME BLUE BALLS!
HA HA HA
I GOT AN IDEA! LET'S TRADE . . . YOU CAN DO POTS N' PANS AND I'LL LOAD UP THE DISH WASHER!
FUCK THAT! I DID 'EM YESTERDAY
YA, YA, I KNOW
THANK YOU, HAVE A LOVELY EVENING
scrub scrub

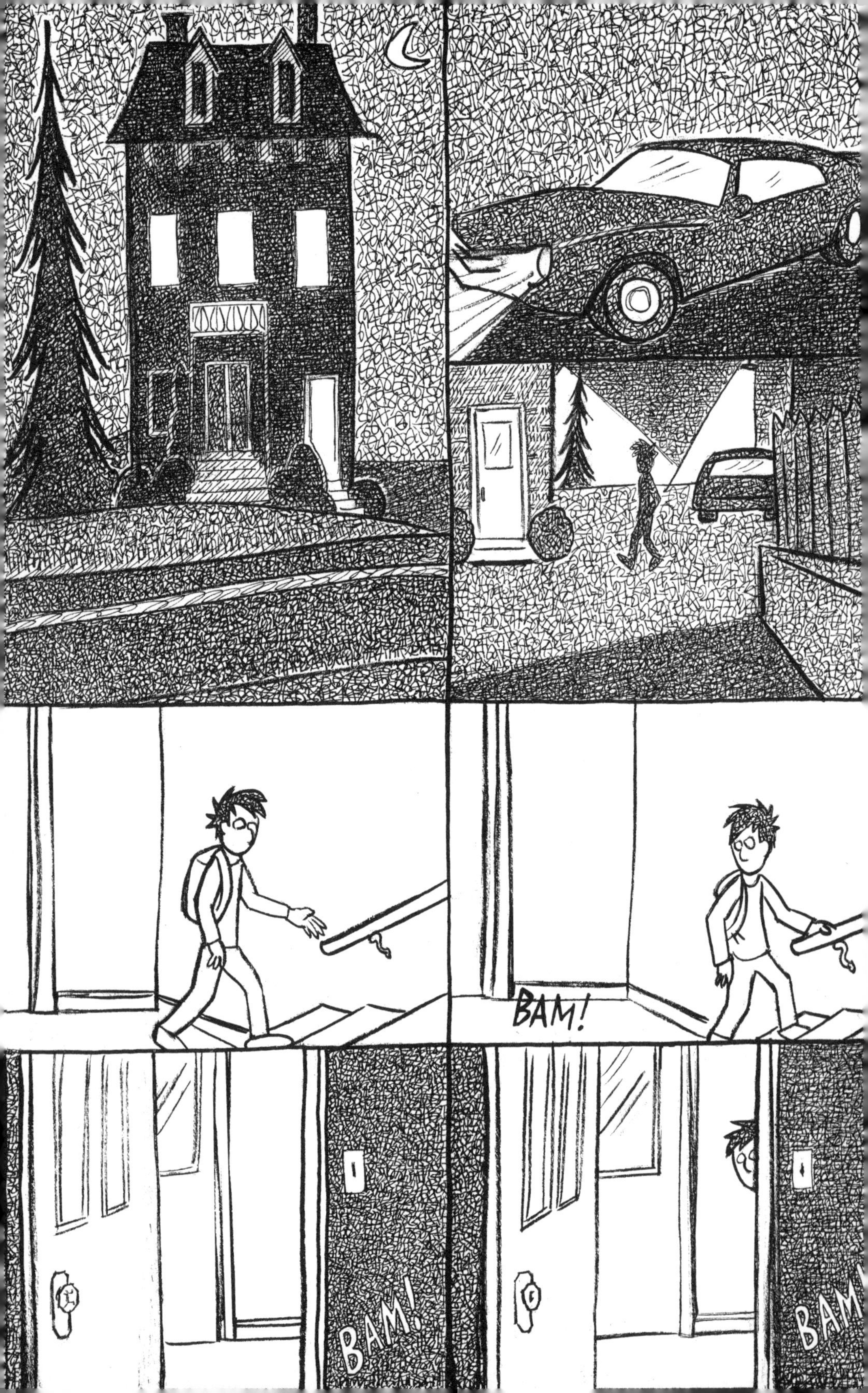
BAM!
BAM!

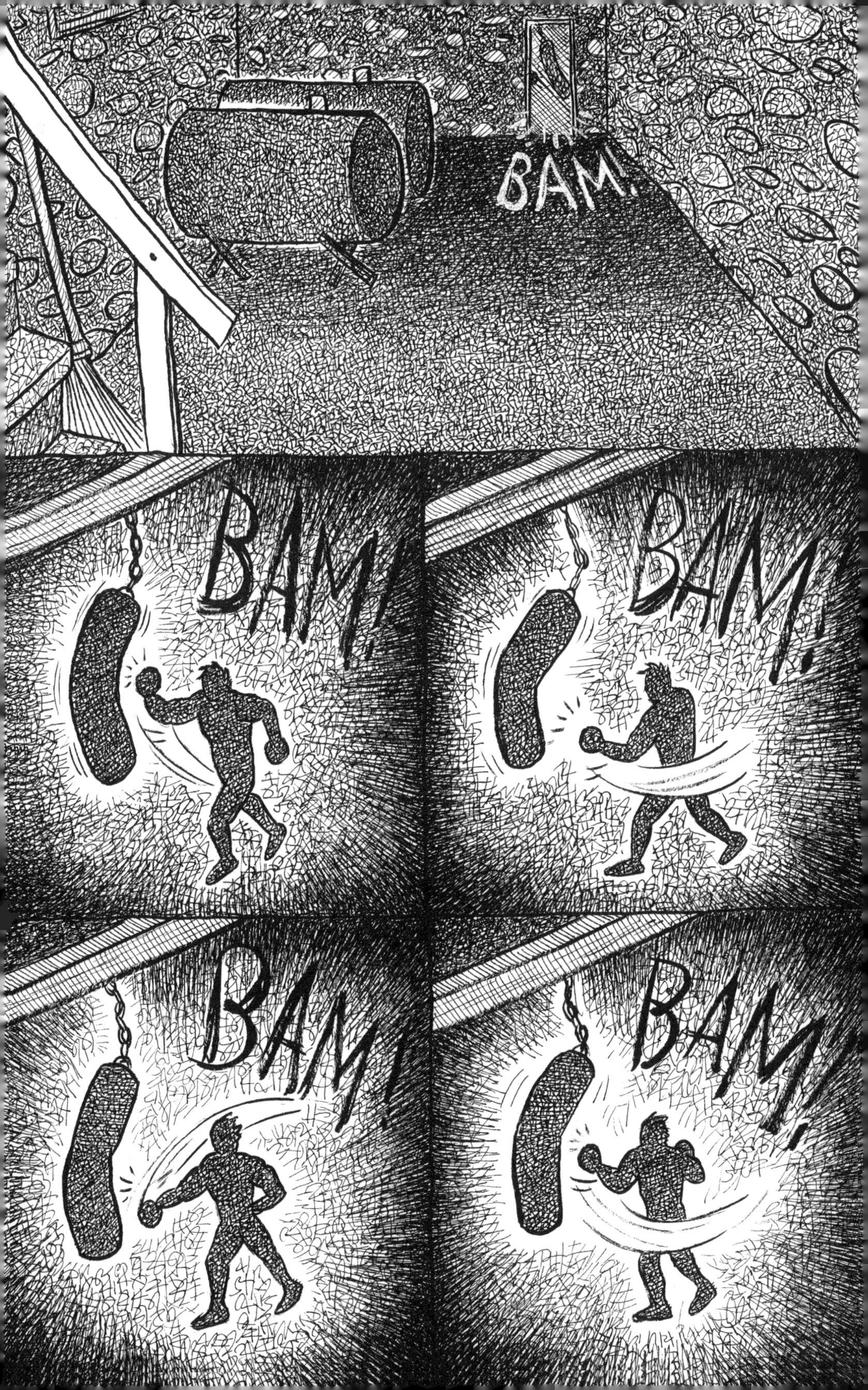
BAM!
BAM!
BAM!
BAM!
BAM!

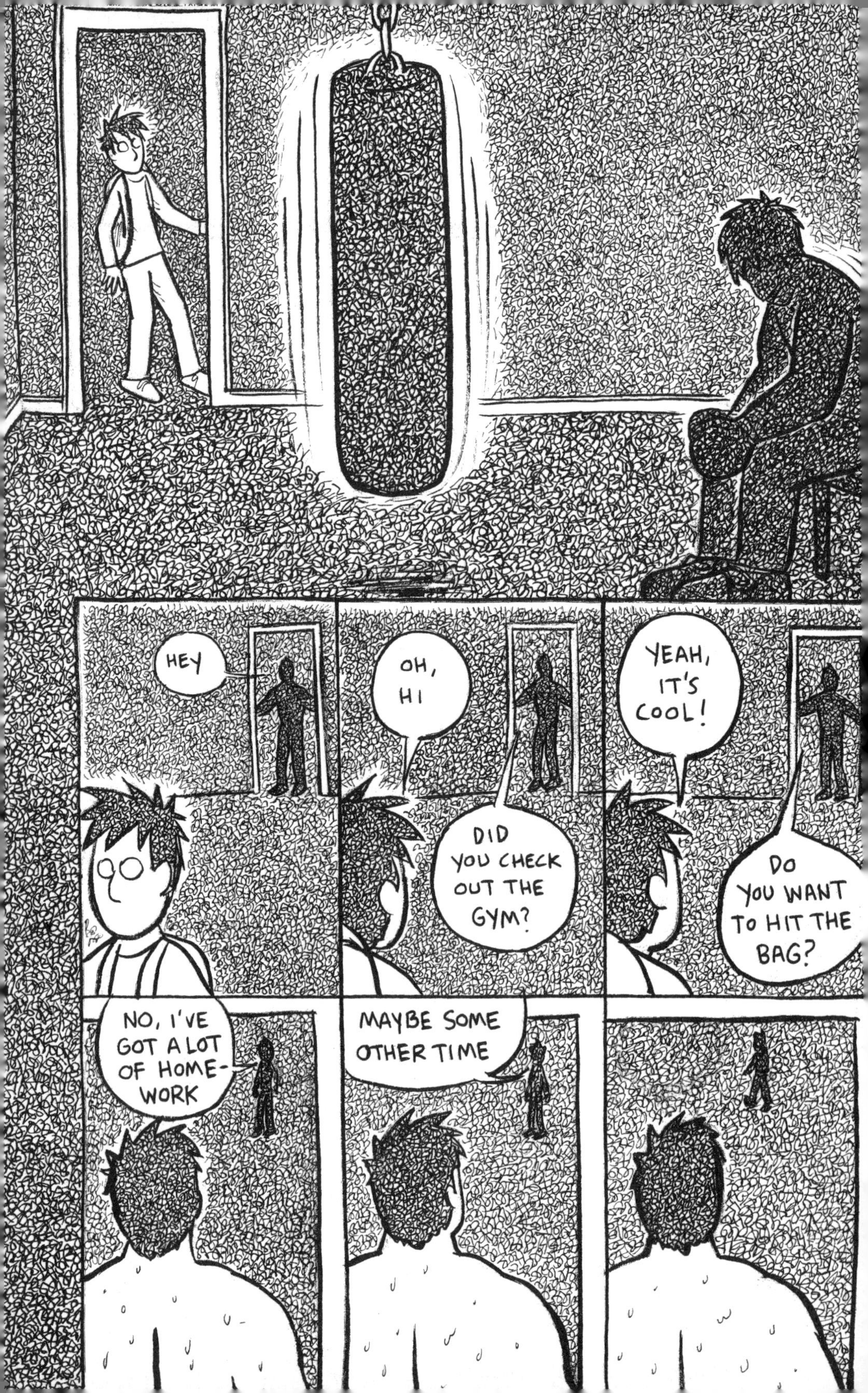
HEY
OH, HI
DID YOU CHECK OUT THE GYM?
YEAH, IT'S COOL!
DO YOU WANT TO HIT THE BAG?
NO, I'VE GOT A LOT OF HOME-WORK
MAYBE SOME OTHER TIME

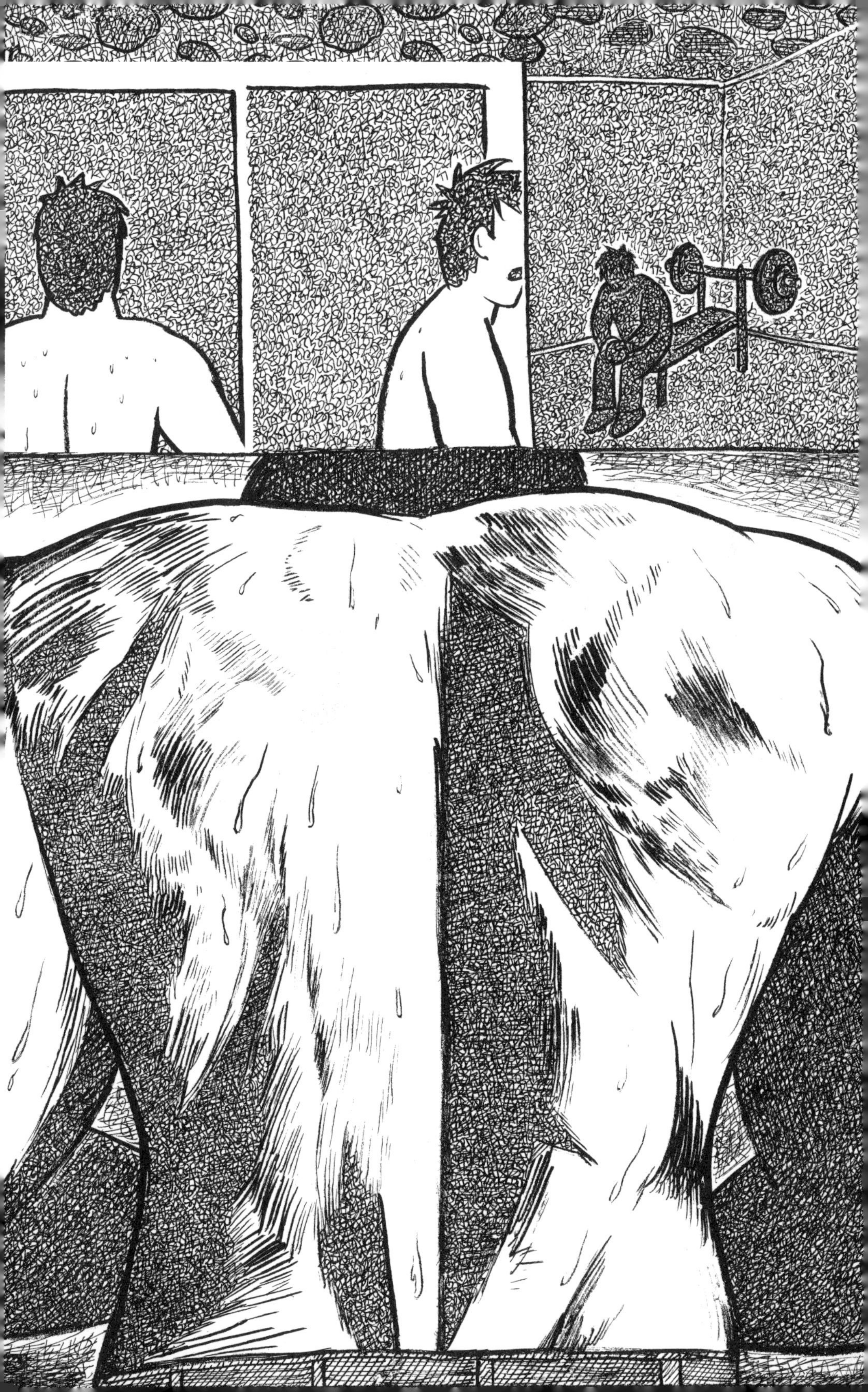

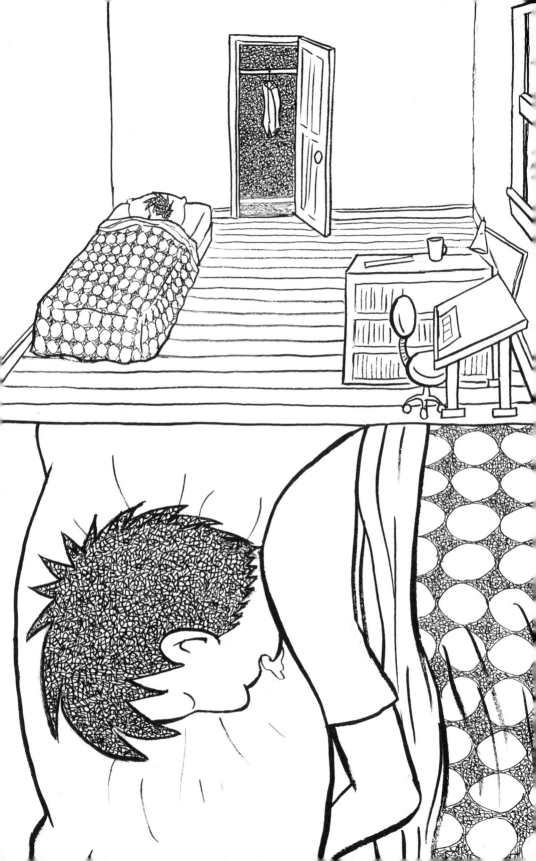

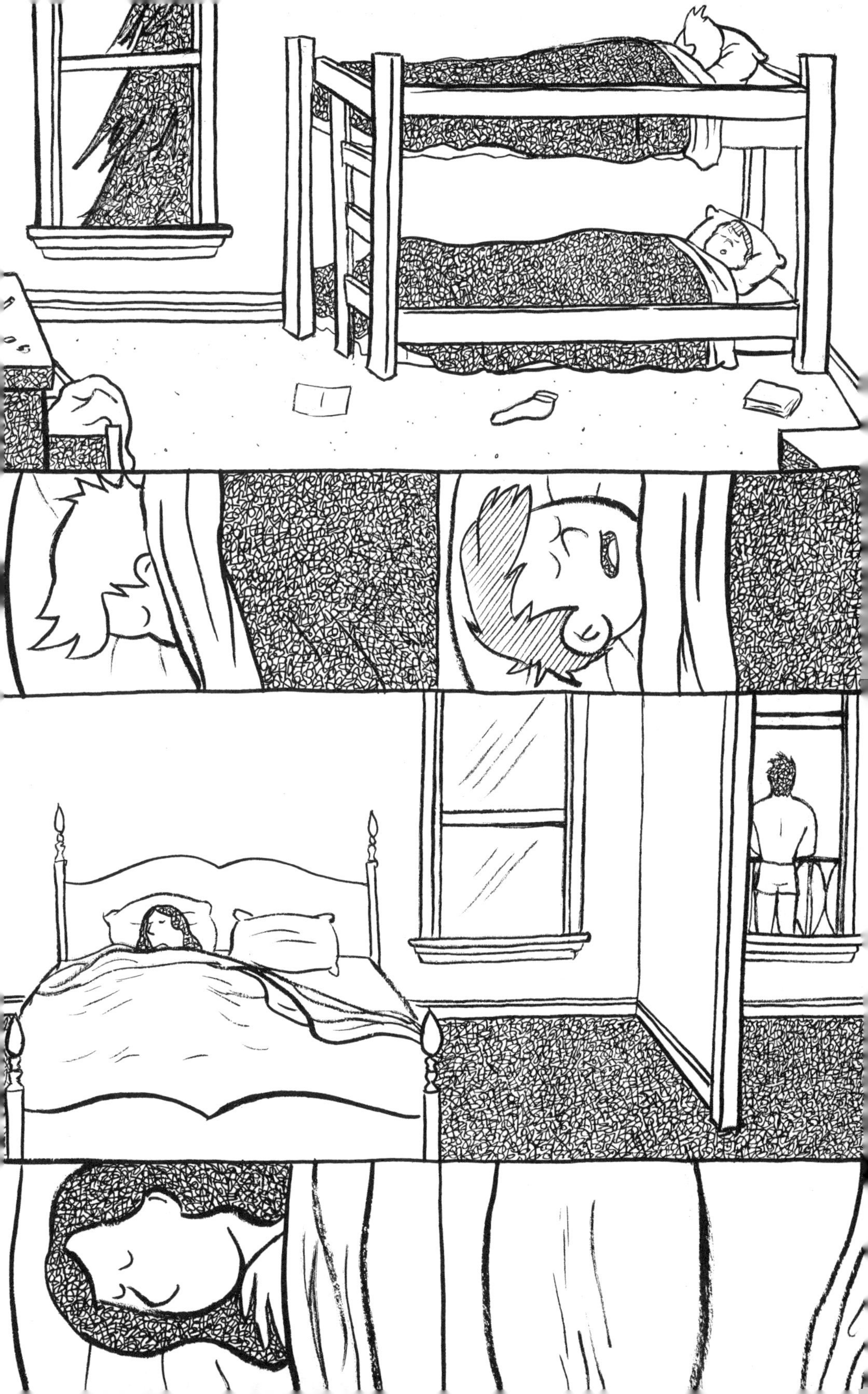

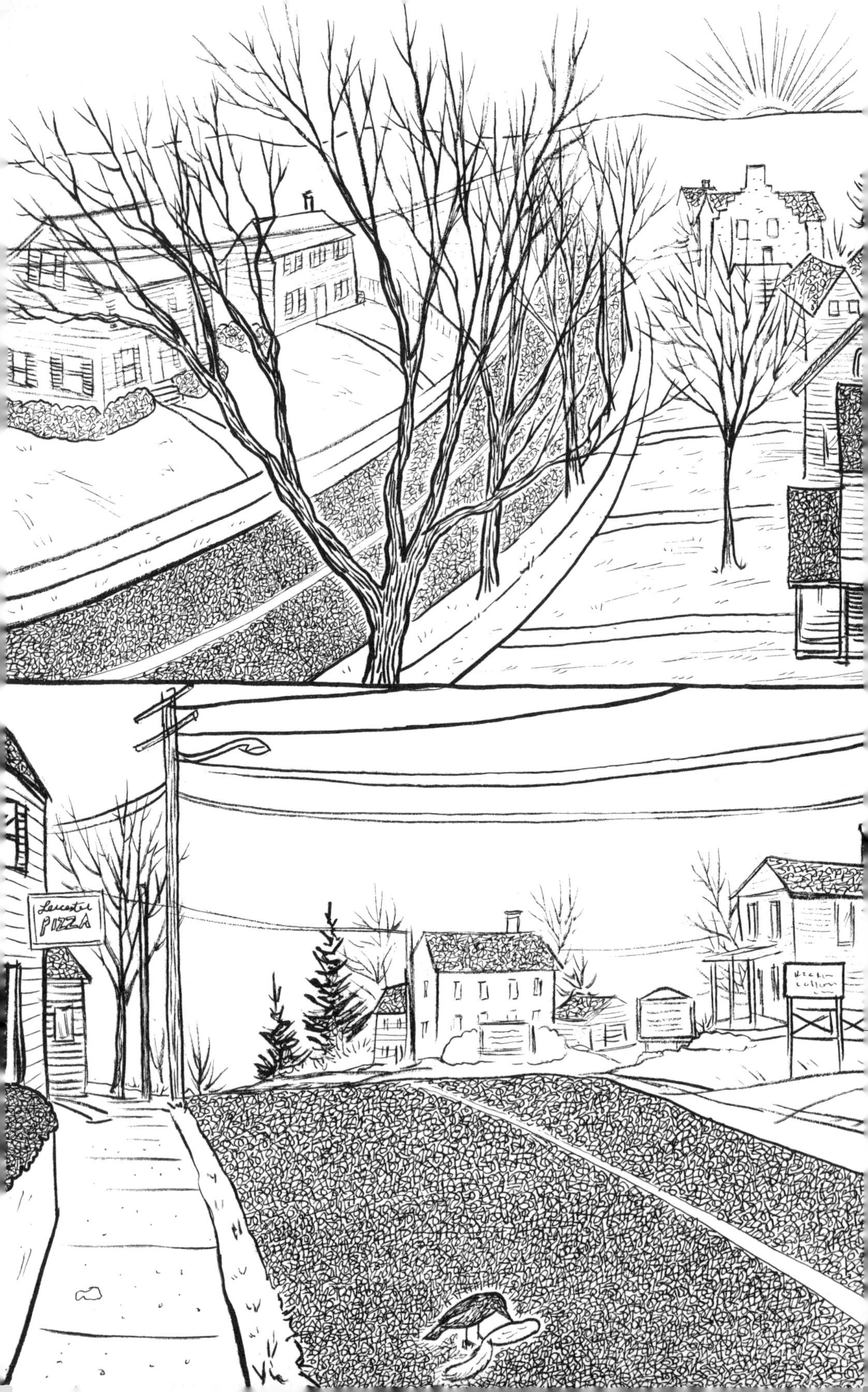
Lancaster
PIZZA

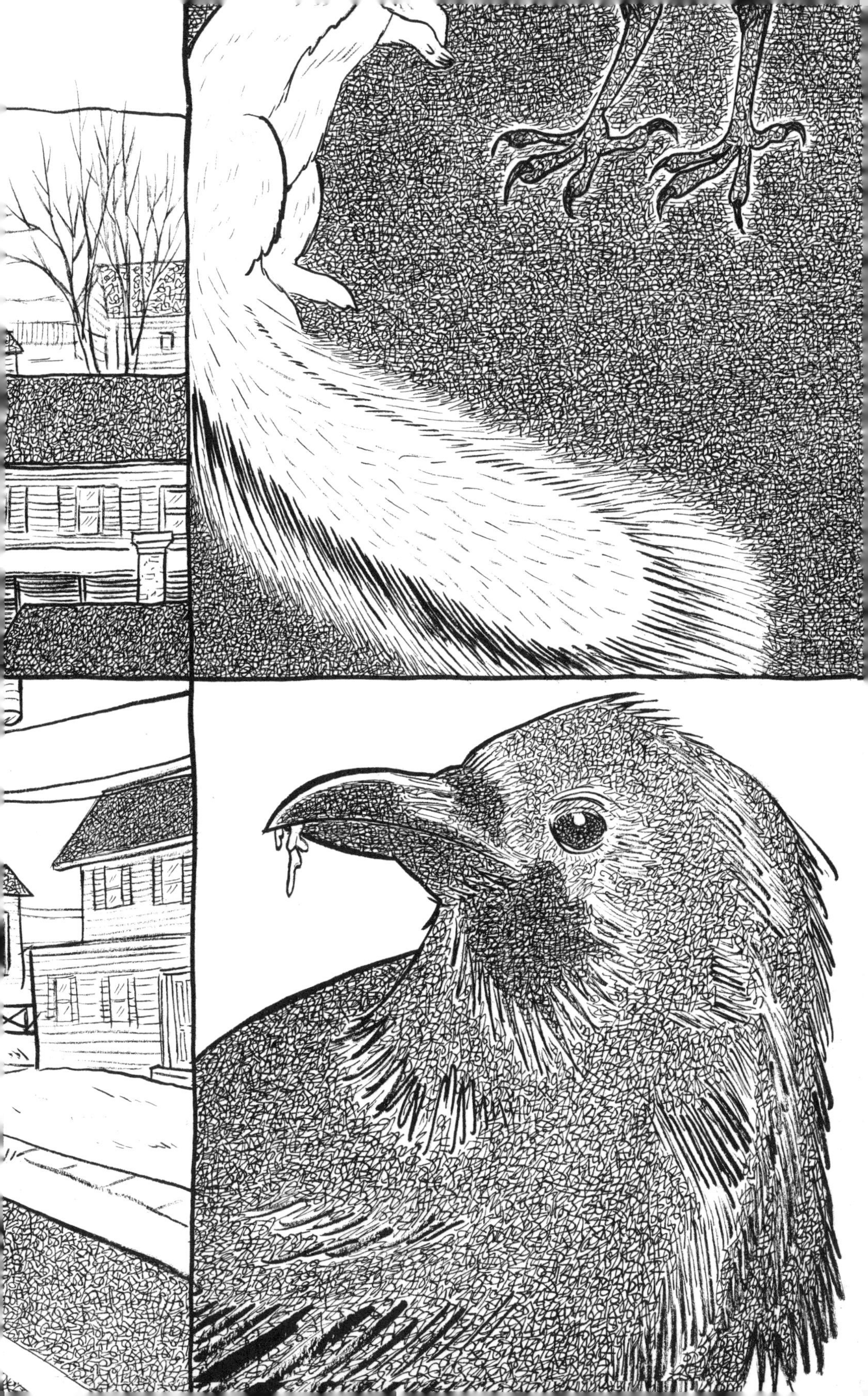

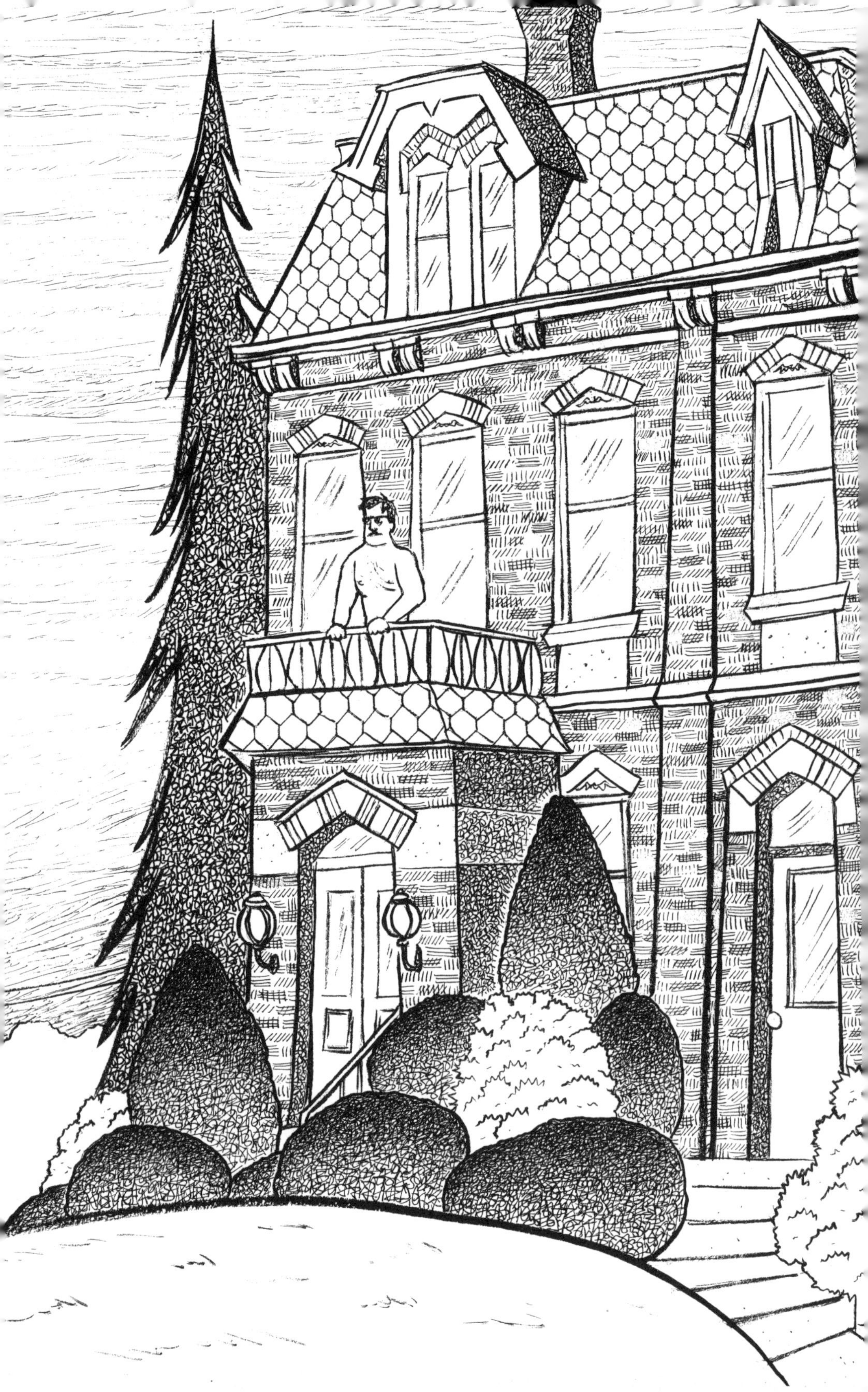

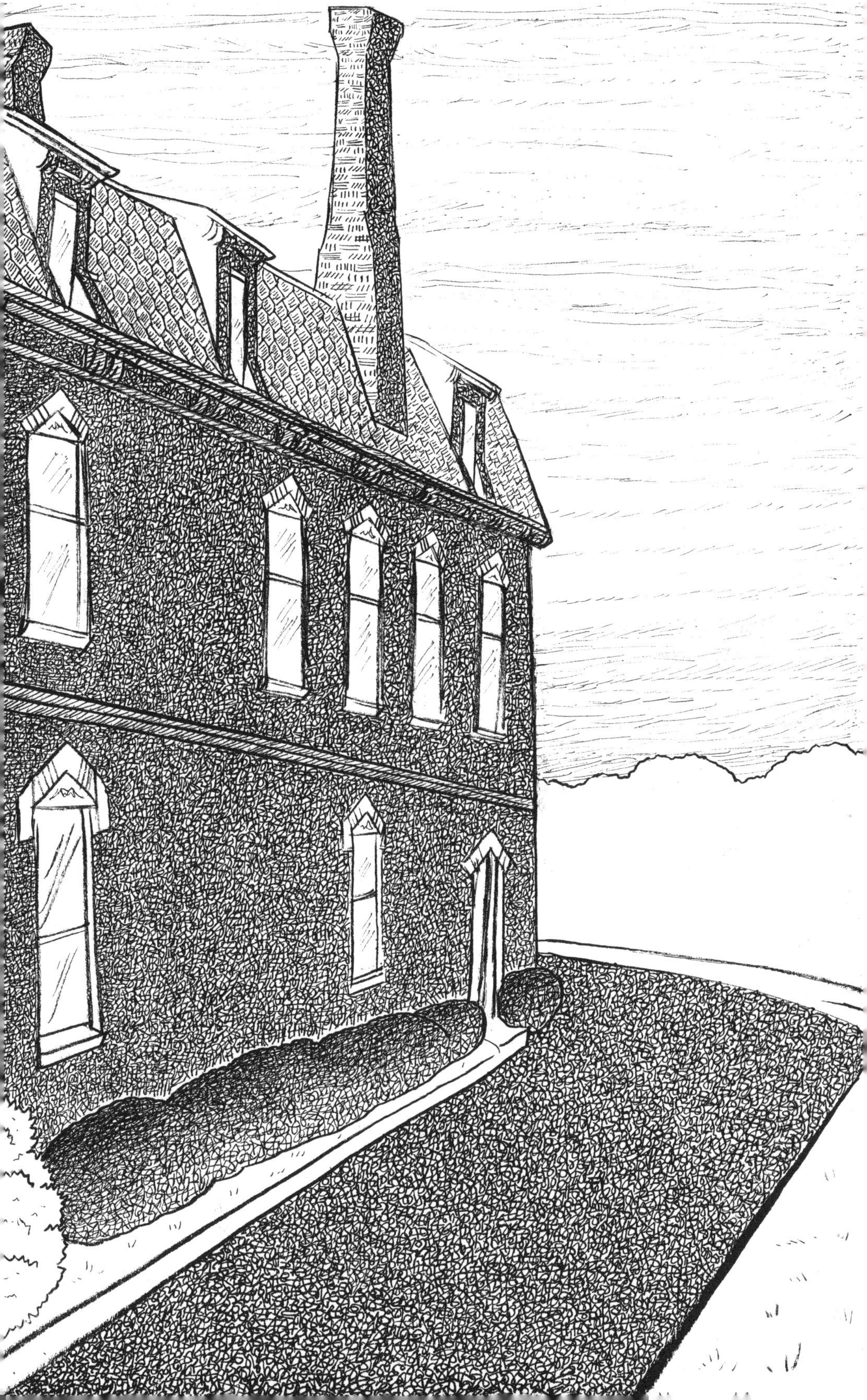

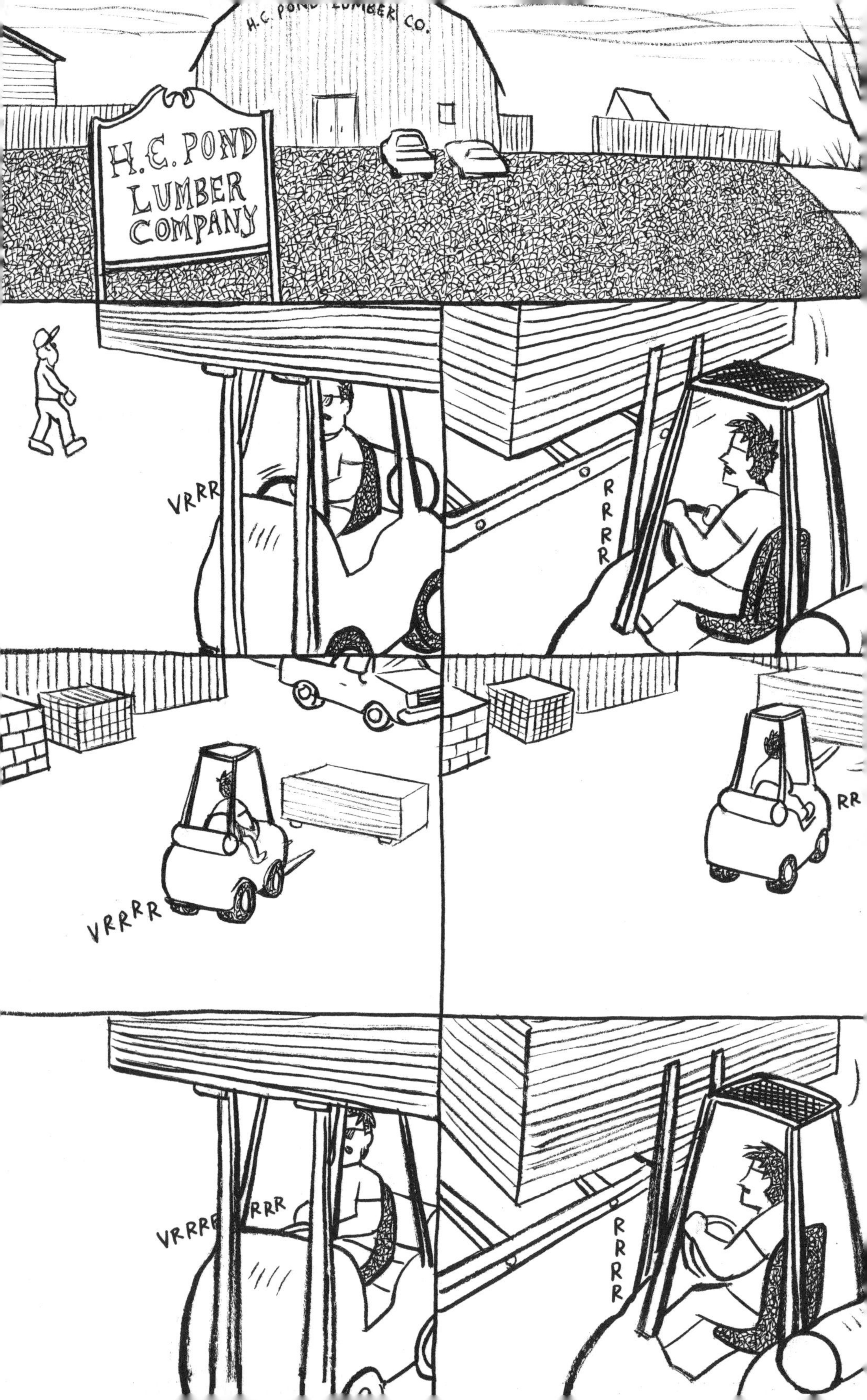
H.C. POND LUMBER CO.
H.C. POND LUMBER COMPANY
VRRR
RRRR
VRRRR
RR
VRRRRRRR
RRRR

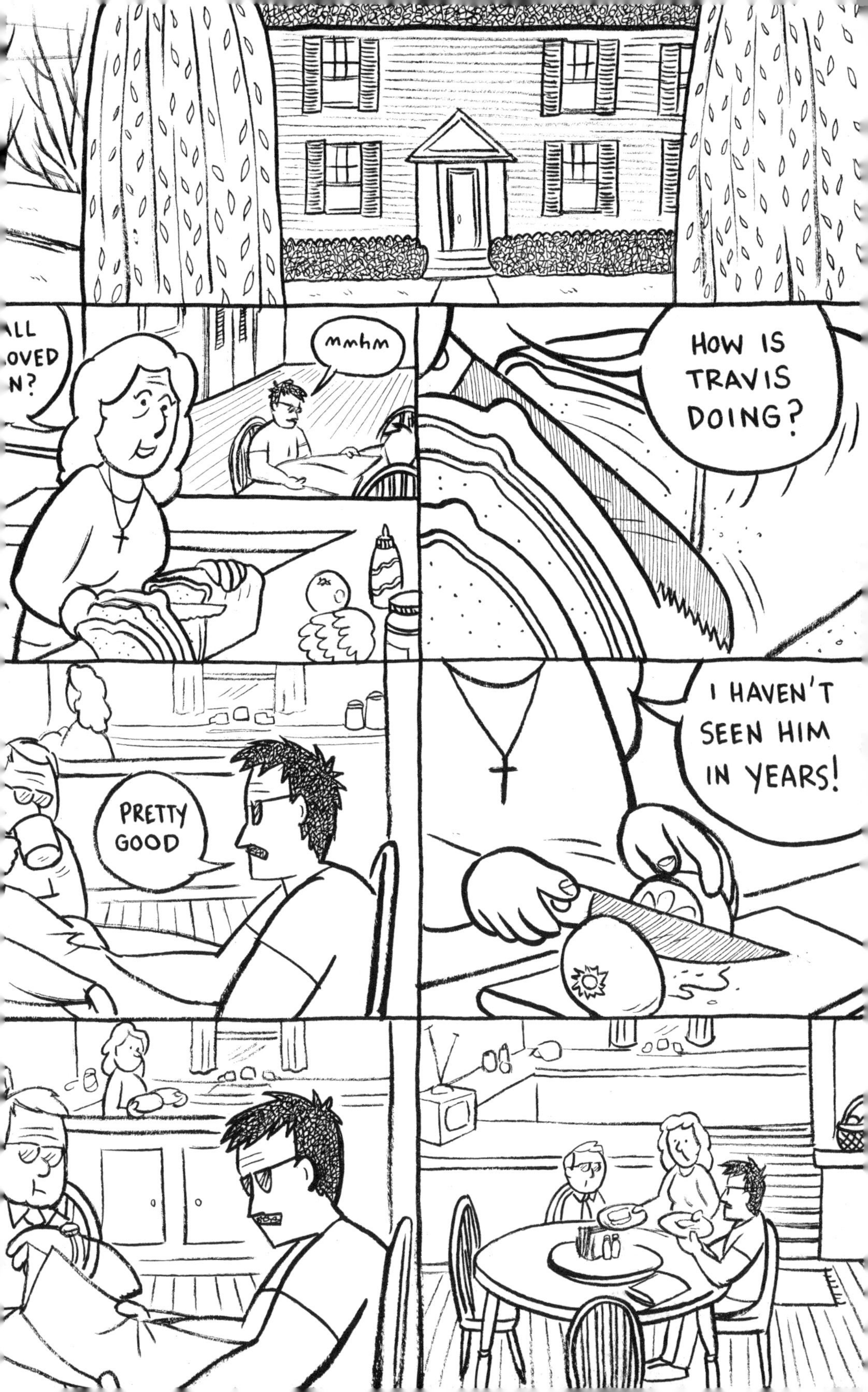

ALL OVED N?
mmhm
HOW IS TRAVIS DOING?
PRETTY GOOD
I HAVEN'T SEEN HIM IN YEARS!

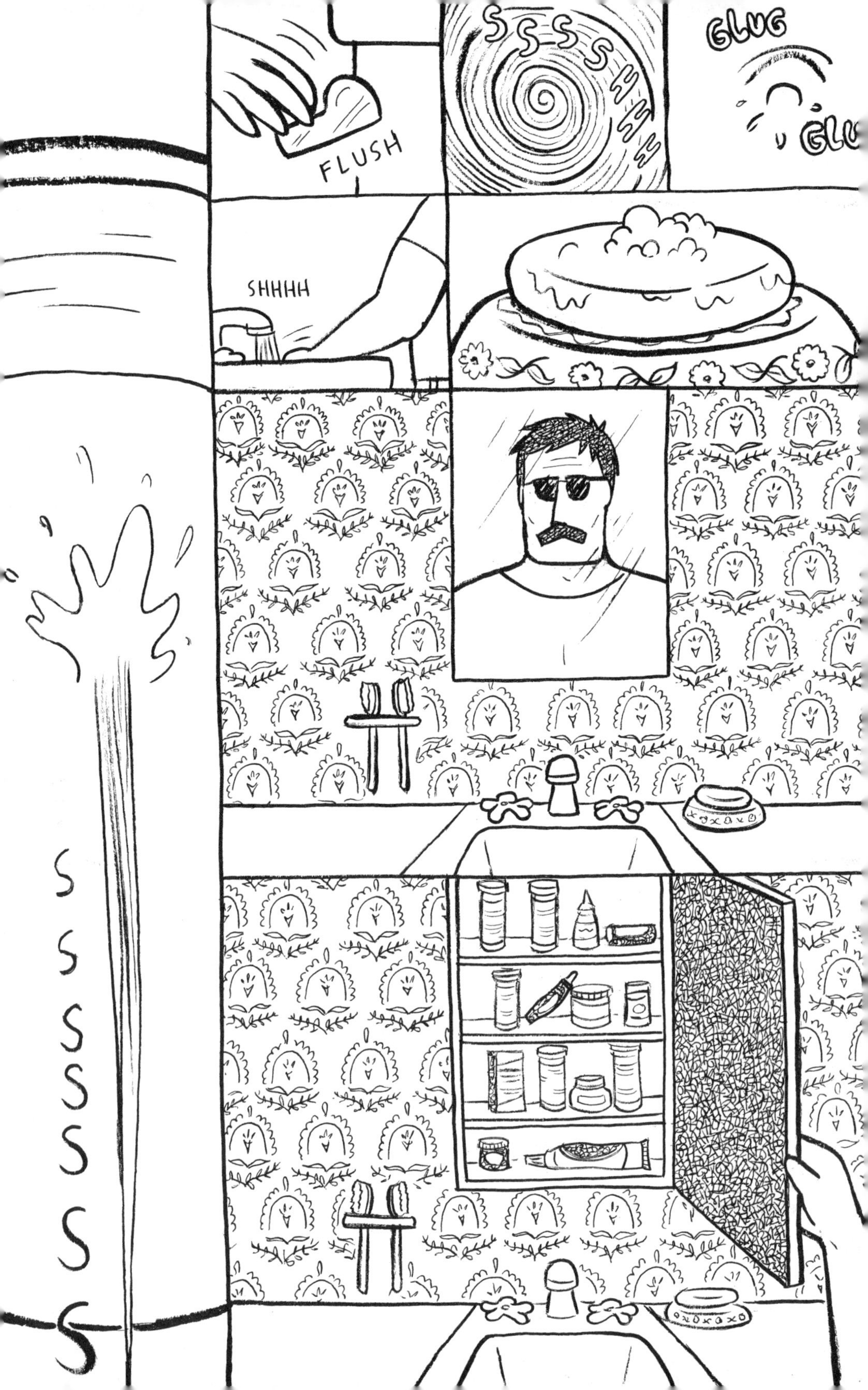
FLUSH
SSSSHHHH
GLUG
GLU
SHHHH
SSSSSSS

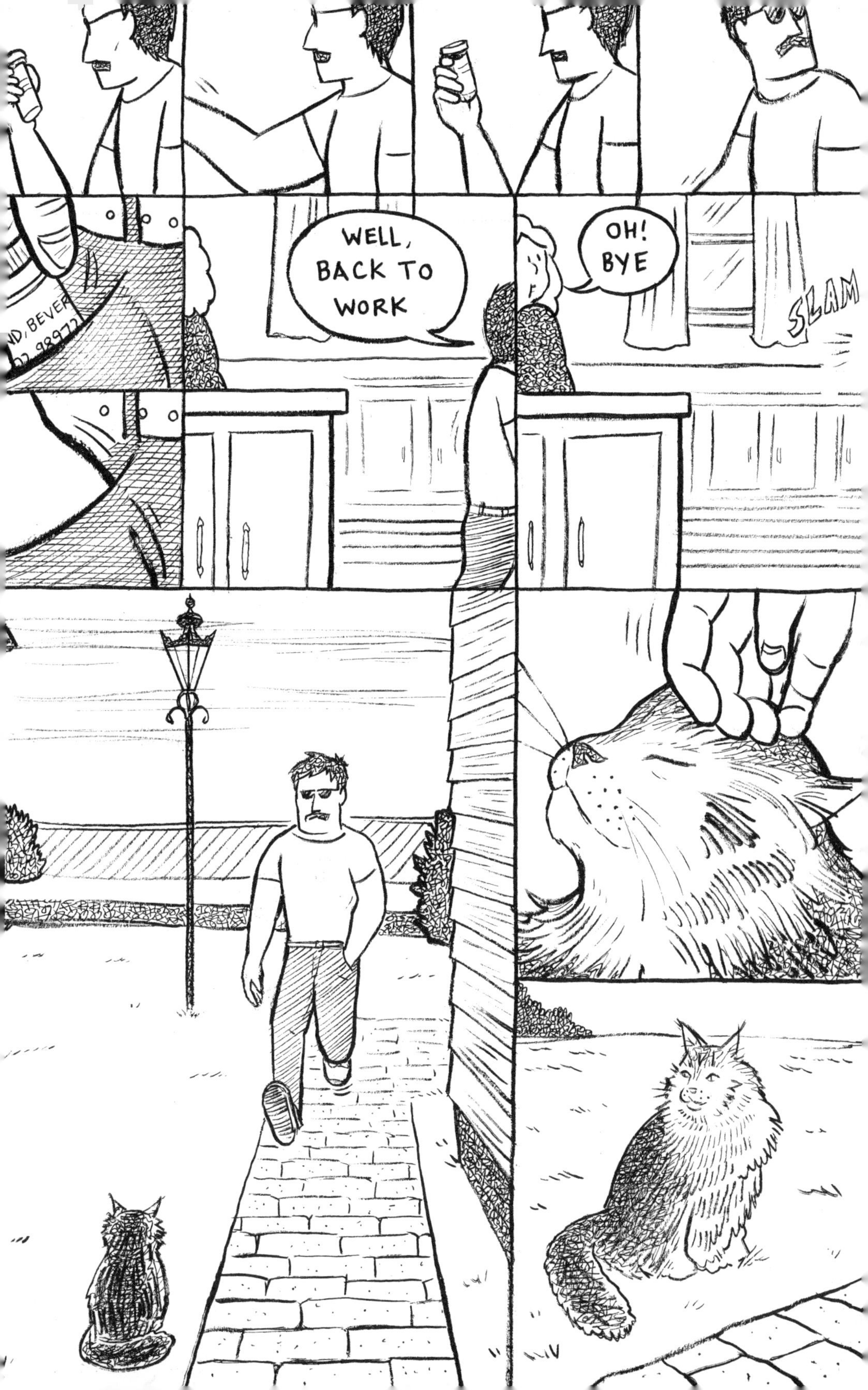
ND, BEVER
WELL, BACK TO WORK
OH! BYE
SLAM

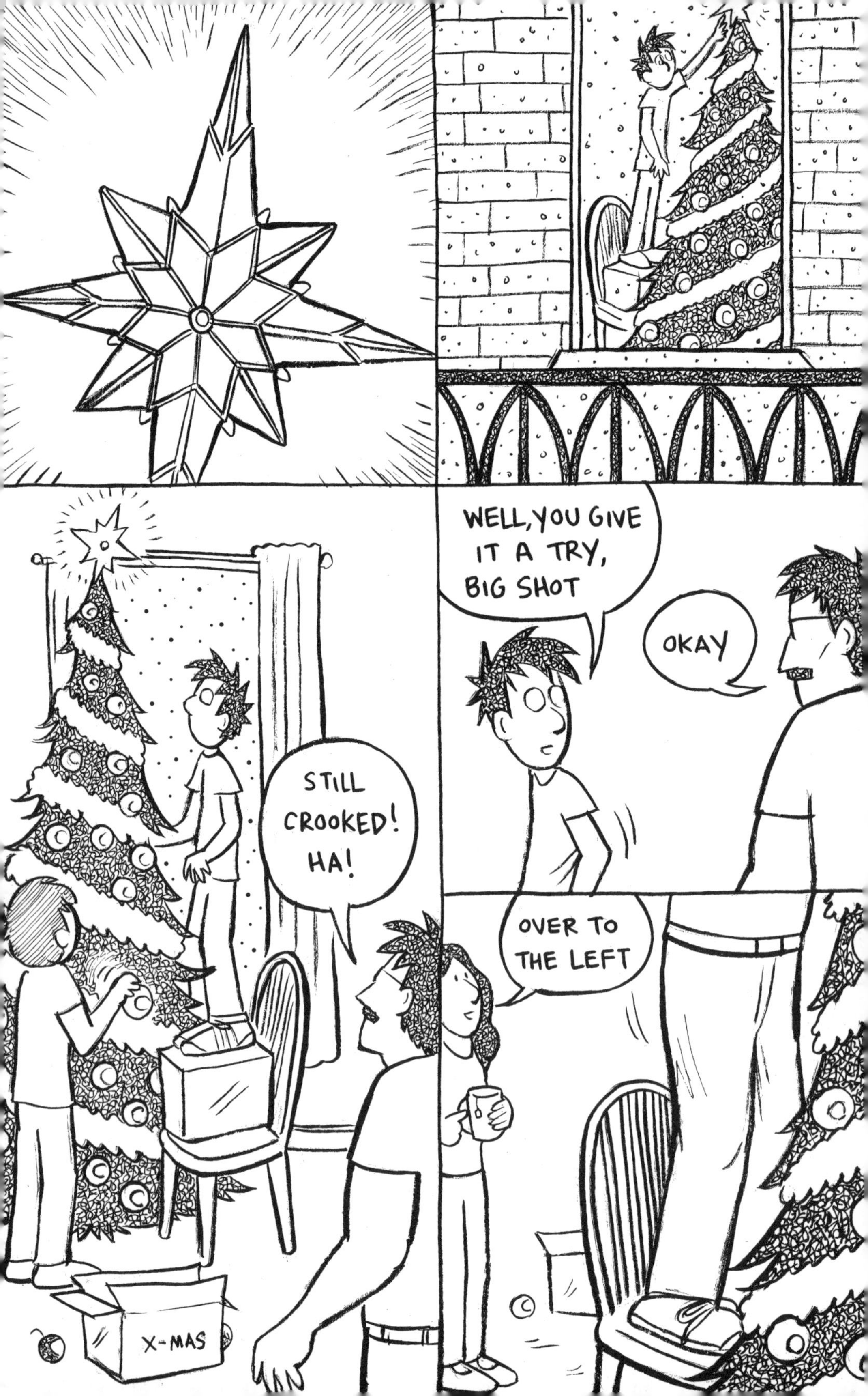
STILL CROOKED! HA!
WELL, YOU GIVE IT A TRY, BIG SHOT
OKAY
OVER TO THE LEFT
X-MAS

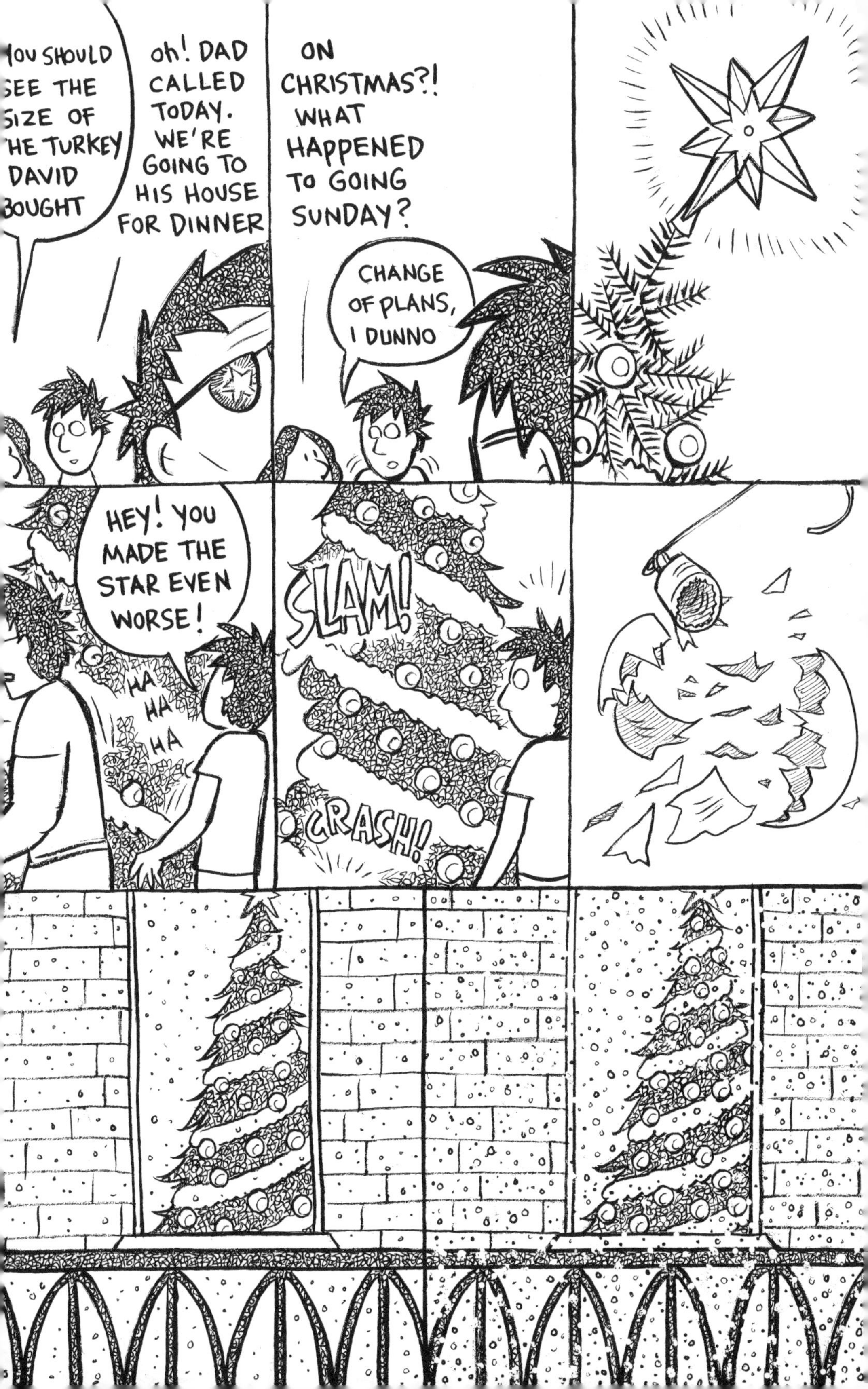
YOU SHOULD SEE THE SIZE OF THE TURKEY DAVID BOUGHT
oh! DAD CALLED TODAY. WE'RE GOING TO HIS HOUSE FOR DINNER
ON CHRISTMAS?! WHAT HAPPENED TO GOING SUNDAY?
CHANGE OF PLANS, I DUNNO
HEY! YOU MADE THE STAR EVEN WORSE!
HA HA HA
SLAM!
CRASH!

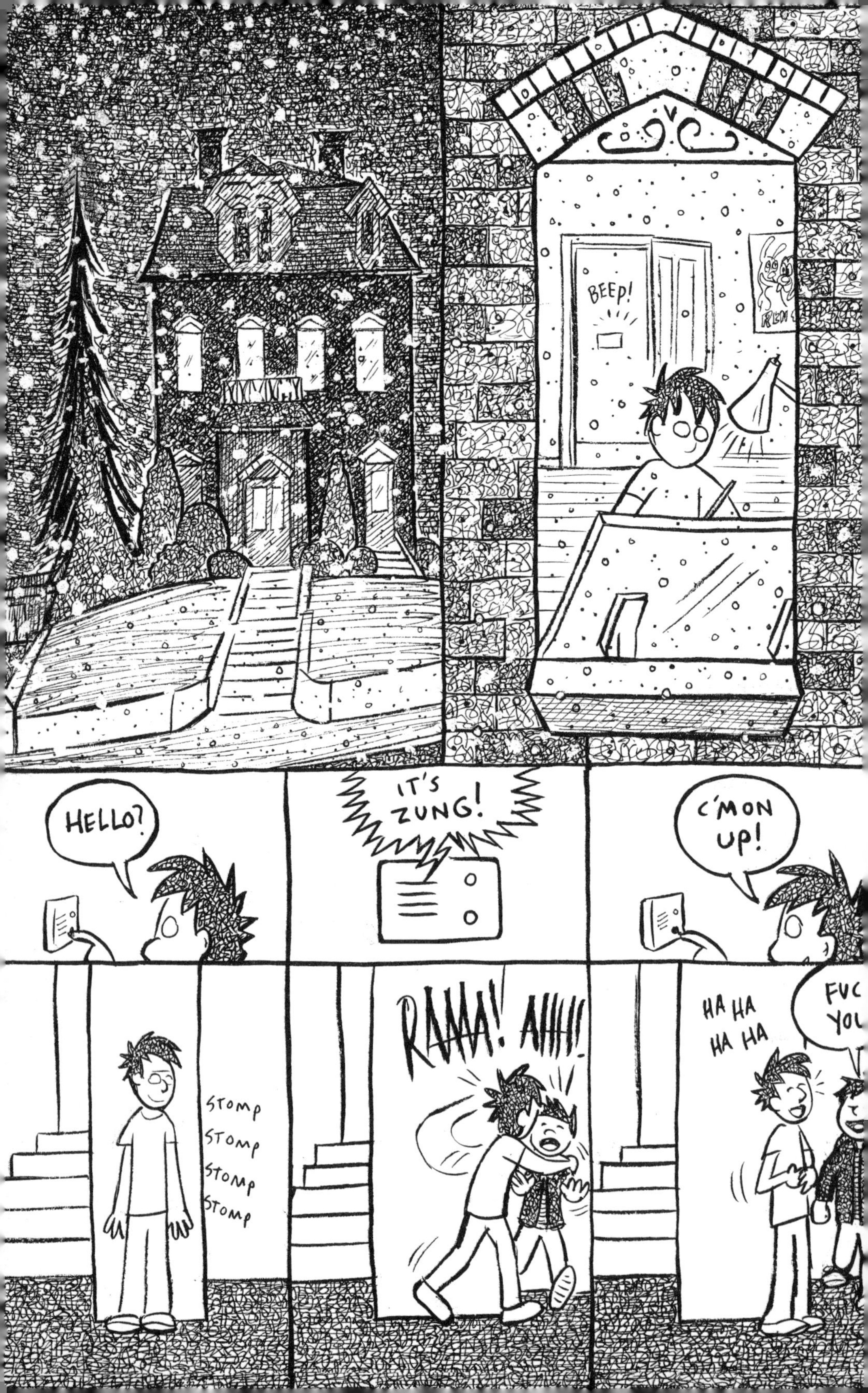
BEEP!
HELLO?
IT'S ZUNG!
C'MON UP!
STOMP
STOMP
STOMP
STOMP
RAAA! AHHH!
HA HA
HA HA
FUC
YOU

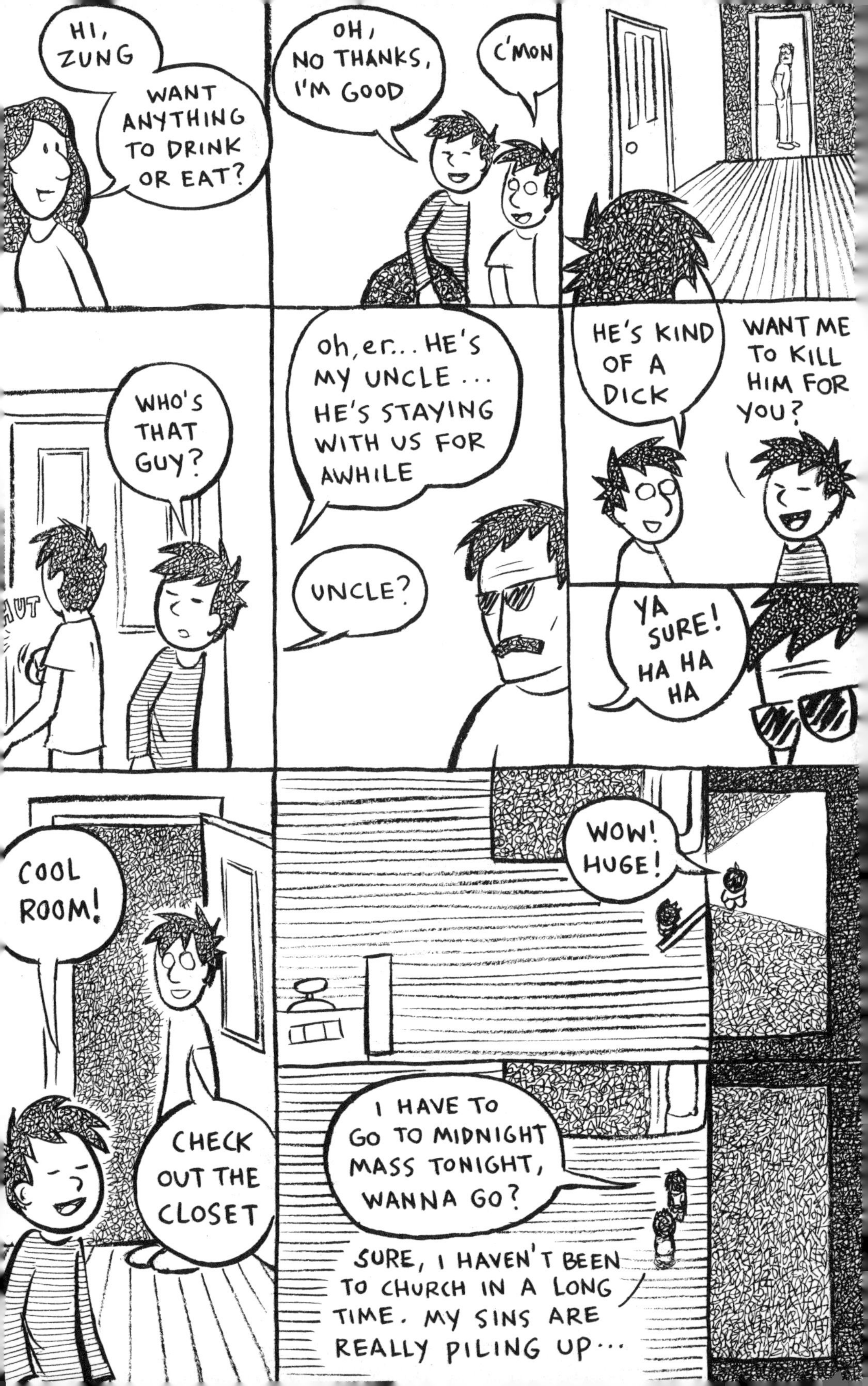
HI, ZUNG
WANT ANYTHING TO DRINK OR EAT?
OH, NO THANKS, I'M GOOD
C'MON
WHO'S THAT GUY?
oh, er... HE'S MY UNCLE... HE'S STAYING WITH US FOR AWHILE
UNCLE?
HE'S KIND OF A DICK
WANT ME TO KILL HIM FOR YOU?
YA SURE! HA HA HA
COOL ROOM!
CHECK OUT THE CLOSET
WOW! HUGE!
I HAVE TO GO TO MIDNIGHT MASS TONIGHT, WANNA GO?
SURE, I HAVEN'T BEEN TO CHURCH IN A LONG TIME. MY SINS ARE REALLY PILING UP...

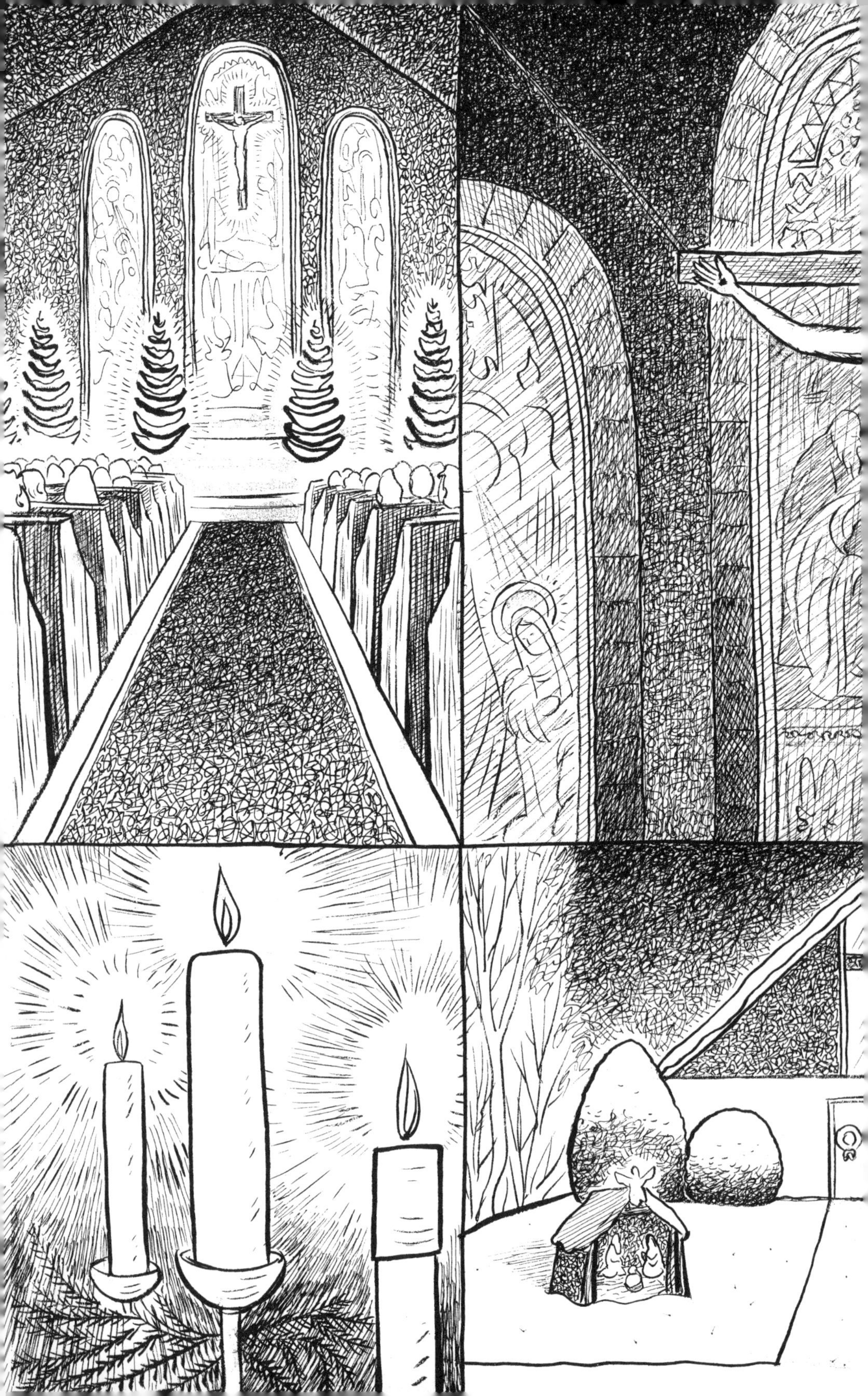

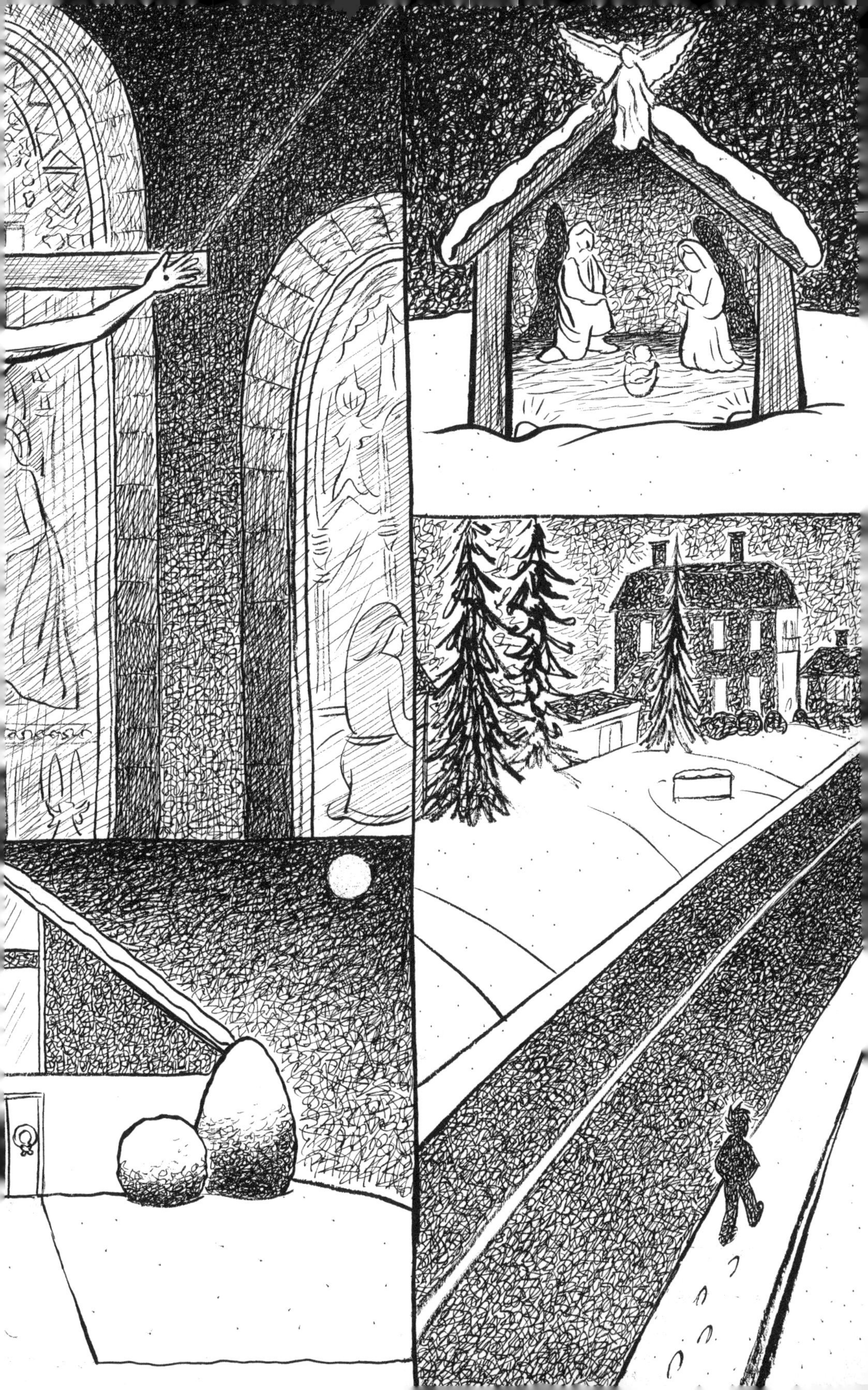

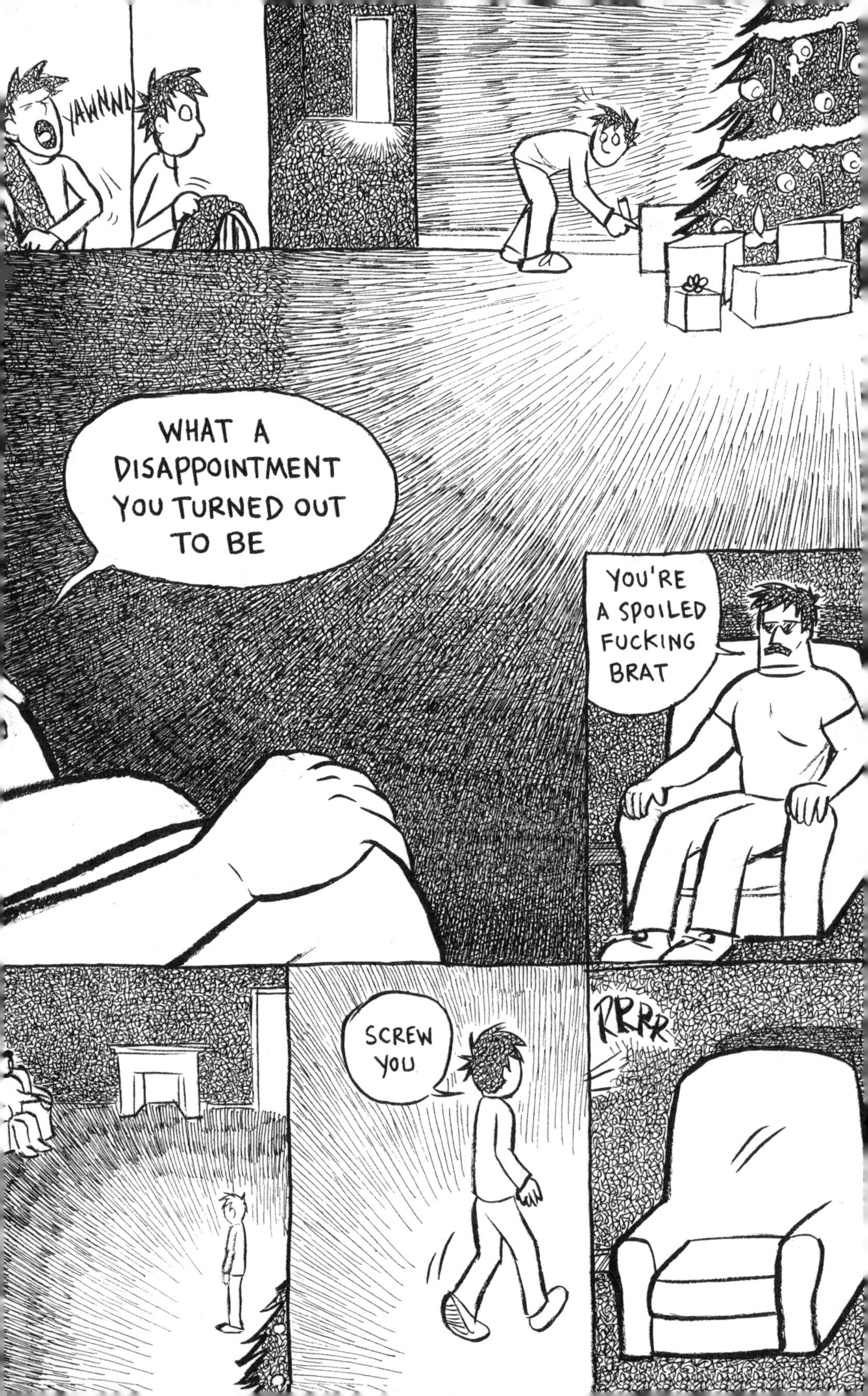
YAWNNN
WHAT A DISAPPOINTMENT YOU TURNED OUT TO BE
YOU'RE A SPOILED FUCKING BRAT
SCREW YOU
RRRR

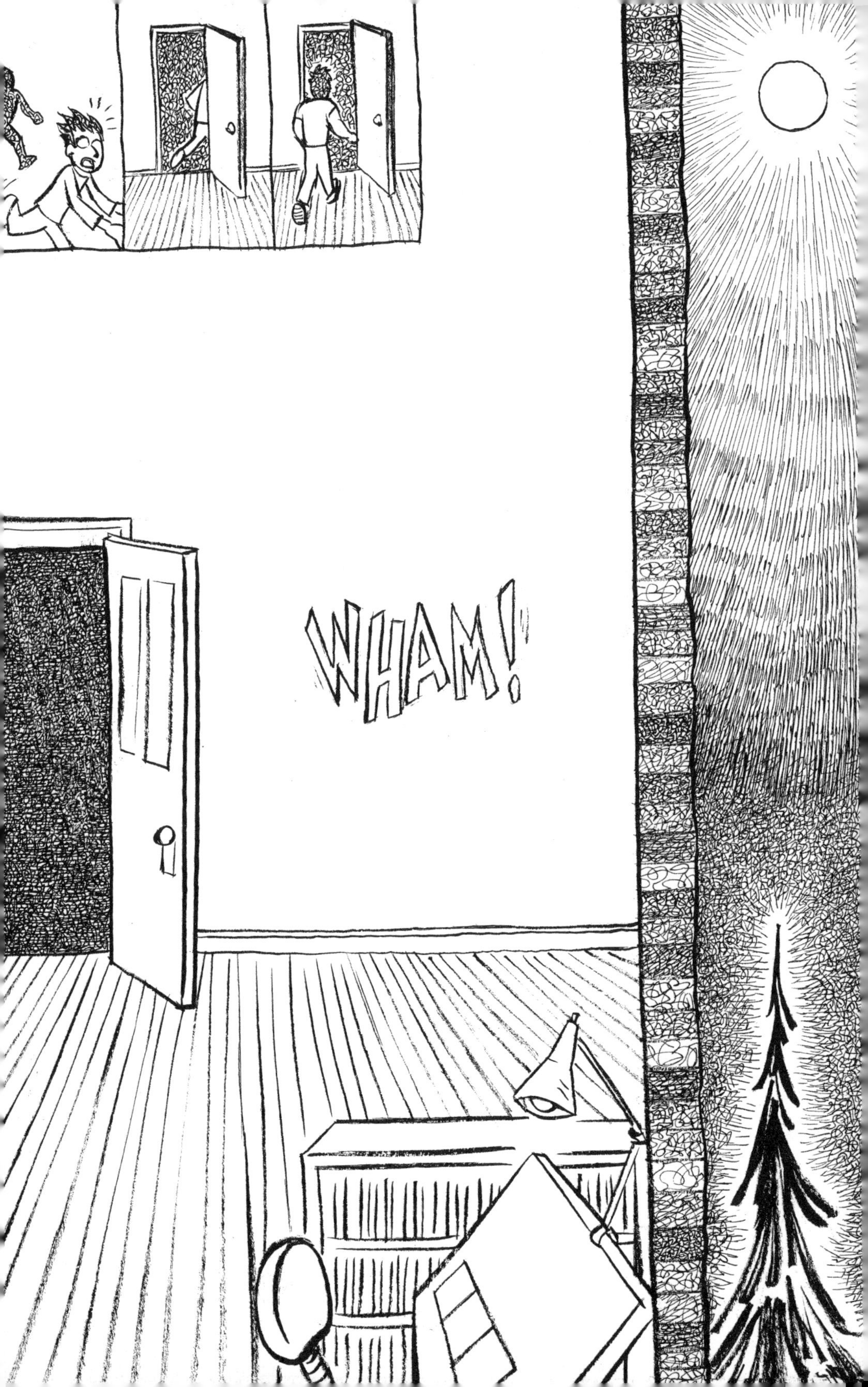
WHAM!

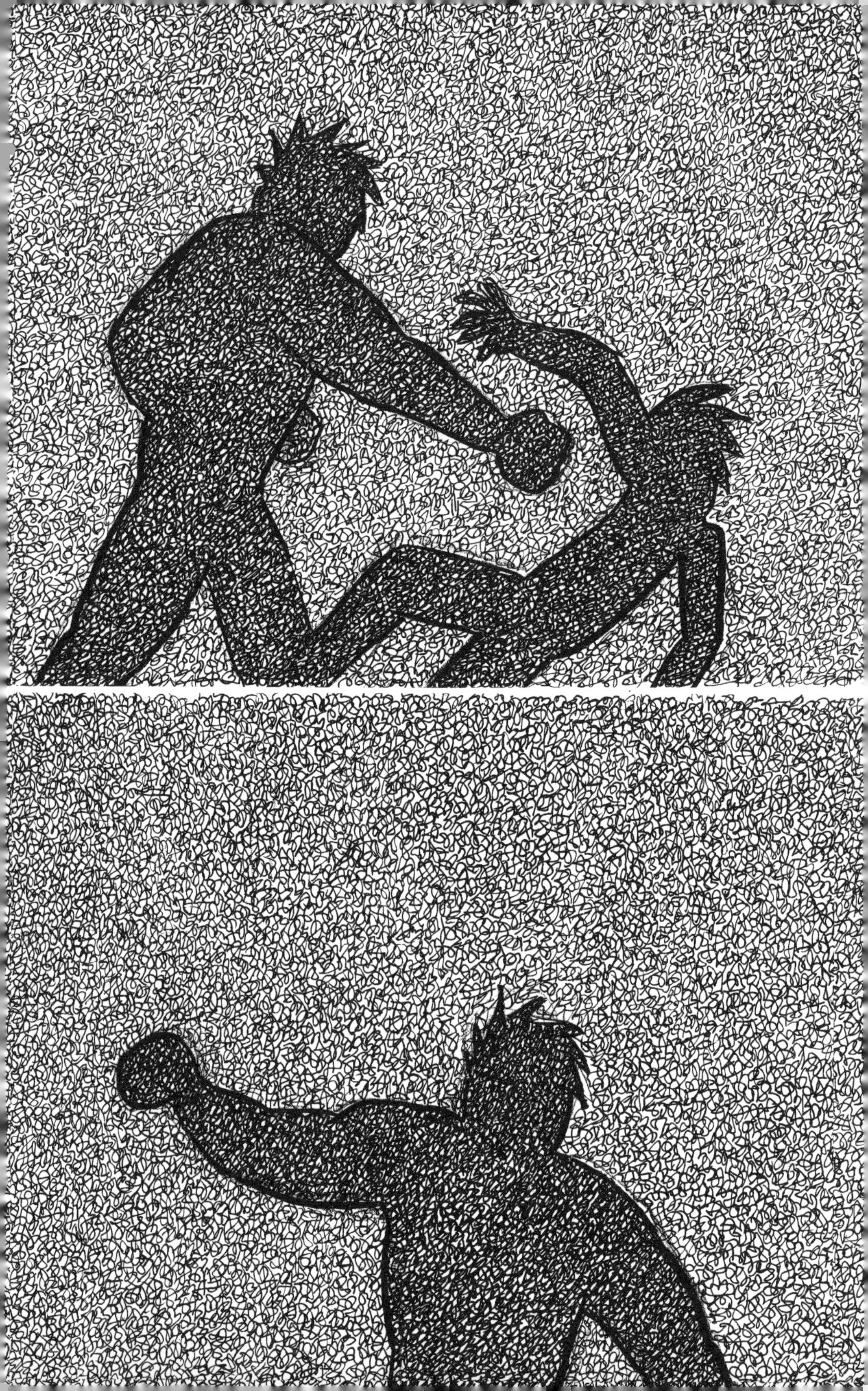

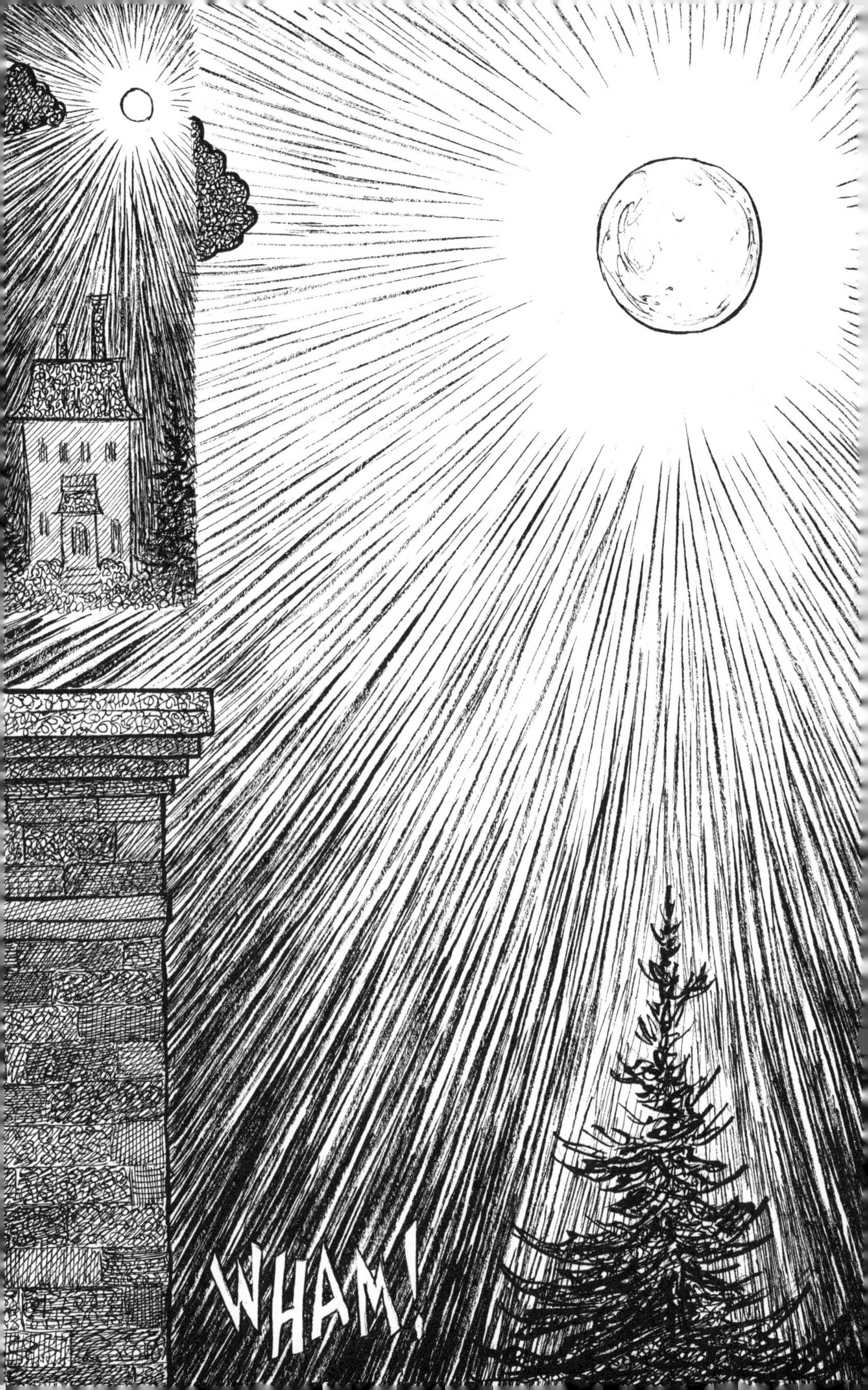
WHAM!

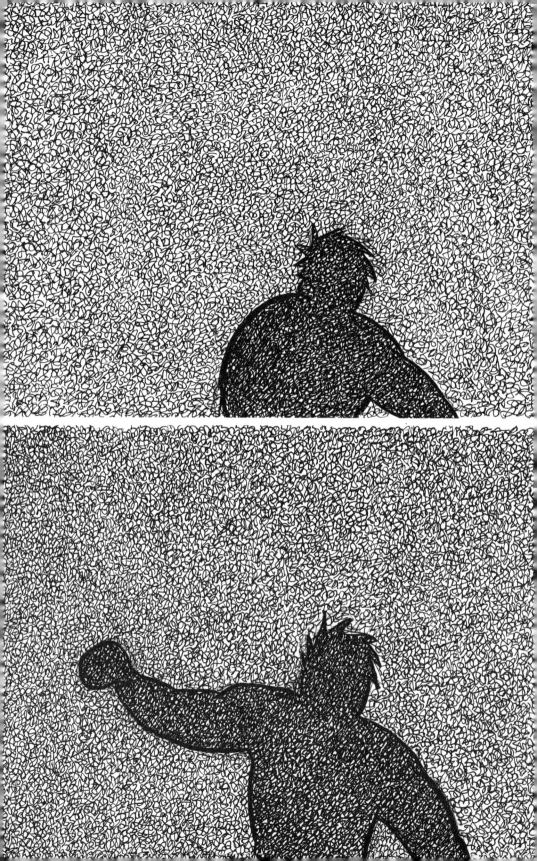

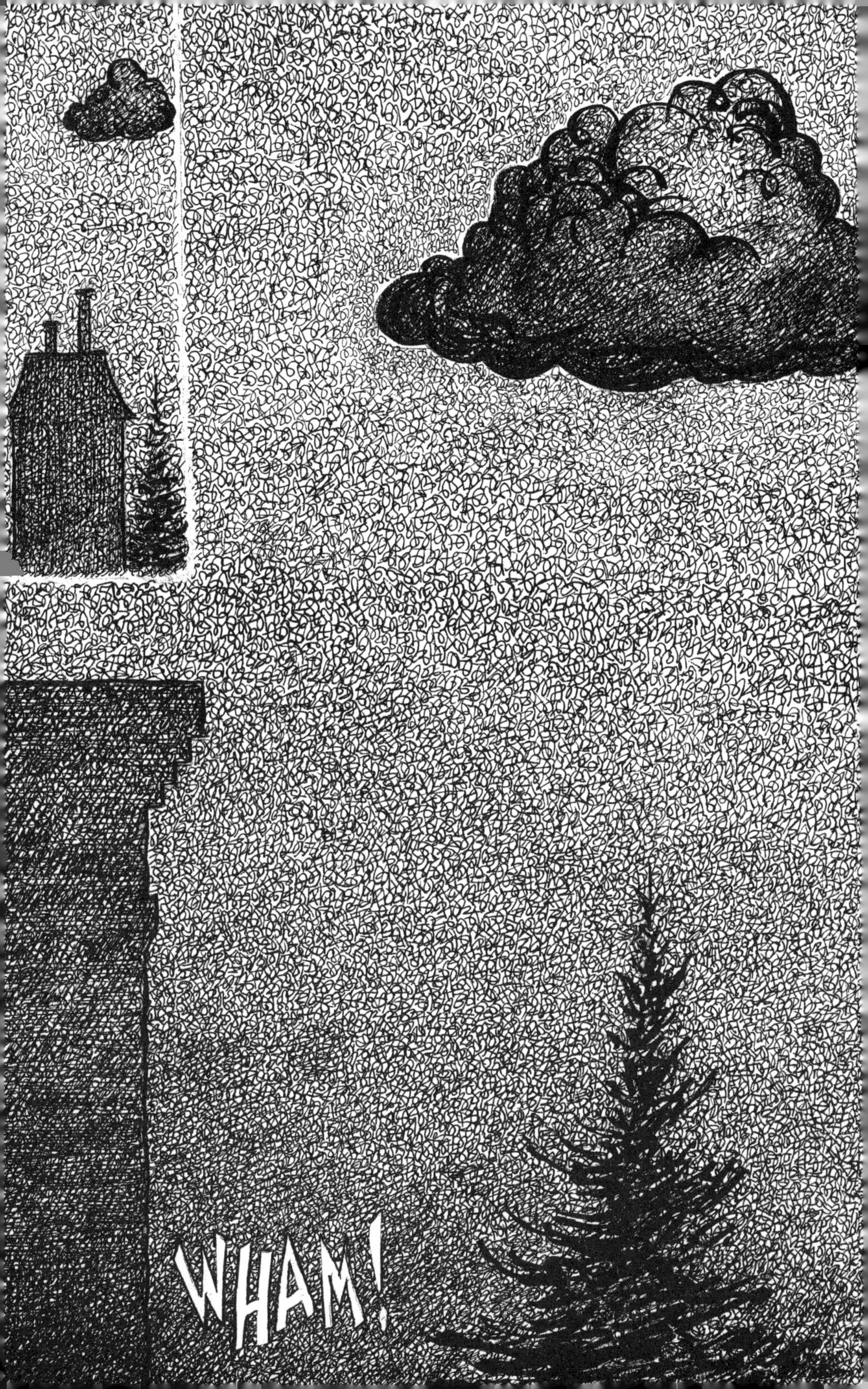
WHAM!

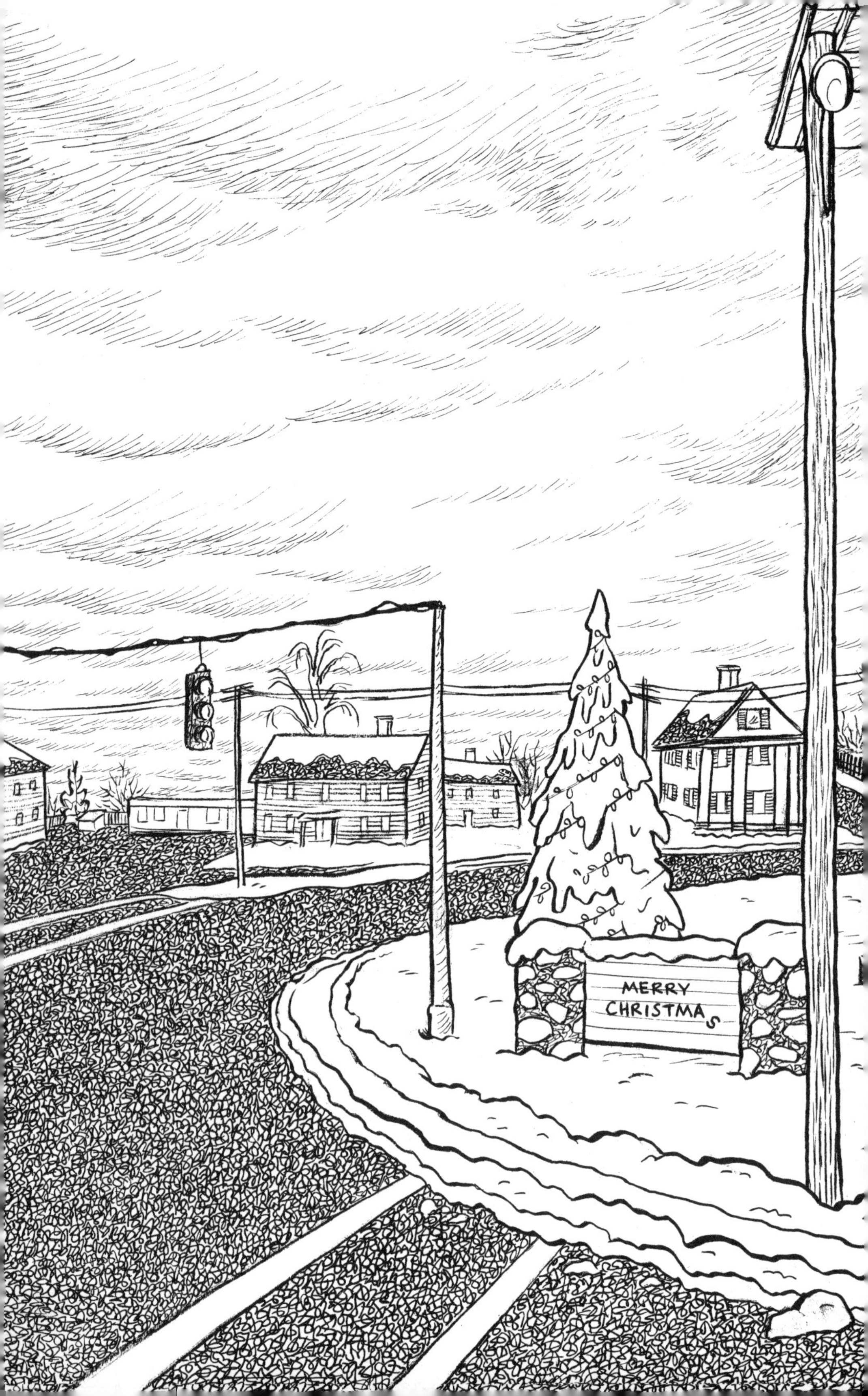
MERRY
CHRISTMAS

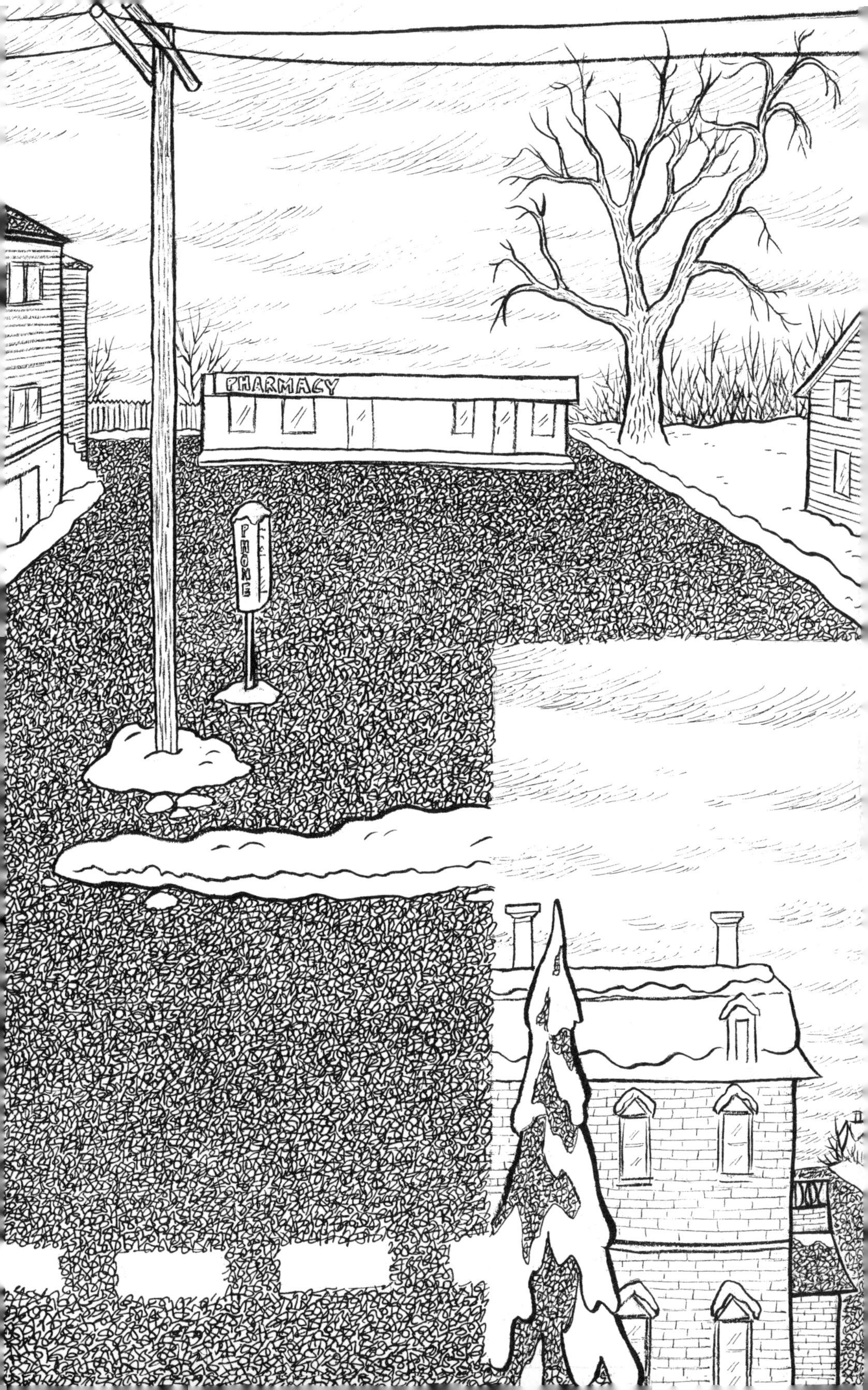
PHARMACY
PHONE

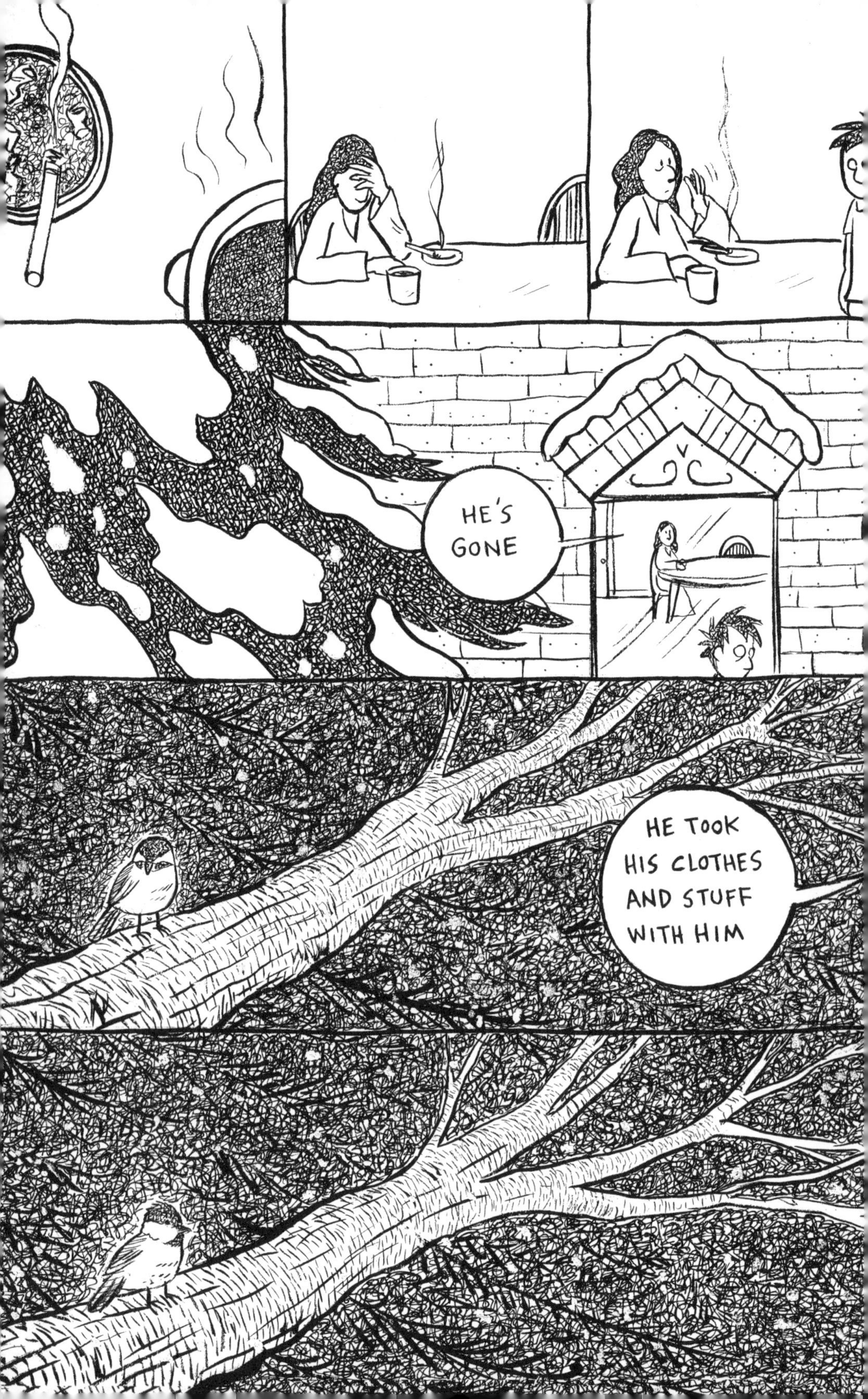
HE'S GONE
HE TOOK HIS CLOTHES AND STUFF WITH HIM

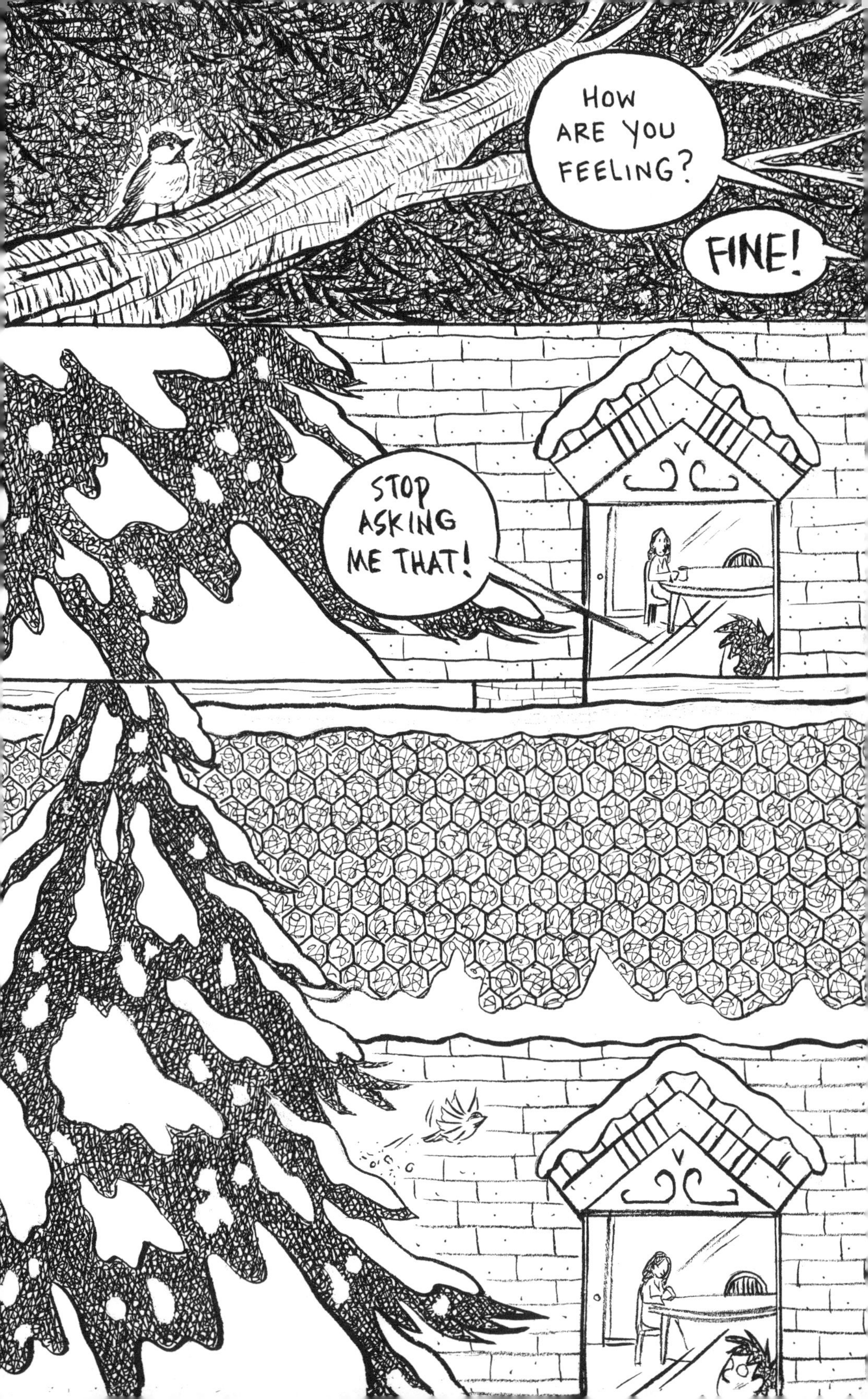
HOW ARE YOU FEELING?
FINE!
STOP ASKING ME THAT!

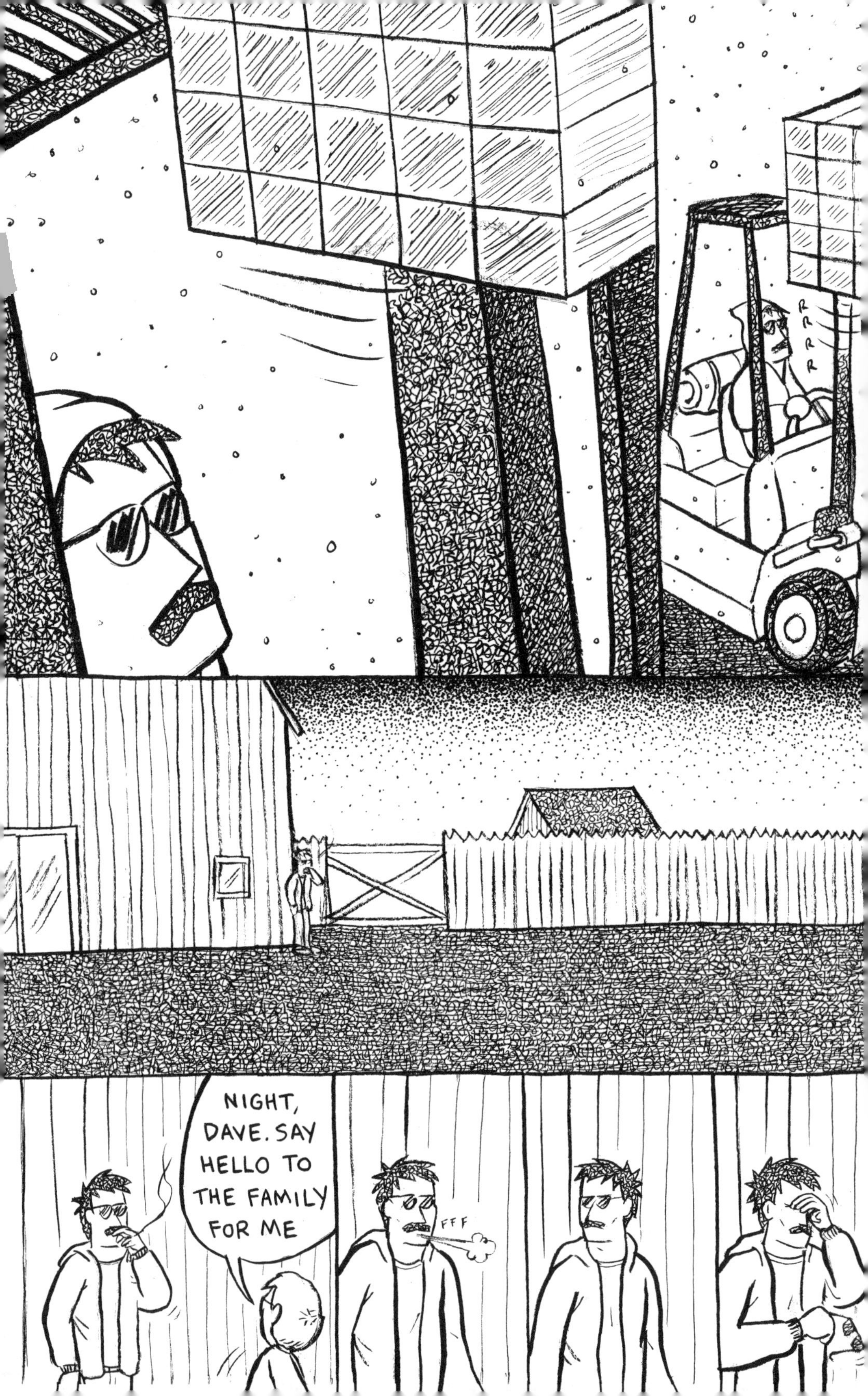
R
R
R
R
NIGHT, DAVE. SAY HELLO TO THE FAMILY FOR ME
FFF

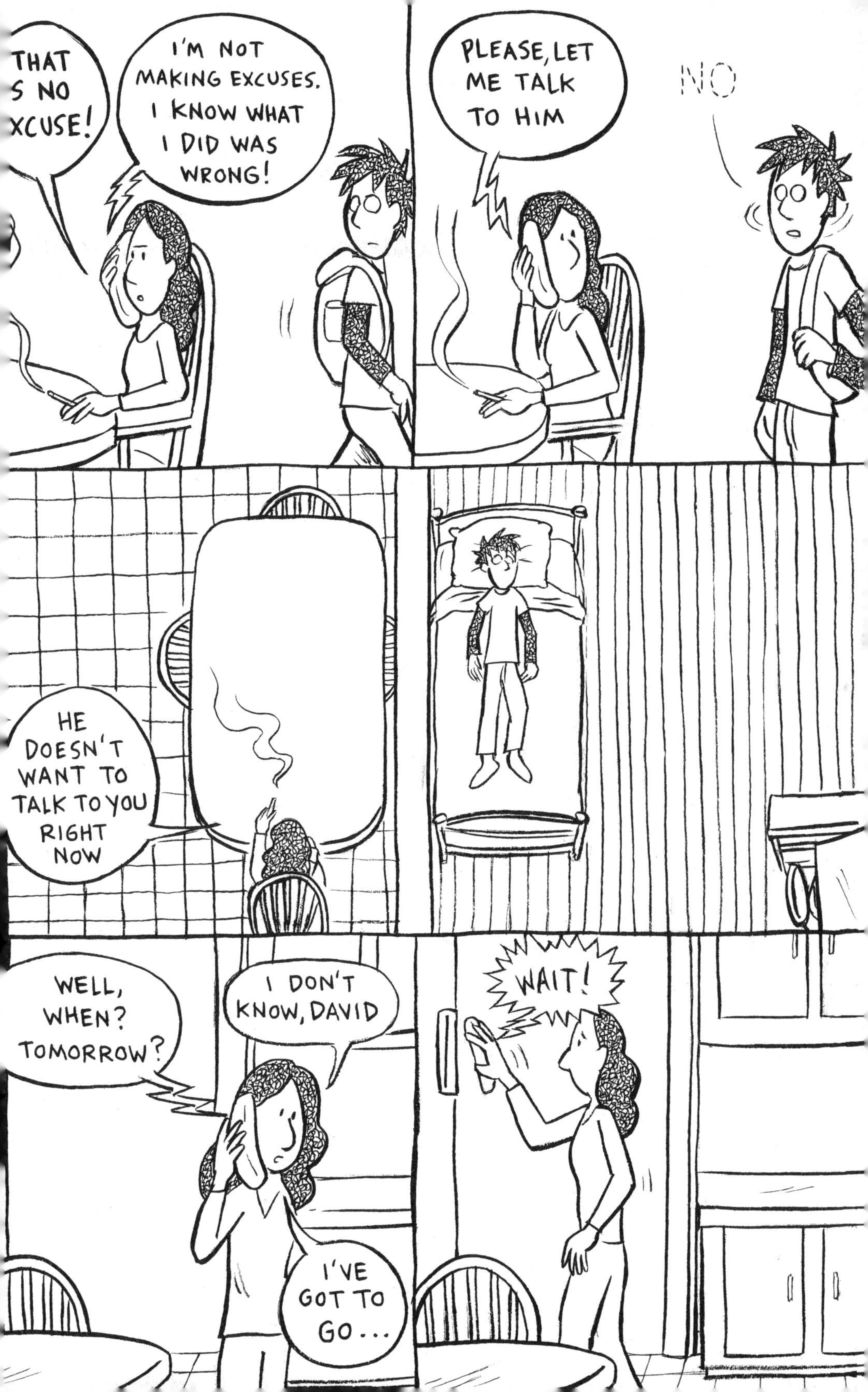
THAT
S NO
XCUSE!
I'M NOT MAKING EXCUSES. I KNOW WHAT I DID WAS WRONG!
PLEASE, LET ME TALK TO HIM
NO
HE DOESN'T WANT TO TALK TO YOU RIGHT NOW
WELL, WHEN? TOMORROW?
I DON'T KNOW, DAVID
I'VE GOT TO GO...
WAIT!

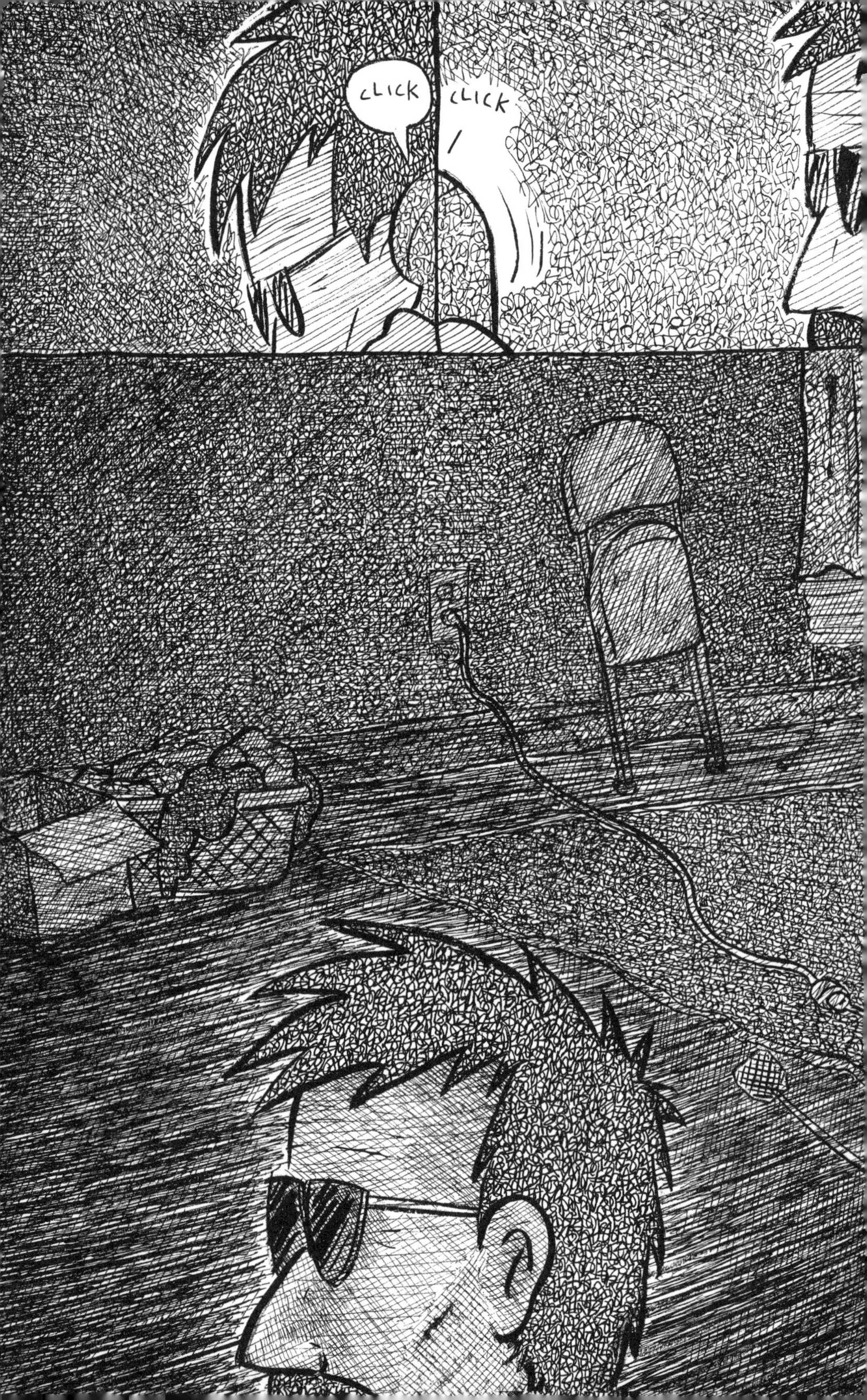
CLICK
CLICK

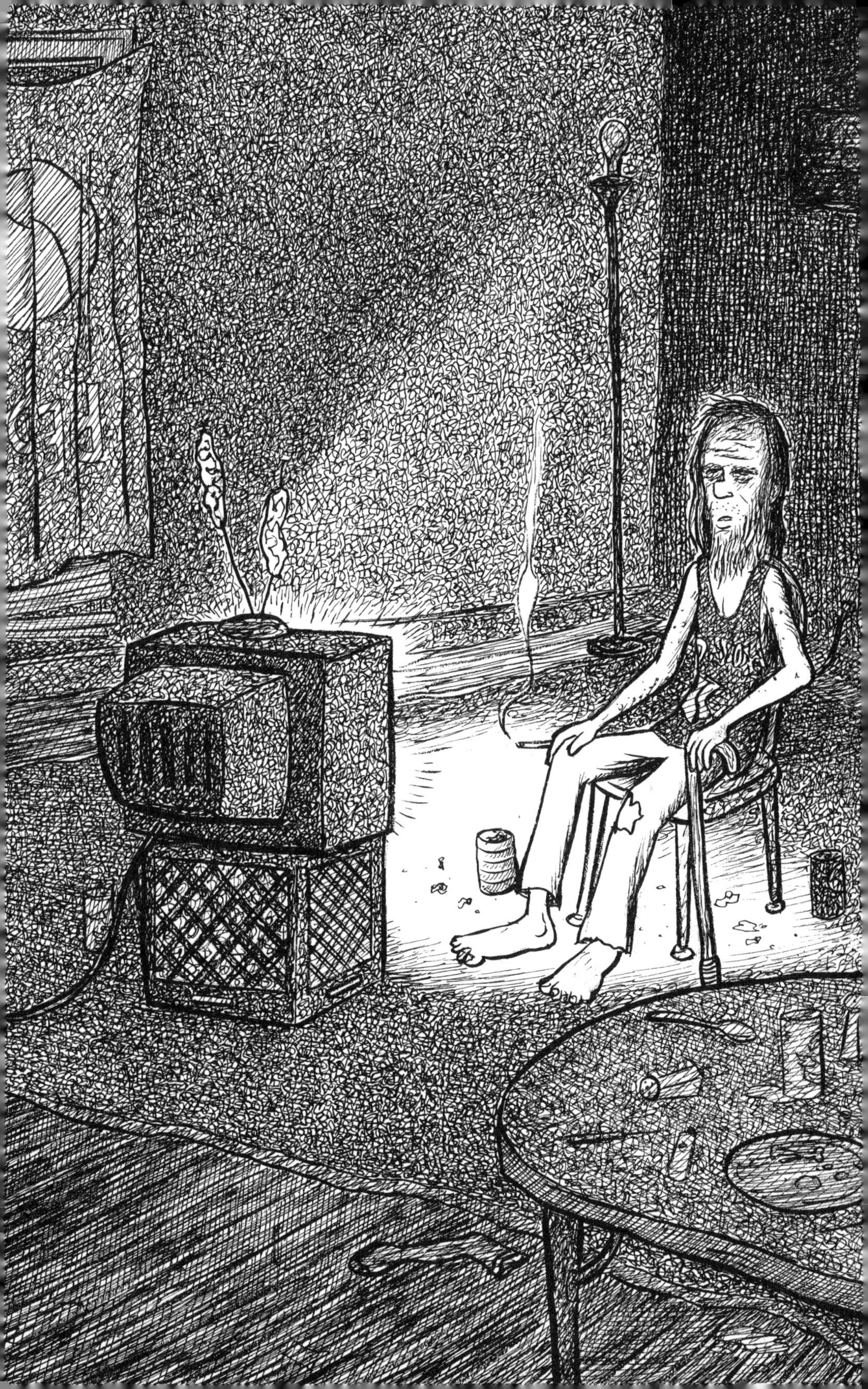

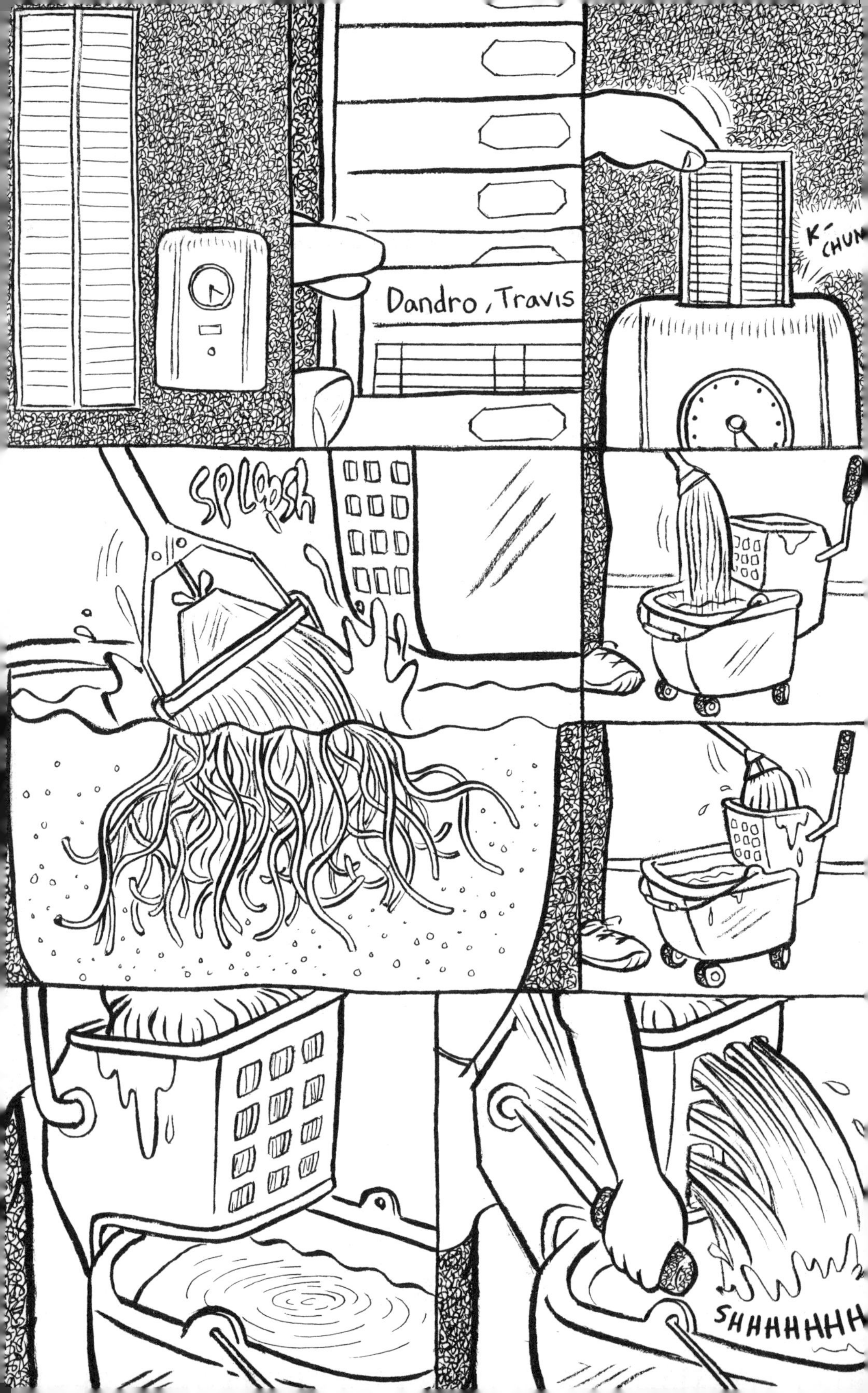
Dandro, Travis
K-CHUN
SPLOOSH
SHHHHHHH

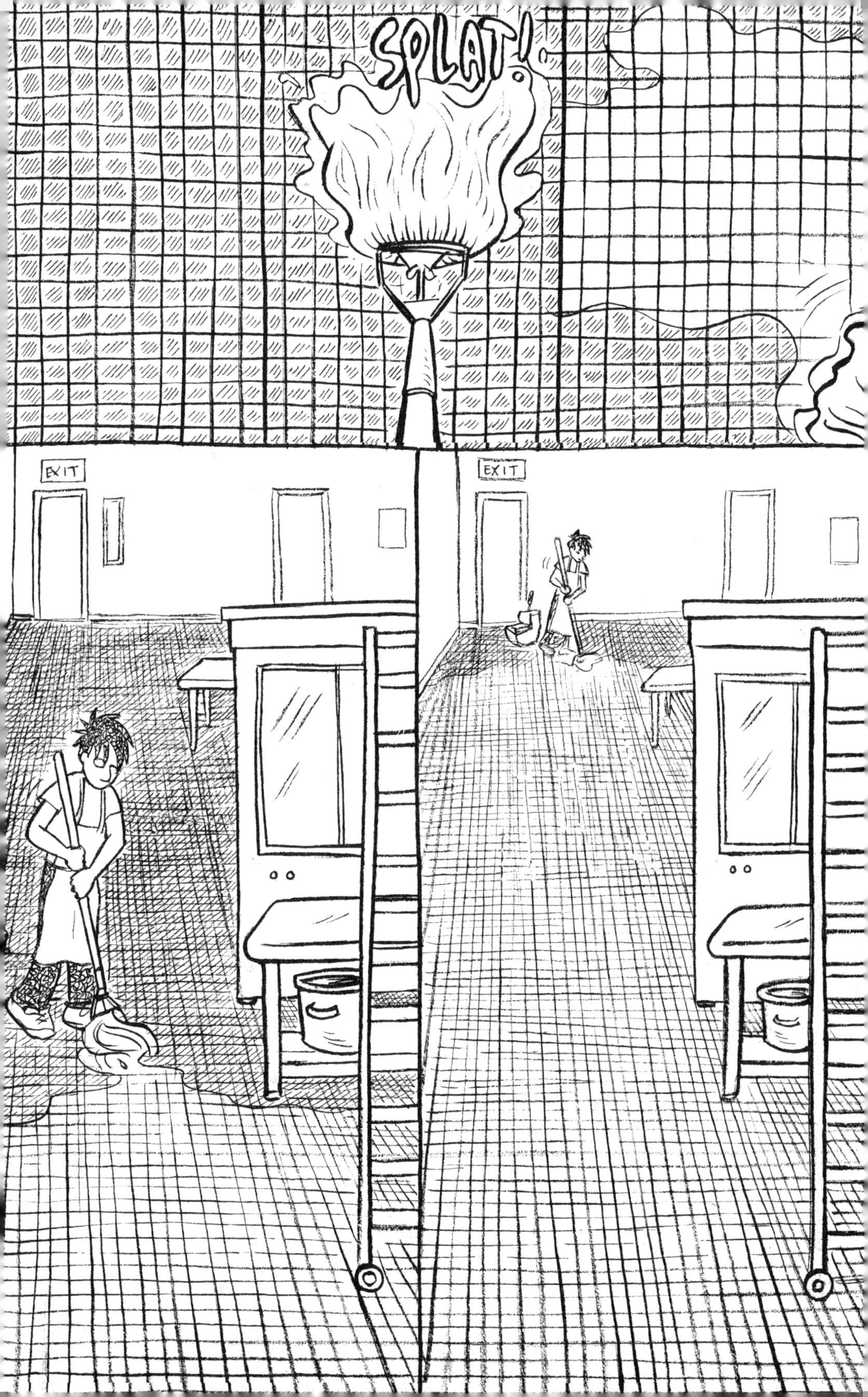
SPLAT!
EXIT
EXIT

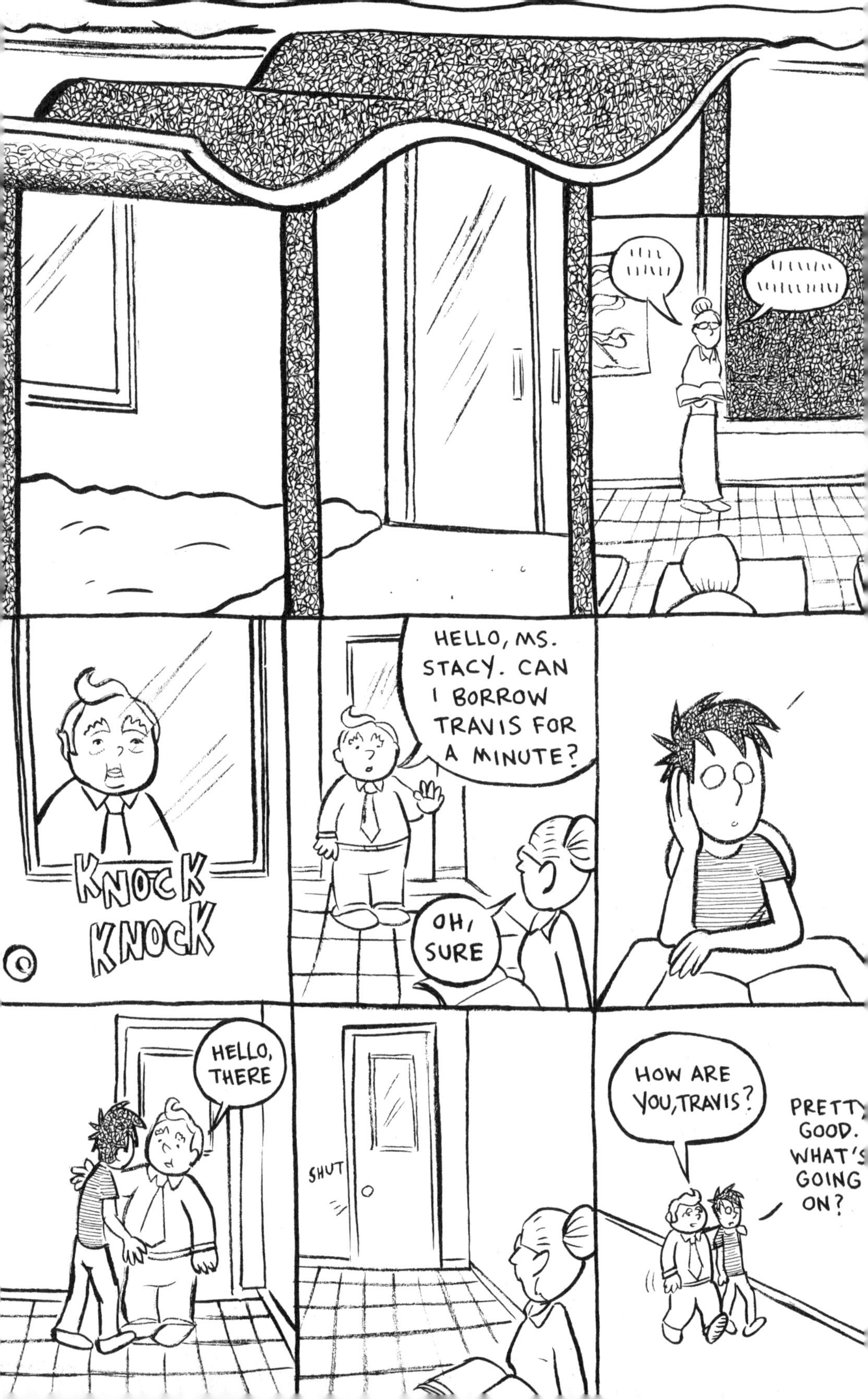

KNOCK KNOCK
HELLO, MS. STACY. CAN I BORROW TRAVIS FOR A MINUTE?
OH, SURE
HELLO, THERE
SHUT
HOW ARE YOU, TRAVIS?
PRETTY GOOD. WHAT'S GOING ON?

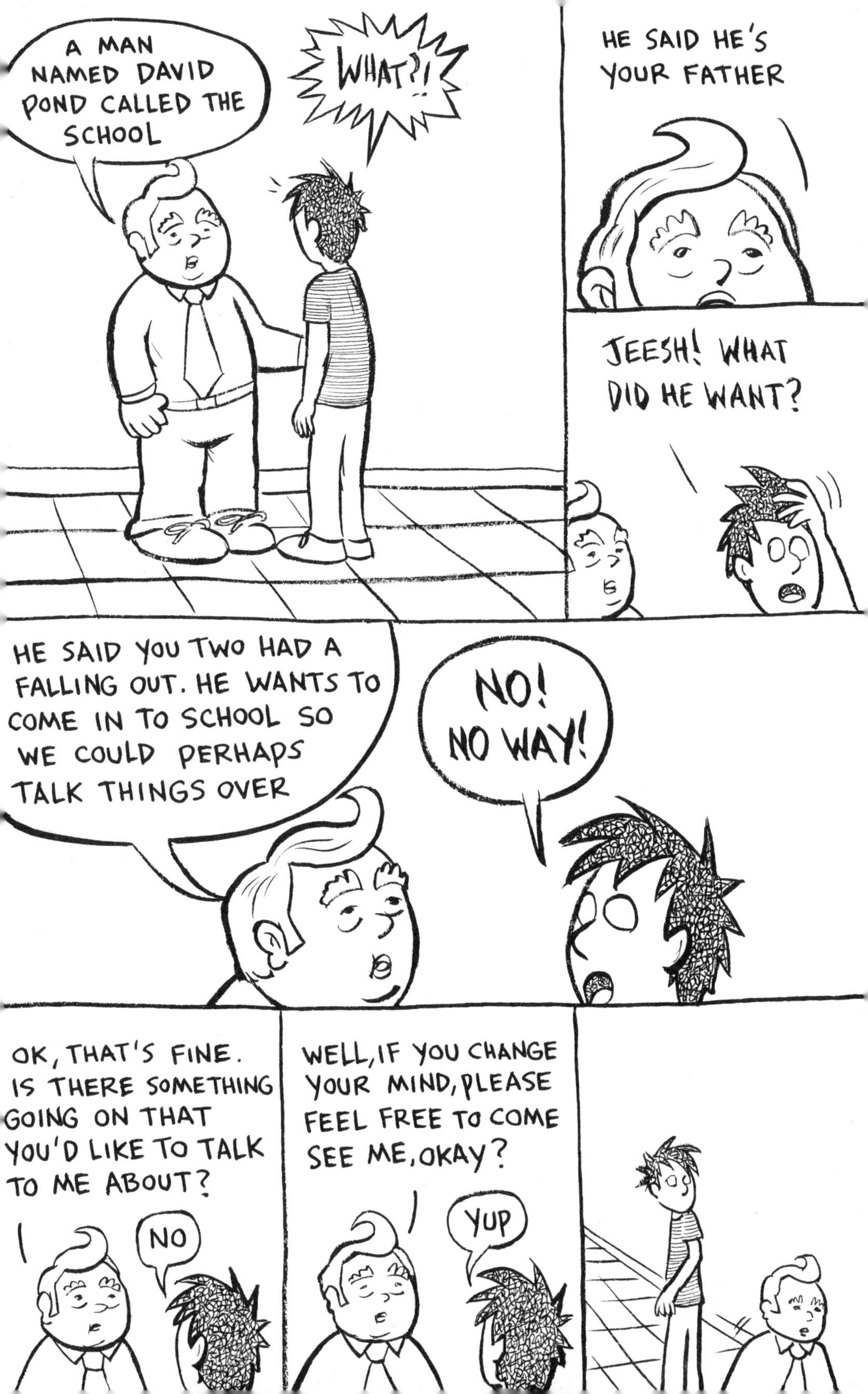
A MAN NAMED DAVID POND CALLED THE SCHOOL
WHAT?!
HE SAID HE'S YOUR FATHER
JEESH! WHAT DID HE WANT?
HE SAID YOU TWO HAD A FALLING OUT. HE WANTS TO COME IN TO SCHOOL SO WE COULD PERHAPS TALK THINGS OVER
NO! NO WAY!
OK, THAT'S FINE. IS THERE SOMETHING GOING ON THAT YOU'D LIKE TO TALK TO ME ABOUT?
NO
WELL, IF YOU CHANGE YOUR MIND, PLEASE FEEL FREE TO COME SEE ME, OKAY?
YUP

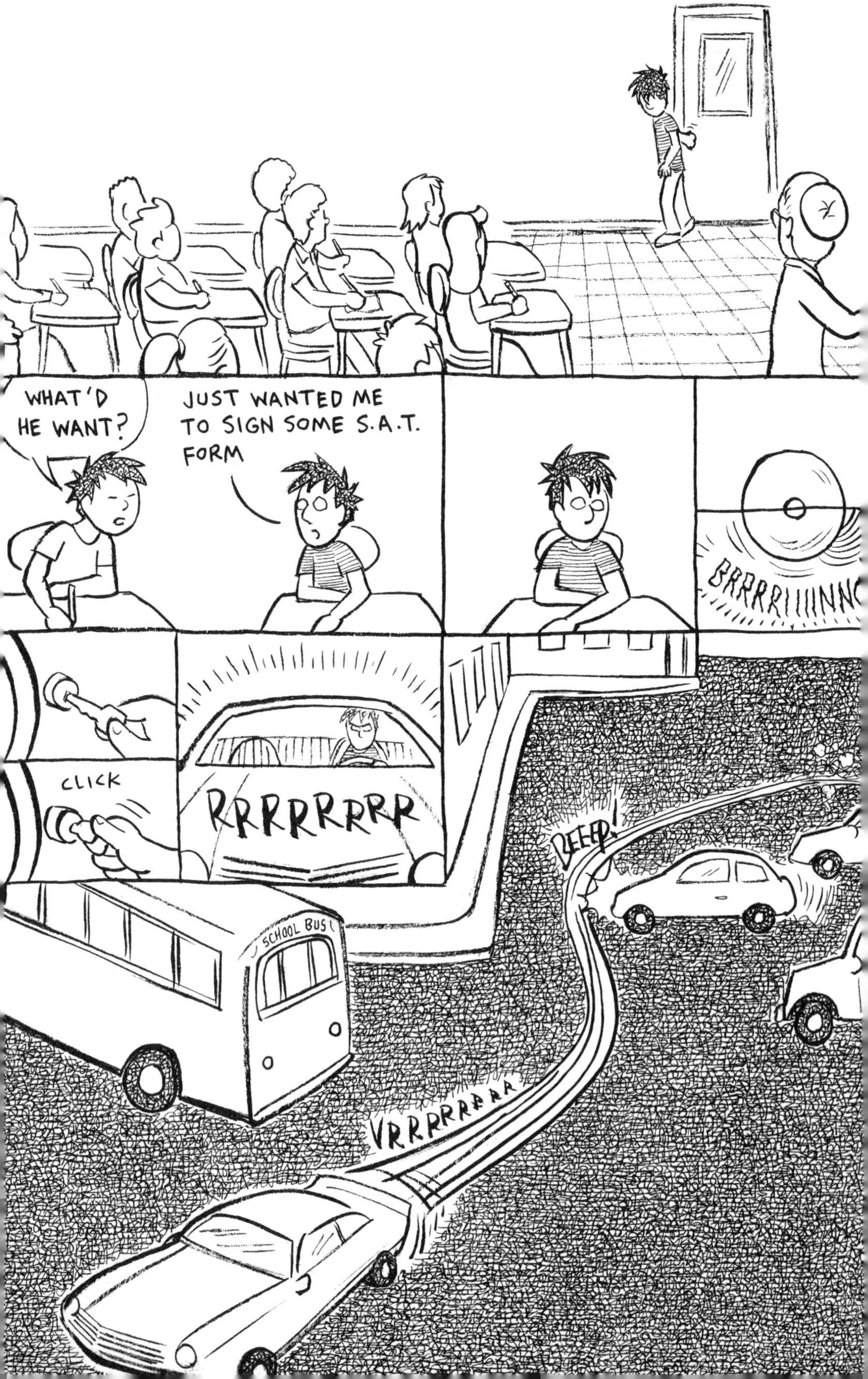

WHAT'D HE WANT?
JUST WANTED ME TO SIGN SOME S.A.T. FORM
BRRRRIIIINNG
CLICK
RRRRRRRRR
SCHOOL BUS
BEEEP!
VRRRRARRA

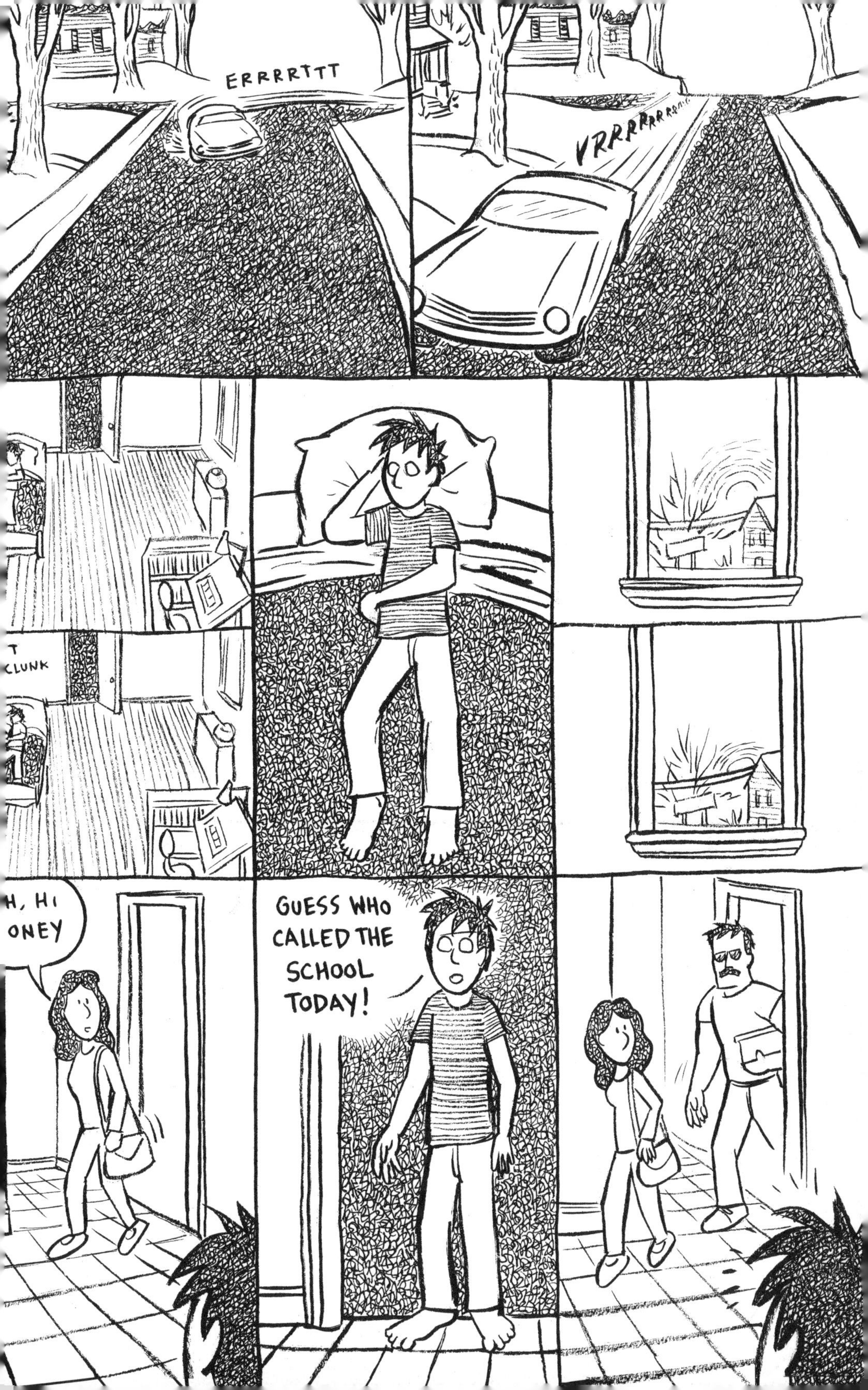
ERRRRTTT
VRRRR
CLUNK
H, HI ONEY
GUESS WHO CALLED THE SCHOOL TODAY!

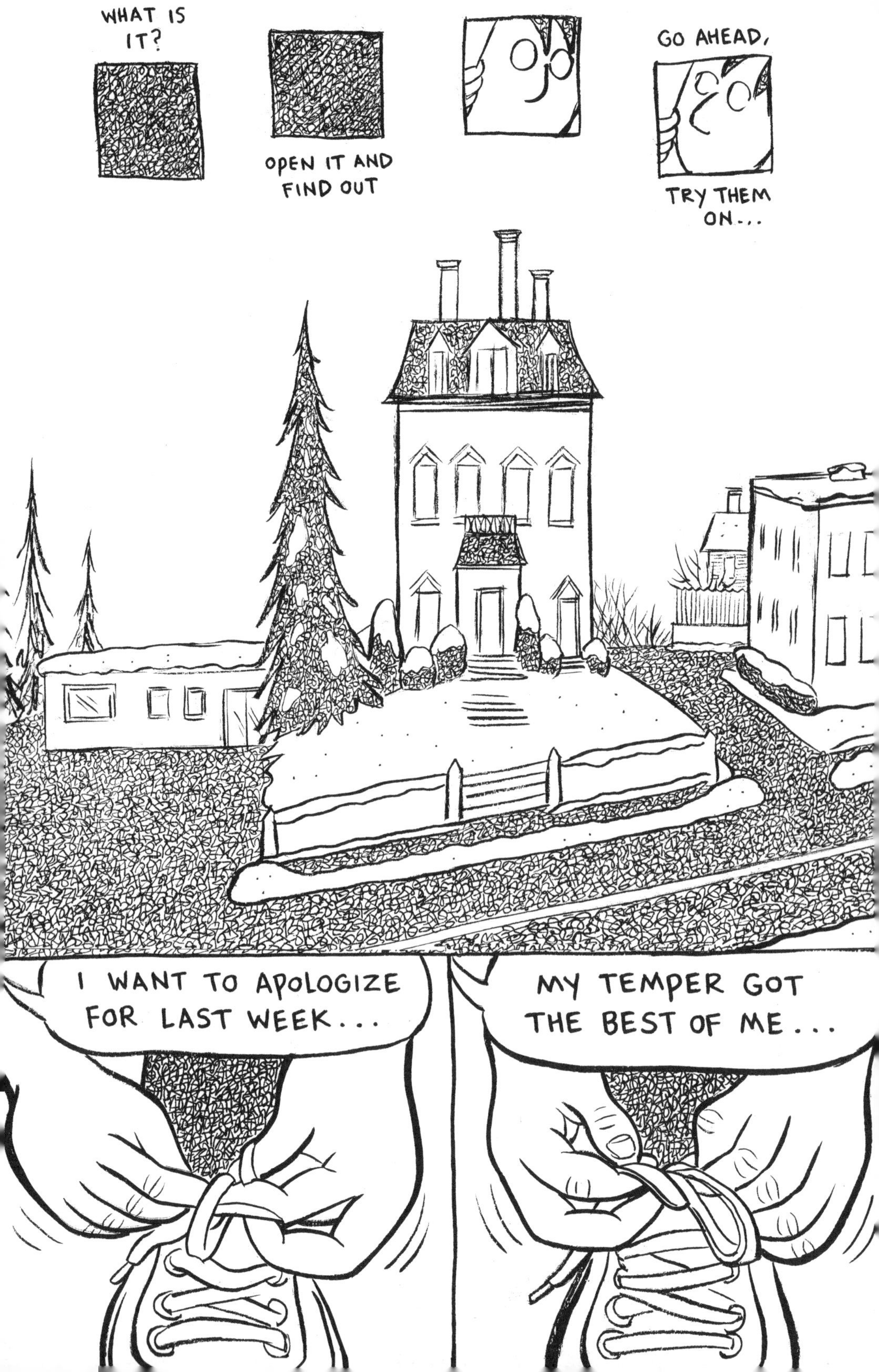
WHAT IS IT?
OPEN IT AND FIND OUT
GO AHEAD,
TRY THEM ON...
I WANT TO APOLOGIZE FOR LAST WEEK...
MY TEMPER GOT THE BEST OF ME...

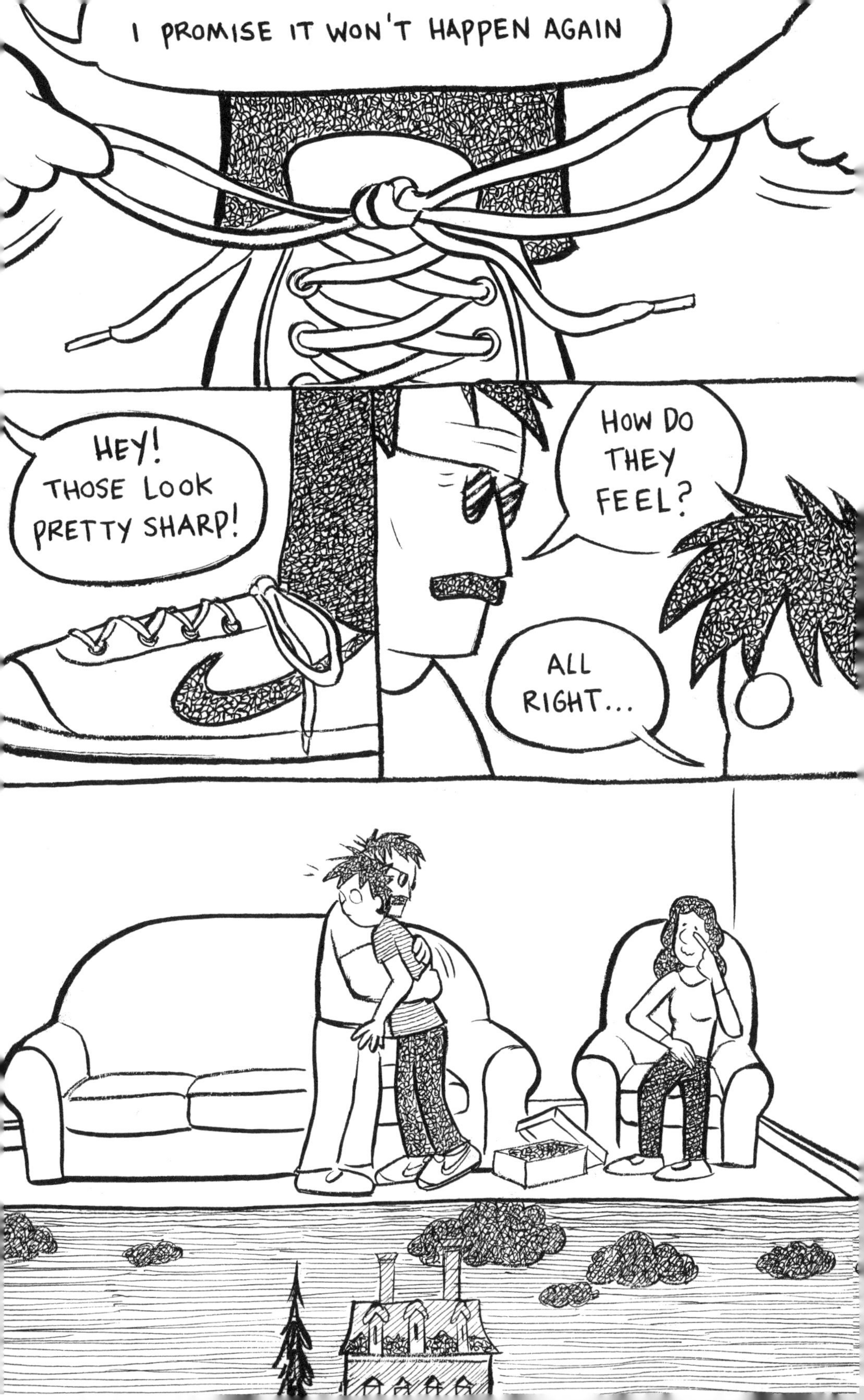
I PROMISE IT WON'T HAPPEN AGAIN
HEY! THOSE LOOK PRETTY SHARP!
HOW DO THEY FEEL?
ALL RIGHT...

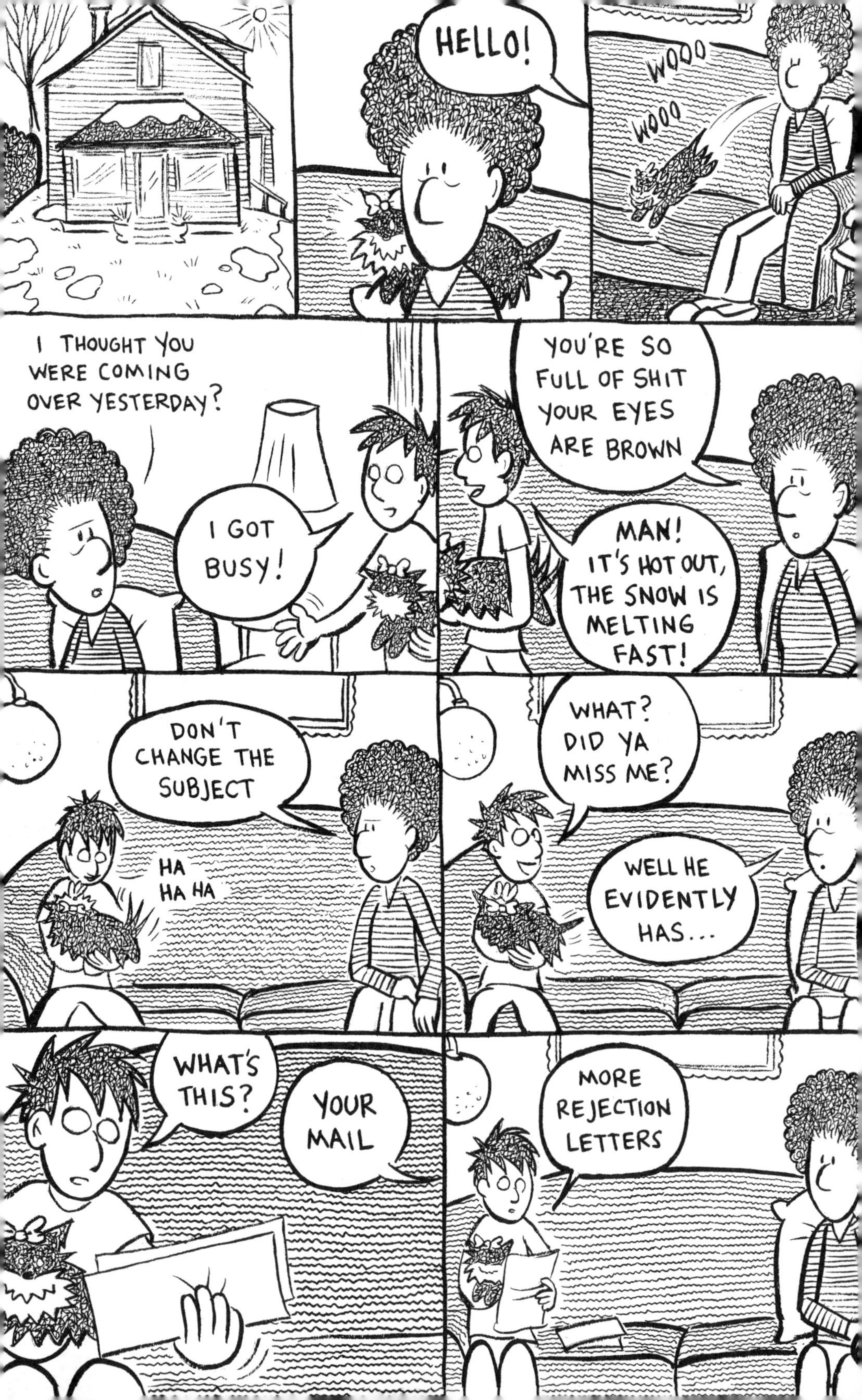
HELLO!
WOOO
WOOO
I THOUGHT YOU WERE COMING OVER YESTERDAY?
I GOT BUSY!
YOU'RE SO FULL OF SHIT YOUR EYES ARE BROWN
MAN! IT'S HOT OUT, THE SNOW IS MELTING FAST!
DON'T CHANGE THE SUBJECT
HA HA HA
WHAT? DID YA MISS ME?
WELL HE EVIDENTLY HAS...
WHAT'S THIS?
YOUR MAIL
MORE REJECTION LETTERS

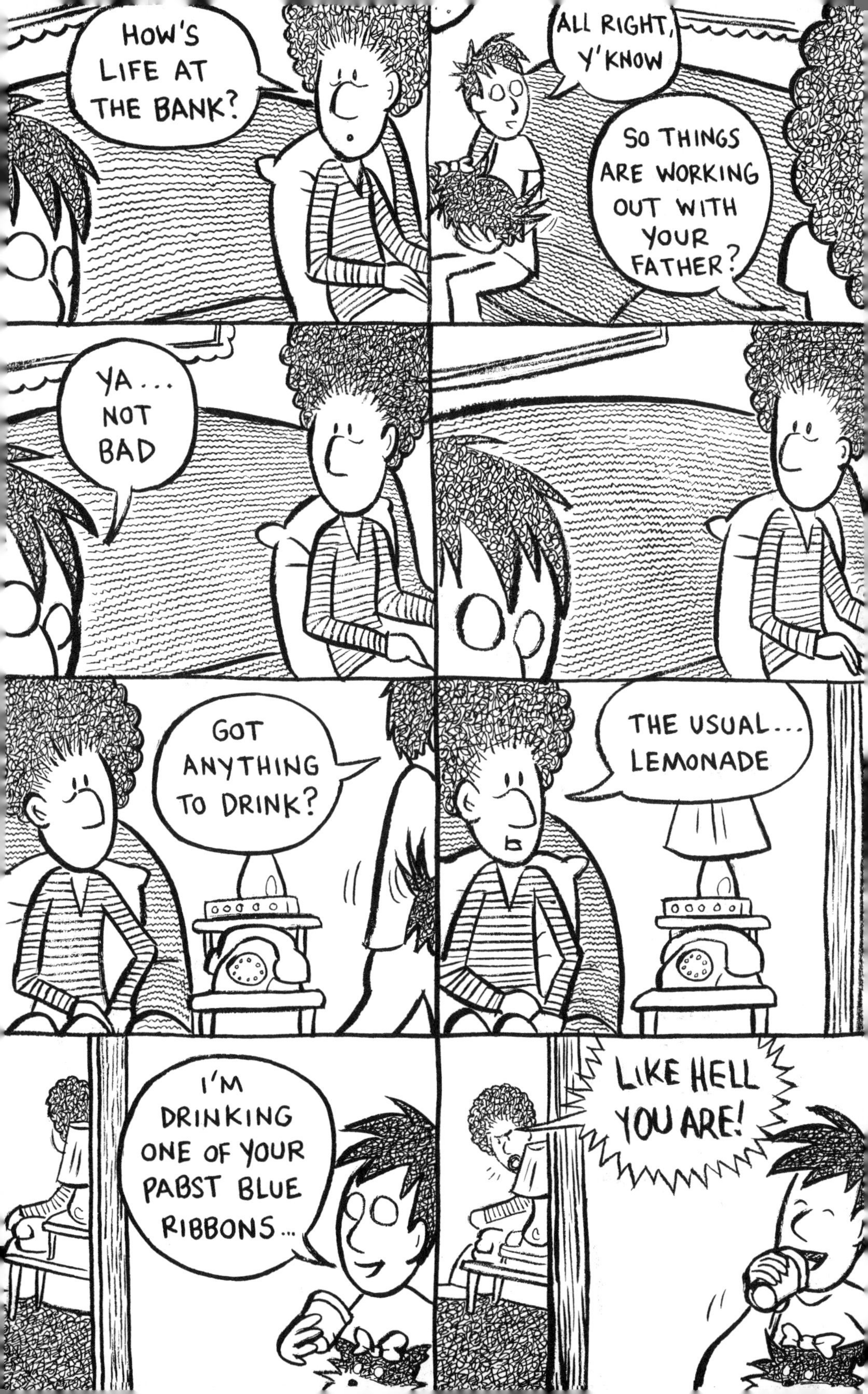
HOW'S LIFE AT THE BANK?
ALL RIGHT, Y'KNOW
SO THINGS ARE WORKING OUT WITH YOUR FATHER?
YA... NOT BAD
GOT ANYTHING TO DRINK?
THE USUAL... LEMONADE
I'M DRINKING ONE OF YOUR PABST BLUE RIBBONS...
LIKE HELL YOU ARE!

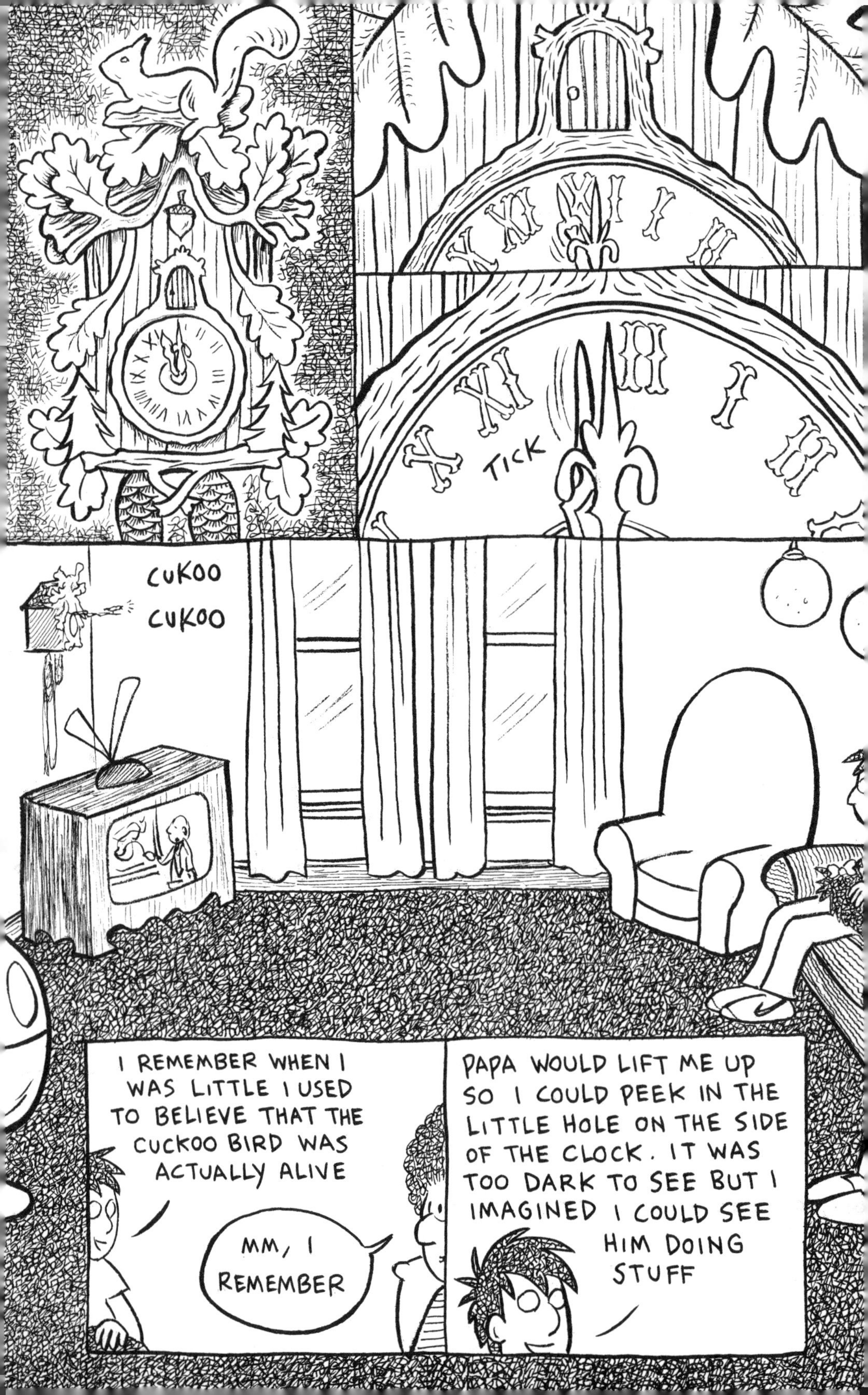
TICK
CUKOO
CUKOO
I REMEMBER WHEN I WAS LITTLE I USED TO BELIEVE THAT THE CUCKOO BIRD WAS ACTUALLY ALIVE
MM, I REMEMBER
PAPA WOULD LIFT ME UP SO I COULD PEEK IN THE LITTLE HOLE ON THE SIDE OF THE CLOCK. IT WAS TOO DARK TO SEE BUT I IMAGINED I COULD SEE HIM DOING STUFF

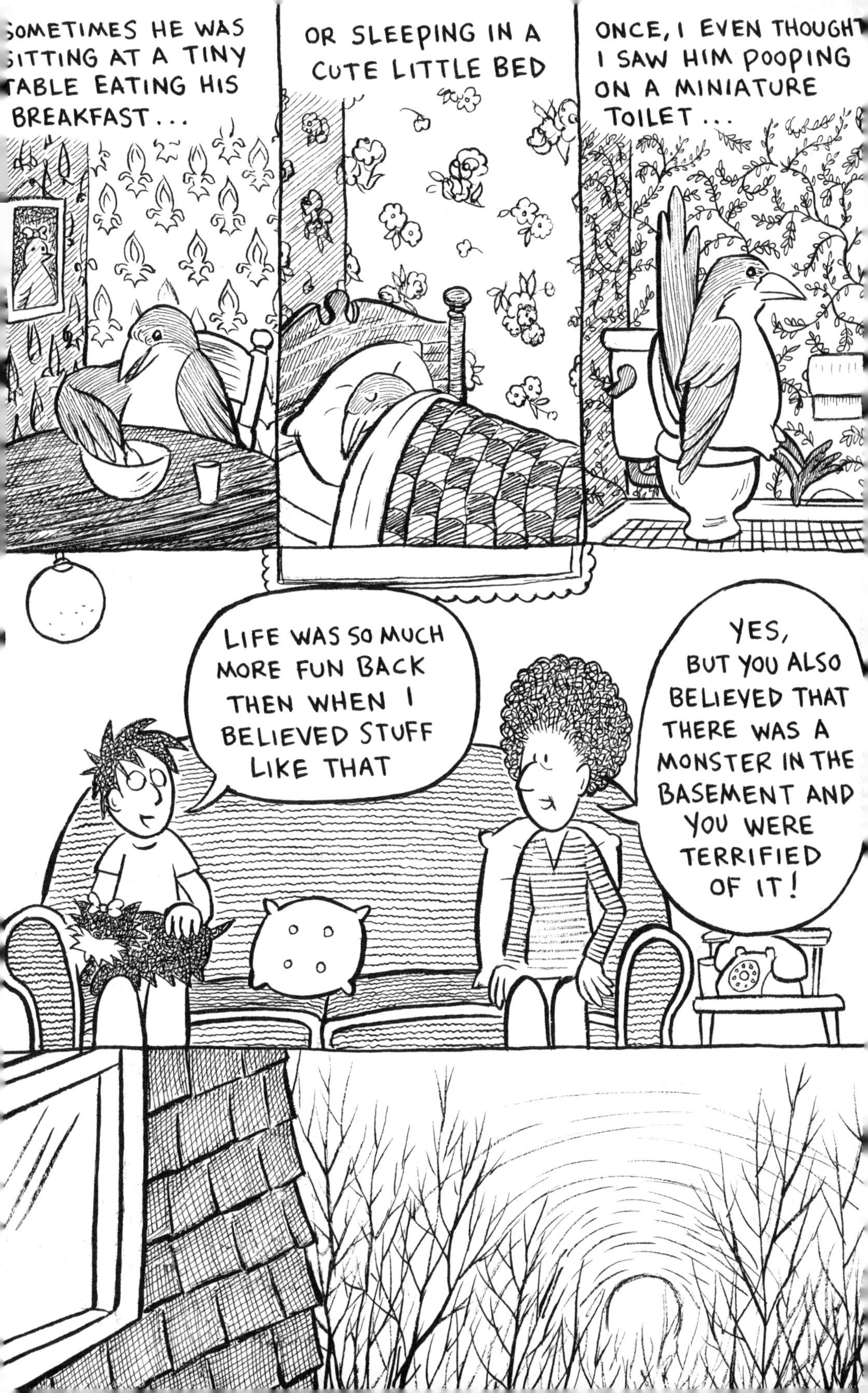
SOMETIMES HE WAS SITTING AT A TINY TABLE EATING HIS BREAKFAST...
OR SLEEPING IN A CUTE LITTLE BED
ONCE, I EVEN THOUGHT I SAW HIM POOPING ON A MINIATURE TOILET...
LIFE WAS SO MUCH MORE FUN BACK THEN WHEN I BELIEVED STUFF LIKE THAT
YES, BUT YOU ALSO BELIEVED THAT THERE WAS A MONSTER IN THE BASEMENT AND YOU WERE TERRIFIED OF IT!

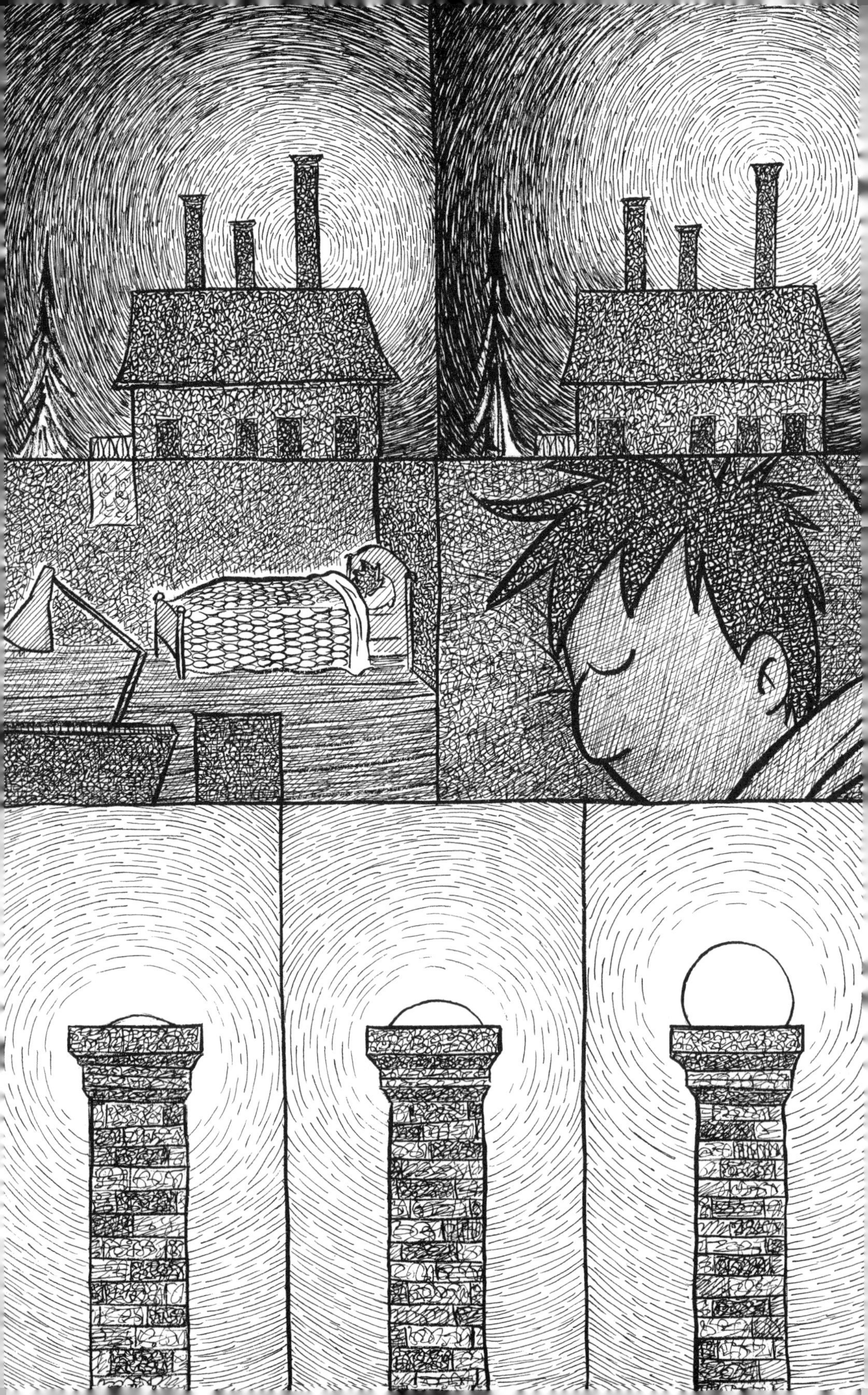

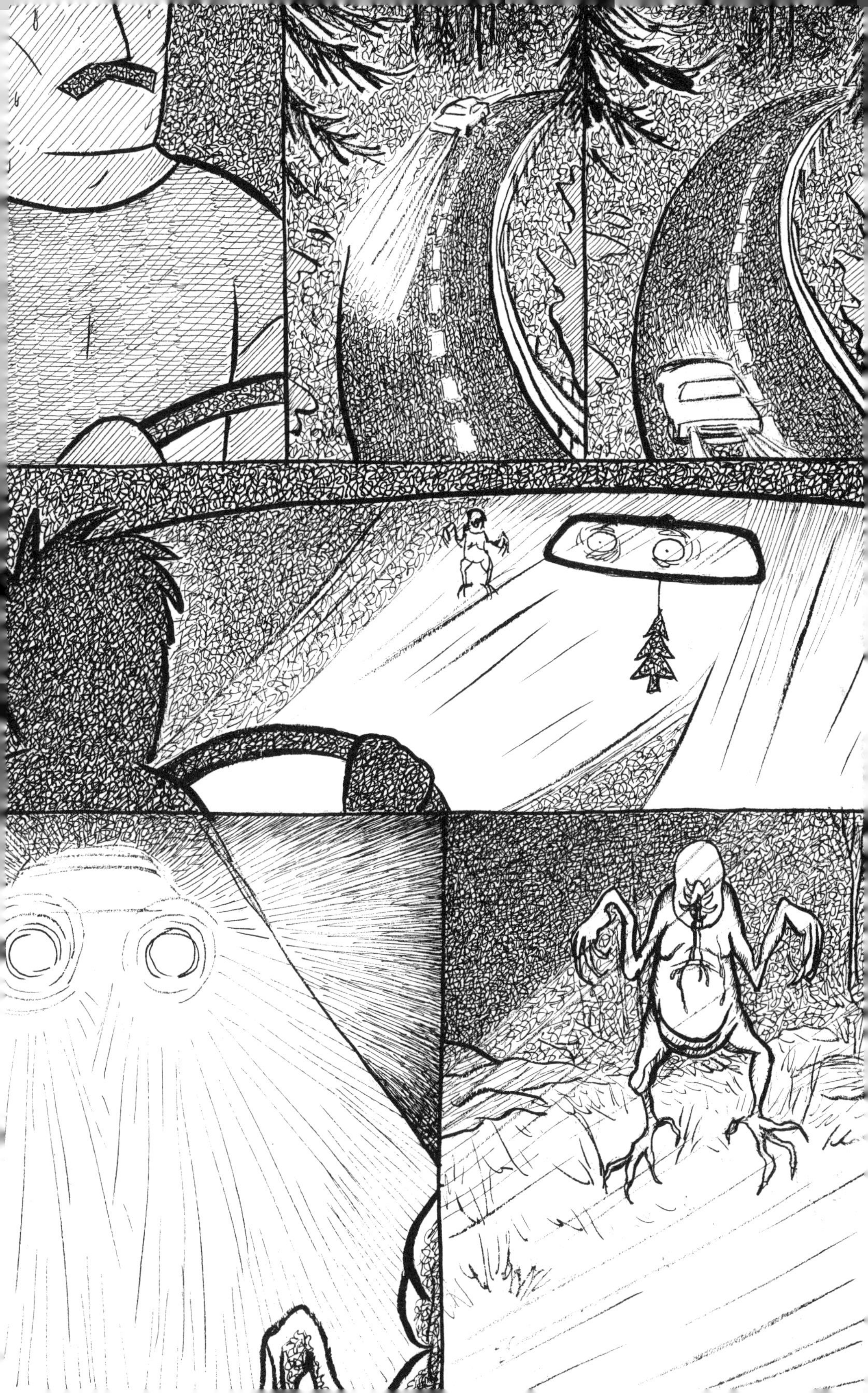

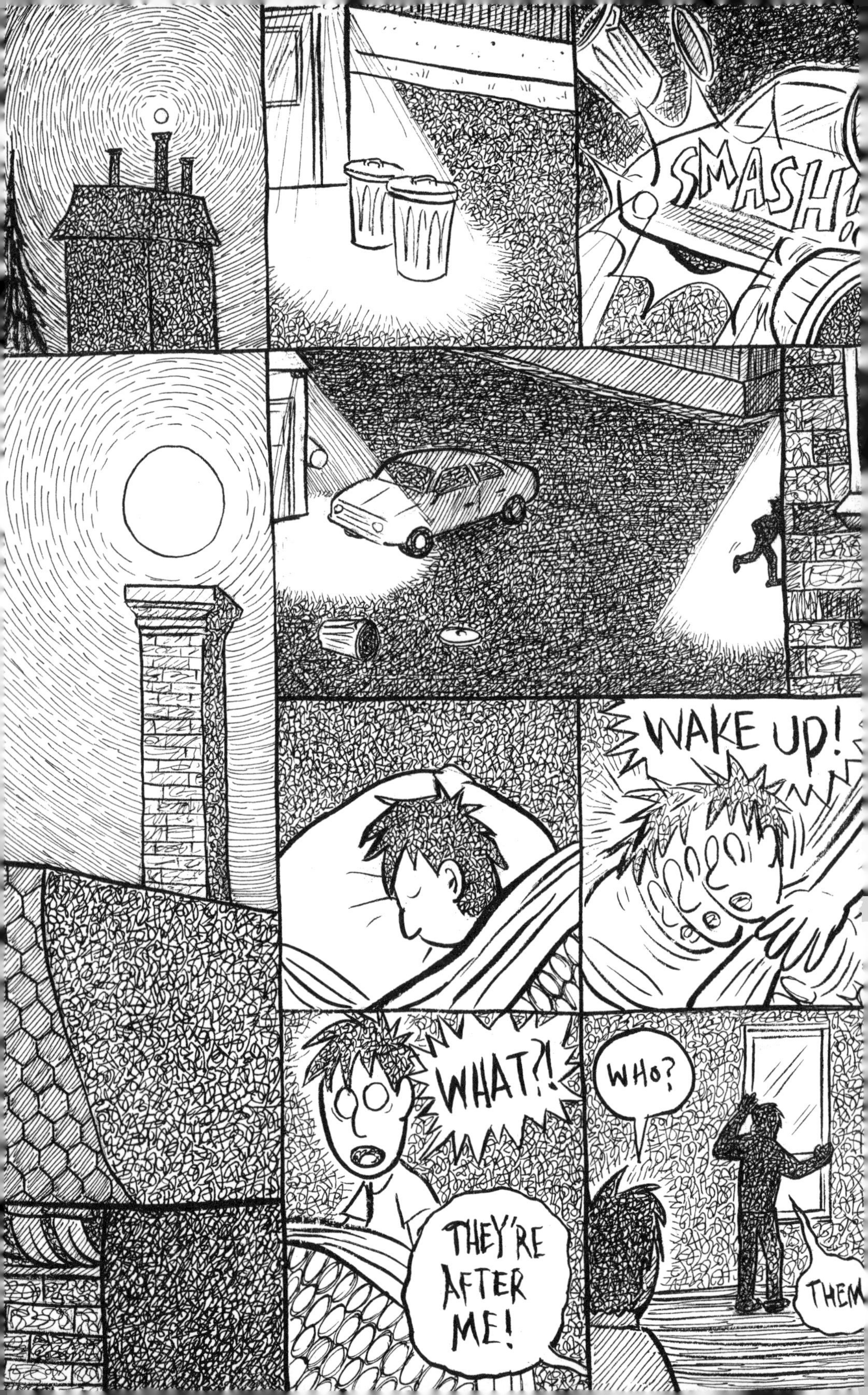
SMASH!
WAKE UP!
WHAT?!
THEY'RE AFTER ME!
WHO?
THEM

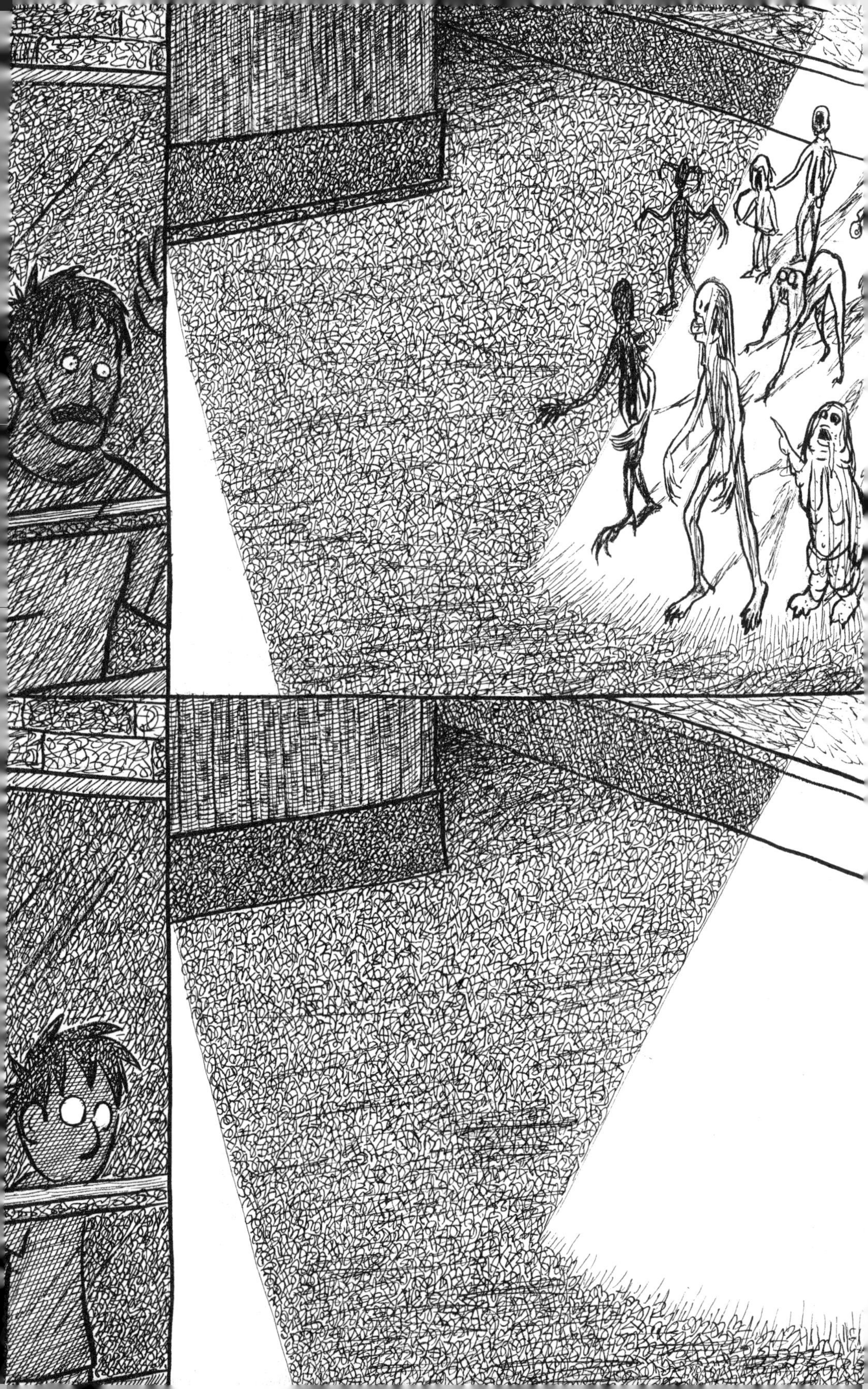

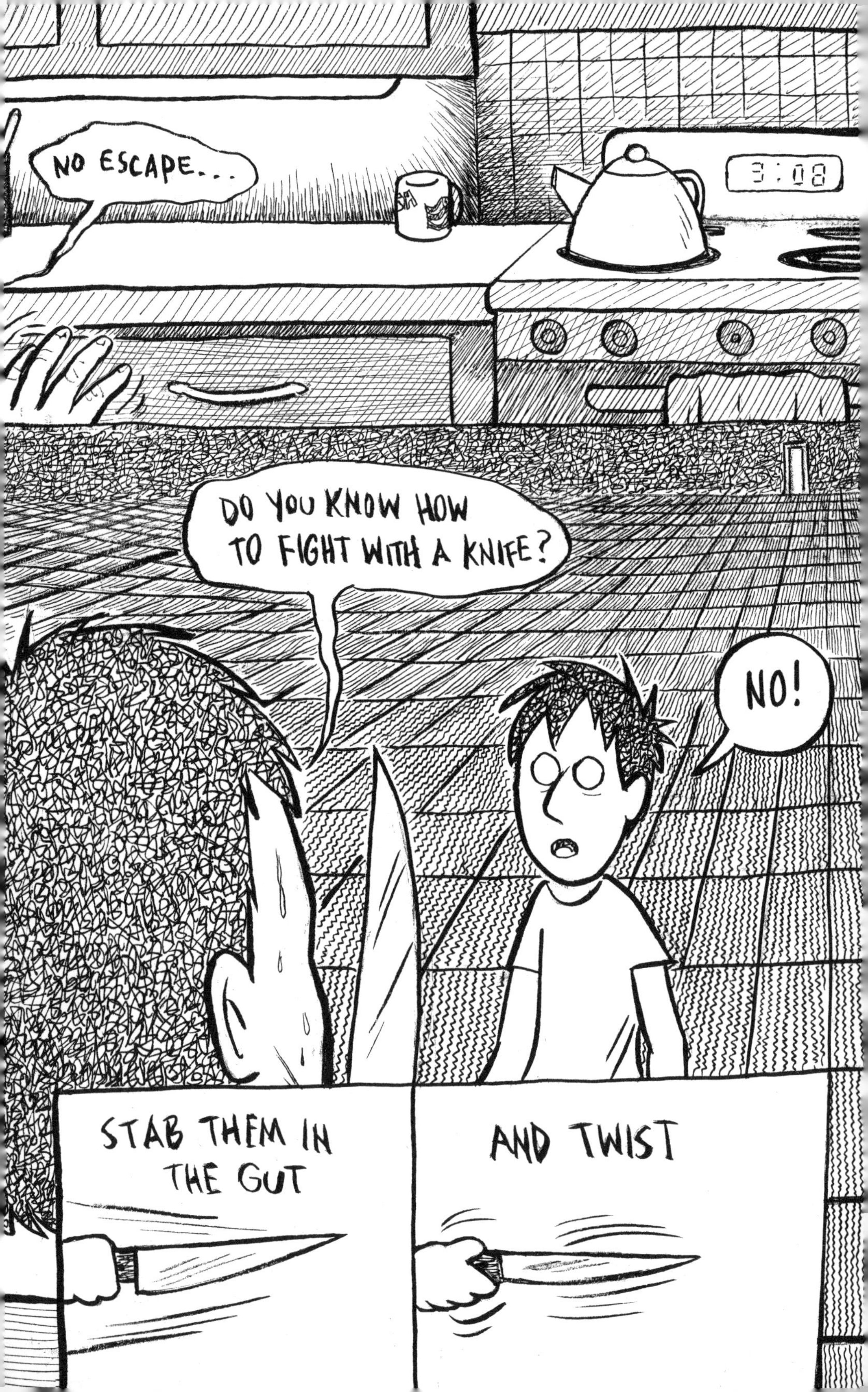
NO ESCAPE...
3:08
DO YOU KNOW HOW TO FIGHT WITH A KNIFE?
NO!
STAB THEM IN THE GUT
AND TWIST

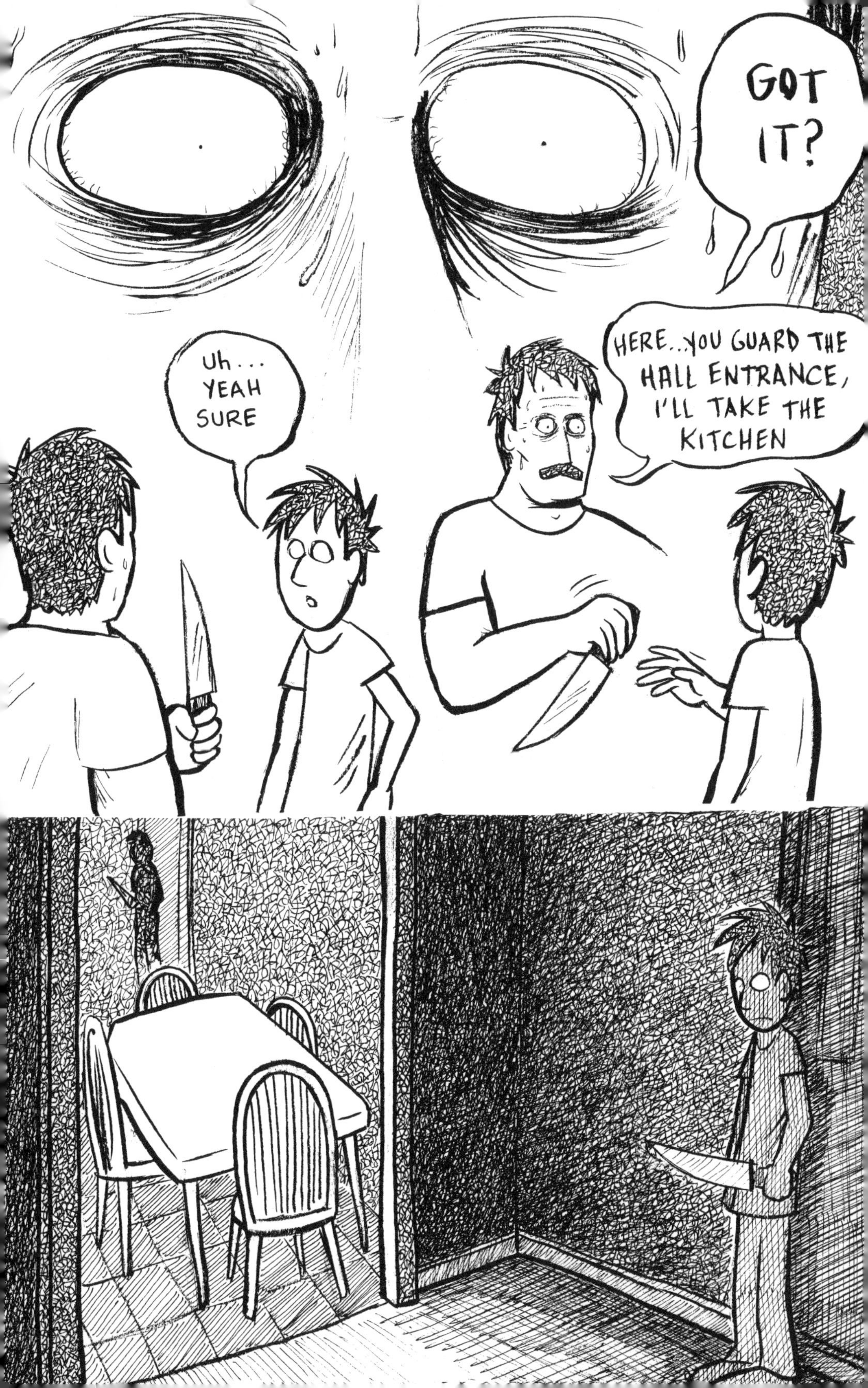
GOT IT?
Uh... YEAH SURE
HERE..YOU GUARD THE HALL ENTRANCE, I'LL TAKE THE KITCHEN

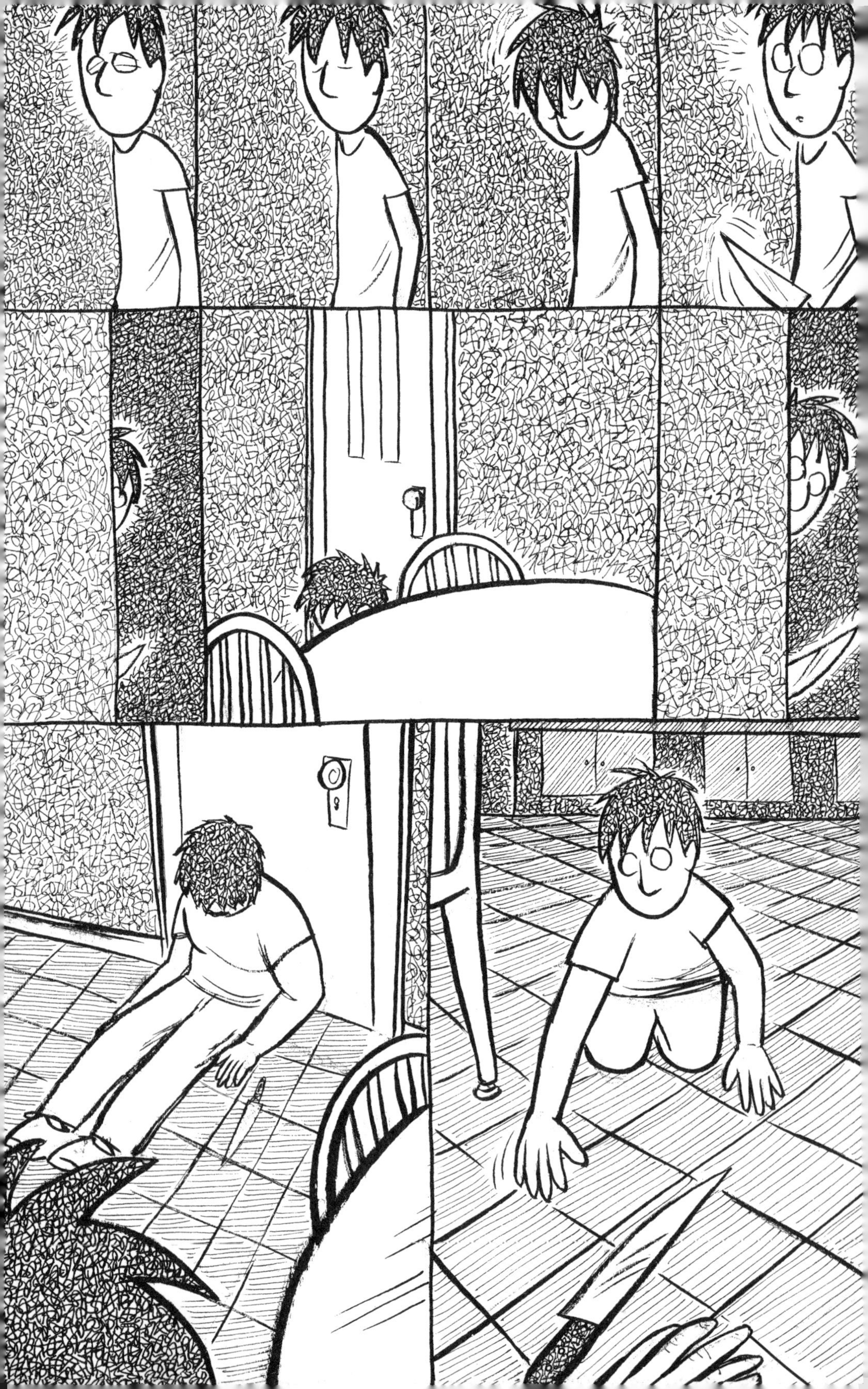

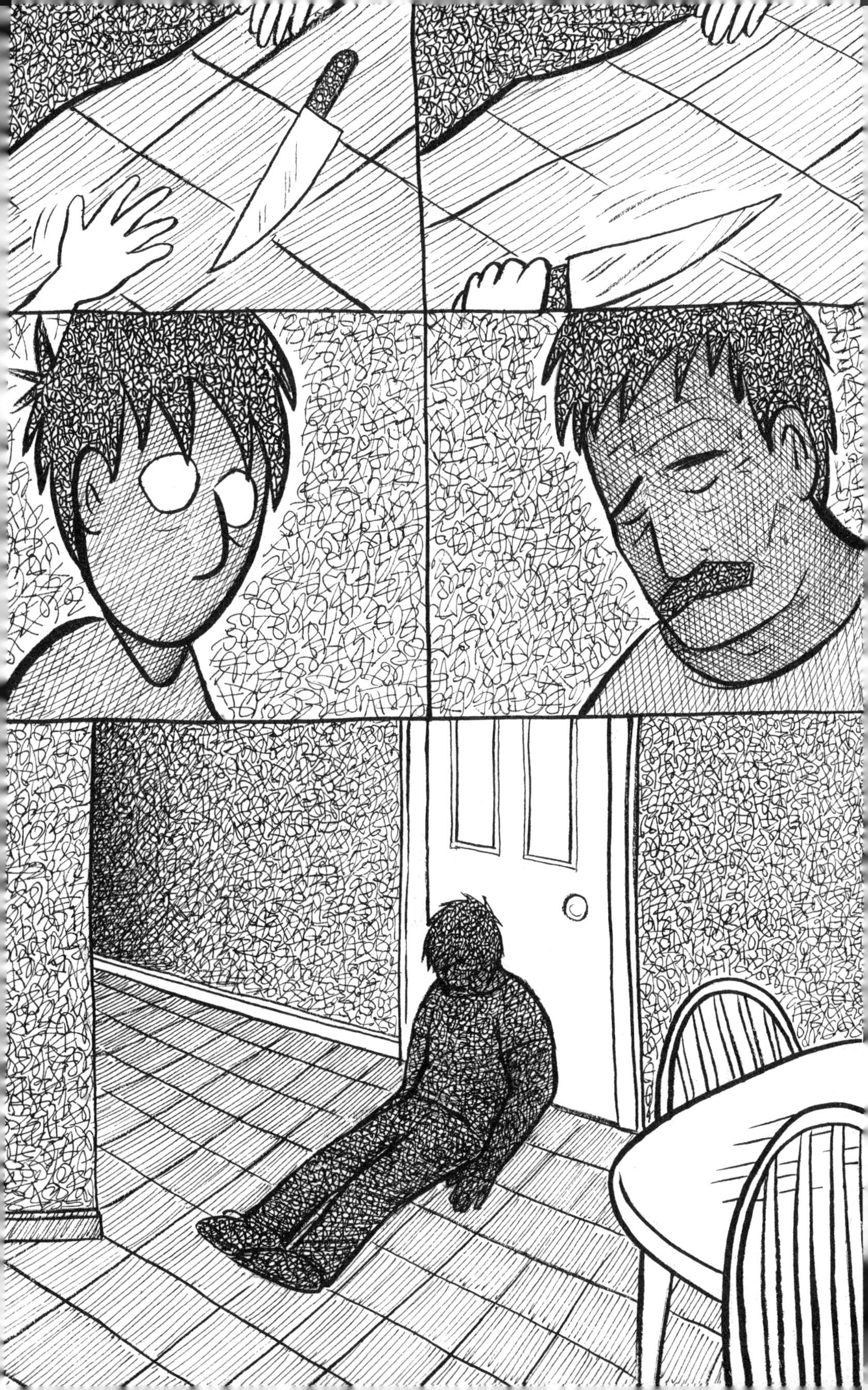

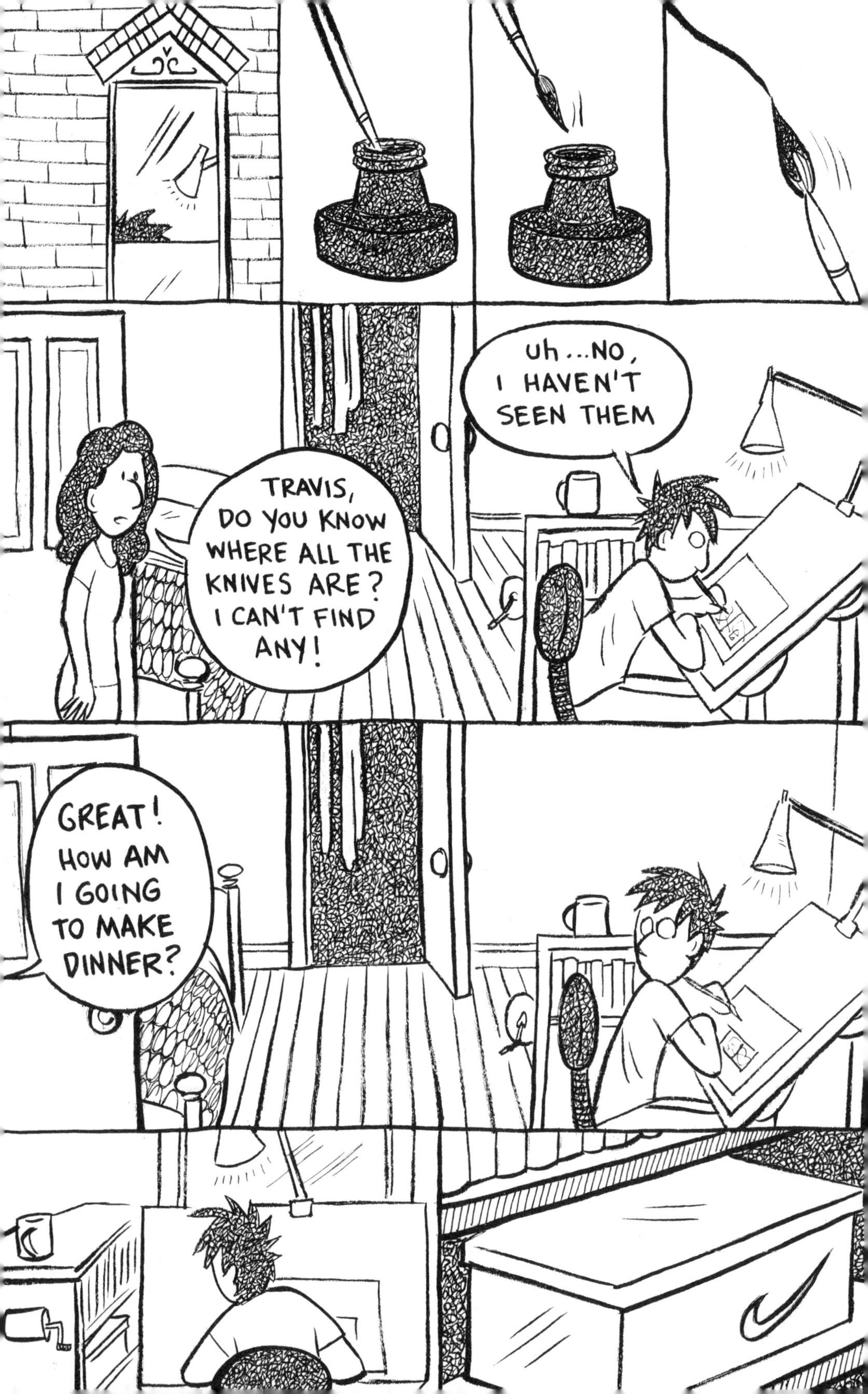
TRAVIS, DO YOU KNOW WHERE ALL THE KNIVES ARE? I CAN'T FIND ANY!
uh...NO, I HAVEN'T SEEN THEM
GREAT! HOW AM I GOING TO MAKE DINNER?

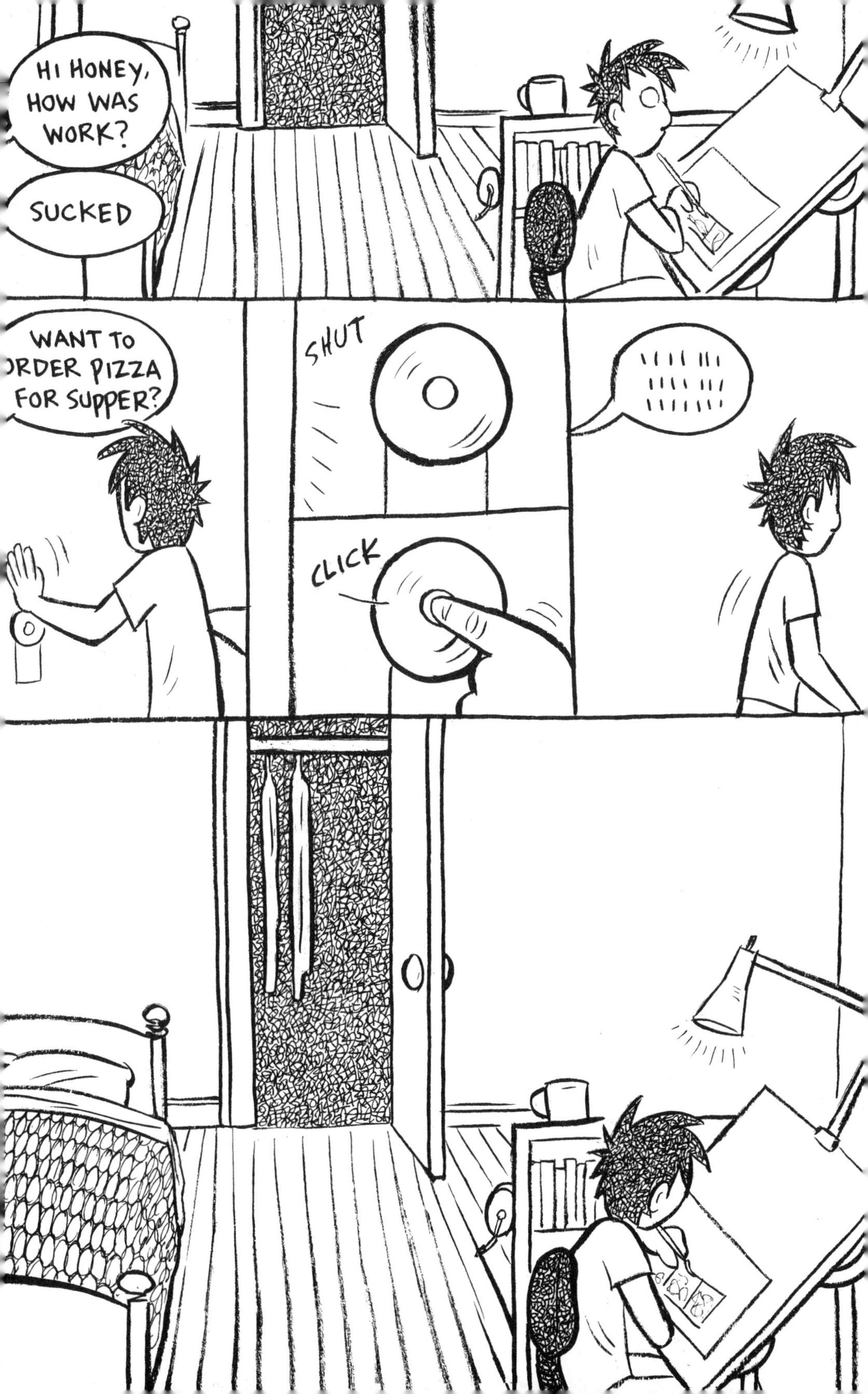
HI HONEY, HOW WAS WORK?
SUCKED
WANT TO ORDER PIZZA FOR SUPPER?
SHUT
CLICK

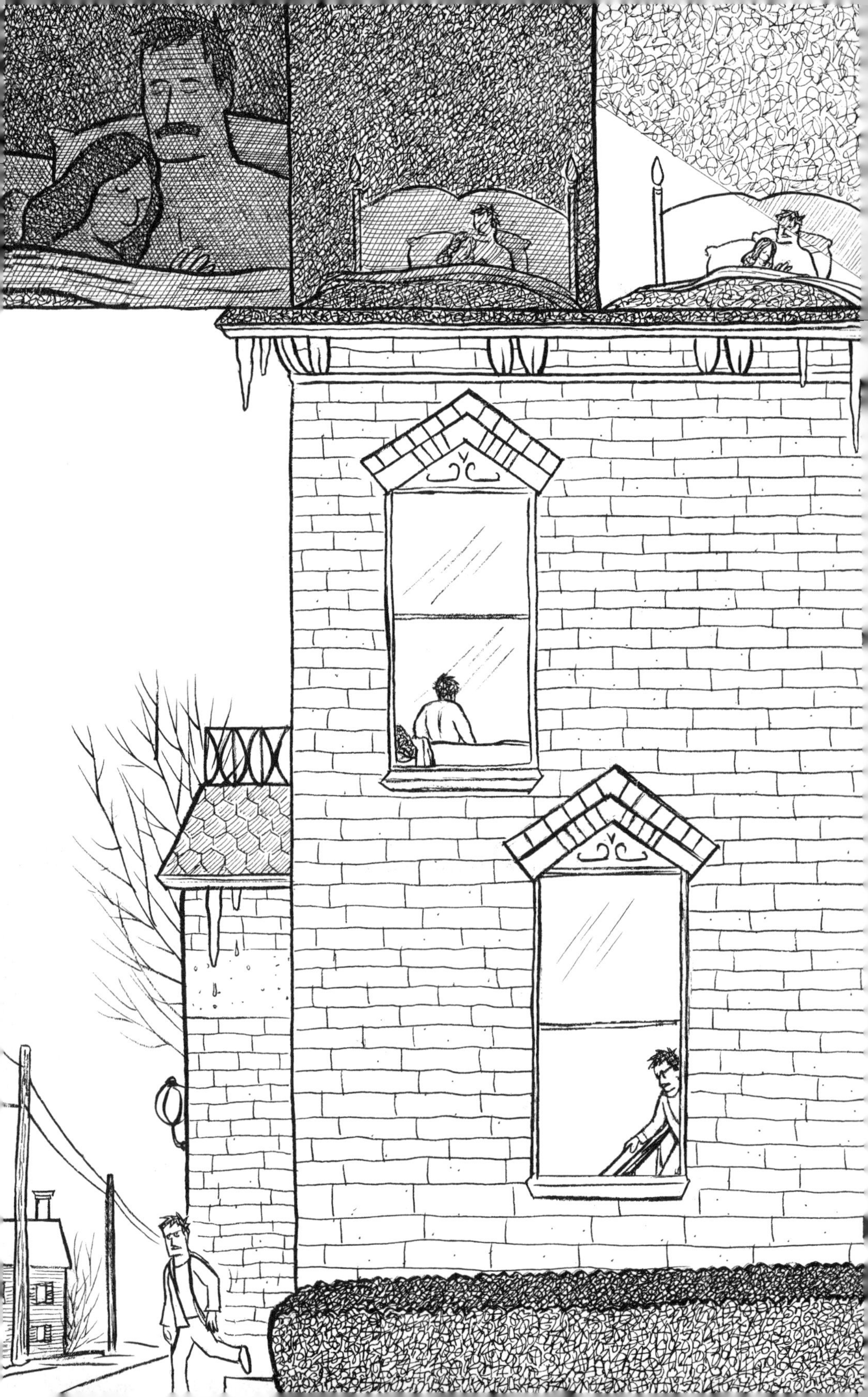

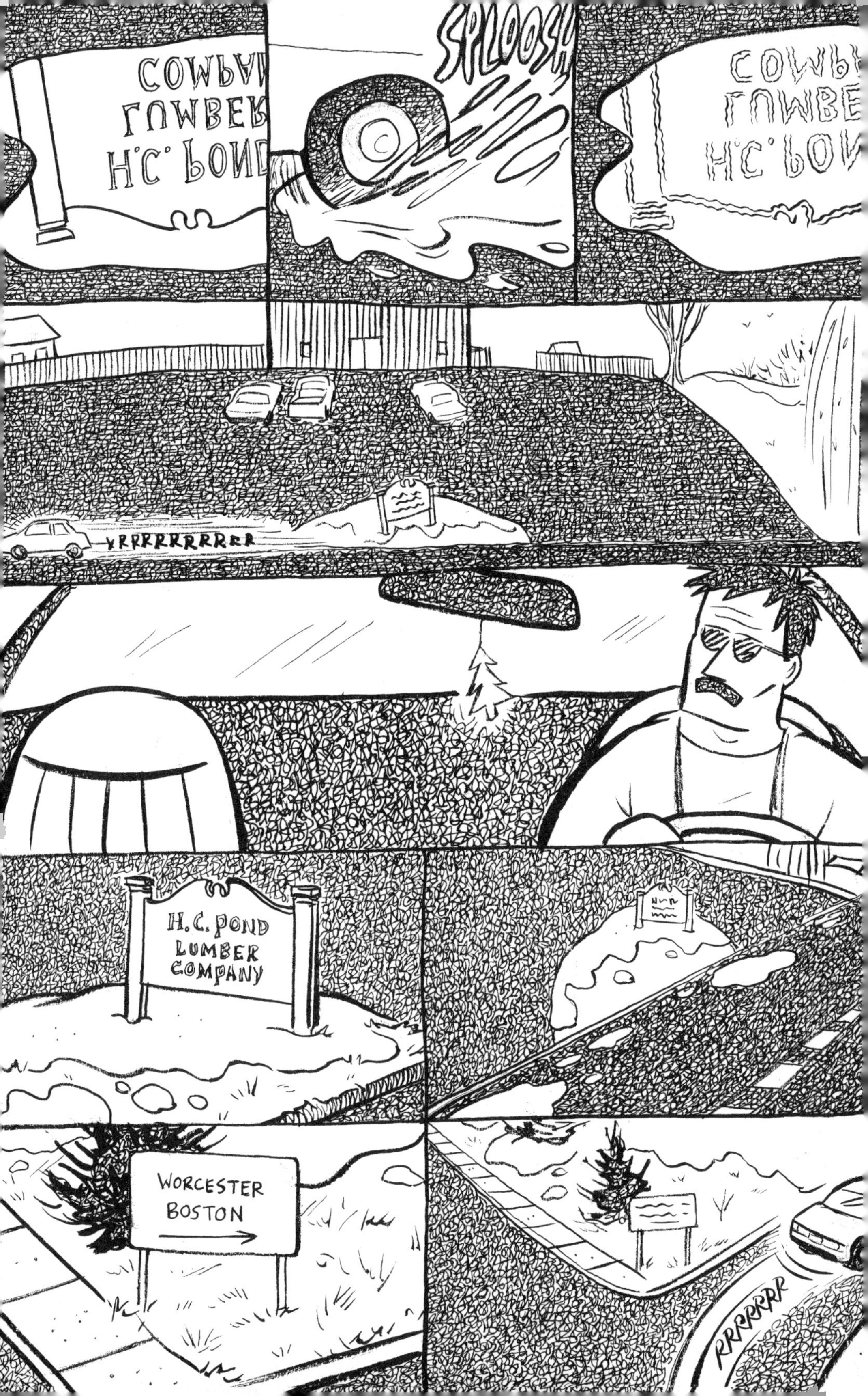
SPLOOSH
VRRRRRRRRRR
H.C. POND
LUMBER
COMPANY
WORCESTER
BOSTON
RRRRRR

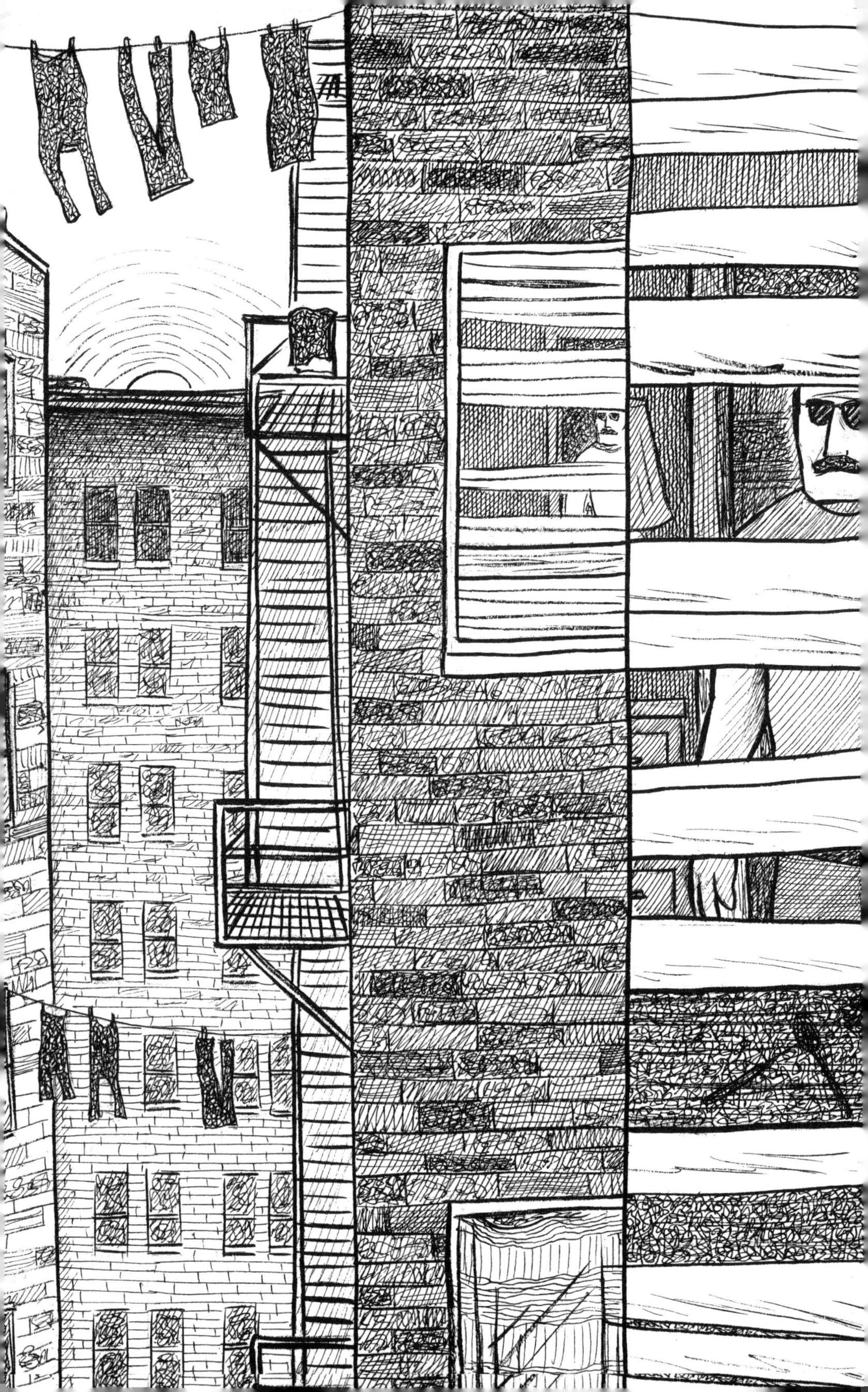

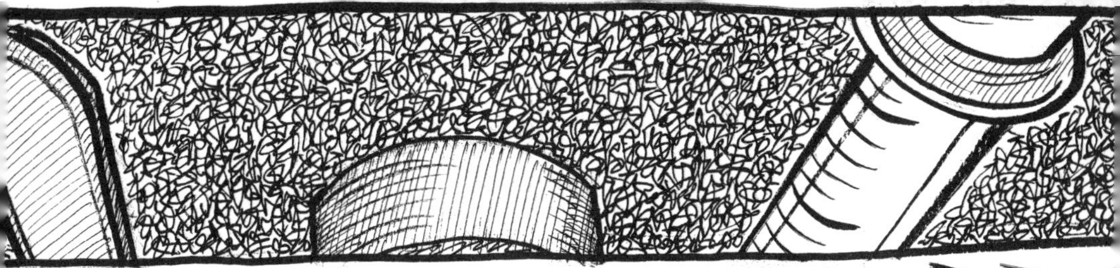
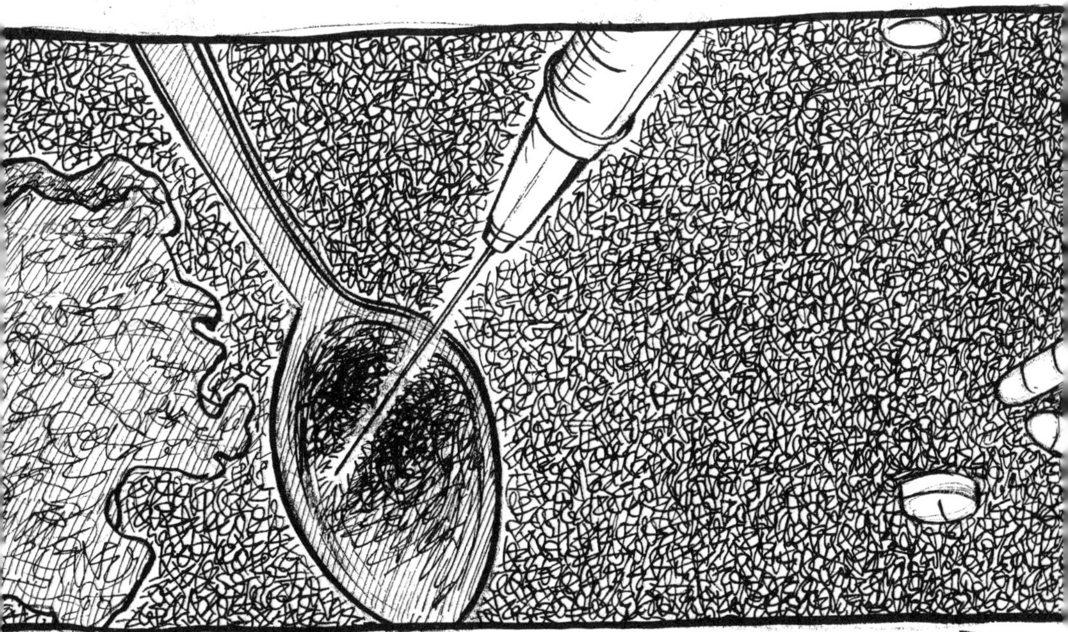
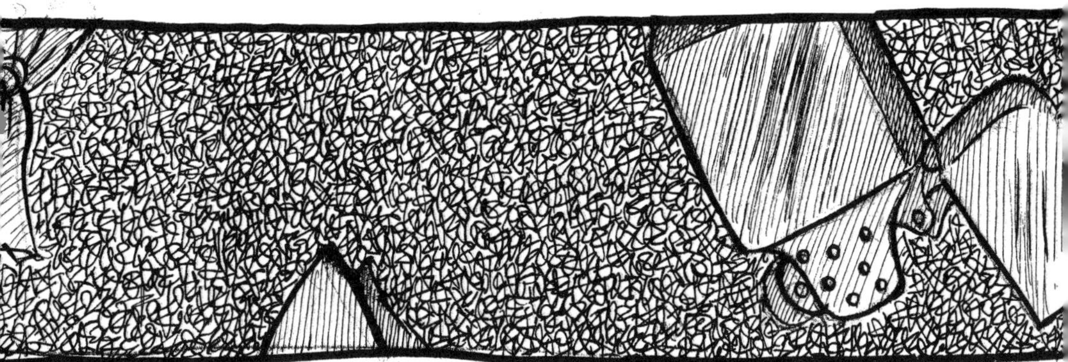

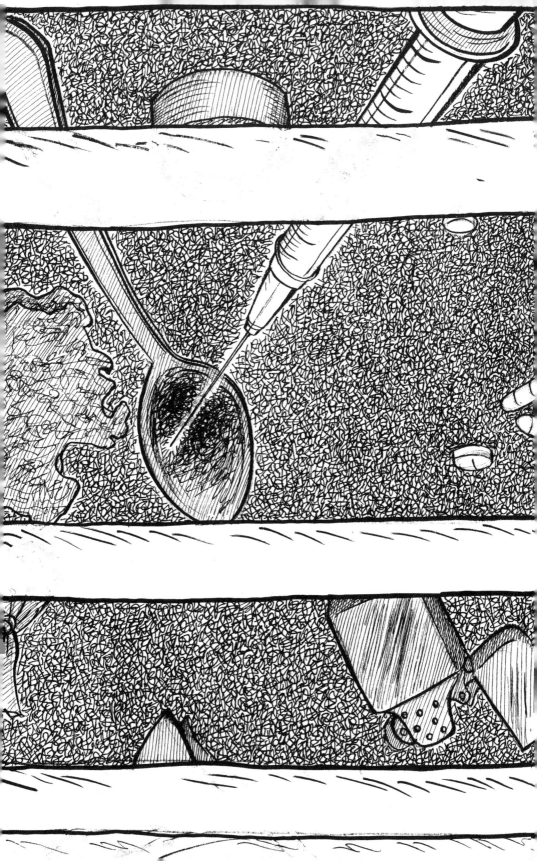

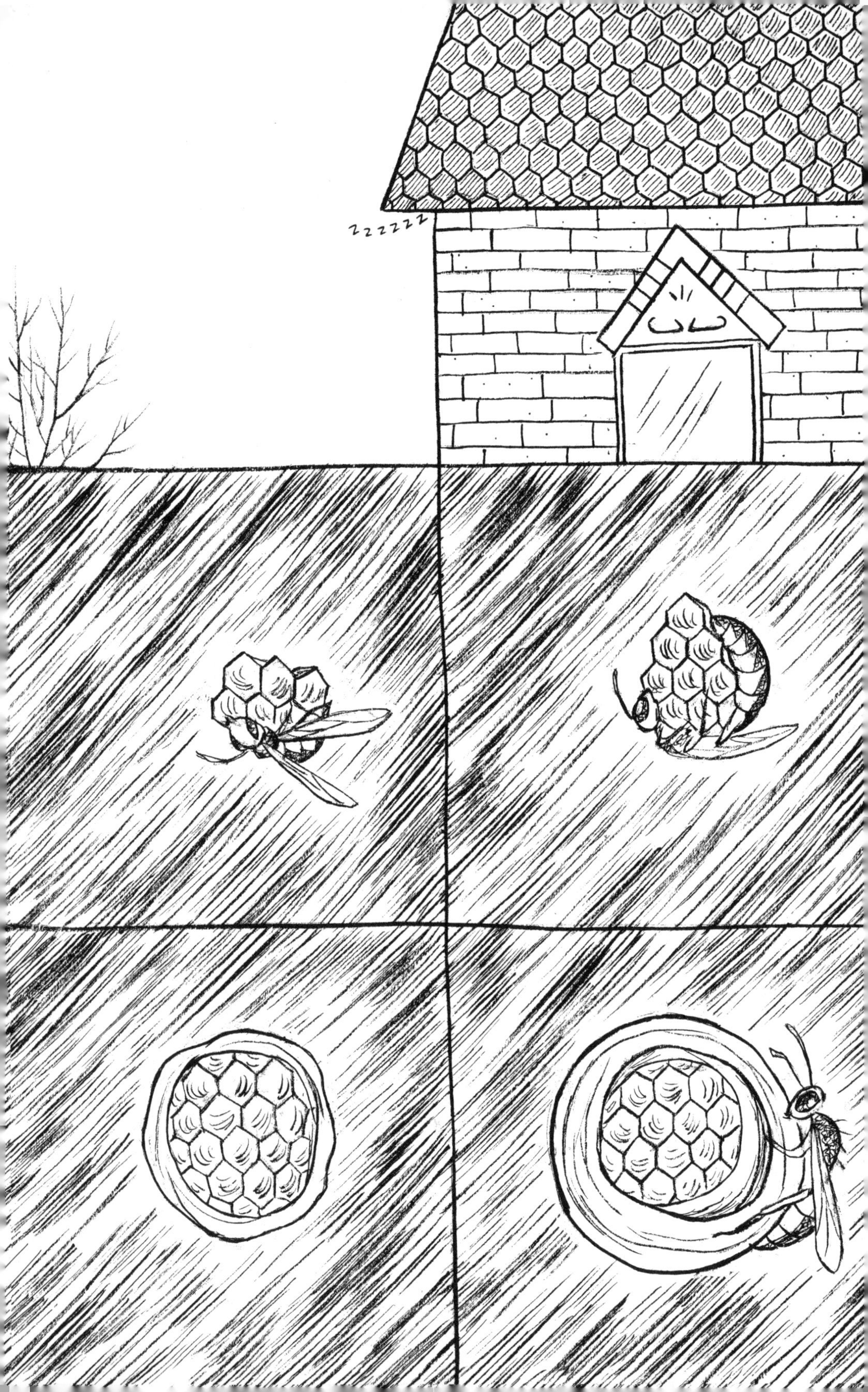
zzzzzz

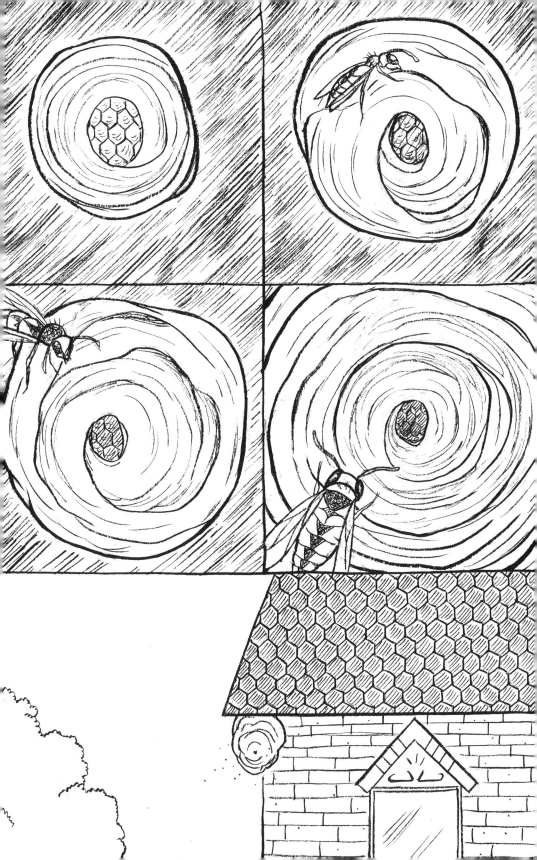

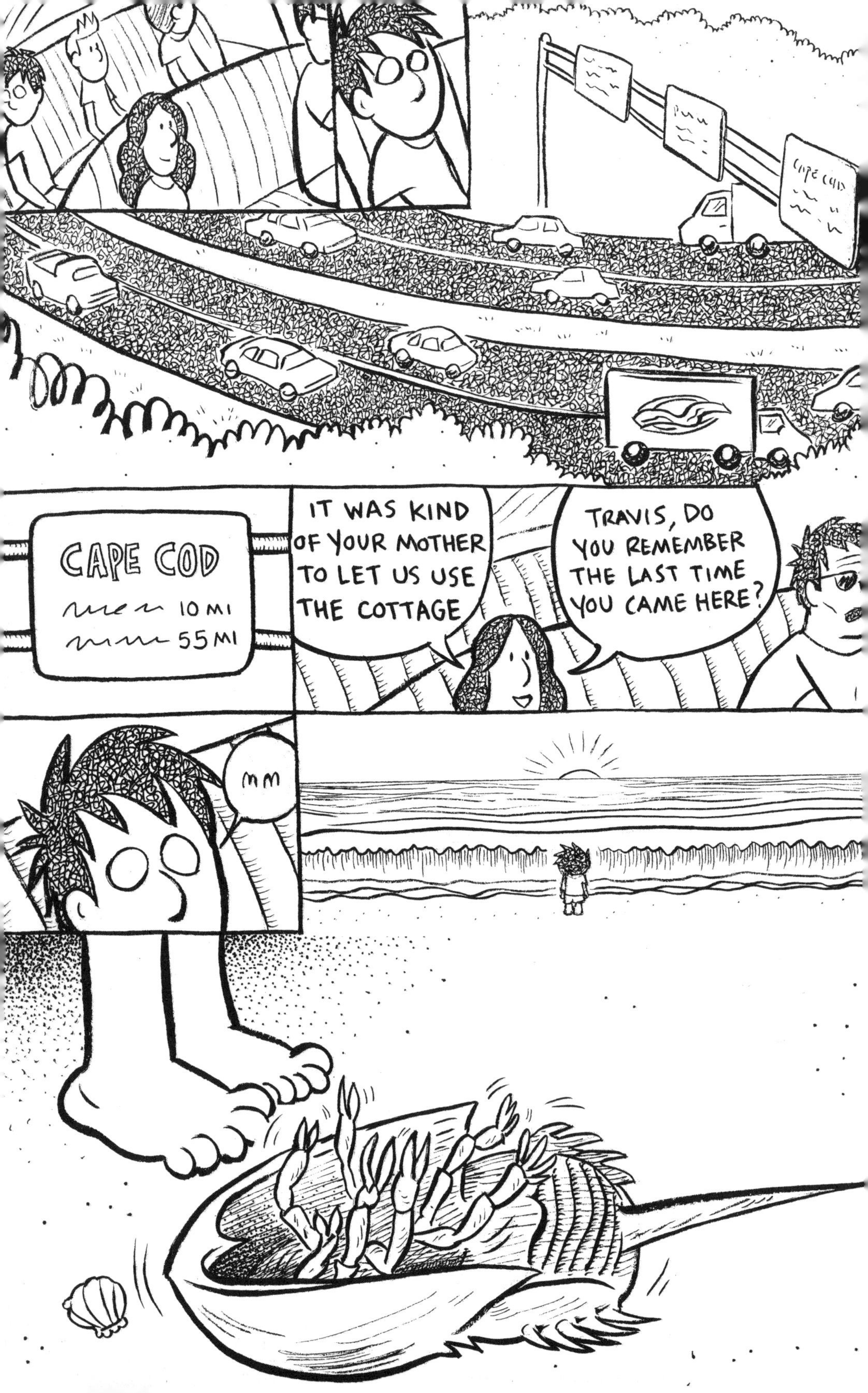
CAPE COD
10 MI
55 MI
IT WAS KIND OF YOUR MOTHER TO LET US USE THE COTTAGE
TRAVIS, DO YOU REMEMBER THE LAST TIME YOU CAME HERE?
MM

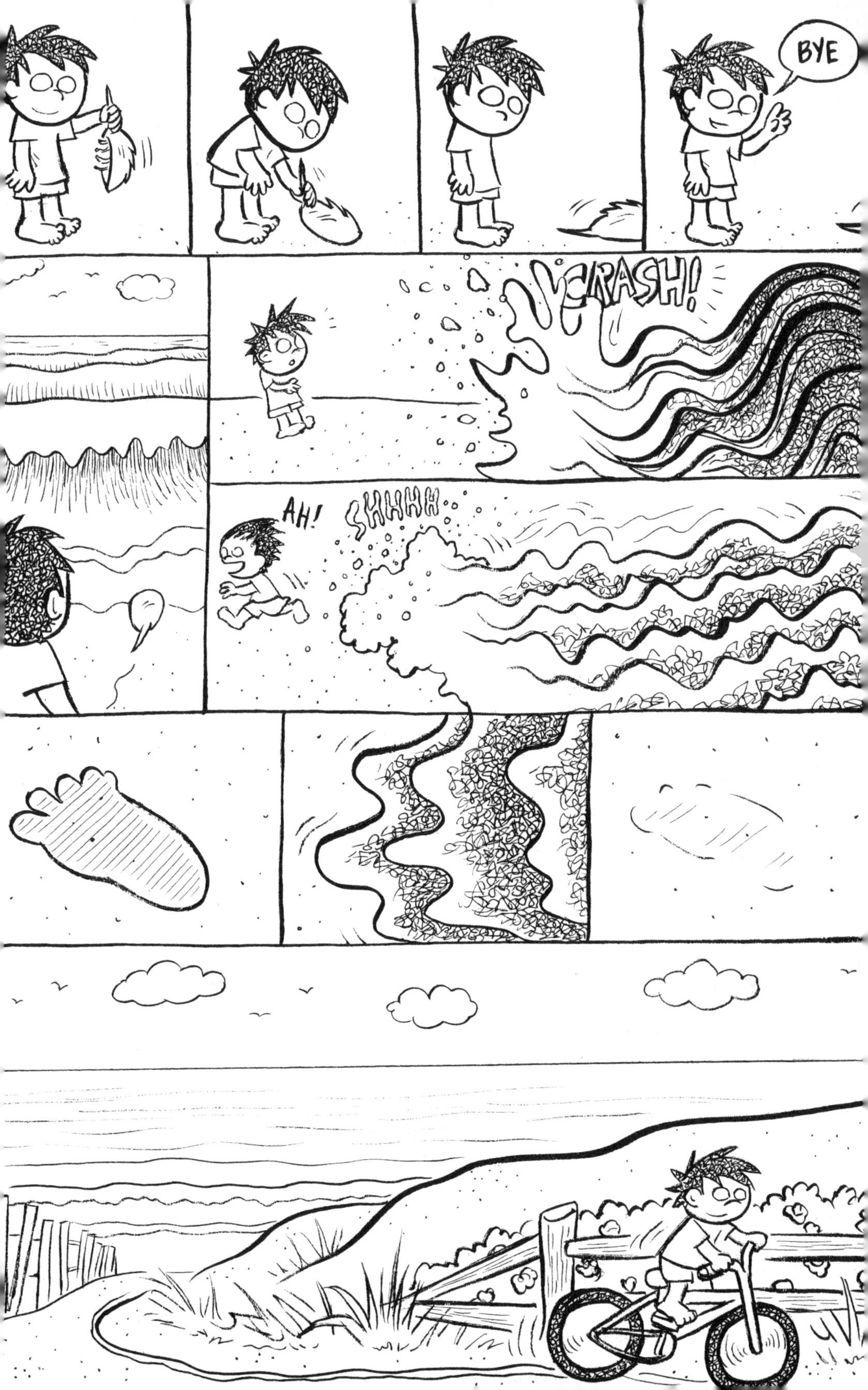
BYE
CRASH!
AH!
SHHHH

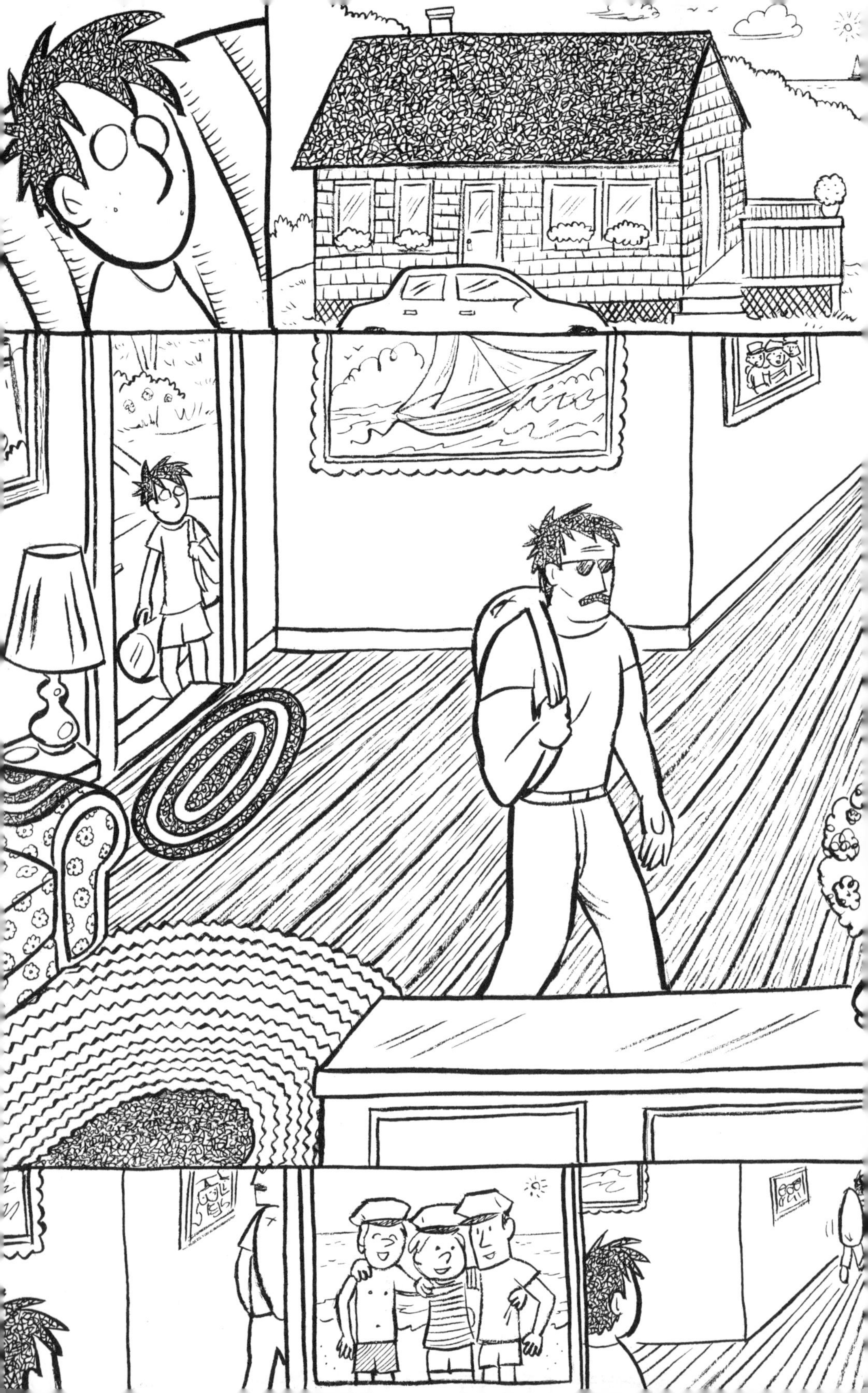

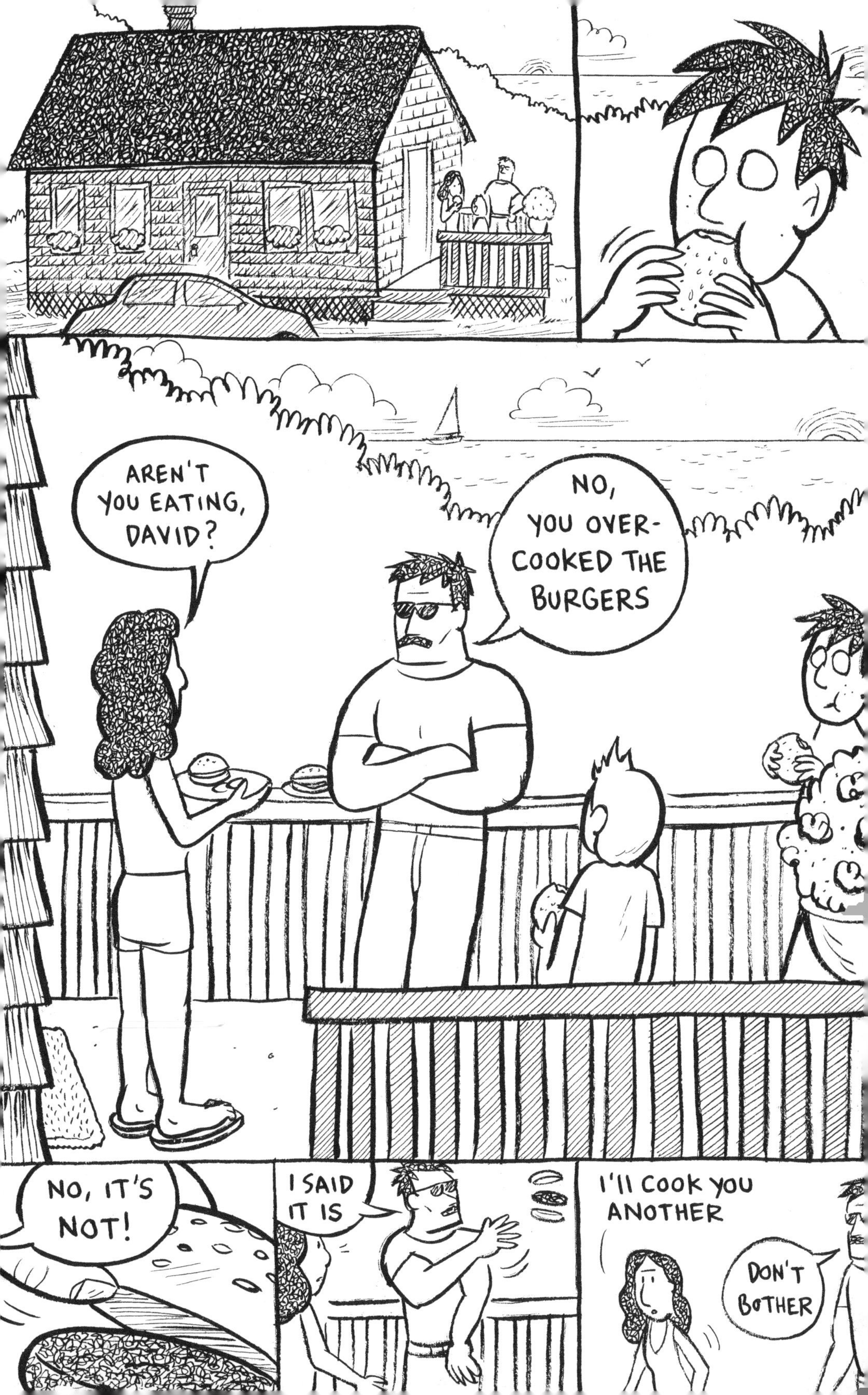
AREN'T YOU EATING, DAVID?
NO, YOU OVER-COOKED THE BURGERS
NO, IT'S NOT!
I SAID IT IS
I'll COOK YOU ANOTHER
DON'T BOTHER

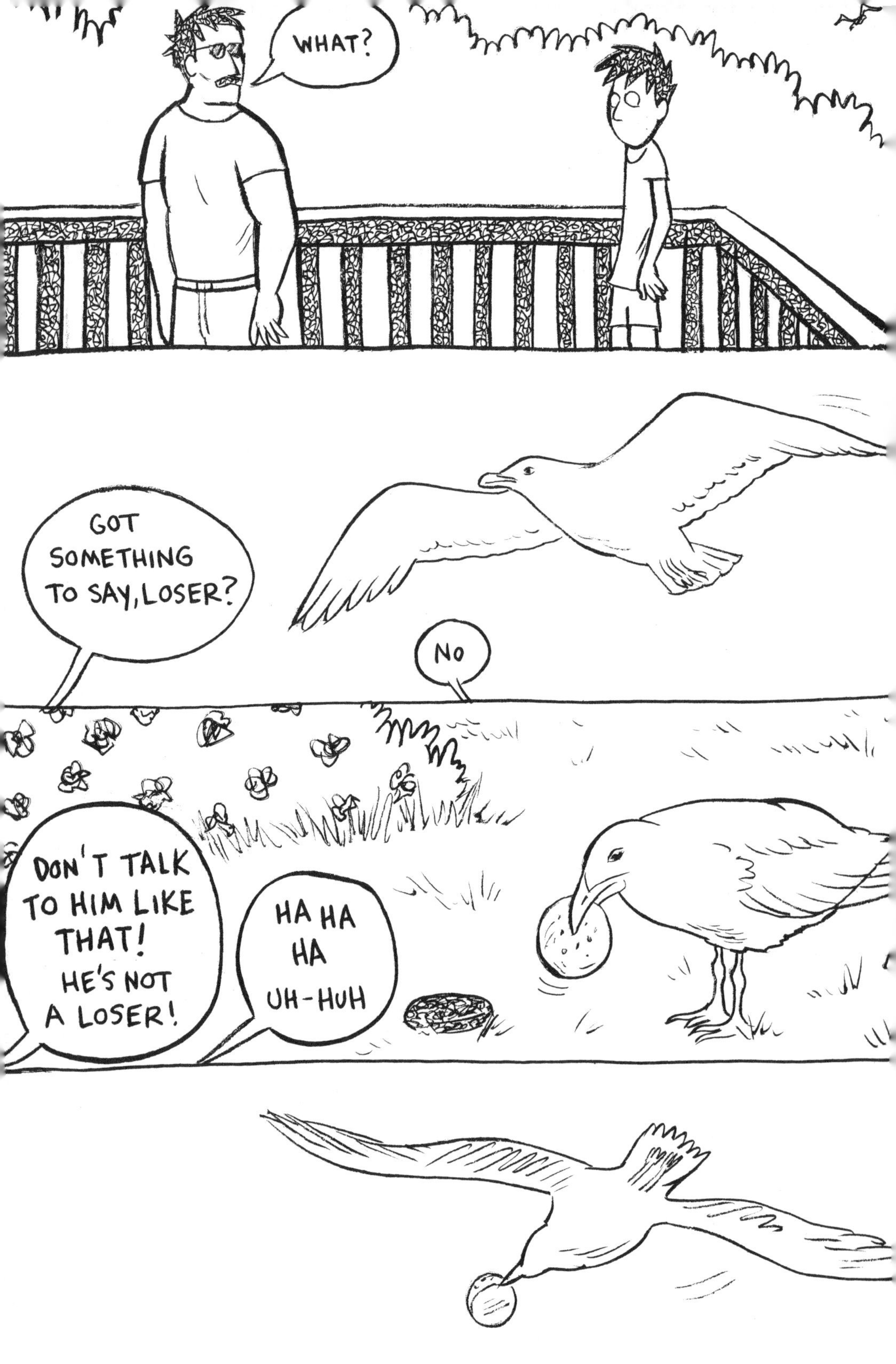
WHAT?
GOT SOMETHING TO SAY, LOSER?
NO
DON'T TALK TO HIM LIKE THAT! HE'S NOT A LOSER!
HA HA HA UH-HUH

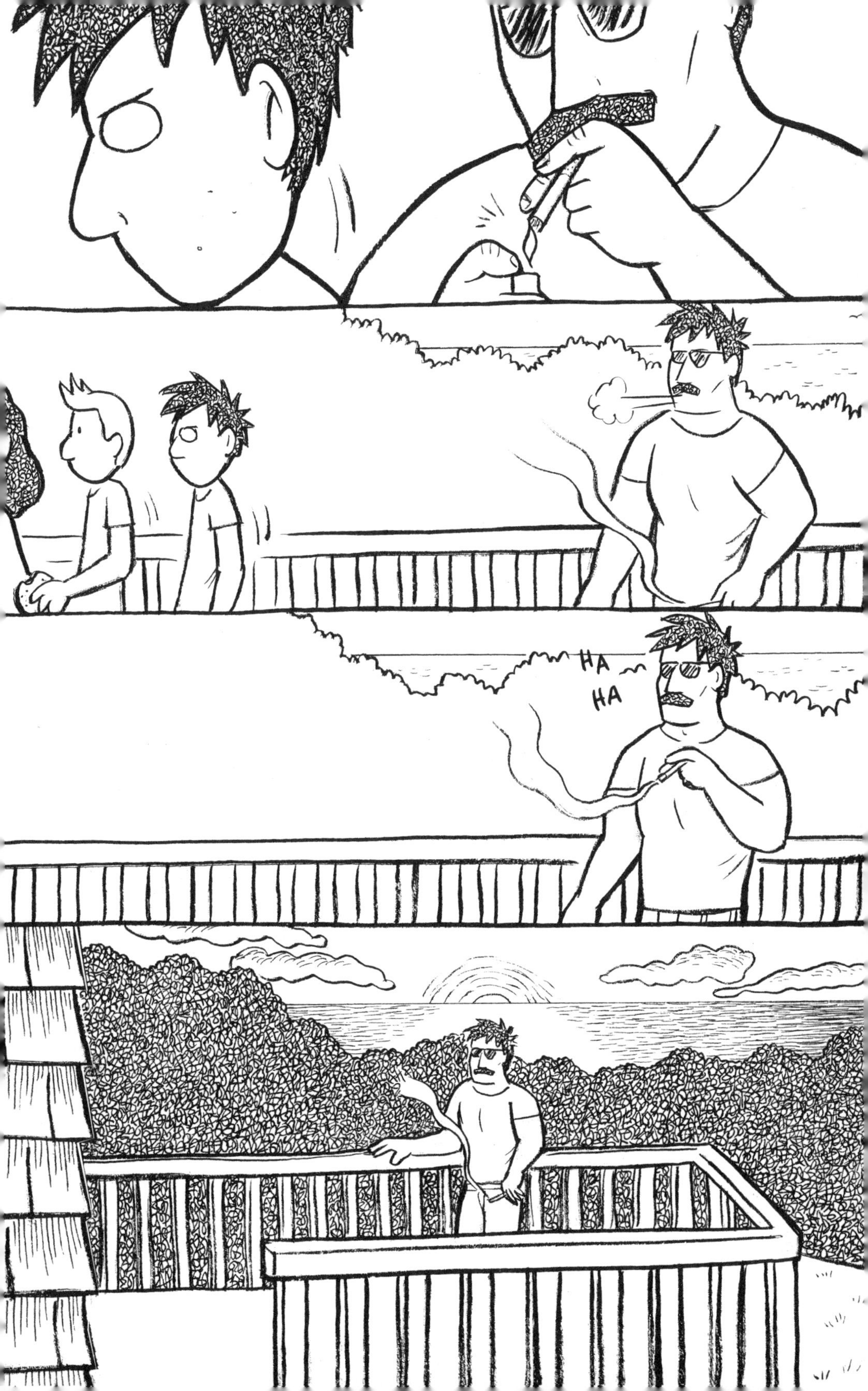
HA
HA

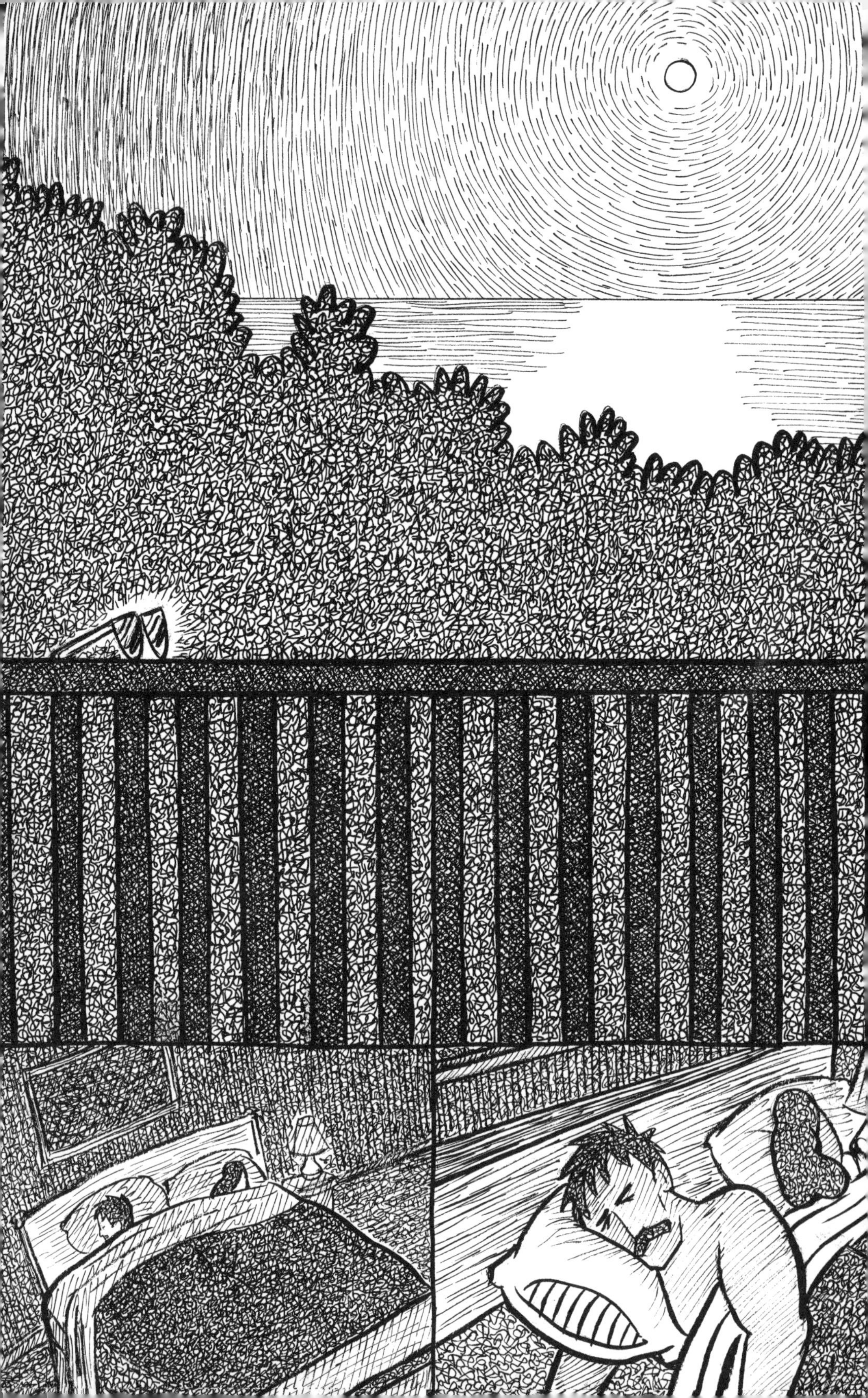

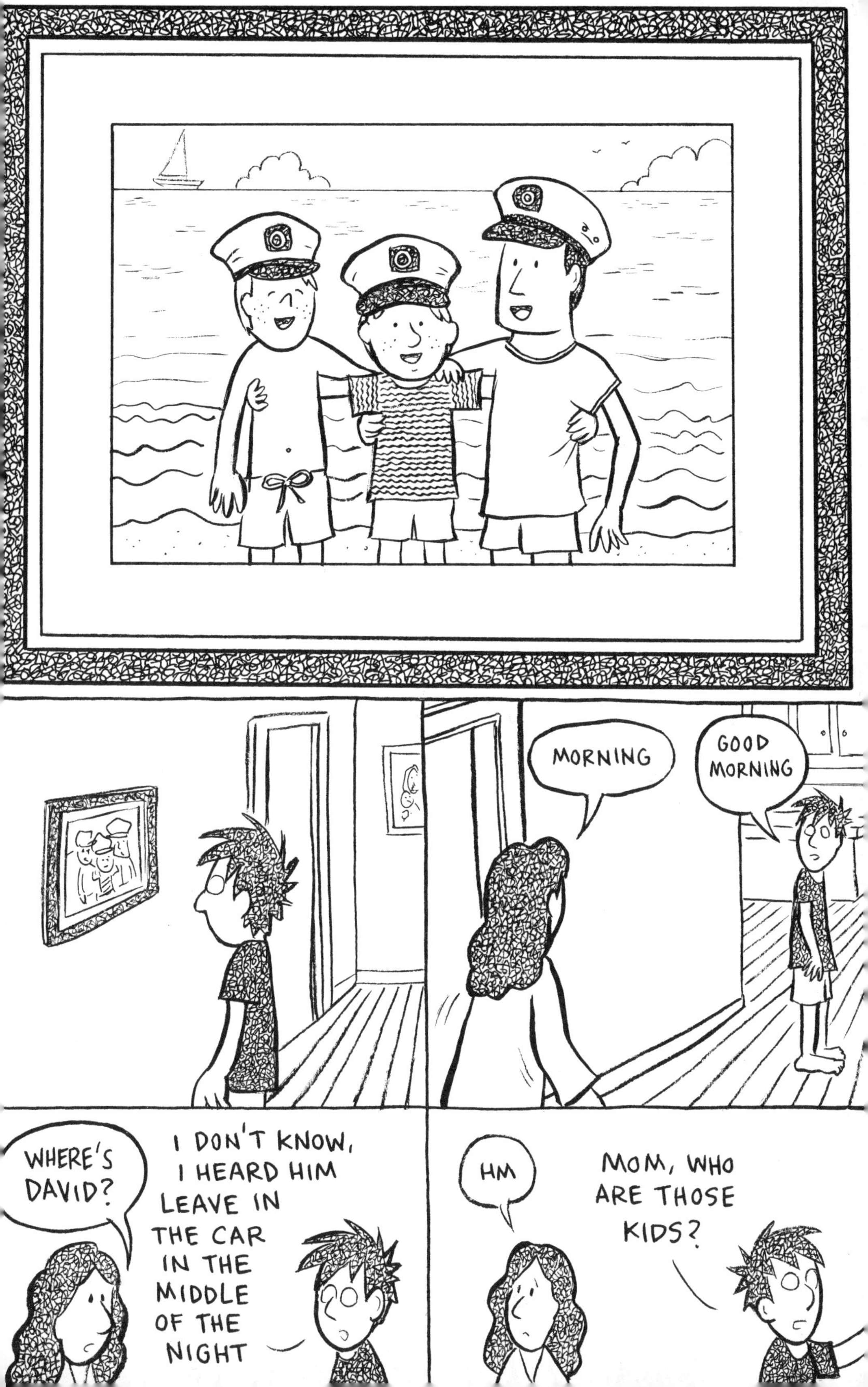
MORNING
GOOD MORNING
WHERE'S DAVID?
I DON'T KNOW, I HEARD HIM LEAVE IN THE CAR IN THE MIDDLE OF THE NIGHT
HM
MOM, WHO ARE THOSE KIDS?

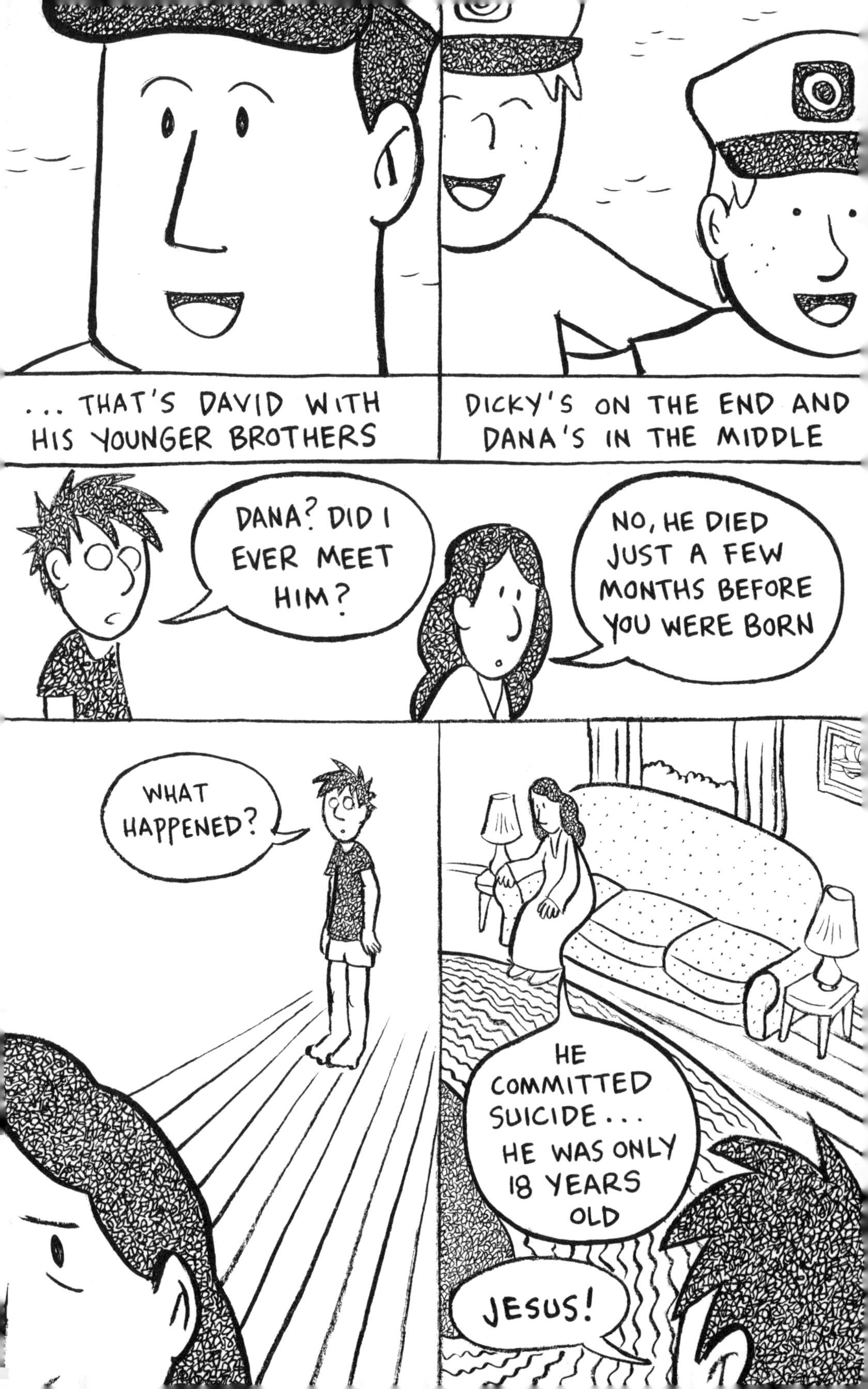
... THAT'S DAVID WITH HIS YOUNGER BROTHERS
DICKY'S ON THE END AND DANA'S IN THE MIDDLE
DANA? DID I EVER MEET HIM?
NO, HE DIED JUST A FEW MONTHS BEFORE YOU WERE BORN
WHAT HAPPENED?
HE COMMITTED SUICIDE... HE WAS ONLY 18 YEARS OLD
JESUS!

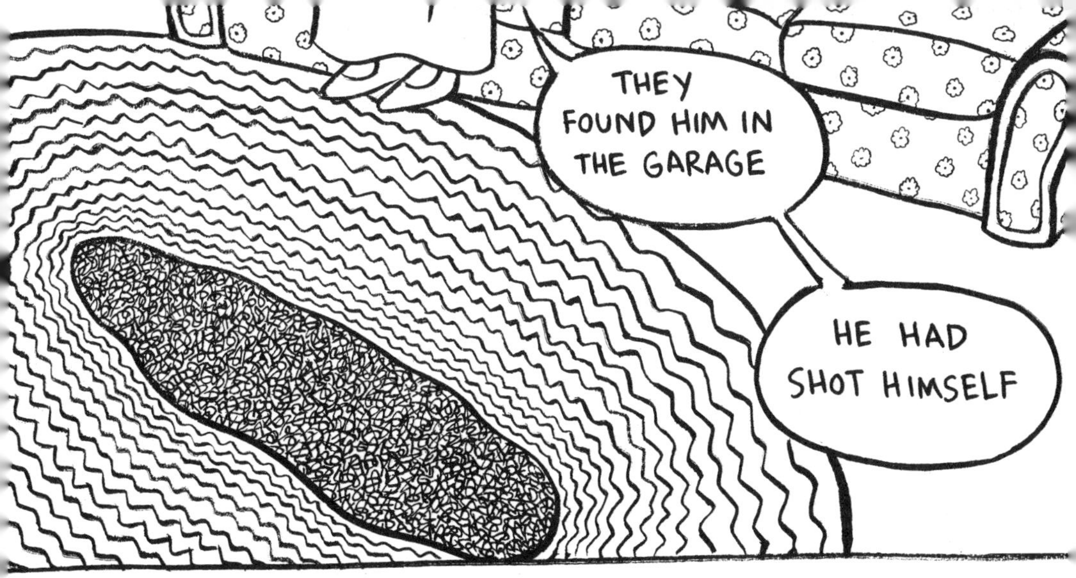
THEY FOUND HIM IN THE GARAGE
HE HAD SHOT HIMSELF

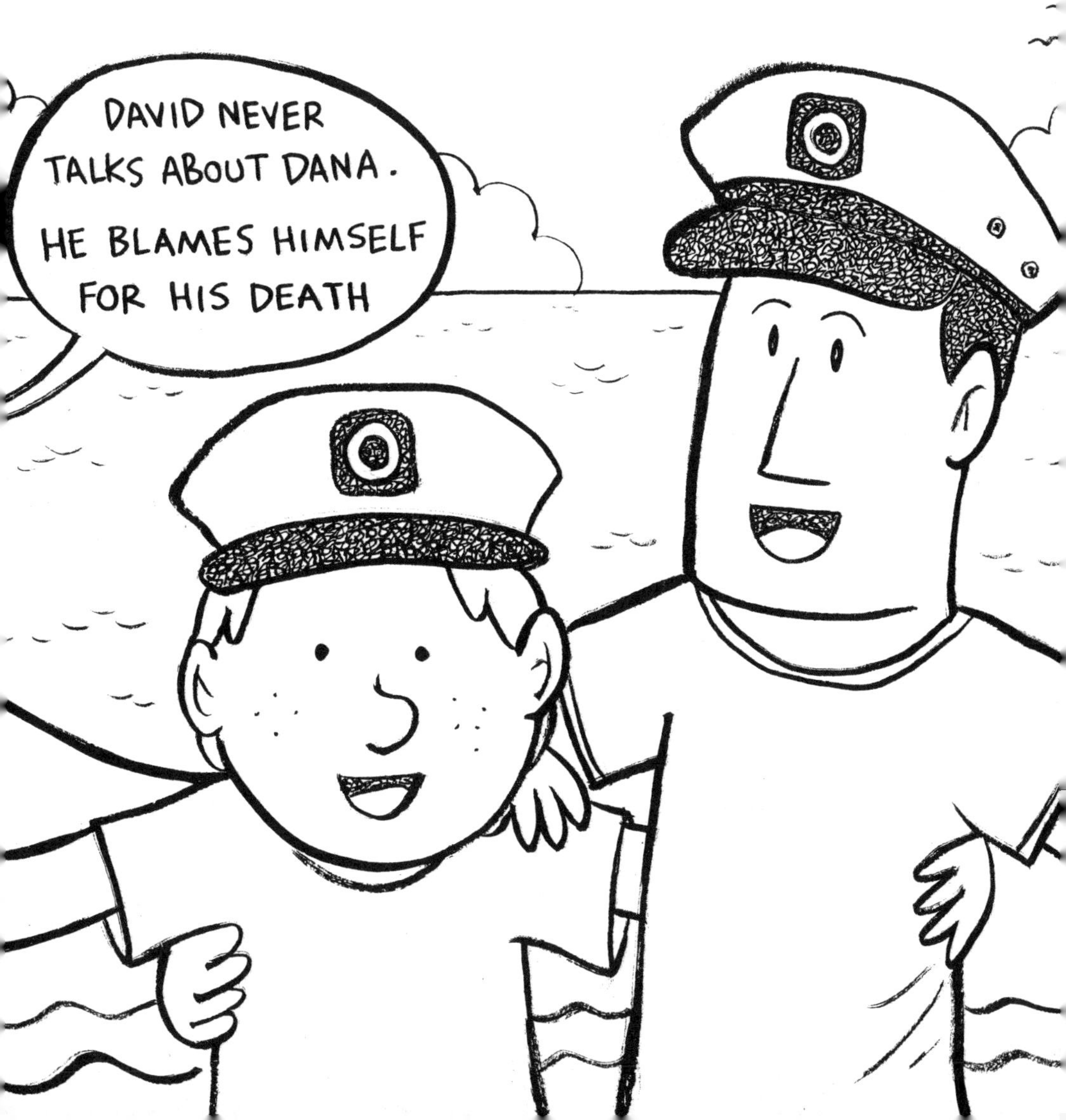
DAVID NEVER TALKS ABOUT DANA.
HE BLAMES HIMSELF FOR HIS DEATH

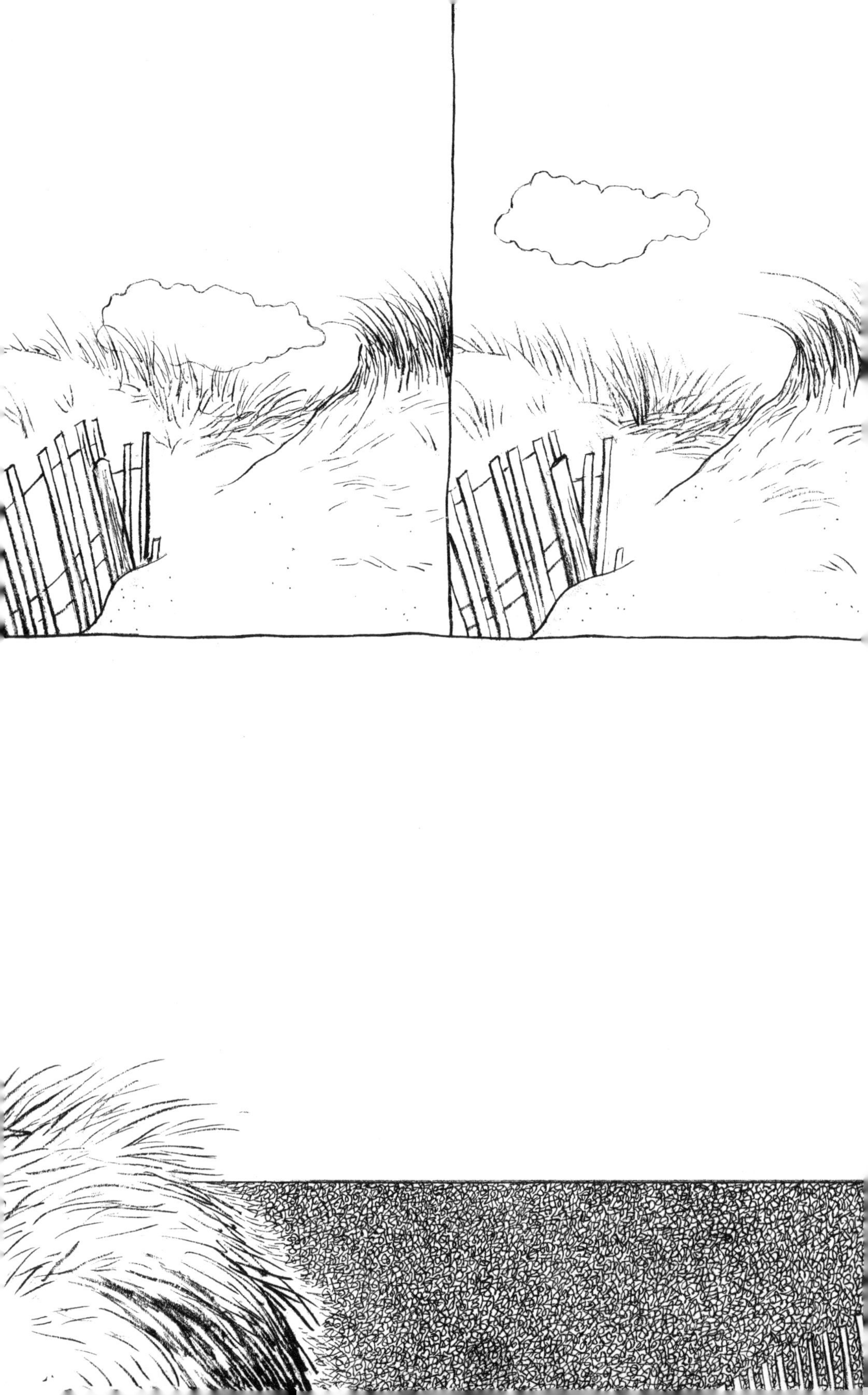

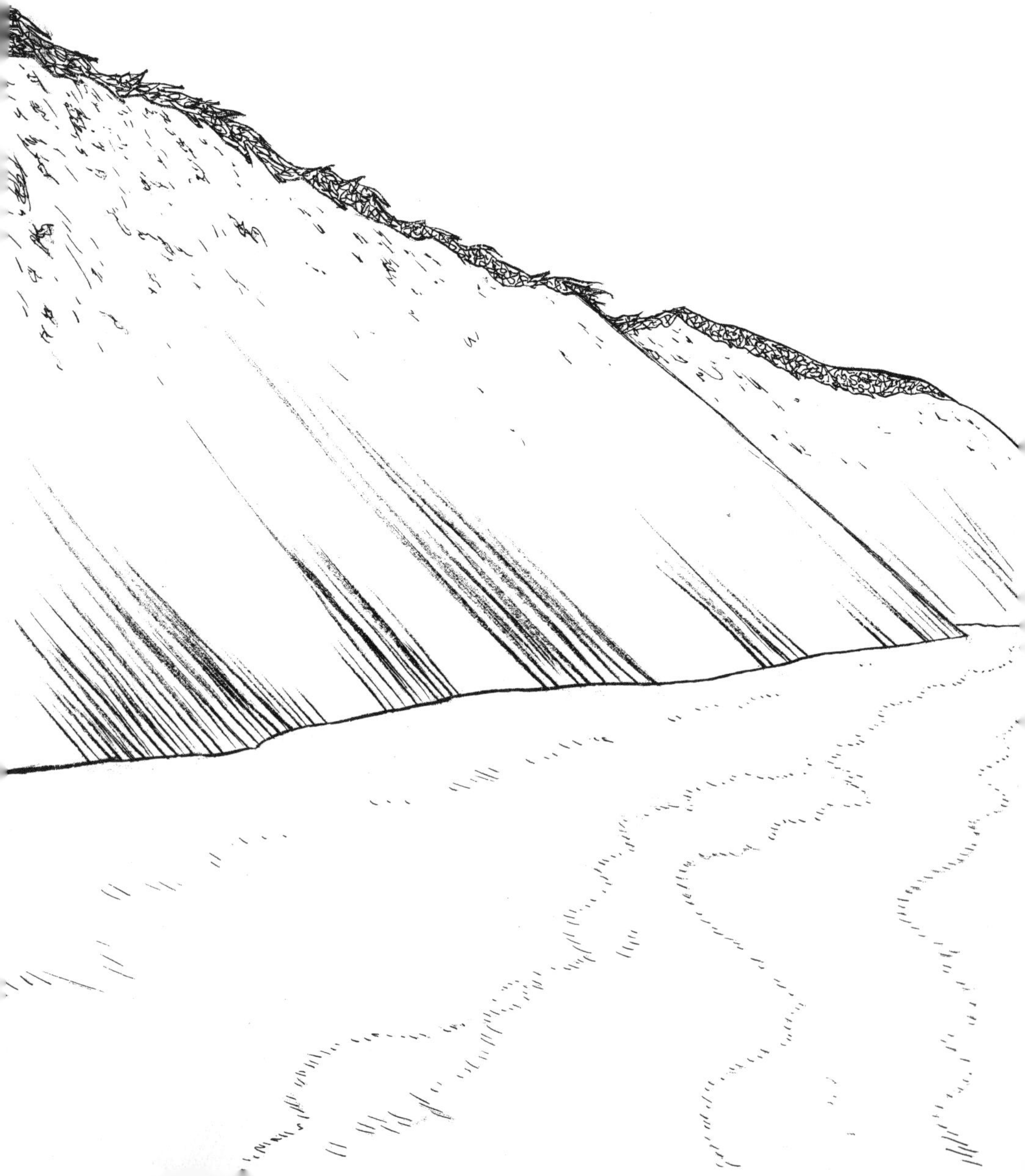

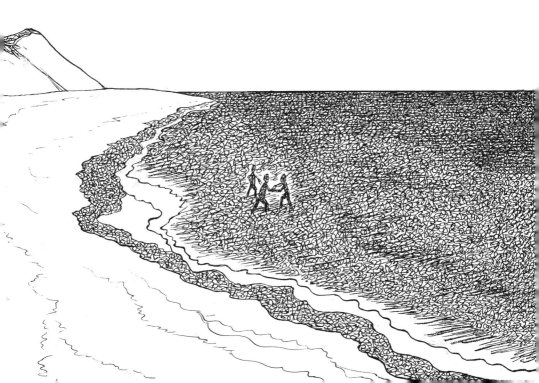

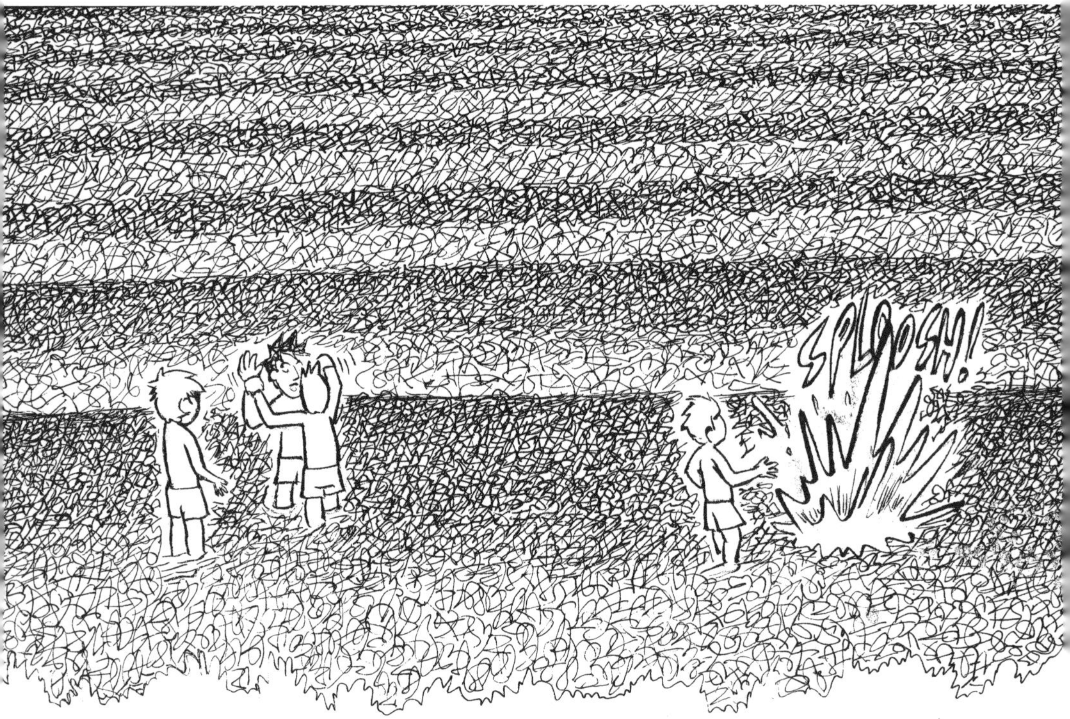
SPLOOSH!

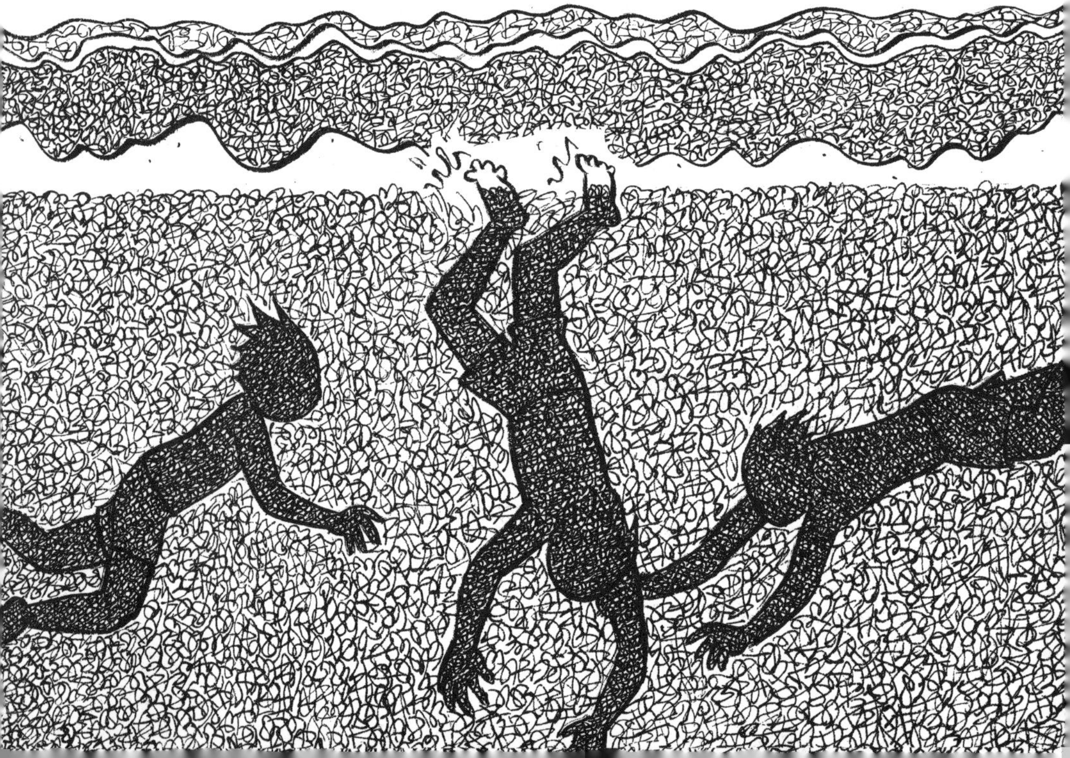

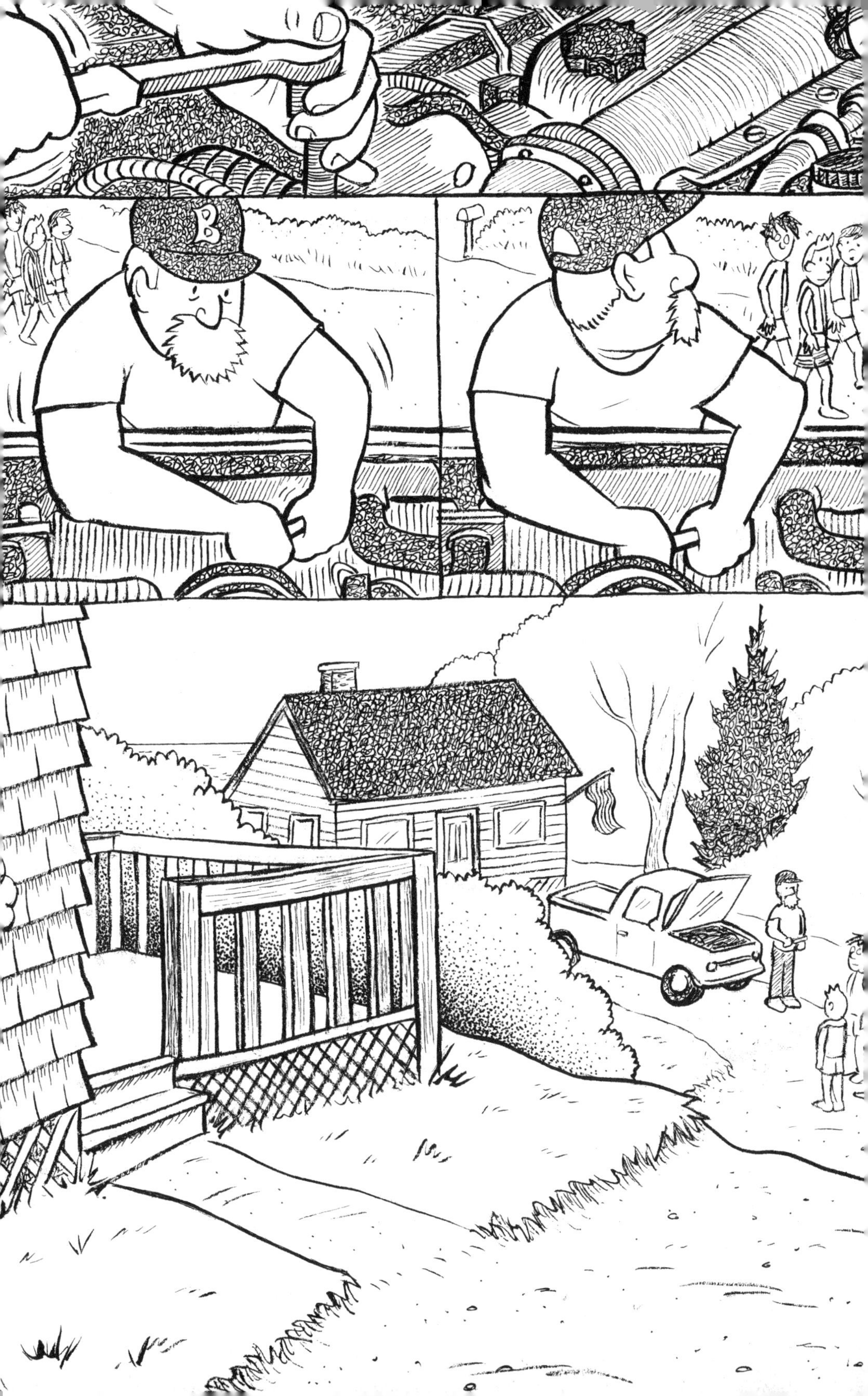

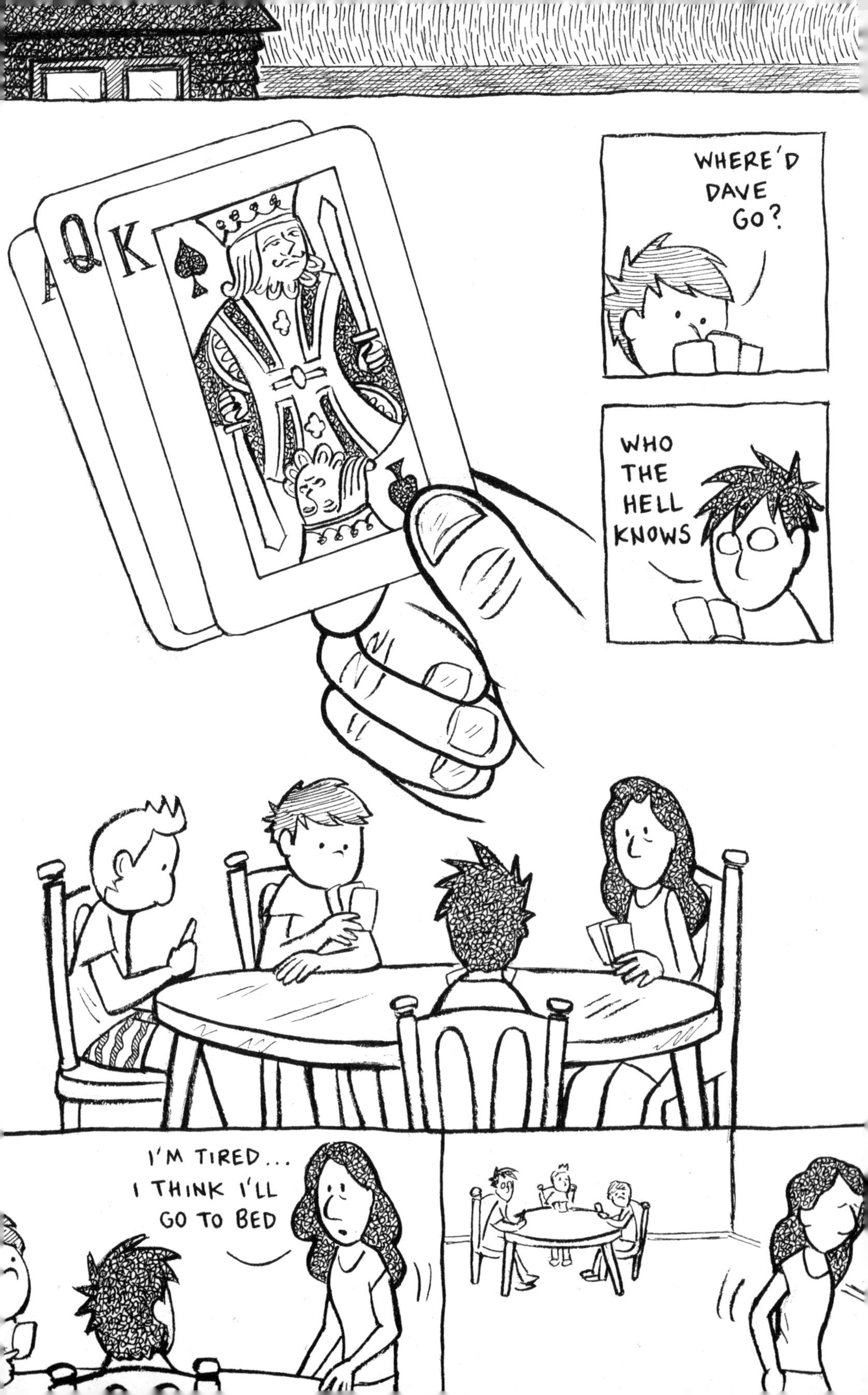
WHERE'D DAVE GO?
WHO THE HELL KNOWS
I'M TIRED... I THINK I'LL GO TO BED

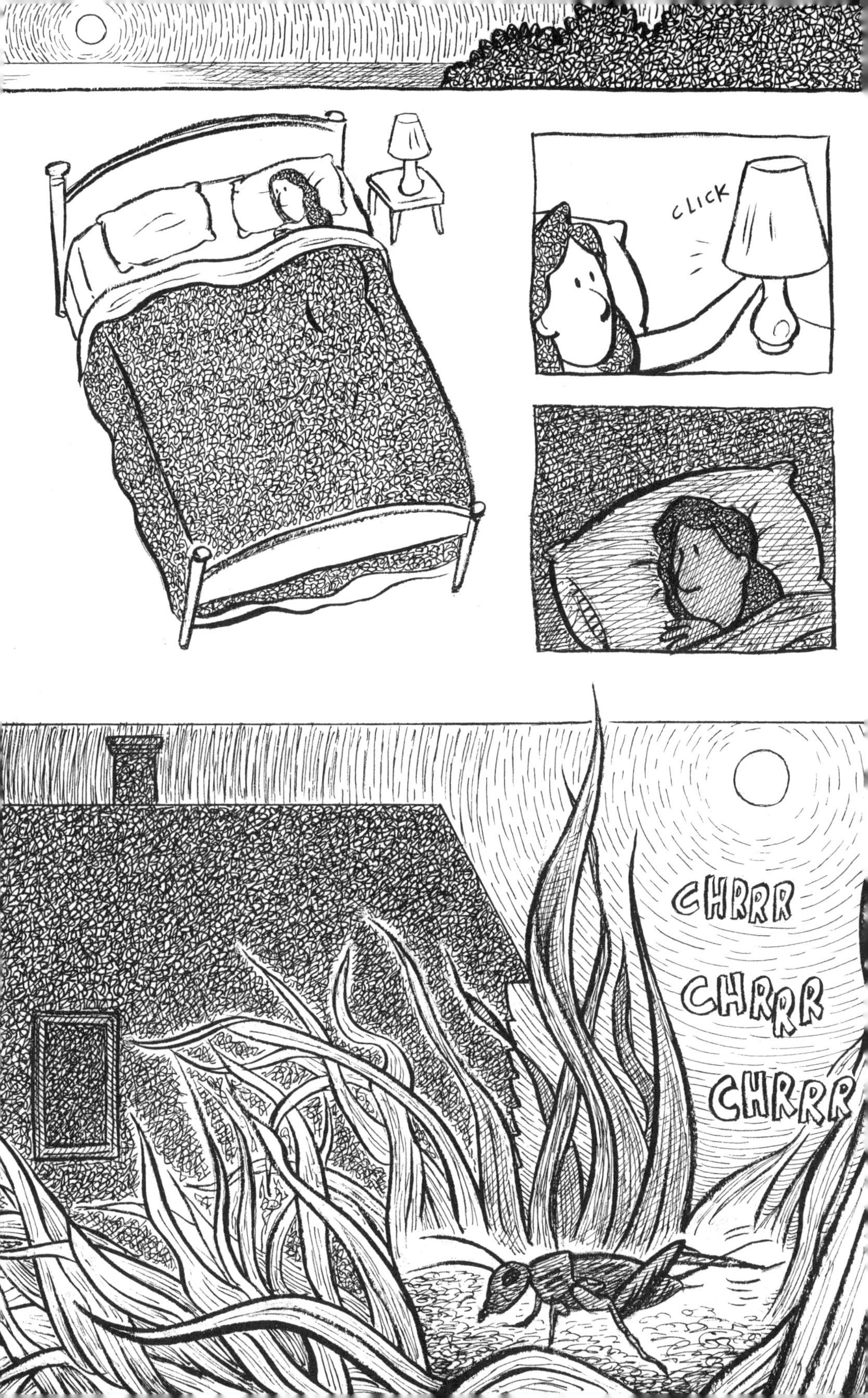
CLICK
CHRRR
CHRRR
CHRRR

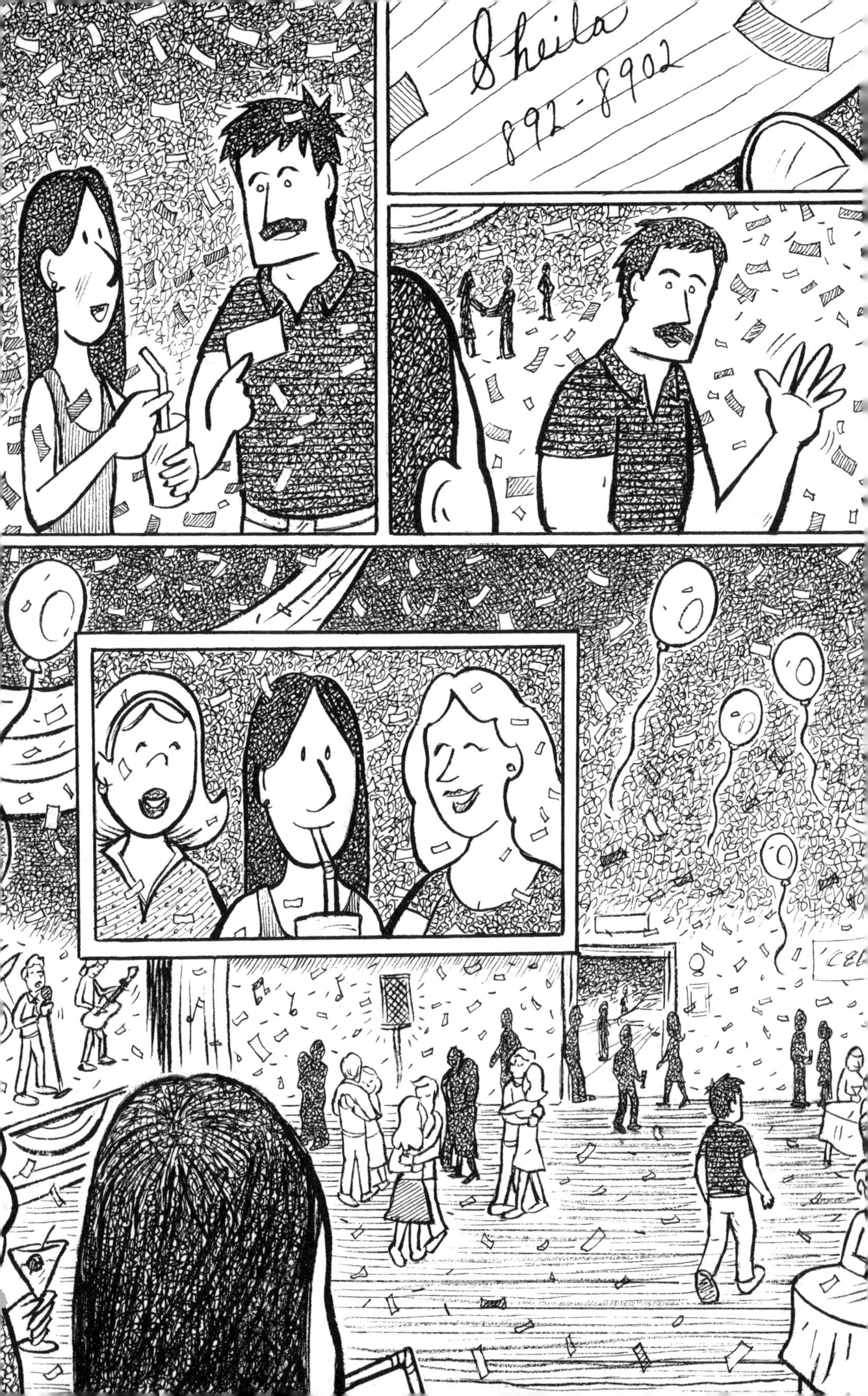
Sheila
892-8902

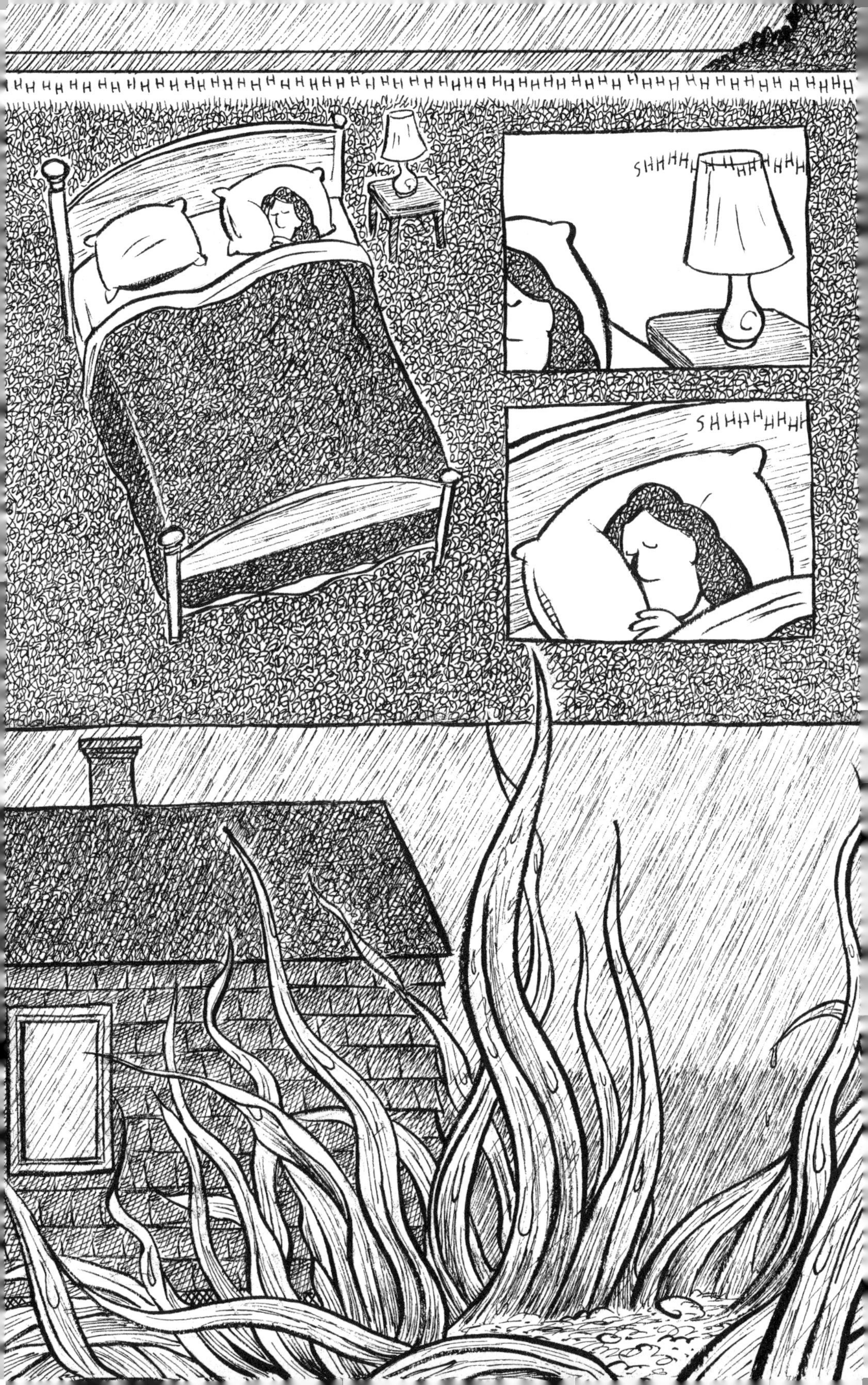
HHHHHHHHHHHHHHHHHHHHHHHHHHHHHHHHHHHHHHHHHHHHHHHHHHHHHHHHHHH
SHHHHHHHHHHHHHH
SHHHHHHHH

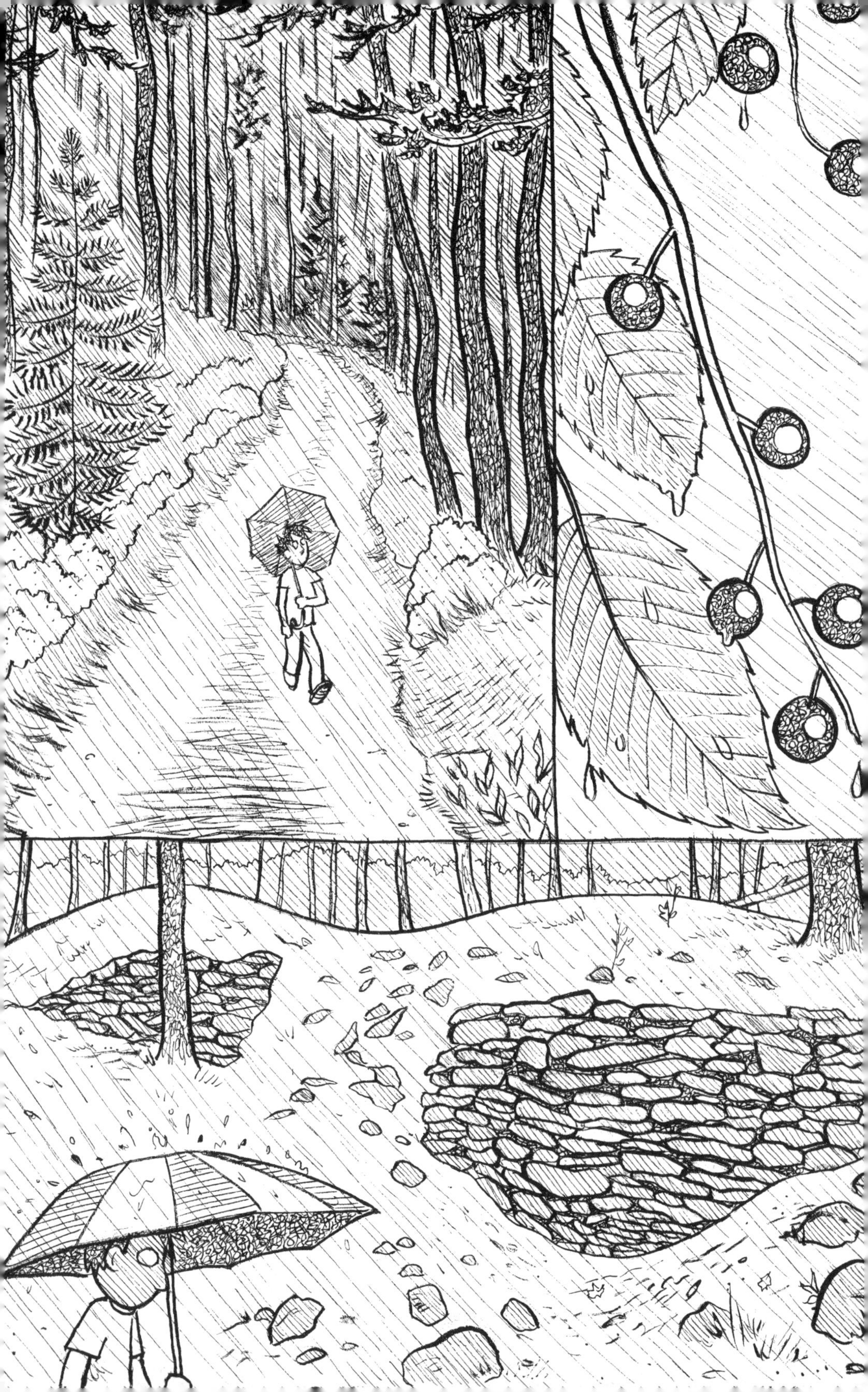

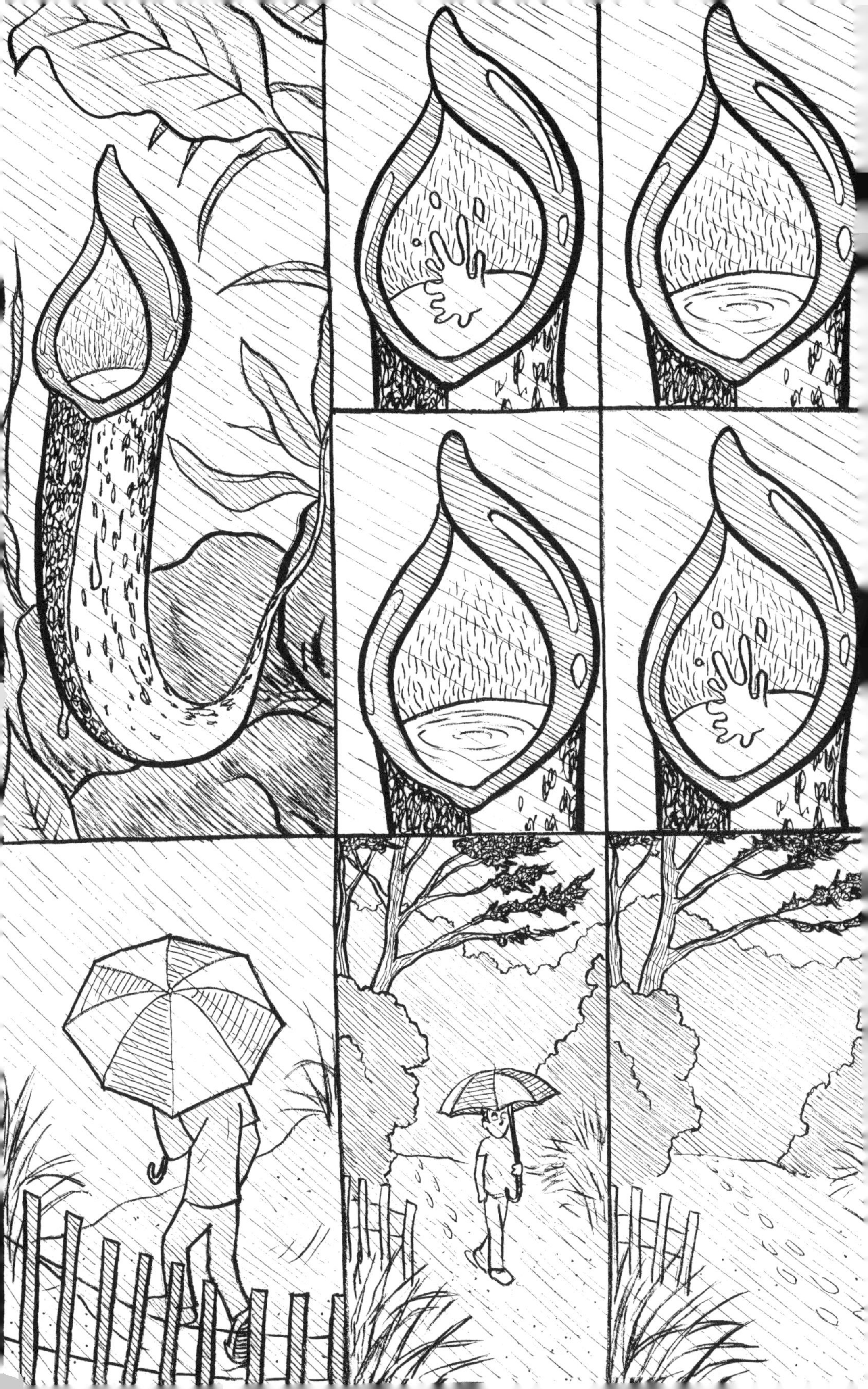

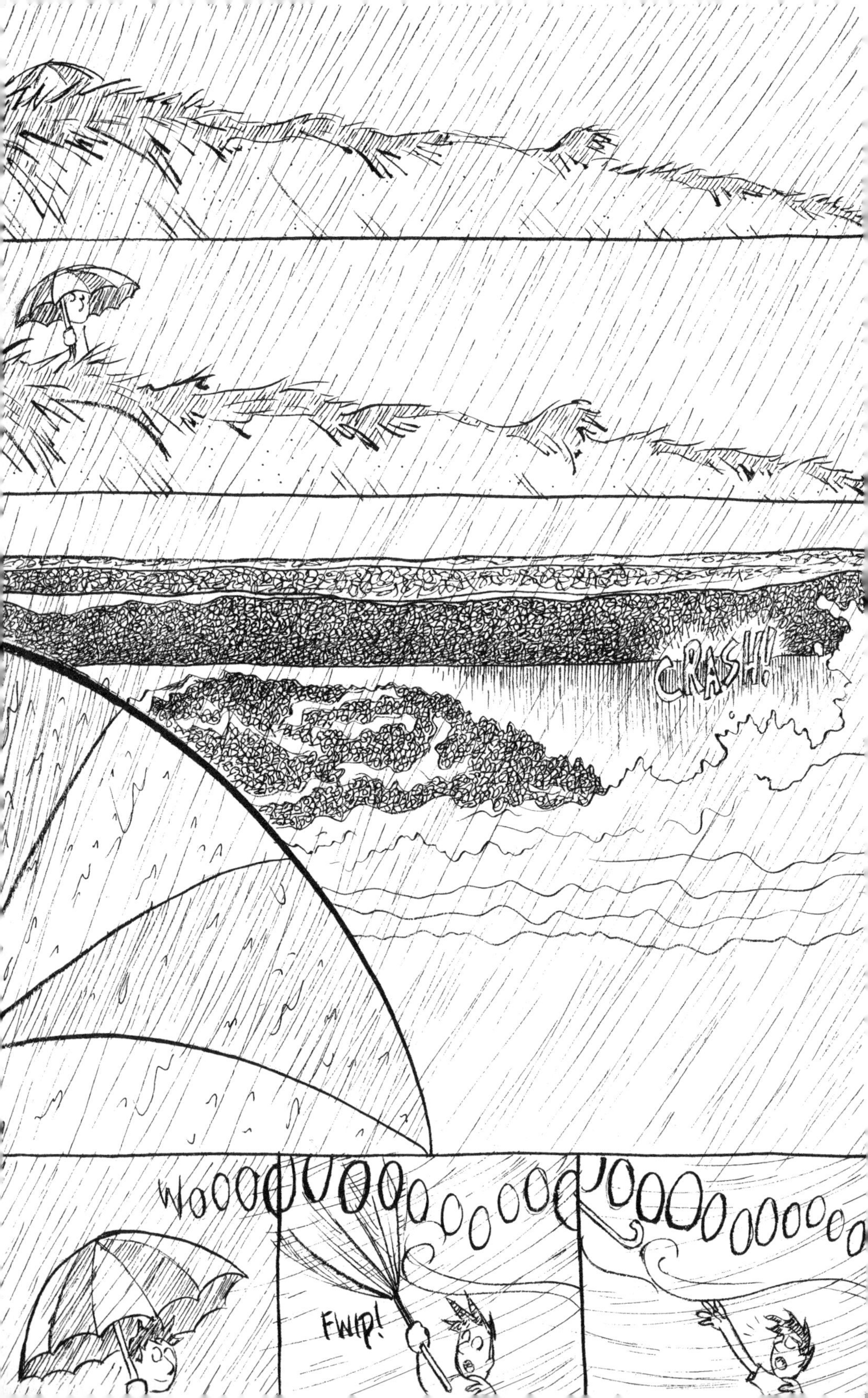
CRASH!
WOOOOOOOOOOOOOOOOOOOOOOOOOO
FWIP!

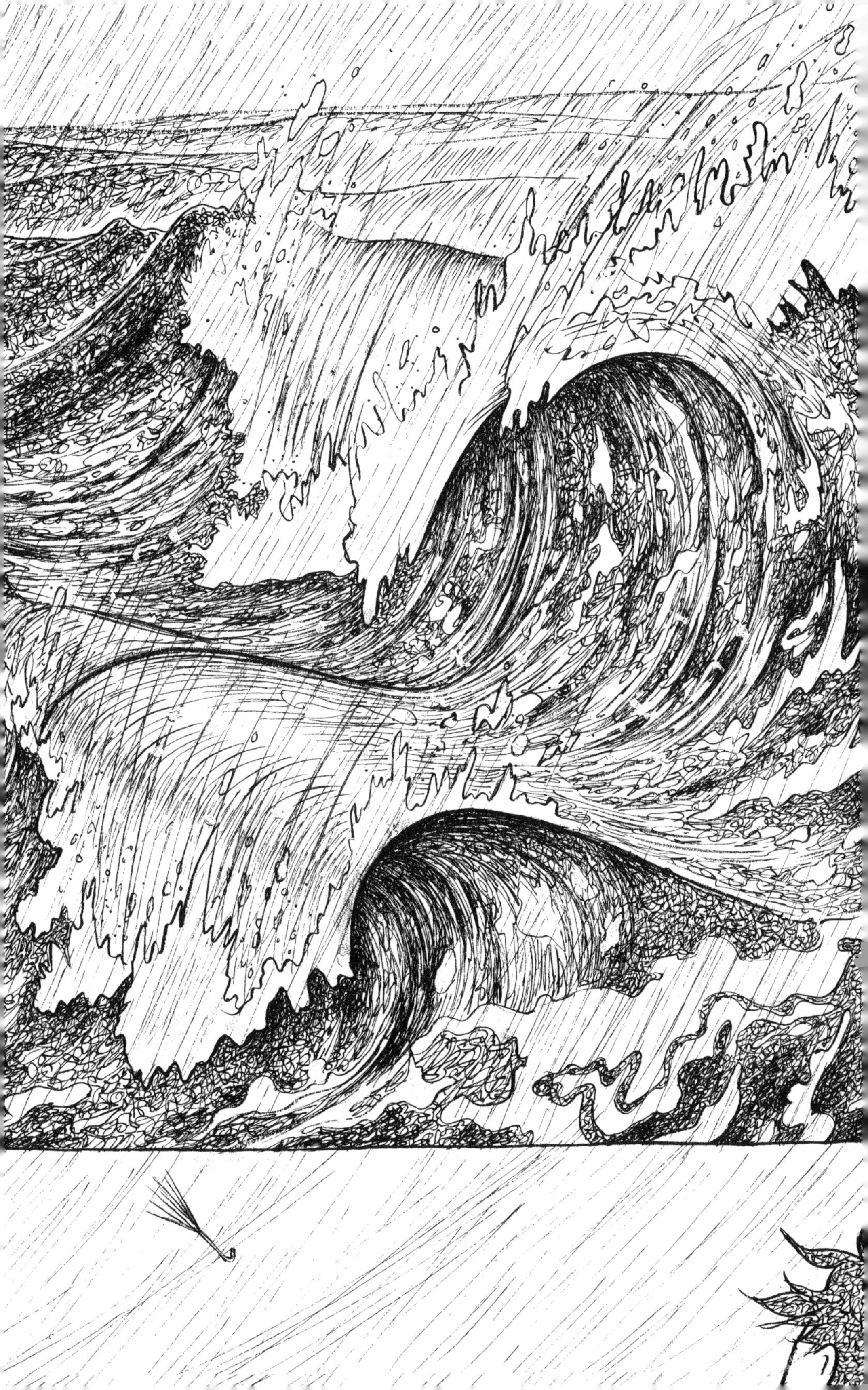

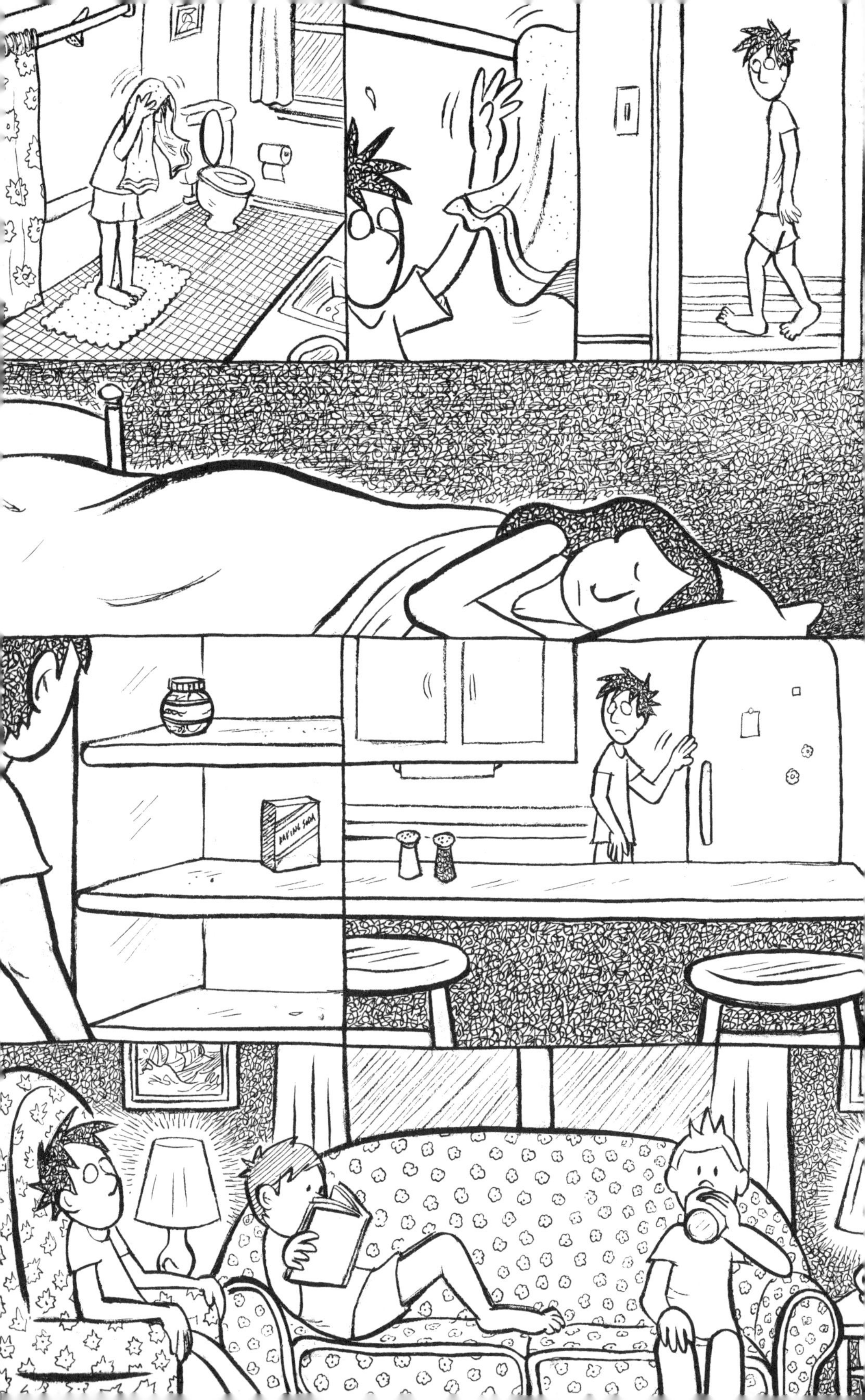
BAKING SODA

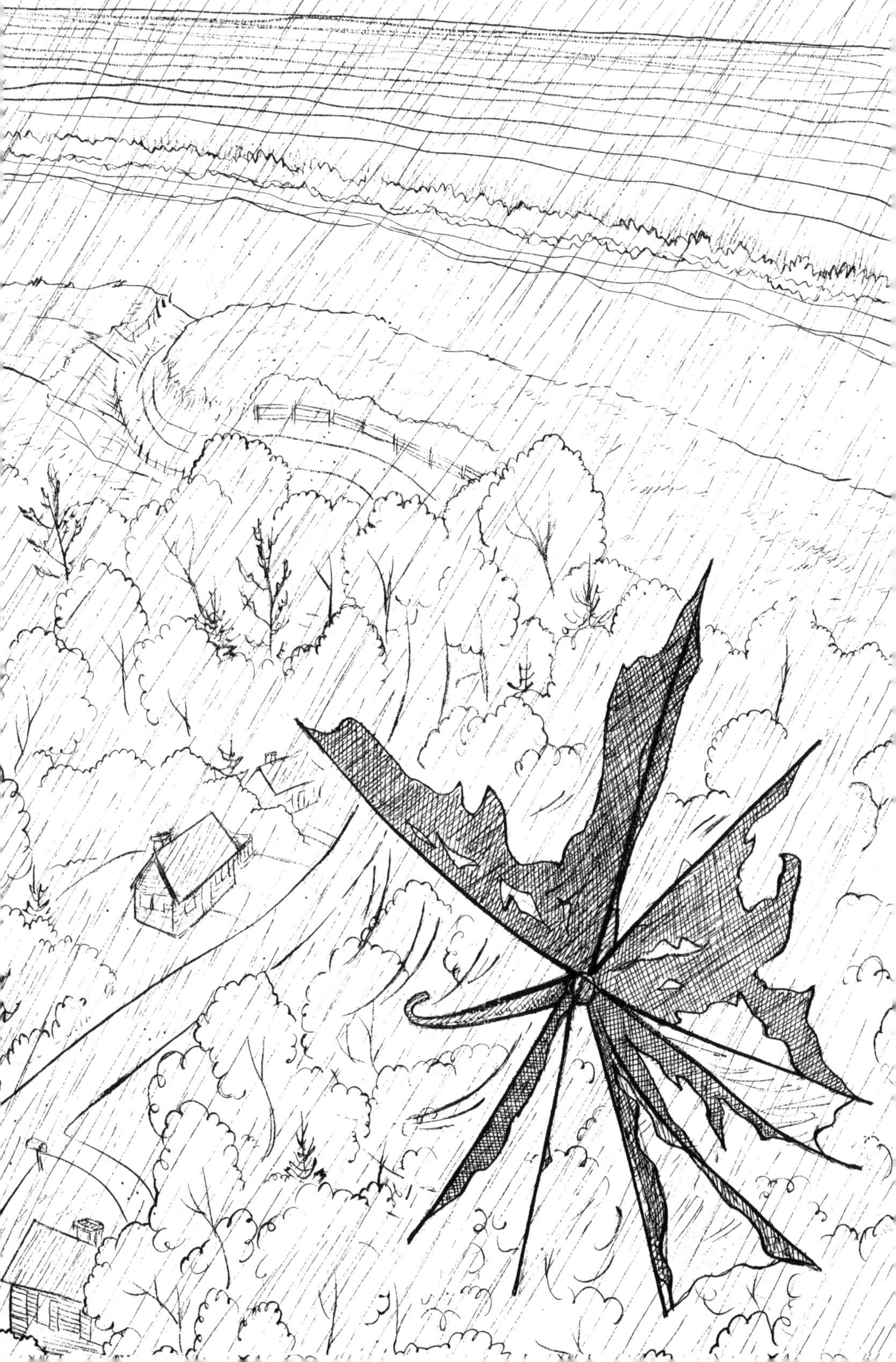

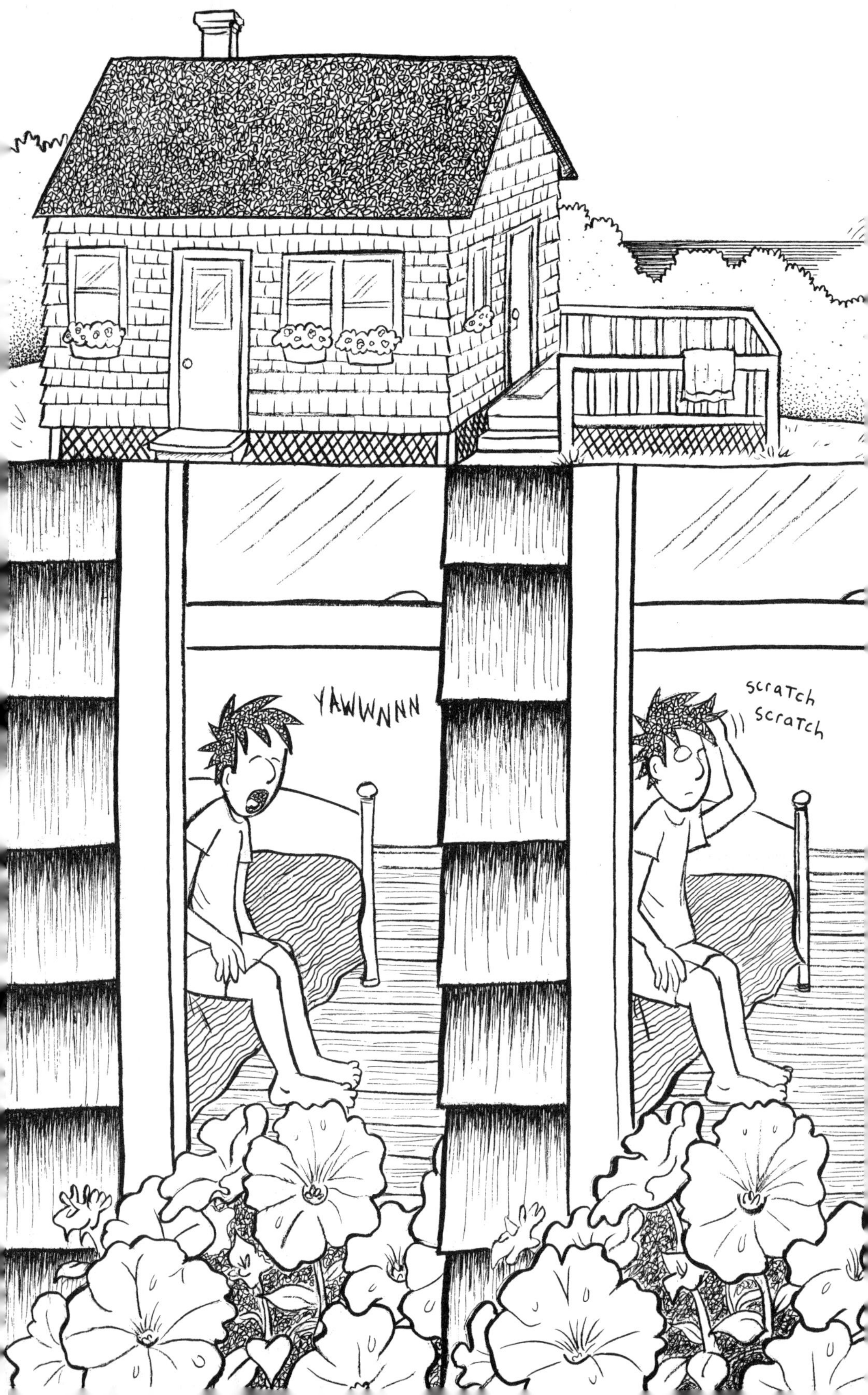
YAWWNNN
scratch scratch

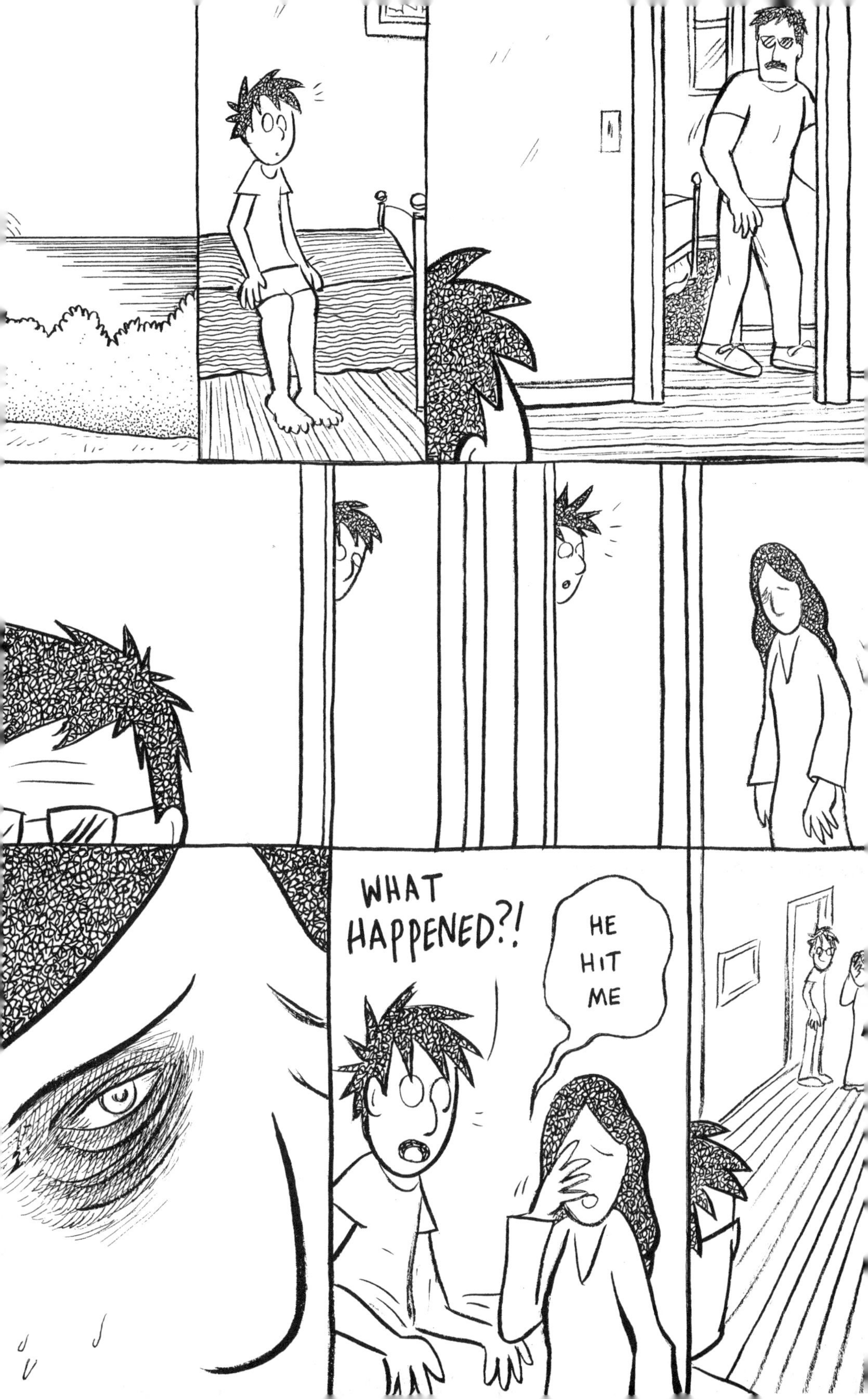
WHAT HAPPENED?!
HE HIT ME

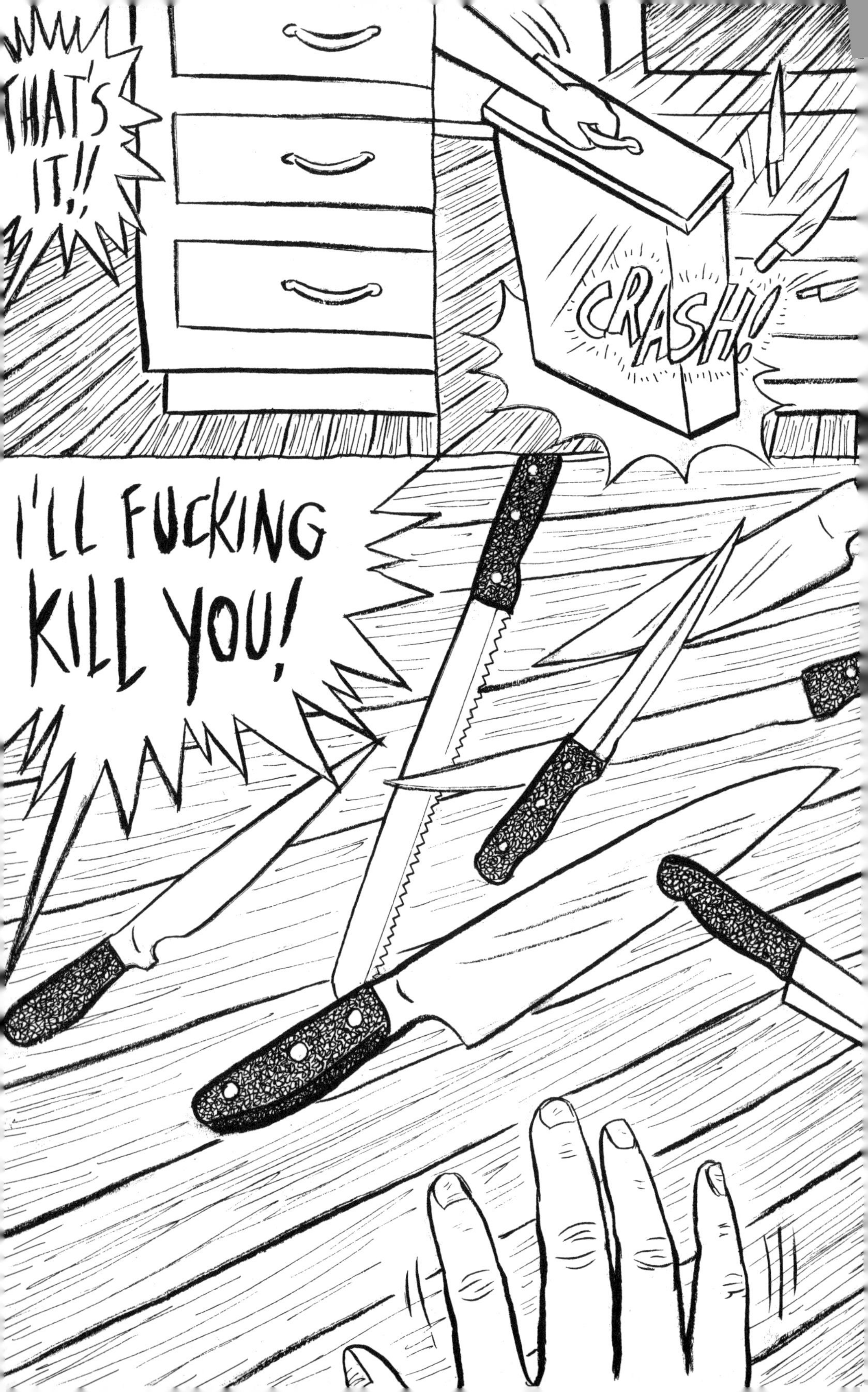
THAT'S IT!!
CRASH!
I'LL FUCKING KILL YOU!

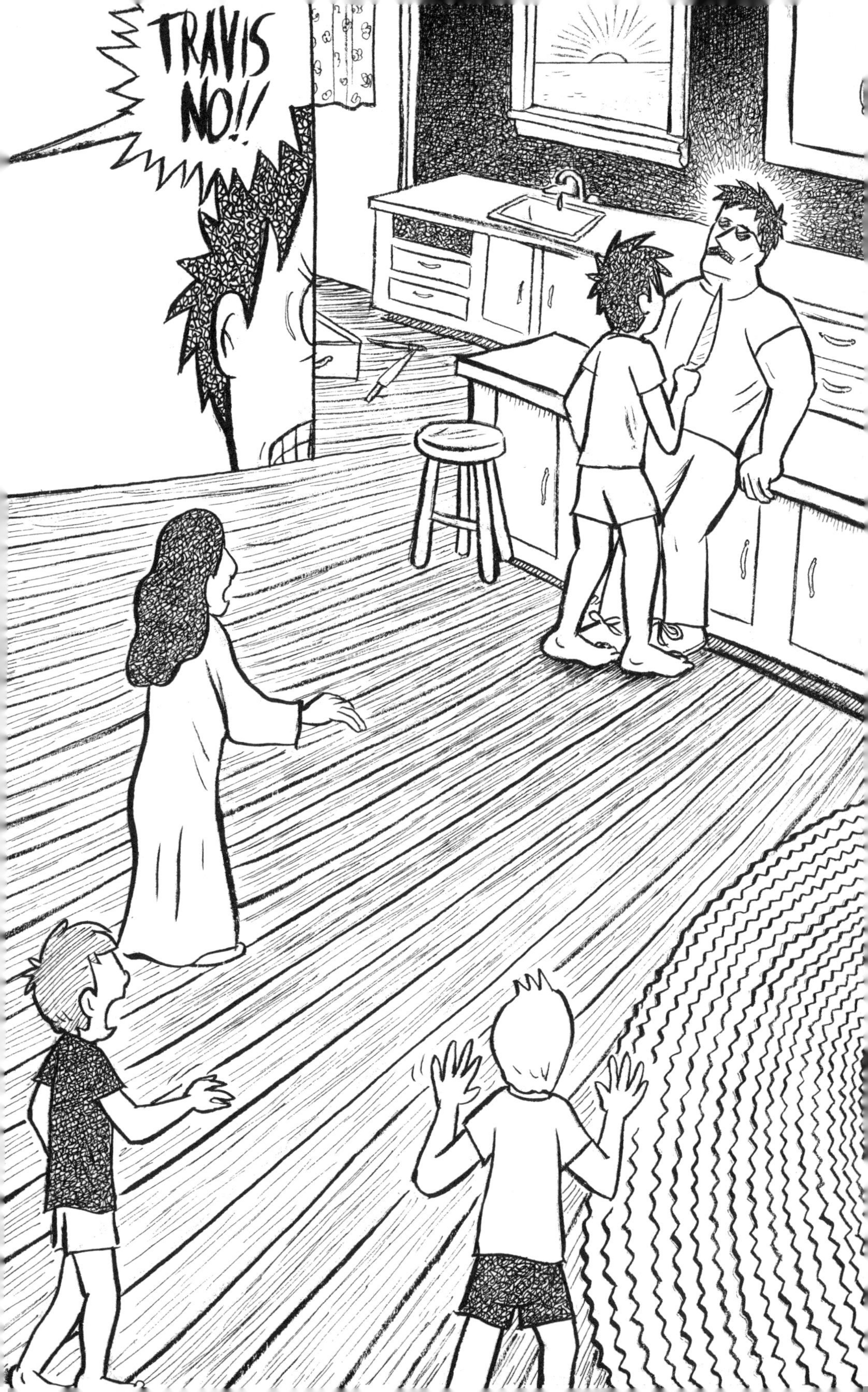
TRAVIS NO!!

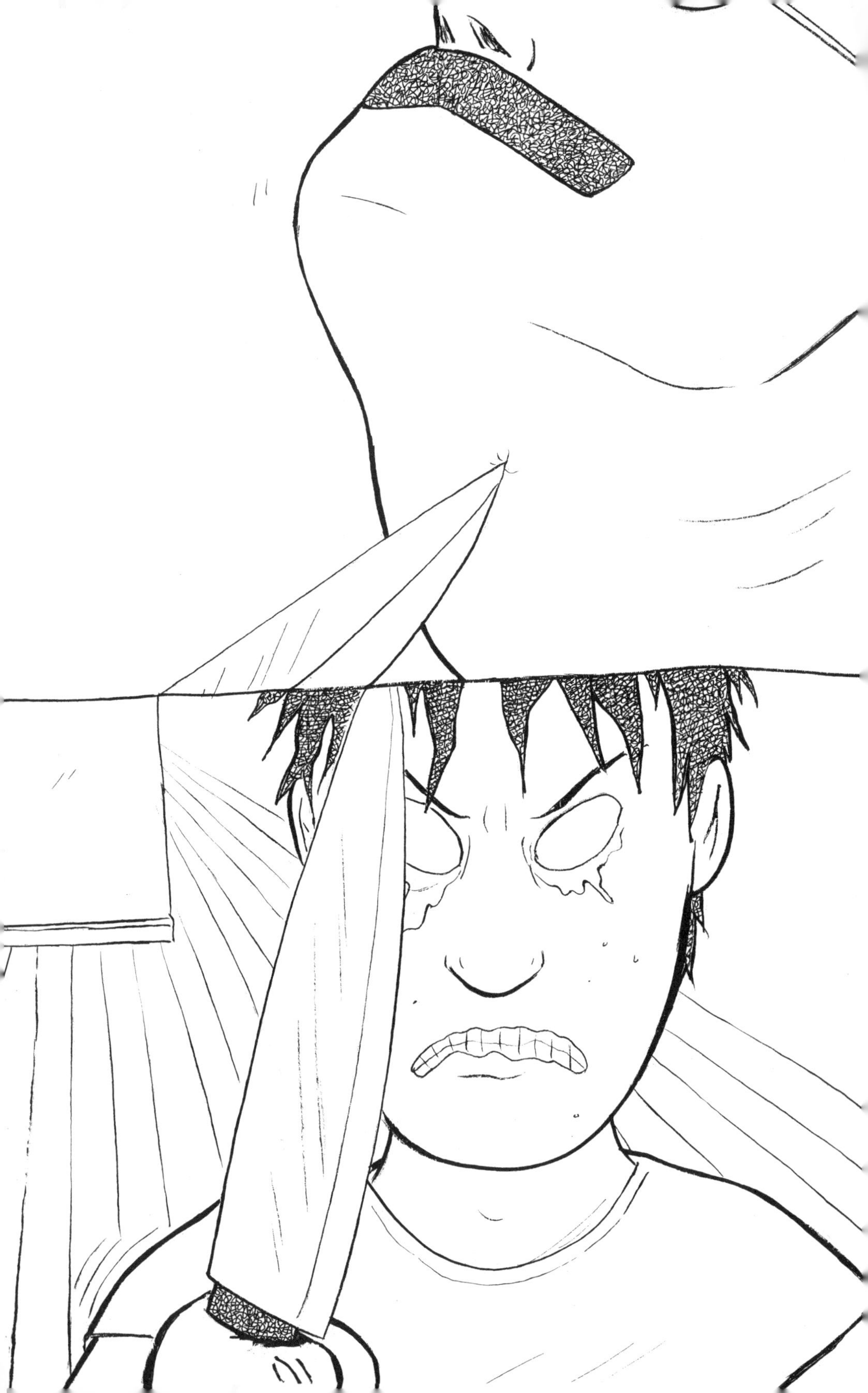

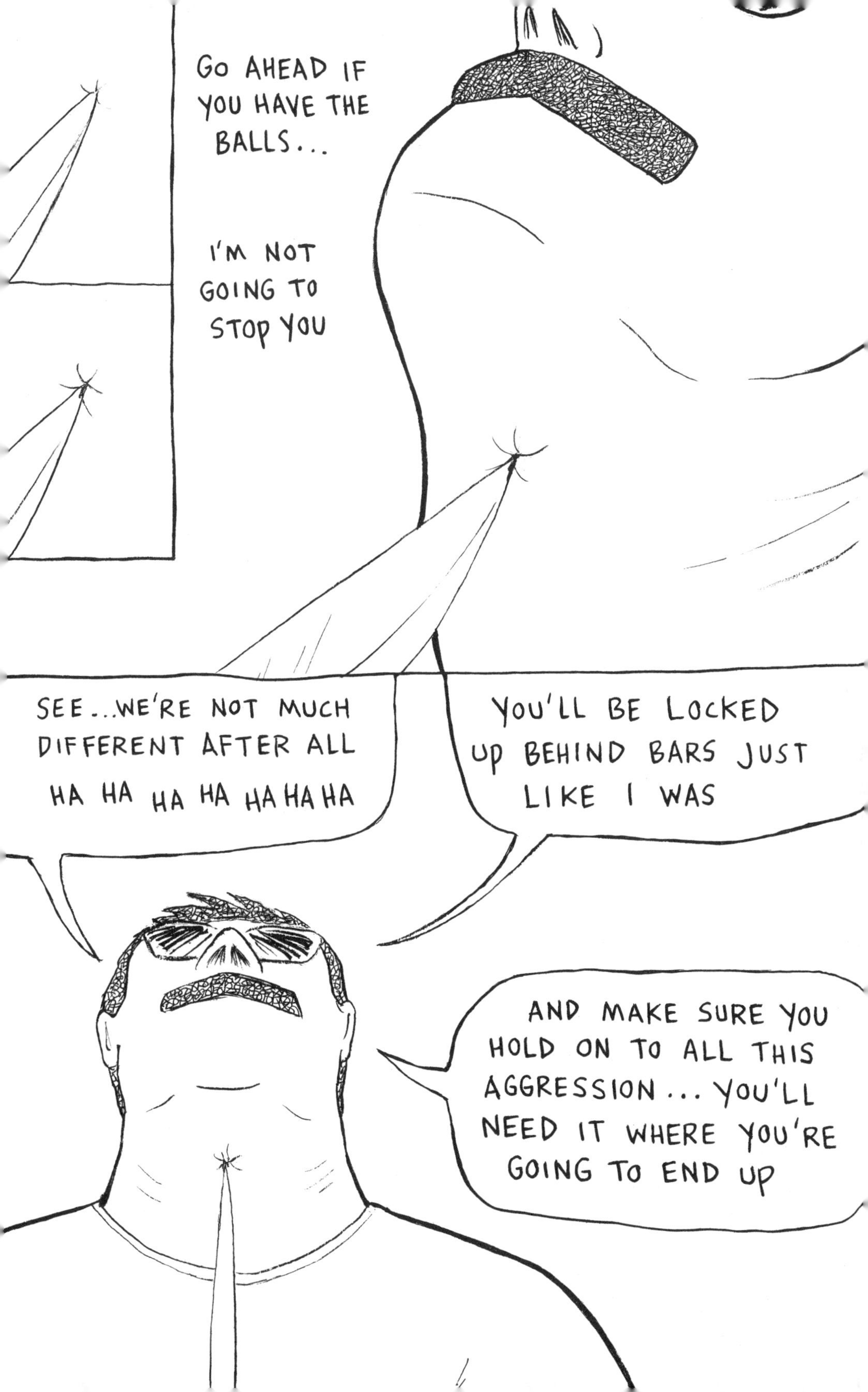
GO AHEAD IF YOU HAVE THE BALLS...
I'M NOT GOING TO STOP YOU
SEE...WE'RE NOT MUCH DIFFERENT AFTER ALL
HA HA HA HA HA HA HA
YOU'LL BE LOCKED UP BEHIND BARS JUST LIKE I WAS
AND MAKE SURE YOU HOLD ON TO ALL THIS AGGRESSION... YOU'LL NEED IT WHERE YOU'RE GOING TO END UP

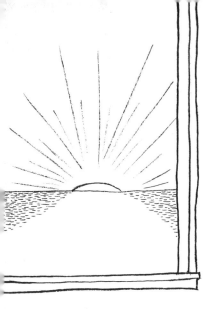

WELL, WHAT ARE
YOU WAITING
FOR, BIG MAN?

I WANT TO DIE

I WANT YOU TO DO IT

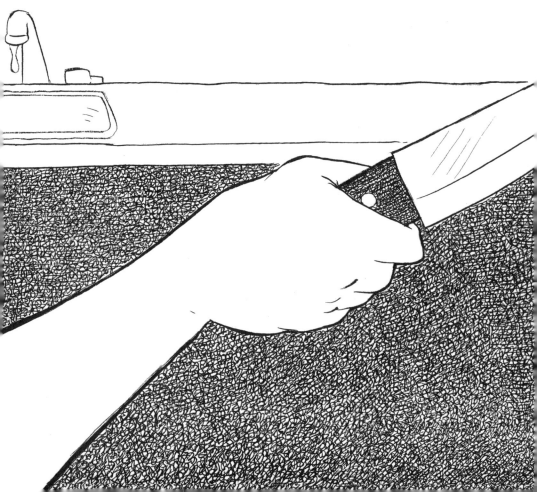

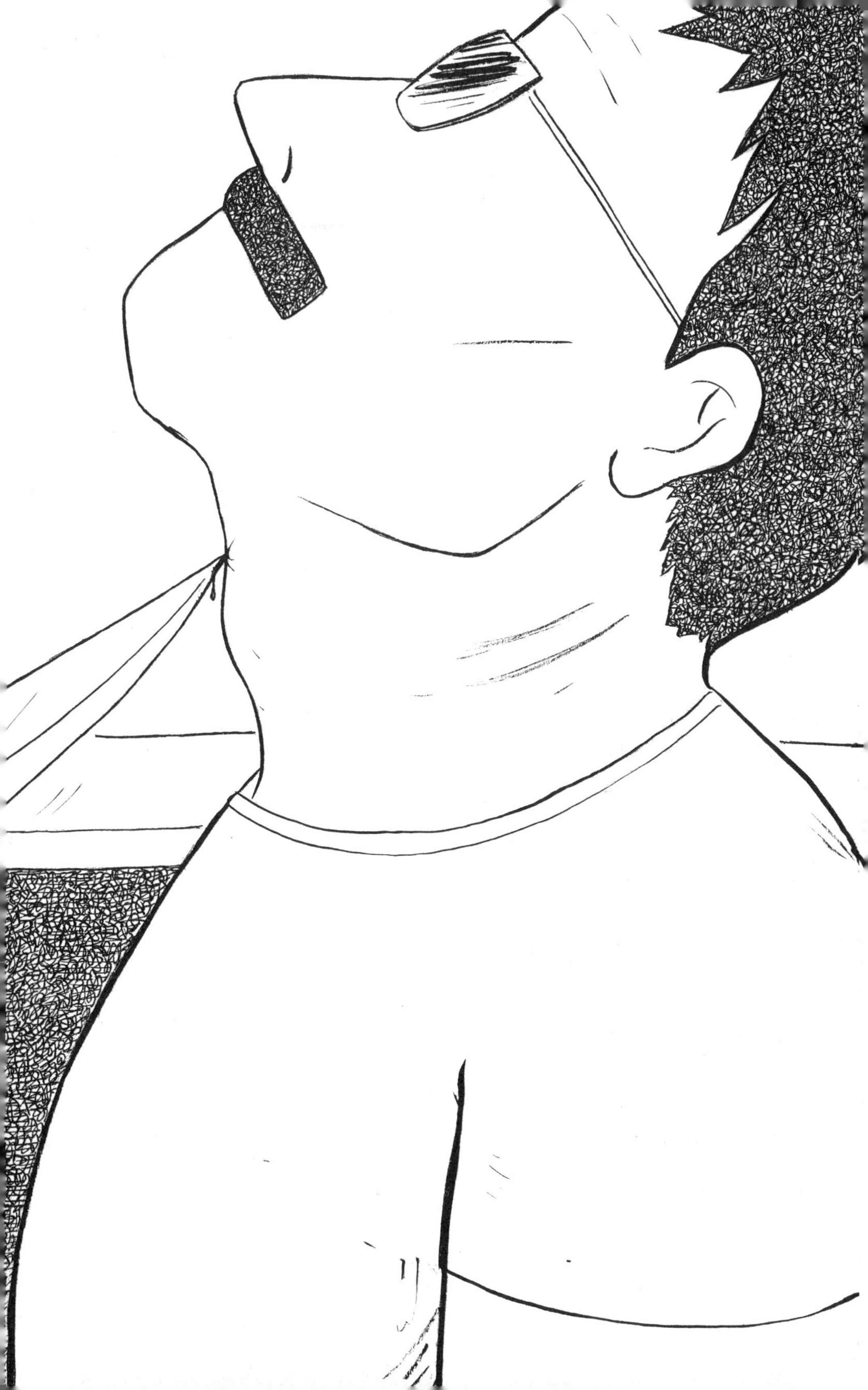

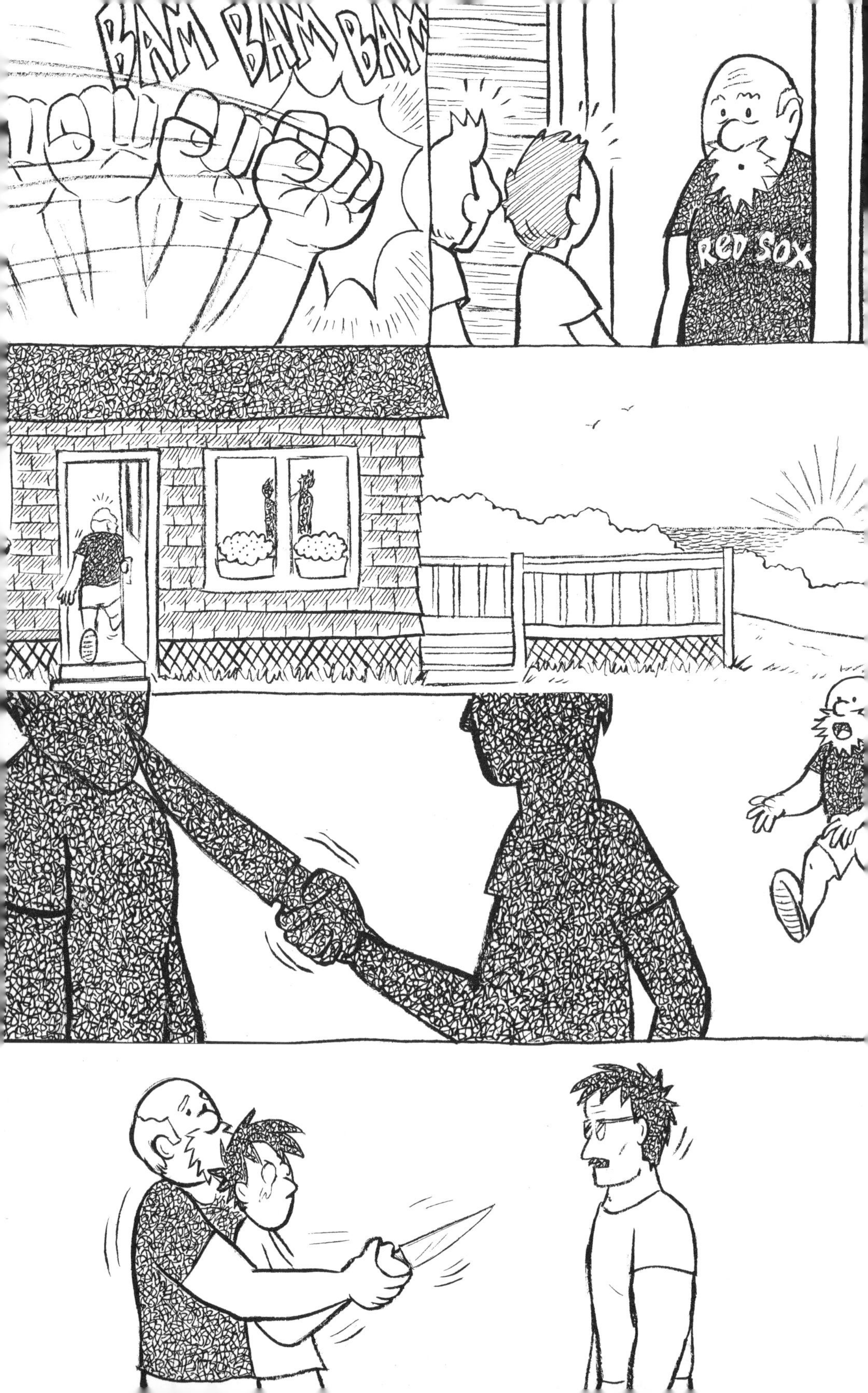
BAM BAM BAM
RED SOX

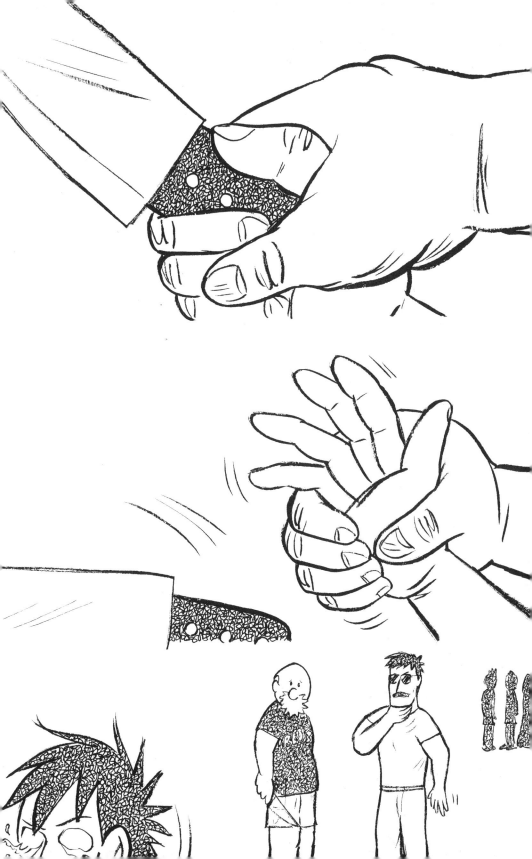

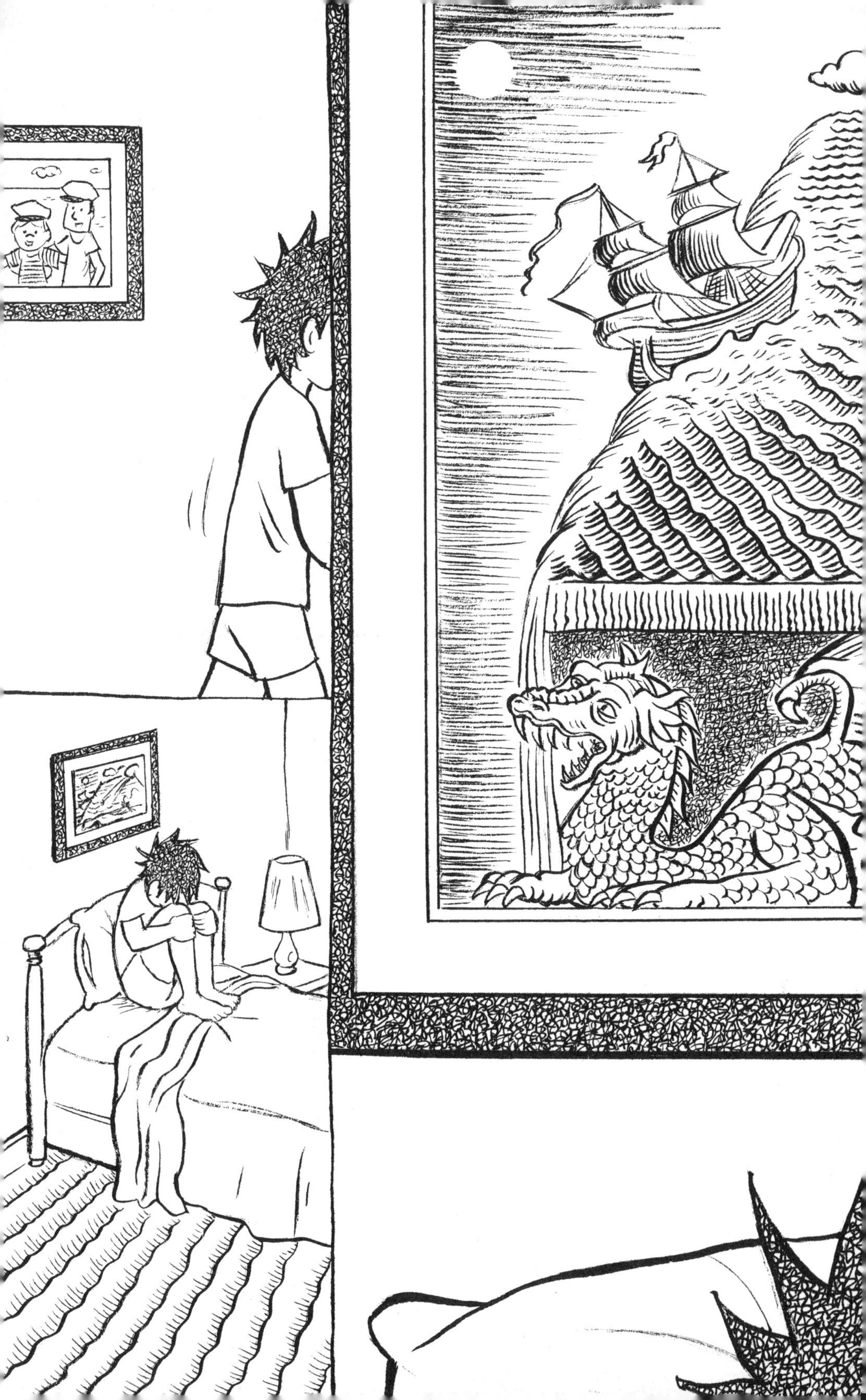

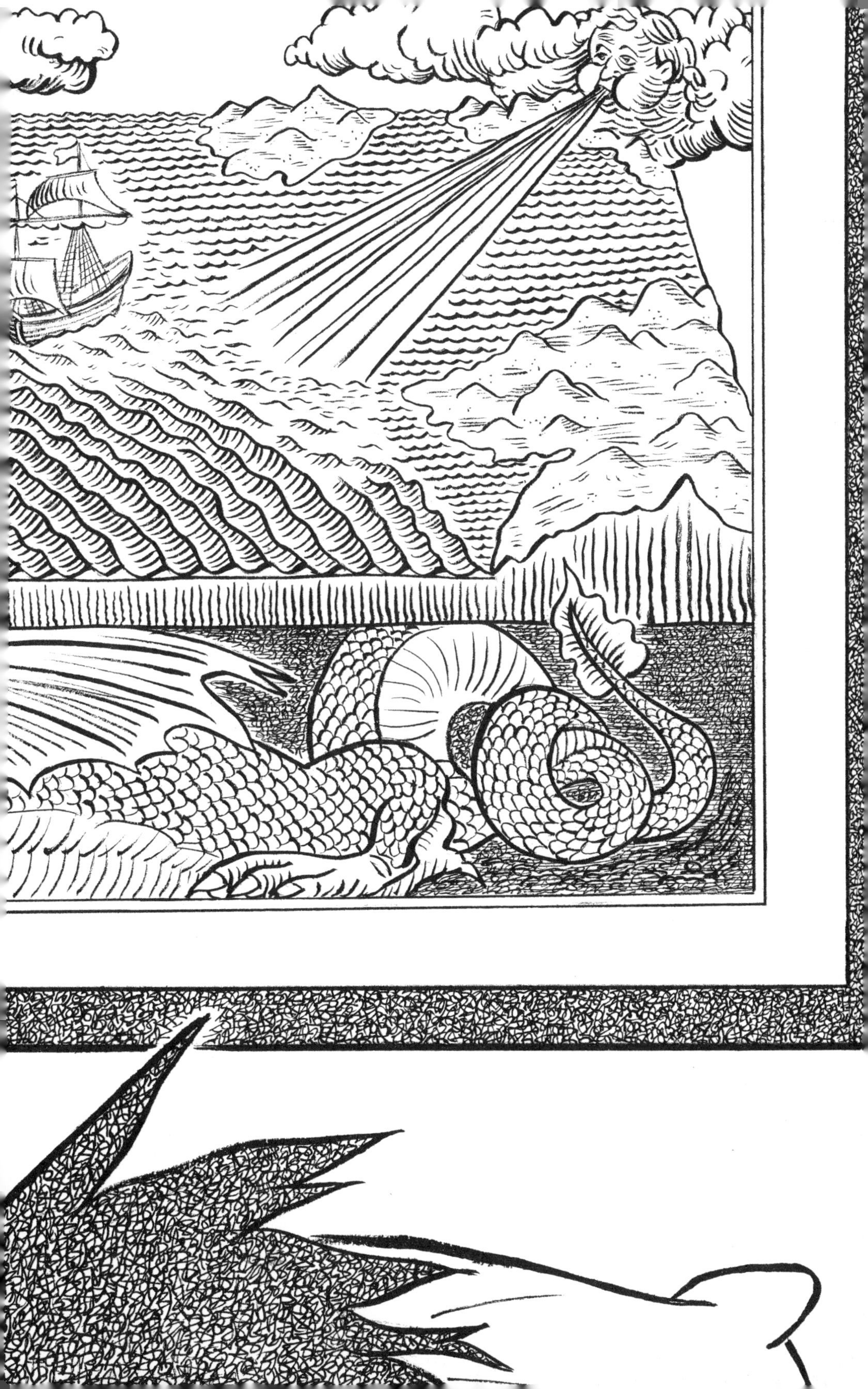

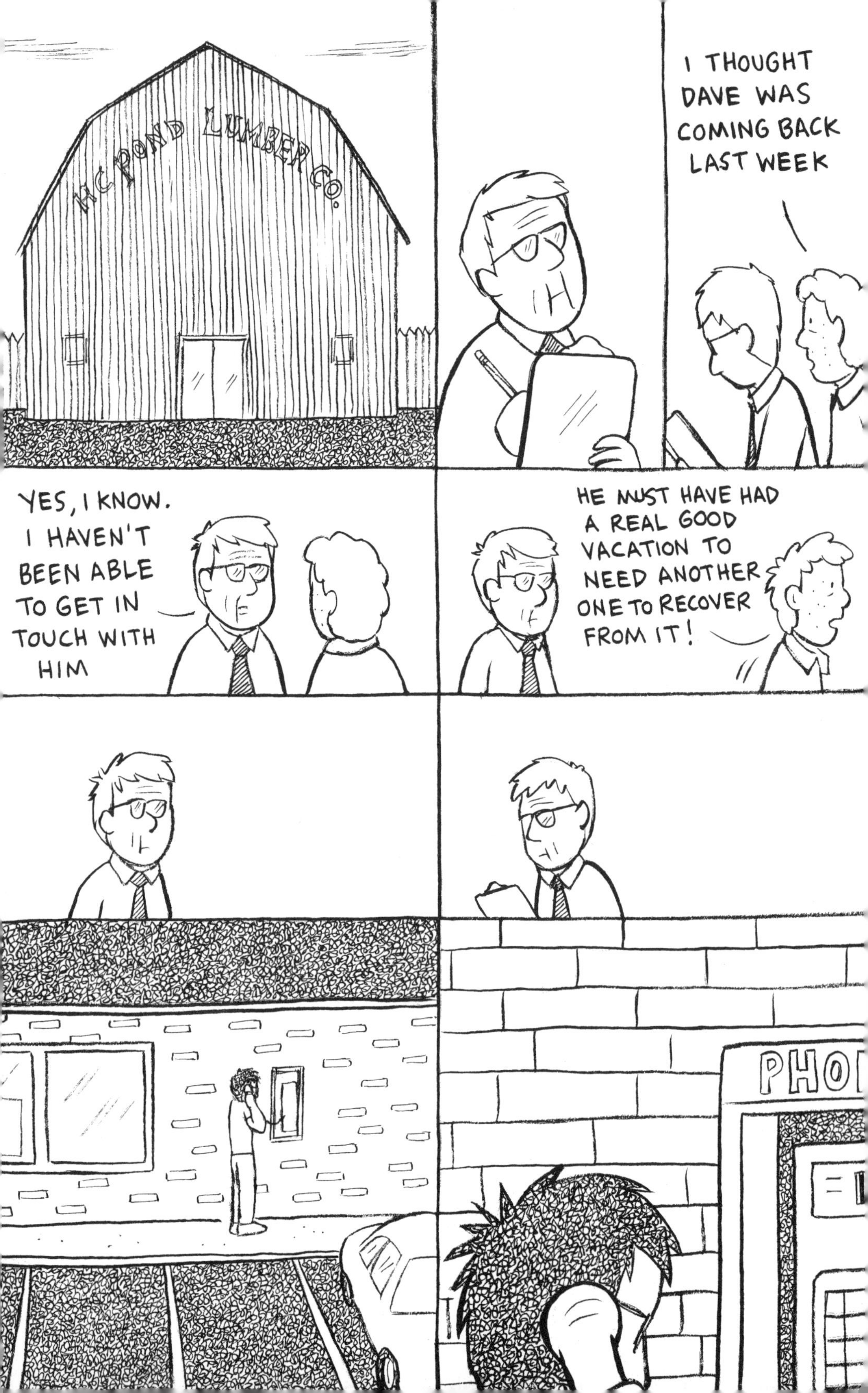
HC POND LUMBER CO.
I THOUGHT DAVE WAS COMING BACK LAST WEEK
YES, I KNOW. I HAVEN'T BEEN ABLE TO GET IN TOUCH WITH HIM
HE MUST HAVE HAD A REAL GOOD VACATION TO NEED ANOTHER ONE TO RECOVER FROM IT!
PHO

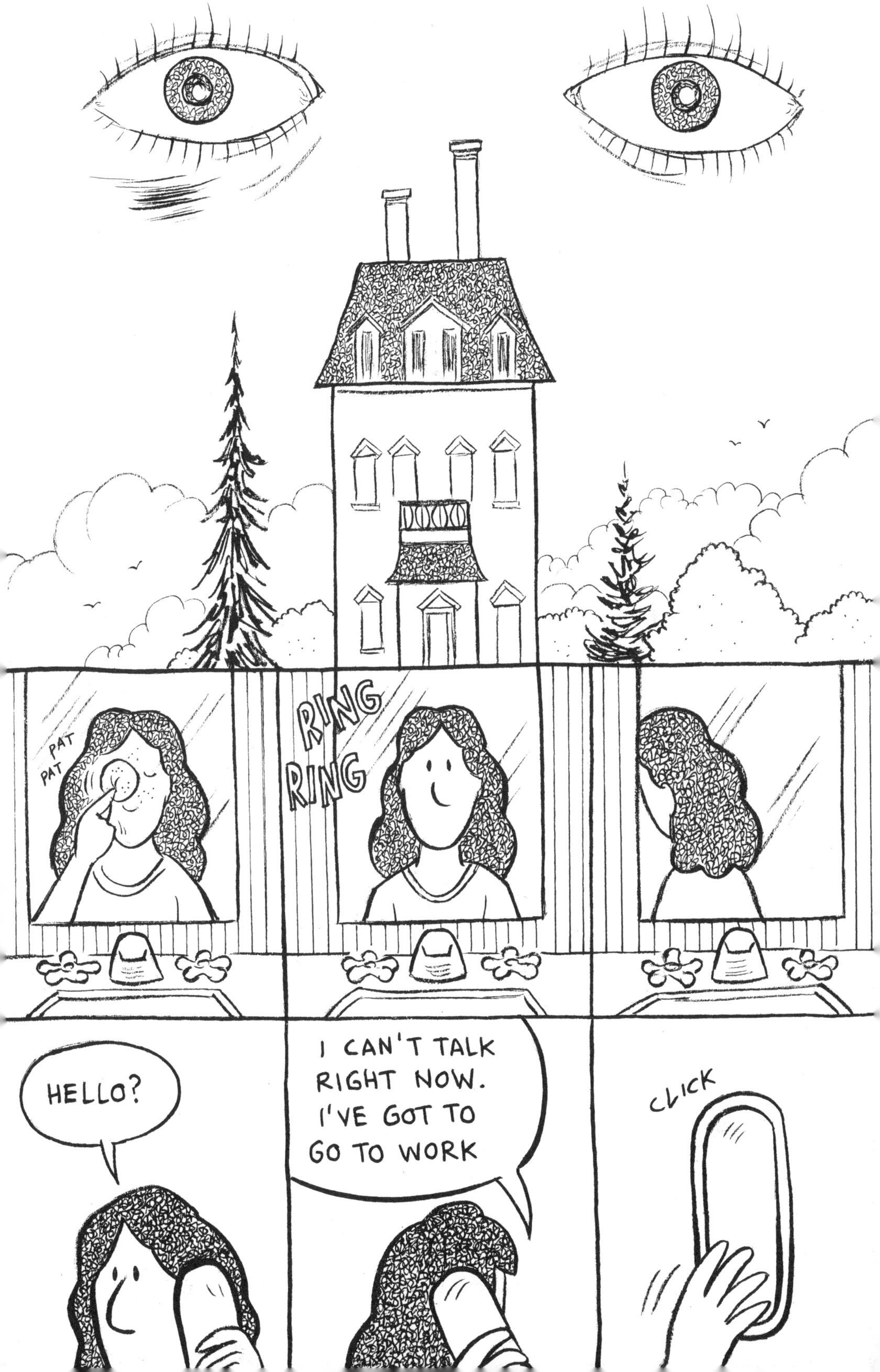
PAT
PAT
RING
RING
HELLO?
I CAN'T TALK RIGHT NOW. I'VE GOT TO GO TO WORK
CLICK

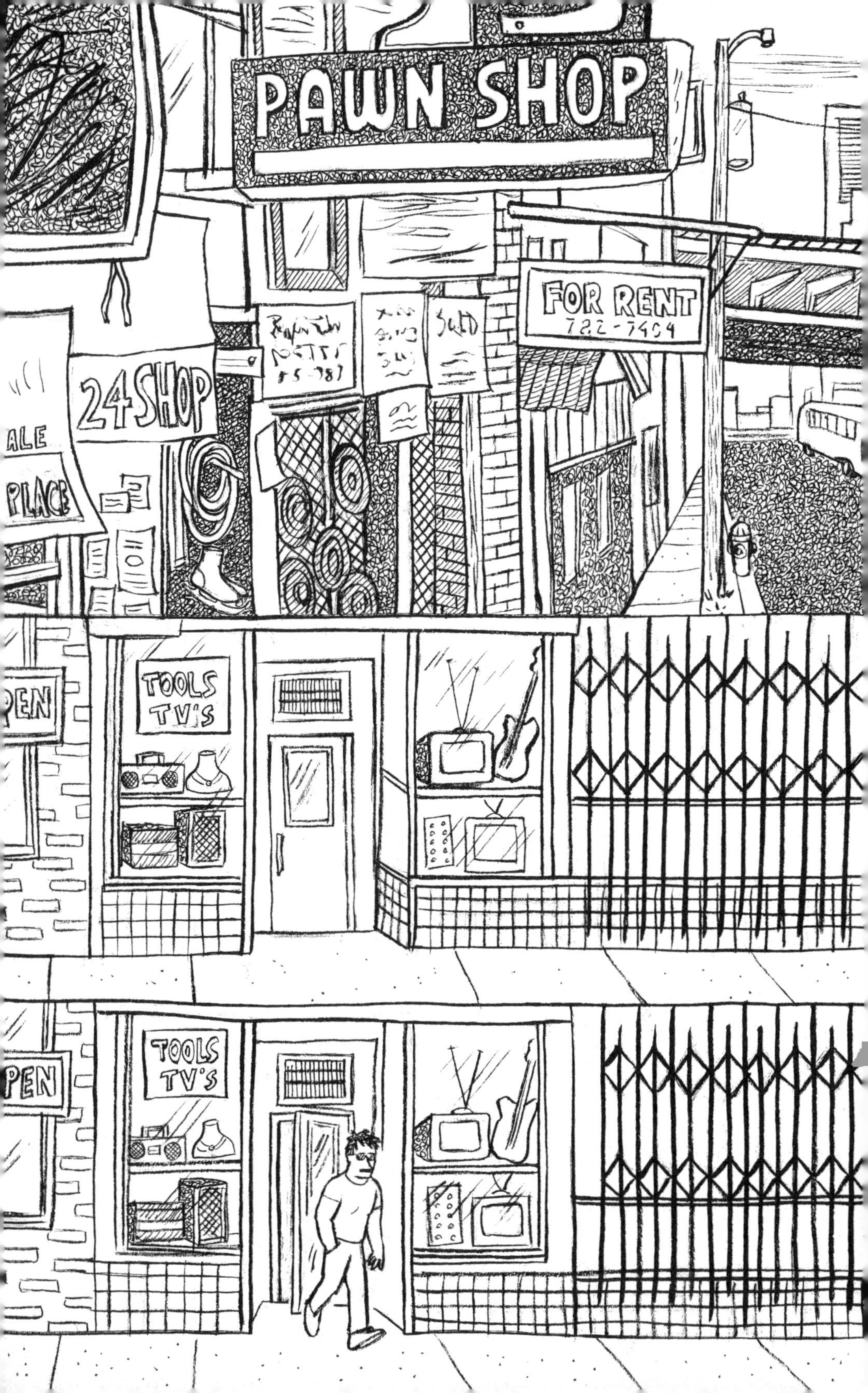
PAWN SHOP
FOR RENT
24SHOP
TOOLS TV'S
TOOLS TV'S

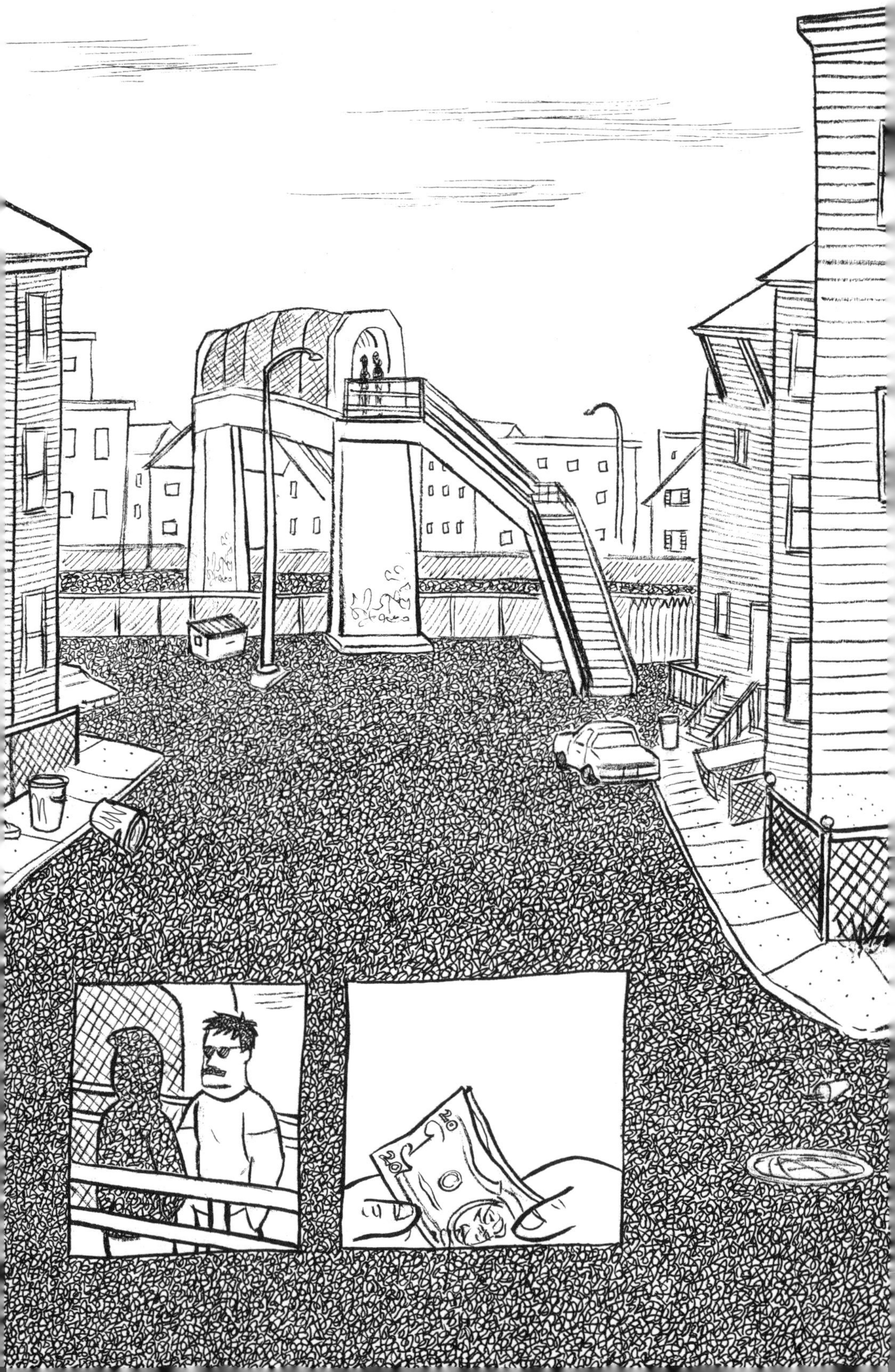

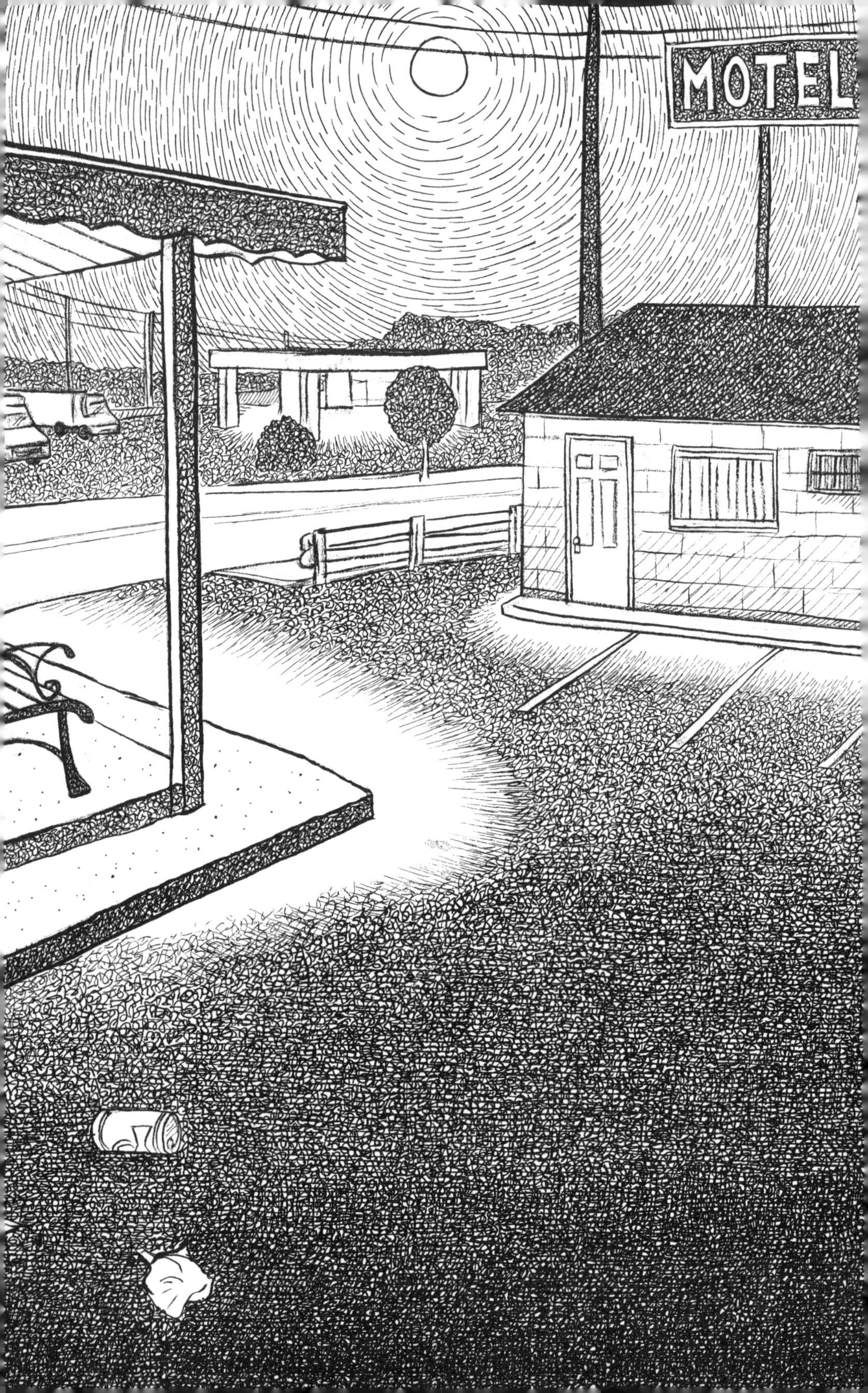
MOTEL

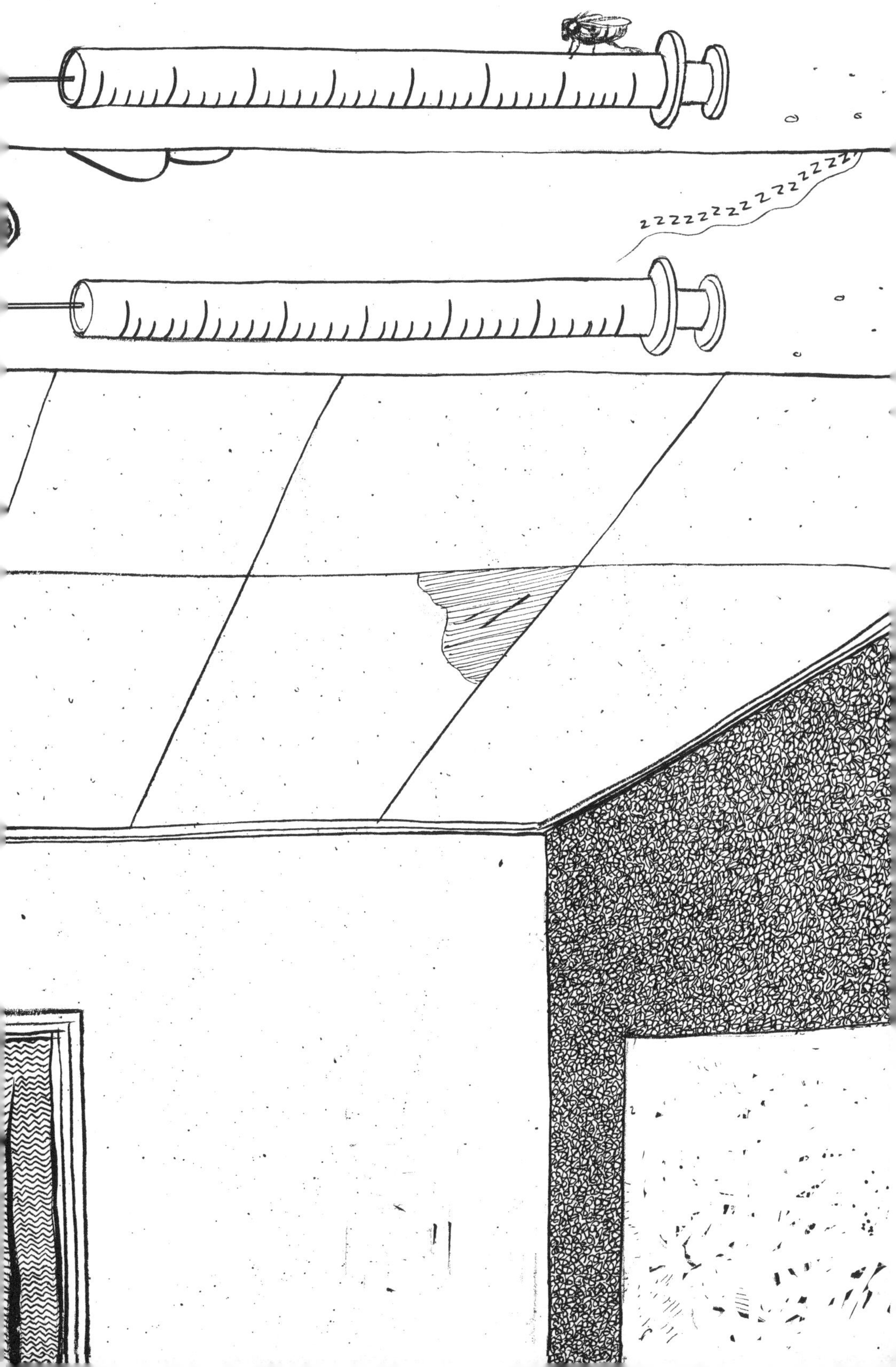

zzzzzzzzzzzzzzzz

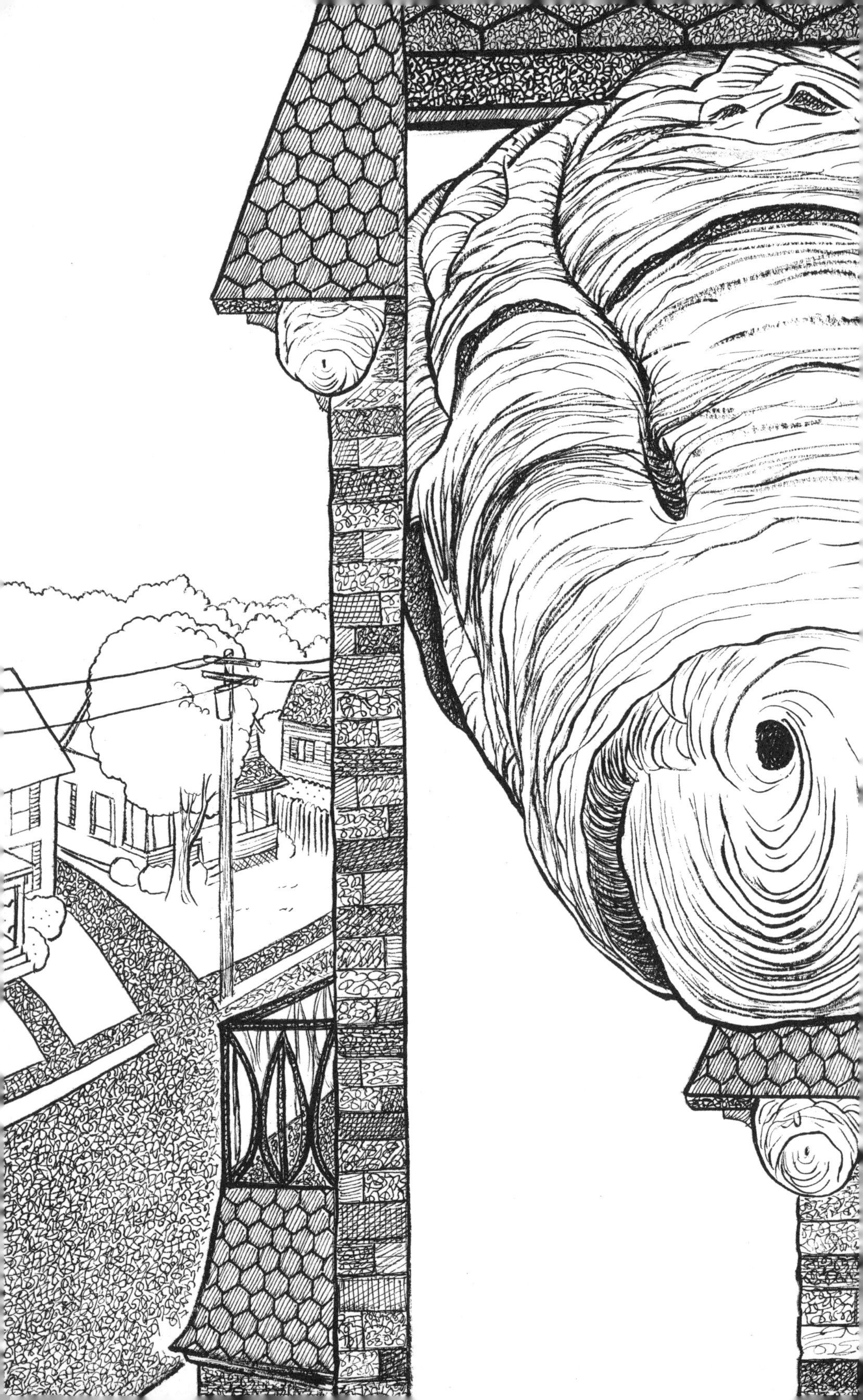

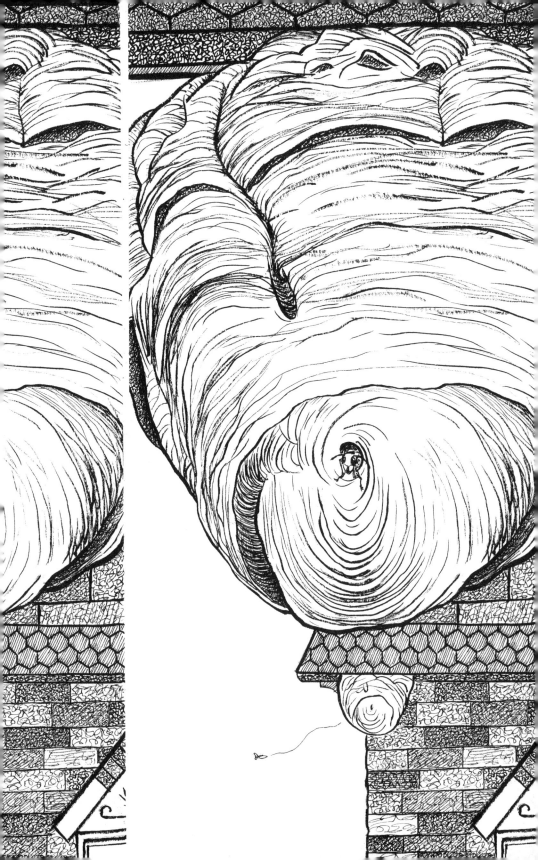

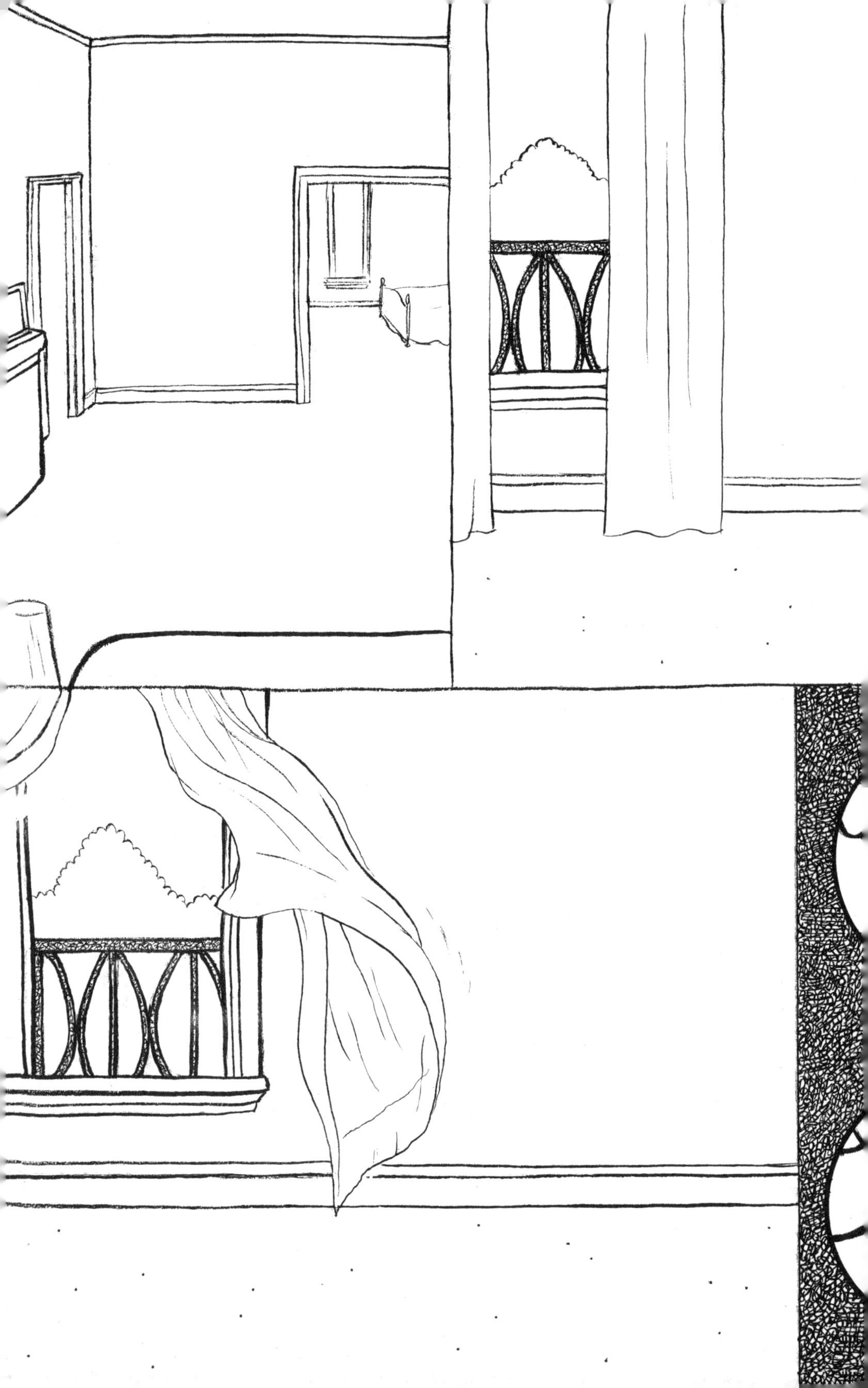

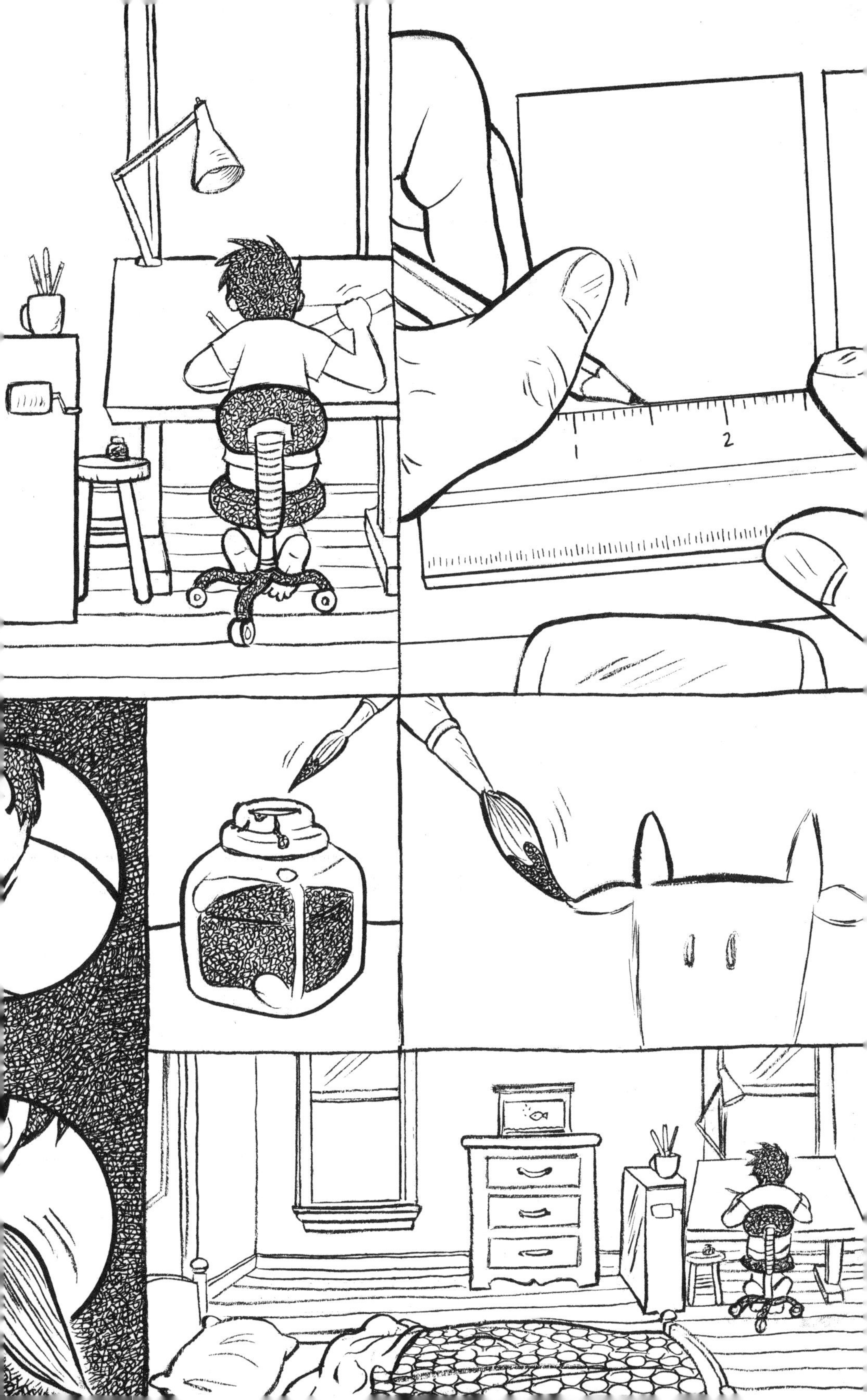
1
2

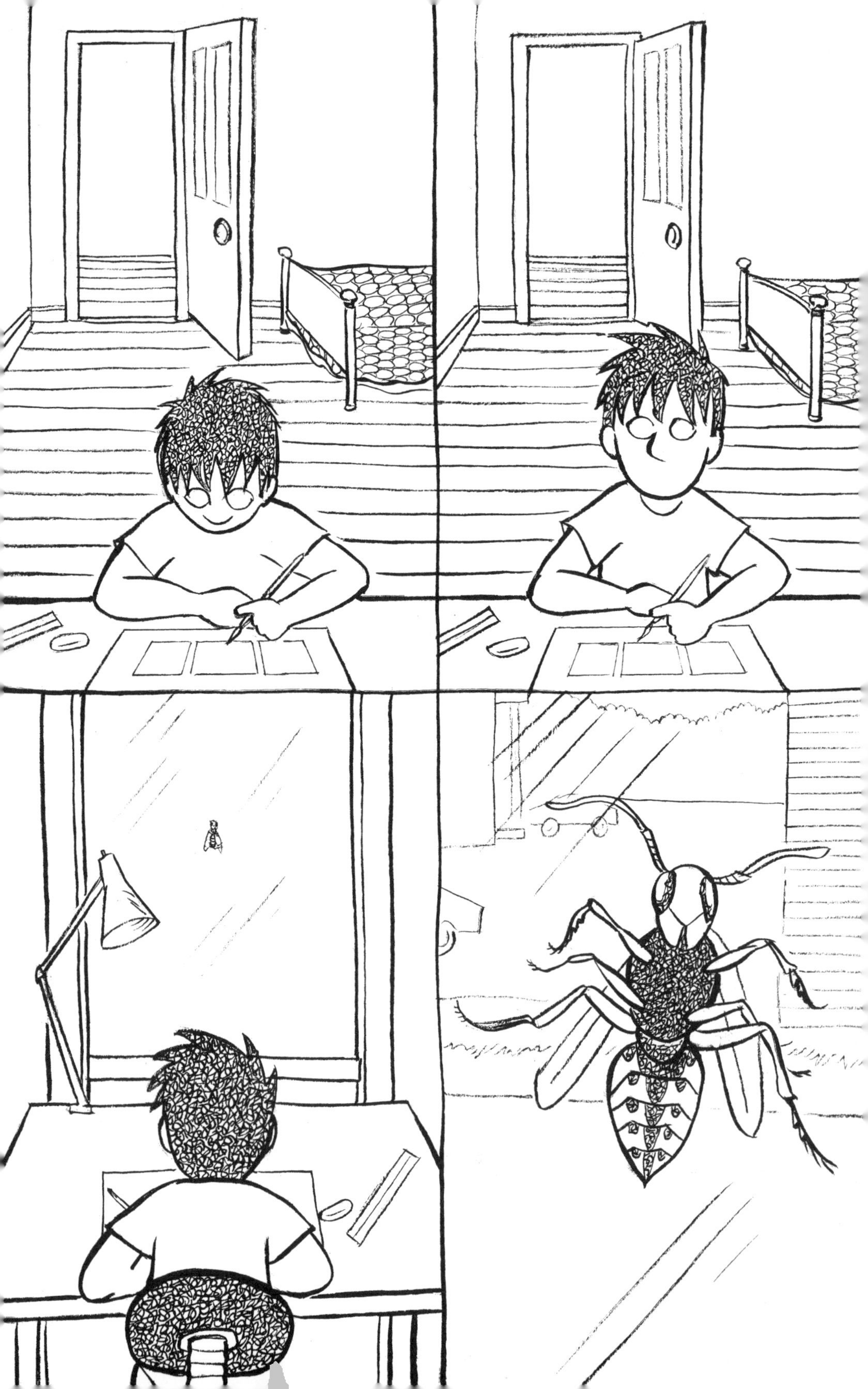

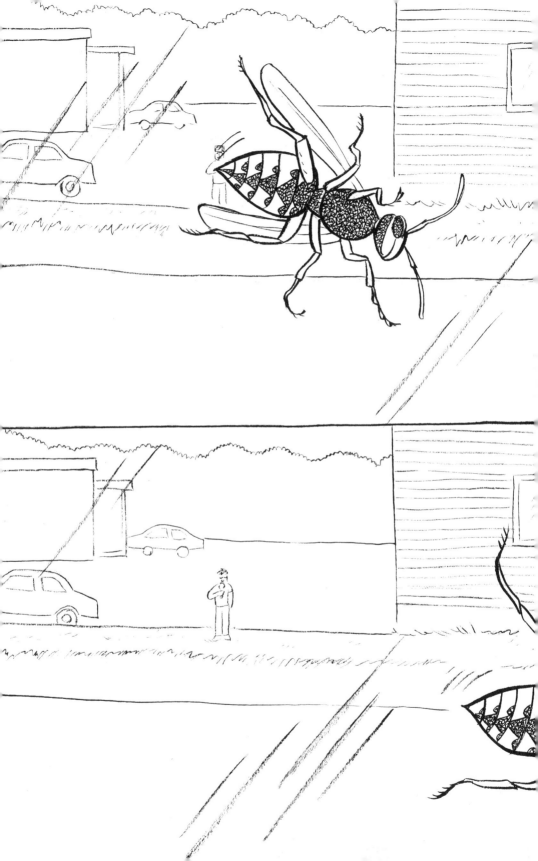

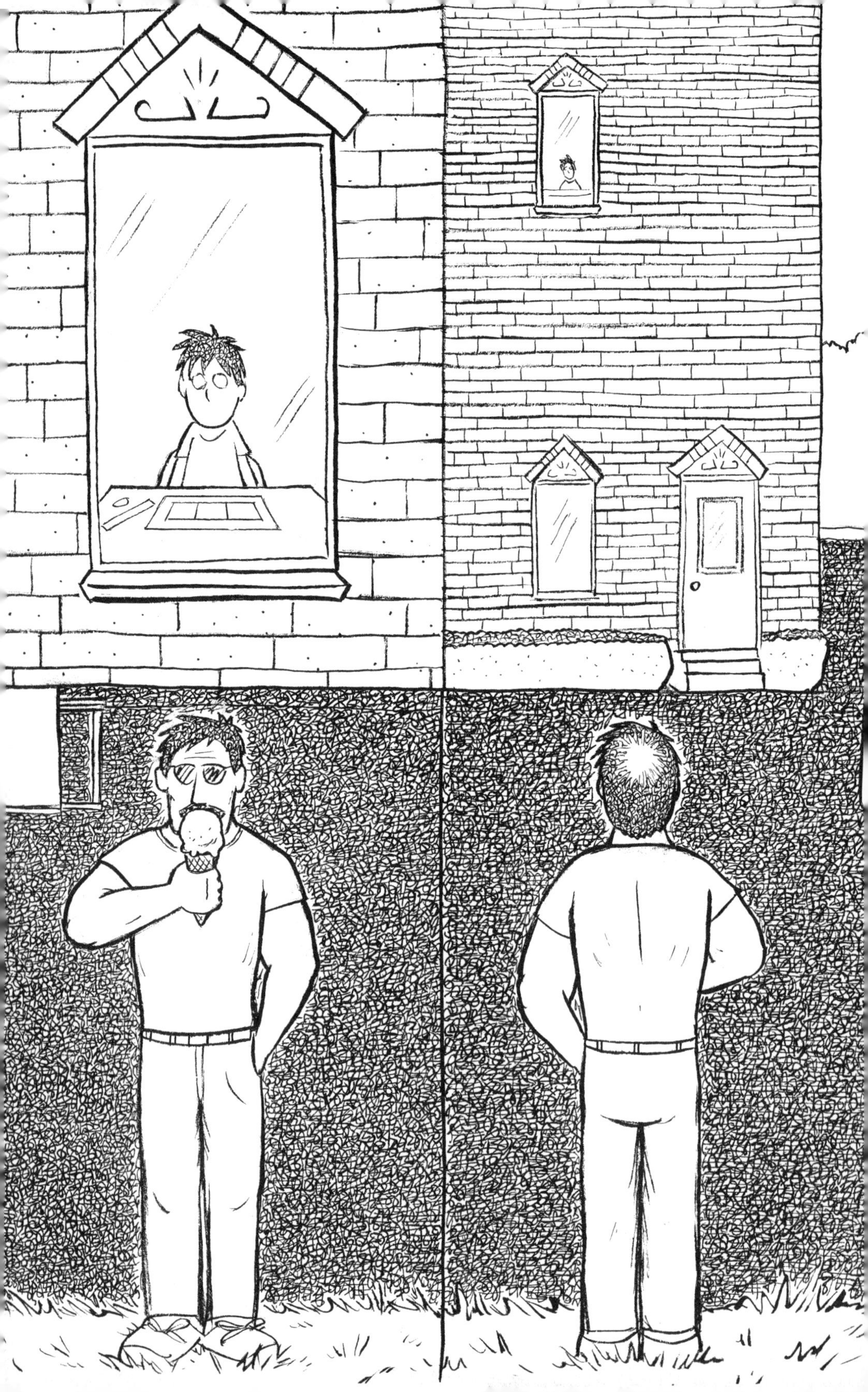

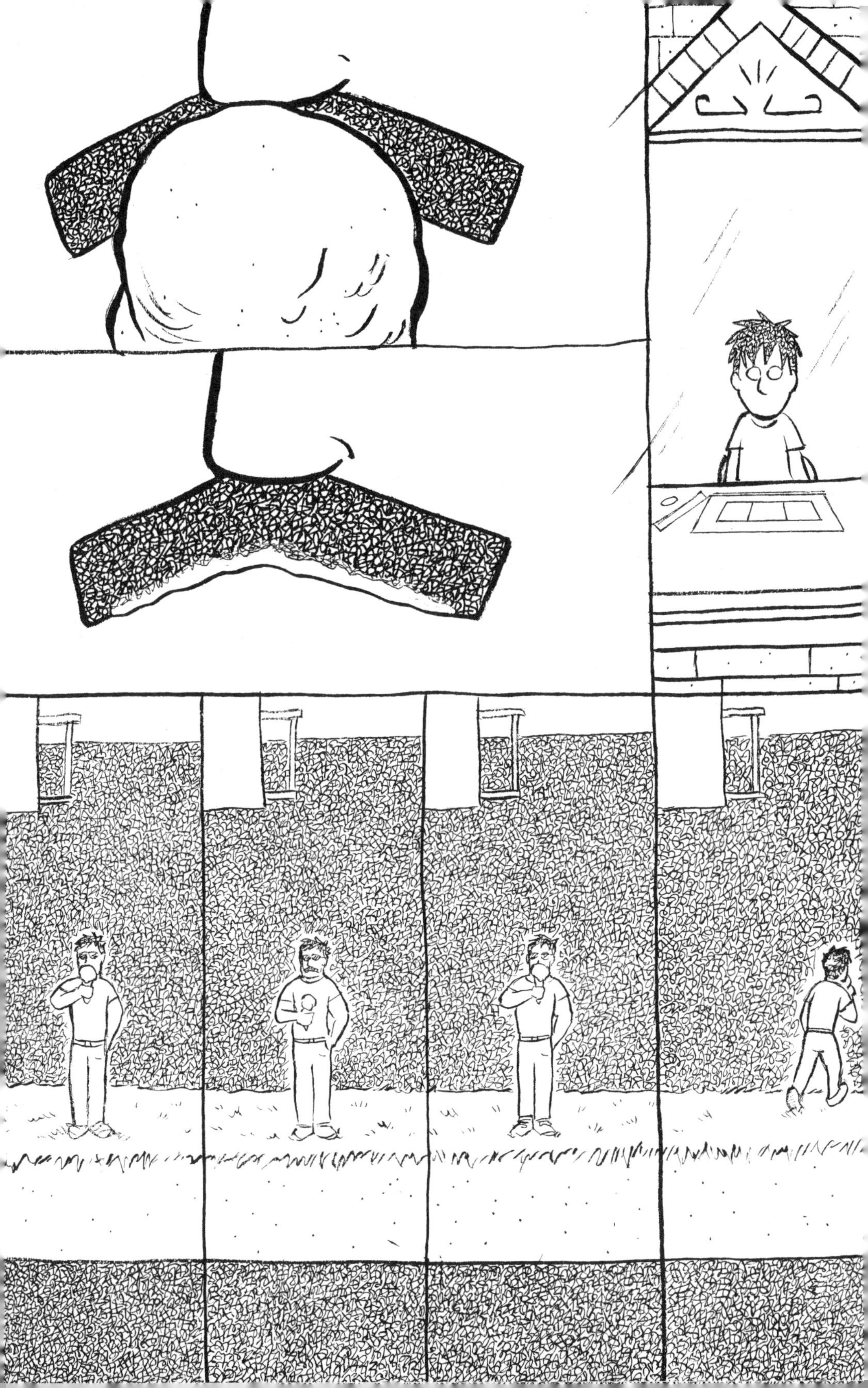

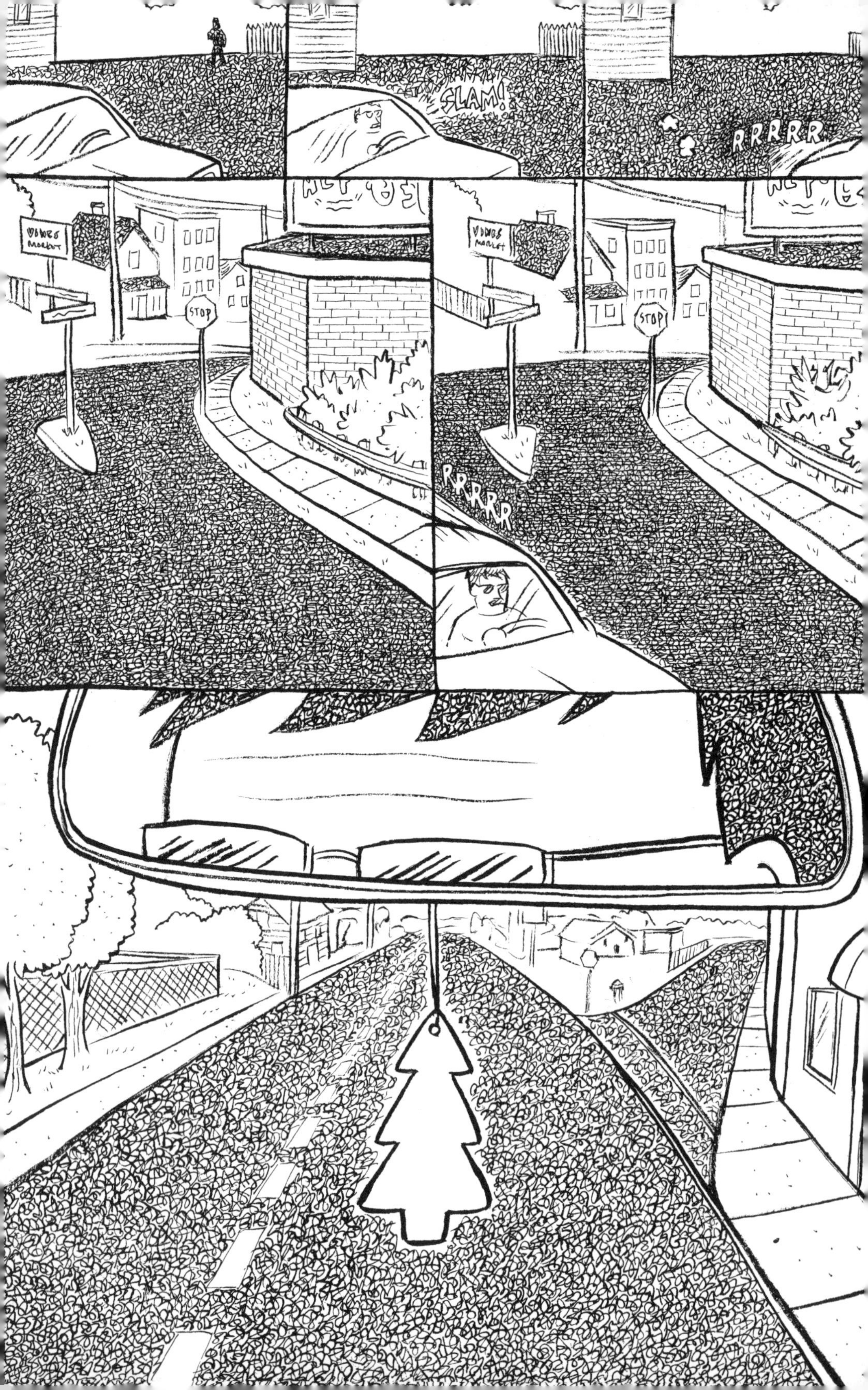
SLAM!
RRRRR
STOP
STOP
RRRRRR

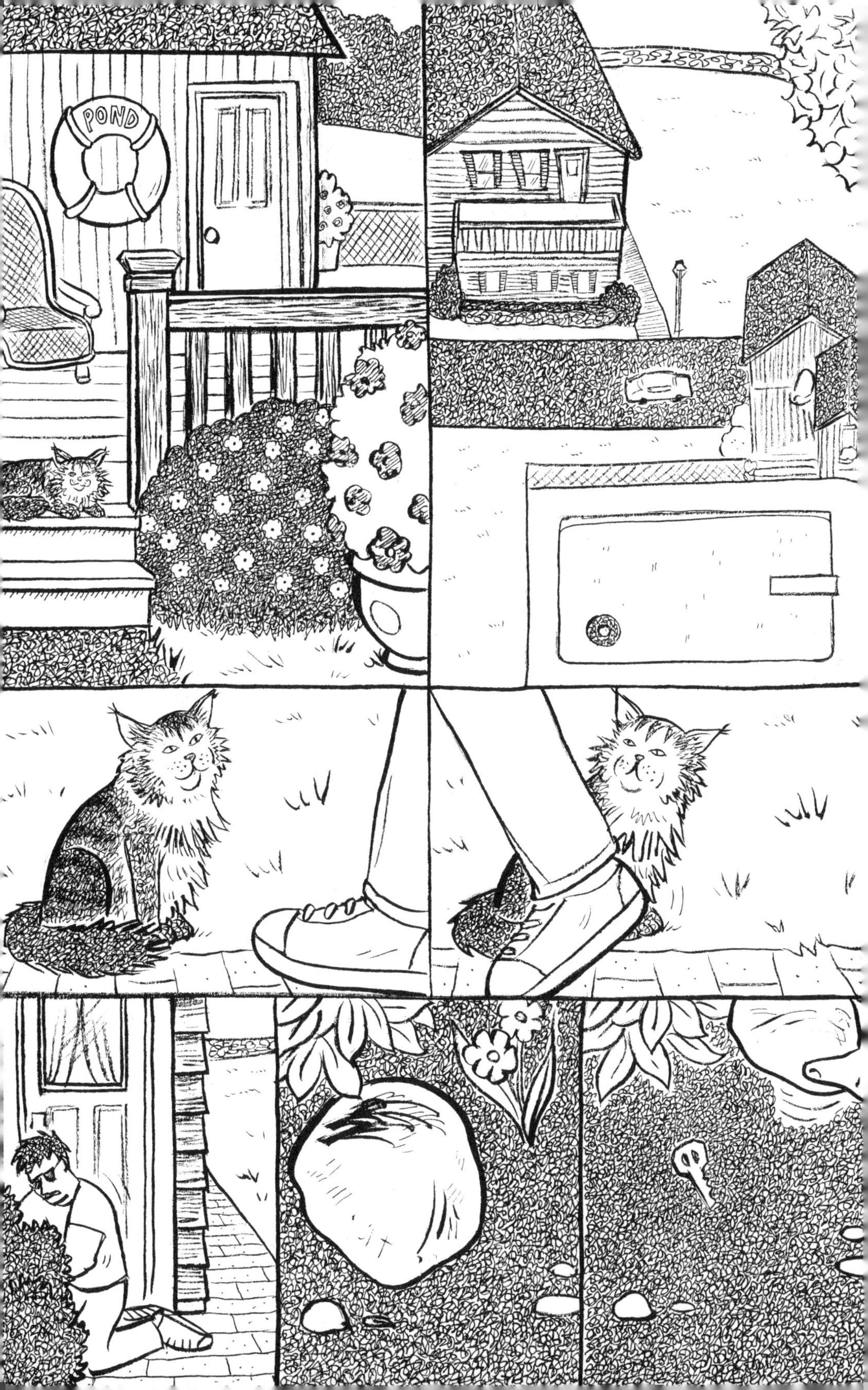
POND

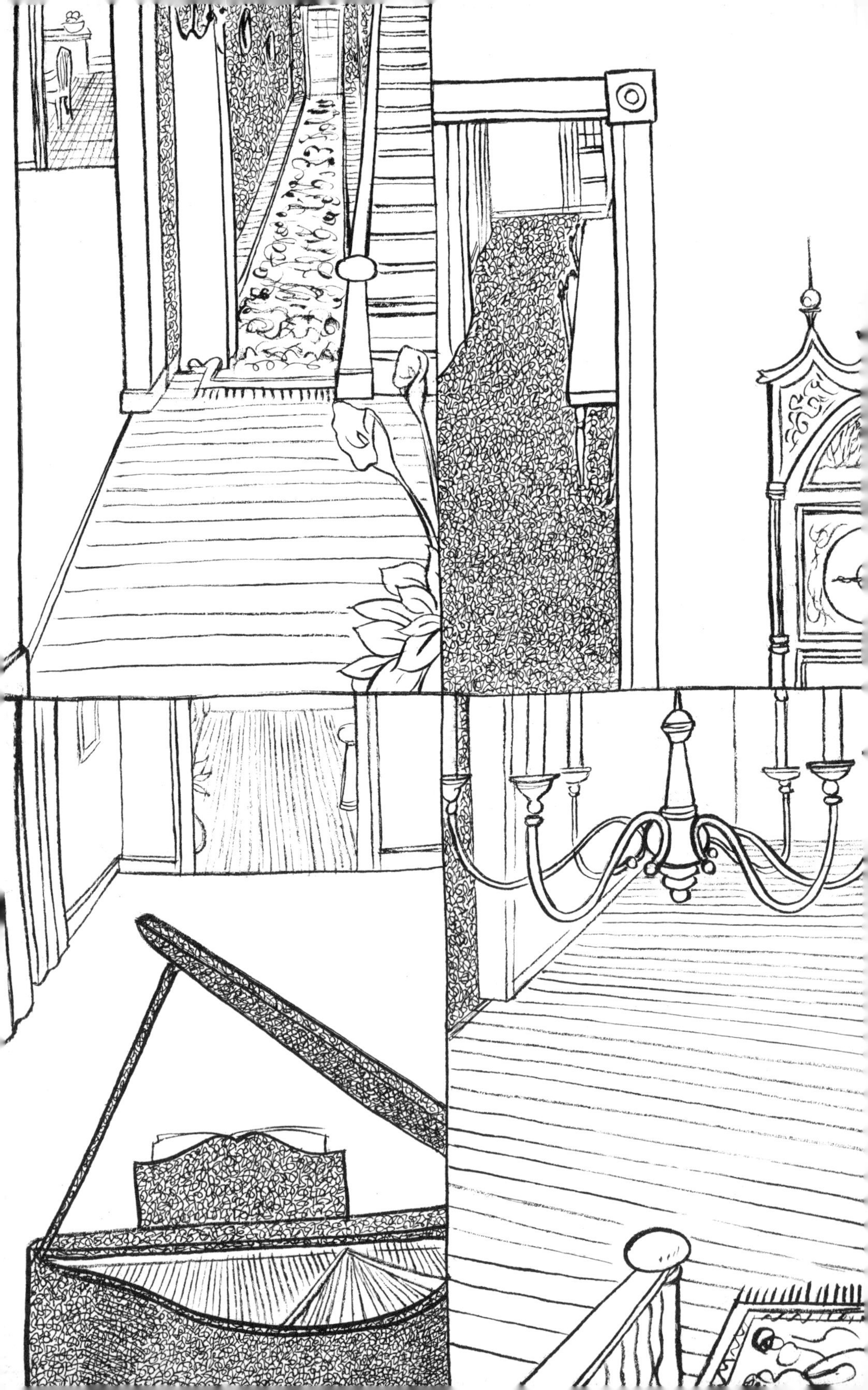

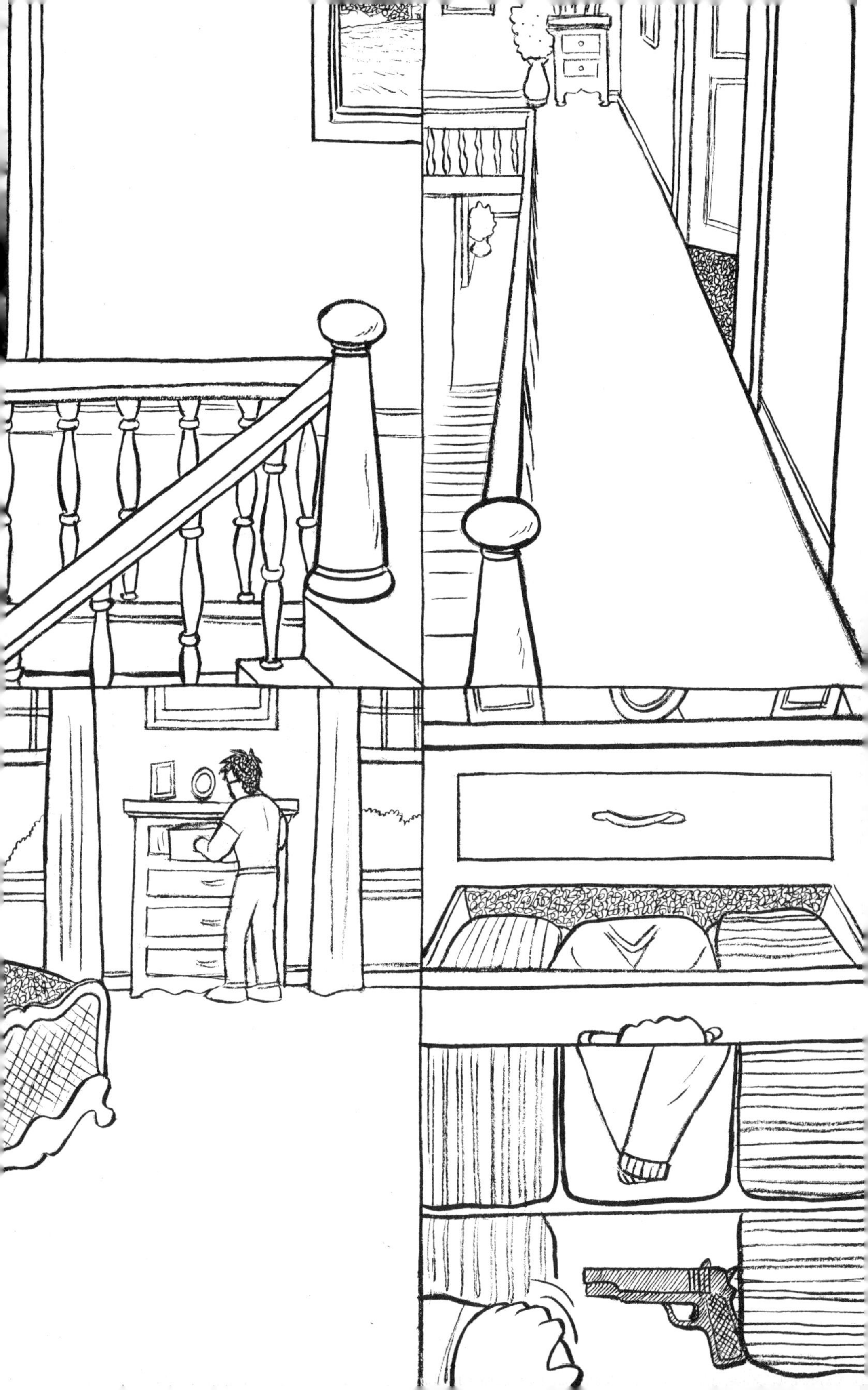

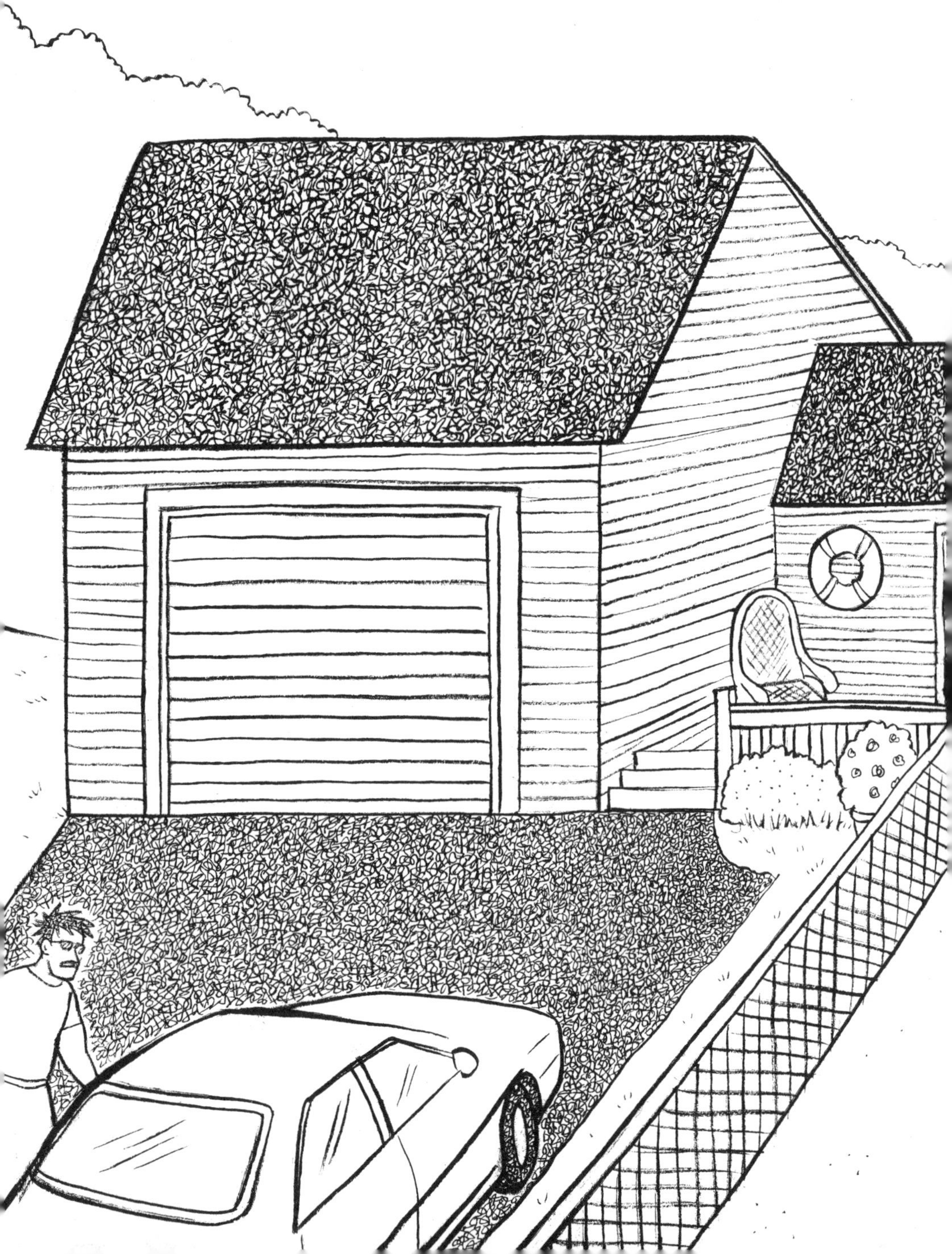

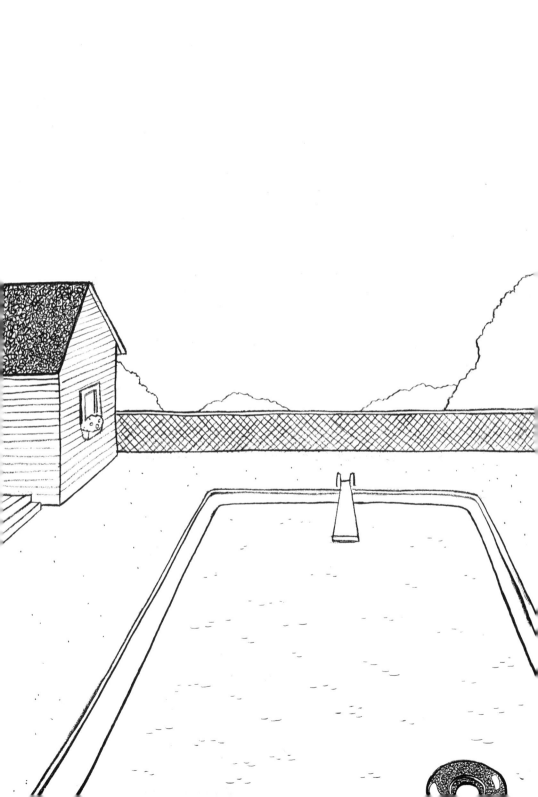

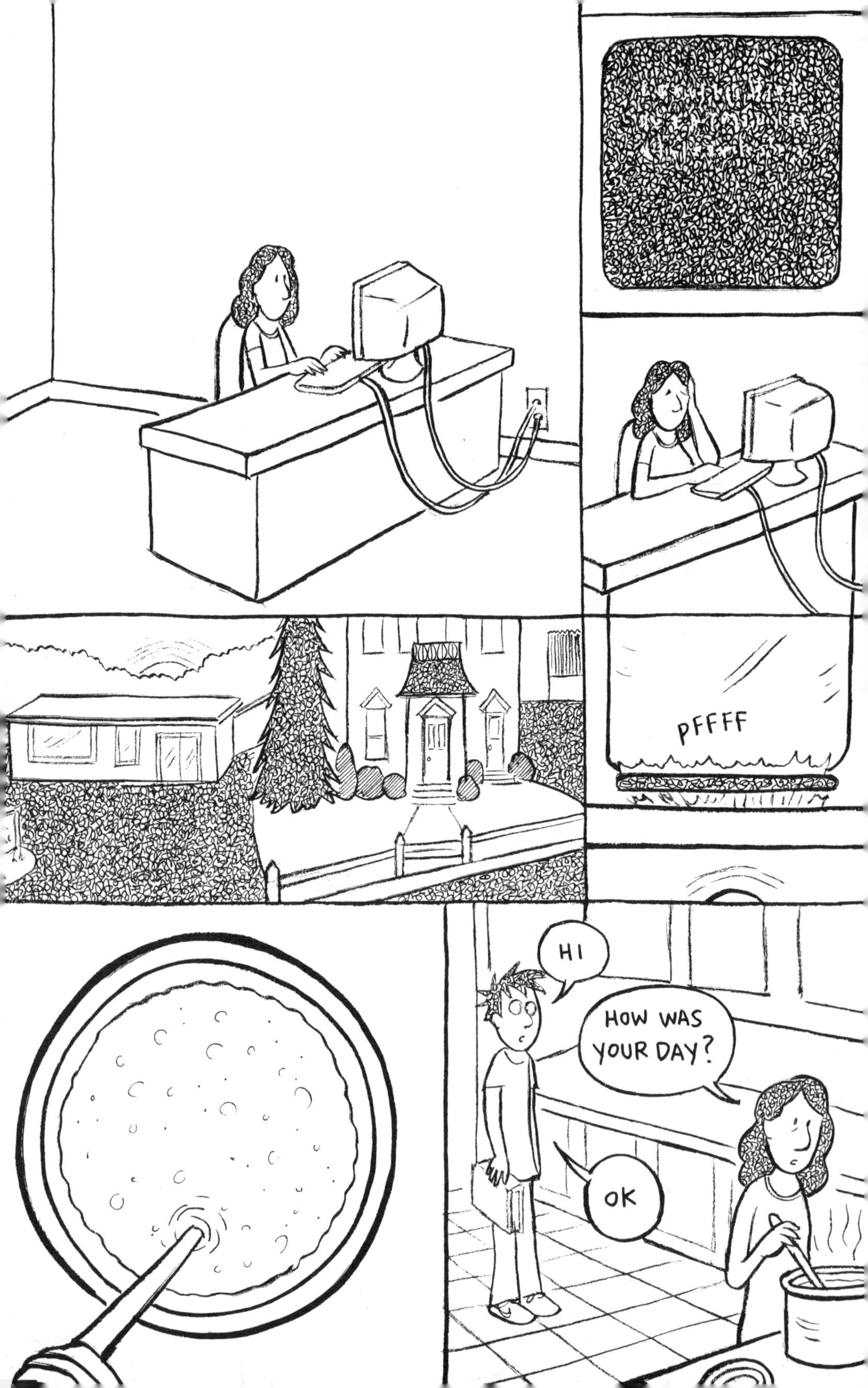
PFFFF
HI
HOW WAS YOUR DAY?
OK

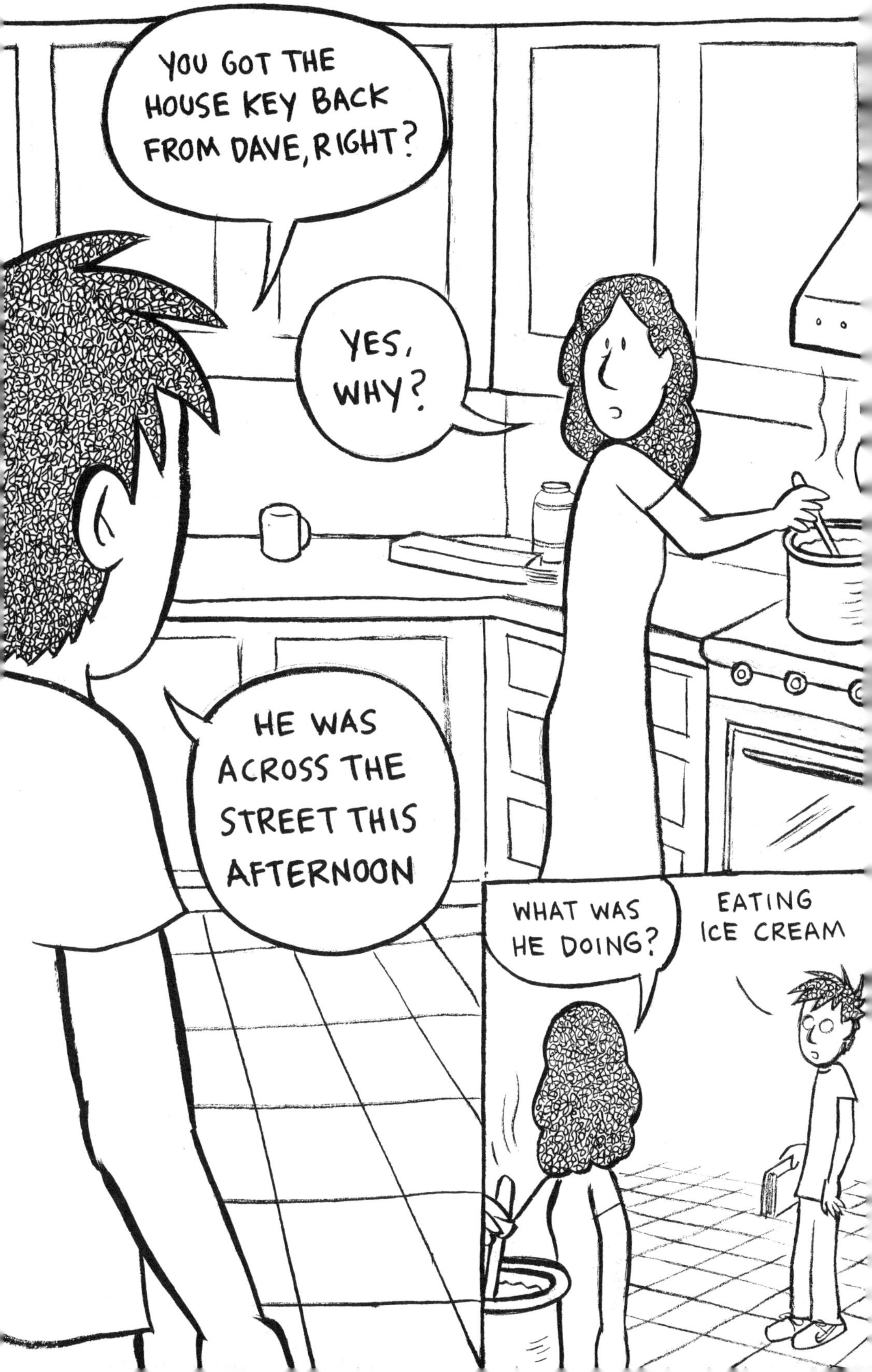
YOU GOT THE HOUSE KEY BACK FROM DAVE, RIGHT?
YES, WHY?
HE WAS ACROSS THE STREET THIS AFTERNOON
WHAT WAS HE DOING?
EATING ICE CREAM

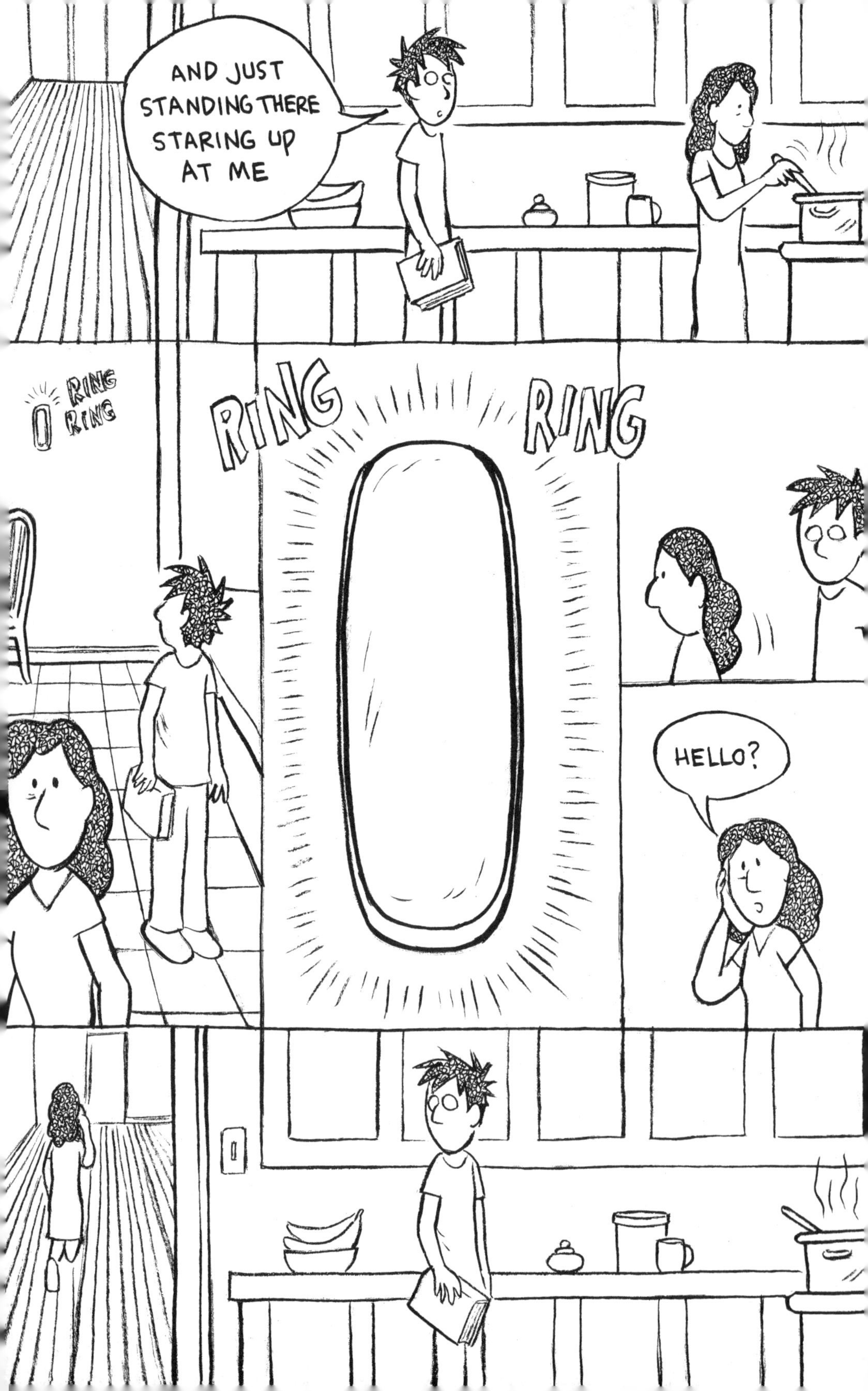
AND JUST STANDING THERE STARING UP AT ME
RING RING
RING
RING
HELLO?

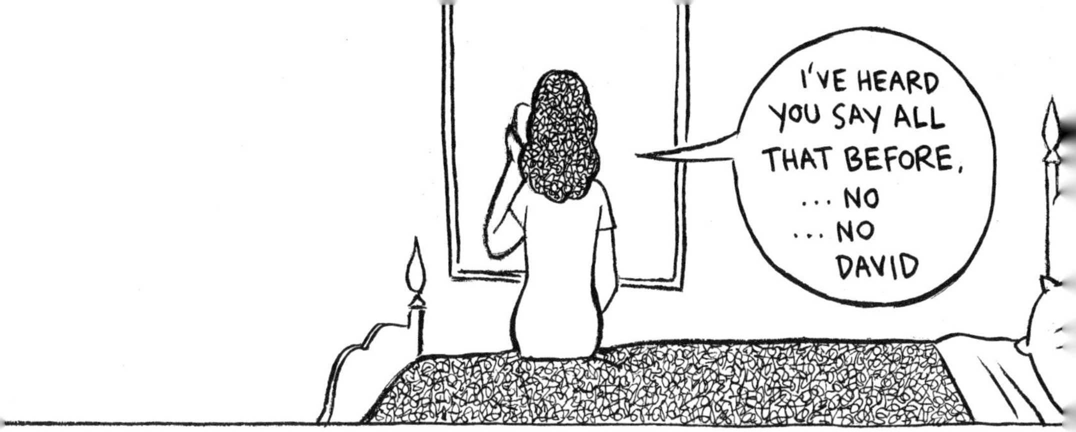
I'VE HEARD YOU SAY ALL THAT BEFORE, ... NO ... NO DAVID

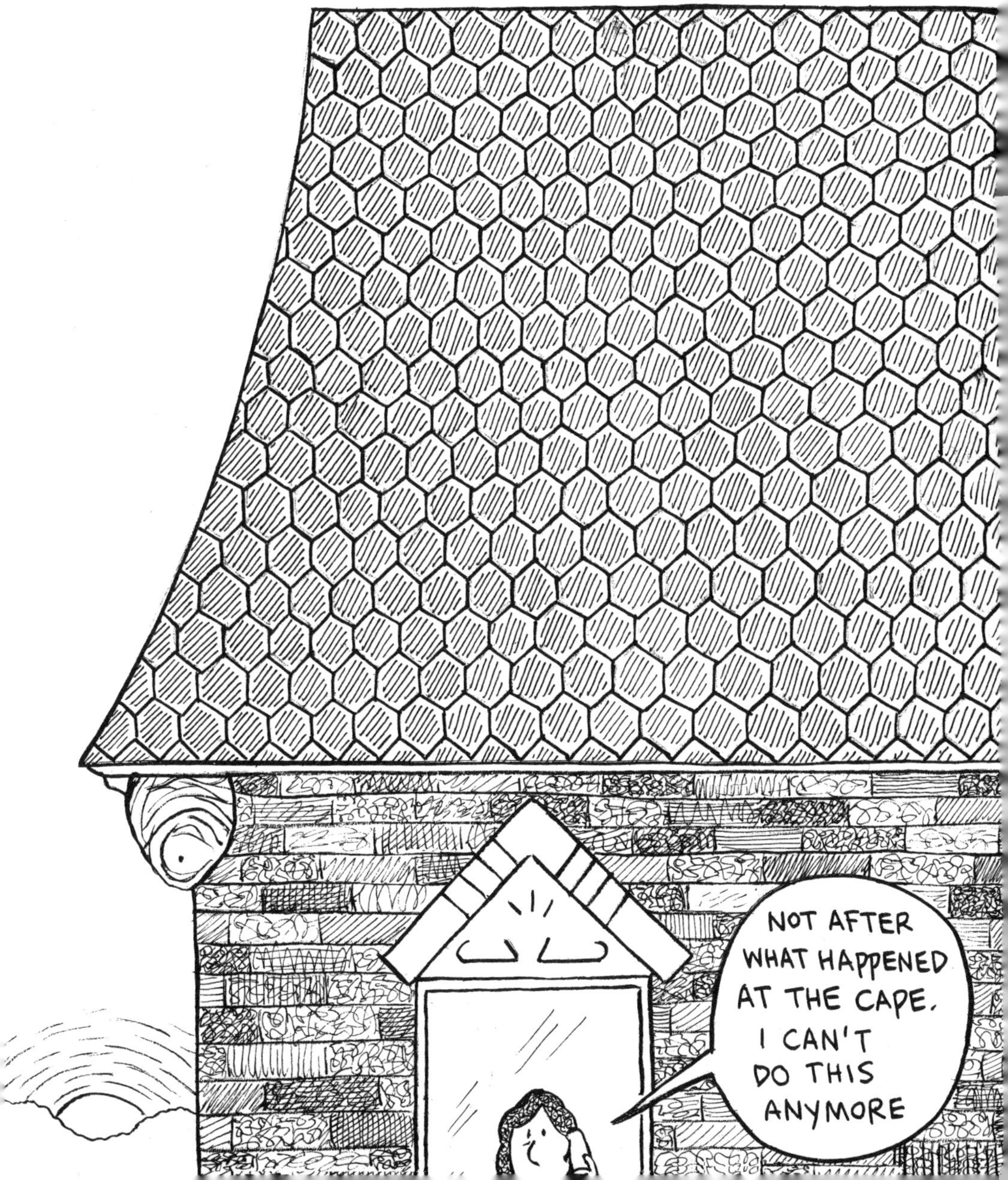
NOT AFTER WHAT HAPPENED AT THE CAPE. I CAN'T DO THIS ANYMORE

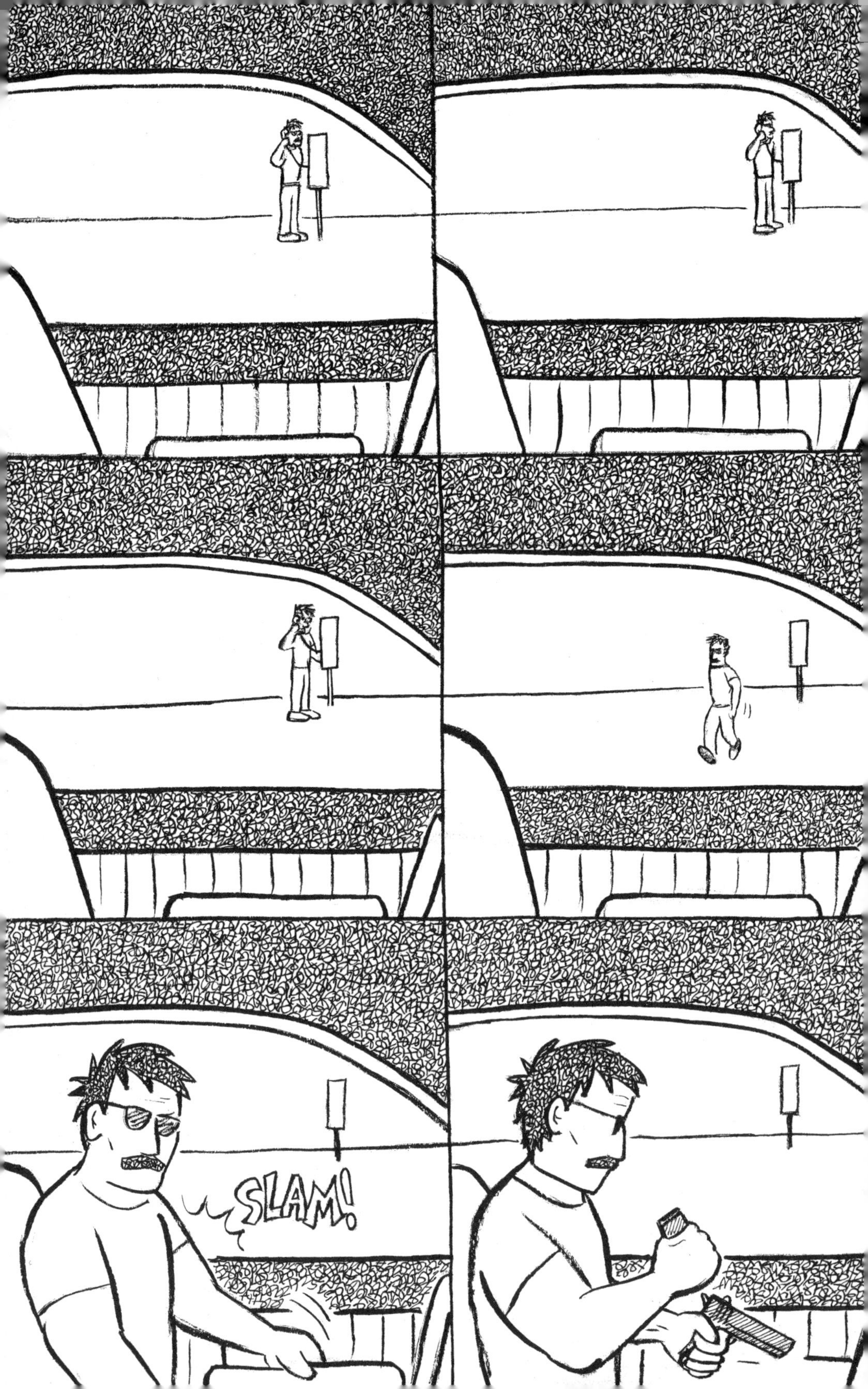
SLAM!

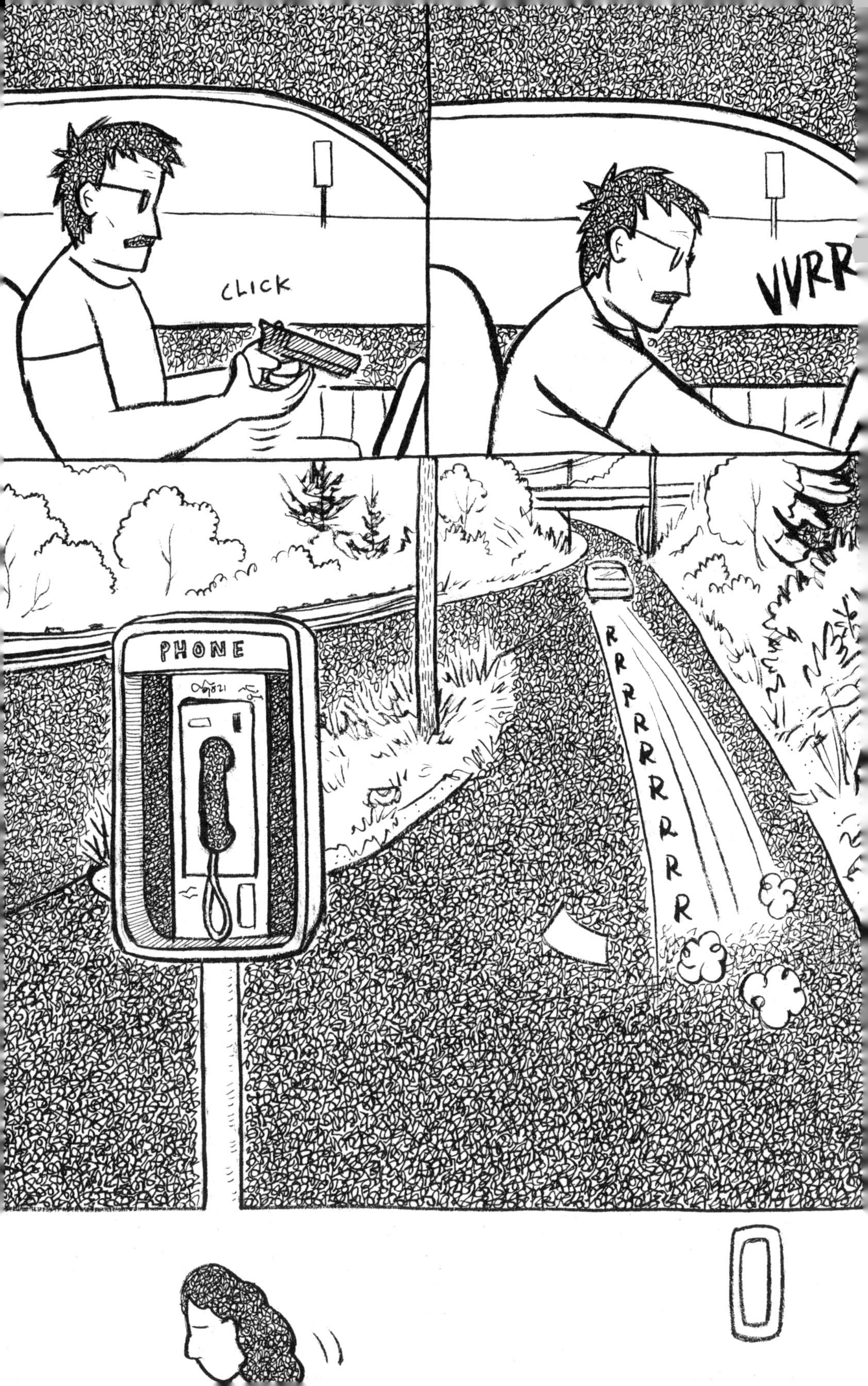
CLICK
VVRR
PHONE
RRRRRRRRR

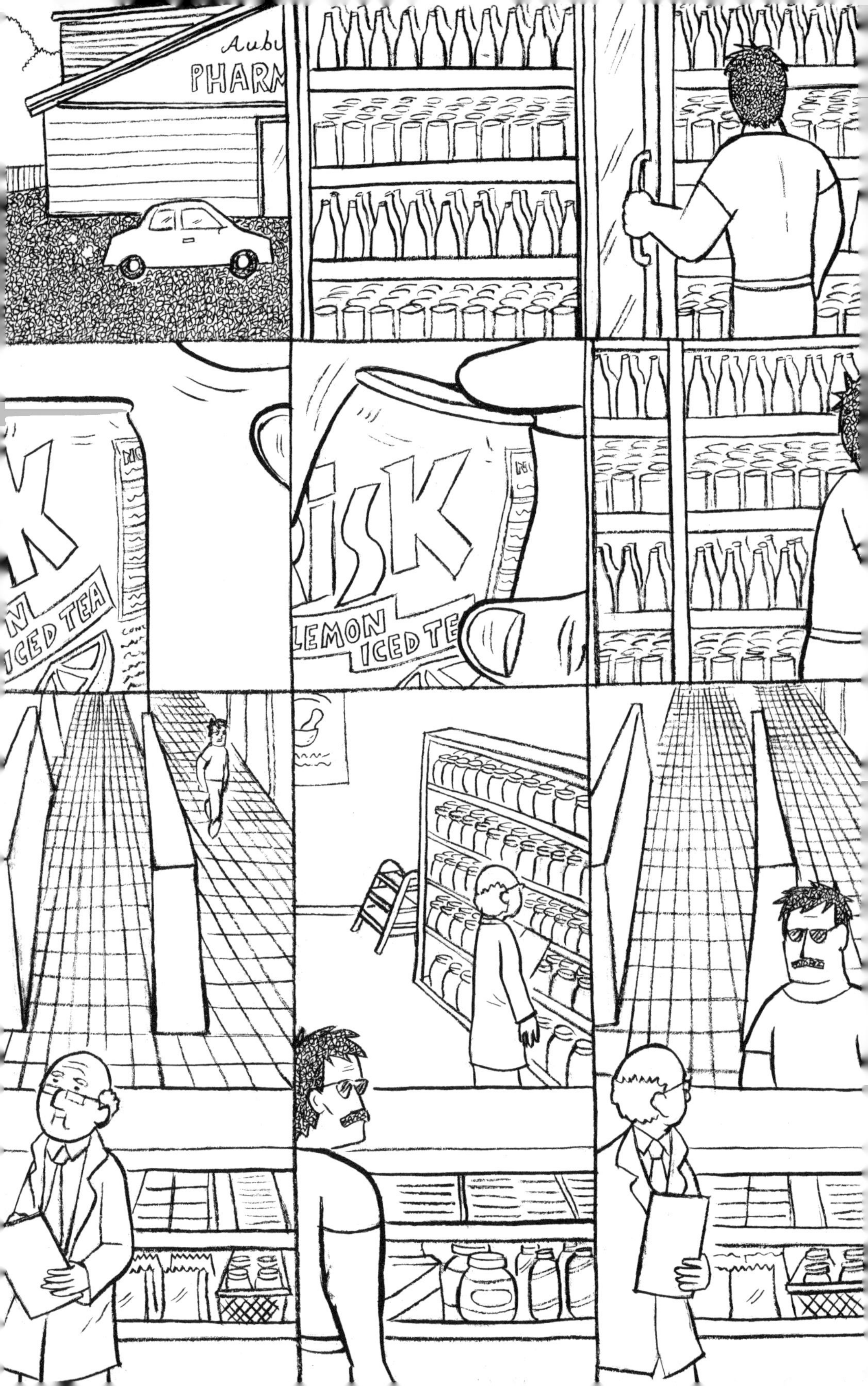
Aubu
PHARM
ICED TEA
LEMON
ICED TE

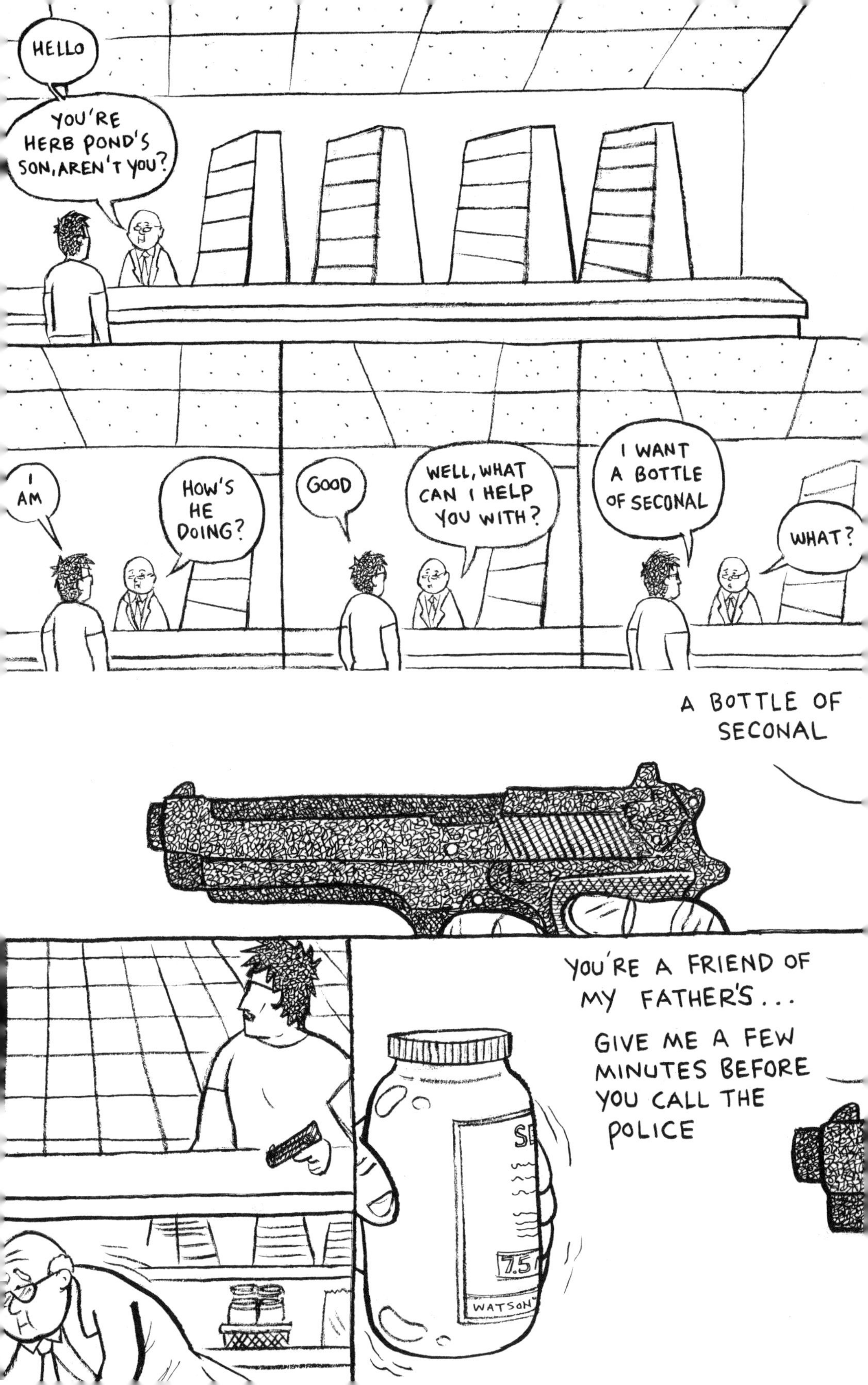
HELLO
YOU'RE HERB POND'S SON, AREN'T YOU?
I AM
HOW'S HE DOING?
GOOD
WELL, WHAT CAN I HELP YOU WITH?
I WANT A BOTTLE OF SECONAL
WHAT?
A BOTTLE OF SECONAL
YOU'RE A FRIEND OF MY FATHER'S...
GIVE ME A FEW MINUTES BEFORE YOU CALL THE POLICE
7.5
WATSON

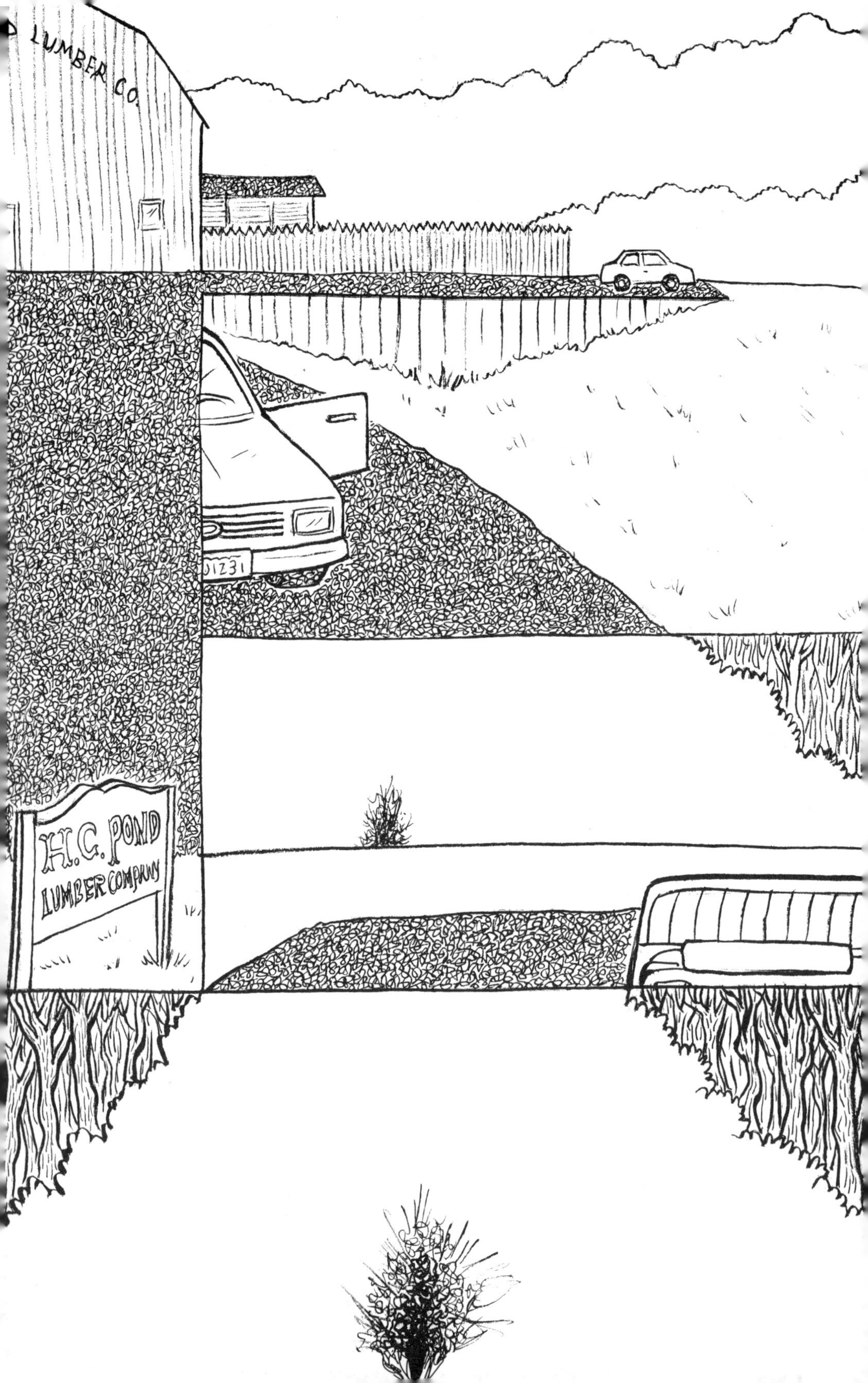
D LUMBER CO.
H.G. POND
LUMBER COMPANY

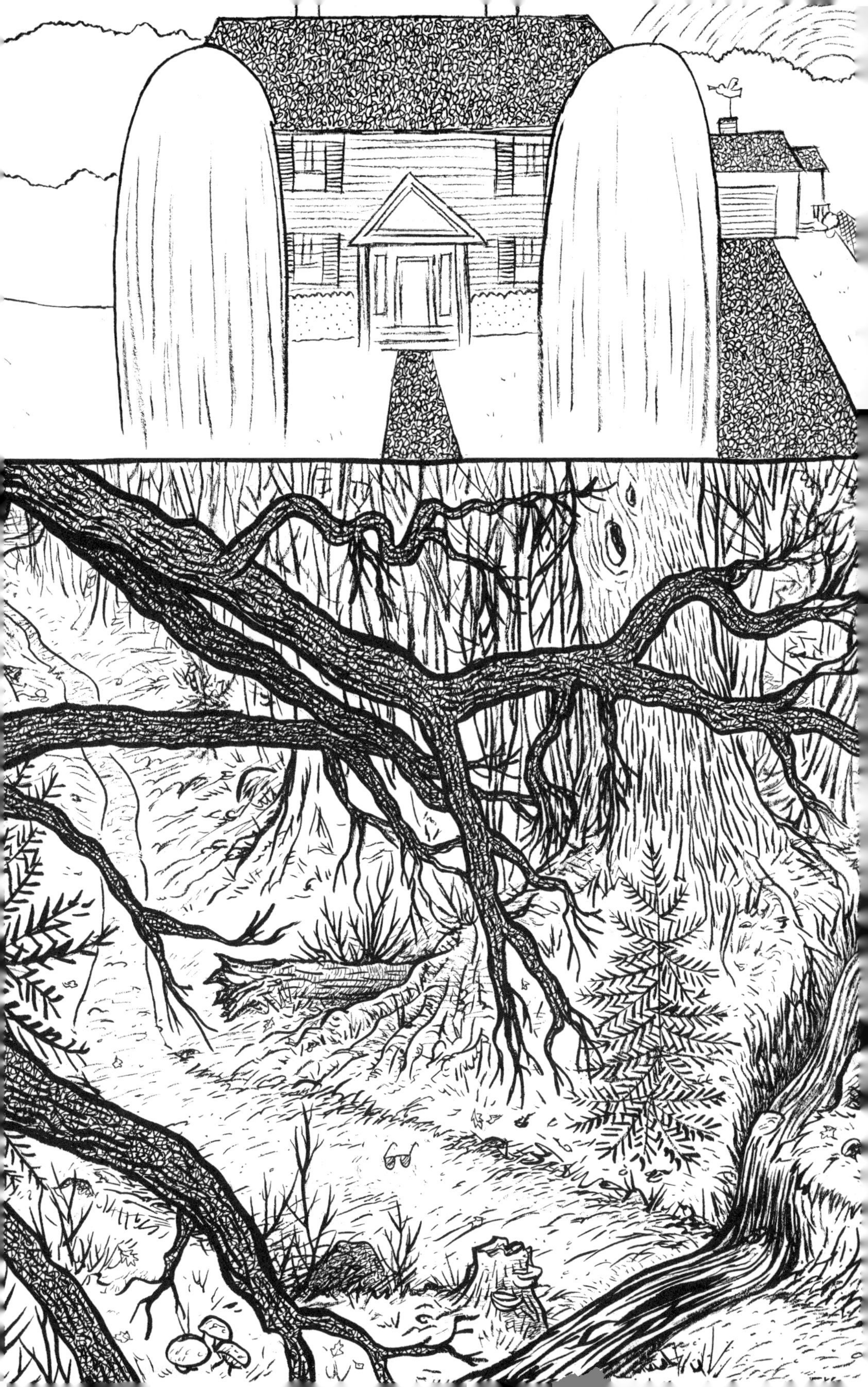

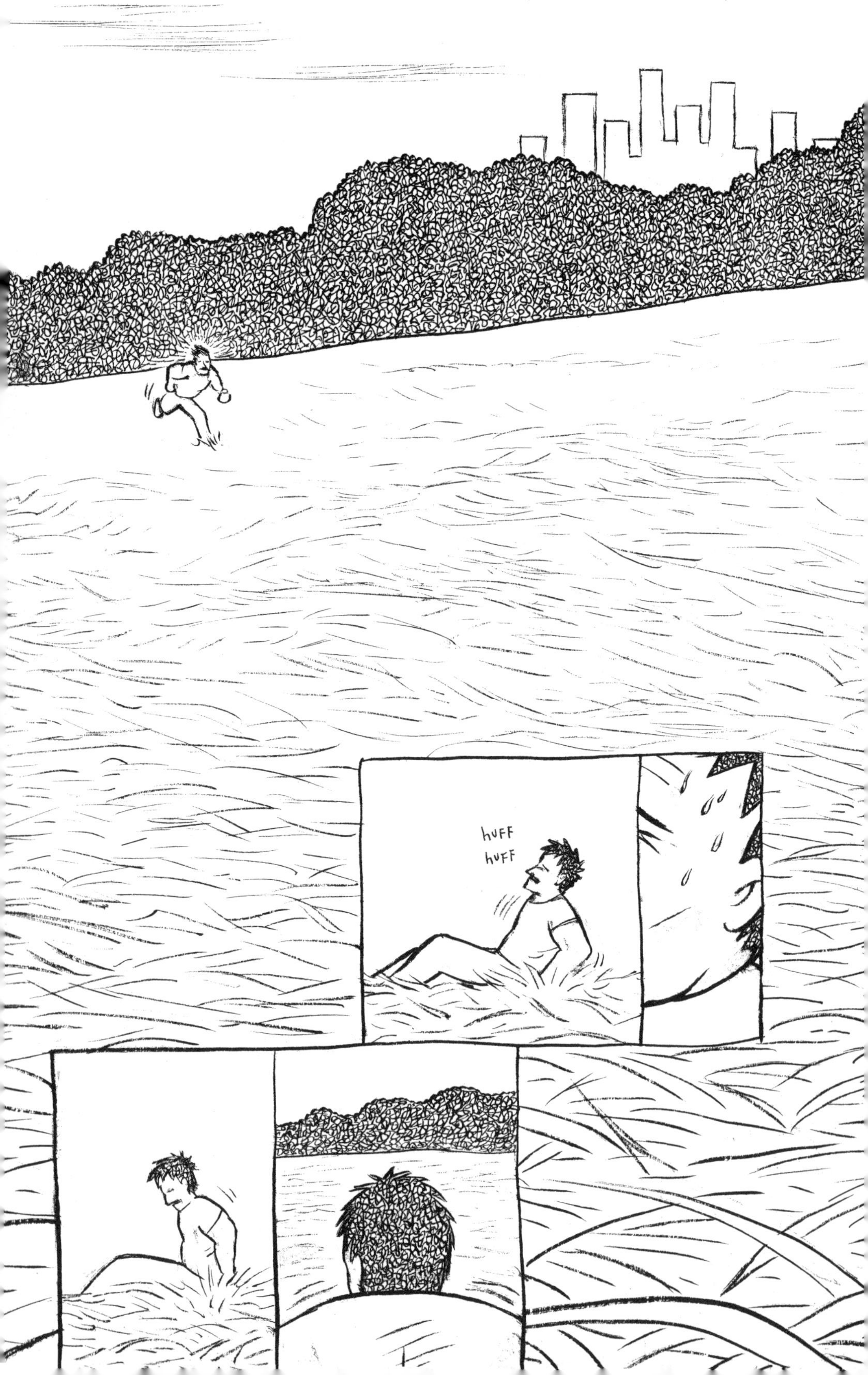
huff
huff

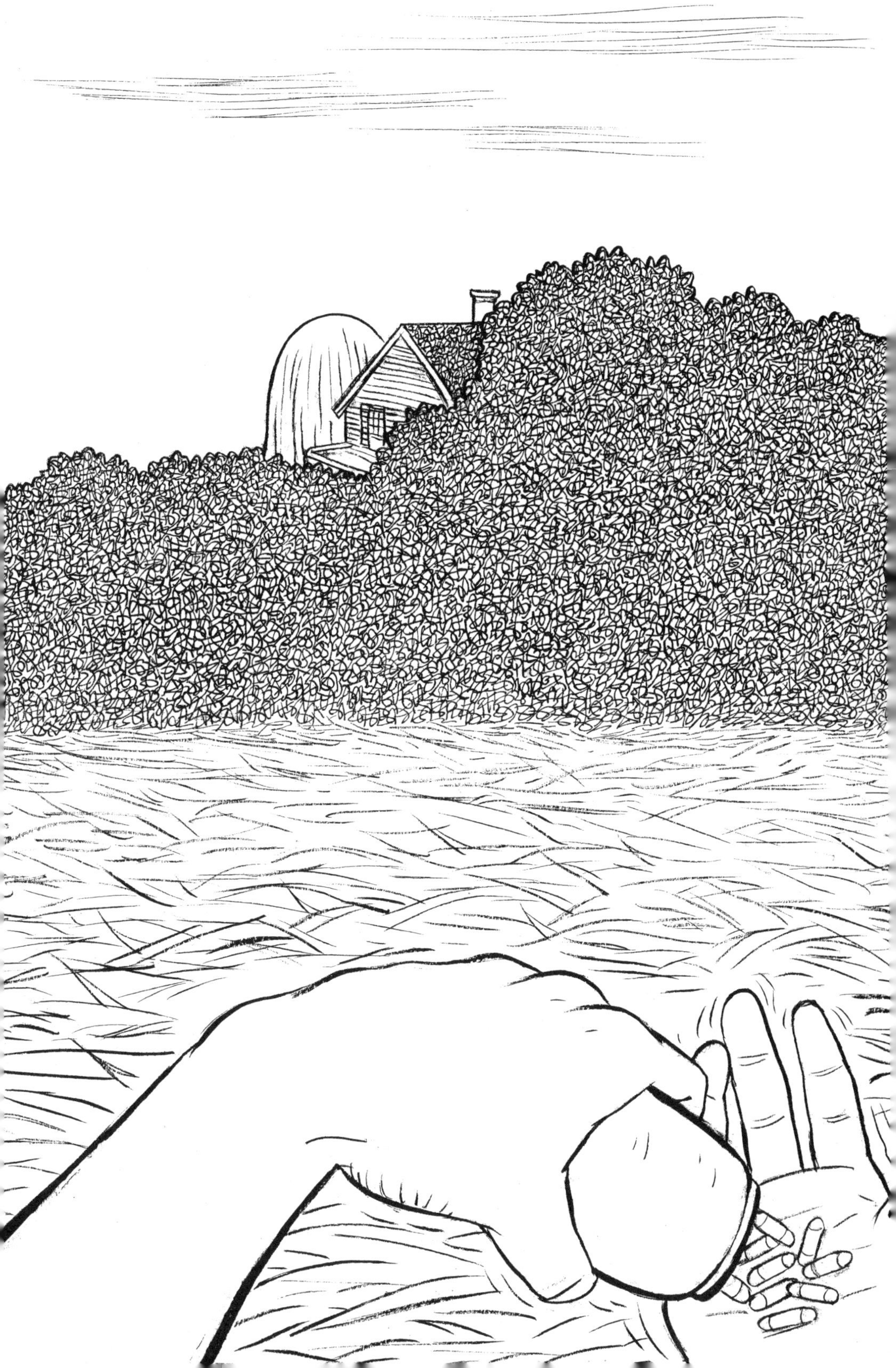

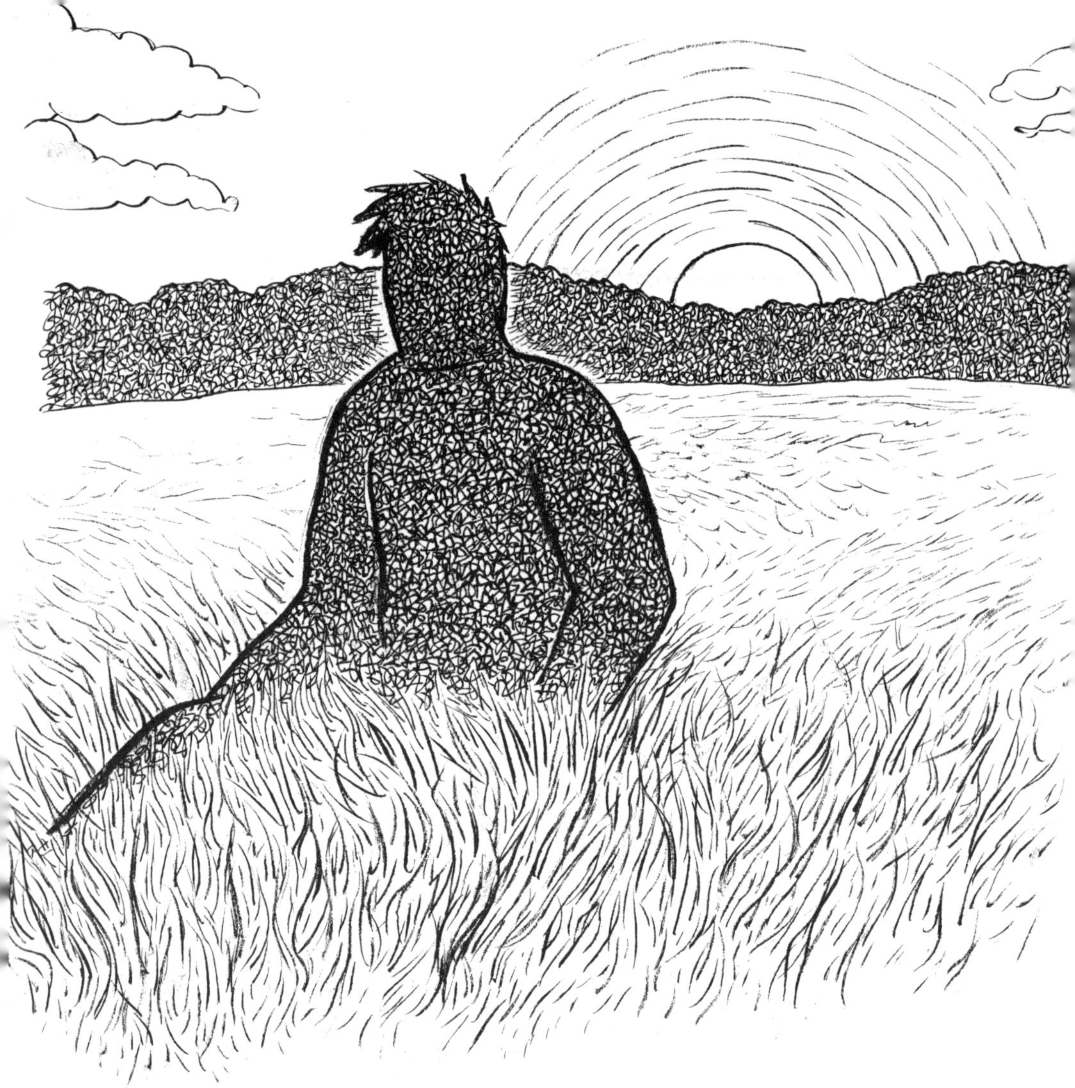

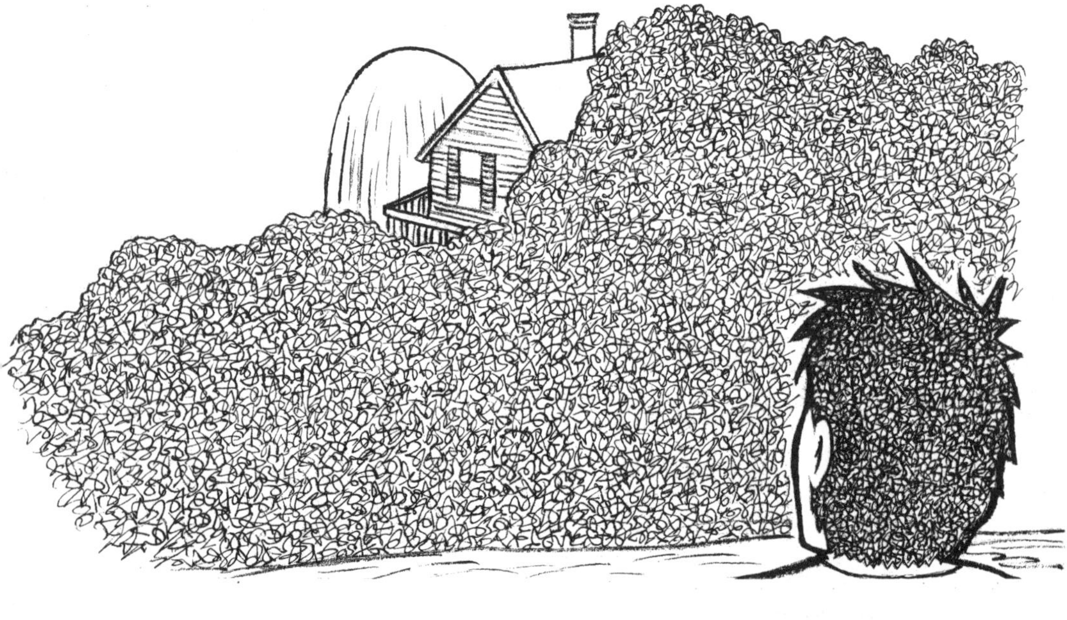

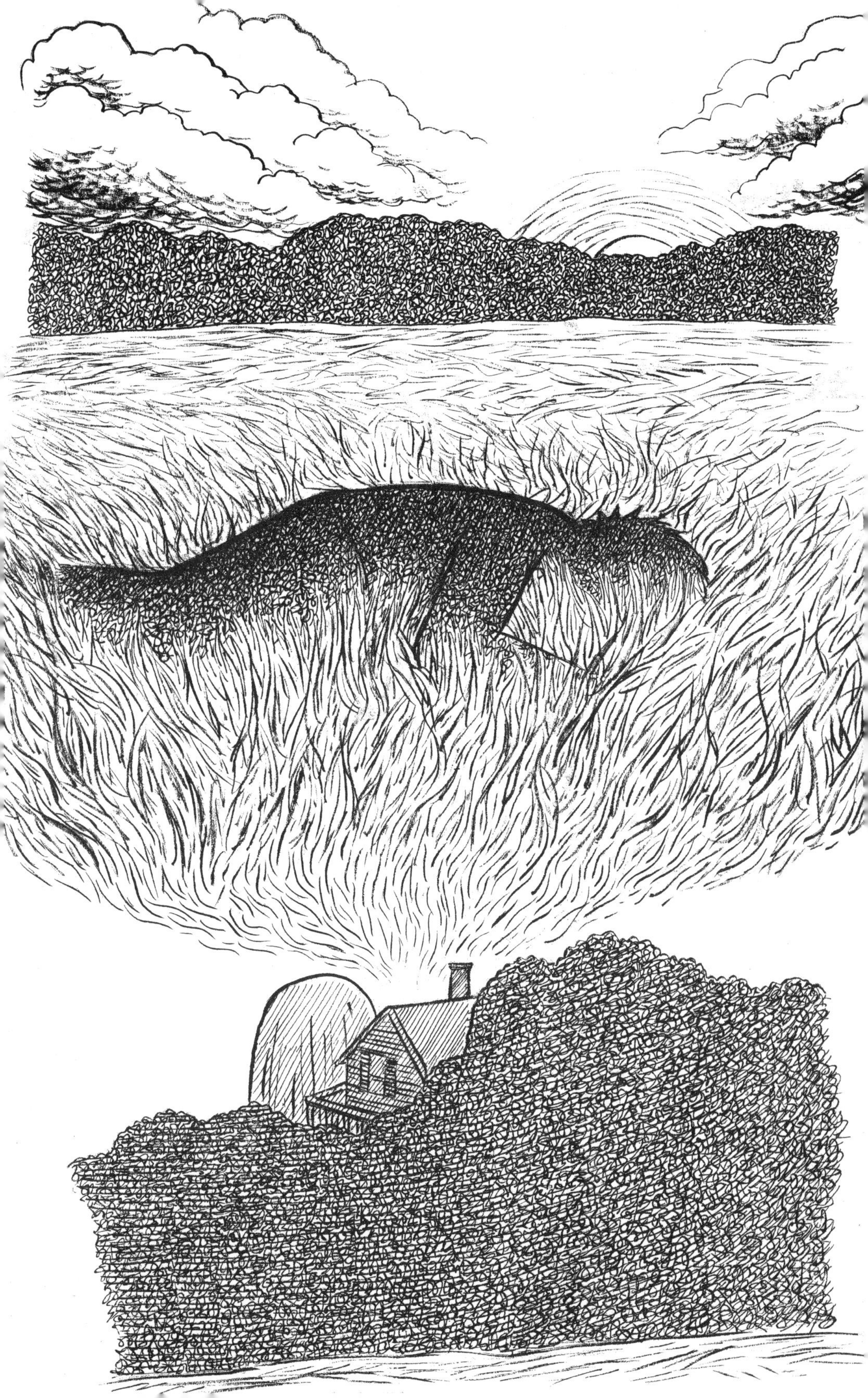

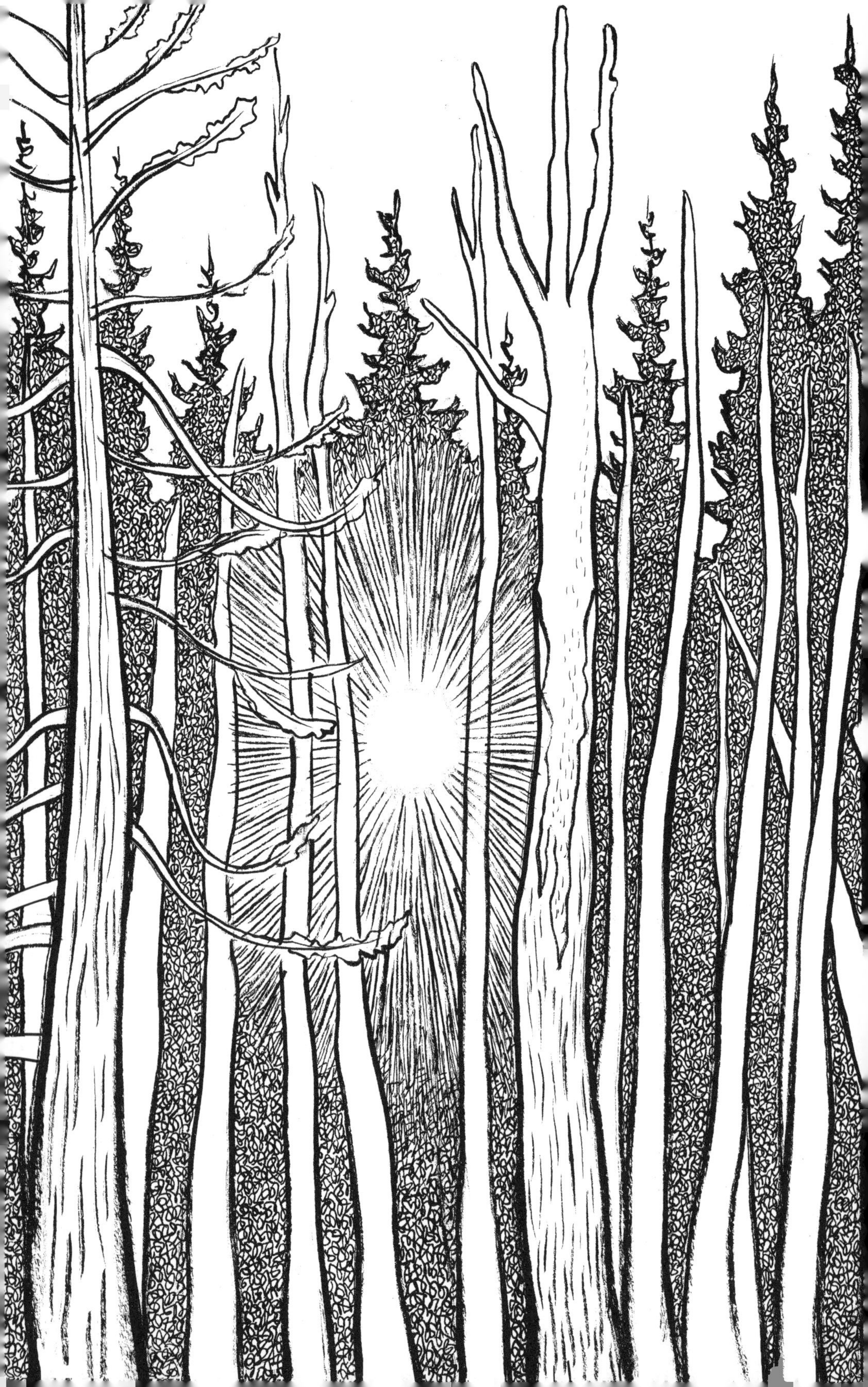

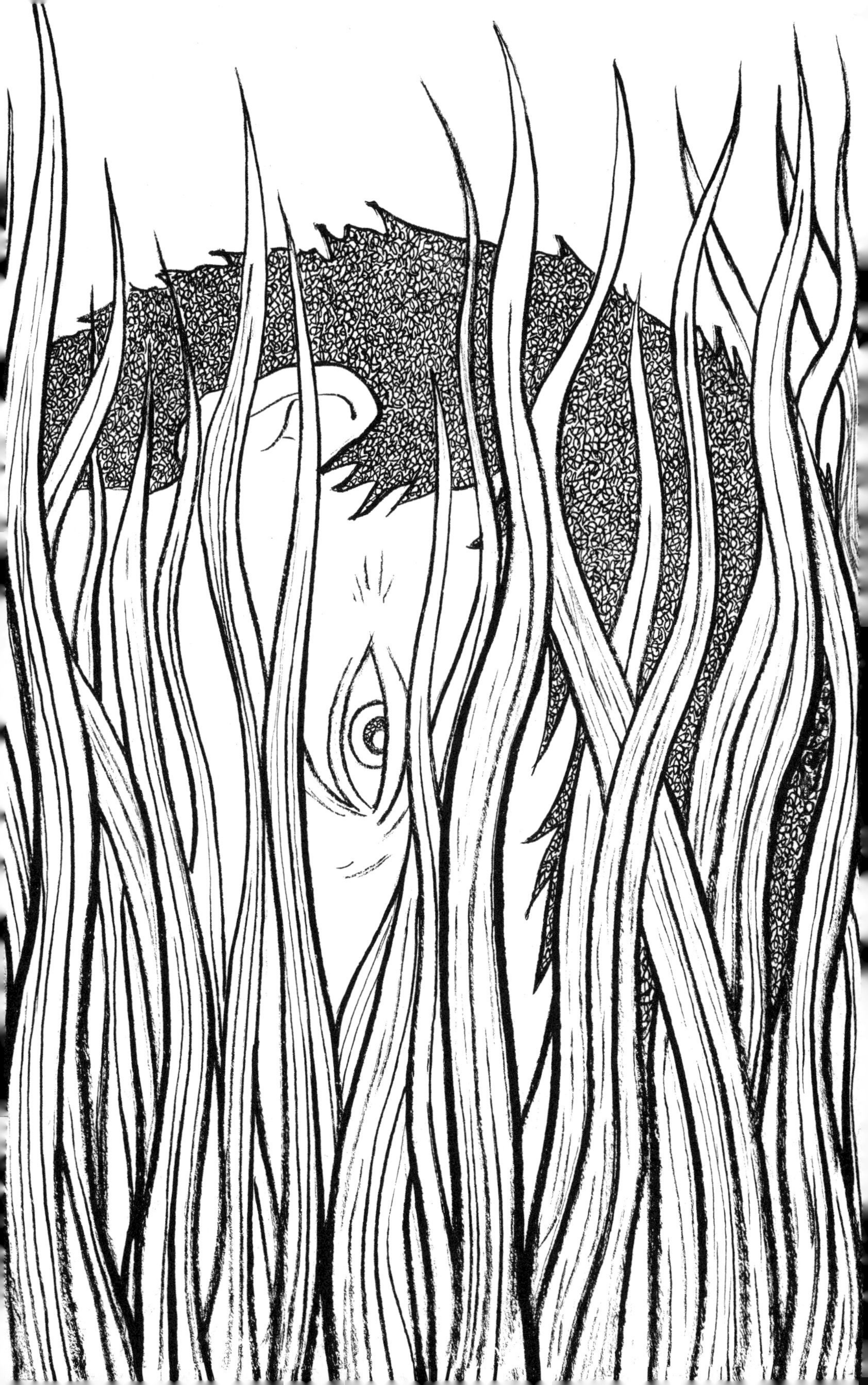

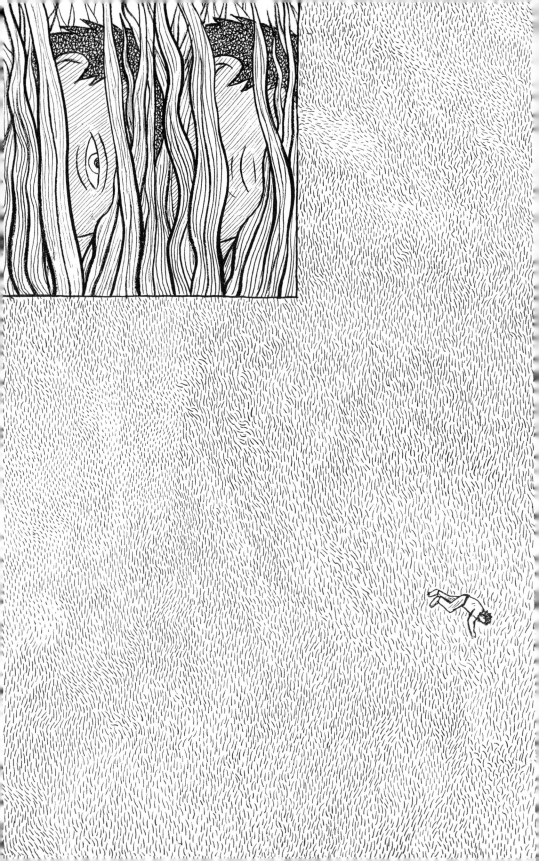

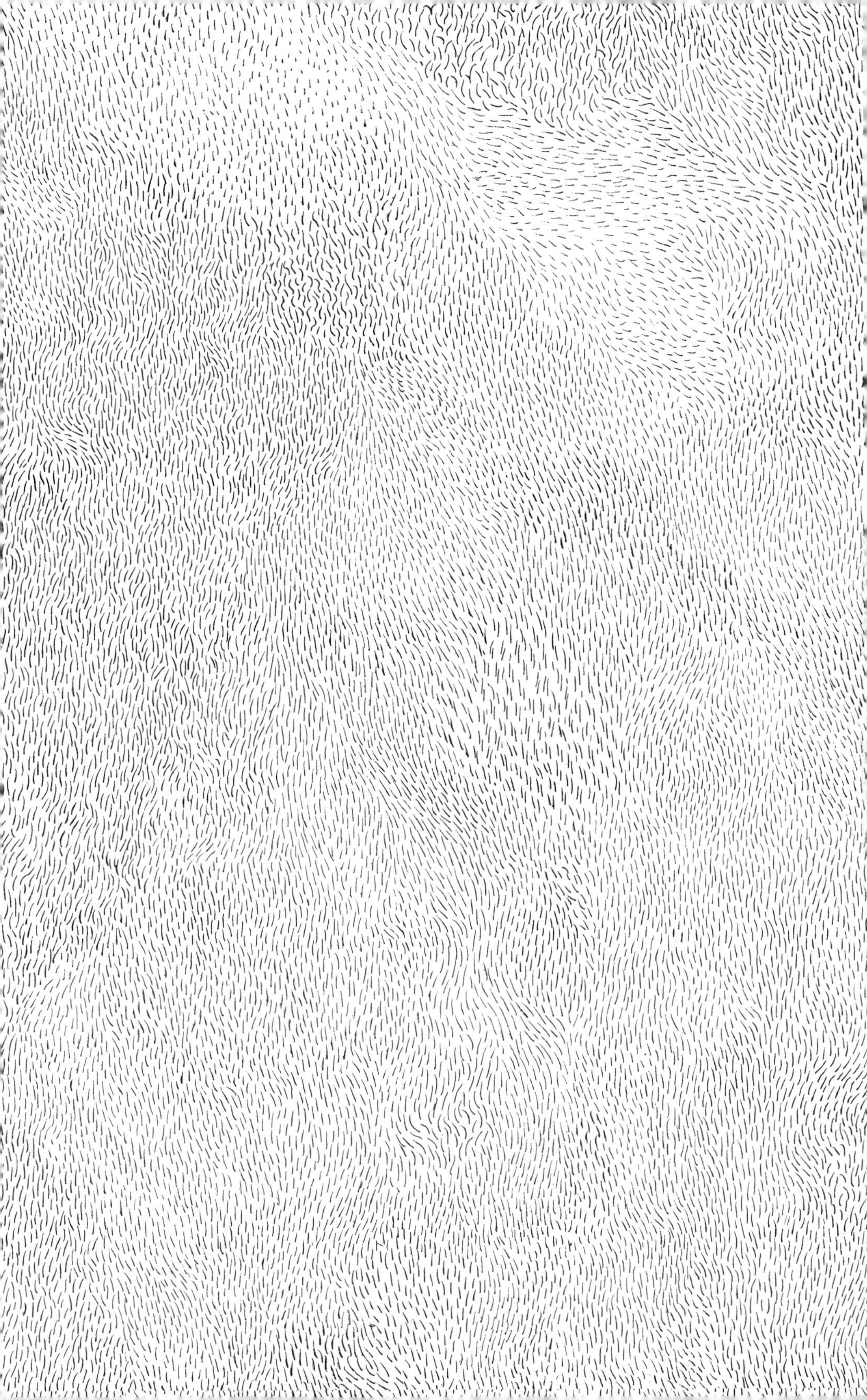

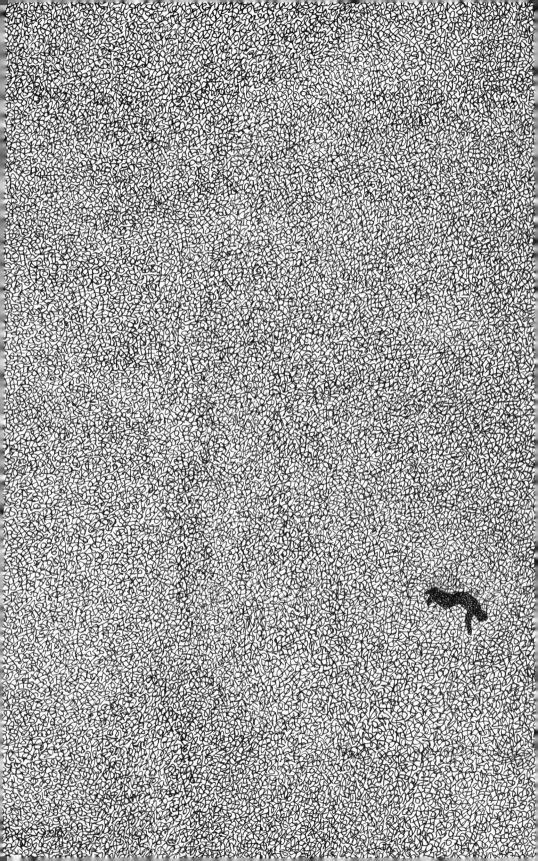

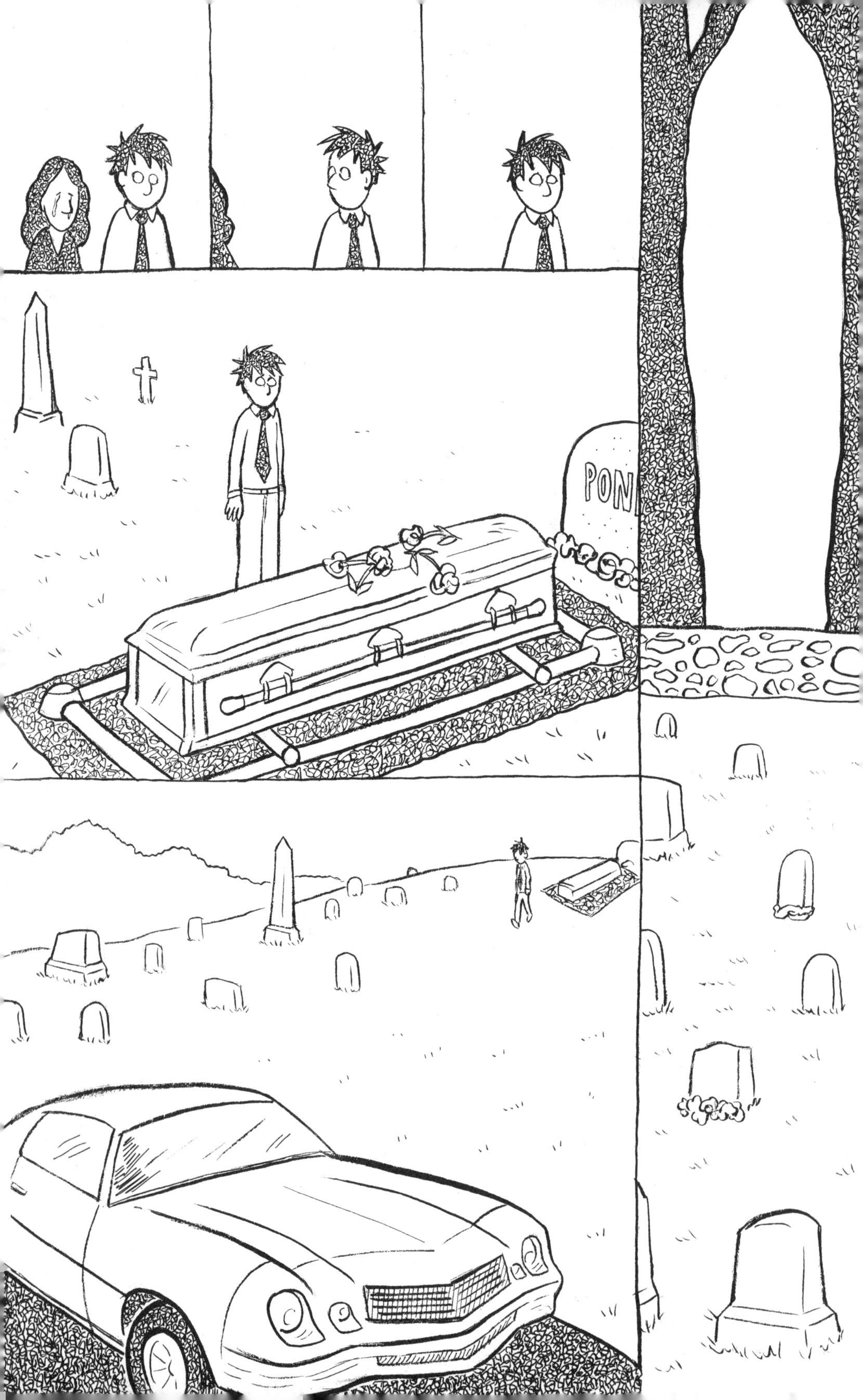
PON

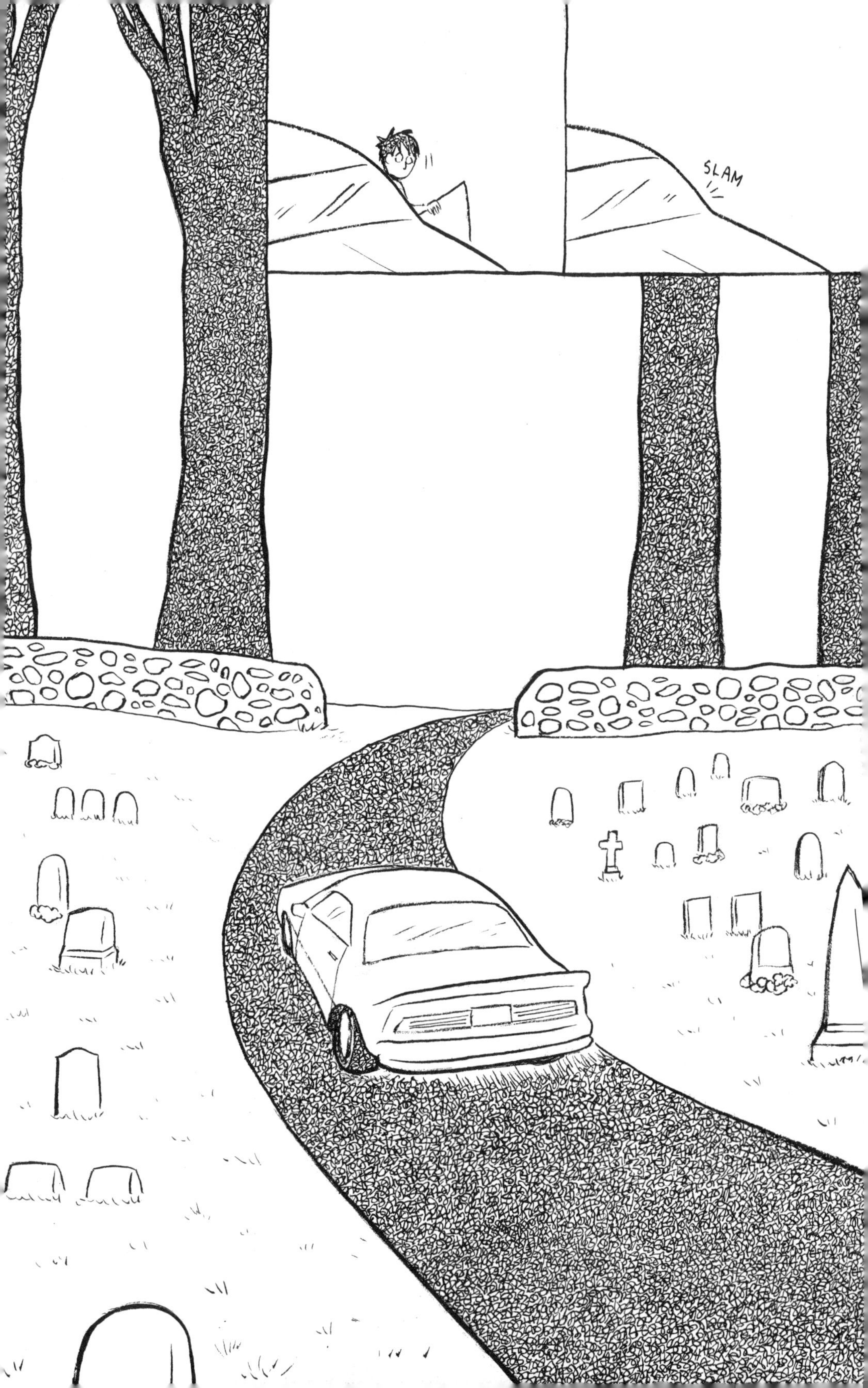
SLAM

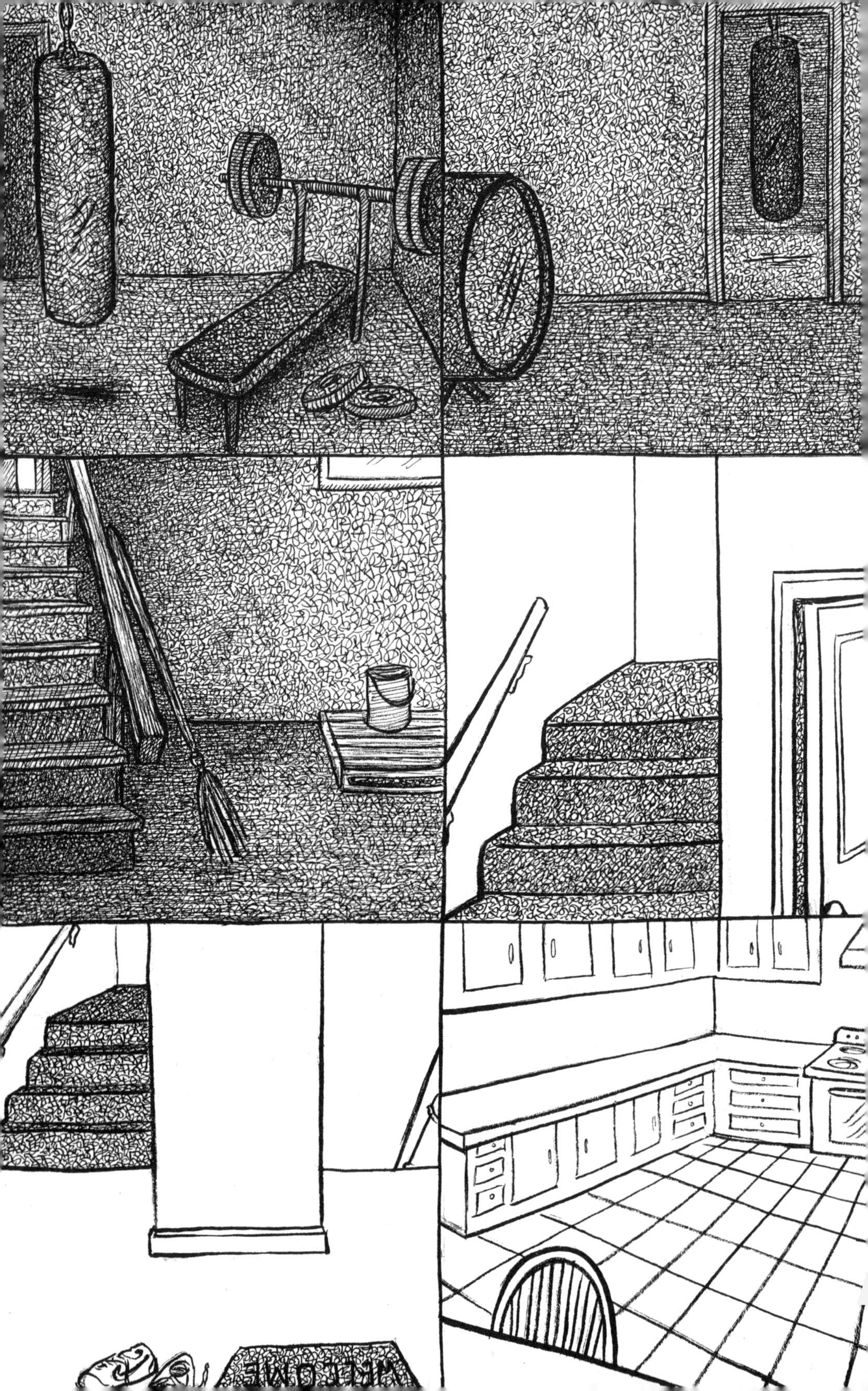
WELCOME

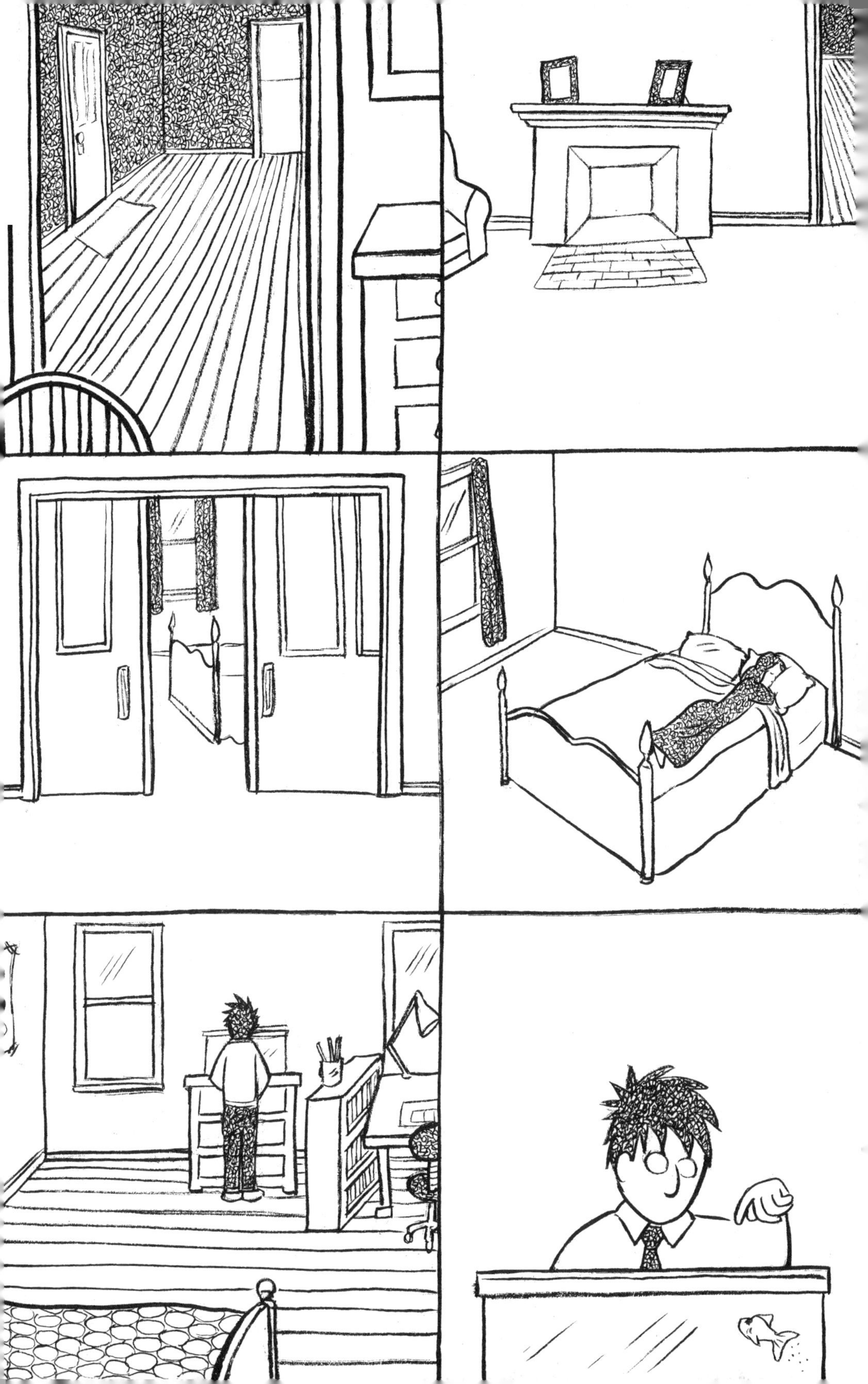

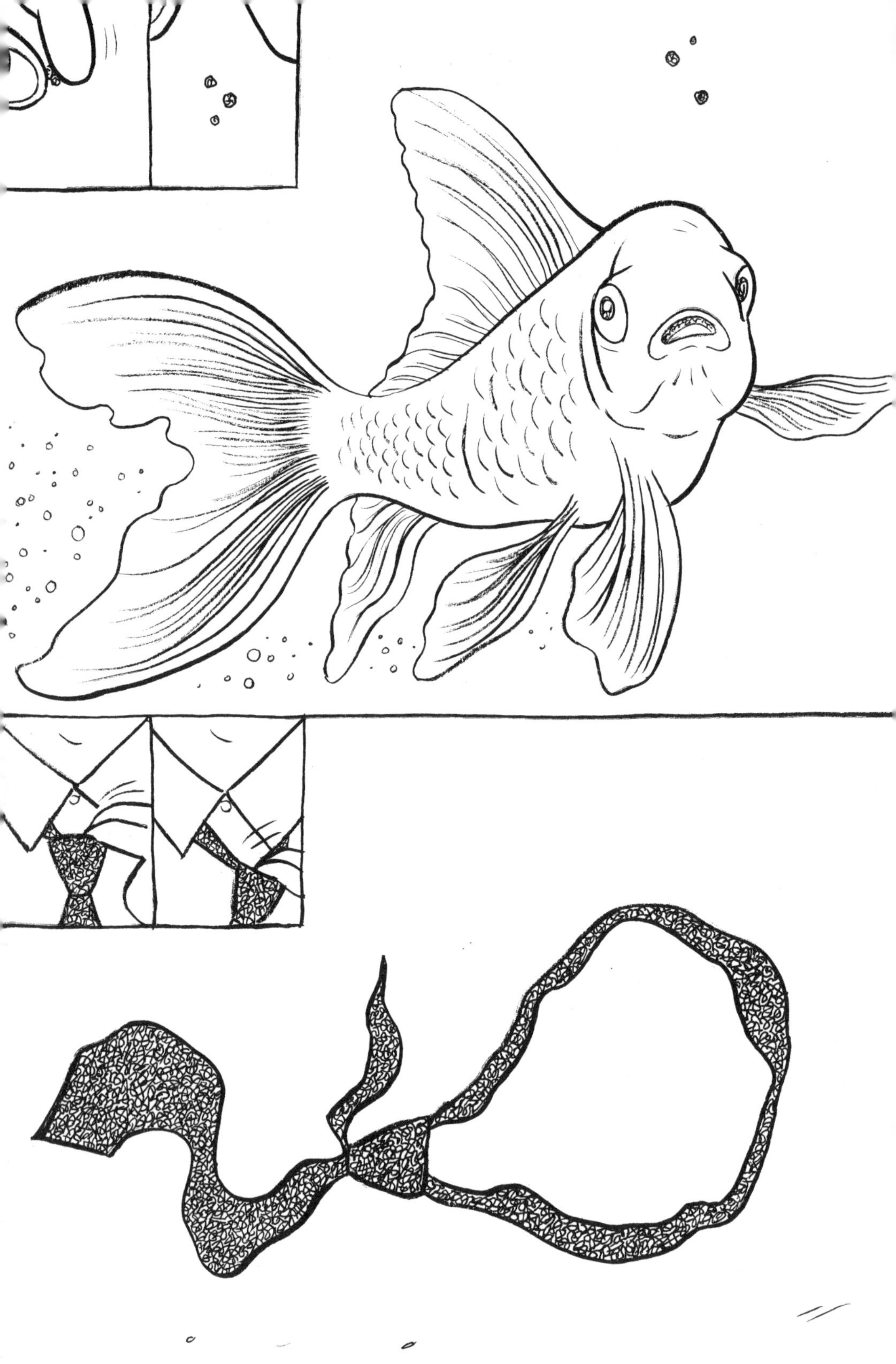

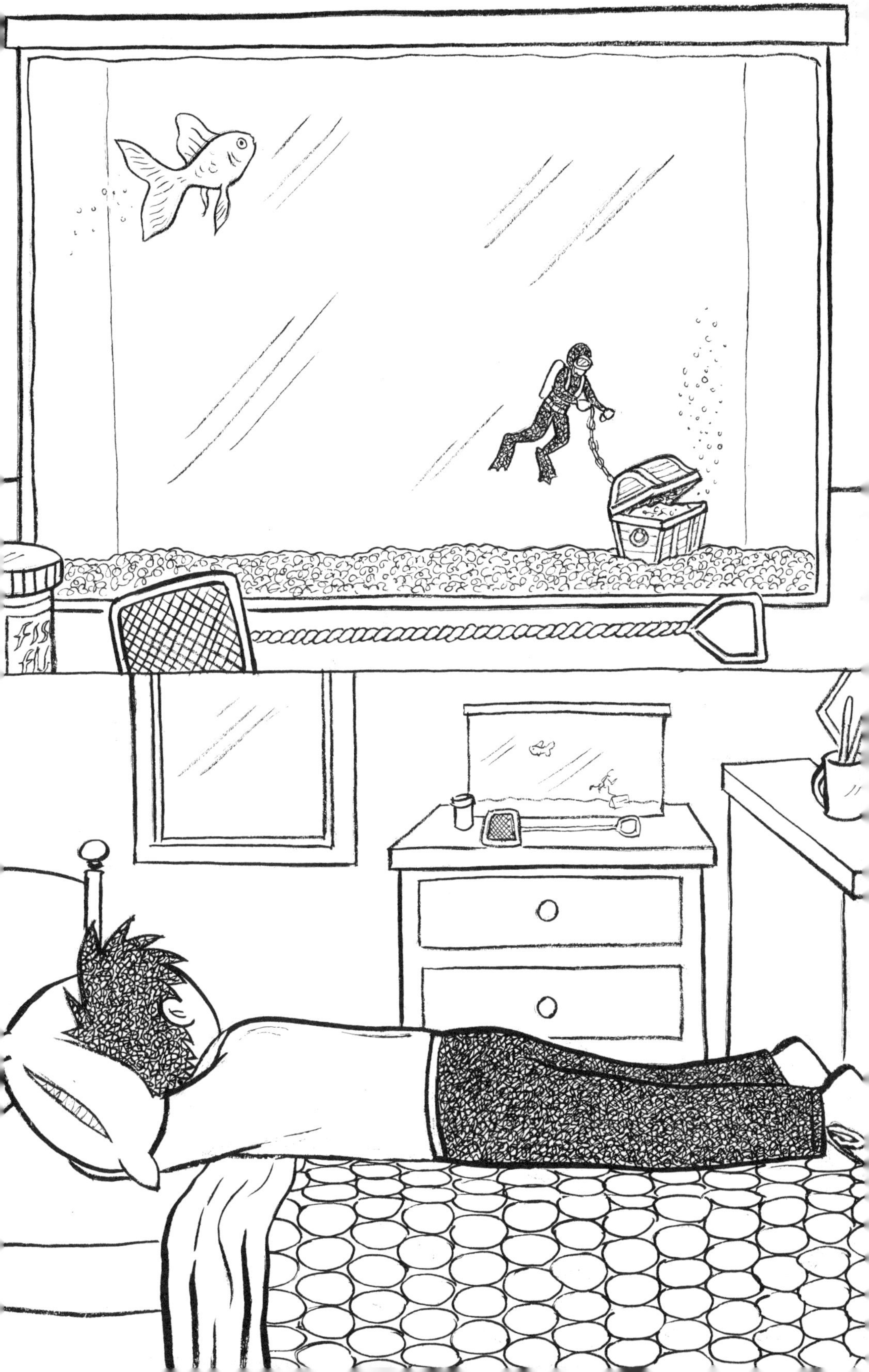

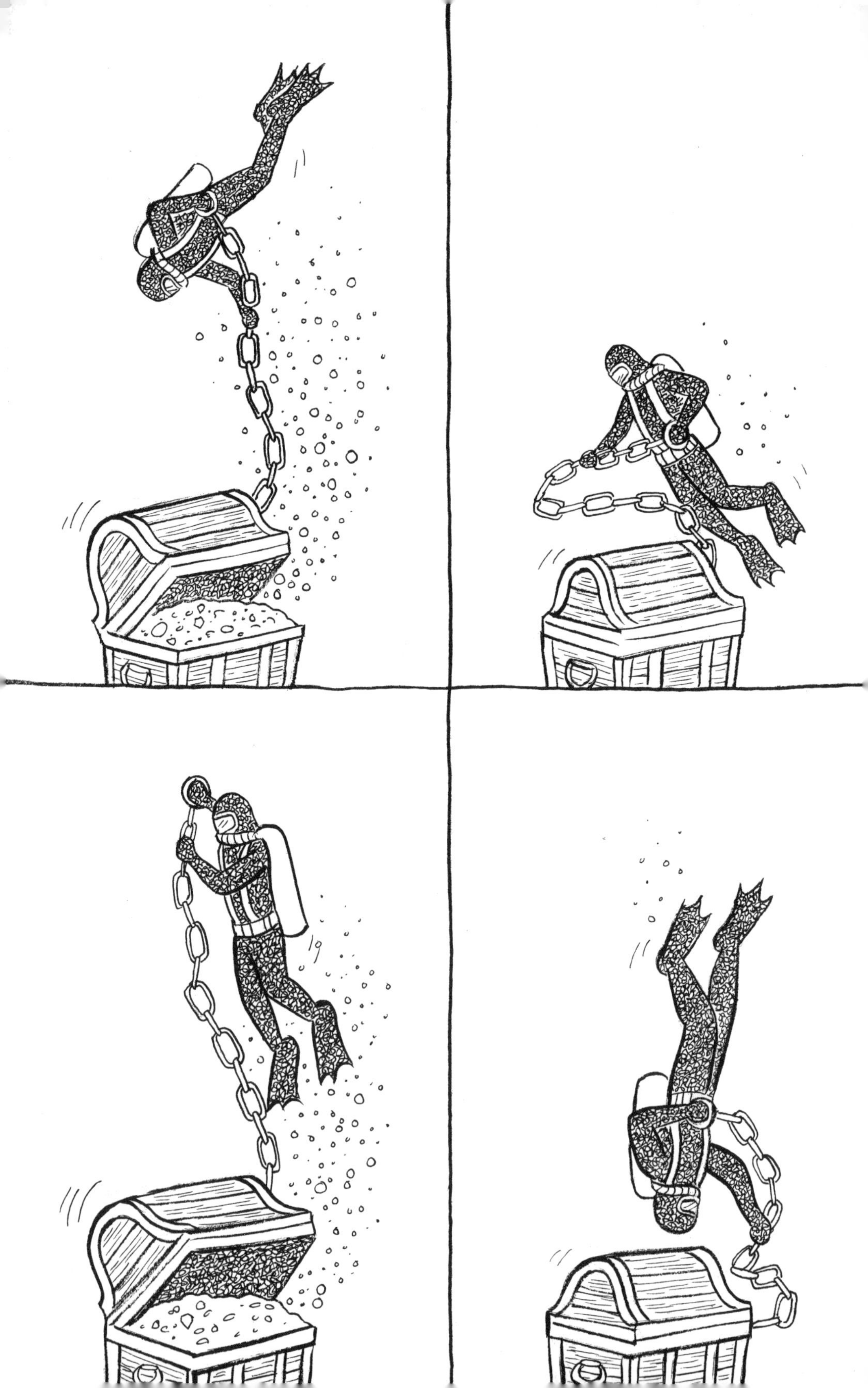

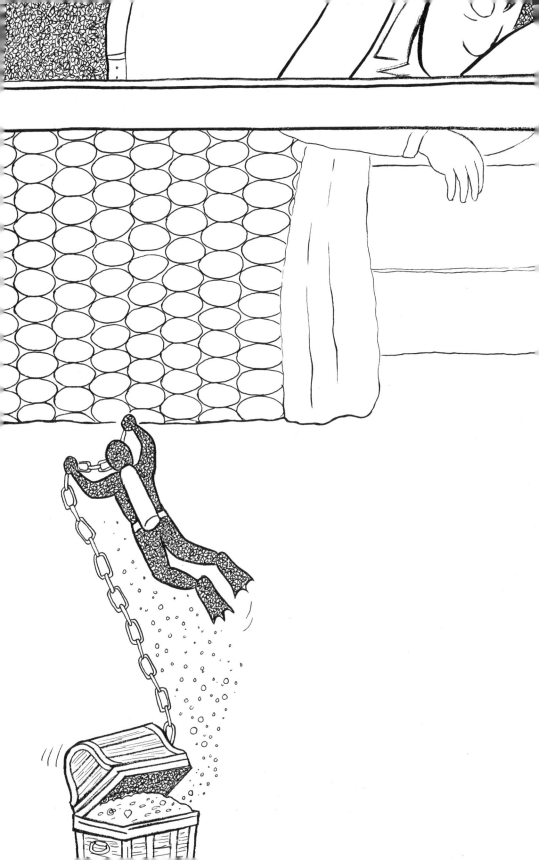

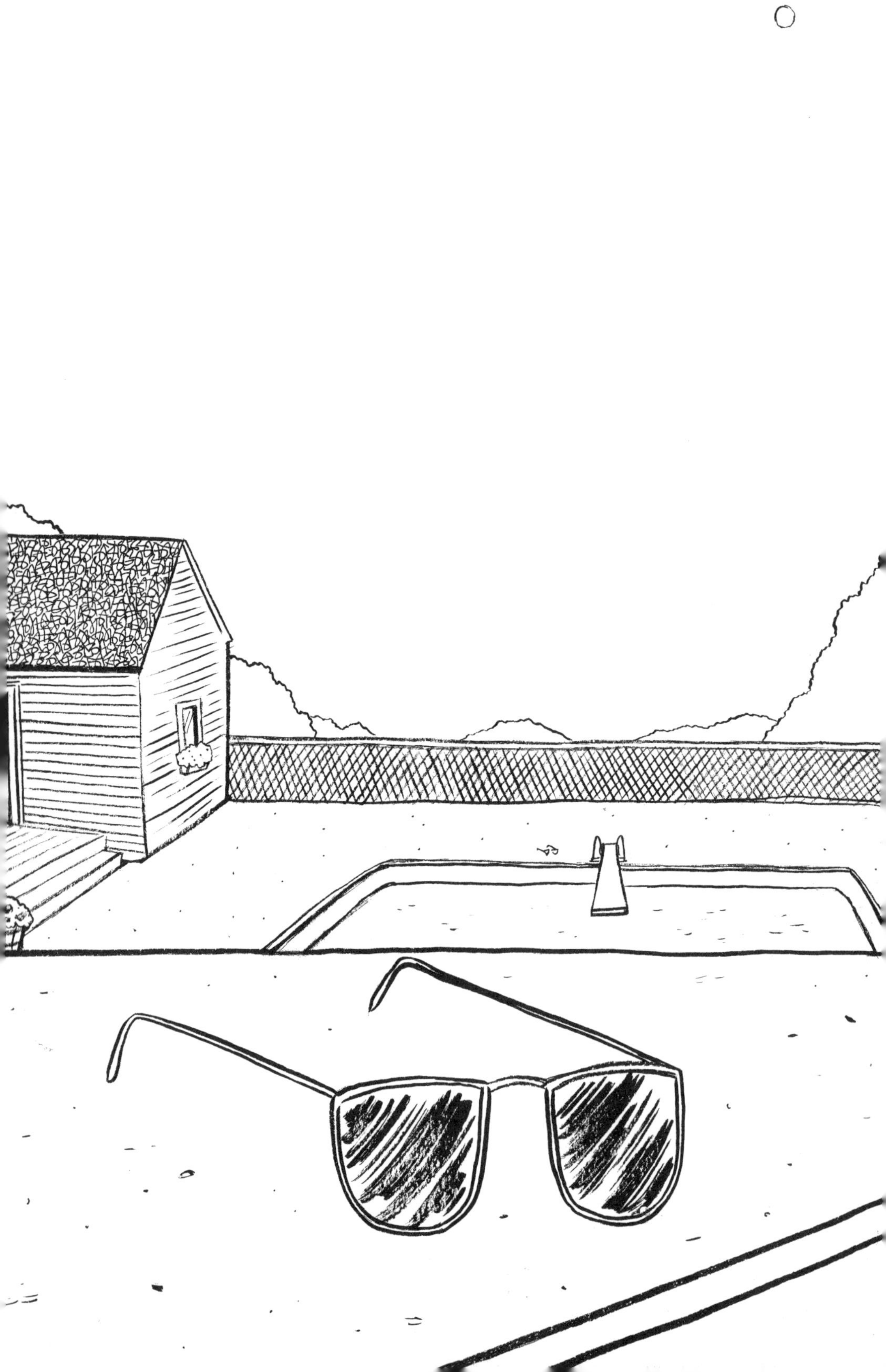

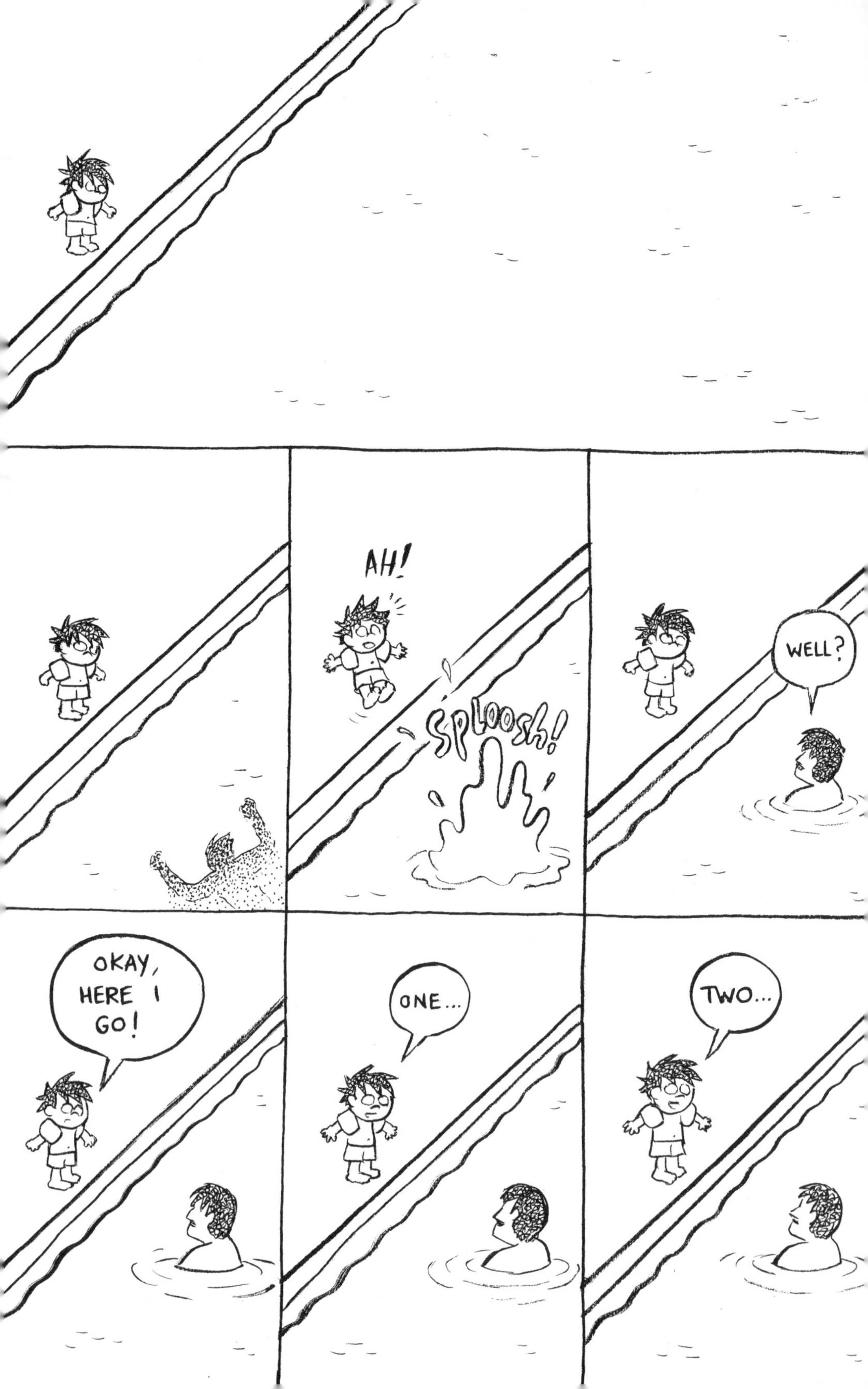
AH!
SPLOOSH!
WELL?
OKAY, HERE I GO!
ONE...
TWO...

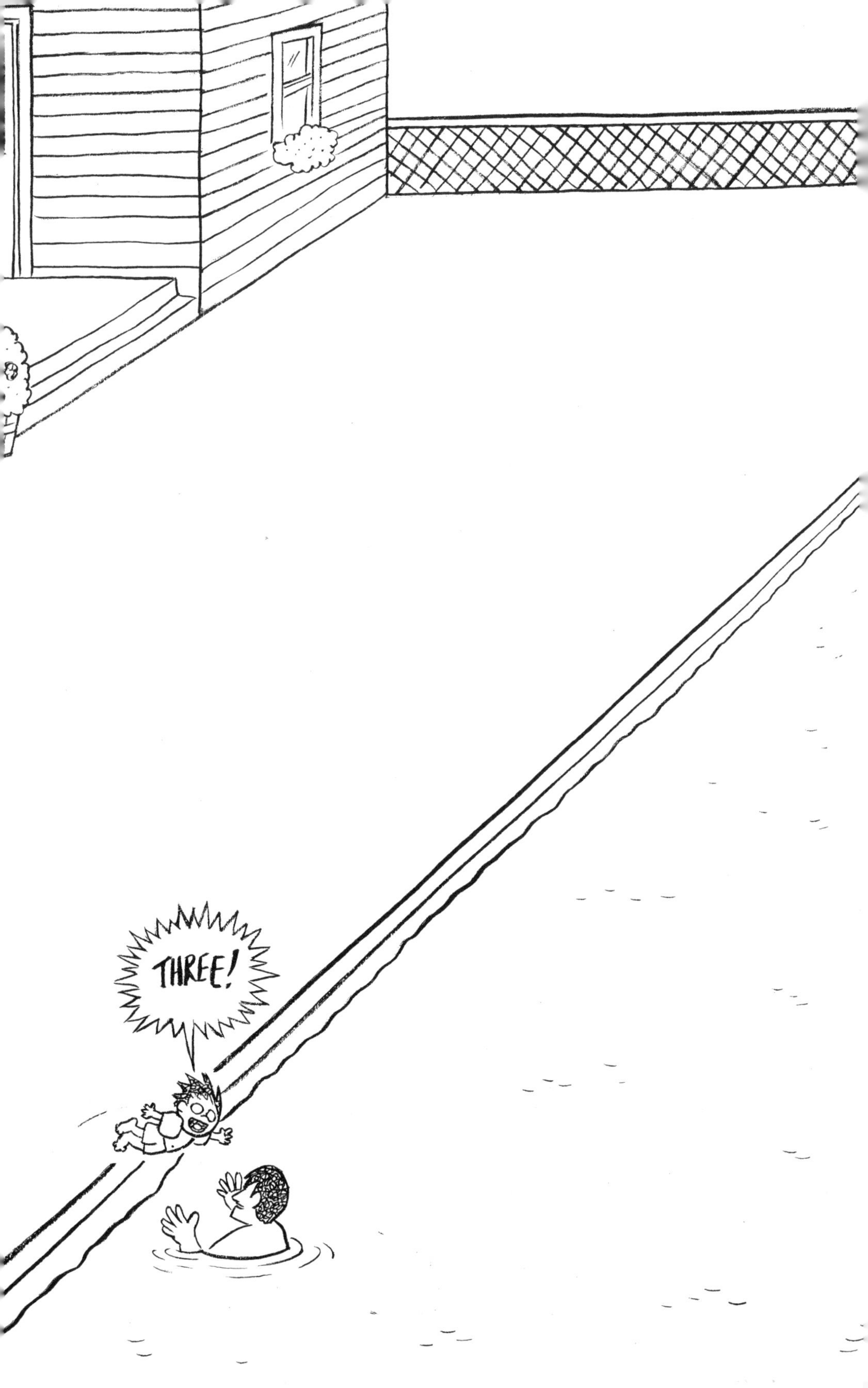
THREE!

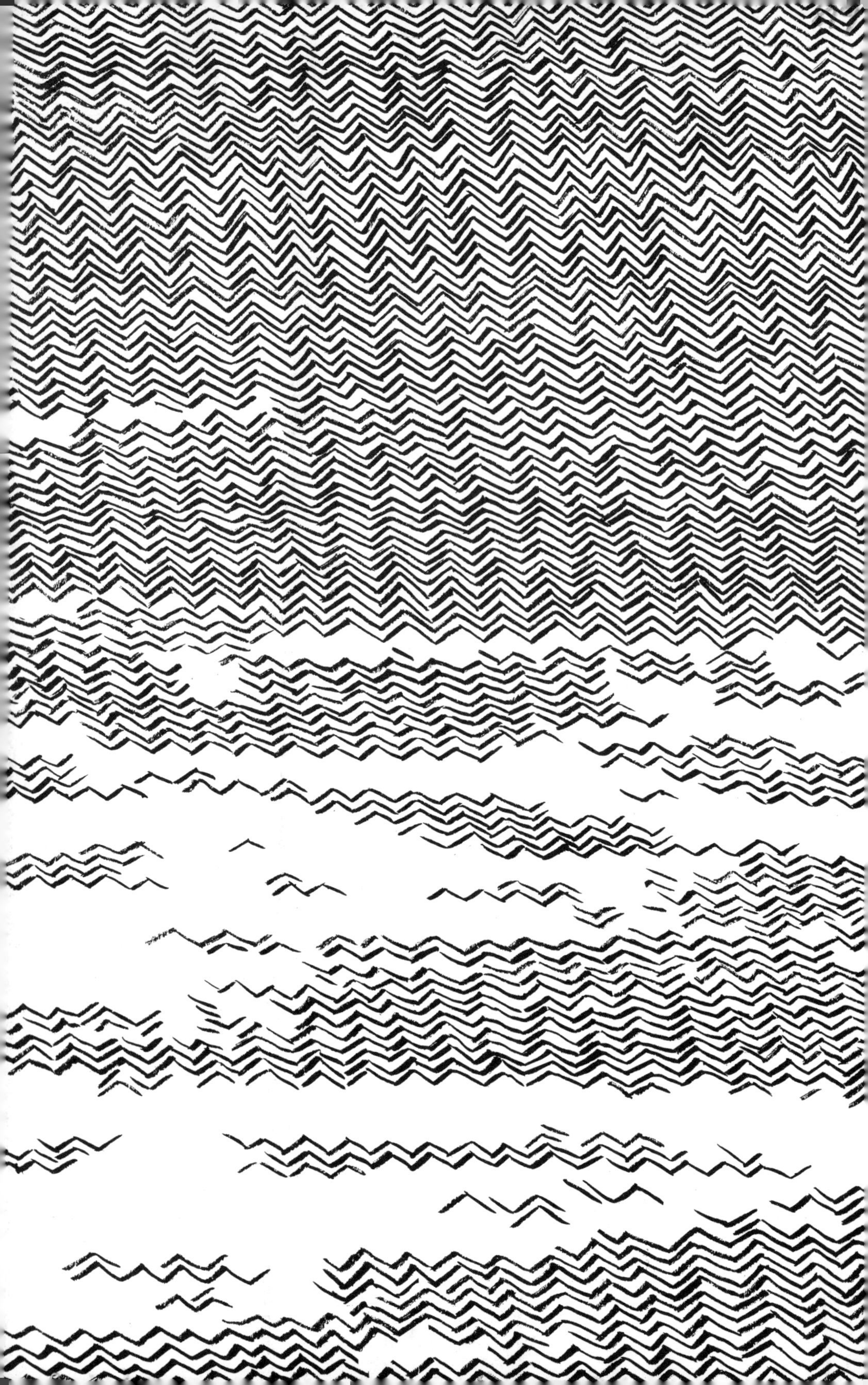